IN THE LANGUAGE
of REMEMBERING

Praise for *In the Language of Remembering*

'*In the Language of Remembering* is two things at once: a subtle, restrained memoir, where the author's own inner journey and questions make themselves heard, but, in the main, also an anthology that brings together the voices, memories, regrets and emotional peregrinations of so many others. Yet again, Aanchal Malhotra lifts Partition from disembodied numbers and statistics, from maps and borders, to highlight the very *human* nature of the tragedy, opening to us layer upon layer, and stories within stories. Featuring with honesty and respect the inner worlds of many who had sealed away their tales, *In the Language of Remembering* often brings a tear to the eye. But more importantly, it generates a sense of awe at the strength of which human beings are capable despite surviving the most wrenching misfortunes – even in loss they are able to find themselves and carry on.' – Manu S. Pillai, author and historian

'Compassionate, caring and insightful, Aanchal Malhotra's deeply personal enquiry traces a complex and multi-layered history to reflect on and come to terms with its many legacies. The narrative – always reflective, always questioning – stretches and crosses the boundaries of nations and politics as only stories can do, and even as it traces loss, pain and grief, and the profound impress of histories through generations, it offers that precious thing: hope.' – Urvashi Butalia, author and publisher

'It is at the intersection of history and memory – national, familial, individual – that we get an insight into how trauma unfolds over time. In this unique intergenerational account, Aanchal has given us a sensitive and precious archive.' – Ritu Menon, author and publisher

'A work of immense courage and grace. It deftly locates the intertwined personal and political traumas, both lived and inherited. Aanchal delicately redirects our gaze and imagination to generations which continue to be affected from the horrors of displacement during Partition that haunt the subcontinent to date.' – Farah Bashir, author

'This is a valuable collection of memories – and memories of memories – skillfully woven into a narrative thread that animates how much the past illuminates and intrudes into the present. The 1947 and 1971 partitions and divisions in South Asia acquire in Aanchal Malhotra's sensitive prose an immediacy and a pressing relevance, two and even three generations after the actual events. The book is a worthy sequel to *Remnants of a Separation.*' – T.C.A. Raghavan, author and former diplomat

'Aanchal Malhotra has written a deeply thoughtful and original work which grapples with the poignant and multiple ways that Partition memories still animate later generations. A moving and emotional meditation on South Asia's history and the way that Partition still resonates in the present.' – Yasmin Khan, author and historian

Select Praise for *Remnants of a Separation*

'In this book, the Partition is not just a memory but also a museum of loss.' – *Scroll*

'A seminal piece of work indicative of an un-learning of the clichéd rhetoric on the genocide that has intellectually imprisoned generations of Indians and Pakistanis alike.' – *The Tribune*

'A different approach from the vast and well-mined documentary archive available on the subject.' – *The Hindu*

'One could call Malhotra's writing evocative, or immersive, or enchanting, but none of that would fully encompass just how sensory the experience of reading these stories is … these memories imprint you with the dawning realization of just what it means to be born of this subcontinent.' – *The Daily Star*, Bangladesh

'Aanchal Malhotra's work shines a light onto a shadowy world and in so doing her book becomes a passport to another landscape, where tragedy, loss, memory and grief are slowly replaced with wonder.' – *Asian Affairs*

AANCHAL MALHOTRA

IN THE LANGUAGE
of REMEMBERING
THE INHERITANCE OF PARTITION

HarperCollins *Publishers* India

First published in India in hardback by
HarperCollins *Publishers* 2022
Building 10, Tower A, 4th Floor, DLF Cyber City, Phase II,
Gurugram Haryana 122002, India
www.harpercollins.co.in

2 4 6 8 10 9 7 5 3 1

P-ISBN: 978-93-5489-891-4
E-ISBN: 978-93-5489-914-0

Typeset in 11/15.1 Sabon LT Std at
Manipal Technologies Limited, Manipal

Printed and bound at
Thomson Press (India) Ltd

For my siblings, Aashna and Aaditya
and
all the inheritors of Partition

'We never wanted to burden them with our memories ... we wanted the sadness to end with us, to remain in our generation, to never be passed down.'

— Bhag Malhotra, Partition survivor

'History does not give you leave to forget so easily.'

— Urvashi Butalia, *The Other Side of Silence*

Contents

Foreword

TAKING THE METAPHOR OF a banyan tree, whose roots hang in the air, Nina, one of Aanchal's interviewees, tells her that 'when there is no land for the roots to grow out of ... you are the outcome of a fractured history'. It is this fractured history of the subcontinent – felt, embodied and inherited, owned and disowned, across geographies and generations – that Aanchal attempts to map in *In the Language of Remembering*.

In her first book, *Remnants of a Separation*, Aanchal compellingly showed us the ways in which the material memory of Partition is carried across borders; in a powerful sequel to her debut book, she emphasizes that this memory, material or otherwise, is not confined to Partition survivors. The memory is passed on, shaping and reshaping the ways in which Indians, Pakistanis and Bangladeshis continue to understand their past and give meaning to their present. In doing so, Aanchal builds on the work of scholars who have long indicated that Partition is far from a frozen event, or an event of the past. Partition remains ongoing.

A decade earlier, as I began speaking with Indians and Pakistanis for my book *The Footprints of Partition*, exploring the journey of Partition after Partition, studying the ways in which the memory of 1947 had transformed over generations, it was this ongoing facet of Partition that emerged in countless conversations. Whether in India or Pakistan, or later in Kashmir and Bangladesh, the ways in which people related to Partition, spoke of it, remembered it, silenced or cast it away signified that 1947 was not a static event.

Sometimes I came across third generations, as Aanchal does, who became intrigued in researching Partition because of the silencing they had experienced growing up. Their parents, their grandparents never spoke of it, never wanted to delve into it, pushing the younger generations to find their own meaning of home, loss, belonging. Others had family members across lines of division, and continued to be deeply impacted by visa restrictions, bureaucratic hurdles, Indo-Pak hostilities and warmongering. Some conversations symbolized how post-Partition events had left deep imprints on people's understanding of 1947, informing the ways in which they saw themselves and the 'other' – whether Muslim, Hindu or Sikh – within our countries, or Indians and Pakistanis across the border.

While some post-Partition events, such as the birth of Bangladesh in 1971, have overshadowed the events of 1947 in the collective and national imaginations, through her conversations, Aanchal shows that in other cases, such as the anti-Sikh pogrom of 1984, the demolition of the Babri Masjid in 1992, or the more recent Citizenship Amendment Act in India, Partition itself becomes a reference. It has the potential to evoke a re-experiencing: of fear, of uncertainty, of anxieties experienced by communities in 1947. And for some families, it was this post-Partition violence that made Partition ever more relevant, immediate and palpable even decades after Partition.

By conducting interviews across generations, and collecting stories spanning the vast geography from Afghanistan to Burma, Kashmir to Karnataka, Aanchal is able to indicate the moments at which Partition, and the memory thereof, emerges and re-emerges. But these are not political or macro moments alone. Rather, her conversations powerfully also depict the presence of Partition in our everyday. Partition and the pre-Partition are evoked not just in political rhetoric by nation-states or during periods of war and violence but also in the most mundane moments within families: in a whiff of recipe carried over, a word spoken here or there, an accent or dialect, a name of a street or neighbourhood representing the pre-Partition past of its residents, a tradition sustained, or the piercing silences, the memories pushed aside, the practices abandoned. The presence and absence, the remembering and forgetting, linger on, each in its own way a response to Partition and its impacts seventy-five years on.

Aanchal begins her interviews by asking her respondents not only when they first heard about their family's stories of Partition but also how old they were and what meaning they gave to those initial fragments of information. In doing so, she creates a canvas of what she calls 'second-hand' memories, showing us the connections and disconnections, the continuity and rupture, and the intricate ways in which Partition emerges and re-emerges across families, communities and generations. As one of her respondents powerfully summarizes:

> In a single second, Partition can transform from an event in history to a feeling in the present day. In a single bite, you can be transported to a land you've never seen but your family belongs to. When the food we are eating, the language we are speaking are all remnants of this division, it feels like Partition is woven into our everyday life, and it may remain that way, no matter how many generations come after us.

Given the breadth of interviews in this book, the thoughtful way in which the narratives have been stitched together itself symbolizes the felt-sense, the visceral and the embodied experiences embedded in relation to Partition, making the chapters deeply engaging. Though Aanchal speaks to people across age groups, ethnicities, nationalities and religions, the narratives are gently woven together in a way that cuts across these lines. Titled as Love, Loss, Pain, Regret, Fear and so on, it is emotions that guide these chapters. In thematizing the narratives this way, Aanchal is able to bring together varied experiences across borders and convincingly show us how, regardless of where one might be placed, whether in terms of geography or religion, human emotions triggered by Partition and its memory are shared.

There are recurring themes – such as relationships to ancestral lands or the desire to travel across – that are common across interviewees. And yet, Aanchal is also acutely aware of the dangers of homogenizing the stories. And so, within each chapter, within each emotion, she creates space for the nuances and uniqueness of each person's story, their memory, their relationship to Partition, reminding us that no matter how much is written about Partition, there is always still so much more to be unearthed.

As a parting note, it remains significant to me that Partition remains so significant to Aanchal. There is an urgency, a quest, a desire to document, to preserve, to archive the memory of Partition. It is an urgency I share; it is an urgency many other South Asians share. The numbers of projects, archives, museums and literary works on Partition that have come to the fore over the last two decades are a testament to this. As a third-generation Indian, and as a third-generation Pakistani, we recognize that time is not on our side. The nuanced stories and experiences of Partition survivors offer an essential lens into our past and present. It is a lens that, for me, provides the only hope to move beyond distorted, jingoistic and censored state histories. But we remain on the brink of losing those who lived through Partition. Countless stories will go unarchived, undocumented. By turning the lens on generational history, we can, however, begin to understand how that memory may be memorialized in other ways, taking on new meanings across families, across borders. In doing so, we can begin to scratch the surface of the long legacy of Partition. The stories and emotions that Aanchal has given a home to are a great service in this direction.

Anam Zakaria
March 2022

Introduction

THE MEMORY OF ONE'S origin is never erased.

On a winter afternoon in Jaipur, the journalist Kavita Puri and I decided to explore the city. As we climbed into an autorickshaw, I greeted the Sikh driver. '*Sat Sri Akal*,' I said, and he looked at me in his rear-view mirror, surprised to hear the familiar greeting so far away from its original landscape. '*Tussi Punjabi ho?*' he asked and, nodding, I asked where his family was from. His response was extraordinary, for he didn't take the name of any city or village in Indian Punjab, as I'd expected, but directly transported me across the border to Pakistan, where his family originated.

'*Assi pichho se*,' he began with a broad smile, speaking in Punjabi, telling me that way back, in the past, they were from Lahore, where his maternal grandfather used to run a mint outside the city. For the rest of our rickshaw ride, as an amused Kavita looked on at us, we chatted about how, during Partition, his grandfather's small money-printing machine was thrown into the nearby river, presumably the Ravi, by rioters. Fleeing the violence, the family migrated to the Indian desert state of Rajasthan, making it home. Born in India and having never stepped foot across the border, our driver still considered his origin to be in the land of his ancestors, for so visceral had been the intergenerational transference of its memory.

I have spent the better part of the last decade recording eyewitness accounts of Partition, across the subcontinent and through its diaspora, where I am often told that the impact of Partition remains largely limited to those who witnessed it. That memory ends with the first generation. However, if this brief interaction in Jaipur demonstrated anything – not to mention, my own efforts as a member of the third generation – it is that familial roots run deep, as does the impact of those being suddenly uprooted.

THE WITHDRAWAL OF the British Empire from India in August 1947 led to the drawing of the Radcliffe Line between the now-independent nations of India and Pakistan. It forced Hindus and Sikhs to migrate eastward to India, and Muslims westward to Pakistan, which had been further bifurcated into East and West. In 1971, East Pakistan became the independent state of Bangladesh. The Partition is known to be the largest mass migration in human history to date, resulting in the displacement of approximately 14 million people, and the death of a million more.

The generation that witnessed the division of a previously undivided land is now in its twilight years. Soon, it may not be in our midst and our direct ties to this lived history will be severed. But due to the sheer breadth of memory that still remains, Partition retreats into the past and extends into the future, even touching generations far removed from the original state of trauma. For most South Asians, it fundamentally anchors our collective experiences and how we perceive and understand the world – it populates our histories and defines our relationships with our neighbouring nations; it may build our characteristics or augment our fears. Particularly for those of us born with a personal history of Partition, the year 1947 reverberates, even though we may not understand why. We subliminally direct an acute attentiveness towards it, for it is a part of our very being. The purpose of this book is to illuminate the ways in which the Partition of British India into the independent nations of India, Pakistan and, later, Bangladesh continues to shape and inform the identity of multiple generations of South Asians today.

THE BEGINNING

THE HISTORY OF all four of my grandparents can be traced back to what is now Pakistan. In 2013, as a graduate student, led mostly by curiosity and lack of awareness, I began speaking to eyewitnesses to know what had happened during Partition. Like others, I had inherited a history that had defined the generation of my ancestors, displacing them from their homes and lands. But for too long, the politics of Partition had overshadowed the individuality of the survivors, their particular stories, their extraordinary losses. When I began these informal explorations, my understanding was limited to the condensed version of events in my school curriculum, and the fact that in 1953 my paternal grandfather had set up a bookshop in Delhi's Khan Market – then a refugee market, created as a commercial initiative for those who had migrated from the other side.

At the time I felt that Partition was a word which had receded in public memory and yet had continued to quietly and painfully linger in private discourses. I hadn't grown up with stories of it, though there had been casual mentions of how much the families had left behind, or what they had been reduced to after. But questions about this part of the past weren't always welcome, and often met with more questions. My grandparents and their siblings would ask me why I wanted to know, if it would change anything, how knowing their tale would affect me, and if the past would have any impact on the future. The expression on their faces would become unrecognizable if I probed, their words replaced by long and solemn silences. The anecdotes that did reveal themselves were ones of nostalgia, sentimentality or lament – my dada recalled the mango grove and cotton fields of his early life; my dadi, the *zenana* in her family haveli; my nana's eldest brother could see the street they lived on; my nani's sister, the stepwell behind their home.

But anything that touched on the brutality of Partition proved inaccessible, for remembering was quite difficult, especially if the story had remained unspoken for a long time. Added to this was the fact that I didn't know how to ask the questions. How could I begin gently, what topics were off limits, and where was the boundary I had to maintain while asking my questions? Should I call them refugees? Should I use the word Pakistan? Was it *home*? Could I ask about the violence, *was* there violence? My heart would pound as I approached these subjects. And whenever my questions were met with silence, the process began to feel invasive, urging me to look for other forms of remembrance.

Eventually, I used the aid of migratory objects to carve a pathway into the pre-Partition past. From Dera Ismail Khan, my dadi had carried a small hand-held knife, and her mother had brought a stunning piece of jewellery that they had initially thought of selling in order to get by in the new country. My dada owned a set of ordinary kitchen utensils, engraved with his and his father's initials, which he had travelled with from Malakwal. My nani's family had carried jewellery bought in Lahore in the 1930s, and my nana's family had brought the yardstick from their clothing shop in Anarkali Bazar and a vessel in which they made lassi. These objects became portals for them to 'return' to the landscape of their homeland, and encouraged a deeper conversation, extending beyond nostalgia or lament. But in those early months what I didn't realize was that we were actually constructing a new language to speak about a definitive and historic loss – a language that did not allow the lived experience of Partition to remain confined to my grandparents' past, establishing it as an event that held emotional influence over my present.

I broadened my study to include others who had carried objects across the newly formed border, using them to understand the myriad experiences from Partition. This became the first and only material archive of the time, and included things ranging from books, utensils, weapons, textiles, jewellery, religious artefacts, documents, photographs and toys to altogether unique items such as a taxidermized, mounted crocodile head – each containing stories of migration and displacement, the only belongings from a time unmarked by borders. This form of remembrance was known as 'Material Memory'.

Like with my grandparents, the physicality of the object paved the way for the memories of an erstwhile home to resurface. I cannot generalize, though, for several people spoke about Partition willingly and openly. But, for most, the questions that may have felt too direct to be asked without aid were now accompanied with less direct enquiries about where an object was from, why it was carried, how it made it across, whether it was cherished. These conversations regularly extended beyond the realm of the material and into the sensorial and linguistic, illuminating how the refugee heart continued to hold on to the intangibles as a way of returning to the undivided land. It was a space where people often said things for the first time – they discussed what had happened to them and their families decades ago; they reminisced about lost friendships and loves, homes and landscapes; they mourned, ruminated and unburdened. It was not just about archiving the object via the personal experience, but also the diversity of experiences. For communities that had been marginalized, overlooked or rendered invisible, this collection of oral history allowed their stories to be heard and preserved. In that sense, these interviews were sacred and served as primary research both for my graduate thesis and first book, *Remnants of a Separation: A History of the Partition Through Material Memory* – published internationally as *Remnants of Partition* (Hurst Publishers, 2019).

It was in 2014, on my maiden trip to Lahore, that the generational unfolding of Partition first became apparent. Shehrbano Raza Rizvi had invited me to speak with her maternal grandmother, Narjis Khatun, about her migration as a ten-year-old from Samana in Patiala state, India, to Multan in Pakistan. Objects of cultural significance, like an age-old *khaas-daan*, *paan-daan* and *sarota*, that had been brought across on this journey, were the topic of our conversation. Both Bano and her mother, Lisa, had joined in, asking questions about things they were hearing for the first time, or interjecting with reactions of shock or sadness, or contributing parts of the story that the other had forgotten. Bano had held the ornate dome-shaped *khaas-daan* and, while remembering her first visit to Samana, she called it a homecoming.

What I witnessed that evening was an extraordinary tapestry of Partition memory, collectively embroidered by three generations. Remembering had become a collaborative act. Here, the conversation gained a new dimension, and the beginning of this project started to take shape.

MEMORY – GENERATIONAL, INHERITED, BEQUEATHED

AFTER *REMNANTS* WAS published in 2017, I travelled across the world with it, presenting its research in the form of papers, exhibitions and interactive lectures, and was pleasantly surprised by the attention it garnered amongst people who had been born decades after Partition. Inevitably, they would come up to me to speak about their family members – what had happened to them, how they had either made it safely across the border or not, who had been left behind, how the stories had either been passed down in the family or not, and, of course, what they had carried. Sometimes, the impenetrable silence surrounding personal history became their reason to reach out; unsure of how to begin the conversation at home, they would request for help. Other times, it was to know why someone as young as me spent her days thinking about something as old as Partition. Many times, these were people who had already embarked on the exploration of their personal histories, some by employing the strategy from *Remnants* of using an object as a catalyst. But most times, if the original bearer of the story was still alive, it was to invite me to speak with them. I would always agree, my only condition being that I would want to document both the first-hand experience at Partition, and *their* second-hand understanding of it.

In these meetings, where several generations interacted, new landscapes of memory would emerge. Some preconceived notions would be shattered, others affirmed. I have seen anger and sadness in equal measure; I have seen guilt for never asking before; I have also seen pain. But most of all, I have witnessed immediate ownership of an often previously unknown history or unknown parts of that history. I don't remember my original intention as wanting to compile these interviews in book form, but rather to simply understand whether, like me, other people too felt an inextricable link to a tragedy they had not witnessed.

IN 1992, MARIANNE Hirsch, the Professor of English and Comparative Literature at Columbia University, while writing about the transmission of memories of violence across generations, coined the term 'postmemory', feeling 'the need for a term that would describe the *quality* of [her] relationship to [her] parents' daily stories of danger and survival during the Second World War … and the ways in which their accounts dominated [her] postwar childhood in Bucharest'.[1] In speaking to children of fellow Holocaust survivors, she realized that they seemed to share certain qualities and symptoms, making them a 'postgeneration'. She describes the term postmemory as a 'relationship that the "generation after" bears to the personal, collective and cultural trauma of those who came before' and how these experiences can be 'transmitted to them so deeply and affectively as to *seem* to constitute memories in their own right'.[2]

To my knowledge, there is no such term coined for the experiences of the subsequent generations of Partition-affected families whose lives have been shaped in some way by their ancestors' pasts, though the term postmemory has been cited in various studies and books, including my own. However, the terms I find myself naturally gravitating to are 'generational', 'inherited' or 'bequeathed', using them often interchangeably to talk about the memory of Partition and its associated emotions that have been passed down. In the same vein, my research participants are referred to as 'descendants', 'subsequent generations', 'inheritors' or simply 'interviewees' across the chapters of this book.

Eva Hoffman, the Polish-American writer-academic known for her work on exile, historical memory and the loss of culture and language, often writes about the impact of Holocaust memory on the children of survivors. Hoffman was born months after the end of the Second World War to Jewish parents who survived in hiding. In *After Such Knowledge*, she acknowledges that the received memory of an event is distinct from the participation in and witnessing of that event, asserting that 'the *generation after* receives its first knowledge of the terrible events with only childish instruments of perception, and as a kind of fable'.[3]

What is interesting to note here is that though the Holocaust and Partition are widely different in historical context, their memories may be transmitted to subsequent generations in similar ways. For the children or grandchildren of Partition, the stories of 1947 hardly ever begin to be passed down as personal history but rather as story – a quality that can be noted in several conversations in this book. The memory of a divided land is first presented in the form of storytelling, often quite innocently. The mention of villages or cities on the other side, the recollection of a childhood landscape, or the food one used to eat are common introductions to what we later recognize as nostalgic elements of Partition memory. However, initial interactions on the subject almost never begin with great intensity or touch upon loss, for that requires time and effort to be exhumed and permitted utterance.

While I understand that we may never be able to fully comprehend the magnitude or landscape of Partition through second-hand memory, what we may receive are vignettes of the past that can be stitched together to create an outline. But to encourage an ancestor to descend into a place of deeper recollection, in order to confront what may be long-suppressed emotions of belonging, identity, grief or even silence, requires continual intervention on the part of the descendants. And it is in this moment of intergenerational interaction that memories, traumatic or otherwise, transform from innocent stories into a construction of personal history.

THE VOCABULARY OF PARTITION

I HAVE ALREADY touched upon the initial discomfort of verbal language that permeated the first few conversations with my grandparents. But I want to propose the idea that, for the most part, we find ourselves unequipped to address the enormity of trauma caused by Partition. It seems that where there is space in language to be found for nostalgia, other things remain mostly absent or disassociated, until exhumed with delicacy over a period of time. There is not only the difficulty on the part of the survivor in uttering what happened and has gradually been rendered unspeakable, but also the incapability of the descendant to demand the immense emotional sedimentation of Partition.

Often, I find myself replaying the earliest audio recordings of my research to understand the hesitation in speaking about the past directly, as opposed to later ones where an object catalyst was introduced, making it the focus of our conversation, *through* which the past would be drawn out. I pay attention to the questions I reflexively asked in English – the language I think and write in – to the questions I later learnt to ask in Hindi, Urdu or Punjabi, or the ones my translators asked in Bangla, Gujarati or Sindhi, eventually understanding that the landscape of this divided past may reside in the mother tongue. The words and phrases people use in their respective languages to describe the days of Partition emerge from their specific historical circumstances. When finally uttered, these words reveal a kind of depth that makes them reverberate across the decades, transforming into physical entitles that can be felt, touched and indeed 'passed on' to subsequent generations.

In these recordings, I notice that my dada speaks to my dadi only in Punjabi – the language of their past, and to me in English – the language of our present. I wonder why so many interviewees are more comfortable saying the names of the cities and villages they left rather than naming the country of Pakistan or India that these are now a part of. I recall many repeating how no one had ever asked about this time in their lives, or how no one cared enough about it.

Perhaps this was one of the reasons why my own grandparents had initially retained their silence, for I had never asked.

Paying attention to the parlance of these eyewitness interviews, I also pick up on painful terms like 'discard', often used for abandoning the body of a family member who had succumbed to the journey of migration, or the bitter helplessness and sorrow with which people spoke of their new status as 'refugees' or '*muhajirs*' or '*sharnarthis*'. This leads me to the words we use to describe this aged trauma, to talk about division, to render emotional and physical loss, and encapsulate belonging or lament. 'The relation between Partition and language is complicated,' author and translator Rita Kothari writes in a piece titled 'Speaking about Partition'. Poignantly, she asks:

> Were languages capable of bearing the burden of words that could capture the enormity of partition? Words such as *bantwara* or *vibhajan* (both connoting division in Hindi); *ladpalayan* (migration and exodus) or *virhango* (separation in Sindhi) appear too quotidian to fully capture the trauma of this experience. The incommensurability of language and experience characterises the human condition, and may not be by itself a unique situation. However, loss or inadequacy of words accompanied – at the time of partition – other forms of tangible and intangible losses such as home, territory, faith, friendships and, at times, self-esteem.[4]

Clearly, the burden is not just of memory but also of articulating it, which in turn affects how and if at all this memory is passed on. Silence can also be a carrier, and one that is practised by many, and augmented by gestures of pain and sorrow. But, ultimately, there remains something extraordinary about Partition that refuses South Asians the luxury of either ignoring or moving past it, forbidding it from withdrawing from the realm of private conversations to enter the public domain so that it may be discussed and reconciled with. For many, the subject is viscerally enfolded in shame and fear, anger and bitterness, adding to the difficulty of its utterance. As a result, we largely accept the unspeakable version of Partition, dubbing it an old wound, enabling it to remain shrouded. Yet, it is only when we shed this historical unwillingness to engage with it and confront the ways in which it unsparingly severed the lives of millions that we will be able to consider it an event of generational significance.

IN THE LANGUAGE OF REMEMBERING

DAN BAR-ON, THE Israeli psychologist and Holocaust, conflict and peace researcher, asserts that 'there are "historical truths" that explain "what happened" but there are also "narrative truths" that depict "how someone tells what happened". It is through such "intergenerational transmission" that one generation's story can influence and shape the stories of the next generation.'[5]

The language used to transmit such stories, *the language of remembering*, extends to the descendants of Partition survivors. What is important to note is that this isn't the language used to remember the experience of Partition, but the language used to remember the recollection of the experience of Partition. It is a language removed from the original experience, and this space created by removal is occupied by the ability to reflect. Each interview in this book contributes to the construction of a generational parlance, but what I was often intrigued to find was that the intensity with which descendants described inherited stories seemed as visceral as the way these would have been described to them. Their second-hand connections to these lived traumas and histories went well beyond a surface telling into something that had become *intrinsically theirs*. They interwove the strands of collected memory and lived reality to present a version which drew a direct line from their ancestors' experience to theirs, articulating it through means linguistic and gestural, practical and emotional. As an example, I turn to a conversation from my fieldwork.

The Indian-Canadian author-actor Lisa Ray, while narrating her father Salil Ray's journey of migrating as a fourteen-year-old from East to West Bengal one hour before midnight on 15 August 1947, admitted the visceral connection she felt towards Partition as an inheritor of her family's experiences. Her grandfather, Santosh Babu, was an anglicized Bengali judge, who carried a cane and wore a monocle, and had an unassailable reputation for honesty and integrity. With news of Partition looming, he had applied for transfer to the Calcutta courts, but his papers had not arrived, even by Independence Day.

'The tensions were growing, the whispers were growing, the underlying panic had started to manifest into its own kind of ... monster, almost,' Lisa says, with wide eyes. 'My father was the third of eight children and, with his family, he waited. My grandfather had refused to migrate until the papers for his transfer arrived, and apparently those papers came on *the* day Partition was announced, and the family pretty much wrapped their lives up and caught the last train to Calcutta.

'My father remembers reaching India with a jumble of suitcases and bags. It was quite a culture shock to arrive at Sealdah station in Calcutta, because though they were originally from there, they'd previously only lived in smaller towns. Here, there was complete commotion and an influx of population, not to mention the communal anxiety and fear surrounding Partition ... I can't even imagine,' she shudders. 'So, the family gets into a taxi, but they cannot all fit along with the luggage, so my father and his elder brother are made to wait with the suitcases until everyone is ferried to the house, and then someone would return to pick up the boys and the remaining bags.

'There is this distinctive memory of my father's, of sitting with his brother in the confusion, and – now imagine this, it's sheer grace – a Sikh taxi driver approaches the boys and asks if they're okay, and where their parents are. They obviously looked very out of place, sitting all by themselves, filled with fear for what was unfolding around them. So, they narrate what had happened, and the Sikh driver offers to drive them to their grandmother's house.

And, can you imagine, they just got into his taxi, he piled up all of their belongings, drove the boys to Kalighat, and refused to accept any payment apparently. It was just sheer goodness on the part of the Sikh gentleman. I'm sure there are many stories of this nature, but this is our personal history of Partition. So many people discuss losing everything, and here everything arrived intact. And in fact, the family were beneficiaries of incredible grace. It never lets me forget the fact that along with violence and brutality, humanity and kindness too thrived in those days.'[6]

I smile. 'Were these stories told to you often?'

'Partition was not greatly discussed. It's only my curiosity that has led my father and me to have such conversations more often in these last few years. But it's not a lived experience. Mine, I mean. What I feel when I hear these stories is a kind of ... I suppose, grieving.' She places both hands over her heart.

'A grieving?' I ask.

'A grieving for the enormity of loss,' Lisa explains. 'I know that there's a generation of Indians today who don't want to look back but, for me, the past has always been essential. It's essential in understanding our present, even our future. Even when I was younger, I sought out people much older than me, to listen to their stories and learn from them. The past both fascinates and consumes me. And when it comes to Partition, I feel that resonance to the other side, by simply being in places like Amritsar, which is so close to the border with Pakistan. There's such a pull, and I think I've absorbed something, but I can't really...' She searches for the right words and continues, 'It's not rational – obviously it's not rational – and can't be pinpointed to a particular rational reason.'

'It may be rational, but it just may not have a language yet,' I offer.

'It may not have a language yet,' Lisa repeats, mulling over this thought. 'It is like a phantom language. You're right.' She looks at me and smiles. 'Our first reaction is always to assume that if we can't explain something rationally, then it must naturally fall into the irrational. But this is not the same. What I feel about Partition, even though I haven't lived through it, is real. It's very, very real.'

And I, who had by this time neared the end of my fieldwork, began to recognize the sentiments of many other interviewees in this interaction. 'It can't be a purely verbal or discernible language, because its resonance can also be found in the things you *aren't* saying – in your movements, in your eyes...'

'It's embedded in the body. Our history is embedded in the body,' she affirms.

⁊

TO WRITE ON the subject of Partition, and other events of similar nature, means to acquaint yourself with the hugely adaptable nature of the human condition. But because apart from material losses Partition left such a considerable emotional imprint, it becomes difficult to gauge just how deeply it is woven into the fabric of one's life or lineage. There are numerous testimony projects[7] working to preserve eyewitness memory, but hardly any that shed light on the descendants of Partition survivors. This realization, along with the conversation with Bano's family in Lahore, encouraged me to consider the subject further.

The very bequeathment of memory is to remove it from its original state, to allow it to be impacted and altered by the realities of the present world. But what also interests me is the process of the *passage of memory* – the relationship between a generation that has lived through a historical trauma and a generation that has inherited the memory of that trauma. And while we assert the importance of eyewitness accounts, we may not necessarily attribute the same seriousness to the testimonies of subsequent generations, due to the distance they have from the site of memory. Yet it is important for this archive to grow as well, to see the ways in which the consequences of Partition are disseminated and manifested.

More often than not, the initial discovery of a family history of Partition leads – first and foremost – to more questions amongst subsequent generations. There is curiosity and confusion as to how it happened, bafflement and shock at the scale of violence and migration, and eventually perhaps sorrow and anger begin to take firm shape as long-term twin reactions. Sometimes, the more we ask, the more we are told. Sometimes, our questions are met with silence. When there is no one left to recall the days, we dive into written and recorded material, beginning a patchwork of research with scraps of information like the names of villages and cities that may have now been renamed. We want to make sense of what happened, but eventually we realize that it is difficult to make sense of something so belatedly, particularly when the event itself seems devoid of all sense.

So, how and why are stories of an aged trauma transmitted and received? Are they offered with intention, or need to be exhumed? Have they always been present and gone unnoticed? Do they cause pain in their retelling – both to the ancestor and the descendant? Is there any point at all in resuscitating this part of the past? And though I've often found myself repeating that Partition was not yet an event of the past, that its legacy was threaded into our daily lives, I had never spent time to investigate how exactly that was or wasn't. This book is a product of that exploration.

THE INHERITORS

THE CONVERSATIONS IN this anthology – with Indians, Pakistanis, Bangladeshis, their respective diaspora, and others who find themselves directly or indirectly connected to the legacy of Partition – were recorded over a period of many years. They, *we*, are the inheritors. The eldest are in their nineties, having experienced the events of 1947, and the youngest are teenagers, physically untouched by Partition yet emotionally drawn to it. The testimonies range across generations, once, twice, sometimes thrice removed, though the majority is made up of the third generation or the grandchild. In several chapters, I have attempted to illustrate why this may be and why remembrance sometimes omits generations.

The conversations have been conducted in person, over video calls and phone calls, through emails, letters and text messages. Sometimes they began as side research or offshoots from other projects, but most commonly as conversation starters with South Asians I would meet across the world. *Did your grandparents or parents witness Partition? What do you know of their memories? Tell me more.* Fragments of memory led to larger stories, which led to complete and incomplete histories of arduous migrations across a man-made border.

I have to admit that talking about a subject this intimate via computers and phones, across different time zones and countries, is a strange thing. Oral history is as much about what is said as it is about what is left verbally unsaid, what is manifested through the body in gesture and movement. I would have thought that the sanctity of these recollections would be somewhat distorted by the use of technology, but, in fact, the conversation remains just as intimate, and the dialogue just as poignant. The absence of physical proximity was felt, of course, but a virtual interview is not better or worse, it is just different. On the other hand, technology has granted me access to stories that I may not be able to record otherwise, across borders I may not be able to cross as easily.

Several of my interviewees have been in touch since the time I was working on *Remnants*. Several more are creative individuals, who have engaged with the theme of Partition in some form or the other in their work. Many are children and grandchildren of Partition survivors still learning to speak about this topic. Some have wanted to talk about it for a while without knowing who they can reach out to; some don't understand why they want to speak about it; and then there are some who are unable to speak about it, despite deeply wanting to. Included also are conversations that have either extended on from *Remnants,* descending the generations, or offer different perspectives of the same story. A number of conversations are with friends, old and new. And lastly, members of my own family – paternal and maternal – find a place in several chapters.

THE CONVERSATIONS

WITHIN THE CROSS-SECTION of just my family, violence alone has never been the primary anchor to remember Partition. It is slowly woven into the conversations over time, *through* emotions like pain or bitterness, economic difficulty or loss, which more appropriately represent their unique experience. The darkness and turmoil are remembered, of course, but these are never the first stories offered.

Why then has the mainstream understanding of Partition remained confined, for the most part, to the realm of violence? The very word has become synonymous with images of refugee-laden trains and blood-soaked lands, murder and arson. And though all this constitutes *a* landscape of Partition, it does not represent its entirety. Popular media has perpetuated and reinforced the idea of the stark dichotomy between communities, good against bad, us against them, non-Muslim against Muslim, but the reality is far more complex.[8] The survivors' memory of that time is not vague or sweeping, but nuanced and detailed. Generations of close relations with friends, neighbours and acquaintances from different religions and ethnicities were essentially severed by a cleave through the land. With the announcement of Partition, difference was created where there may not have been any before, or it was exacerbated where it may have existed latently, or it was propagated and practised where it had always been blatant, leading, inevitably, to violence.

But to confine these conversations to violence alone is to misrepresent the highly complex emotional and ethnographic landscape of the time. If the hours I spent with survivors had demonstrated the subtlety and diversity of lived experiences, then the hours spent with their descendants did quite the same. Thus, in order to liberate my research from any structure that may be further divisive, I chose not to arrange the book according to geography, religion or nationality. Instead, each of the twenty-four chapters is inspired by certain emotions or actions that appeared emblematic of the conversations.

These are conversations on Beginning, Belonging, Borderlands, Discovery, Family, Fear, Friendship, Grief, Hope, Identity, Legacy, Loss, Love, Memory, Material Memory, Migration, No Man's Land, Pain, Regret, Returning, Separation and Reunion, Silence, The Other, and The Quotidian. This unique way of presenting the work, while highlighting the diversity of experience, also allows the testimonies of various nationalities, ethnicities, religions and social and age groups to be nestled close to one another, without discrimination. It enables us to follow how the same event could impact various groups in similar or different ways. The geography of these stories extends from Afghanistan in the west to Burma in the east, from Kashmir in the north to Karnataka in the south, swallowing the better part of South Asia. There are numerous interviews from the diaspora, and of families that have faced multiple displacements and migrations.

However, despite being thematically categorized, almost all chapters do overlap in terms of what they reveal. No story can be completely isolated or distilled into a single emotion. I may broadly be able to say that one story is about loss, another about grief and a third about hope, but, even so, the story about grief can also exemplify loss, and the story about loss can also reveal hope. There may be moments in the book when testimonies contradict one another, but this is the nature of human experiences, for they are complex, manifold and cannot fully be contained. But what comes to light quite naturally is that if everything we know about Partition is defined by our version of events, by our family's experiences, or by whatever side of the border we find ourselves on and its specific allegiances, then we must remember that the very opposite of our perspective exists as well.

Each chapter is arranged as a collection of conversations, lending to its structure, and attempts to present the voice of the descendant as the primary source of information and reflection. These conversations are deeply inward, intuitive and often surprising. And though they may be emotionally demanding, the texture of each is determined by what is revealed. Some conversations have illuminated the differences between me and my participants, formed either by personal opinion or how the consequences of history were meted out to each of the countries involved in Partition. But together, they embody the power of cross-border testimonies, and answer questions on why the past should be remembered, why it has not been remembered, and what may happen to future remembrances if it is allowed to endure in silence.

The impact of many stories is augmented due to present-day events, simply because they are being told from the perspective of someone who exists in this present world. Their experiences, biases, hopes, fears, confusions all find a way in, depositing another layer over that of historical memory. But one will find no chapters on politics or trauma alone, for these can be felt within every single story about Partition – reverberating across generations, infiltrating memory in a way that they become incidental and almost routine. If politics or trauma are alluded to, then it is done in the context of the narrative, and it is done often. Inevitably, descendants make mention of political or violent forces that had at Partition or have continued since to perpetuate a divisive society.

Thus, along with the brutality of 1947, the four wars fought between India and Pakistan – in 1947-48, 1965, 1971 and 1999 – are repeatedly brought up; some stories also make mention of the 2001-02 stand-off at the Line of Control (LoC) and the ceasefire in 2003. The creation of Bangladesh in 1971 holds prominence in several conversations. The 1960 Bongal Kheda movement and 1983 Nellie massacre in Assam are discussed, as are the 1964 riots and ethnic cleansings in East Pakistan, the 1984 Sikh massacre, and the 1992 demolition of the Babri Masjid in Ayodhya. In addition, the political consequences of more recent years surrounding refugees and immigrants, like the National Register of Citizens (NRC) and Citizenship Amendment Act (CAA) in India, and Brexit in the United Kingdom, are brought up from time to time. Lastly, the political leaders and parties from the time of Partition are less frequently discussed, but mention is made of the current leadership of India, Pakistan, Bangladesh, the UK and the US, wherever relevant.

❧

THERE ARE ALSO some recurring themes to be found throughout the chapters.

The first is the question of the village or ancestral land, and as many of us are born on the opposite side of the border in relation to our ancestors, the answer lies in inaccessibility. Personally, as someone raised in the city of Delhi with no association to ancestral land or *pind*, any time this subject was raised, there was a painful resonance. Sometimes, my friend, the Hindi writer Pranav Misra, and I would discuss this aspect through the stories we wrote. Able to trace several generations from both sides of his family to Uttar Pradesh, all of his stories were about being rooted, and all of mine were about rootlessness. He wrote about *going home* and I wrote about *discovering home*. He wrote from memory and I wrote from longing. He was able to see his ancestral land and walk in the shade of the trees that his great-grandfather had once planted, whereas I didn't even have vague coordinates of the homes my grandparents once lived in. There was an uncomplicated ownership of earth and soil, water and sky that I could never discern in my voice or the voices of my interviewees.

The second is the identity of being a refugee – a status that many families were forced to bear post their migration to either India or Pakistan (East and West). My paternal grandfather had spat out this word, 'refugee', in disdain when we had first spoken, for he had spent decades disassociating himself from it. My aunts, too, touch on this detachment from the refugee experience in our conversations. Several interviewees make mention of the neighbourhoods they or their families live in as 'refugee colonies' and 'camps', or how this status had either once defined or continues to define their social and/or economic relationships.

Perhaps the most poignant aspect that appears in some form in nearly every single conversation is the desire to travel to the other side. This is expressed sincerely, painfully, through the recollection of dreams or the production of art and literary work, through melancholy and hope, as an aspiration for many descendants. It is the simple desire to see where their ancestors came from, to associate an image to a memory, to set foot on the soil of their origin. I cannot say whether this will ever happen, whether subcontinental politics will ever allow for unrestricted or easier travel between the three nations. But in the hearts of many, there remains hope.

On the other hand, however, I am struck by how few interviews make mention of the process and legacy of decolonization. The hasty departure of the British from India is often eclipsed, if not fully obfuscated, by the complicated relationships that have emerged between the countries of the erstwhile Empire. If the role of the British or animosity towards the colonizer are alluded to, it is generally in conversations with those who currently reside in the diaspora. But, for citizens of the subcontinent, the past seven and a half decades of intricate and deep-rooted historical, political, military, geographical, social, familial, ethnic and emotional discord seem to have largely rendered the original cause almost inconsequential.

PART OF THE reason to embark on this project was a personal one. The questions I was asking my interviewees were questions I had asked myself over the years. At times, their answers concurred with how I felt, and at other times offered perspectives I hadn't previously considered. Often, I would invite them to ask me questions – I felt it fair, after all – but very few would accept. Most were partaking in this kind of unusual 'interview-conversation' for the first time and were unsure of what the protocol was.

While there may have been initial hesitation on *how* to tell an inherited story, for the most part, people wanted to share. They wanted their ancestors' stories to be heard and understood, to be learnt from, to be individualized and not clumped into the 'data' of Partition migration. The subject was not removed from them, no matter how removed they may have been from the site of its occurrence. Each chapter varies in length as well as in terms of the numbers of interviews it carries. Much to my surprise, the chapter I had assumed would be the most populated – Silence, due to the sheer enormity of unspoken residual memory – has ended up being the shortest. Whereas chapters that deal with the everydayness of Partition inheritance, where it is lived or performed or evoked even through the most banal of activities or conversations – chapters like Family, Identity or The Quotidian – are the lengthiest. And where there was space for sentimentality and nostalgia in the eyewitness experience, this was less noticeable in the narrations of subsequent generations. There were, of course, traces of lament and longing, but not in the same way, for these were mediated by temporal distance from the actual event.

I have emerged from these conversations with enormous respect for each of my interviewees, for they have answered sincerely and deeply, allowing their vulnerabilities to be recorded and written in a way that may not have happened had our roles been reversed.

THE TESTAMENT OF A GENERATION

OVER THE LAST few years, I have thought a lot about how and why we hold on to the past we cannot change, and the heaviness that accompanies this 'keeping' – a sense of accumulation and preservation. I have wondered why those who have a family history of Partition inevitably, and sometimes even unknowingly, carve a path to an unpartitioned land. I don't have a definitive explanation for this, but in recording the many, many stories that fill these pages, I have begun to feel like a palimpsest of Partition memory.

The truth is, I was searching for the reasons why I had been unable to let go of this historic event, why I keep returning to it in the form of personal history, literary inspiration or academic exploration. Somehow, I felt certain that all these conversations with people who were either similar or different from me would lead to a reasonable explanation. Thus, in every conversation, I searched for the answer to my obsession, but all I found was more questions, or iterations of my questions that others were also asking.

Where ordinarily I would try to keep a certain distance from the subjects of my work, this time it seemed impossible and also futile. By adapting the formal interview into an informal conversation,

I automatically made myself a participant in the process. Each conversation has become as much about me as it is about the interviewee, and in each interview I have found shades of myself and my family.

Many times, I have wondered about who would read a book like this – a book that attempts to make meaning of a time devoid of all rationality, a time of madness. And, to add to that, a book of second-handedness – second-hand sadness, second-hand loss, second-hand pain. Can all these emotions still be felt in their second-handedness? Sometimes I would find myself asking this question and, at other times, answering it. But, as I stand at the project's completion now, looking at it in its totality, the question itself feels irrelevant, unnecessary. An interviewee once said to me that he felt 'seen' after our conversation. And so I have deduced that there is no need to gauge the veracity of emotion or experience, neither eyewitness nor second-hand. The point is to have an archive of memory and visibility: the testament of a generation.

Though this book is comprehensive, it is by no means an exhaustive record of the inherited memory of Partition. For any omissions that may remain in my research, I ask you to forgive me. For everyone who was willing to talk, there were more who chose to speak off record and even more who wished to say nothing at all. This only means that beyond the scope of these conversations, there remains a reservoir of memory – unwritten, unrecorded, unspoken, perhaps even unwanted. And though there is nothing I can do about this unrecorded memory, I can only hope that there may come a day when the pain of Partition is no longer veiled by fear or shame or anger but is replaced by a sense of survival over what is undeniably the most cataclysmic event in the contemporary history of the subcontinent.

Author's Note

EVERY CHAPTER OF THIS book is a world in itself and each section within it is akin to a separate essay. As these essays sit next to one another and form connections, the geography of the chapter extends across regions and religions, seasons and time zones, the personal and the political. Weaving these narratives into a coherent form has been an emotionally demanding process, so I cannot imagine its reading to be an undemanding activity. I urge the reader to give each chapter the attention, time and consideration it deserves. Read slowly, delve deeply and absorb wholly these stories that together hold the shape of a once-unpartitioned land.

1

Beginning

∽

M Y FIRST QUESTION IS always about the beginning. *When did you first hear about your family's story of Partition? How old were you, and did you understand what it meant?* The answers, naturally, vary. Some stories emerge when family members get together and reminisce about the past or speak about the economic and social losses that occurred. Some stories are exhumed because of objects and heirlooms carried across during Partition. Some stories begin with semantics – the word refugee, the use of a language never passed down, the mention of birthplaces now on the other side. Some stories begin with the concept of home or belonging – *where are we from*, many of my interviewees have asked their families, *where is our ancestral village?*

Therefore, in this book, the term *beginning* is not defined as the origin of memory but, rather, the inheritance of memory. A story *begins* when a memory of Partition is bequeathed from one person to another, or one generation to the next.

Over the last few years, I have journeyed through many *beginnings* – that moment when someone first learns that their family was affected by Partition, that moment of transference, of transmission. When a personal relationship with a collective history is established. At times, this moment is a product of gentle prodding or casual curiosity. Other times, it is brought on unexpectedly by events in the present day. Sometimes, it is purposefully passed down to ensure that subsequent generations are fully aware of the past. Then there are times when it is never even mentioned, consciously silenced, leading to discoveries by subsequent generations years later when there is no one left to ask. In any case, there is no one beginning, and no means to predict its arrival. It is different for every person and is often quite removed from the actual sites of Partition.

Through the course of this book, we will encounter many *beginnings*, but in this chapter I turn to my paternal family, whose stories have dominated my understanding of the depth of Partition, to know how the memory of that time was passed down the generations.

⌒

'SO THEN, WHEN did you first talk to someone about Partition?' I ask my grandmother, Bhag Malhotra, one evening. She is peeling an orange with great concentration and, for a second, she pauses to look at me. It has been seven years since we first spoke about her experiences of migrating from D.I. Khan to Delhi in 1947 and I am curious about whether there has been a memory keeper in the family before me.

'When *you* asked about it all those years ago,' she answers nonchalantly, dunking a slice of the orange into some black salt.

My mouth drops open slightly. Surely, that couldn't be the case. Surely, sixty-six years couldn't have passed before she began talking candidly about possibly the most devastating event of her life. I knit my eyebrows together and cup my face in my palms, unsure of how to continue the conversation. Then my eye catches the wedding portraits of my grandparents hung above her bed.

Several years ago, at a conference in Bangalore, I had seen a presentation about how men and women who had been part of the Italian Resistance during World War II often ended up marrying one another, for no one else could understand what they had been through. 'Who else can I speak to about this?' they asked.[1] At the time, this had left a deep impression on me, and I wondered whether couples who had both lived through Partition found solace in the fact that they could speak to one another about it, that the other would understand.

When I ask my grandmother if this was the case – my grandparents had met in the Kingsway refugee camp in 1948, after all – she dismisses it with a click of her tongue. 'Partition happened, we came from D.I. Khan, they came from Malakwal. He was in college at the time, I know this much. But I never asked how he felt about it, and neither did he.' I try to enquire further, but this is not a topic she wants to discuss, so I veer towards the second generation, their children.

'No, never. What would they know about what Partition was?' she scoffs. 'They were so young.'

'But did they never ask where you were from even once they were older?'

'*Beta*,' she begins, almost frustrated with the line of questioning. She cannot understand why I want to know these things. '*Subah kaam ke liye niklo, raat ko wapas late aao.* I had to work, there was no choice in the matter. I used to wake up at 4 a.m., wash and dry the clothes, do any sewing that needed to be done. Then I would get the children ready for school, make all our lunches. Then your grandfather and I would get ready and leave for work. I would take an autorickshaw from Netaji Nagar to the Ministry – it would cost only one rupee – and he would take his scooter to Khan Market. Then in the evening, I'd have to prepare dinner, make sure things were laid out for the next day, check the children's homework. And that's how it continued. There was no time for questions, for reminiscing or remembering. Where was the leisure? There was no time for children, even. They never asked, "Mummy, where are you from?" or "Where is papa from?" and we never told them. How could I speak to the children about...' she pauses before uttering, '...Partition? Yes, sometimes when I met my family, we would talk about D.I. Khan and our life there, but nowhere else.' Her frustration has dissolved into pain. She breathes in deeply, sniffling.

'But if they had asked, would you have told them?'

'*Zaroor*, why not. Just like you ask me questions, if they had asked, I would have told them. Maybe they did ask once they were older. But Partition was not a subject spoken about in our home,' she says with finality.

Later that night, I think about the difficulty in having conversations about Partition, how the very mention of the word can lead to extreme reactions, ranging from deep nostalgia to acute bitterness. By all accounts, it is a fragile, often uncharted territory, and I wonder if, like me, my father or his siblings ever set out on *beginnings* of their own.

MY PATERNAL GRANDPARENTS have three children: my eldest aunt, Neeraj, born in 1957, my second aunt, Tanuj, born in 1960, and my father, Anuj, born in 1962. On a crisp winter afternoon, Tanuj bhua and I sit in her rooftop garden to talk about the past. There are things that she recalls which have evaded my grandmother's memory. Bhua has prepared notes for our conversation, and as we settle into the lawn chairs, she begins to skim through them.

'Whatever I know about that time is from my mother. I never had any conversations with my father about Partition. And my mother, too, would never speak to us about it directly. Maybe the only times I heard her talking about her birthplace were when she went to visit her maternal family. Sisters, aunts, cousins, even her mother and ailing grandmother would discuss the life they had lived before Partition. As teenagers, we would overhear little snatches of conversation. My mother would come alive during this time, speaking in her own language, the *boli* of Derawali, and this is how I learnt that she came to Delhi from a place called D.I. Khan.' She smiles to herself and continues, 'See, when they were all together, the conversation quite naturally found its way across the border. This time was a hiatus from their refugee life in India, the only time they didn't think about their worries or losses, about money or jobs, about married life and its responsibilities. This time was private and precious and dedicated to the past. Perhaps it was a way to relive or even reclaim their identity.'

'You mean the identity left behind on the other side?'

'Yes, a way to remember who they had once been, because here they became somebody else, they were forced to.' She pauses for a few seconds and then repeats herself, 'But mummy never spoke on her own about Partition, and I don't believe I asked either. Ever. And the reason was probably that they always seemed happy. My parents never seemed sad or bothered about the life they were living, so we had no reason to ask. We knew from the age of seven or eight, because of the Independence Day celebrations at school, that *batwara* had happened, but we didn't really understand its horrors.'

'Do you think that your parents ever spoke to each other about it?'

'Not to my knowledge, no. I personally feel that, as a family, we are not so...' Her voice trails off.

'Open?' I offer.

'Open, yes. And we don't indulge in the past or share our problems, especially resentments, although they may affect our attitudes. We harden up to a particular incident or person; it goes deep down and it bothers us from within, though we may never speak of it. As I grew older, she talked about the camp and how her own family refused to accommodate them. Sometimes, she went further back into her childhood, the death of her father, and how her mother, bibiji, began teaching and earning as a single mother. She was never emotional or sad, and it was never one long story; always sporadic and in bits and pieces if ever anything related came up. But these exchanges were brief, she hardly ever elaborated and we never probed further.'

'Do you regret not asking –' Before I can finish, she nods in agreement.

'Yes, yes I do...'

'– at a time when she would have remembered more?'

'But I don't know if she would have opened up to me then. I think the decision was very firmly to move on. There was so much for them to do, so much to rebuild – both at work and at home. My parents were always working, so where was the time to lament the past? I understand their decision to look forward, but when you ask me now, of course I regret not asking more, because I think it would have brought me closer to my parents.'

My aunt reminds me that because their living relied entirely on her mother's income, my grandmother did not have the choice of staying at home to raise her children. In 1955, when my grandparents got married, she was working as a junior clerk at the Ministry of Rehabilitation and it had been two years since he had established the Bahrisons bookshop in Khan Market. They lived in a small, allotted flat in north Delhi's refugee colony of Hakikat Nagar, with my grandfather's parents, elder brother and sister-in-law. Gradually, the family grew, space became sparser, and ends harder to meet. In 1958, a year after my eldest aunt was born, my grandmother took up government accommodation in Netaji Nagar, south Delhi. The house was run with her salary, and all profits that came in were put back into the business for expansion.* Sunday was the only day taken off work – alternate Sundays were reserved either to visit the family in Hakikat Nagar and my grandmother's mother in Vijay Nagar, or picnics at Buddha Jayanti Park or to watch a children's film. In 1977, my grandmother took early retirement from her government job and then divided her time between the bookshop and home.

As she recounts all this, tears well up in my aunt's eyes. 'See, it is the sacrifices that are difficult to talk about. They could not afford to take days off, or enjoy their youth, or even splurge on themselves, because every paisa was saved. *Koi fazool ka kharcha nahi.* Papa invested in property to multiply the wealth and now, if I think about it, it seems that they were in a hurry to restore what had been lost during Partition. I have not faced a single hardship because of how my parents provided for me and my siblings.'

I remark on how she is more emotional about her parents' life in post-Partition India than about them having to witness the violent

---

* Today, sixty-eight years after its establishment, Bahrisons Booksellers is considered a Delhi landmark.

process of Partition itself. Not once have we discussed the train station in Delhi where her maternal grandmother stood on 16 August 1947, resolute to take her children *back* to what became Pakistan. Nor has she mentioned how her paternal grandfather was dragged off the train and held back in Mandi Bahauddin for over six months after Partition.

She inhales sharply. 'I think when you are witnessing something like Partition, everything is robotic. There is no time to think or weep or even plan. When I now look back, I think about the chaos and unplanned migration. *Chalo, chalo, chalo,*' she says, moving her arms by her side, as if herding a crowd. 'There was no time to think, there was no control over the circumstances. All their actions were mechanical, on autopilot, which lasted some years, I'd say. But after Partition, their difficulties in India – economic and social – had to be overcome through scrupulous planning and saving, and working tirelessly.'

I nod. 'I always think about how if something like this were to happen today, we may not have a contingency plan. We have no structure in place for this magnitude of man-made tragedy. We just don't expect it and so we don't prepare for it ... just like in 1947.'

A silence lingers for a few seconds, and just when I think the conversation has come to an end, she speaks again. Her eyes are distant but her words are precise. 'I feel as though the Partition made my parents harden up, in the same way a child does when an entire childhood is snatched away from them violently overnight. I think that's what they did; they shut their feelings deep inside their hearts. It may not have appeared obvious on the surface, but now when I think about their manner of being, it was toughened by an unthinkable experience.'[2]

That afternoon, my aunt leaves me with a memory both sad and beautiful. In 1999, the first bus service, *Sada-e-Sarhad*, Call of the Frontier, between India and Pakistan was launched in an effort by both governments to improve relationships. Running between Delhi and Lahore, on its inaugural trip in February, the bus carried the then Prime Minister of India, Atal Bihari Vajpayee, who travelled to attend a summit in Lahore and was received at Wagah by his counterpart, Nawaz Sharif. Passenger journeys began in March, and my aunt remembers watching this on the news with my grandmother.

'The first passenger got off the bus and walked over to the border. And when he stepped over onto the other side, he got down on his knees and touched his head to the ground. *Mattha zameen pe teka.* He must have migrated from that side in 1947 and this was the first time he was able to return to his soil. Suddenly, I realized that mummy was crying. She was watching the news very intently and there were tears flowing down her face. I remember asking her what happened, and through her tears she had said, "*Mein kadey jawaangi apni dharti?* When will I be able to visit my land?" That was the first time I realized that there was so much in her heart that had not been expressed. Probably the longing for that happy childhood ... I can spend a lot of time thinking about all the things her silence about Partition meant, but it was this one incident that encapsulated it for me.'

'SOMETIMES, I USED to overhear conversations between my mother and bhuaji, fleeting conversations. I don't think I was older than ten or eleven, but I did ask at the time and she wasn't very open to talking.'

I am on a video call with my eldest aunt, Neeraj, who has lived in Montreal since she was married in 1977. Every memory she recounts from her childhood includes bhuaji – Swaran Lata, my grandfather's adoptive sister and my grandmother's closest confidante.*

'I would ask my mother whether she had come from Pakistan...'

'Did you know that the two countries had once been one?' I ask.

'Well, not really. I just knew that it was our neighbour, but nothing about the animosity between the two countries. She never

---

* A brief description of my grandparents' friendship with bhuaji can be found in Chapter 7, '*Friendship*'.

wanted to talk about it, and I remember the expression on her face changing immediately. It would become a very stern look, and as a child I was very afraid that these kinds of conversations would lead to her temper flaring or mood changing. Then the mood changes would always become migraines...' She looks into the distance and I follow her gaze to the edge of my computer screen. 'You see, when something enters her mind, something serious, something deep, it doesn't leave easily. She keeps thinking about it, obsessing over it. And at the age of ten, I couldn't understand that my seemingly innocent question could cause her long-term pain. At that age, all I understood was that if I continued to ask these questions, then her mood would go sour and she would get a migraine and then I would have to massage her head and she wouldn't make dinner and we would go hungry!' she laughs. 'That was my complete thought process, and so I learnt this way not to probe further.'

I begin to ask my next question, but she has an interesting observation to add.

'I remember my mother's family – my aunts, my grandmother – they all had the same stern look on their faces constantly. And as a child, I always used to think, "Why are they so unhappy, *itne dukhi kyu rehte hain saare time?*" I never knew what kind of hardships they had seen growing up. But I know that I would've crumbled if such a thing happened to me. I think that their defence mechanism – the only way they knew to protect themselves from feeling anything about Partition – was to build a wall around themselves. They distanced themselves, even from its memory, from any utterance of it. This is what I feel my mother's family did. They all built a wall around themselves so that nothing would affect them further. And that gave them that sternness, that severity.'

'Did your father have that sternness?' I ask, curious.

My aunt smiles at the mention of her father. She and I were part of the final moments of his life; we were both in the hospital when he passed – she by his bedside, I standing at the threshold of the room, unable to enter. When I was born, my grandfather was sixty-two years old. When I got to know him, he barely had any years left.

When I really understood him, he was gone within months. From everybody's memory of him as a young man, I have learnt that he was hot-headed, he had a fire in him. But in my memory, he is a gentle and hard-working man, completely self-made. A man I cannot write about without breaking down.

'I always found that I could have a better conversation with my father when he was in his bookshop,' she says through her smile. 'He was always more relaxed there, more open. And though he never volunteered information either, I did ask him a couple of times and he always answered me briefly. He told me that they used to live in Pakistan and had to come to Delhi during Partition.

'But the person who was most open with me was bhuaji. Our parents were always working and so it was she who took care of us, basically raised us. When I was in high school, I started having real conversations with her about my parents' experiences of migrating to India; it was she who told me about the hardships. But the conversations never began with the word Partition. Curiously, they always began with the importance of education and how courageous my great-grandmother was to have, even as a single mother at that time, focused on educating her daughters rather than marrying them off at young ages. From there, we segued into Partition, the uprootedness, and their life in the camp.'

'Did your mother's reluctance to talk about that time make more sense to you, then?'

She thinks about this for a few seconds, as if making sure that she remembers rightly. 'I truly understood it only when I got married and moved to Canada. I was older and more mature, of course, but I was also away from my own country, and that changed the way I looked at where my parents were born – the fact that there was now a border between them and their homeland. At the age of ten, you don't understand the implication of a border: so they took a train and came to India, I couldn't see the big deal in it.'

She smiles sadly, and I replicate it. I already know what she is going to say and it's already breaking my heart. So often in childhood we are cruel to our parents, so quickly we judge their behaviours, so little we comprehend their histories – in some cases, as in this, histories complex and suppressed.

With a deep sigh, she continues, 'After marriage, I used to relish the joy of going back to India, back home – to family, to land. That's when I understood that they could never experience that, they would never be able to go back and see their land. And I also feel that when you *visit* your parents, and not *live* with them, they begin seeing you differently. They open up more, begin sharing, as my mother did. But this came very slowly and gradually.'

There is a seriousness to these conversations, a space that is new and unfamiliar, particularly when put in the context of the extent of intimacy found in South Asian families. The wall between generations is gradually dissolving and, through my questions, emotions that are usually concealed deep within come to the surface. I want to be able to look at my family objectively, trace the storylines and connect the dots in a way that any researcher would do with a family they are working with. But it is too difficult not to be subjective. Their history is my history, and somewhere down the line in their stories begins my story.

'Do you think certain habits or qualities of your parents have been shaped by Partition?' I am tempted to contribute my own observations on the subject, but I am interested in what she may say.

'Yes, for sure. My mother never trusts anyone, from the outset. And it definitely comes from the fact that just before and during Partition her family could rely on no one but themselves to survive. You must know this, that after her father passed away, her mother was cheated out of family property, had to leave the ancestral house, and had to begin working to support her children. My mother once said this to me too, that if one's whole childhood has been shaped by mistrust, it becomes your default. And the second is her tendency to hoard things, just in case she may need them later. This stems purely from lack of resources, because when you don't have enough, you have a propensity to hoard what you do have, not let go of even the smallest thing – be it food or extra cloth or wool or even buttons. Even if you are not in that position any more, the habit has become your nature so that you cannot throw away anything. Even now, when I open her box bed, I find sweaters she used to wear to office in the '50s. If I tell her that she needs to throw them, she always responds with, "*Jab mein mar jaoongi toh phenk dena*, you can throw them when I die."'

I nod vigorously, all too familiar with the office sweaters, crepe saris and handmade woollen coats from her Ministry days, wrapped in old blankets and peppered with naphthalene balls.

'When you understood the sheer scale of Partition,' I advance towards a more serious question, 'how many people it affected, how many families it tore apart, the violence, the trauma, the immensity of loss on both sides – how did it make you feel to know that both your parents had witnessed it?'

'I felt horrible,' she answers in a small voice, 'horrible for having judged them growing up. They inherited habits they could not have helped.'

'And do you think your childhood was shaped by the after-effects of Partition?' She was born a decade after Partition, at a time when her parents had only just begun getting back on their feet.

There is a long pause.

'I don't know how to answer that, *beta*. Our parents were always very strict with us...'

She thinks about this some more and then continues, 'Well, the word was never spoken in our house, not even in passing. My parents never talked about it amongst themselves. But my father's mother, mataji, would speak about it, the loss, the sadness, *kitna dukh dekha batware ke dauran*. She would talk about it when all of us cousins got together – Deepali, Rashmi, I, we were the grown-up cousins. And when you're together, you probe more, you feel more confident asking things. And anyway, you have a different kind of affinity with your grandparents. So, she would tell us these stories.'

I think about the relationship I have with my grandmother and the ease and deftness with which I can ask her questions about her life, and this makes sense. I think about the impending conversation with my father – the sheer fact that I have left it for last, even though he is the most accessible to me.

Somewhere, somehow, a generation is always bypassed.

To bring our conversation to a close, I ask my aunt what she feels when she thinks of Partition.

'Anger,' she answers, without missing a beat.

'Because of the suffering your parents had to endure?'

'No, because of the fact that Indians killed Indians, under someone else's direction.' Suddenly she breaks down and I am taken aback. She has remained so calm throughout our entire conversation that I am completely unprepared for this.

'It's like a family,' she says, tears streaming down her face. 'How can I betray my family? Were we that weak as a society?'

She pauses to wipe her eyes and I stare at the screen.

'This is what I fail to understand. How did it happen? It was Indians against Indians. Us against us, under the direction of a foreign rule, and that I will never understand. I just fail to understand. Even more so now when there is no foreign rule and such violence keeps happening in the country.'

There is silence for a few seconds before I respond, 'I thought you would say something more personal.'

'Isn't this the heart of it, though? How did it happen? We were *so* many!' Her voice is passionate and exasperated. 'We could have prevented this, could have stood up against it. Anyway, this is what has stayed with me to date. Of course, all the suffering of my own family pains me, but *this* is incomprehensible.'

'So the anger begins with the conquest, the colonization.'

'Yes, and to get personal, my parents and so many others – Hindus, Muslims, Sikhs, friends, neighbours, brothers – became puppets in the hands of the British. *How* did it happen, *why* did it happen?'

In the journal that the Urdu satirist and columnist Fikr Taunsvi kept while continuing to live in Lahore as a Hindu for four months after Partition, he writes about rivers of blood and days of darkness, how both parts of the Punjab had become the battlefields of Cain and Abel, for Partition had separated one brother from another. On 2 September 1947, with anguish and bewilderment, he asks, '*Why* is this happening? Why is *this* happening? Why *is* this happening?'[3]

'PARTITION WAS JUST a word for us. It never meant anything, at least not to me.'

My father, Anuj, is matter-of-fact, always has been.

'My parents never gave me any reason to ask anything. They never called it "the other side" or "*sarhad paar*", or "*uss taraf*", but just the name of the city or village they had come from. Partition was not a subject discussed at home, but if they did ever talk about the past, it was with bhuaji. This is how my sisters have collected stories: from her, woman to woman. But Partition has not shaped my life in any way, except that it brought my parents to achievements that would have otherwise been unachievable. They truly never gave us a reason to ask about it, though.'

He ends this sentence in a way that makes me think he has concluded our conversation, and goes back to removing the skins off a bowl of peanuts kept before him on the table, rubbing a few together between his palms. As I watch this, it strikes me that maybe I am looking for answers where there are none. Why does Partition affect me more than it does my father – both my parents, actually. Why should a decades-old event that impacted both their parents bypass their generation altogether and find its way to me, becoming almost an obsession? I don't have the answer yet.

'When you started your publishing house in 2002, you commissioned a fair bit on Partition,' I remark.

From 1978 onwards, while he was still in school, my father began working with his father at our bookshop. In 2002, along with that, he began a niche publishing house called India Research Press, which published non-fiction, primarily academic works on politics, culture, history and socio-economic and ecological issues affecting the subcontinent. In its early years, the press produced a staggeringly large number of books on the Partition of India.

'Yes,' he replies coolly, 'because that's the time my curiosity grew. All of a sudden, everyone around me was talking about Partition.'

'Did something happen for them to be doing that?'

He shrugs. 'It just so happened that the kind of books that came my way were on Partition, and it was something I enjoyed working on. As simple as that.'

But it really wasn't as simple, and so I prod further. 'The very first book you did...'

'*Lahore 1947*, edited by Ahmad Salim.[4] Stories and essays by all the wonderful Lahoris!' My father recounts the details of the book with ease, his eyes twinkling. 'There was an excerpt from Fikr Taunsvi's journal; Alys Faiz wrote about her journey from Srinagar to Lahore; B.C. Sanyal wrote about leaving Lahore; Satish Gujral wrote about Lahore burning; there were pieces by Khushwant Singh, Pran Nevile, Amrita Pritam, Jahanara Shah Nawaz. We did a lot of research for this book. I mean, it was not the kind of research *you* do, mine was very cursory in comparison. But I did it so that I could understand the subject of Partition better ... for the purpose of the book.'

I nod and make a note. Later, as I flip through the pages of the book, I realize that the dedication is written by him as the publisher. Fairly unusual, as this beloved task is generally assumed by the author or the editor of an anthology. But perhaps given that this was his very first book, my father felt compelled to write it. The words stare up at me, and I think about how matter-of-fact our conversation was, how I grasped at the ends of something, *anything* emotional. My thumb caresses the page as I whisper the dedication that perhaps reveals more than anything that he says ever will: '*To the people of India and Pakistan, for whom, in search of hope, time has remained still and memories grown deeper* – Anuj Bahri, Publisher.'

'While working on this book, then, did you feel the need to know more about your own family?'

'Well, that is how it started.' His tone is softer now. 'That's why I began recording my father, that's how the idea of the book came into being.'

The book.

In 2002, my father was forty years old, and my grandfather was seventy-four. The next year, 2003, would be my grandfather's seventy-fifth birthday and the fiftieth anniversary of the bookshop. My father decided that a gift befitting the occasion would be a biography of my grandfather – from Malakwal to Delhi, college student to bookseller, refugee to entrepreneur – and so he began to ask him about his life.

'I asked where they had come from, and he wouldn't really indulge me. He would say "we had so-and-so canals of land" or "my father was a bank manager" but nothing deeper, and certainly nothing about the actual process of migration during Partition.'

I ask why my grandfather didn't answer any of his questions.

'I don't know. These things take time. You see, like us, here, you have the patience to persist on while I continue to eat peanuts throughout our conversation,' he laughs. 'So my father would also do similar things when I tried to have a serious conversation, and then I would get irritated and...' He trails off.

'Do you think it was a way of deflection?'

'Of course, completely. He answered to an extent, but then he brushed the topic aside. So, I decided that if he wouldn't speak to me, maybe he would speak to someone else, and I requested my editor at the time, Debbie, to interview him. And sure enough, he began talking to her, filling tape after tape with details of his life before and after Partition. He talked to her, but not to me.'

As he says this, there is no sadness or bitterness to be found in his voice. It was what it was. When I ask him if this hurt him, he scoffs. 'Not at all, it was understandable. Because they were unpleasant memories. If it were me, I wouldn't want to give such memories to you...'

He clears his throat and continues, 'So Debbie would record him on these little Dictaphone tapes, and at night I would listen, transcribe, write, and then in the morning I would give her a new set of questions to ask. I think she must have spoken to him for thirty or forty days.'

'In fact, I actually remember reading what you wrote each morning,' my mother, Rajni, chimes in.

The thought of collaborative manuscript writing makes me smile. 'Where are the tapes?'

My parents begin discussing whether the tapes are in some old drawer at the bookshop, or could they possibly be somewhere at home, or if the transcripts are on the computer, or if an original draft of the biography is lying somewhere. I am anxious, I *need* to listen to these tapes. In the months before my grandfather died, I interviewed him extensively as well. He was reluctant at first, but he gave in eventually. He softened, he relented, offering his history to me without much fuss. It was not over thirty or forty days, but I think he provided a complete history. Now, I wonder, *what more will I find out from these tapes, how much more complete can a complete history be? What all do I not know? How will I feel listening to his voice again?* Meanwhile, my parents have arrived at the conclusion that no one knows where the tapes are, and I am torn between regret and relief. Perhaps they will turn up when we least expect them to.

'So ... uh, when you were listening to the tapes, could you envision their journey to India?'

'I could connect the dots, yes,' my father says. 'The one scene I could see before my eyes was when the traders barged into the halted train at Mandi Bahauddin station and dragged my grandfather off, keeping him in Pakistan for the next six months so that he could train new employees in the running of the bank. He used to be its manager before Partition. In that scene, I could imagine my father repeating the words animatedly, "Daryay Lal, Daryay Lal, Daryay Lal *kahan hai*?" When you listen to him on the tapes, you can imagine him telling the story, sitting with his arms folded and eyes closed. "Well, you know" – he would start every answer this way. You get an idea of what his feelings are through the tapes. But he never once cried during the entire recording, he wasn't emotional. Very matter-of-fact.'

A family trait, then.

'Did they make you see your own family differently?'

'No, it was just history – someone having lived their life and then recreating it through memory.'

'But it did make you understand their adversity once in India,' my mother says to my father, 'Like how mataji had to sell her bangles so that he could buy the Khan Market shop, or all the odd jobs he was forced to do at the beginning just so they could survive. When I was reading the manuscript, I certainly thought about these things. I would get torn up reading what you wrote; I'd never thought about them before.'

'It was the situation they were in, Rajni, it was the circumstance, and what they could do to make it better. What I do remember clearly from the tapes was the section about the food they cooked in the communal kitchen at the camp. How they would celebrate when there was more than one dish made, maybe a dal *and* vegetables on a special occasion.'

'I don't remember that section being very long in the book,'[5] I say, wrinkling my eyebrows.

'It was condensed to a paragraph or two, but in the tapes it was a long-drawn-out section. My father elaborated on this quite a bit: how every day his mother would speak to the family over food. It made emotional sense to me. That no matter what is available, the woman actually has a way of satisfying everybody in the family, how she elevates even that meagre meal to the status of a feast. She convinces everybody that, "Look, this is what we have today, maybe tomorrow will be better. Not maybe, tomorrow *will* be better." It's always the woman, you must understand. A woman works very hard and has great power to keep the family together. Post Partition, it was women who kept the family structure intact. It is an important part of womanhood; men just don't have it.'

I bite my lip, wishing these parts had been in the book.

Bahrisons: Chronicle of a Bookshop was ultimately published as a rather slim book, one hundred and seven pages. It was presented to my grandfather on his seventy-fifth birthday in October 2003 at a big event on the lawns of the Ambassador hotel. Mrs Sheila Dixit, the chief minister of Delhi at the time, released the book. The night was alive with the songs of qawwali-wallahs, and my grandfather was incredibly pleased. A life had been deservingly commemorated. But my father tells me that the original manuscript was nearly four or five hundred pages and then they cut it down as per editorial suggestions. More general, more impersonal. When I ask him why, he is quick to admit that it was bad judgement, for it became very distanced. He didn't think at the time that people would be drawn to such a personal biography or memoir.

'In hindsight, I think I was wrong. It is these very personal, nuanced details that build the landscape of Partition. I should find those tapes and rewrite it. Maybe I can do it again. Maybe you can?'

My final question to my father is less a question and more a confirmation.

'Do you have any regrets that your father chose not to speak to you about Partition, and spoke to Debbie instead?' This question is more personal than any other, because I wonder now how I would feel if all the family members I had interviewed for my work over the years had preferred speaking to a scholar or a stranger.

'No, he wouldn't talk to me. How can I regret something I can't help?'

'You don't speak to your children about these things, though,' my mother offers, 'because, well, I've never asked my parents anything about Lahore either...'

'And, Aanchal,' my father adds, 'have you ever asked me about my childhood?'

'Well, no...' I reply in a small voice. Perhaps they have a point.

'I think there is an intrigue about your grandparents that your parents don't possess.' My mother is thinking out loud. 'I don't know if we consider our roots to begin from our parents. We always want them to go further back into our ancestry – grandparents, great-grandparents...'

When I ask my parents what they say if someone asks where they are from, they both agree that where you are born is where you are from. By that standard, my father is from Delhi and my mother is from Toronto, even though his parents are from D.I. Khan and Malakwal, and hers are from Lahore and Amritsar. So why do I feel conflicted about where I am from? This is a vast question, and I am daunted by this sense of belonging to several places at once, places on this side and that side of the Radcliffe Line, places that I was born and grew up in, places my grandparents were born in and fled from. I feel as though I am casting a very large, very fragile net across the expanse of my ancestry, claiming several places as my own.

AT THE END, I return, overwhelmed with information, to where I began. When I tell my grandmother I have been speaking to her children about Partition for the last several weeks, she raises her eyebrows to say, '*Yeh kaisi research thi*, what kind of research was this?'

I laugh and sit down next to her on the bed. She does not understand my obsession with talking about Partition and, truth be told, nor do I. Part of me is ashamed of bringing up the subject again, but these conversations with my father and his siblings have led me to ponder something crucial.

'Did you think,' I ask my grandmother, 'that subsequent generations of your family would ever be interested in knowing about your experiences of Partition?'

I am not surprised when she answers very quickly in the negative. 'I didn't think the event would matter after it happened, or that anyone would put it in books or interview the people who had lived through it. I couldn't even imagine any of our children or grandchildren asking, thinking or writing about Partition.' When she looks at me, I am unable to read her face. This is an expression I don't recognize.

'We never wanted to burden them with our memories. *Jo humara dukh tha woh humare tak hi rehta*, we wanted the sadness to end with us, to remain in our generation, to never be passed down.'

2
Belonging

⚘

IN 1909, THE FOUNDATION for a three-storey haveli called Shams Manzil was laid in Jullundur. Built as a corner home in Ali Mohalla, off G.T. Road, it was where Mian Faiz Rabbani was born in 1931. Sixteen years later, in 1947, he and his family migrated with much difficulty to Lyallpur (now Faisalabad) in Pakistan. The sprawling haveli of Shams Manzil was left behind in a now independent India, and eventually divided into four sections. Three of those, purchased by the Thakur brothers, were renamed as Durga Bhavan. Then, in the late 1950s, Prem Kaur Anand purchased the fourth – what was originally the front of Shams Manzil – and kept the original name intact. Twenty-five years after Partition, Faiz Rabbani, now in his early forties, filled with longing for his homeland, travelled to India to visit Shams Manzil and was delighted to find the building still standing.

He was invited in for breakfast by Prem Kaur Anand's son, Upkar Singh Anand, then in his mid-forties, who, on learning the identity of Rabbani sahib, referred to him as '*ghar de maalik*', owner of the home, and proudly pointed to the stone plaque at the entrance still bearing its name. Overcome with emotion, Faiz Rabbani returned to Pakistan with the assurance that the home his grandfather had built was still loved and cared for. In 2007, Shams Manzil was sold and, in 2008, ninety-nine years after it was first built, the semi-demolished site was visited by his niece, Samar, and her husband,

Air Commodore Kaiser Tufail. On the phone, they spoke with Upkar Anand, who allowed them to carry the still-intact name plaque of the house back to Lahore with them. In this way, a part of Shams Manzil, a part of Jullundur, was returned to Mian Faiz Rabbani, who in turn showed it to me during my visit to Lahore in 2014.[1]

Several years after that, in late 2020, I receive an email from New Jersey-based sisters Amneet and Puneet Anand. Puneet had just purchased a copy of the American edition of *Remnants* for her grandfather, Upkar Singh Anand, whom they call nanapapa. While skimming through my book, he came across a photograph of the plaque of Shams Manzil and recognized it immediately. His daughter, Jasjot, or Joti, did not initially believe him, but he was insistent that this was, indeed, the plaque from their home.

When I receive their email, I am filled with awe at the power of the internet, and find myself hoping that this is the Sikh gentleman who welcomed Mian Faiz Rabbani during his visit. The sisters send me a photograph of a page from their grandfather's old journal that bears Air Commodore Kaiser Tufail's address in Lahore. The coincidences are overwhelming, and I propose that we set up a video call with their grandfather, who is now ninety-three and living with them in New Jersey.

In November 2020, I finally speak to Upkar Singh Anand, who migrated from Rawalpindi during Partition as a nineteen-year-old in his second year of college. He recalls how his elder brother, who had retired from the army, came running home one day in March 1947 – the days of which would ultimately be known as the Rape of Rawalpindi – to tell the family that they must be ready to fight: "*Muqabale ke liye tayyar raho.*" But the family only migrated in July 1947, travelling from Rawalpindi to Ferozepur, and further to Dehra Dun, where his cousin was a divisional forest officer. Eventually, they settled in Jalandhar and were allocated a property near Ali Mohalla, and nearly a decade later is when Shams Manzil was purchased by Prem Kaur Anand. It was in this way that the stone plaque of Mian Faiz Rabbani came to share its ownership with Upkar Singh Anand.

When I ask him about the photograph of the plaque in my book, he says in Urdu that not only has he seen the haveli with his eyes, but has also lived his life in it. *'Humne toh apni aankhon se dekhi hai, apni zindagi issi mein guzari hai.'* From memory, he recites some broken verses written on the plaque.

In the far end of the room sit his granddaughters, Puneet, born in 1990, and Amneet, born in 1993. Beside him is his daughter, Joti. I ask about Mian Faiz Rabbani's visit, and he begins to search for any record of it in the pile of old journals on the table. He holds up Kaiser Tufail's Lahori address, for now his memory is betraying him with age. But Joti, who was around ten years old at the time, reminds her father of the visit, and it becomes clear that the Sikh gentleman who welcomed Mian Faiz Rabbani back into his home was indeed Upkar Singh. She confirms that it happened in the same way as described in my book, that not only did a Pakistani gentleman visit the haveli but also, years later, when they no longer lived in the house, they received a phone call seeking permission to carry the plaque to Pakistan. Then, awash with emotion, she tells me that she and her brother were born in that house.

'Everything goes back to Shams Manzil,' she says lovingly.

For the next two hours, the conversation spans Partition and migration, memory and home, continuing in Urdu for the most part, for I am told that it's his mother tongue. Upkar Singh speaks slowly and softly, as much with his voice as with his hands. When I ask him whether he has told his granddaughters about Partition, he sighs and says that though he has, the days are not worth remembering. His family didn't think that Partition would be permanent and took only a suitcase of summer clothes. He later lamented that Rawalpindi had been left behind and that India had been so brutally divided. But reminiscing the days now, he tells me that he belongs to the undivided land and cannot forget those memories.

'Hindustan aur Pakistan alag thodi na ho sakte hain. Yeh yaadein toh apni jaan ke saath hi jayengi.'

The old journals on the table are his pride – some belonging to him and some to his father – and can be traced back to before his childhood. He tells me there is a *shajra-e-nasab*, a family tree, written by his grandfather in 1908, and describes how his walid sahib was tall and regal, '*shandaar*', and his walida was demure and beautiful. Recalling life through poetry, he embroiders much of our conversation with it.

This interview has enlivened him and charmed me, and beaming directly into the camera he says with contentment, '*Aaj kisi ne apne paimane se pehchana hai.*' When his granddaughters, who understand bits of Urdu, ask what that means, I mirror his smile and reply, 'Today someone has recognized him by his own measure.'

We talk past midnight in Delhi and midday in New Jersey, and before we disconnect the call he pensively states that the career path I have chosen – in writing about Partition – is a gravely difficult one. '*Jo raasta aapne pakda hai woh bohot muskhil hai.*'

'Why do you say that?' I ask, though I too feel this every day.

'*Duniya dekh ke keh raha hoon,*' he says sincerely, having seen the depths of the world.

WEEKS LATER, I receive an email from his elder granddaughter, Puneet, who works as an English educator in New Jersey. During one of our earlier conversations, she had mentioned that Partition often finds its way into her writing and mediations:

> How has Partition shaped me? Partition has completely changed me … I started to become aware of just how much the trauma externally shaped the countries of India, Pakistan and Bangladesh, but I was just not yet aware of the internal trauma carried by the silences of generations past, by our families, by our own parents even. My body became more aware of just how deep the undercurrents of this trauma ran, when specifically exposed to literature of Partition.

It was the haunting stories of Saadat Hasan Manto – 'Khol Do', 'Toba Tek Singh', 'Thanda Ghosht' – that left a deep impact, a feeling of hollowness within her, and enabled her to ask her grandfather questions.

> I started understanding why Nanapapa's mother tongue was Urdu. He spoke once when I was in high school, of his family thinking he was dead. It wasn't until I read about the ghost trains that I realized just what had happened. His family had a funeral for him. He never spoke of it again. I couldn't find the words to ask again.

Upon reading this, I am filled with terror, for despite everything we ventured into during our interview, he never mentioned anything of this sort. When I ask her about it, she tells me that the miscommunication happened during the migration to India, and though she can carefully ask her grandfather again, it is the sole detail that he has always remained very quiet about. So, I probe no further. But several weeks later, she sends me a video of her grandfather where he is seated in a chair and Joti is asking him about the days of Partition. It takes him a few moments to locate himself back in time; he is confused by her questions at first but eventually arrives at the moment of migration, switching between Urdu and English.

'I sent everyone from Rawalpindi and came later, with my grandfather and a few other people, on a train that was full of Muslims. Barely any Hindu–Sikhs. The train passed through Gujrat and Gujranwala and, on the way, we saw Muslims fleeing from the Hindu–Sikh areas. *Fleeing, just fleeing*.' He repeats this loudly, with his arms stretched above his head and eyes faraway, as if looking out the train and into the distance.

With measured words, Joti reminds him that he was supposed to have boarded an earlier train, in which no one finally survived, and her father listens to her, eyes still faraway. There is dread in her voice, and even while watching this on video I can understand what she means. Suddenly, Upkar Singh too picks up on it.

'Ohhhh,' he says slowly, 'yes.'

'What happened, everyone was ... slaughtered on it?'

'The train we boarded at Mano Majra – uh … no, the name, I cannot…' He moves his fingers in the air as if trying to physically grasp the name of a village. Listening to him breaks my heart, for lived and collected memory has intersected in a way that is indistinguishable from each other, creating a new genre – Mano Majra is the fictional village in Khushwant Singh's *Train to Pakistan*. But setting the detail aside, Upkar Singh continues his story about the train they were lucky to not have boarded. 'This train was full of … what happened? Everybody was slaughtered. The people inside the train, they were…'

'The train going from Pakistan to India? *Uss train ich*, most of them were Hindu–Sikh…' Joti confirms.

'*Uss train ich…*' her father repeats slowly, trying to recall.

'*Kisi ne aake maar ditta saari train nu?*' she asks, now in Punjabi, whether everyone was killed.

'*Maar diya, Hindu–Sikha nu maar diya,*' he confirms.

'But your family was expecting you, and when you did not reach, they assumed you had died.'

'Family was in Ferozepur at the time, and they found out we were late, and thought we had died. *Kriya karam bhi kar ditta sada, mera khayal hai,*' he recalls how they had indeed had a funeral.

'*Ardas kar ditta.*' There is a heaviness to Joti's voice as she asks about the final prayer performed at the end of a life.

'They thought *ke yeh ab swaranvaasi ho gaye hain.*' He folds his hands and gestures to heaven.

As the video concludes, Upkar Singh narrates how they finally reached Ferozepur, where someone provided them shelter for a little while, after which they travelled to Dehra Dun and were united with the rest of his family.

In her email, Puneet maintains that even now she continues the dialogue with her nanapapa, collecting 'snippets of memories'. She is particular about telling me that they speak not when he is in a good mood or a bad mood, but in an 'open mood', for he is the type of person 'who narrates the breadth of his feelings, emotions or losses through the realm of Urdu poetry'. When I read this, I smile, for I am witness to it. Sometimes Puneet understands the words and at other times her mother steps in as the in-between generation, translating the Urdu to Punjabi or Hindi in a way that offers her more insight. And there it is – 'three generations of understanding, spanned over two different continents, mulling over one concept'. Asserting that these memories and visions are so powerful, she writes,

> ...people may die, but the lives they created do not. Those lives are preserved in the essence of everything they touched, every place they passed. At some point, Shams Manzil, India, the history of Partition, Pakistan, new borders, old borders, all of this blurs. When I connect, I am there. When I connect, I am with them. When I connect, I am a fuller me. This is my rendering of just how much the Partition has shaped me. My nanapapa is and has always been a gateway – and gatekeeper – of my history, identity, and ancestors, and I revere him for that ... If I can keep even a little bit of these truths – these memories – alive, I have done right by him and right by myself. I am rooted to him, to our lands, to our history, and to these lost stories. I remember, so future generations can remember.

As a South Asian educator, Puneet often discusses Partition with her students. And while showing them the maps of Pakistan and India, she feels that she does not just point to Rawalpindi as 'an external location on a two-dimensional plain', but points just as much inwards, to herself. 'The more I read the map, understanding it so that I can further pass on the understanding to my students, the clearer my internal coordinates become.' Her sense of belonging runs deeper than the creation of nation states and frontiers; it is tethered to soil and its inherited memory. There is a calling that pulls her closer to the 'roots bound to Rawalpindi, to a space and time before borders, to the true "home" of [her] ancestors'.[2]

⟆

TO SAY THAT Puneet's words resonate would be an understatement, for too many times have I pored over old maps with great investment and intrigue to see where my grandparents migrated from. I grew up in the metropolis of Delhi, laying claim to no village, no ancestral land, no place of origin in the country where I was born, for all that now lay across the border. My grandparents' houses were the ones they had built post-Partition, in refugee rehabilitation colonies. In that sense, there is something fundamentally binding when I see the places once associated with them – Lahore, Muryali, Dera Ismail Khan, Malakwal, Qadirabad – printed anywhere, even in this inanimate way, for they are my origin. There is an urge to graze my fingers over the words, claim them, even though I know deep down that they are already mine.

Some time in the early months of 2020, my mother discovered a stack of certificates belonging to my father's great-grandfather, Lala Bidhi Chand, who worked in the Indian Imperial Police. Based on his police records, we can trace his three-decade-long career – from a Sergeant 2nd grade in 1874 to a full Deputy Inspector in 1904, appointed to census duty in 1891 and to plague duty in 1898. The son of Atma Ram, a Hindu Pathan of Qadirabad, Bidhi Chand's documents show him serving across undivided Punjab, in the districts of Sargodha, Mandi Bahauddin, Gujranwala, Jhelum and Rawalpindi.[3] But it was in the most mundane details of these commendation certificates – lines that read 'Resident of Qadirabad, Gujrat' – that I found solace. It was the first time I had seen the place where my paternal grandfather's family hailed from documented formally, and it filled me with an indescribably strong sense of belonging.

The only other moment when I had felt this connection to Qadirabad was in February 2016, when my grandfather passed away and we travelled to Haridwar to immerse his ashes in the Ganga. At Har ki Pauri, we looked for a small hut with a red flag to visit the priest who kept our family records, so that we could perform the *pind-daan* ceremony for my grandfather, as an homage to his departed soul.

'The Malhotras from Qadirabad,' my father announced once we entered the hut, and it was the first time I had heard him claim a place with such conviction. Suddenly, all borders lay invalid, even the most militarized ones, for when it came to origin, my father had crossed the Radcliffe Line within seconds, and arrived at the home of his ancestors.

From a corner of the hut, a priest only a few years older than myself retrieved a large oval-shaped bundle covered in dark grey cloth and further protected with a red cloth. When he unravelled it, the object within resembled the inside of tree bark, whose every line was a separate sheet of paper. This was called a *pothi* or a *panda-pothi*, a record which may go back up to two or three centuries. He turned page after page, trying to find our family tree, and then pausing on a deep mustard coloured sheet with Devanagari text across it, he asked my father to confirm the names of his forefathers.

'Anuj Bahri, *Delhi*. Balraj Bahri, *Malakwal*. Daryayl Lal, *Qadirabad*. Bidhi Chand, *Qadirabad*. Atma Ram, *Qadirabad*,' my father listed five generations and nearly a hundred and fifty years of family history with ease. But the further back he went in our genealogy, the deeper into an undivided India he traversed. And with each name, the priest nodded, checking the *pothi*. Satisfied, he made the notation of my grandfather's demise right next to his elder brothers', reuniting them once again in death.

'The Malhotras from Qadirabad,' the priest stated, rolling the *pothi* up into its oval, bark shape again.

That was the moment I realized it – that my connection to independent India, to Delhi, could be traced back to only *one* generation. My father. The birthplace of every generation before him, the heart of their belonging, lay now in a land called Pakistan.

BUT FOR MANY, this sense of belonging to a borderless land is brought on by conversations that prompt them to descend deeper into themselves. Belonging, thus, is not always looming on the surface, but can be embedded deep within, and emerges only when exhumed.

It is only after a while in our conversation that Ali Abbasi, born in the late 1980s and based in Ireland, even arrives at the condition that belonging may not be a physical place but a sense we carry in our bodies and pass down the generations. Having grown up in Dubai with friends from the three countries of erstwhile British India, Ali recalls the casual nature with which he was told about how Pakistan and India were once one, after which Pakistan and Bangladesh were once one, until they all became separate, independent states. The tangible link to Partition was his maternal grandmother, Hashmat Siddiqui, whom he would visit during holidays in Pakistan. The youngest of nine siblings, she was born in 1938 in Delhi.

'I don't think I would have asked her anything about it, but it was such an important part of her life that she felt the need to tell us about Delhi and her migration from there during Partition. It is an identifying moment for her, when they *chose* to become Pakistani. And even though it was a choice, all her stories betrayed a sense of sacrifice for what had been left behind.'

'What do you mean?' I ask.

'Well, she would always tell me stories about how her family – whose last name is Taimuri – are direct descendants of the Mughals. I don't talk about this a lot, since I couldn't gauge the veracity of her stories, but the moment of migration due to Partition was also a moment of great loss for her. It was a fall from grace; a denial of lifestyle and land…' He thinks about this for a few seconds before continuing, 'You see, I haven't ever put much faith into the established structures of power or identity. So, when I was young and living in Dubai, my being Pakistani was not an active part of my identity, because there was so much amalgamation between people there. You could dissolve into a general subcontinental identity, and it was extraordinary. Of course, I thought it was cool that my nani descended from nobility, but it ended at that. Perhaps if I was raised in Pakistan, it may have been different, the enormity of Partition may have affected me more, as would its losses.'

As I listen to Ali, I feel almost envious of how nonchalant he is, and part of me immediately cringes at how seriously I take my ancestry. Notwithstanding his matter-of-factness, I wonder whether he has ever felt a kinship towards Delhi, the city of his grandmother's birth.

He smiles widely. 'It was in my early twenties that I realized that we were different from other people in Pakistan. That we were not Punjabi, or Sindhi, or Balochi. So, who were *my* people and what was *our* legacy? We were *muhajir*,[4] and that naturally brought me back to India. I suppose that Partition is the starting point – both the beginning and the end of something...

'Both sides of my family come from India – my paternal side were from Amroha in present-day Uttar Pradesh; they migrated to Lahore and were able to assimilate into the culture and land. They very much became Lahoris. My maternal side came from Delhi to Lahore, then continued on to Karachi, and it is on this side that there is a sense of belonging elsewhere, to a land across the border ... Actually, I found this photograph of my mother and her siblings in Delhi in the '80s, and I wondered how they were able to travel to India during that time, because Pakistan was under martial law until the middle of that decade.[5] Eventually, this feeling became more pronounced.'

'What feeling?' I ask, able to discern the nonchalance fading away from his voice, replaced by a sense of ownership.

Ali is contemplative as he says, 'Everyone is concerned about their history – you know, where you're from, who you are, your land, your language. In Pakistan, I have no village, no place that is my own, no place that I can trace the roots of my family to. For the Hindustanis in Pakistan, everything before Partition is now unreachable.' He takes a deep breath. 'And I felt it very clearly when I saw that photograph of my mother and her siblings in Delhi. I thought, "*Oh right, you got to go*," knowing full well that I may never be able to.'

✑

OVER THE LAST several years, anything uncomplicated about 'home' that I may have accepted as a part of my upbringing has been rendered insufficient. By exhuming the days of Partition, I have come to understand that the term 'belonging' is both complex and multidimensional. It comprises not only physical belonging – a sense of ownership over land and tangible space – but also cognitive belonging, a psychological landscape of solace and familiarity, which is not necessarily always within reach.[6] But the physical distance Partition created from one's homeland was often mutually exclusive to the longing that grew for that homeland within those who had migrated, despite the difficult circumstances of their journeys. And now, over seven decades after Partition, I am curious whether this longing for a land left behind by one's ancestors translates into a feeling of belonging to that land within subsequent generations.

When I speak with Kolkata-based Kastury Ghosh, born in the late '50s, and her son, Jashaswi, born in the early '90s, the attachment to the land across the border – *opar Bangla*, the other Bengal – is resonant. Jashaswi is not only the storyteller out of the two but also the story-collector, for he has carefully preserved the history of his family. The stories are plenty, he warns me in advance, and they extend deep into the heart of an undivided Bengal.

'I will begin with my mother's paternal side,' he says, 'who were zamindars and moneylenders in Binajhuri Gram village in Chittagong, and hence were given the title of Mahajan. After Partition in 1947, everyone remained in what became East Pakistan and only my mother's granduncle, Joy Mohan Chowdhury, and his family migrated across. His in-laws, called Sarkar-Majumdar, were very popular pharmacists in Chittagong and, once in India, his brother-in-law, Bibhuti Sarkar, started the Krishna Glass factory in Kazipara on the outskirts of Kolkata. Not only is the glass factory a landmark, but Bibhuti Sarkar is also an important figure because he later joined the Congress and helped in the transfer of population from East Pakistan to India. So, this was the first wave of migration from my mother's paternal family.'

Jashaswi is very careful to proceed chronologically, checking his notes time and again to make sure he hasn't left any details out. 'The next important year is 1950. Until then, my mother's paternal grandfather and parents were still in East Pakistan.[7] But in February 1950, the Sitakunda massacre happened, where pilgrims from all over East Bengal, Tripura and Assam were on their way to Sitakunda for the festival of Maha Shivratri and were violently attacked by communal mobs and massacred at the railway station. Several houses near the station were also set on fire.'[8]

'Very traumatic riots,' Kastury adds and, nodding, her son says, 'It led to grave fear among the Hindus who had remained in Chittagong. My mother's grandfather, Nutan Chandra Chowdhury, and parents, Sukhendu Bikash Chowdhury and Arati Chowdhury (neé Dewanji) – my grandparents – fled to India. My grandmother often recalled how they barely escaped with their lives, leaving everything behind. There is this one story she told again and again about how because Chittagong was in the interior of East Bengal and the family was fairly wealthy, they could afford to take a plane to India. But while they were at the airport, she was in a complete daze, leaving the only land she called home to go to a foreign place...'

'Carried nothing, everything she left there,' Kastury says, sadly, 'just one sari, nothing else. *Amara ek kapore chole elam shob chere.*'

'We had to leave everything behind, with the exception of just the clothes we were wearing,' Jashaswi translates, telling me that this is something his grandmother often repeated. 'Another incident she'd recall was that at the airport, her ticket fell out of her hand and on to the ground, but she didn't realize it. The pilot then said to her, "*Ma, tomar ticket ta nao. Tomai ebar odeshe jete hobe,*" which means, hold on to your ticket, it is time for you to go to *that* country now. She was crying so much, weeping that she had to leave *this* familiar land and go to *that* foreign one. The pilot picked up the ticket and handed it back to her.'

With sadness, I meet their gaze and ask, 'How old would she have been then?'

Kastury thinks, 'In her early twenties – married, but with no children. My eldest sister was born in 1952.' She then begins to speak to her son in Bangla, and after a few minutes of listening and nodding, he translates, 'My mother tells me that in those days, they had mud ovens for cooking and my grandmother had buried all her jewellery under the oven in the ground. She never thought this would be a permanent move, she always expected to return. She also specifically remembered distributing ten Akbari mohurs amongst her relatives who were also fleeing, as she did not want to keep all the valuables on her person, but nobody knows what became of this wealth. She maintained that because it was a financially difficult time for everyone, the relatives must have kept them or used them once in India.'

'What did the family do once here? So much of their wealth must have been left behind,' I observe.

'Indeed,' Jashaswi agrees, 'but because my great-grandfather's brother had already been in Calcutta for three years, they stayed with him in Kazipara and many men of their family were employed at the Krishna Glass factory. They set up operations in Calcutta, Bombay, Madras, and various uncles were sent to various parts of India to manage these branches. But the main business – moneylending – could no longer be practised. With the money they had carried, they bought shops in a pharmaceutical wholesale market in Calcutta called Bagri Market.

'Of all the memories that my grandmother recounted from those early days in India, there was one that she kept returning to, to tell us about the back-breaking poverty caused by Partition. She would recall it with horror and sadness...' Jashaswi takes a deep breath in before narrating. 'One afternoon, she was in the kitchen with the other ladies of the house, preparing rice. In those days, the kitchen was on the ground level, and the drain from the house led to an open drain in the street. As the excess starchy water from the rice was drained out into the street, my grandmother watched from an open window as a refugee woman stood there, seeking permission to collect and essentially drink it. She was hungry and had no money and had resorted to, well...' His voice trails off. 'My grandmother couldn't believe the destitute state that people had been reduced to. This is what had happened to them. They had lands taken away, their money taken away ... and had no choice but to stand by a drain, collecting starch water to survive.'

Then as the two again speak in Bangla amongst themselves, I am left in the grave second-hand memories of rice water. The image of a woman standing by an open drain is vivid enough to make my heart sink. A few minutes later, Jashaswi clears his throat. 'I should mention that even after their migration to India, my mother's grandfather, Nutan Chandra Chowdhury, kept going back and forth between Calcutta and Chittagong for years. He had a brother and several sons, but he never let any of them make the journey across or risk anything.'

'How come he travelled back and forth?' I ask, eyebrows raised. 'Was it ... easy?'

'I don't know whether it was easy, but he made several trips to retrieve their belongings – never found the jewellery, and the house had been burned down completely. My grandmother, in fact, remembers that as they were escaping to the airport, the pillars of the house were being set on fire by rioters. So, though the house could not be saved, the family had other properties and my great-grandfather tried to sell them all off little by little. It is quite incredible that even after the border had been established between India and East Pakistan, he was able to make so many trips between 1950 and 1974, which was when he passed away. And this becomes another important date, because it was after the 1971 war.

'His final trip to what now became Bangladesh was in 1974, when he sent across a sum of 40,000 rupees. My middle aunt, Arundhati, was to be married and my grandfather had fallen ill and his father was extremely worried, should anything happen to his son. So, he travelled to Chittagong again to sell off whatever remaining property he could. From there, he phoned the family to tell them to go ahead with the wedding plans as he was sending the money. Then in Chittagong city, he suddenly felt unwell and found his way to my grandmother's maternal family's home – basically, his daughter-in-law Arati's childhood home. My mother's grandmother looked after him in his final days and he died there.'

I am poring over my notes, trying to draw the lines between Kastury's maternal and paternal sides, but I feel overwhelmed. Apologetically, I ask Jashaswi to repeat the details and he laughs.

'It is very complicated, and there are multiple migrations happening. I will get to my mother's maternal side later, but in 1974, the only person who was in Chittagong was my mother's maternal grandmother, Pushpa Lata Dewanji, and it was by her side that my mother's paternal grandfather, Nutan Chandra Chowdhury, died.'

I nod, diligently noting down names and dates until Jashaswi says something that makes me look up.

'He did always want to die there. There was this strong urge to retain some part of the land, which is perhaps why he was the only one who did all the travelling there. One of the main reasons was his attachment to Binajhuri Gram, his paternal land, and he wanted to maintain that relationship to his birthplace. I think he always hoped that after settling his children in India, he would return to Chittagong.'

'I have a question…' I begin hesitantly. 'In 1950, his family had to flee because of the terrible massacre against Hindus and they barely managed to save their lives. When you are made to go through something so traumatic, what is the desire to keep returning to that place?'

Mother and son speak at the same time, and as a result I hear only half of what each of them says. Smiling, Jashaswi gestures for his mother to begin.

'In India, we have nothing. We left everything,' she states, both sparingly and heartbreakingly.

Picking up the thread, he continues, 'They always considered the move temporary. If you remember, my grandmother actually buried her jewels in the ground. I don't think they ever expected to be separated from their land so finitely … and so my great-grandfather held on to every last bit of Chittagong that he could.'

I smile, for this is a sentiment that many who survived Partition still feel. I ask them both whether the stories of migration were told to them in their respective childhoods.

'My grandmother, *her* mother,' Jashaswi says, gesturing to Kastury, 'would speak about Partition constantly. Actually, a lot of extended family remained in Bangladesh, but they would visit and keep us informed of what was happening. So, Bangladesh was and continues to be something we regularly discuss. Even now, because there is family there, it will always be relevant.

'But I also want to mention that my grandmother talked often about the atrocities that happened to them, and there was almost a hatred towards the other community and a sense of distrust, which percolated across every conversation. For instance, if we ever spoke about politics in West Bengal, she would immediately say how we needed the Bharatiya Janata Party in power as they reflected a Hindu nationalist position...' He pauses and then clarifies, 'We didn't all support her feelings, but she was speaking from a very particular experience.'

'Of surviving Partition, you mean?' I ask.

'Yes, it stemmed from the pain of having to flee your home due to violence and persecution.'

Here, Kastury reminds her son of a detail she wants him to add. He encourages her to speak, but she shies away. *You tell her*, she mouths, and he nods respectfully.

'With my grandmother, somehow every conversation would become about Partition. She would always assert that we didn't understand what had happened to them, and we couldn't empathize with what they had been through. There would be sudden throwbacks to her childhood in Chittagong, and even though she did not really see any misfortune, she always lamented. She compared the then and now, and all her problems would begin and end at Partition.'

I smile. 'Well, did you ask her questions about the past?'

'Oh yes, we both did, which is how we know what we do,' he replies. 'But by the time I really got intrigued, it was too late. She had already passed.' Then brightening up, he continues, 'As a member of the third generation, I have distance from Partition and am able to appreciate the extraordinary nature of these stories – the resilience, the struggle. And there are intangible remnants from that time that still remain: for instance, the language of Chittagong called Chatgaya,[9] which to date my mother and her sisters understand and use certain words of. Or even the food that they cook at home is different from the Bengali food of West Bengal. My mother's childhood was always influenced by Bangladesh – from both sides of her family – and some part of them always remained on that side. Regardless of how many generations pass, it is difficult to sever ties even with the memory of homeland.'

Kastury beams widely, agreeing with her son.

'What happened on your maternal side?' I ask Kastury as I flip through my notebook. 'How come your grandmother, Pushpa Lata Dewanji, was in Chittagong in the '70s?'

'It is complicated,' she states simply and then encourages her son to continue.

'In the last few weeks, we have both ventured deep into this side of my mother's family, talking to her aunts and uncles ... and the sheer hesitation to even discuss the days of Partition and thereafter is astounding. They kept asking us why we wanted to know and became very disturbed trying to recall the past. This was quite a revelation for me, because I never thought there would be so much hesitation, particularly among family. Many of them simply refused.'

'*Nahi baat karna*,' Kastury says, 'they don't want to talk.'

'There was, how do I put it ... a hostility. A very strong wish to end the conversation. The migrations on this side of the family are even more complicated and continued for decades after Partition.' He checks his watch and asks me, 'Are you sure you have the time? This is a long story.'

'I'm listening,' I reply and bring my pen to my notebook.

'My grandmother, Arati Chowdhury (neé Dewanji), was born to Upendra Lal and Pushpa Lata in Chittagong City. The family were diwans of Chittagong who used to work with the East India Company as collectors and hence were given the title of Dewanji.

My grandmother grew up very wealthy, for the family had many businesses of import–export, oil mills, and even bakeries, all named after Arati.

'After Partition, this family also lived through the Sitakunda Massacre in 1950, but they were resolute to remain in East Pakistan. *This* is one thing we need to establish at the beginning – that Upendra Lal and Pushpa Lata Dewanji did not want to leave Chittagong under any circumstances. Yes, they wanted to establish a base in India for some security but had no interest in leaving East Pakistan at that point of time. Now, the period between 1950 and 1965 is important, because during this time they travelled extensively between India and East Pakistan, buying land in the same area of Calcutta where my grandmother, their daughter, was married. They wanted property in India that they could escape to or send their children to, if needed. But this couple was very, very resolute in remaining in East Pakistan. They were wealthy and possessed a large amount of land, and this land was something Pushpa almost revered. Her sense of belonging to it was so deep that no amount of religious or political conflict would persuade her to leave it.

'The first time the family was forced to take such a call was in 1964, when Upendra Lal Dewanji died, leaving his wife to single-handedly take care of the home, business, land and family. They had seven children, four sons and three daughters, and many of them are already married by this time. My mother actually remembers travelling to Chittagong for her grandfather's funeral. Now, Pushpa Lata Dewanji becomes the matriarch of the family, just as the 1965 war happens. And this is the moment when the many, many complicated migrations of the Dewanji family truly begin.'

As Jashaswi begins to list the extensive travel across the border, I find myself making migration routes and taking detailed notes. As years and events are added, I make addendums to those notes, and keys for how to read the many addendums. By the end, the pages of my notebook transform into documents of migration and resistance, and the sheer porosity of India's eastern border is not lost on me.

In 1965, as India and Pakistan are at war, Pushpa Lata Dewanji sends her eldest son and his wife to Agartala in Tripura to set up a business. Their children remain with their grandmother in Chittagong. Simultaneously, the youngest son and daughter are sent to Calcutta to live with Arati and her family. It is at this time that the family also begins to construct a home in Calcutta. By the 1971 war, one daughter has been married in East Pakistan itself. During the war, Pushpa Lata, her two sons and unmarried daughter remain in what will now become Bangladesh, and she sends her four granddaughters across the border into India. The tone in which Jashaswi describes the days of war is chilling; after much struggle, the girls were sent across on foot, shrouded in black burqas. The family witnesses a daughter-in-law's father being murdered before their eyes during the riots, and Jashaswi and his mother have often heard of the violence that ensued against the community at the time. Once in India, the four granddaughters – Kastury's cousins – would tell her about the horrible circumstances in which they fled.

When the war is over, Pushpa Lata remains in Bangladesh, but realizes that she may not be able to stay on much longer. She now finally begins to sell off her properties, spending more time in Calcutta. I am in awe of her resilience, for every single difficult decision she has taken to protect her family has been after the death of her husband. In that sense, she was a true matriarch.

'The next important date I have written down is 1982,' Jashaswi reads from his notes. 'Pushpa Lata was in India, but she had not given up the home in Chittagong yet, still making trips back and forth. But in 1982 she became paralysed and was treated for two years in India. In 1984, she stayed on for my mother's wedding, which was the last major event she attended here. In fact, the only photograph my mother has with her grandmother is from this time.'

'How did she get paralysed?' I ask, cutting his thoughts short.

'Oh … uh, a cerebral attack that left the entire right side of her body paralysed,' he tells me.

'She could talk,' Kastury adds, 'her memory was also intact, but couldn't move on the right side.'

Jashaswi now returns to the chronology. 'Now, some time between 1984 and 1990 – we are not certain of these dates – she declared that she no longer wanted to stay in India.'

'She wanted to return ... to Bangladesh? Despite everything the family had witnessed?'

'Despite it all,' he concurred. 'She felt her health deteriorating and, because of the paralysis, didn't think she would live much longer. But she did not want to die in India. The phrase she kept repeating was, "*Amake bari niye chol. Ami amar potir bhite te morte chai.* Take me home, I want to die in my husband's homeland." Do you see what she meant by this?' Jashaswi looks at me squarely now. 'That despite establishing a home and safe life here in India, she did not consider the land her own. She did not want to die on a foreign land. She begged her sons to take her home, and they actually flew her back to Chittagong.'

I notice how Jashaswi uses the word *home* with utmost care, for in the context of Pushpa Lata Dewanji it was always the other side, *opar bangla*, the other Bengal.[10] I wonder if in India she thought she was in a kind of exile, 'the unhealable rift forced between a human being and a native place, between the self and its true home'.[11]

'In 1990, Pushpa Lata's grandson got married in India, but she did not attend the wedding. In 1991, the newlywed couple went to visit her in Bangladesh. And though she welcomed the new bride happily into her home, she was adamant that she would not leave with them. "*Ami aar pherot jaabo naa* ... I will not go back." She was firm, her last wish was to die in Chittagong.'

'Did she?' I ask in a low voice.

He shakes his head sadly. 'In 1992, the Babri Masjid demolition happened, which again gave rise to violence against Hindu Bengalis and other minorities in Bangladesh,[12] continuing until 1993. *This* would be the event that would send the entire family across the border once and for all. My mother's uncle felt that they would not survive those riots and sold whatever they could at whatever price they could, even if it was at a loss, and began to send family members across to India. But this too happened in phases and Pushpa Lata was very particular that everyone had to get out safely and only then would she leave. See, she was so concerned for the well-being of her children, and despite nearing ninety she very much controlled the decision-making powers in the house. So, strategically, things were sold off and she came to India in 1993. The last people to leave were two of her sons, who arranged a seller for the house, went to the courthouse, signed across the property and directly went to the airport from there. That was it, they never returned – 1993 was the family's final migration.'

He heaves a deep sigh and places the handwritten pages on his lap.

'Pushpa Lata Dewanji finally died in 1995 in a land she considered to be foreign. And what I find unimaginable is the sheer insistence – that whatever the circumstance, whatever the new name of the land, whatever the political party in power, she wanted to remain in Chittagong. East Bengal, East Pakistan, Bangladesh, none of these names changed her relationship with the land. That was sacrosanct.'

'Mrs Ghosh,' I say, now turning to Kastury, 'how do these stories make you feel?'

Kastury speaks inaudibly in Bangla for a few minutes and then Jashaswi translates, 'She says that she learnt determination from her grandmother, and these are values she wants to live by.' He smiles. 'I will tell you how I first heard this story. See, my grandmother, Arati, was also paralysed for the last five years of her life. Being in Kolkata, we thought it would be easier for her to move into our home. But she refused, and quoted exactly the same lines that *her* mother had once said – *I will die in my own home, I will die in the home my husband died in.* This story then continued with my mother, for after my father died a few years ago she too refused to leave this home. *I will die in my own home*, she maintained, *I will die in the home my husband died in.* These are things one has heard so much now that they almost feel like they are in your blood.'

I nod and then ask, 'Do you think that your great-grandmother ever feared the fact that she was a Hindu minority living in Bangladesh? Did the riots or –' but even before I am able to finish, I find him shaking his head from side to side.

'My mother is saying that she never feared that. For her, that was her land and she wasn't going there illegally. No one could take away something that already belonged to her. But it was sad that she couldn't remain there till the end, as she would have liked to.'

I skim the pages of notes, consumed by the deluge of dates and details.

'When you asked me to talk about Partition,' Jashaswi says, smiling, 'I could have never imagined just how long the consequences of Partition would extend. That resistance to the partitioning of land and identity would become a way of life. My ancestors' actions show me that some things – like belonging to a place – cannot be retracted by merely drawing a line. And for forty-six years, from 1947 to 1993, the Dewanji family held on to the right to belong to a land they had been born on and raised their family on.'

'In that way, both sides of your mother's family are quite similar...' I begin.

'...where ties to the land are revered over all else,' he completes my sentence.

'You hold on to as much as you can, or as little as you can ... until you can,' I say.

'This symbol of soil,' Jashaswi says, cupping his hands as if holding an imaginary pile of loose soil, 'is something that has been embedded into my mind. I feel that generations of my family, both paternal and maternal, have held on to this concept of soil, of what becomes a house, of what you can call a home. Even now in Chittagong, a Devanji Lane, a Devanji ghat remain in memory of the family. Belonging goes deeper than the name of a place or a stamp on a passport. It is as deep as the deepest soil of the earth.'

'*Sheita bolo je ekhono loke oi desher mati niyeashe*,' Kastury says.

'Ah yes, my mother is saying that over the years several members of her family have carried the soil of Chittagong with them and worshipped it. As if a part of Chittagong had been transported and recreated wherever they went. In this way, they have carried their home with them.'

3

Borderlands

∽

'DID YOU KNOW,' HARLEEN Bedi asks me as we stand in front of the old Sher-e-Punjab restaurant in Dalhousie's Gandhi Chowk, 'that the flag of Pakistan was hoisted here in August 1947?'

Dalhousie is located in a tight corner where the states of Punjab and Kashmir meet the international border with Pakistan.[1] It is the autumn of 2017 and I have travelled to write a story about a cottage named Kehkashan, constructed by Mian Afzal Husain, the first Muslim vice-chancellor of Punjab University, Lahore. During Partition, his family fled from Dalhousie, leaving behind their beloved cottage. Over time, it became home to the Bedis, who had also been displaced from their ancestral lands in Kallar Syedan.[2] Harleen says nothing more about the flag, but that evening she and I are invited to tea at a neighbour's cottage. There, from the residents of Upper Bakrota, I learn of what happened during Partition.

The quaint hill town used to be a popular destination for Punjabi aristocracy,[3] and in the summer months many families like Mian Afzal Husain's retreated up to the hills. On 14 August 1947, when the state of Pakistan came into being, it was simply assumed that Gurdaspur district, under which Dalhousie fell, would be part of it, because of the narrow Muslim majority.* Hence, for three days, there

---

* According to the 1941 census, Gurdaspur district had a 51.14 per cent Muslim majority.

fluttered in Dalhousie's Gandhi Chowk the flag of Pakistan – hoisted by the Muslim postmaster.[4] But on 17 August, when Radcliffe's final boundary was announced, the tricolour took its place as Gurdaspur was awarded to India, forcing Muslims to flee without any prior notice or planning.

The next morning, Harleen and I return to Gandhi Chowk, and I try to imagine a *kaafila* of Muslim families leaving in haste the picturesque hill town they were certain would be a part of Pakistan. I look around the former General Post Office, now a promenade of shops with identically peaked green roofs, betraying no evidence of such a migration. And yet, now that I know its peculiar history, the ghostly presence of Partition is undeniable.

SIR CYRIL RADCLIFFE'S boundary awards in Punjab and Bengal were anything but uncomplicated. The hoisting of the Pakistani flag in Dalhousie in present-day Himachal Pradesh is just one such example of the often-perplexing nature of the award. It is famously said that Radcliffe had never been east of Gibraltar. However, at the time, it was argued that his *absence* of knowledge and apolitical attitude about India would make him an unbiased map-maker. His appointment as Joint Chairman of the Boundary Commission was an altogether unenviable position, where he was aided by eight judges – four each for Punjab and Bengal, as nominated by the Congress and the Muslim League[5] – a private secretary and an assistant secretary. Radcliffe arrived in India on 8 July 1947 and was asked to submit the award by 15 August, giving him approximately five weeks to draw a line that would decide the fate of millions – a feat that would, in any and all circumstances, make him a complicated figure in the legacy of India's partitioning. His time in the subcontinent was difficult as he struggled with both political and natural elements. And although he submitted his report to the government on 12 August, the Radcliffe Line was not revealed to the public until *after* Independence. As a result, Indians and Pakistanis awoke in newly independent nations without actual clarity on which side their homelands now fell. When the border was finally announced on 17 August, it not only led to large-scale migration, violent riots and disturbances across both sides but bestowed, according to the historian Yasmin Khan,

> a variety of eccentric features on the subcontinent's political geography. East and West Pakistan were separated over a thousand miles, and travelling by sea over the country's two major ports, Karachi and Chittagong, took approximately five days ... The inevitable result, particularly in the most contested districts in Punjab – Lahore, Amritsar, Gurdaspur, Hoshiarpur and Jullundur – and in parts of Bengal, was dire confusion.[6]

In several border districts of Bengal, as in Dalhousie, the Pakistani flag also flew for a few days until it was replaced by the tricolour. This happened in Nadia district – in the towns of Shantipur, Bongaon, Kalyani, Ranaghar, Krishnagar, Shikarpur and Karimpur[7] – and the Muslim-majority districts of Murshidabad and Malda.

In a travel piece titled 'Trailing Blood from the Swan's Belly', the journalist and author Bishwanath Ghosh writes about how the map of West Bengal 'resembles a crudely drawn swan', with Malda right in the centre of 'the swan's throat, separating Bihar from Bangladesh. Had Malda been separated from India during Partition, West Bengal would have been completely cut off from its picturesque northern parts such as Darjeeling, Siliguri and Cooch Behar.'[8]

IT IS FROM Malda – where Independence Day is celebrated not on 15 August, like in the rest of India, but a few days later – that Abhishek Acharyya speaks to me. Having just moved there for work, he begins the conversation by telling me that the border with Bangladesh is barely 3 kilometres away. 'I will go there for a walk this evening,' he says in a way that makes me imagine standing at the edge of a country, where a single foot on the other side is a foot in a foreign land.[9]

Bangladesh is not exactly foreign for Abhishek as that is the land of his ancestors. But his story is unusual – though he is of Bengali descent, he lays proud claim to both the divided provinces of Bengal and Punjab. It is in this way that he connects the east and west of Radcliffe's line.

'Both my parents' families came from East Bengal, which became East Pakistan and now Bangladesh. My paternal grandfather is from Barisal, where he used to be in the business of German inks, and continued to stay there until 1952, when he had money issues because of a shipment stranded in a port somewhere and had to make a run for it. My paternal grandmother migrated from East Bengal, though her extended family was from Naihati in West Bengal. Naihati has two sides, divided by a railway line – the western side is old, established in 1869, but the eastern side developed after Partition with the influx of refugees. Each of these localities became like a separate district of East Bengal, and people who came across the border together in convoys ended up living there together.

'My mother's family came from Netrakona district and settled near Ranaghat in Cooper's Camp, which is perhaps the subcontinent's oldest and least-known refugee camp.[10] My maternal grandfather knew no one on this side of the border and so the process of resettlement was tremendously difficult – living in tin shacks with no resources – and though he managed to eventually find work in the railways and restart his life, the families that still live in Cooper's Camp are defined by the horrors of Partition.'

I ask him whether that is how he first learnt of Partition, and he laughs.

'Far from it. I first learnt about Partition in Punjab. While my grandparents lived in West Bengal, my parents moved to Punjab for work. I grew up in Rupnagar in a neighbourhood called Ali Mohalla, with the knowledge that our local gurudwara used to be a mosque before Partition. It was like an open secret.'

I smile at the thought that instead of being demolished, a house of worship from before Partition was repurposed as another house of worship.

Abhishek continues his story. 'Then, when I was ten or twelve years old, this woman in our building began telling stories about how she came from West Punjab to East at the time of Partition. They were always train stories, and I really love trains! So, she would tell us about how, during the journey, their train stopped near a pond and Muslim rioters got on. Out of fear, families began throwing the young girls off the train and into the pond. It was better to die than be assaulted, out of concern for their *izzat*. She would tell the stories with such passion and fear as if she could see the scene before her eyes. When her turn came, the train suddenly began moving and that was how she survived being thrown off and left behind. Now...' He pauses and brings his palm to his chin. 'I don't know how much was exaggerated and how much was the truth, but this was the beginning of my knowledge of Partition – these stories from Punjab, mostly around trains.'

'When you visited your grandparents in Bengal, did you ask them if they'd had similar experiences?'

'Yes, but by then three of my grandparents had already passed. So, most of my stories are from my eldest uncle, born in 1944. He talks a lot about the past, and there is a noticeable difference in the childhoods of my parents' siblings born in East Bengal and those of my parents, who are younger and were born in West Bengal. When their older siblings are gone, the memory of Partition will disappear with them, and so I do as much as I can to record these stories for posterity. For this uncle of mine, there is still deep pain associated with Partition and the ownership over land and home...'

'How so?' I ask, for over seven decades have now passed. Land has changed not just ownership but also identity.

'Well, when conversations around the National Register of Citizens (NRC) began and people feared that it may lead to another Partition-like situation or conflict, or people could be sent back to where they had come from decades ago – the checking of documents and papers, the very question of identity – I think that's when conversations around Partition really began in our home. And no matter how long it has been for my family, no matter how stable their life is here in India, no matter how cemented citizenship may now be, the very discussions aroused fear and reminded them of what they had once been through. Partition still felt too recent, too immediate, too traumatic, even seventy years later.'

THE STORIES OF flags and borderlands follow me throughout my research. Saffron, white, green and red. Twenty-four-spoke chakras, stars and crescent moons, and a rising sun. The undivided boundless sky, the divided dusty land. Days of celebration and of sorrow, of independence and of partition. Fragments of memories passed down the generations, snatches of conversation. A word here, a word there, a whisper, a wail. All in unison telling the story of one country, colonized, plundered, divided in two, then in three.

ON A MAP, Amrita Das shows me that her ancestral home in Karimganj, present-day Assam, is only 365 metres from the international border with Bangladesh. The structure, built by her great-grandfather, Rai Bahadur Ramani Mohan Das, is a magnificent brick mansion, with rows of arched pillars running along both sides of the *dalan*. Its rounded driveway is elegantly old-fashioned, and right beside the home is a small pond surrounded by lush greenery. She proudly tells me that for the past 158 years, her family has hosted a Durga Puja gathering in the house. Karimganj was once a part of Sylhet district and was eventually awarded to India. Since generations of Amrita's maternal family have populated this borderland, I ask her what they recall of August 1947.

'It was a time of uncertainty and fear. And though the more prominent incidents took place in 1971, when East Pakistan became Bangladesh, the 1947 Partition was a time when my ancestors feared becoming refugees themselves. What I have gathered from my elders is that in the early morning of 15 August 1947, my grandfather, Seetendra Mohan Das, and his three brothers, Ranendra, Shashanka and Rithendra, arose to learn that someone had put the flags of Pakistan on the main gate and the *dalan* of the house. Even though the official demarcation hadn't yet been announced, this sight devastated their morale. My uncles tell me that the flags remained there for two whole days. At that time, not everyone had access to a radio; the closest one was about a kilometre or so away, in a bank near the Kali Bari. There, on the third day, they heard the announcement of the Radcliffe Line on All India Radio and discovered that the centre point of River Kushiyara would be the border between India and East Pakistan.'

But how can you tell a border over a river, I think to myself.

'The news spread like a wave of joy among the people of Karimganj. The Pakistani flags were removed and Indian flags were hoisted in the house and on top of the *dalan*. My grandfather and his brothers sat on the iron bench beside the pond and, in sheer joy, played the *bigul*. A small celebration was held to rejoice the fact that Karimganj would remain a part of India. And though post-Partition life brought its own set of challenges and the family lost their properties in East Bengal, I think they were relieved that they would not be uprooted, as they knew so many people on both sides who were.'

'They felt the economic loss, then. The properties in East Pakistan...' I say.

'During the unrest of 1947, my grandfather was in the Kumarshail Tea Estate – managed by the family – and had to return home immediately. The property remains in Bangladesh and is still owned by us even today. There is a story that my grandfather narrated quite fondly to his children. The estate had elephants to manage it, and my grandfather's most beloved one was named Jayatara. She was like his pet. When he left the estate, he sadly also had to leave the elephant behind. After Partition, when things were calmer and people could still move across borders without passports, he went to meet her. By then, she was put into hard labour by the new managers of the property. But when he called out her name, she immediately recognized his voice and came running to greet him. Jayatara and her *mahut*, Nalini, only came once to the Indian side, to bid adieu to my grandfather, and then they went back.'

We often forget that in the cruel division of Undivided India, it was not only people or land that were affected but also animals and the elements. Pets abandoned; rivers divided.

'So, what does the border near your home look like?' I ask her, imagining a green luscious riverbed.

'I've walked to the border a few times while visiting Karimganj. You can stand on the banks of the river and look at Bangladesh. In some places, it isn't even very wide, and you can see the day-to-day lives of the people on the other side. During any procession or festival, you can hear the ongoing celebrations. To be honest, if someone didn't have prior knowledge of the river being a border, they would assume that the other side was part of the same land.'

In my notebook, I draw the snaking river, Kushiyara. As I do, I am reminded of the words of poet-novelist Karuna Ezara Parikh: 'Decades spent watching a border that was more snake than cement, more river than rope.'[11] In the centre of the river, I draw a dissolving border, and then turn my attention back to Amrita's words.

'Everything is the same,' she stresses, 'only the acknowledgement of the fact makes it a different country.'

THE BORDER BETWEEN India and Bangladesh is the fifth longest land border in the world, measuring 4,096 kilometres, touching the Indian states of Assam, West Bengal, Mizoram, Meghalaya and Tripura. But it is also the most segmented land border between any two countries in the world, with nearly 199 enclaves – the territory of one state enclosed within the territory of another state. In Bangladesh, there once were 102 Indian enclaves, which in turn contained twenty-one Bangladeshi counter-enclaves. In India, there were seventy-one Bangladeshi enclaves, containing three Indian counter-enclaves.

Dahala Khagrabari was once the world's only third-order enclave in the Indian district of Cooch Behar. In an altogether perplexing situation, it was completely encircled by the Bangladeshi village of Upanchowki Bhajni, which was further encircled by the Indian village of Balapara Khagrabari, which was still further encircled by Debiganj in the Rangpur district of Bangladesh.[12] In 2015, Dahala Khagrabari was ceded to Bangladesh in the Land Boundary Agreement, which finally arrived at a comprehensive settlement of the land boundary issue that had existed between India and Bangladesh since 1947.[13]

For lateral movement between the two countries only, the India–Bangladesh passport was introduced as a special travel document in August 1972. The light blue passport was issued by the Republic of India, and on its third page were stamped the words 'Emigration Clearance Not Required'. After being issued for forty years, it was eventually discontinued in 2013.[14]

NOT ALL MEMORIES of borders emerge from those whose families once crossed it. In fact, for Mayukh Bhattacharya, who grew up in the mid-90s in Agartala, Tripura, the border with Bangladesh is not only a common but a rather nostalgic sight. Contrary to the usual feelings evoked by a country's frontier, this one reminds him only of his childhood.

'In Kasba Kalibari, there is a rather famous temple dedicated to the goddess Kali, which my family frequented when I was young. We would offer prayers at the temple and then picnic somewhere nearby. Because it was far from Agartala, we'd hire cars to take us there, and I would revel in this temporary escape from the city. The temple itself, interestingly, is located on a tilla, a tiny hill just by the border. From the temple you can see the farmers of both nations sowing the rice fields divided by barbed wire, people fishing in the ponds nearby, and even the railway station of Akhaura in Bangladesh.'

There is a refreshing innocence to his memories, a lightness that cannot easily be found in stories of divided lands. He tells me that Agartala received metre gauge rail connectivity in 2008 and it was only in 2016 that it was converted to broad gauge. So, the allure of a train ride as this luxury for which the family had to travel to either Assam or West Bengal always existed. 'As a child, I would stand on the hilltop and watch the trains go by across the border in Bangladesh, dreaming of what a train journey might be like.'

WHEN I LISTEN to stories from India's eastern border with Bangladesh, I cannot help but notice its porous nature – undulating, segmented, made of rivers and green fields – and compare it with experiences of crossing the border on the western side with Pakistan. Narjis Khatun, who migrated from Patiala to Multan, mentioned when I interviewed her in 2014 in Lahore how at the time of Partition this border was so primitive and unmanned, wholly identical on both sides in a way that one could hardly make out the moment they crossed over into Pakistan, the moment they adopted a new identity:

> But the strangest thing was that we never realized when it happened, *kab ek mulk khatam hua aur doosra shuru* ... when India ended and Pakistan began. There were no obvious differences between one land and its conjoined neighbour, and so I suspect that we gained our new citizenship in a moment curiously lost on us. Tucked away in a corner of an overcrowded train, we had quietly become Pakistani.[15]

In his memoir *Tales of Two Cities*, co-written with the Indian journalist Kuldip Nayar, Pakistani journalist Asif Noorani writes a short passage about Abdur Rahman, the friend of a family friend. Rahman, who died in his eighties, often recalled that until the

Radcliffe Award was announced, no one was sure whether Lahore would be part of India or Pakistan. Strong rumours even suggested that the city itself would be partitioned between the two nations – the part on one side of the canal that bifurcated Lahore would go to India and the other to Pakistan. Rahman and his best friend, Chhabra, who eventually settled in Lucknow, decided that if this were to happen then every morning, at an agreed time, they would each stand on one bank of the canal and speak to one another. Chhabra was certain that the countries would unite once again after Partition, but this was not to be. They did, however, remain friends and Chhabra visited Rahman just before his eighty-first birthday, when the pair stayed together in Model Town and reminisced about the days of the past.[16]

INDIA'S BORDER WITH Pakistan is 3,323 kilometres long, spanning the Indian states of Jammu and Kashmir, Rajasthan, Gujarat and Punjab, cutting through glaciers, plains and desert land. Apart from being one of the heaviest militarized borders in the world, it is also lit up by hundreds of kilometres of floodlights, making it visible even from space. Every evening before the borders close for the day, the security forces on both sides perform the customary lowering of the flags, a ceremony called Beating the Retreat, for which the Attari–Wagah post is undoubtedly most famous.* There, the Indian Border Security Force (BSF) and Pakistan Rangers have been carrying out the elaborate performance of, ironically, both brotherhood and rivalry since 1959. Their actions are mirrored, for they are conjoined twins after all.

Each time I attend this ceremony at Attari, I am both moved and conflicted by how close Pakistan physically feels but how far it truly is. Often, people who attend this ceremony are, for the most part, there for the pomp and show, the extreme display of nationalism and superiority, the patriotic song and dance and hype of it all. Of being divided, being independent. But there is hardly any evidence

---

* The story of the establishment of this border post in October 1947 can be found in the chapter 17, 'No Man's Land'.

of once being one. Perhaps the only moment of peace found is at the end of the ceremony, when as both the flags are slowly lowered, they intersect. It is a brief interlude, a moment of rare oneness, which cannot otherwise be found throughout the evening.

I have never attended this ceremony from the Wagah side, and so I wonder if India feels just as similar – so close, yet so far. But if ever we were to fathom the depths of shared pain among those who visit this border from either side, we needn't look any further than the stories told[17] of citizens carrying posters bearing the Punjabi poet Ustad Daman's heart-wrenching verses, written after Partition and recited at a *mushaira* in Delhi:

> *Barbad ihna azadian ton hoye tussi vi ho, assi vi haan,*
> *Akhiyan di lali dasdi hai, roye tussi wi ho, roye assi wi haan*
> You were ruined in the name of freedom, and so were we.
> The redness of our eyes reveals that you have wept, and so have we.

During Partition, Daman's house in Lahore was burnt down as he was taken to be a Congress supporter. Jawaharlal Nehru – who had once famously bestowed Daman with the title of 'Poet of Freedom' when he recited a poem at a public gathering in 1930 where Nehru was present, forming a long friendship between the two – offered Daman Indian citizenship. This he refused, saying that he could live nowhere else but his birthplace of Lahore,[18] where he was born in 1911 and died in 1984.

THE CONVERSATIONS I have had about borderlands over the last several years clearly reveal a feeling of a land being within sight, yet definitely unattainable. The documentary photographer Roshan Abbas Naqvi narrates his experiences at the Attari–Wagah ceremony. 'Amidst the colliding patriotic egos in the air,' he recalls, 'I saw a milestone which mentioned that Lahore was just 22 kilometres ahead.

There it was, within reach. I wanted to visit Lahore but I knew I couldn't. It felt cleaved, divided, but also oddly fascinating, how we had made our peace with this fact.'

As Roshan rightly observes, it is exceptionally difficult for ordinary Indians and Pakistanis to move back and forth between the two lands, for visas are now sparingly granted. However, after Partition, documents were issued to assist in movement between the newly separated nations. Like the India–Bangladesh passport, there was also an India–Pakistan passport given by the Republic of India. An old-fashioned cardboard booklet covered with brilliant red cloth was issued to migrants to enable them to visit family, friends and ancestral homes located on the other side of the Radcliffe Line. It was also granted for single visits to religious sites such as the Nankana Sahib Gurudwara, or for sporting events.

The writer and artist Saaz Agarwal, best known for her work on the Sindhi experience of Partition, once wrote about discovering an India–Pakistan passport issued to her father in his early twenties to travel to Karachi for work while he was employed with Franco Indian, a pharmaceutical company in Bombay:

> Along with the passport was the correspondence which gave us some background: an application had been made on 20 June 1957 and the passport was issued less than a month later, on 16 July 1957. It was valid for one year ... [and] for only Karachi.[19]

It is hard to gauge when this document was discontinued, but perhaps the circumstances after the 1965 war made the movement of people across the border difficult, and the document was withdrawn.

CALIFORNIA-BASED SANJIV NANDA has a history of Partition on his father's side – the family migrated from Quetta to Dehradun – but it is his mother's side that we speak about. She hails from the border town of Ferozepur, where all of Sanjiv's summer holidays were spent. He and his cousin Rashmi, who now lives in Ohio, often reminisce about how in their childhood in the 1970s, the border wasn't quite like how it is today – no hawkers and vendors, no crowds and no elaborate show for tourists.

'Our grandfather, Dr Sadhu Chand Vinayek,[20] was a larger-than-life presence in Ferozepur as a physician for the rich and poor in the town and the district. We were one of the few families to own a car, a white Fiat, in which eight or nine cousins would often pile for an outing once a week, typically to the children's park in Ferozepur Cantt. Adjacent was the Barki Memorial, where a Pakistani tank captured at Barki during the 1965 war was placed on a raised platform. The Urdu numerals used to fascinate us.

'Then a couple of times during the summer, we'd have longer outings with a picnic. The border was around 10 kilometres from Ferozepur but was hardly visited by any tourists in the '70s as rickshaws were the only means of transport available. We would visit the Martyrs' Memorial, where the revolutionaries Bhagat Singh, Sukhdev and Rajguru were cremated on 23 March 1931, and explore the old crumbling fort walls around it. As the day came to a close, we would inevitably head to the border, where the village of Hussainniwala in Ferozepur, India, meets the village of Ganda Singh Wala in Kasur, Pakistan.

'I remember a rail line ending abruptly short of the border. Cultivated fields were all around, on either side. There were no barbed wires, just two checkpoint barriers on the road separated by approximately 25 yards of "no man's land" in between, a term that fascinated us. *Whose land, then?* Flag raising at sunrise and lowering at sunset were conducted solemnly, with Indian and Pakistani soldiers crossing over to the other side to raise and lower their respective flags, a lone bugle providing the soundtrack. Before and after the ceremony, we would see the soldiers engage in idle chatter.

'When we returned from our outing, Biji, our grandmother, would delve into her own personal recollections of learning about the surreptitious, late-night hanging of Bhagat Singh, Sukhdev and Rajguru, the transportation of the remains from Lahore and burning at this remote site near Ferozepur.'

The Pakistani oral historian Anam Zakaria writes about this border from the Kasur side in her book *The Footprints of Partition: Narratives of Four Generations of Pakistanis and Indians*: 'Standing here at the border ... where the only visible lines of division are a distant wire or plants that would usually be found in people's homes, distorts the fine separation.'[21] She is told by her guide that sometimes people even cross over accidentally, and until 1986 there was no line or wire demarcating the border. As he points out to her where Pakistan ends and India begins, she realizes that it is merely 'inches away' from the other side.[22]

HUSSAIN KHALID, BORN in the early 1990s in Karachi, went to a border ceremony for the first time only after reading a significant amount of Partition literature. He travelled to Wagah, 'searching for familiar faces on the other side, for anyone with similar emotions to his'.

Just the thought itself creates warmth in my heart. I ask him what this means.

'I mean anyone who is looking beyond the religious symbolism in the architecture of both sides, or listening to sounds smaller than the collision of national songs. I remember, after leaving the pavilion, looking back at the landscape of the Wagah–Attari border and seeing no border. Green fields extended into the blue sky without any divide.'

In this, we understand one another well. Indeed, the sky, the fields, the birds that fly from one side to the other, the trees that grow from Pakistan into India, the wind that blows from India into Pakistan – what is the nationality of this natural world grown and nurtured at the borderland?

As our conversation shifts to nature, Hussain relays a memory of the monsoon.

'Growing up, we used to visit our village, Behlolpur, located on the bank of the river Chenab in district Gujrat, which is very close to the border. Every time after it rained, the sky cleared up, revealing the Himalayan mountain range in India, and we could see lights from a temple nestled within those mountains. Then, during the 1999 Kargil war, the villagers used to make up stories about how the Indian Army was monitoring our moves from the temple, and tell us to keep all lights off after sunset. So, for the longest time, the sight of that temple was a source of insecurity for me. It was also during the war that I kept wondering why, of all places, we lived so close to the border. Otherwise, India always felt very distant...

'As we are speaking now, I have this view of India flashing before my eyes. So, the city of Gujrat and Sialkot are divided physically by the river Chenab and connected by Marala dam, where usually you can see water just extending into a smoky horizon. But in 2013, as I was travelling from my village to Lahore, I crossed Headmarala in Sialkot and the sky was so clear that I saw these gigantic mountains on the horizon. There was India, gently reminding me that something which was mostly forgotten about existed beyond the haze.'

'Did you ever figure out which temple it was?' I ask.

'Yes, much later. In 2017, on a trip to Azad Kashmir [as Pakistan-administered Kashmir is called in Pakistan] with a friend, I saw the temple again, and my friend told me that was India. Immediately, because I was older now, my mind began trying to map out the arduous routes through mountains that people would have taken before Partition to reach their house of worship. It is exactly three hours from my village, and is a rather famous temple too, Vaishno Devi. Each time I speak to my father about it now, he recalls it not with fear or any ill sentiment, as I used to, but with joy.'

'How come?'

'Well, my ancestors are originally from Jammu in India. They migrated in September 1947 and the men of the family even went back during the 1965 war in the hope of borders tumbling down. I'm told they kept riding their horses back and forth for nearly three months until they realized that the border now was indeed a hard fact of life.'

'Is that when you first learned of Partition?' As always, I'm curious about beginnings.

'I think I would have learnt of it first in our grade 9 Pakistan Studies textbook. We had a section on the Two Nation theory, which explained why Pakistan was the need of the time, and it followed several subheadings like religious beliefs, different cultures and traditions, different customs and values, so on. In the exam, we were encouraged to write down as many differences as possible to score higher marks.'

'So, what *was* your perception of India at the time? You mentioned your village and its proximity to the border, even the fear you felt during Kargil.'

'Well, if I had to look at it objectively, I suppose the perception was rather complex and even contradictory. On one hand, yes, the villagers feared being watched by India, and I too questioned why we lived so close to a border during wartime. But at the same time, we would watch Indian TV shows on DD National – I can still hear the sound from that 14-inch black-and-white TV! – and there was a warmth when people spoke about Indian shows and movies: the characters felt familiar, they felt our own. And then, because my village is on the bank of the Chenab, during summertime when the sun was scorching, the river used to be our refuge. The Chenab flows from Akhnoor in India into the Sialkot district in Pakistan. Very often, villagers used to find objects – little pieces of wood or pine cones mostly – as their feet would hit the water. They'd pull the object out of the river and yell in excitement, "*Ooh, India tun lakri aayi ae*" – Oh, look, a piece of wood has come floating from India!'

Though I chuckle at the preciousness of the memory, it reminds me of all those times when the first generations who witnessed Partition would tell me to get them a fistful of soil or stones the next time I was in the land of their birth – either India or Pakistan. How something as ordinary as a piece of wood or a pine cone could encapsulate the entire physical memory of home.

As our conversation comes to a close, Hussain admits, 'That extraordinary view of the Indian mountains from Headmarala, that is the hardest to forget. It felt extremely personal to me; I never told anyone about it, never returned to it either. Similarly, all these recollections about India and the border … it's like being in a strange state of longing.'

There is deep lament to be heard in his words, which is perhaps the most appropriate legacy of the horsemen from Jammu wishing to go back to their land, knowing well that it would not look, sound, smell or feel the same as when they once inhabited it.

'The generation that has hatred for the other side has not known the other side at all,' he concludes.

4

Discovery

✑

'GROWING UP, I DIDN'T know there was a Punjab on the other side of the border!' Amitoj Singh tells me when I ask him when he first understood the word Partition. 'Maybe it was this tiny discovery which made me re-evaluate what I thought of Pakistan.'

I smile. A Punjab here, a Punjab there. A Gujarat here, a Gujrat there. A Hyderabad here, a Hyderabad there. Delhi Gate in Lahore, Lahori Gate in Delhi. A Karachi Bakery here, a Bombay Bakery there. So many halves of a once whole.

Some discoveries are small and innocent; they appear as quietly as wrinkles in our understanding of the past – like opening the passport of a grandparent to discover their birthplace lies in a land now separated by a border, or hearing them speak in fragments of a language lost during migration. Amitoj's discovery was somewhat like this – hiding in plain sight. That Punjab was violently divided during Partition meant that, naturally, one half remained in Pakistan. And yet, unfortunately, in our popular imaginations in India, Punjab is so intrinsic to the nation state that generations far removed from a pre-independent India cannot imagine that we claim ownership over only half. But I am not surprised by his confession, for it's not the first time I have heard this.

Nodding, I ask how his perception of Pakistan changed after this discovery.

He laughs. 'I can't deny the animosity towards Pakistan growing up – because of cricket matches, media or politics, but eventually the reading of history made this feeling difficult to maintain. You see, I studied in Delhi at a Christian high school and it was only when I went to a Sikh college in my early twenties that I realized the enormity of Partition. There I learnt about the kingdom of Maharaja Ranjit Singh, and was intrigued by the diversity in his courts and armies. I found myself wondering how Sikhs and Muslims, Hindus and Christians never fought under his rule. He was arguably the greatest leader of undivided Punjab and I suppose I was trying to understand why such a way of governance was not possible now...'

His voice trails off for a minute, then he continues, 'Reading about Ranjit Singh's empire led me to his great capital, Lahore, which brought me to a book, *City of Sin and Splendour: Writings on Lahore*,[1] edited by Bapsi Sidhwa. Each story revealed how syncretic the city had once been, and how that syncretism was eventually consumed by the violence of Partition. From thereon, I began probing at home, only to realize that Lahore was closer to me than I'd imagined. My nani was born there, in Bhati Gate's Waan-wali Galli.'

The lure of family history is perhaps greater than that of national politics, even. When Amitoj talks about Lahore, he casually calls it '*saada* Lahore', our Lahore, and this little detail reveals how easy it is to erase the distance between him and the city across the border. Conversations with his nani, Surjit Kaur, take him back in time to when she was a student at Victoria High School, located in the haveli of prince Nau Nihal Singh, built during the reign of his grandfather, Maharaja Ranjit Singh.[2] This school was not far from her own home in Bhati Gate, built by her grandfather in the late 1800s, five storeys tall, including a basement, a roof and a connecting wall they shared with their Muslim neighbour. When the rumours of Partition began, the families made a pact that neither would harm the other,[3] and the structure was such that because the roofs of the buildings were connected, the women would often walk to the terrace and talk to one another from across the partitions. He stresses on the fact that though this situation was amicable and the families were close, there were always fault lines.

'They would never eat at each other's houses but would often share dry ration. At school, there were separate *matkas* of water for Hindus and Muslims. I was shocked to learn that even water was divided.'

'And did your grandmother tell you these stories readily?' I ask.

'Oh no, one had to pry them out of her; she didn't want to talk about this time. She made Partition out to be a very normal event in her life; according to her, because everyone went through it, there was nothing extraordinary about her experience. There is history of Partition on both sides of my family – my nana migrated from Gujranwala to Delhi, my dada from Muzaffarabad to Shillong via Gorakhpur – but I am closest to my nani, and so my knowledge of Partition is mostly based on her stories.'

'So, what happened to her family at Partition?'

'They moved in March 1947, when there were riots in the city,[4] but it was done in such haste that they had only an hour to decide whether they would continue to live in Lahore or leave. A relative who worked at the nearby police station informed the family that Partition was imminent and the riots would only get worse. A detail my grandmother mentions again and again is that from their haveli they took a taxi which cost them 26 rupees – a very large sum at the time – to the train station. From Lahore, they migrated to Sangrur – now in India and, at the time, a Muslim-majority town. There, they lived with her uncle who used to be a doctor in Burma. My grandmother describes how she witnessed the Muslims of Sangrur leaving *their* land and I think that's when the reality of Partition dawned on her – she longed for her Lahore as she watched men and women, infants and the elderly walking towards the border in a *kaafila*. She inherently understood the experience of leaving behind land, friends, safety. In fact, even the house they were eventually allotted belonged to a Muslim friend, with whom she used to play while visiting Sangrur and whose family had left for Pakistan...'

We both look at each other in silence. There has been no mention of violence or bloodshed, no refugee trains or *mohallas* set on fire, and yet, even in a story of completely safe migration, one cannot deny the presence of an ache for a home left behind. Though fifteen-year-old Surjit Kaur had made it to Sangrur safely, her pain was surmounting. I ask Amitoj whether she ever went back to Lahore and he brightens up.

'In 1999, my nani-nana went to Pakistan, to Gurudwara Nankana Sahib, Rawalpindi and Lahore, and stories from their trip were part of our dinner-table conversations for a long time. My nani vividly remembered her life there and had a desire to go back. At Lahore's Shahi Qila, they met a tour guide whom they asked about the *galli* where she had grown up. He was eager to help but told them to follow him at a distance so that no one would know he was leaving the premises with Sikhs. And, sure enough, he led them straight to the *galli*! When she walked inside, she was horrified to see that not only had her house burnt down in the fires of Partition but it had also remained in that state since then. She didn't like it and wanted to leave immediately.'

'Do you think it saddened her – the sight?'

'I think so, yes. But I'm not sure whether she left because of the sadness or the fact that she was accompanied by my grandfather, who was wearing a turban. She was probably more afraid for his safety.'

'Well, how do you feel when you listen to her stories?'

Amitoj breathes in deeply. 'There is an urge to go see that place, the other half of Punjab. I feel connected to it, invested in it, even though I've never been there before. I want to see it some day.'

THE CONNECTIONS TO the great city of Lahore run deep in families, trickling down generations eventually. For twenty-one-year-old Rashi Puri, 2020 was a year of discovery and the word Lahore dominated almost every conversation with her grandparents. Earlier on in the year, she came across the transcription of an audio recording she had done in 2013 while travelling on a train with her nani. They had set out from Delhi to Amritsar and, as they were about to reach Jalandhar, her nani, Shashi Bhalla, began narrating the story of how she had migrated during Partition from Lahore to Jalandhar. With great presence of mind, Rashi, all of fourteen, recorded the conversation, mostly because she had never heard anything like that before.

'It came so suddenly, I couldn't have expected it,' she tells me, 'but I didn't really understand it then. It's only when I speak to her now, years later, that I realize Partition is actually my nani's earliest childhood memory; it is the first thing she remembers about her childhood, and that fact in itself is so traumatic. She was eight years old when she migrated to India on the night train with her mother, two sisters and a brother. Her mother had made her sit under the seat, covered her and told her to be quiet throughout the journey, and midway through, she tells me ... well, she had had nothing to eat...' Rashi pauses and sighs, and then looks at me, unsure of how to narrate the story.

'It's okay,' I tell her, recognizing the overwhelmed look on her face, 'memory is not chronological, neither hers, nor yours. Tell the story as you'd like.'

She nods and begins again slowly. 'Things connect eventually. At first, they seem like disconnected habits and quirks, but eventually it all makes sense and somehow finds its way back to Partition. You see, for as long as I can remember, my nani has kept food on the headboard of her bed – boxes of dried fruit, biscuits, other snacks, a bottle of water or two – and I never wondered why that was. But coming back to 1947, when her family was migrating from Lahore to Jalandhar, her mother had tied grains of corn into the dupattas of all her daughters, and somehow the knot in my grandmother's dupatta came loose and the grains fell to the ground. As I mentioned, she was covered and hiding under the seat and she must have fallen asleep there. But when she woke up, she was starving and couldn't find her grains and began crying. That's when her sister had to give her hers, and it is from this moment that the habit of hoarding food, or at least keeping it close, was born. When I heard this little anecdote, something just shifted inside me. Partition was *the* defining memory of my nani's childhood, and it just made me realize how little I knew about it and how soon those memories may dim.'

'So, you began speaking to her about Partition?'

'Well, it began that way: how she came from Lahore to Jalandhar, then moved to Delhi, then to Baroda, and finally to Bombay. But then she started telling me stories about my grandfather's journey to India, and soon I was having conversations with everyone in the family. I was – *I am* still – the first person to ask my grandparents and their siblings about these things.'

'Tell me about your grandfather,' I suggest.

'Well, this is a long story and one that I am still discovering parts of. My nanu, Virender Singh Bhalla, was eleven years old when he lost his father to the riots of 1947. That was all I knew, and I didn't quite understand how to approach him with only those facts. So, one afternoon as I was sitting with my grandparents, my nani helped me by innocently asking nanu what his father's name was. And with that, well, he just took us back to his life in Lahore, which is a topic he approaches with great sadness, if at all. But that day he talked about his father, Anant Singh Bhalla, who was a schoolteacher in Bhagbanpura, and his grandfather, Sardar Prabha Singh Bhalla, who worked under the Maharaja of Bikaner and upon retirement built a home in Model Town,[5] a posh colony outside the walled city of Lahore. He told us how Anant Singh and all the children used to follow a very particular diet – no carbs, only protein, vegetables and fruits – and just basically happy, carefree childhood memories. And that was it, nothing else. But my nanu has an elder brother, Joginder Singh, who's ninety years old now, and I figured maybe he would remember more. On a video call from Bhubaneswar, he started our conversation with the question, "Do you know that my father was murdered in Lahore?" That's the first thing he said.'

The murder of Anant Singh Bhalla took place in broad daylight on 16 June 1947 on Grand Trunk Road, Lahore. It was around noon when he became one of the many casualties of the violent riots engulfing the city.[6] It was an unfair death, and one that Rashi's grandfather has still not gotten over. By evening, the news had reached the family. Anant's mother, Melo Bhalla, was so devastated that she beat her hands on her face – to the point where her bangles broke and shards entered her eyes, blinding her forever. The light had left her life. Through an old letter, Rashi discovered that Anant was cremated the next day. And then she reveals something altogether eerie.

'When I was in Bhubaneswar last, I was looking through old photographs with my nanu's brother and I found something that I didn't and still haven't had the heart to show my nanu. It is a photo of the day my great-grandfather was cremated, so 17 June 1947. It's really strange, because the entire family is at the cremation ground, and he is lying before them, covered in wood. His father, Prabha Singh, is by his side. His mother, Melo, is there, so are my nanu, his siblings and a couple of other relatives. And I ... I don't know what to make of it, to be honest. I don't know who would have taken the photo either.'

'How did you find it?' I ask, unsure of what else to ask.

'Well, my nanu's brother is very meticulous about his photo albums – they are numbered – and I found it in the very first one, maybe it was the oldest one. I asked him about it and he just said, "That's my father a day after he was murdered." He didn't say anything else, and I didn't want to press further.'

I'm at a loss for words, and Rashi can see that. She cracks a small, sad smile.

'Yes, that photograph really sent shivers down my spine. Not only because it's of a cremation, but also the fact that everyone is looking into the camera. Staring, in a very bizarre and uncomfortable way. Their eyes are wide and empty. My nanu's elder brother is crying. Their mother, Savitri, is holding her deceased husband's head. And, well, they're all just staring.'

I want to tell her that maybe their eyes were wide and empty with disbelief. Maybe it was the suddenness of death: that a man could be alive in the morning and dead by that afternoon. That for most people Partition seemed a distant and impossible reality until they were undeservedly paying the price for it. Or maybe their eyes were merely wide and empty with sadness, or trauma, or numbness.

'What did you feel when you found it?' I end up asking her.

'I think it just pained me more than anything else.'

I am wondering whether the incident could have encouraged the family to migrate pre-emptively, before a Partition line was announced. When I ask Rashi this, she shakes her head and tells me that because of the terrible rainfall and floods in Lahore that summer, the family was unable to move until mid-September, an entire month after Pakistan had been created. But from June to September, other strange things ensued.

One month after his father's death, Joginder Singh travelled from Lahore to Delhi, where his maternal grandfather had managed to find him a position in the government. He left behind his widowed mother, grandparents and siblings. Rashi tells me that he remembers how by July, despite the border not having been officially announced, people had begun to migrate to cities where they thought they would be safer. But the Bhalla family believed that a city like Lahore, which had long fostered Hindus, Muslims and Sikhs, would remain as is, that Hindus would continue to live in Pakistan and Muslims in India, for it was merely the system that was changing, not the soil or its people. But in the first week of August, a Muslim family suddenly arrived at their doorstep and moved into the house. It was a large space and so they occupied the empty rooms, and eventually the two families even ended up sharing parts of the house.

As I hear this, I am shocked. I have heard of refugees occupying empty evacuee property, but this is very unusual. I imagine a rather unique patchwork-like joint-family set-up, wondering what all they would have shared – whether they would have divided food in the time of rationing and hunger, whether the Sikh and Muslim families cooked similar or different things, whether they would have protected one another from riots and other harm, whether they were cordial or hostile in the beginning. I wonder how Sardar Prabha Singh would have felt to have people move into his home without invitation. But, most of all, I wonder whether the Muslim family is still living in that Model Town home in Lahore, and what their side of the story would be – for history, particularly the personal histories of Partition, always has two sides to consider.

But this much is clear: the desire for soil and home was greater than all else, for the Bhalla family continued to live in that house with the migrant Muslim family for nearly two months, ironically on a land that was being ripped apart on the basis of religion.

In September, they migrated to Jalandhar, where they lived in a camp. Melo Bhalla died there. Then in mid-November the remaining family members arrived in Delhi and registered themselves at the Purana Qila camp.[7] It appears that one small discovery led to another, which further led to another, and suddenly an entire history Rashi was once unaware of has unravelled itself before her. She tells me that after the conversation with her nanu and his brother, she found an old suitcase full of her great-grandmother's belongings. Inside it, tucked within a *Hindustan Times* edition dated 11 September 1957, were seventy letters written by Savitri Devi Bhalla from 1947 to 1958. They were all addressed to the postmaster general and GPO India, to be further sent to the GPO in Lahore. Each of these detailed the fact that her husband, a schoolmaster, had been murdered during Partition riots in Lahore and that the 4,388 rupees and 14 annas in his bank account were to be transferred to his family in India. Along with copies of the letters that she wrote, Savitri also kept every single letter she received.

Dated 8 April 1949, a letter from the Office of the Director General Posts & Telegraphs addressed to her reads, 'Madam, I am directed to acknowledge the receipt of your letter ... regarding your claim on a savings bank account No. 242654 in Pakistan in the name of your deceased husband. I am further directed to inform you that, as the cases of deceased accounts are fraught with numerous legal and technical difficulties, and as these cannot be overcome without the express concerns of both Dominions, it is feared that further delay will be inescapable.'

'It is the details that I cannot forget,' Rashi admits, '4,388 rupees and 14 annas. Or even her refugee number – she mentions it again and again in the letters – 273949. I can't un-know it, can't forget it.'

Sometimes, when we don't know enough about the past, we cling to all the things we *do* know, wanting to preserve them, retain them, afraid that one day we may forget them. As Rashi shows me letter after letter, I feel as though I have been let in on a family secret. The content of Savitri Bhalla's appeals is heartbreaking and yet I am struck by her might and determination in pursuing both governments for funds that were rightfully hers. Some of the letters have been written on the blank sides of used papers, revealing the dire financial condition of the family at the time. In one, she writes about how she had to delay her daughter's marriage because of a lack of funds. Then finally, in 1959, the governments were able to transfer the funds to Savitri Bhalla, requiring her *'to come down to the P&T office to complete the procedure'*.

Like me, Rashi too thinks often about the plight of her great-grandmother. 'I always read these letters alone, and never more than three or four in a single sitting. It's too much, I'm overcome by emotions for a predicament I didn't experience, and yet these letters have become my link to the family who came before me, to their losses, their sacrifices, their dreams. It's like I've absorbed the details; the dates and numbers are imprinted on my skin. They're with me. I don't know for how long, but for now they are there.'

There is a sadness in her tone, a helplessness, and I ask her whether she has shared these letters with anyone else from her family, her nanu perhaps.

'You are the only person I have ever discussed these letters with. My nanu's silence about Lahore is more revealing than anything he may say. There are many more questions, but for now I'm satisfied with what I have discovered, because it's more than what I knew before, and that is comforting.'

✑

AS I MOVE through the months, interviewing, processing and writing down stories, I become acutely aware of the allure of nostalgia, how cities that ancestors fled from can be steeped in carefree childhood memories, and how descendants willingly adopted these cities as their own. I note how most conversations inevitably mention loss and suffering, displacement and rebuilding. But the stories of violence are divulged carefully, uttered with horror and bewilderment, even if they are recalled by someone who didn't witness the violence first-hand. They are pieced together from scattered incidents and fragments of inherited memory, sometimes followed up by apologies for not knowing exactly when or how something happened or what their ancestor would have felt, or if they spoke about it with anyone. This is revealing of how Partition histories are discovered by subsequent generations. But not all discoveries are pleasant, or even emotional, though.

I have been privy to stories of the victims of trauma for a long time, but never had I heard a first-hand account of a perpetrator. And sometimes I did think about this – that if so many people suffered in the violence that ensued during Partition, then certainly there were people committing those violent acts. A part of me thinks that this is a simplistic and reductive way to think about it, because I wasn't there and I did not see the events unfold, and there are many other facets to consider. But even writing these sentences down is difficult, because for far too long *the mob, the rioter, the violent body* has been a faceless, ambiguous one. But when engaging with an individual's memories of perpetrating violence, we are assigning a face to that violence, no matter how many decades old it may be. And on that note, I have wondered whether and how such a story is passed down the generations, how it is discovered, received, treated. Whether there is any context provided, any reason, or even remorse. But I had never been in a position to ask, and so when I was told such a story, I found myself in difficult, uncharted territory.

When I receive an email from A,* it reads: 'I have a story from Partition. My distant ancestor abducted and sold many women ... a gruesome tale of horror.' It offers no more details, and I am unsure of how to take this conversation forward or even conduct such an interview. There is no rule book for oral history, because every situation is unique. I write back asking whether he feels comfortable telling me about what happened at the time. The reply reads, 'I don't think there is any point in talking about Partition if we cannot speak honestly. I am a servant of truth and of the recording of truth.'

And so it begins. For the next few weeks, A and I exchange emails about his ancestor, P. He starts by admitting he had not thought much about Partition until he discovered the violent acts of his ancestor – he was a child when he first heard passing references to the crimes he had committed. To give some background, he tells me that his family hails from Haryana. During the Great War, his great-grandfather sent three of his four sons – all married – to fight, and when the war was over, only two returned, one had lost his life. As per custom, the widow of the brother who did not return was married to the youngest son. In recognition of their services, all three sons were given land in the newly irrigated canal districts in what is today Pakistan. A tells me that because their village was a semi-dry desert with perpetual water scarcity, the families started a new life in their new lands. Then, inching closer to the story of P, he writes,

> The land grant of the son who died was given to his widow, now married to the youngest son. When years passed and they had no children, the family began looking for another bride who could give the youngest son some heirs. Their attitude towards the first wife became harsh and cruel, and curses of being a barren woman followed her. Eventually, a young girl, my biological grandmother, was married to my grandfather, who was already in his thirties.

---

* Initials have been used to retain anonymity on the individual's request.

A does not write every day, and certainly not chronologically. He writes in the same way that memory unfurls, sporadically, unpredictably, inspired by chance remarks, and the story is revealed fully over the course of many mails. He does not always write about his family either; sometimes we speak about the village and often discuss language and customs:

> I grew up in a Muslim-abandoned village of Haryana. Seen from the roof, the three-domed mosque of our village stands silent with its elegant onion domes ... Growing up, our street was a beehive of Multani people [who had migrated during Partition] with their smooth, refined, pliable dialect and then there were my own people, the Jats of Haryana, with their thick, heavy accents. The two sounds were antipodes to each other and I spent many hours just absorbing these two sounds.

Meandering, he returns to his family. The young bride eventually bore the youngest brother a son, whom his first wife adopted. The couple had three more children, one of whom was A's father. Then in the summer of 1947, by virtue of contacts in the army, the family got news of Partition and decided to migrate back to their village in Haryana as a precaution. The rogue, P, was a distant relative and well known in the area for acts of robbery, strangulating travellers and abducting young women:

> He beguiled them by appearing helpful, gaining confidence of victims, keeping them hopeful, then abducting them by force with his accomplices, and then breaking their resistance. I can go on telling such stories, for such is the evil associated with his name.

Upon receiving this, I think long about how to respond. Because we are not having this conversation in person, it is hard for me to gauge his reactions. I ask whether the stories of his ancestor, P – and, by extension, of Partition – are openly discussed in the family, to which A replies that he has heard about how as a child his uncle used to oppose P's presence in the house. Resenting his devilish ways, he did everything he could to dissuade his parents from inviting him in. One day, P challenged the young boy to a wrestling match, nearly strangling him to death on purpose until two men riding past on camels tore the pair apart:

> This was the first memory I discovered about P, when I was barely ten years old. It was not told to me directly, but I overheard it, which meant that it was discussed at home. Then as I grew older, his legend grew denser and more ominous. See, in the summer of 1947, when the family returned from west Punjab to Haryana, they brought news of attacks on Hindus by Muslims, and this is the dominant memory that has remained in everyone's mind – the story of Muslim mobs setting upon hapless Hindus. And P took his revenge the only way he knew how. During and after Partition, he was involved in a strange business venture, wherein he travelled across the breadth of Haryana looking for girls who had either been left behind or whose families had died in the riots. Almost every other village in those days was a Muslim village, and the names of these villages still bear testimony to their antecedent. So, for several months, P would round up young girls and sell them. Once a girl prisoner ran away and her body was found in our village well. However, it is only my assumption that the girls were Muslim, since they were never identified by their religion.

These stories disturb me deeply, and sometimes I find myself asking too direct a question. Inevitably, a reply arrives, and the horror deepens. But I do consciously need to remind myself that if it is difficult for me to read these stories, then it is even more so for A to tell them, for him to even acknowledge that they exist in his history, for him to resuscitate them to the surface, for him to write them out. There are shades of vulnerability to be felt in every conversation about Partition, and just because this is an interview with a younger person does not make it any less delicate than an interview with an eyewitness.

A tells me that at the time of Partition, neighbours would comment on the number of girls arriving and leaving the premises. He doesn't write much else, but even in the sparseness of detail, one only needs to imagine. That Partition was a gendered event is a fact well established on both sides of the border,[8] but this kind of trade of women as a means of revenge is frightening. A too acknowledges that this was the fate of too many women, and there were others like his ancestor.

As I begin to share what I have written based on our conversations, the barbarianism of it all upsets A deeply. Despite this story being decades removed from his present life, he is affected by it. Perhaps seeing it all down on paper is different from merely knowing of its existence. But I also admit that my first drafts are harsh, they are written from the perspective of a young woman trying to imagine the fate of other young women caught in such a predicament. I find it difficult to write with objectivity; I surprise myself with my wrath. Truth be told, I don't know yet how to take care of this story, and not to let judgement seep through. What I know for certain, though, is that I want to be careful not to exploit this relationship, for A has opened up in a way that is difficult and unusual.

In his final emails on the subject, he tells me that the actions of his ancestor are not representative of the entire family, and were his alone. He reminds me that neither of us was present at the time of Partition, that humans are complicated beings, that some actions cannot be accounted for by anyone else apart from the person who committed them, and so I must not write about this with bias, even though I may want to, due to the cruelness of the memories he is divulging:

> For the sake of human faith, we must not make evil excessively evil … Partition was not a day-long affair, it stretched over several years and P preyed on the displaced population like a monster. I am no one holding the blindfolded scales of justice over him in his absentia. I cannot explain why he did the things

he did, but he met a well-deserved, gory end for what he did to those hapless women.

IT IS NOT unusual for the past to remain undisturbed for great lengths of time, making no effort to reveal or obscure itself, but waiting for the right moment and perhaps the right person to *notice* it. The final section of this chapter is a conversation with two siblings born and raised in England in the '90s, and the many sporadic discoveries that have led them to piece their family history – of Partition and beyond – together.

When I first speak with Chayya Syal, our conversation is brief but revelatory. She was nearly thirty years old when she learnt that her paternal grandmother's family was not originally from the Punjab, as she had always assumed, but from Peshawar in the erstwhile Frontier Province (now Khyber Pakhtunkhwa), with generations going back to Kabul before the Durand Line was even established. The language they speak then is Hindko. Having grown up in London, this discovery makes her re-evaluate her identity, which till now has been understood to be part of the Indian diaspora. The next time we speak is a year later over a video call with her and her younger brother, Bharath, who both live in England.

'I think I was five years old when I heard the word Partition,' Chayya says, as Bharath listens carefully.

'How can you remember so certainly?' I am curious.

'Well, I was told that I was born in exile and naturally, as a child, you don't understand what that means. But those words are imprinted in my memory. In the 1990s and early 2000s, my grandparents would watch films at home – you know, *Kargil, Border, Mission Kashmir* – but I never understood Hindi, so I couldn't completely grasp the films. But what I did notice was that they aroused certain emotions in the adults. They would speak about this Partition, and the relationship between India and Pakistan, and how much the British had looted the subcontinent, taken everything. And I remember thinking that if they'd taken everything from us, then why were we here?' she laughs.

'How and why you ultimately found refuge in the place that once colonized you...' I add.

'Exactly. The two events I grew up hearing quite a lot about were Partition, after which my grandfather migrated from Delhi to Kenya, and the military coup in the 1980s in Kenya,[9] which ultimately sent them from Nairobi to London. But our grandmother, our dadima, always told us that we must never forget where we were from and how we had survived. She said the fact that we were alive was our greatest victory. Now, these are big things to tell a child.'

'But, growing up, did you feel Partition was a part of your history?'

'Oh yes, very much. We didn't understand the extent or severity of it, but we certainly recognized the loss it carried. And for me at least, a lot of this is interwoven – the event of Partition, race, ethnicity, belonging, growing up in the diaspora. These are all interconnected. You see, I've never been to India, nobody apart from our grandmother has. And when our grandfather, our dadaji, died, no one told me about it but someone said that he'd gone back to India, because I was too young at the time to understand death.' Chayya smiles at the innocence of the thought, but her eyes are sad. 'I had a strong connection to being Punjabi, but I never felt patriotic as an Indian because other Indians around me were always telling me that I didn't look like them, or follow the same traditions or customs as them. Growing up, I always got along better with Pakistanis or Afghans than with Indians. And then there was the issue of our surname...'

'What do you mean? The surname Syal?' I raise my eyebrows.

The screen of the video call is split three ways and I see Chayya give a look that is clearly meant for Bharath. He nods to encourage her, and she continues, 'I went to secondary school with a lot of Gujaratis, and they would always look at my surname and ask what my caste was. When I asked my father, he said we had no caste, we were Punjabi and that was that. But I just didn't know any other Indians with our surname, and so I was always accused of being a Muslim spy, because they couldn't place where my surname was from.'

My mouth falls wide open in horror.

'I'm deviating a bit from your topic of Partition, but I assure you it's all connected,' she says to me. 'You see, the understanding of our history from an undivided India has been such a gradual process, where each conversation has led to a tiny, newer discovery; like another layer into ourselves, into figuring out our identities. Anyway, coming back to our surname – we know a little more now, but even while I was at university, we had no knowledge of it.

'There was an incident at university, where a priest was invited to give a talk, and he began talking about the caste system in India, and how one can tell a "good" Hindu from their surname alone. So, he went around the room randomly asking people their surnames. When he came to me, I said my name was Syal, to which he asked where we were originally from, and I didn't know what to say because I didn't know where we came from, and so I just said I'm Punjabi, and he persisted by asking *where* in Punjab, to which I had no answer. He then very publicly said that he thought my family wasn't telling me the truth because my surname wasn't Hindu or Indian. And no one stood up to him, so he just continued on by saying that there were many Muslims with this surname and asked whether I was there to convert people...' She exhales loudly. 'Honestly, I'd never been so humiliated in my life. But I just didn't have any answers, and I think Partition is greatly responsible for this feeling – it is the reason that so many people, particularly those who have grown up in the diaspora, don't know where they are from.'

I'm deeply disturbed by how casually and publicly Chayya's background was not only demanded of her but also insulted. The sheer complexity of religious and ethnic identity was reduced to a baseless and exclusionary classification. The Dalit scholar and activist

Suraj Yengde explains that casteism is 'the world's oldest surviving discrimination. It's personal, but it also is societal.'[10] In South Asia, family history is tied to family name. And merely telling someone your name will hold you to your caste, class, religion and origin. When I mention this to Chayya, she nods, 'That's how it felt. He wanted to hold me to something unknown.'

'Did you speak to anyone at home about this? Or even what it meant to be born in exile?'

'We only began talking about family history this year, never before. And the comment about exile … well, I've never told anyone this, not even Bharath.' She looks into the camera and with a small smile says, 'When I was a child, I used to think it was like in *The Lion King*, where Simba is sent away, and we were like Simba, far, far away from our roots. And the only thing that connected us to those roots was our name, but the irony was that even that was a black hole for us.

'I think, growing up, I never really felt like England was my home, even though I had been born and raised here. Then, when 9/11 happened, suddenly everyone's national allegiance was questioned. I was only ten years old, but I'd already understood that I wasn't really from here, and then all of a sudden everybody else was saying that I wasn't from here either. So, I never felt a sense of ease in England, and I never felt connected to India. Which led me to the question: *where are we from?* And, actually, Bharath is the best person to talk about our origin, because he has done the most research on it in the last few years.'

Bharath, who is seven years younger than Chayya, has only been listening so far. He now enters the conversation. 'I'm a very curious person, I question everything, always have. I think the best way to understand our history is to look at our paternal side – our dadima and dadaji's families. On our maternal side, all we know is that our grandfather's family came from Jalandhar, but it was never spoken about.

'Our dadima's name is Raj Kumari Syal, and several generations ago her family was from Kabul. Then, in the early 1800s, they travelled down to Peshawar, and this really explains a lot of the influence on our upbringing. How the Punjabi we speak now is influenced by Hindko[11] rather than traditional Doabi Punjabi, or how the dishes our grandmother cooked were influenced by a medley of Punjabi and Afghani food, or even the way we looked – the shape of our noses, the colour of our skin – it was all different from the other Punjabis we knew. Then, some time in the 1930s, dadima's family left Peshawar for East Africa, well before Partition, because they witnessed dire economic conditions. Dadima was born in 1941 in Kenya.'

'What was it she always said?' Chayya adds. '"You never leave your land except for poverty or love." It broke my heart that they left because of poverty.'

Bharath nods. 'So, in a sense, dadima's family has no tangible connection to present-day India, really. Our connection to Partition comes from our dadaji, Khushbhakt Syal, who was born in 1934. He was thirteen years old in 1947 and working in the tar pits in north Delhi since the age of twelve; he was in a sense a child slave. He lived extremely close to the violence that erupted in Delhi during Partition, and though he didn't migrate across the border, he witnessed the riots in his city.

'A few years later, in 1954, again because of poverty, our dada's family decided to migrate to Kenya. Dadaji was twenty years old at the time. Our grandparents had an arranged marriage in 1961, in a place called Musoma in Tanzania. Then in 1983, because of the military coup, our grandparents and their children all came to London. Our father was one of the last to escape – he went from Kenya to Egypt to Russia and then on a train to France and, finally, London. Now, we have only one relative left in India, our dadaji's youngest brother. There is no one else.'

'That being said,' Chayya says, 'on our dadaji's side, we *can* go back four or five generations ... I have it documented in a terribly untidy family tree,' she laughs, holding up some pages to the camera. 'What we know for certain is this: at some point in our history, there were two brothers, Roop and Dhoop Chand Lal, who had a business that sent them across the expanse of the north-western region from Lasara in the east all the way to Kabul in the west, and they spoke and read everything from Punjabi to Farsi, Urdu to English. But their origin was a place called Seetpur, in Muzaffargarh district of present-day Pakistan, and they had been there for so long that they were known as Sons of the Soil. Seetpur is where the Indus river meets the Chenab, and because life then was mostly agrarian, the family would travel along the rivers – they went where the river went, and they moved when it dried up. In this way, they ended up travelling from Seetpur to Multan, and all the way up to Jhang, likely along the Chenab.'

'It is only in recent years that we have discovered that the roots of the name Syal,' Bharath adds, 'are from around Multan – it's an indigenous tribal surname that still exists and there are several people in Pakistan who have this surname. We have no connection to them that we know of or, if we do, then we don't know how to find out more. But what's most interesting is that we have no real direct connection to Partition, and yet this border has cut us off from our history, because even the most ancient of our origins are now not in India – as we grew up thinking – but across the border in Pakistan.'

I have mostly listened so far, but I now ask, 'Have you ever seen that document, *A Glossary of the Tribes and Castes of the Punjab and North-West Frontier Province*?' When they both shake their heads, I continue, 'Well, it's an ethnological study of areas of present-day Pakistan and India, compiled by the Indian Civil Service administrator Horace Arthur Rose. Much of it is based on the census reports for the Punjab from 1883 and 1892, and was first published in Lahore in 1911. The edition I have is from 1914[12] and it is an overwhelmingly comprehensive document of castes, sub-castes, origins and histories of tribes, even tangential stories of mythology attached to particular names...'

I search for the document on my computer and share my screen with the Syal siblings. As far as oral history interviews go, this set-up seems very unconventional and futuristic, but I am grateful that despite the oceans between us, the quality of the conversation has remained as authentic and sincere as it would have been in person. I make sure that they can see the document clearly on their respective screens and then search for the surname Syal. Several results appear and I hear one of the siblings gasp. I scroll down to the first result, which appears under the letter M, and take a deep breath. There is complete silence from the other end and the only sounds I can hear are from the traffic outside my own window in Delhi.

'I didn't even know such a resource existed,' Chayya finally whispers, still visibly stunned. Bharath says nothing, but I can see him combing through the text carefully. The surname Syal is listed under the heading of Máchhi, or fisherman, and the text below mentions the Indus river and the area of Multan.[13] The tribe is listed as both Hindu and Muslim.

'Chayya...' Bharath calls out to his sister softly.

'Wait, there appears to be more,' I say distractedly, searching for the name further, using different spellings. When I type in Sial, it brings me to a more comprehensive and specific history of the tribe under the letter S. *Shuni – Siál*, the heading states. I begin to read aloud:

> Siál, Syál, politically one of the most important tribes of the Western Plains. As Mr. E. B. Steedman observed the modern history of the Jhang district is the history of the Siál.[*] They are a tribe of Punwár Rájputs who rose to prominence in the first half of the 18th century.[14]

'Jhang,' Chayya repeats, for it is a word she has come to recognize as her own.

---

[*] A mirási attached to the Dhidoána clan says that Sewa, a Sahgal Khatri, was converted to Islám by Báwa Faríd and was then called Siál.

As we all scan through the next few pages, I cannot help but feel like I'm intruding on the discovery of a very personal history. I wonder if it may have been better to just send them the document and have them find this information on their own. I look at them both, but they are completely engrossed, peering at the tiny, scanned text.

Taking a deep breath in, I summarize my reading so far. 'So, uh ... it appears that Sials or Syals are found in both India and Pakistan, and can be Hindu, Muslim *and* Sikh. The Sials of Jhang had once been nomadic pastoralists. The document breaks the tribe down further by geography ... and the *Tárikh-i-Jhang Syál* narrows its origin to the confluence of the Chenab and Jhelum.[15] The list of its chiefs begins with Mál Khán and puts the establishment of their rule in Jhang in 1477 AD. Apparently, Heer, the heroine from one of the best-known Punjabi legends, *Heer-Ranjha*, was a Siál.'[16]

I look up from the screen and, smiling widely, say, 'So, actually, you had a lot of the pieces already ... but to see the name in this document is quite incredible, I'm sure.'

'This ... all makes so much sense,' Bharath says very slowly, staring at the screen.

I look at Chayya and suddenly notice that tears are falling down her face. 'Chayya, I'm really so sorry, I didn't mean to –' I begin, but she stops me immediately.

'No, please ... I'm so moved,' she says.

Bharath brings both his palms up to his cheeks and exhales. 'Well, now we know.'

Chayya nods, 'It's just so moving because I've never seen our surname anywhere like that before. To see it written down, documented in such a complete and concrete way with actual history tied to a particular land ... the river, the cities, all the names we had heard only in passing or as fragments. You know, after a certain point, because of Partition, there are only so many Indian records you can access. But *there* we are, *we belong*.' She points to her screen and then wipes her eyes dry. 'I'm just an emotional person. Even when I found out recently about our connections to Peshawar and Kabul, I felt so emotional because it was a connection to a real place, which explained a lot of our habits and lifestyle.'

The document brings about a very natural and dense pause to our conversation. Each of us is looking at our screens in silence. My heart is beating with happiness, for the Syal siblings have discovered something tangible about their history – though now I don't quite know how to continue the interview and feel as though I may take away from this moment if I move on to other topics. But Chayya herself breaks the silence after a few seconds.

'I really wish Partition had never happened. There were only losses all around. I am thirty years old and I have discovered my roots just now, *right now*, on a video call with a historian. It's surreal, because every time before this, whenever I looked back to the past, there were no answers, only confusion, only black holes. Whenever I've thought about Punjab, or being Punjabi, it's always been associated with pain. For many years, I couldn't watch films on Partition without crying and I can't explain why that was. I wasn't born during that time, I didn't witness it; actually, neither did any of my grandparents directly. But it was the sheer scale and depth of loss and trauma that it incurred within every single person and each generation that has followed. The creation of this Partition line has made so many people's pasts inaccessible to them.

'Even my dadima who was born and raised in Kenya understood the impact of what Partition meant. She once told me that it was the day the soil lost its heartbeat because everyone was just viciously ripped apart from where they had been – knowing that your home was being carved up and having no say in it, feeling helpless.'

'I feel the same,' I tell her, and then turn to Bharath. 'Chayya mentioned that over the last few years, you'd been doing a fair bit of research on the family. How much does Partition factor into that study?'

Bharath thinks for a few seconds before he says, 'I was familiar with the general backdrop of the British Empire in India, but it was our own family connections that made it real. And, of course, this document today has only added to that. But, as Chayya mentioned earlier, growing up, we constantly felt like we were in exodus. I think our father felt it too. Being a Punjabi man with Peshawari influences, who had grown up surrounded by Gujaratis in Kenya, his identity was quite jumbled. I've come to believe that this is why he would tell us that the world was an ocean.'

'The world is an ocean?'

'Yes, the world is an ocean. Your body is a diving suit – you don't own it, God owns it. It is your job to explore this ocean. It's not tied to any country, any nationality, any flag. That's what he used to tell me when I was a child, and it was so beautiful and facilitated so much exploration for me. That's how we thought of things at a young age. But now, when I look at our family history and Partition, it is with sorrow and pain because it is the severing of a place to which my family once belonged. As I have made these discoveries, the pain has become a little more muted, but even the inheritance has made us second-hand witnesses to Partition.

'We were basically untouched by religious violence on both sides. The argument that Partition is what led to our exodus is only applicable to my grandfather's side. But what is really so painful for me is the fact that I had to spend years painstakingly piecing together where we are from. I felt like I was lied to, like my history had been obfuscated – by family, by government authority, by religious authority. We now know more than we did before, but there is so much to still unearth. I am certain that we are not alone, though. That there are so many children and grandchildren whose histories have been severed and hidden from them in this exact way, where the past is just a black hole.'

'There is solace in knowing where you come from, a sense of belonging to somewhere,' Chayya adds reflectively, 'and we just never had that.'

'And we have lived with Partition in our own ways,' Bharath responds, nodding. 'For me, personally, it is the fact that our ancestral home is now in Pakistan and I am lucky to have realized this at an age where making the journey there is possible. Because of old age, our dadima will never be able to see the land her ancestors once lived in. But I want to go there and experience it.'

Chayya now smiles so widely that even oceans away, and through a computer screen, I am certain I can feel hope radiate out of her. 'I would love to go back to where our family comes from, I would love to just walk on that soil. It sounds really silly but I keep thinking about the soil losing its heartbeat at Partition. And I just want to touch it and tell it that we are still here. We're far away but we're still here. That's why I got so emotional when I saw that document just now, because finally, after so long, it felt like I could go *somewhere* now.'

5
Family

⤲

O NE OF THE FIRST interviews I conduct for this chapter is
with Shafa Tasneem, born in Chattogram (earlier known as
Chittagong), Bangladesh, who tells me proudly that she has family
in Bangladesh, India and Pakistan. At first, this surprises me, but
the more interviews I conduct thereafter, the more I find this to
be a commonality, particularly among families that witnessed the
multiple partitions of the region. But what strikes me during the
conversation with Shafa is her extraordinary tone – she is bereft of
the characteristic sorrow that accompanies stories of separation, and
is quite matter-of-fact while discussing how members of her family
came to gain different nationalities.

Shafa comes from an Urdu-speaking Muslim family from
Rahimabad, Bihar. In 1948, at the age of twenty-four, her paternal
grandfather, Abdul Malik – one of seven siblings – left India for East
Pakistan. He left in anger due to a family matter, but Partition must
have also played a role because Shafa's aunts tell her that he went
wherever all the Muslims were going, and often he would narrate the
tale of when he fled home with only two annas in his pocket. Out of
the siblings he left behind, his two brothers who were still studying
ultimately joined him in East Pakistan. The remainder – two brothers,
two sisters – were married and settled in India.

When Bangladesh was created in 1971, one of the main causes
being the linguistic differences between the Bengali- and Urdu-

speaking communities, one brother migrated to Pakistan. He had worked for the government's Telegraph and Telephone (T&T) Department but now found himself unemployed and being told that he was Pakistani and no longer belonged in Bangladesh. He was held captive multiple times for being 'Bihari', a term that not only refers 'to the people of Bihar alone, but is used for a variety of Urdu-speaking people who migrated to East Pakistan at the time of Partition'.[1] But Shafa's grandfather happened to be close to a 'Bengali' commissioner – the term Bengali 'often used synonymously with Bangladeshi or East Pakistani'[2] – who would come to their aid and save the brother. However, the family's goods were seized several times and their car was also taken away.

Eventually, in 1981, ten years after the first brother left for Pakistan, the second one followed, in hope of better economic opportunities. There, they would be known as *muhajirs*, the term for Urdu-speaking refugees. '*Ab toh jeena-marna yaheen hai,*' is what Malik sahib had said when asked if he would join them, asserting that he would now live and die in Bangladesh. Though he remained disturbed after these incidents, he had a well-established business of iodized edible salt called Malik Sons,* set up in 1952. The brothers remained in touch and, much to my amazement, were somehow even able to meet one another frequently. But, triggered by Partition, a family of seven siblings was dispersed across the three nations that once constituted British India – four died in India, two in Pakistan and one in Bangladesh.

Shafa was born in 1997 and directs our conversations to the ways in which her grandfather's decision to remain in Bangladesh as an Urdu-speaking Muslim continues to carry an undercurrent of the two partitions the land has witnessed. 'Growing up, we were never allowed to speak Urdu outside our homes, particularly near any government areas or buildings. And as a child, I found it somewhat abnormal to see an Urdu-speaking family conversing in Bangla

---

* One of the oldest salt houses in Bangladesh today, it is still run by Shafa's father and uncles.

anywhere outside a household setting. But as a Bangladeshi citizen, these are the underlying effects of Partition, and I've intrinsically understood them since childhood.'

It becomes clear from her words that Partition cannot be understood as a one-dimensional event, for it not only affected the lives of those who fled, but also those who remained. Her grandfather may have stood by his decision to 'live and die in Bangladesh', committed his life to a country that had provided him refuge in 1948, bequeathing this intention to his subsequent generations, who are proud Bangladeshi citizens. But the language politics that compelled him to make a choice and be separated from his family has continued to this very day, carving out a complicated space for his descendants to inhabit. Though there are several incidents she can recall, Shafa tells me that the first time she felt 'attacked' because of her language was five years ago, while she was still a teenager. At the passport office, an official overheard her family speaking to one another in Urdu and began pointing their way, calling them refugees.

'That might have been the very first time I heard the word refugee, and it sounded like slang. He spoke loud enough for us to hear him accuse us of remaining in Bangladesh after the 1971 partition. Most of the time, it is common people who face the consequences of political decisions, and though I did not witness Partition first-hand, I took that incident to heart.'

I understand language to have always played an integral role in Shafa's life, as she recalls an incident from when she hadn't even turned nine years old. 'My father's aunt had come to visit us from Pakistan. One afternoon, I saw her penning a letter in Urdu which left me so in awe that years from then, I, a born Bangladeshi, became a self-taught Urdu reader. In fact, I'd taught myself Hindi way before that as well. And I am proud of it, not just because language is a fascination, but because I felt it was a responsibility towards the sum total of my ancestry.'

Despite her young age, Shafa's outlook is resilient and proud of the multiple nationalities that make up her family. But Partition continues to cause her deep pain, less because of familial separation and more because of how blood-soaked it left the entire subcontinent. She thinks about the common people who laid their lives for freedom, and how those sacrifices are often lost in the celebration of that freedom.

Returning to the moment of her grandfather's initial migration, I ask, 'Does the family speak about it?'

'Though the word Partition is hardly uttered, it is certainly sensed in an impactful and visceral way. It is … an unchangeable, accepted grief. The way we in Bangladesh speak about Pakistan, the way our family in Pakistan speaks about India, the way those in India speak about its neighbours is not in tandem with how the three nations perceive each other politically. Since my grandparents and their siblings were able to meet one another often, I don't know how much of this lament they carry. There aren't many in the family who take this suffering intimately, or even express it, or think about what could have been, but me…'

She need not have said what she says next, for her tone betrays it.

'…these sentiments feel heavy in my heart, occupying a very private space.'

'But it is a rare joy to witness a family made up of Bangladeshis, Indians and Pakistanis,' I say.

'I wish such a reality was witnessed by us all without discrimination. And even though we may have scattered away, I relish the fact that as a family, we did not break apart.'

THE CONVERSATION WITH Shafa not only illuminates the different ways in which families parted after Partition but also the different identities they adopted in their respective nations thereafter. Apart from the conditions of life that the family had once been used to, Partition sometimes changed the very structure of the family itself.

When I speak with Arslan Athar,* a Pakistani writer born in Dubai in 1995, based currently in Lahore, he tells me that for several years

---

* An excerpt on buried objects from Arslan Athar's interview appears in Chapter 15, 'Material Memory'.

he has been trying to understand how and why his family came to be divided in the decade following Partition.

'For a long time, we never spoke about when my paternal side left Hyderabad,' he recalls, 'and why only half came to Pakistan and the other half remained in India.'

'But did you always know of your family in India?' I ask.

'Migration is present on both sides of my family,' he says, patiently laying down both context and chronology, 'but the only distinction is that my mother belongs to a Punjabi Muslim family that came from Hoshiarpur, India, to Faisalabad (then Lyallpur), Pakistan, during Partition and left no family member behind. Their migration was singular and complete. On my father's side, however, the migrations are not only belated but also lack clarity on the when, how and why.

'Ever since childhood, I knew that part of my paternal family was still in Hyderabad – it's very common for *muhajir* families in Pakistan to have relatives in India. But at some point, either I or a cousin asked my grandfather about where we were originally from, and he said that the generations before him were Afghani and had been employed as guards at the palace of the Nizam of Hyderabad. Over time, the family mixed with the local population, married, and settled in the state. During Partition, Hyderabad state chose to join neither India nor Pakistan, retaining its sovereignty. It was only after Operation Polo in 1948 that the last and seventh Nizam, Mir Osman Ali Khan, acceded to India, ending his dynasty.'[3]

Here, Arslan is careful to add the disclaimer that memory eludes corroboration. 'In the few conversations I had with my grandfather on the subject, he recalled that post 1948, it became difficult for middle-class Muslims to remain in Hyderabad, which had a Hindu-majority population even under the last Nizam. They were crushed, couldn't find employment. But what ultimately drove them to migrate to Pakistan was that they could no longer be a part of an India that was fighting with itself.'

'What did he mean?'

'Well, he said that in the years following Partition, India was still fighting with its own Muslim brothers. I think there's more to this move than he ever spoke about with anyone, but the idea of a Muslim nation, the need for freedom, concern for his growing family, and the economic opportunities all paved the way for their migration to Pakistan.'

'But half the family remained in India…'

'That's correct, so my grandparents left each of their parents and several siblings behind. One of my father's sisters was adopted by my grandfather's sister and her husband because they had no children of their own, and so she was left behind. Once in Pakistan, my grandparents first stayed in Peshawar, where my grandmother's brother was the dean at the university, and then later my grandfather joined the army. When they settled in Karachi, he called two of his brothers from Hyderabad to join him. It was only when I spoke with my aunt who had been left behind that I learnt my father was actually born in Hyderabad in 1959, and only after that did the family migrate.'

'But why leave family?' I ask, trying to understand.

Arslan looks at me and shrugs helplessly. 'There are a lot of big questions in my mind that I wish could ask my grandparents, but now it's too late. So, I have to do my own research, put the pieces together about what may have happened. If I could, I would have asked them – why did you move so late, why were you unable to convince your parents, your other siblings and, of course, the bigger question –' he pauses, '– the permanent trauma around separation itself.'

This, I think, cuts at the heart of the tragedy of divided families – that it is not always only about the parting of ways but also the space that is formed in between. What fills the void after family has left for a land that's often inaccessible?

Gently, I ask Arslan if he wants to discuss this, and he takes a breath in. 'I have felt a deep pain while speaking with my aunt who was initially left in India. But the story is more complicated, because long after her birth parents – my grandparents – migrated to Pakistan, she too was brought over. But by then, she'd spent a good part of her life in India and couldn't go back easily, and missed everyone *she* had left behind, including her adoptive parents, whom she'd been close with. She couldn't see them grow old and I distinctly remember her sadness. Similarly, my grandparents had to live away from their siblings and not see their nieces or nephews grow up, or attend weddings or funerals. They couldn't be with family in either happiness or grief.

'But I also think that there was a sense of abandonment in the family that remained in India. Again, I don't know why they stayed, so I can't fully explain this feeling, but for a long time, even if any of them came across to Pakistan when travel was easier, this pain was never discussed, it remained buried. Only now, post my grandparents' death, some of these quiet, festering grievances have emerged. *Aap chhod ke chale gaye*, you've left us behind, and things like that.' After a few minutes, he adds, 'Is it animosity or anger? Is it just pain or a feeling of desertion? It may be all these things, but it's definitely a wound.'

He takes time to construct his thoughts.

'The thing is, you see your family go through this pain, but you brush it off. There is an acceptance of sorts, because … what else can you do?' His question is sincere but rhetorical. 'You can't unmake the border. And if the family in India struggled with separation, the family in Pakistan struggled to rebuild their life. They came here with nothing, and in that sense any trauma they endured or memories they left behind became secondary to survival. They didn't talk about loss or sadness; they didn't talk about anything; they just persevered because all the trauma *had to be* worth something. My parents' generation were taught that they must be grateful they had a homeland for Muslims. A land that was their own. My father was raised in a Pakistan of extreme nationalism, where there was a definite understanding of what was Pakistan and what was India, and what they meant to one another. Enemies.'

'But wasn't that complicated, having family in India? How can your family be your enemy?'

'How indeed. But in that sense, aren't India and Pakistan born from the same land, also siblings?' he asks with a smile. 'Partition and the migrations after it led to many relationships being severed and many others being created, sometimes without choice. It is ... very complicated, and I'm sure it couldn't have been easy. But there's been a fair bit of disassociation for my father now, and he really wants to visit Hyderabad – to see the city where his parents grew up, the city where he was born.'

'And do *you* feel a pull towards Hyderabad?' I ask.

His face breaks into a warm smile as he says, 'Of course, very often. There are many Hyderabadi customs that we practise to date in our family. For instance, in Pakistan, you ordinarily don't touch your elders' feet, as I've seen most Hindus do, as a sign of respect. But this is common to Hyderabadi Muslim families, where you can either bow your head in a gesture of *adaab*, or touch your grandparents' feet or, as my Pakistani cousins who have been raised in the traditional Hyderabadi way do, prostate on the ground!' he laughs. 'In return, the elder will give their blessing by placing their hands on your head.'[4]

'Exactly as we do, then,' I note, and then, returning now to the beginning of our conversation, I ask, 'Arslan, when you think of all the unanswered questions about your family history, do you find that path leading to Partition?'

'That is *the* moment, the trigger, no?' he asks me.

'The very word feels like a dismemberment to me,' I admit.

He nods. 'Exactly, when I think of Partition, all that comes to mind is a complete departure. Sometimes I feel my identity was created *because* of this departure and the migrations that followed. Sometimes it bothers me that my family has chosen to speak so little about what happened, because I want to know both sides of my family – the Indian and the Pakistani. But then fragments of memory suddenly emerge in Dakhni Urdu, or tales about Hyderabad and the family that still lives there are told with nostalgia, and this is how you can be certain that the legacy of Partition continues to hold within it the stories of many generations.'

༄

A FEW WEEKS after this conversation, I speak with Z, who seems to pick up from where Arslan has left off – Hyderabad. Born into a north Indian Muslim family in 1997, Z moved to the City of Nizams nearly a decade ago, and only then realized just how many people came from divided families like hers. In the years following Partition, both sides of her extended family migrated to Karachi. While her father was able to keep in touch with his relatives, on her mother's side contact became sparser as time passed.

To begin, I ask Z the same question I had posed to Arslan: 'Growing up, did you know you had family in Pakistan?'

'In school, we read about Independence and Partition, but I never thought they had affected us personally, because my grandparents hadn't been displaced. It was only much later that I learnt about the consequences, about how my maternal grandfather was separated from his sibling...' She looks at me now. 'They are Pakistani and we are Indian, but the blood which runs in their veins and in mine is the same, so how different can we be? My father always says, "*Jo apne hain, woh toh apne hi rahenge, na?*"'

I smile.

'Forty years ago, when my mother was a child, her cousin from Karachi came to meet the family, and after that there was no contact. For forty years, there was no contact until my father was able to find him again on Facebook. He introduced himself and said that his wife was longing to speak to her family and reconnected them. They spoke over a video call, and it was very emotional, because though they were family, they were seeing each other for the first time in decades. And, you won't believe it, he distinctly resembled my mother's father!' A wide smile appears on Z's face.

'Is that the only way you can now speak?' I ask. 'On phone calls or social media?'

'With the younger generation who are comfortable with technology, yes. But with travel being so difficult between the two countries, there are older family members who will never be reunited,' she says and goes on to narrate the tale of her mother's aunt.

In the decades after Partition, before Z's mother was even born, her father's sister migrated to Karachi for a better life. Life in India post Partition became difficult. She had hoped that Pakistan would provide a better future for her family, but this was not to be, and life remained difficult there too. Every night, she would sleep holding her daughters tight, doors locked out of the fear that came with being in a new country. Ashamed at what her extended family in Pakistan would think of her financial status, she slowly distanced herself, until there was no contact at all. Z's family in India, for whom she was a blood relative, could not keep in touch either, due to cross-border restrictions. As a result, Z's mother, one of the youngest siblings, never met her aunt, yet was raised on a healthy diet of her stories. These stories she further passed down to Z. But no one ever managed to contact the aunt, and it was only when she passed in 2020 that Z's mother felt an inconsolable sadness for a family member she had never met.

'It was as if part of her had died,' Z says, helplessly gesturing to her body, as if a leg or an arm had been amputated. 'She had only ever met her through other people's stories and memories, but she felt that loss … and *through her*, so did I. Seeing her mourn, not once did the question of Indian or Pakistani cross my mind. In fact, it just confirmed that blood is thicker and runs deeper than any man-made border ever will.' Tears have begun flowing down her cheeks and she apologizes, gently wiping them away.

This helplessness often serves as a companion to the fate of divided families. Generations are raised on mere memory – sometimes once removed and, as in the case of Z, even twice removed – about relatives they may never get to meet physically, except perhaps in a third land. The realization that your own are geographically so close, yet so far, on the other side of an unsurpassable border, can be overwhelmingly tragic. In this sense, even consanguineous relationships appear at the mercy of the two states, their scrutiny and their restrictions.

The historian Vazira Fazila-Yacoobali Zamindar dedicates her book *The Long Partition and the Making of Modern South Asia* to 'all our divided families', where one of the lasting arguments is to show,

> ...that families became divided not because members of a family chose to live in one country or move to another. They became divided because of the way the Indo-Pak border came to be constructed as an outcome of a long, drawn-out process of Partition.[5]

When Z returns to the subject of her family, it is with a more sanguine disposition. 'Our generation needs to look at history with the knowledge that we were once one, because there *has* to be some solution for this, there *has* to be the hope that things will get better. Because I truly feel for my parents and their parents, who have spent their childhoods with family members they can no longer meet.'

'I MUST HAVE been as young as twelve when I first learned that my maternal side, the Nakais, came from Lahore and still had family on the other side,' Gurmeet Sangha Rai, the conservation architect, recalls, taking off her thick-rimmed spectacles and resting them on her forehead. It's a late autumn afternoon in Delhi and we are seated on either side of her desk at the Mehrauli office she shares with her husband, the photographer Raghu Rai.* Ornately carved doors lead from one room to the next, and the walls are fitted with cabinets and bookshelves.

'Was Partition spoken about openly in your home?'

She clicks her tongue. 'No, never. My maternal grandfather, my nanaji, never talked about Partition or its trauma, so I never looked at it through the lens of distress, or even rebuilding. All I knew was that they had come to India in 1947 and were comfortable here. I grew up in a household of five sisters, of whom I was the only one

---

* An interview with Raghu Rai about his hometown of Jhang can be found in Chapter 20, 'Returning'.

interested in culture. We lived in Delhi till 1978, and one of my earliest memories is driving down from Delhi to Punjab during the summer holidays, and my father quizzing us. He would say to my sisters and me, "If you can name all the Gurus, then I'll give you two rupees!" I was probably the only one who made an effort and felt an enormous sense of pride when I won that quiz,' she chuckles.

'The second memory that connects me to undivided Punjab came in 1982, when we were reunited with our family from Pakistan. That year, the Asian Games took place in Delhi,[6] and we received our first visitors from across the border. An uncle, Zahid Nakai – well, he's really a grandfather, a nana by relation, but he is close to my parents' age – had come with a group of family members, and they'd looked up my nana in Kotkapura, and later come up to Gurdaspur to see my mother. I would have been about sixteen years old at this time, and I remember them well – beautiful people with lovely big cheeks.'

'Are you saying,' I now ask, 'that between 1947 and 1982, there was no contact between your family in India and that in Pakistan?'

Gurmeet shakes her head. 'I don't this so.' And after a moment of thought she repeats, 'I don't think so.'

'What happened for them to be divided this way?'

A smile now appears on her face. 'After the Asian Games had reunited the family, they began going back and forth – for weddings, engagements. Anyone who could go went. But my personal relationship with Pakistan developed only in 1995, when I was doing a project mapping the historic buildings along the Grand Trunk Road and the Mughal Imperial Highway through Punjab.'

As I follow her professional trajectory, I learn that one year after the Asian Games took place, seventeen-year-old Gurmeet enrolled in a Bachelors of Architecture programme at the Chandigarh College of Architecture. It was here that she first encountered the word conservation, understanding it to be design in a historic setting, which laid the foundation for her life's work. She graduated in 1988 and was married the following year. From 1989 to 1991, she worked on a master's degree in architectural conversation at the School of Planning and Architecture in Delhi. The couples' two daughters,

Avani and Purvai, who join us towards the end of this conversation, were born in 1992 and 1994 respectively. In an interview, she recalls taking both girls with her for a survey of the G.T. Road project, and how, as it unfolded, it became the 'milestone to understand Punjab', the root of her identity. By 1996, at the age of thirty, Gurmeet had set up the Cultural Resource Conservation Initiative (CRCI),[7] a conservation consultancy firm. From the very beginning, her work was no less than social action or cultural activism, striving to conserve sites of historical significance.[8]

Taking me back to the winter of 1995, Gurmeet recalls, 'We travelled to every village along the Grand Trunk Road in Punjab, starting from the eastern border near Ambala, and by summertime we had reached the western extent in Amritsar. As we got to the border, we saw a *kos minar* on the Radcliffe Line but couldn't go across to Lahore, where the historic road led. Now, this is the early '90s, when it's still relatively easier to be going back and forth between India and Pakistan, and we were adamant to go across, so we came back to Delhi to apply for visas. I have to say, though, that until then I thought the Nakais were the odd ones to have family on both sides of the border, but later I was surprised to find that this is common.'

'But yours is not just a family divided between India and Pakistan,' I note. 'It's also a family that, as the generations progress through history, branches off into both Sikh and Muslim Nakais.'

'That's right,' she nods.

Printed in 1865 and compiled by Sir Lepel Henry Griffin, a civil servant and then Assistant Commissioner of Lahore, *The Punjab Chiefs* traces the history of the 'Nakkai' family to its earliest ancestor, Chowdhri Hemraj.

About the year 1595, the Sikh Guru Arjan, travelling with a few followers in the Lahore district, reached the little town of Bahrwal[*] ... He was not received with hospitality, and passed

---

[*] The village is presently known as Baherwal (or Beharwal) Kalan, and falls in the Kasur District of Punjab, Pakistan.

on to the neighbouring village of Jambar, where, tired and foot-sore, he begged for the loan of a charpai (native bedstead), and lying down in the shade of a tree, went to sleep. By this time *Hemraj*, a Sindhu Jat, chowdhri or headman of Bahrwal, who was absent when the Guru passed through ... heard of what had occurred, and, ashamed of his townsmen's inhospitability, set off to Jambar to try to induce the holy man to return. Upon arrival at the village he found the Guru asleep ... He dared not wake the saint ... [and] being a man of resource and some physical strength, he lifted the charpai and the Guru together on his head and carried him away to Bahrwal. When Arjan woke he was much pleased with *Hemraj's* attention and called for water to drink [but] was told that the water of their only well was brackish. The Guru then directed *Hemraj* to throw some sweet cakes down the well ... the water immediately became sweet and pure. [He] also blessed *Hemraj* and prophesied that he would have a son, by the name *Hira Singh*, who would be a great and powerful Chief.[9]

And so it came to be that Sardar Hira Singh, born in 1706, took possession of the 'Nakka' country – lying between Lahore and Gogera with its headquarters at village Baherwal – lending its name to the family of Hira Singh and the *misl* he commanded, which was one of the twelve that later formed the Sikh Empire. It descended from Hira Singh Nakai to Sardar Nar Singh to Sardar Ran Singh, who would ultimately become the father-in-law of Maharaja Ranjit Singh, marrying his youngest daughter, Raj Kaur, to the future king.[10] The command of the Nakai *misl* was handed down the generations to Kahan Singh in 1807, after which it was absorbed into the Sikh Empire in 1810.[11]

As the decades passed, Sardar Ishar Singh Nakai, one of the descendants of Kahan Singh, converted to Islam in 1879, adopting the name Abdul Aziz Nakai, and married Umar Bibi. However, before conversion, his first marriage had already borne him a son named Nihal Singh, who continued to be raised as a Sikh by his relatives.

It is at this moment that the Nakai family bifurcates, and the reason why at Partition one section remains in Pakistan while the other must migrate to India. The Sikh lineage continued down to Gurmeet's great-grandfather, Pratap Singh, her grandfather, Boota Singh, and mother Satwant Kaur, who were all born in an undivided Punjab. Meanwhile, the Muslim lineage descended from Abdul Aziz Nakai to Sardar Muhammad Arif Nakai, who served as the Chief Minister of Punjab (Pakistan) in 1995-96, and further down to Zahid Nakai, and his brother, Ishtiaq Nakai.

'My friend Shalini accompanied me, and we decided to take the train across, the Samjhauta Express,' Gurmeet says excitedly. 'In those days, the train would run twice a week, Mondays and Thursdays.[12] So, we began from Amritsar at 8 a.m. and reached Attari by about 3 p.m. We changed platforms and around 4 p.m., a green-coloured train arrived, all the passengers clambered in, and it soon left for Pakistan. After much protocol between the border police personnel, the train chugged to the first station of Wagah in Pakistan, located probably about 500 metres into the country from the international border. From there, the passengers were taken to a warehouse- or hangar-type enclosure, where all the customs and immigration formalities took place before anyone was allowed into Pakistan.

'It was during this process that Shalini and I were asked where we're going and who we're going to see. I promptly said that we were going to meet the chief minister of Punjab, Arif Nakai. "*Hum chief minister sahib ke ghar ja rahe hain*," she chuckles. 'To my surprise, they actually believed us and we were sent to the first-class compartment of the train, which was completely empty. From the window, we spotted this young boy in a shalwar-kurta, maybe ten or twelve years old, selling chai. We had a cup of tea and then decided to go back towards the second-class compartment, for which we had tickets, as we were quite overwhelmed by this empty coach. It had already started to get dark, and there was a zero-watt blue bulb in the train. All the passengers were still being questioned, you know – "What are you bringing into Pakistan?" – bags were being opened and checked. People were carrying boxes of Hajmola, coconut oil, bundles of paan leaves. There was a fight in the compartment as well, because apparently someone had stolen someone else's paan leaves and...' Her voice dissolves into peals of laughter and I join in.

My older interviewees would often tell me that travel between the two border cities took only a half hour in the years before Partition. One had even recalled how they would cut school in Lahore to go watch films in an Amritsar theatre. With this in mind, I ask Gurmeet when they finally reached their destination.

'From there the train took an hour or so to reach Lahore. We had left Amritsar at 8 a.m. and reached Lahore by late evening, and Ishtiaq Nakai, the younger brother of Zahid Nakai, the gentleman who had come to Delhi for the Asian Games, was there to pick us up.'

I nod slowly. 'And ... well, what did you think it was going to be like? Pakistan.'

'I never really thought about that, actually,' she admits, sitting back in her seat. 'I was so preoccupied with my Grand Trunk Road project. I wanted to go across and look at a few things – Lahore as a historic city, as Maharaja Ranjit Singh's capital, I wanted to see his *samadhi*, I wanted to see the Lahore Fort. We had been documenting craft as part of the project, so I was interested in that. And, of course, I wanted to see my grandfather's village. I was very keen to know – will the Punjab of Pakistan look the same as the Punjab of India?'

'How did your nanaji feel about you going across?'

She takes a deep breath in. 'I wasn't expecting anything there, either. When the family started visiting one another, he had also gone back to Pakistan. But I never knew how he felt about it, nor did I grow up with him talking about Lahore. We never sat down and asked him to tell us stories, because in my memory my nanaji was a very hard-working farmer. I remember him as a man of the soil, he had so many *murabbas* of land.* What I'm trying to say is that I never realized that he came from such an important family in the narrative of undivided Punjab and was part of the making of history...'

---

* 1 *murabba* equals a land block of 25 acres.

'From whatever I saw of Lahore, the people were warm. They would tell me what good Urdu I spoke, and I would tell them what good Hindi they spoke!' she laughs, for the languages feel almost seamless sometimes. 'How they indulged us with food, shopping, sightseeing. And then, Ishtiaq nana and his wife, Noni nani, took us to the ancestral villages, which now fall in the Kasur district. Their village is called Wan Adhan, and right next to that is my nanaji's village, which to this day is known as Pratapgarh, named after his father, Pratap Singh Nakai.'

'That must have been so moving,' I say with a wide smile.

She beams. 'What we didn't realize is that the abandoned villages on that side were populated by refugees, just as they were here, and my nanaji's home had been divided between two families. In one part of the house lived a weaver, a *julaha*, this old man, and he remembered how in the '80s my grandfather came to Pakistan for a wedding, after which he went to his village to see his home; "*Meinu yaad hai, Sardar Boota Singh aaye si, mere bade jigri yaar si.*" He presented me with a shawl he'd handwoven.

'Of course, by now, everyone learnt that Sardar Boota Singh's granddaughter had come to the village from India. So, there was a whole procession on the road, a *baraat*, calling us to their homes. One of them even said that he thought we had come to take back the land. Can you imagine that? I told him, "*Tussi ghabrao na, twadi zameen wapas nahi leyange.*" They actually thought that we could claim the land, that land was stronger than the strongest Partition Line. At this, both Shalini and I had tears in our eyes … though we were overwhelmed with their love, we realized their vulnerability. And this is as recent as 1996.'

'I can imagine,' I say sadly. 'For people who have been so violently displaced once, there is always the fear that it could happen again.'

'There was gratitude that we were not going to take the land away.' Her eyes are wide with disbelief. 'That really saddened me.'

'Tell me about the house … how did you feel when you saw it still standing?'

'To be honest, I didn't feel this overwhelming emotion when I saw the house. I looked at it first as a piece of architecture, and then as a piece of memory. Shalini and I were more in tears when speaking to the people of the village, with human contact, rather than property. I understood the importance of oral history, of storytelling, of memory keeping because of that trip and its experiences.' She pauses, interlacing her palms and placing them on the table, and then says, 'When I came back to India, I went to see my nanaji in Kasauli and I gave him the shawl. I said to him, "*Woh aapko bada yaad kar rahe si*," that he was being remembered by his friend. And I'm saying this with a sense of achievement, that look, I've done this, I've touched the land where you came from, I'm beaming as I say it ... and he just begins to weep. He was crying. I couldn't believe that I was seeing my grandfather cry. I felt ... terrible. All this, all these emotions had been buried so deep within him.'

'What happened to him at Partition?' I ask.

Slowly, she begins, 'My nanaji was such a jovial man, so full of energy and joy that I never realized there was a sadder side to things. Like the house they lived in, in Kotkapura, Faridkot, was evacuee property, which they later demolished and rebuilt, but I was born in that house – the only one of my siblings to have been born at home and in Punjab, in that house, connected to Partition.'

The more we speak about the past, the more Gurmeet's tone becomes laden with sadness.

'In 1947, my nani was expecting a baby and had gone back to her parents' home in Patiala. Her older brother, Rajbir Kang, was part of the Indian Civil Service, and would later be put in charge of the rehabilitation efforts in the area. So, she was in Patiala, while my nanaji, a young man in his twenties, and my mother – their eldest child, born in 1944 – were in Lahore. When the riots began in the city, he thought that they would be able to protect themselves. But then he saw a train full of murdered passengers and decided it would be best if he and my mother came to Patiala. But they always thought they'd return to Lahore, so they never carried even their jewellery or anything of real value. Even today, when my Ishtiaq nana talks about how the land came to be allocated in Indian Punjab after Partition, there was so much that fell in Pakistan and so little in India that he is in awe of how my nanaji began his life again from nothing. He left so much behind, and Ishtiaq nana always says that had it been him, he may not have been able to survive. But then, there are snippets of conversation I've heard over the years where my nanaji is asking his elders, "Why did you let me go?" to which they replied, "We would not have been able to guarantee your safety ... so we let you leave."'

Like butter, Gurmeet's voice slowly melts into silence.

Tears sting my eyes. 'Did anyone else from the family migrate to India?'

'As far as I know, my nanaji was the only one. The family had told him that he should go because it was no longer safe for him in Lahore. And after what he saw, the train full of bodies...'

After a few seconds, she adds, 'Interestingly, the direct impact of Partition can be felt within my mother's generation. Shortly after this, she was sent to boarding school at Oak Grove in Mussoorie, and this left a very lasting impact because she saw her parents only once a year. So, it was not only the loss of home and that displacement, but also this immediate separation from family. My mother grew up like quite a brown lady, culturally disconnected from the Punjab narrative. Actually, most of us became disconnected from our roots because of the impact of Partition. I didn't even get Punjabi as my language. Neither I nor my sisters got any of the stories or cultural lore of Punjab – whether it's history, religion or mythology. We became disconnected because of how Punjab was fractured during Partition.'

'And today – does Partition continue to impact you today?'

She smiles. 'Today, I am so connected with my family in Pakistan that in my head I don't create a division between the two Punjabs. For me, Punjab is a single, continuous cultural entity rather than fragments with administrative and political boundaries. I try not to navigate it through the lens of pre and post 1947.'

Just then, Avani appears at the door and gives both her mother and me a hug. Pulling up a chair, she says that she vividly remembers her first trip to Pakistan. Avani is a photographer, and so much of her memory is visual that she recalls the predawn darkness of the morning when they assembled in Ambedkar Stadium to board the bus to Lahore.

Gurmeet nods and begins to collect the papers on her desk into a neat pile. 'I took them all, the girls and my mother, in 2007. You must also speak to them about it, record their stories.' She is due for a meeting in the other room and leaves me with these parting words, 'People celebrate Independence Day across India and Pakistan, but in our family we lament it. It comes with too much pain.'

I look at Avani, and she nods knowingly. 'Come,' she says, now leading me to the next room, where her younger sister, Purvai, is painting a canvas laid flat on the ground. Seating myself cross-legged next to her, I take out my recorder, but before I can ask any questions, the two break into conversation themselves: the fear they felt before going across, the similarities of landscape and the grand welcome they received.

'The village in Pakistan was exactly like the one in Gurdaspur,' Purvai says. 'The villagers greeted us the same way, except that they were meeting us for the first time. I remember sitting on a *charpai* and drinking a tall glass of milk and endless cups of tea. I have many food-related memories,' she laughs.

I smile. 'Do you ever think about the fact that the family got divided because of Partition?'

'But I don't feel divided,' Purvai stresses. 'I just feel like we are a family that doesn't meet very often. We see it as something we can return to, family we can be reunited with, whenever possible. And luckily, we also come from older generations who found a way not to feel divided within themselves. When the Kartarpur corridor opened in 2019, all the grandparents from both sides met there. They stay in touch.'

'At the end of the day,' Avani says, 'every family conversation is eventually aimed towards when we can meet again and how.'

'Within the political framework of the two nations, you mean?' I ask.

The sisters nod in unison.

'Avani, as a photographer, you've often dealt with borderlands.' I allude to her work in Kashmir, capturing a landscape cloaked in the long shadow of Partition, resulting in images both tender and haunting. 'What about emotional borderlands? Do you feel the resonance of Partition, as a fourth generation?'

She thinks about this for a few seconds and eventually says, 'I am trying to articulate it in words, but I'm better with images.'

'Do you want to draw it instead?'

'May I?' she asks, and I offer her my pen and notebook.

On a blank page, she writes '1947'. Two arrows emerge upwards on either side, halting abruptly at two dots. She tells me that this is the generation of her grandparents. Continuing the arrows further up, she pauses, draws two more dots and tells me that this is the generation of her parents. Her father was born in Jhang-Maghiana, her mother's roots can be traced to the outskirts of Lahore. These two generations have seen war, the first has witnessed it, the second has inherited memories of it. Both have felt some form of loss. Putting pen to paper again, she extends the arrows further until they almost intersect, and draws a circle within them. 'This is us,' she says and points the pen around the room, 'our generation.' She splits the circle in half, and outside the two semicircles writes 'India' and 'Pakistan'. The arrows curl inwards towards the circle, not meeting, but not separating either.

'This is the political scenario in which we have to find a way to remain connected. It is rare for someone like you to sit down and talk to us, who have not witnessed Partition, to ask us what we feel about carrying it as a legacy. It is rare, because this is not a conversation that people want to have any longer.' She taps the paper with her forefinger. 'Because this is our family, we feel this connect to the past. But this is not an active conversation, and that's the sad part.'

'We need conversations of empathy,' Purvai adds softly.

I nod. 'How empathy withstands politics, how humanity withstands politics.'

'The conversation about Partition can no longer remain a conversation of victimhood,' Avani concludes. 'It has to transform into a conversation of rebuilding. Not only for divided families like ours, but also for India and Pakistan, who are, in a way, also a divided family.'

✍

'I'D DIVIDE MY family's story of Partition into different experiences,' says the journalist and writer Aatish Taseer, methodically embarking on a three-tiered conversation.

'On one hand is my mother's Sikh family, who left Gujranwala during Partition and, losing everything in the process, reached Delhi and were given compensation near Karnal. They never quite got over the reality of what had happened. Then, there is my father's Pakistani Muslim family, where my paternal grandfather was one of the proponents of Partition. He was a renowned Urdu poet and very close to Iqbal.[13] At Partition, the family was obviously affected by violence and destruction, but they were inheritors of the new state of Pakistan.

'And then there's the third strand, which is my own – the experience of having an Indian and a Pakistani parent in real time, and reckoning with Partition and its legacy as a fact of one's life. For a long time, I thought it was a luxury or privilege to have this connection to both sides of Punjab, when Punjab had been torn asunder. But I realized over time that it would never have occurred to me to feel at home in Pakistan – I was always a visitor, and happy to be there and happy to have friends and family there, but I certainly grew up thinking of India as home, and...' He pauses, letting his sentence trail off. 'In fact, this divided identity was more of a liability than I realized, because it has forced me in the direction of a third country, whether it was the UK, where I was born, or America, where I now live.'

I first meet Aatish in 2019 in Delhi over lunch. *Remnants* has been out for over a year, and his new book, *The Twice Born:*

Life and Death on the Ganges, is due to release in a few weeks. Though we have never met before, I feel an immediate kinship to him as someone who shares a part of my history, and much of our conversation revolves around Partition, Punjabi families in Delhi, and our respective travels across Pakistan. Aatish is the son of an Indian journalist and a Pakistani politician, born in 1980, and holds British and American citizenship. But much of what I know about his complicated and divided personal history, and his parents' relationship, is through his powerful book *Stranger to History: A Son's Journey Through Islamic Lands*, which begins as a quest for his estranged Pakistani father.

In the book, Aatish writes that during his childhood, when people asked whether he was being raised as a Sikh or a Muslim, his maternal grandfather would assert that he was being 'brought up to be a human being'.[14] From the age of two, he was raised by his single mother in Delhi, and he sought out his father for the first time in 2002 at the age of twenty-one. But in late 2019, the Government of India revoked his status as an Overseas Citizen of India (OCI) on the grounds that he had 'concealed the fact that his late father was of Pakistani origin'.[15] This came merely months after he had written an article critical of Prime Minister Narendra Modi for *Time* magazine at the height of India's general election. This revocation of his OCI – which is akin to a permanent visa for persons of Indian origin, and a substitute for dual citizenship – felt more like a severance to Aatish, for he now found himself living life in his adopted country, the United States, not merely an immigrant but an exile.[16]

It is this thread along which he continues the conversation, a year on from the revocation, drawing the consequences of his cross-border identity from Partition to the present day. 'Now, I almost cling to this life in America as a form of protection from the situation at home. I don't want to spend my life repeating to people that I really *am* Indian,' he says, giving me a sad smile. 'Asserting your identity with such vehemence is exhausting, and you don't want to be shaped by *just* that. Maybe if I held an Indian passport, it would have been different. But across South Asia, the relationship with the father is still given dominance – father's profession, father's religion, father's nationality – regardless of whether the father is present or absent. So, that's really the third strand of Partition, which is actually living with a divided identity.'

After a few seconds of silence, I finally say, 'Tell me about your maternal family's migration.'

'Well, they just had no idea what Partition would mean,' he admits. 'My grandfather's brother, whose name was Jindo, used to say that first it had been the rule of the Muslims, then the English and now once again it would be the Muslims, making no difference to them. "*Saanu ki?*" They hadn't read to the bottom of the desire articulated by Iqbal and carried forward by Jinnah, and truly believed that it would be quite easy for them to continue living where they were. There was an absolute sense of security, particularly since they were a landowning family, of rootedness and connectedness, to their soil.

'My grandfather's regiment, Probyn's Horse, was just back from fighting the Japanese in Burma during World War II and, though temporarily stationed in south India, was going to Pakistan, and so the family quite simply opted for Pakistan. He never changed his decision but started to feel the difference in the Muslim soldiers, where they began to exclude him from discussions and things like that. It was probably his only real intimation of what was to come. Meanwhile, my great-grandmother, a young widow, had spent the summer in Mussoorie with my great-uncle, and came back to Lahore to find it in flames. At the railway station itself, their Muslim estate manager found them and said that it was no longer safe for them to stay. They were made to board a train to Amritsar, the first border town on the Indian side, but it never left the platform. They waited in the heat and monsoon, and eventually disembarked and caught another train, which took them across. When they reached Amritsar, they learnt that everyone on the train they'd initially been on had been massacred. Bibiji never spoke about Partition, nor did she get over it. She just couldn't speak about what had happened, and remained very bitter and resentful against Muslims.

'But her son, my grandfather, on the other hand, was full of longing, and not once thought that the people he'd grown up with, or the Muslim community, were to blame for anything. He was almost disdainful of being on the Indian side of Punjab, actually – always felt tethered to the Punjab of *that* side, to the people of *that* side, the manners of *that* side, and the emotional bonds that still remained. Till the day he died, he saw his life in Delhi with my grandmother as very provisional. Anything to do with Pakistan would lure him into this kind of ecstasy state. The tragedy of Partition had just settled into him very deeply.'

'He eventually joined the Indian Army, then?' I confirm, and Aatish nods.

'But that's ... that's complicated. To fight in World War II *alongside* men who eventually became Pakistani, and then to fight *against* those same men in the '65 or '71 wars.'

With a sigh, he says, 'My grandfather believed Partition to be a cruel trick of history. When he was in Burma fighting the Japanese, one of his most painful experiences was finding this dead Japanese soldier whose samurai sword my grandfather eventually brought back to India. When they found him, he had these love letters tucked into his uniform – these letters written between him and someone back in Japan. But they were in English, and my grandfather was very struck by them, because he realized that this soldier had been someone who was educated and refined, and had succumbed to the war in this inhuman way. So, he quite naturally deemed soldiering as a futile business. And then, to suddenly be at battle with men he considered *his own* – Pakistanis from his old regiment – would have been confirmation of why war was tragic and how it only appeased governments and not individual people.'[17]

'And did your mother inherit any of these qualities – the bitterness of her grandmother or the longing of her father?'

'Neither,' he says instinctively. 'With her, there was a near complete amnesia because nothing had been passed on. This is also a testament to how well India had been able to assimilate much of its refugee population. There's a story about her and a friend travelling to England in the '70s, when she would have been in her twenties, and there were some Pakistanis around. To avoid being understood by them, my mother and her friend spoke in Punjabi.'

I smile, part amused, part surprised.

'*I know*,' Aatish smiles broadly as well. 'It hadn't even occurred to them that Punjab – and naturally its language – had been partitioned between the two countries. It was *that* far away – the idea of what Pakistan was. And I think that it was only when she met my father at the age of twenty-nine, and they had this passionate love affair, that a curiosity around Partition was aroused, and she began making sense of what had happened historically … She became aware of that history very late in life. It was on the fortieth anniversary of Partition that my mother actually asked her grandmother, bibiji, about what had happened. Bibiji lamented the loss of land and material wealth, but what really pained her was to think about how the beautiful Jamavar shawls that she'd left behind were now being adorned by strangers in Pakistan. This small detail upset her and she took it very personally.'[18]

I lean back in my seat and am quiet for a few minutes before Aatish asks what I'm thinking about.

'Well, I'm thinking about your mother growing up never asking these questions, the amnesia, and comparing it to your exploration of the reasons and consequences of Partition, both personal and political, which leads me to the fact that remembrance sometimes skips generations and requires effort,' I offer.

'I don't think I was asking these questions until I met my father, to be honest,' he admits. 'And then I was asking them a lot, because it became a very real thing. In travelling to Pakistan in 2002, I had gone where my grandfather could not go. But I do also think about how there's a natural delay when something as historic as Partition occurs – there is a delay as people come to terms with the trauma that has happened. And then, thirty, forty, fifty years later, there's an awakening.'

Turning to the associations that Aatish ultimately made on the Pakistani side, I keep in mind his earlier comment on the tearing apart of the two Punjabs. In many ways, his parents' relationship felt like a belated wave carried on from Partition, where, though an Indian Punjabi and a Pakistani Punjabi had very briefly come together, their union was already bound by precedent. But from the beginning, Aatish's mother had been clear on who his father was, where he was from, and why it would have been impossible for him to be in his life. His grandfather, on the other hand, 'made it seem like [another] chapter in the Partition saga he had lived through',[19] and on this Aatish writes:

> And though it could be suggested that the same charlatan god who had put up what seemed like absurd divisions between my grandfather and his country was also responsible for landing him, after all the violence, with a half-Pakistani grandson, he would not have seen it that way … In his hands, the peculiar circumstances of my birth were not strange, unworkable facts, but a kind of recompense for all that had been lost.[20]

Aatish tells me that his grandfather was very comfortable with the idea of his father, remaining his advocate till the end of his life. An anecdote that he liked to tell was how when Aatish was born, he made a trunk call to inform his father, which was when he first heard the Punjabi from the other side. He thought it musical and very disturbing, for it struck him immediately that he was speaking to 'his own person'.

'Apart from parentage, does Partition factor into the understanding of your identity?' I ask.

He brings his hands to his chin, grazing the stubble. 'Well, I think of Partition as an iteration of a deeper and older drama. What are we to do with the survival of the Hindu past into the present? What are we to do with the coming of Muslim rule? What are we to do with whatever's left of Britain and British influence over India? This three-tiered history of India, which is still vibrating and has fairly dangerous repercussions – of which I see Partition as an expression – is very important as a mediation. What it means for history to roil under the surface, for it to be resolved, to go quiet, and then enter a phase of reawakening. India is like the ultimate laboratory to study those cycles of repeated disruption and healing.'

Nodding, I zero in. 'But what about for *you*? What does this legacy of Partition mean for *you*?'

There is a short pause, and I watch him in silence.

'Well, there's the incredible music and art and writing – all the creativity on the front line born out of Partition – but, you know,' he says, shrugging his shoulders, 'it's like a pain that won't go away, and the exhaustion that comes from that pain of seeing people mired in history. You see Indians and Pakistanis, and you think to yourself, "My god, you are so alike!" and it's tragic because the differences are so small in comparison to the gain, which can ultimately be so meaningful, and in that sense the solution *seems* easy. But in this atmosphere, everything is difficult; Kashmir is difficult, a discussion on minority populations on both sides is difficult...' he scoffs.

'This is what breaks my heart sometimes – that it feels so much within grasp, and yet so distant,' I say.

'It breaks mine too,' Aatish agrees sadly. 'But nothing is possible until we reach a frame of mind where we look one another in the face, and – you know, what Baldwin says about how we think our pain and heartbreak are unprecedented, but then we realize that this has always happened in the history of the world. Indians and Pakistanis need to understand that we are just part of a larger thousand-year drama, and must find a creative resolution from what has become an enduringly hostile situation. Otherwise, there is no growth or survival for either community. And so, to answer your question, it's not so much *Partition* but the greater extending background that I live with far more.'

'But to have an Indian mother and a Pakistani father is not complicated for you?'

'I've never found it hard,' Aatish replies almost immediately. 'For me, Pakistan felt like you were in a place where some key components had been taken out; it immediately struck me as that. What I do take seriously, though, is the commonality of the Punjabi culture, or what a shared subcontinental culture stands for.

'A lot of people assume that I am very confused when it comes to my identity, but in fact there is no confusion. It's very easy to be both Indian and Pakistani because the illusion of difference could not be more real. I don't have the religious problem that Muslims, to an extent, must answer when it comes to the way that faith influences their history. Even largely secular people like my father succumbed to this question of faith. But the only worship I ever had in my life was related to a Hindu past, and it's a glorious thing to have that bedrock of classical Hindu history living on in India.'

'I feel rather embarrassed to admit that I thought the threads would be more complicated,' I say softly.

Aatish smiles warmly. 'You shouldn't be. It was very unformed and heavy and mangled as I was growing up. But I really considered a part of my becoming a writer as resolving these things, finding ways to speak about them, to write about them, to kind of move past them. I think that that was a very conscious decision to resolve a personal history.'

'So then, what *do* you think of when you think of Partition?'

'Futility,' he says without missing a breath.

'I would have thought you'd say family.'

He chuckles. 'No, just futility. I find it completely exhausting, because its effects are ongoing and I feel them on a personal, emotional level. And also because one just wants for things to somehow be better between the two countries.'

I take a deep breath. 'I couldn't agree with you more.'

'When I think of Partition, all I feel is a mixture of futility and fatigue,' Aatish concludes.

IT IS ONLY after I speak to Mrs Sidhu that I begin to understand that if Partition was responsible for the violent eradication of some families, it was equally responsible for the creation of others, as a means of extrication from that violence.

Her son, who lives overseas, has set up a phone call between us, leaving me with the words, 'There is a story you need to hear.'

Mrs Sidhu and I begin our conversation with pleasantries, but because this isn't a video call, it feels even more distant than some of the longer-distance calls. Though her son has explained the nature of my work, she has questions about why I spend my days listening to stories about a past I can't undo. I tell her it's so that there remains a record of what happened, in people's own words.

'*Seedhi si baat hai, beta*,' she says matter-of-factly, 'it is important to remember, but it is also very painful,' and then narrates the story of her paternal aunt and what happened to her in a town of present-day Haryana during the days of Partition.

'Muslim families were massacred in the village. In one such family, two girls managed to survive but everyone else was killed before their eyes – father, mother, uncle, brother, everyone. The villagers had heard stories of Sikh girls being raped and abused in West Punjab, and as retaliation they did the same here with Muslim girls. One of the sisters was sent off to the next village, married into a Sikh family there. But the other was paraded around, abused by many men.' She pauses and then adds quietly, 'At times, by our own extended family. *Unki izzat baar baar looti gayi, kabhi yeh le jata, kabhi woh le jata.* For about six long months, men continued to take advantage of her, one would keep her for ten days, another for a week, a third...' Her voice trails off.

I exhale deeply, a sharp pain rising in my chest.

'Until one day, my eldest uncle, tayaji, came back to India from overseas, where he was working as an irrigation officer. His wife had died and his young son became motherless. So tayaji returned home, learnt of the young girl and what had happened, and he married her. Despite knowing that his own extended family had taken advantage of her, he made her his wife. When I told my son this story, I said, "Your life can be bad for one day, two days, a week, a month, but it cannot be bad forever." Imagine what she must have thought in those months, after watching her parents die in front of her eyes, after being paraded from house to house, man to man, she must have felt like a living corpse. She must have willed for death to take her, maybe even tried to end it all herself. But there was a better future for her, because she eventually lived a long life with my tayaji. They had four beautiful children, three daughters and a son.'

I have questions, but they all bear shades of intrusion. As I'm contemplating what I can ask, she continues, 'After he married her, the same people who had taken advantage of her didn't dare look at her any more. She was no longer a "*Musalmaan*'s daughter", she was now their elder brother's wife. Everything else became irrelevant. And tayaji didn't care about what anyone would say, he accepted her completely. *Lekin inn baato ka zikr unhone kabhi nahi kiya*, she never talked about what happened,' Mrs Sidhu stresses.

'When did you first find out that this had happened?' I ask quietly.

'The elders of the family would talk, so we all knew about it. Sometimes tayiji would cry because she'd miss her parents, or remember the way they'd been killed. Despite living a very good life with my tayaji, there were some things that she would never be able to get back. For instance, she didn't have a maternal home, a *maika*. Tayaji was a very wealthy man, he had acres and acres of land, but she lived her whole life in that same house. We would all come home to our *maika* to see our parents and our siblings, but she could never go anywhere. She didn't have anyone else.'

'Did she ever see her sister again?'

'I don't think so. She'd also gotten married to a Sikh man, but from what I know, the sisters never met again. Or if they did, then tayiji never told anyone about it.'

For a while, the phone line goes quiet and I wonder if this suggests a natural end to our conversation. But when Mrs Sidhu talks again, it is from the lens of not just perception but deep sensitivity. 'What I cannot stop thinking about is her witnessing the massacre of her entire family before her eyes. To that, add the disadvantage of being a woman with no agency. When I used to imagine all that she had endured in those months after Partition, it would really pain me.

I was very close to her, we spent a lot of time together, and often my heart would want to talk to her about this. But I'd always stop myself, afraid to pick at her wounds. I hoped that if ever she wanted to talk about something, she would bring it up, but she never did. She just became completely devoted to her husband and their children, and then passed away in 1994...'

'What was she like?'

'Very particular,' she recalls, 'Tayiji was very particular about her habits and personal hygiene. Whenever she'd come to stay with us, the very first thing she'd do was bathe and then fold the clothes she'd travelled in, and take out a new pair to wear. She carried her own towel, toothbrush, hairbrush, never asked for any of these things. Then she would eat lunch, then have a cup of tea and nap until 5 p.m. If she had to go and meet the neighbours or any family, she'd do it in the evening, and when she came home, she'd immediately bathe again. Three *salwar-kameez* suits, she would easily change three suits a day. She was also very particular about having a clean environment, the house was always spotless.'

'Do you think it was because of her experiences that she became so particular about hygiene?' I wonder.

'*Yeh ho sakta hai*, maybe you're right...' she muses. 'She never spoke much either, mostly only answered what she'd been asked. Sometimes, when I was younger, I used to think that tayiji spoke less so that no one would ask her anything. *Toh jaan boojh ke unhone apna nature hi reserved sa bana liya tha*, she'd moulded herself into a person who wouldn't be asked any unnecessary questions. I would think this a lot when I was younger. You'd just be sitting next to her and she would say nothing at all, and only when you would ask, "*Tayiji tussi kaise ho, ki haal chal hai?*" that she would respond, "*Sab theek hai, bete, sab theek.*" That was the extent, though she was very close to my mother, so I wonder if they ever spoke about the past. But now they're both gone and I still feel the suffering of '47.'

'Did she know that you knew?'

'Yes, she knew that we all knew.'

When I ask her to tell me about tayaji and tayiji's relationship, I hear her smiling even over the phone. 'They were very much in love. After Partition, they just started afresh and never looked back. They took care of one another their whole lives. I wonder,' she offers a thought, 'if initially she must have feared that he too would treat her the way others had. But he came like a *farishta*, an angel in her life. Maybe she thought that she had lived through a very bad dream for a very long time, and then she suddenly woke up.'

'So many others weren't as lucky,' I say softly.

'*Bilkul*, this is what my son and I talk about. She was lucky, and eventually she lived a good life. My tayaji respected her.'

Something Mrs Sidhu mentioned earlier has been gnawing at me throughout our conversation. I need to confirm it, but just thinking about it makes me feel uneasy. 'You mentioned that it was members of your family who had taken advantage of her after Partition?'

'Yes,' she replies instantly, 'they did it to many girls on *this* side of the border, after they learnt of what had happened on *that* side to Sikh girls. But tayaji just put an end to it. He declared that the girl be handed over and he married her. He asked no questions. But the same people, the same cousins, the same family who had assaulted her never looked at her again. My grandfather had five brothers, and those brothers all had several sons. Tayaji was the oldest of them all. The moment tayiji became their older brother's wife, the behaviour of these extended family members towards her completely changed.'

I want to ask whether she thinks the couple ever spoke about it between themselves, but I cannot get myself to form the words. Already grateful to have been let in on such an intimate and unspoken part of someone's life, I meekly inquire about her tayiji's religion after marriage.

She clicks her tongue. '*Mazhab se badi insaniyat hoti hai*, humanity is greater than religion, so it didn't matter to him. They married and she changed her name. Those who have lived through '47 have seen more than their share of trauma. With my tayiji, no one knew what went on inside her. Maybe she kept fighting her own emotions her whole life – she got married, raised children, led her life till an old age, but maybe that grief never left. Maybe every Raksha Bandhan, when she would see us all tie rakhis on our brothers, she would remember her own, remember his face, remember his lifeless body, his blood … I think about these things now. I think about how difficult it may have been for her to endure or forget or suppress these thoughts.'

She ends with these words: 'Partition was the reason she both lost and gained family. But whatever was in her heart was carried in silence to her death. Can you ever imagine being in her place?'

6
Fear

⤬

EVEN THOUGH IT'S DAYTIME, the heavy curtains of the room I'm waiting in have been drawn, and everything is blanketed in shadow, save a single flicker of sunlight peeking in from where the two curtains meet. After a few minutes, a small woman with hunched shoulders is led into the room by her son and daughter-in-law. I can't see her face clearly, but I can tell she is wearing a pink salwar-kameez too big for her bony frame, and her grey hair is tied in a bun. Her nose pin sparkles even in the dark. It is September 2018 and I've been in Jammu for over a week now, interviewing eyewitnesses about what they remember of Partition.

When I begin by asking her birthplace, her son promptly replies that she is from Mirpur city, in present-day Pakistan-administered Kashmir. But the woman says nothing, so I try again, this time asking how old she was in 1947. Again, her son most naturally answers on her behalf but I politely tell him that I'd like to hear from her. Sliding my recorder closer, I ask the question again. Her hands are folded neatly in her lap and she looks through me and beyond, but begins to speak. She doesn't remember her age but knows that her eldest son was one year old at the time. Out of the corner of my eye, I watch as her son sits up straighter at the edge of his seat; though he doesn't look old enough to be the child that she speaks of, he pays attention to her every word. The woman's mouth is soft and toothless, and her voice is raspy. She speaks Pothwari, and that too very quickly, making all the gummy words bleed into one another. My understanding of the language is already weak, and I worry I may miss out or misunderstand.

'It was 25 November, the festival of Gurupurab, when the attack happened in Mirpur. We fled in different directions … we ran in a maddening crowd of hundreds. I was separated from my whole family, even my husband, and the only person with me was my son – he clung to me and I clung to him. He had been wounded, and I'd torn my *dupatta* and tied it across the wound to stop the bleeding. For a while it seemed I was running away from the bullets, away from the firing, away from the houses that had caught fire, running away from the armed men. I was just running, but I didn't know where I was going until I found my mother. I saw her lying on the ground, and I reached out to help her, but it was too late. They came with their guns and their sticks and they climbed on her neck and broke it. They killed her in front of my eyes and there was nothing I could do about it.'

'They?' I ask softly, 'wh-who is they?'

Her son quietly clicks his tongue and she chooses not to answer the question, but continues the story. Because I am sitting so close to her, even in the dim light I can see that tears have formed in the corners of her eyes. She wears two necklaces – one, a fine rosary, and the other of small pearls, and fidgets with them as she speaks.

'After killing my mother, they grabbed my son and me, and carried us on camels into the depths of Gujrat and then further to D.I. Khan. We stayed there for six months with other women who had been abducted. Some, like me, had children; others could have been children themselves. Six months, no one knew where we were. I can still see it before my eyes, all of us in that room. Then on the tenth day of Maghar, the police showed up and we were finally retrieved and taken to the Kurukshetra camp.'

With every word she utters, I feel myself biting down on my lower lip until I hurt myself. I am struck by how she remembers the dates. According to the Nanakshahi calendar used in Sikhism, the month of Maghar coincides with November in the Gregorian calendar, which would mean that she stayed there not for six months, as she recalls, but in fact a whole year.

I want to ask her more, but her son tells me that this is enough. He begins to stand up and expects me to do the same, and I scramble with my recorder and notebook and pen. I look at the woman, still sitting, still touching her necklaces, and ask him whether I can photograph her. He is quick to tell me that she doesn't like to be photographed, but I tell him how I am interested in her hands – the way they sit folded in her lap, the way they find their way to her necklaces, the way they reveal. There is beauty in her hands, I say, and rather unenthusiastically he agrees. I lead her into the light of the veranda right by the front door. She walks slowly, hunched over, gently placing one step after another. When she sinks into the beige plastic lawn chair, she lets out a sigh.

Your hands, I gesture to her, *can I see your hands.*

She humours me by stretching them out, turning them around as my camera captures the fine lines. She is watching me intently as I move from wrinkle to wrinkle, finger to thumb. Her hands remind me of my grandmother's, for they have the same soft-to-the-touch-lathered-daily-with-Ponds-cold-cream feel. I smile as I think about this. Then catching me completely off guard, she grabs my forearm and looks straight at me. Her grip is urgent, and a thin film of cataract has begun to appear on her lenses, making her eyes partly cloudy. My heart is beating very fast, and my immediate assumption is that I have either offended her in some way or have awoken some painful dormant memories that she would rather not have remembered.

But it is neither, for she leans in closer.

'Many years after it happened,' she whispers each word slowly, 'a letter arrived addressed to me. It wasn't a bill or a notice, but a letter. An envelope with my name on it, and as soon as I saw it, my heart just stopped. No one had ever sent me a letter before. *What if, what if*, I kept thinking as I held it in my hand. I was so afraid, I didn't even dare to open it. I just tore it up and threw it away. Who knows, what if it had been from one of my abductors? What if...'

❦

THREE YEARS HAVE now passed since this interview and two observations have remained with me – the first is her confession itself. I had wondered even then whether it was the first time she had told anyone about the envelope. I never got a chance to ask her this, but the layers of silence it was made to embed itself under was made clear by her son's intervention during our interview. This confession, then, was perhaps her *speaking for herself*. And the second is how my arm still remembers the urgency of her touch. Somehow, the memory of her skin on mine, coupled with the raspy aged fear in her voice, was so strong that it still makes my heart stop when I think about it. The body remembers fear, even when it is inherited.

IN OCTOBER 1984, Prime Minister of India Indira Gandhi was assassinated by her Sikh security guards, and for days after, Sikhs across the country were brutally attacked and their homes and neighbourhoods pillaged and burned. My own paternal family remembers blackening the name plates of all the houses in their lane in south-west Delhi in order to protect the Sikh families who lived there. My aunt recalls the shrill cries of mobs that resounded in the air and the fiery sticks they carried as they marched. In *The Other Side of Silence*, Urvashi Butalia writes about how she was among the hundreds of volunteers working to provide resources and shelter to those who had suffered. They distributed food and blankets, compiled lists of the dead and missing, and listened to their stories. She writes that 'often older people, who had come to Delhi as refugees in 1947, would remember that they had been through a similar terror before. "We didn't think it could happen to us in our own country … This is like Partition again."'[1]

It is this re-emergence of the fear evoked at Partition – when viewed through the prism of violence in 1984 – that Kuldeep Kaur speaks to me about. Our mutual connection is my father, for Kuldeep and her siblings went to the same school in Delhi as he did, Air Force Bal Bharti, around the same time. That morning, I meet her at

Serendipity Delhi, the travel-inspired lifestyle store she established with her brother in 2014 after restoring a dilapidated haveli in Jonapur village. She leads me to the roof, where pink and haldi-coloured bougainvillea flowers line the walls, and we momentarily escape the noises of the city. A striped cat deftly scales the wall, a lone kite is hurled into the sky from a neighbouring rooftop, and we settle into cane chairs with piping hot cups of tea in our hands.

'Both sides of my family come from Nawabshah, in Sindh, and migrated only in 1948,' she begins. 'My father was eleven years old and my mother would have been just two, but they have heard stories from their elders. They managed to remain in Sindh as long as they could, but a feeling of insecurity and fear had settled in, not only because of the violence but also widespread forceful conversions to Islam. So, they came by ship to India and settled in Alwar, in Rajasthan.'

'I'm a bit embarrassed now, because I always thought your family migrated from West Punjab,' I admit.

She laughs and tells me that it's a common mistake, for they are a small group. When I read about the community further, I learn that Sindhi Sikhs may indeed only number between 18,000 and 20,000 in India. According to the 1941 census in Pakistan, there were approximately 32,000 Sikhs in Sindh prior to Partition[2] and, for the most part, they have remained 'the missing people' when it comes to scholarship on Sikhism, Sindh or Partition.[3]

'Stories of Partition peppered our childhood, but I do think that it was in the aftermath of 1984 that Partition was actively remembered and discussed, both in the house and at school. I was in Grade 11, and I remember how on the day of the assassination, 31 October 1984, we were all sent back home from school. My cousin's wife had just given birth to a baby boy that morning, and my mother's sister was due to be married days later, on 4 November. So, there was naturally an atmosphere of festivity at home. But her fiancé's family lived in west Delhi, which would, in the days to come, become the epicentre of the violence in the city.

'In the evening of the same day, we saw hordes and hordes of people collecting on the street in front of our neighbourhood of Bharti Nagar. No one knew the extent of the violence or the riots, but I remember my father, who was a senior officer in the air force, calling home and telling my mother to keep a suitcase ready. I couldn't understand what was going on, but my mother began pulling out all the important papers and items we may need – *just in case* – and packing them...'

'...reminiscent of Partition,' I say.

'Exactly in the same vein as Partition. And the sheer act in itself was ridden with anxiety. We were going through the motions in the same way the family must have when they migrated from Pakistan to India. *Just keep the suitcase ready*, my father kept saying, *just be ready, just in case*. At the same time, we were still quite certain that my aunt's wedding would happen four days later, talking about how the guests would reach if there was curfew or roadblocks, very much still preparing for a wedding. But by 1 November, no one was able to contact the groom...' Her voice suddenly drops, and each word is uttered carefully, '...we later learnt that his entire family was burnt alive.'

'What?' I ask in horror.

'They were all burnt alive in the riots – parents and two sons, all burnt alive.'

She divulges no more details, but she doesn't really need to. I feel as though I am listening to a story from the days of Partition, and it frightens me to learn what human beings are capable of doing to one another.

'The escalation of violence in those days found precedent only in Partition. I remember the air force trucks picking up people from across the city and taking them to gurudwaras and makeshift camps for shelter. It felt like people had become refugees in their own country. Our entire extended family in Delhi was camping out in our home, in a single building, out of fear for the outside. I remember an older relative, who may have been in her thirties at the time of Partition, comparing the days to 1947, and you could sense the fear in her voice; it was palpable and defining, both physically and subliminally...' She exhales and then adds softly, 'When anything of this nature or scale happens, you become very conscious of your identity as a minority, which should not happen in a country that is constitutionally bound to embrace it.'

She pauses for several minutes, and I think that she is waiting for me to finish my notes, but when I look up, she is lost in thought, gazing at the white stone wall behind me. After collecting her thoughts, she speaks, 'You know, Aanchal, I was a teenager in 1984 and even though I lived through it, I don't really think I fully understood what was happening. But I keep returning to its connection to Partition, and how it reminded people of what it felt like to be targeted and displaced from their own homes. In that sense, Partition feels very close to me on a human level...'

I nod, not wanting to interrupt her flow of thoughts.

'When we eventually went back to school, several of the Sikh boys had cut their hair off.' She raises her hands to her head, and the silver bangles on her wrists jingle.

Tears sting my eyes.

Her voice is now sadder as she continues, 'We were teenagers, so young, and would joke around about it. We didn't ... we didn't understand the enormity of what it meant to cut your hair as a Sikh. And then, interestingly, among my friends, Partition remained a topic of conversation for months after. These two girls kept talking about where their families had come from, and how they'd fled to India.'

'Why do you think that was?' I asked.

'Well, the riots had happened and obviously they were connecting the two incidents. There was a definite reverberation of what Partition had felt like; 1984 merely refreshed its memory, even for the generation that did not witness Partition first-hand. There was something so visceral about the fear and violence of the 1984 riots that had only ever been seen at Partition.'

I am unable to get the image of the charred family out of my mind, of the wedding that never was. Regardless of anything else she says, that image – like all the images of violence that I have collected from

1947 – is now imprinted in my memory. I feel saturated, despite the many degrees of separation. When I tell Kuldeep this, she nods like she understands.

'You are an invisible witness to a real memory. Sometimes, I think traumatic memories carry a certain forbearance to themselves. Whether eyewitness or inherited, they remind us of the boundaries we have to live within. They establish the cost of freedom.'

OVER THE YEARS, I have heard several stories from those whose ancestors were not directly affected by Partition but were impacted by the scenes they witnessed in their own home towns. Then, decades later, when questioned and aided by their subsequent generations, they recall them with the same instinctual dread that can be found in narratives of displacement.

'*Toofan* is the typical Gujarati term my grandmother used to describe Partition. A storm, a tempest,' Rukaiya Idrish Siamwala, who was born in the late '90s in Visakhapatnam, says. She belongs to the Bohra Muslim community of Siddhpur, Gujarat, and her maternal grandmother, Sakina Hasan Ali Shahpurwala (now Sakina Nurruddin Khorakiwala), was four years old in 1947. Despite the young age, some images have remained imprinted in her mind and she relayed these to Rukaiya.

'She remembers groups of people coming from the Hindu parts of Siddhpur village with long wooden sticks, the ends of which were tied with cloth and lit with fire. They also had stones and long knives, threatening the people of Bohra Mohalla to migrate to Pakistan. This was the *toofan*. My grandmother also tells me about the *nirashrits*, a refugee or someone without a home, who had begun migrating to Gujarat after Partition. But because she was very young at the time, she couldn't pronounce the word properly and called them *nirashi*, which means dejected or without hope! They were allotted the homes of those who had migrated to Pakistan.'

'How have these little details remained lodged in her memory?' I ask Rukaiya with fascination.

'I've thought about this a few times as well, and I suppose it is because of the terror and discomfort attached to them – the fact that people marched into the Bohra Mohalla to set it ablaze or to intimidate people into fleeing. But my grandparents tell me that the thought of migrating to Pakistan never even crossed their minds, and if I can speak for myself, as an Indian Muslim, the idea of not being able to call India home is unacceptable to me. So, I understand why they remained on their land, their soil. And perhaps at the time they thought, like every other riot, which they call a *chamakla*, this too would end soon.

'But it certainly triggered something in my grandmother and her family, and this is why it has remained in their memories so strongly. She had four elder brothers, who were all married with children at the time, and they must have discussed the situation at home. However, she does always maintain that if there were Hindu Gujaratis coming towards the Muslim homes in Siddhpur, there must have also been Muslims going towards Hindu homes as well. It is this is very madness of the time that she attributes to the *toofan*.'

Just because Partition did not impact them directly does not mean that its consequences do not define their relationships, and this is the heartbreaking legacy of the Partition line. Rukaiya tells me that her grandmother's sister migrated to Pakistan in the 1960s after she was married, and they were unable to meet. 'Even as a child, I never quite understood the reasons for Partition. I know this is a simplistic way of thinking, but the image of an undivided land is so powerful and poignant. Now, Visakhapatnam to Karachi, my grandmother to her sister, I feel like India and Pakistan are siblings torn apart by an unfair history. My heart really breaks for them, they can never find their horizon, never meet with dignity. There is a dull ache in my chest each time I think about this.'

I ask Rukaiya how these stories of Partition were first told to her, since I am curious about what becomes the anchor to recall the days of the divide when there is no physical displacement or migration, no sense of longing or loss for a land left behind.

'These stories are never told on their own,' she is quick to say, 'their traumas are hidden behind several walls, maybe even deep in our genes, and require effort to emerge. But the intensity with which my grandmother remembered Partition, despite being a child at the time, should demonstrate just how unforgettable the days still are. I once asked her why these memories were still so vivid, and she said, "How can one possibly forget something like that? It created terror *inside* the body." Actually, she used the word *dehshat*, panic, recalling how while she and several other children played in their *mohalla* in Siddhpur, a group of men – young and middle-aged – ran towards them with knives, stones, long wooden sticks lit with blazing fire, screaming that all the *Musalmaans* had to be killed. This deep-rooted terror is what her body remembers.'

After a few moments of reflection, Rukaiya adds, 'I would not be able to forget that kind of fear either.'

'MY MATERNAL GRANDMOTHER'S family walked to India after Partition,' Priyanka Pathania tells me as she mixes a spoonful of brown sugar into her coffee. She was born in 1982 in Pathankot and works as a scriptwriter and producer in Bollywood. As I uncap my pen to take notes, she chuckles. Because Priyanka is a very close friend, this scholarly seriousness takes a few minutes for her to get used to, but she soon settles into the conversation and I find myself interrupting very little throughout.

'Her name was Nirmala, and she was the youngest daughter of a family that owned orange fields in Kashmir and Punjab. We were inseparable; I was raised on her stories, and many of them happened to be about a life before Partition. She would tell me about Mirpur, where she grew up, or her father's orange fields, or about their visits to the Katas Raj Temples, where, among the cluster of temples and ruins, sits an iridescent pool of water. According to the Puranas, this pool was created from a teardrop of Lord Shiva as he flew across the sky carrying the body of his beloved wife, Sati. His tears resulted in the creation of two magnificent pools on Earth. One fell in Katas, Pakistan, and the other – as if foretelling the Partition of the subcontinent – fell in Pushkar, India.[4] Sometimes when I close my eyes, I feel like I can see Katas, even though I've never been there. This was the power of her stories.'

She makes a rippling motion with her fingers on the table as if moving across a magical waterbody.

'Then, when I was in Grade 5, I saw a map of the subcontinent somewhere which showed Kashmir divided between India and Pakistan, and I remember crying for two days after that. My mother has no memory of this, but the incident is imprinted in my mind because I felt like I had been lied to. Why had no one told me that Mirpur was now in Pakistan? Of course, because of all of my grandmother's stories, I knew that she had come to India at Partition, but somehow as a child I didn't register that her birthplace was now...' Her voice trails off, looking for words.

'...on the other side?' I finish.

She sighs. 'Yes, and there was something about not being prepared enough to see it there. Printed officially on paper, dislocated from India. It was hard to comprehend, and I just felt like I had been lied to.'

'But you weren't lied to,' I say with a smile. 'These are just difficult things to explain to children. Why homeland is now inaccessible, why a border stands between you and it.'

Priyanka's expression is soft and almost childlike now. Though there are tears welling up in her hazel-brown eyes, she becomes conscious of the fact that we are sitting in a public place and, with a tissue, wipes her face. 'I tried to ask my teacher about it in school,' she speaks through sniffles, 'about the divided Kashmir. She tried to explain, but couldn't...'

As I ask how her grandmother came to India, the bright background of the café we are sitting in seems suddenly juxtaposed against the seriousness of the memories that Priyanka now unravels.

'After the violence occurred in Mirpur at the end of 1947, her family walked either to Sialkot to their relatives' or elsewhere in Punjab, and then into India. She was in her late teens, and I think she tried to forget much of that time because of an incident that happened with her best friend. It could have happened in Mirpur itself, or later on during their journey – she was never clear about any of the details, and mentioned this only once and never again.

'She remembered clearly that there were riots, that mobs had entered the village and were looting and plundering, killing people and abducting women. My grandmother somehow found a safe place to hide, but from there happened to watch her best friend being picked up and taken by the rioters. She could do nothing about it, because if she'd tried to save her, then they would have abducted her as well. But she told me that she could never forget the look in her friends' eyes – helplessness, despair, panic, fear – she could never unsee it. That incident embedded so much fear in her that I think she carried it throughout her life.'

Neither of us says anything, and the chatter from the café surrounds us.

'I wonder if she felt any guilt...' I say finally, in a small voice.

'Yes, perhaps that too,' Priyanka exhales, and then, gathering her thoughts, says, 'You know, as a child, I learnt of the happiness that came before Partition and the hardships after. I accepted these as stories, as something that happened decades ago and could no longer impact anyone. But it was only when I grew older that I realized how much unspoken trauma it had given birth to. My grandmother loved telling me stories, but there were things she could never say to me, never speak about. Her friends' eyes ... she may have mentioned them only once, but I think she thought about that moment every day of her life.'

'Why do you think that?'

'I know this is my grandmother's story, and I am only putting the pieces together. But, in 2008, when my grandfather died and they took his body for cremation, I didn't go – I was in their house, clearing up, laying the food, making the beds. Under the mattress on both sides, I found meat cleavers. I was shocked, and it immediately filled me with terror.' She pauses for a few seconds. 'I suppose, when you have lived through something as unfathomable as Partition, your defences are forged and heightened by the experience. You plan for the worst. Maybe you keep a suitcase ready. Maybe you gather together the things you'd need in an emergency. *Just in case.* My grandmother slept with a knife under her mattress. The incident of witnessing her friends' abduction, of walking days amidst the violence, of losing home and comfort, had instilled in her such tremendous fear. And I don't think I ever understood this until I found that knife.'

I take a deep breath in.

Her hands fidget with a paper napkin, folding and refolding it. 'There are other things too … like, when I was young I dated a Muslim boy, and when my grandmother found out about it, she was furious and forbade it. I think witnessing the riots, particularly the incident with her friend, made her feel very strongly against the community. But then she also had this other side, where she would visit mosques and dargahs and never seemed to have a problem with the religion. It was very odd, and I could never understand these great contradictions in her behaviour. But because my childhood was spent mostly with her, I too inherited a lot of this mindset, and have had to work on myself every day to unlearn these prejudices. Only now, in hindsight, can I see that they were born from a very particular experience at Partition. I wonder if she knew that similar acts of violence had happened against Muslims on the Indian side…' Priyanka begins to tear the paper napkin in her hands.

'The dichotomy is very complicated, though. Anytime my grandmother spoke of an undivided India, it was always happier memories. They were nostalgic conversations full of longing for the childhood home and landscape. But everything that couldn't be verbally said, particularly about the scale of religious violence or the losses that followed, was manifested in this way of othering, in this feeling of fear.'

She looks down at the table, eyes still wide with thought. This conversation between friends has become sombre and heavy; the second-hand memories of an aged fear have saturated it. Our coffees have gone cold, and the paper napkin has been ripped into many small pieces and divided into two piles. She now collects and arranges them all in the diamond-like shape of the unbroken subcontinent.

Then, looking up at me, Priyanka says, 'It's remarkable how a single incident can impact so much of a person's life and generations beyond. Because this line is still drawn, this pain will always remain. And the more I learn about it, the more I wish it had never happened … I wish Partition had never happened. I want to be a citizen of an unpartitioned India. *That* should be a thing.'

SINJINI MAJUMDAR, A corporate lawyer born in 1994, is based out of Mumbai but spends time at her maternal grandparents' house in Kolkata, where the stories of her dadun and didan have shaped her understanding of Partition.

'My dadun, Narayan Chandra Pal, was born in 1926 in his maternal home at Dinhata, which is today part of the Cooch Behar district of India. But since his family lived in Ramdia, Faridpur, he grew up there until Grade 6, when he was sent to Dinhata for high school and then to Calcutta. Because he is now in his nineties, the specific dates are a little difficult to extract. But I have tried to create a timeline for you of his formative years during the Independence struggle.' She smiles, shuffling through her notes.

'So dadun arrived in Calcutta fresh out of high school in 1942 and was staying in a hostel of the National Medical College at 21 Linton Street, Beniapukur, near Park Circus,[5] when he found himself witness to Direct Action Day. The streets of Calcutta were empty on the morning of 16 August 1946, and over the next few days thousands of the city's residents would be killed and wounded.[6] Dadun's neighbourhood and the surrounding areas saw terrible disturbances and rioting, and he, along with his roommates, was stranded on the topmost floor of this three-storey hostel. Everyone staying on the floors below had fled, leaving just a few Hindu boys to fend for themselves. Dadun tells me that because they knew the area to be a predominantly Muslim one, they decided to remain in the hostel, for fear of being killed or wounded as tensions flared across the city. They had no food, apart from dried *chanas* and *muri*.'

'How long did they remain stranded there?' I ask.

'For a week,' she sighs. 'They were there for the entire duration of what came to be known as The Week of Long Knives.'[7]

'How could they have survived on such meagre food for a week?'

'So, there are interesting details about this week that dadun tells me – for instance, the neighbours who lived around the hostel knew that there were Hindu boys stranded there and would bring them food like biscuits and condensed milk that they had looted from the Hindu shops. It was quite ironic. Dadun was obviously afraid, but because the neighbours knew them – even though they were Muslim and these boys were Hindu – they decided to help rather than harm them. They felt a strange sense of protectiveness towards them, even though the entire city was burning on these very religious lines. So, when mobs or rioters would come to search the area, these neighbours would claim that all the hostel buildings were empty.'

When I ask her why she thinks that was, she shrugs her shoulders. 'Perhaps othering is only possible when the other is faceless, nameless? I think that because they knew these boys – saw them every day, spoke to them, were acquainted with them – their conscience was awakened.' Sinjini takes a sharp breath in and then continues, 'There was a horrific incident that took place during this week that is imprinted in my grandfather's memory, where some local boys murdered an innocent passer-by in broad daylight. Someone put their hands over dadun's eyes while the man was killed, and then everyone just carried on as he lay there in a pool of his blood.'

I gasp.

She exhales loudly. 'Yes. Dadun asked why they weren't killing him, since he was also Hindu, and they all simply said that they knew him, so it was different.'

'Well, how did your grandfather finally leave the hostel?'

'They were rescued by British soldiers who came in a truck and asked the boys to pack their belongings – beddings, clothes, books – and come with them. They were told that they need to go back to their home towns and were taken to Kalighat, where the military had a short-term luggage storage facility for those evacuated from Calcutta.[8] Each of the boys was given a slip for his belongings, and upon their return to the city, they could show it and pick up their luggage. Most of them didn't have relatives in the city, which is why they were staying in a hostel. They were then dropped off at Sealdah station, the other major train station apart from Howrah. Dadun said the military was patrolling the entire premises, and from there he and a senior who lived in a village close by caught the Dhaka Mail. It dropped them off at … wait, I have this written down somewhere,' she pauses and again looks through her notes. 'They got off at a station called Belgachi, and dadun tells me that he purposely got off from the wrong side of the train. Basically, he jumped off on the railway track rather than the platform.'

'How come?'

'After what he had witnessed in Calcutta, he was afraid that he may encounter a mob … so he got off on the railway track and began walking home. Ramdia also had a train station, but the Dhaka Mail did not pass through it. Dadun would have had to wait for another train, which he did not want to do in the circumstances. On the way, he encountered someone from his village who was shocked to see him there and told him to tell nobody that he had come from Calcutta, or what he had seen in the city, as there was a lot of fear among the villagers. Even once he was home, I don't think his parents let him leave the house and he just kept to himself. In fact, my mother has heard from her grandmother that during the month that dadun was home, he would have constant nightmares and throw up everything he ate. But dadun himself has never confessed this to me.' She closes her eyes in sadness. 'I guess it was post-traumatic stress, and fear. An enormous amount of fear had settled into him. Dadun said that even when the British soldiers evacuated them, his hands were shaking out of fear – he didn't know who was coming to get them, what would happen next, whether he would live or die. Those were the worst days of his life.'

'Did this incident define any part of his life?' I ask Sinjini, noticing how deflated her body language has become. The deeper she has travelled into the heart of the story, the deeper the story seems to have settled into her. I can hear a knot in her voice.

'When dadun tells this story, I can sense no inkling of pain in his voice. It's as if he is telling me an electrifying fictional tale, casually narrating a near-death experience. Even today, he is possibly the most positive and motivated person I know … Maybe forgetting it or supressing the trauma was his way of moving past it.'

'How does it make you feel?' I ask, settling back into my seat.

'Well, these stories affect me a lot because I am generally an emotional person,' she smiles. 'I don't think I would have been able to witness what he did and then come back to the same place. He spent one month in Faridpur, and then had to return to Calcutta to continue his education at medical school. But it had only been a month, how could one just forget all the violence that they had witnessed and return to normalcy? Maybe he has a stronger personality and was able to overcome it, but I don't think I could.

'I would never be able to forget the image of dead bodies littered across the roads.[9] He tells me how on their way to the station, both sides of the pavement were soaked red with blood, and the entire city was reeking of death. Every time he tells this story, he mentions the smell, the stench, the foul odour of bodies. This is something that's etched in his memory, the smell. But the thing I keep thinking to myself is this – what if the Muslim neighbours hadn't cared enough about these boys to protect them? Dadun would have died, he would have been killed like everyone else. He would have never survived.'

Her voice quivers and her eyes betray that she has often imagined this landscape of violence and terror. Fear emanates from her every word, and so I ask, 'Do you feel scared *for* him?'

'*Of course*, yes. Sometimes I feel like I'm there, I'm at the hostel, I'm on the train with him, I'm looking at the city being swallowed by violence. Maybe I have internalized this too much. But if he had been killed, then none of us – my mother, me – would be here. A single instance is the difference between life and death.'

'Sinjini,' I begin softly, 'when did you first hear these stories?'

'I have heard these stories over many years since I was a young girl, but I am still learning different parts of them, for there are always more details added. And I want to be able to hold on to these memories, but I am also afraid of them. They are scary and unfathomable. It's different when you read about Partition violence in books or academic papers. You may feel some sadness or empathy, but it is still removed from you. The minute you learn that your family witnessed something so traumatic during the days of Partition, it immediately becomes your own. This fear, this grief, this pain, it is mine. It is my family's. But even within families, I suppose generations are impacted differently by it.'

Since this is at the heart of my study, I ask her to elaborate.

'Well, my mother doesn't feel as affected by these memories. She does not engage in second-hand nostalgia or fear. She is a practical person. But I can't explain why the stories of Partition impact me so much.' As Sinjini continues to speak, the sadness surmounts, until it eventually overwhelms her. 'I think what I find difficult to understand is how people can overcome the gravity of the losses they endured and the violence they witnessed. They had to carry on, bearing these invisible scars that they never talked about or even faced. But I can't be the only person who feels this pain, can I?'

With that, she breaks down, tears gently gliding down her face. 'See, I told myself I wouldn't be too emotional when I spoke to you, but I can't help it...'

'Well, there is no singular, acceptable way to understand trauma, lived or inherited. We can only do it in the way we know how,' I say, speaking both from personal experience and other such conversations.

Her face is coloured by the sunshine spilling in from the window, and she wipes her eyes dry. 'I'm still a bit embarrassed by how I can have such an emotional perspective on an event I have only heard stories about. Anyway...' she breathes out, 'dadun returned to Calcutta after a month in Faridpur, and the hostel was no longer a hostel. He managed to rent a flat with some friends on Convent Road nearby, in a building that used to be a hostel for Muslim boys. They would commute to the National Medical College from there but had to cross their old residence every day. Naturally, it must have affected them to pass by the place where they were nearly killed. It was a reminder of what had happened. But they maintained a low profile.

'Dadun lived on in Calcutta after Partition, but his family remained in Faridpur, which became a part of East Pakistan, as there was no violence in his village. Eventually, they also migrated to India. The story that my mother has heard from her grandmother is that dadun's father used to work in a British jute mill; he was a jute tester and knew the different types of jute and their qualities. But when the Swadeshi movement began, he resigned from his job. He came back home without his shoes, and then pulled out all my great-grandmother's saris which had been made with cloth from England, started a big bonfire, and burnt everything. Apparently, she was crying, but he declared that he had resigned and would never again work for the British. After that, he spent his days cultivating plots of agricultural land he owned.

'Gradually, the atmosphere changed and my great-grandmother, who was a very practical lady, wanted to be closer to her son, my dadun, and also understood that things could politically worsen. In 1965, when they were visiting Calcutta, the borders closed in the aftermath of the Indo-Pak war and they never went back. I have checked all the visa stamps in their passport. Eventually, they became Indian citizens but learnt that their house in Faridpur, which still stands, was looted and the property was taken over by the Pakistan government...'

'Your dadun never returned?' I ask.

'He would go back and forth when his family still lived in Faridpur, but not after they migrated to India. It is only in the last decade or so that he's been thinking about the other side.'

I nod, and then skim through the many pages of notes I've taken. 'Sinjini, you mentioned both your grandparents were from East Bengal, but we haven't spoken about your grandmother yet.'

'Well, hers is a very different story to my grandfather's, where though there was no physical trauma, the unspoken, mental impact caused by Partition was ever present,' Sinjini says in a voice suddenly transformed, softened as if to take care of whatever she will now divulge. There is something about this change that causes my heart to feel uneasy.

'My didan was ten or eleven years old when her family migrated from a place called Natore in the Rajshahi district of East Bengal. But she doesn't have a lot of memories about that time, because she never wanted to discuss this phase of her life. She had happy memories from the time she began college, but everything before that is quite bleak. During Partition, her eldest sister was already married, and she had three elder brothers and a younger brother who was born just after Independence. The family came from Rajshahi to Calcutta, which is what her refugee certificate says, and then went further to Puri in Orissa. The family suffered tremendous financial losses; they had virtually nothing to their name, and my grandmother was given away to an orphanage shortly after.'

I open my mouth to say something, but no words emerge. Sinjini knowingly nods and continues.

'She stayed there for about six months before her grandfather took her away and raised her along with her three older brothers. He was a schoolteacher and would take the three boys along with him to school, but my grandmother remained at home and was homeschooled by him. She was quite a small child, and would cook and clean and study by herself throughout the day. He was quite a strict man and the children led a very regimented life with him. There were schedules – study time, sleep time, mealtime – everything was fixed, and she had a very unhappy childhood.' She hesitates momentarily. 'It's just … I feel very strongly about this entire episode in my grandmother's life, because it really defined her.'

I ask her if she'd rather not talk about her grandmother, and she shakes her head.

'The first thing that strikes me is why her parents only gave away the daughter, why not the sons. I understand that the family had financial difficulties, but how could they just give a child away? Maybe it was a temporary thing, maybe they were figuring things out. But they just left her at the orphanage until her grandfather brought her home to a town called Kalna in West Bengal. She remained affected by the experience and was never close to her parents, who continued to live in Puri.

'I found all this out from my mother, because my grandmother never wanted to discuss this. She suffered from anxiety her entire life, which stemmed from this moment – first, she was displaced from her home during Partition, then made to migrate to a whole new land, and then had to undergo this kind of abandonment and betrayal by her own parents. It was true that she stayed with family, her grandfather and brothers, but she was hungry for love and tenderness. There was no female figure in her life, no one to help her through the things that a mother would ordinarily help her daughter through…' Her voice trails off.

'Did it affect the relationships she had with people in the later phases of her life?' I ask.

'She was generally fearful of everything. She suffered from ill health and was often in the hospital. Anytime I speak to my mother about this, it is clear that the experiences of my grandmother were unfairly traumatic. There was so much sadness, and it was mostly from being misunderstood and unloved. As a little girl, she couldn't go out, didn't have any friends, and didn't live a normal childhood. I was sixteen years old when she died, but I remember her as a fragile person, both physically and emotionally, who could never be told much. Everyone was always telling her not to worry about her children or grandchildren, because she was so affected by the world around her.'

Sinjini then remains quiet for several minutes, as do I. There is a deluge of sadness surrounding us, and it is so tangible that I almost feel like I can touch it. Truth be told, I don't know what to ask any longer, for the stories of her grandparents have overwhelmed me. But then I think about the fact that if I'm hearing these stories for the first time, then Sinjini has heard them since childhood and her grandparents have further lived and possessed them every single day. Maybe she picks up on these thoughts, maybe she feels them too, for when she looks at me again, I recognize the sadness on her face.

'There are things from these stories that have stayed with me. My didan always told this to my mother, who has further told me that I must be prepared for everything in life, because of how unexpectedly the generation before her was uprooted. The future is unforeseen and out of your control, so I must be prepared for any upheaval. I think *this* is really how Partition has created long-term emotional insecurities and fears within people and their subsequent generations.

'With both my grandparents' experiences, there was so much trauma and horror. But when I listen to my grandmother's story, it just affects me in a...' She brings her left palm up to her heart and breathes in deeply. 'It's so personal. I don't have any words ... I don't have the words to explain how I feel, so how could she? I do understand why she would want to bury that entire part of her life. Suffocate all the memories of that time.'

'Would you have wanted to speak to her about it?' I ask hesitantly and, to my surprise, Sinjini nods.

'If she was ever willing, I would have wanted her to share what she went through. I know I may not have been able to help her in any way, but it could have made her lighter. Even if she couldn't let go of the past, at least she could share it. I would have happily taken her sadness, her heaviness, her pain, her fears. I would have borne the entire weight of her memories.'

7

Friendship

'IT MAY BE UNUSUAL to say this in the context of Partition, but from whatever I have heard in my own family, there was an energy during those months of turmoil, of helping others, of resilience and friendship. I cannot describe it in any other way,' Rabeya Sen tells me. Her family migrated from India to the United States when she was four years old in 1981 and is now based in Los Angeles.

'I knew that though my family was not displaced during Partition, they'd witnessed its horrors in Delhi. But it was only when I heard this story from my mother that it confirmed what I'd always hoped to be true. That in the face of unthinkable violence, my family had the courage to commit themselves to acts of kindness and love. That, in some cases, the forces of separation were not as strong or emphatic. I believe this to be my legacy of Partition, not one of rupture, but one of unity, of friendship.'[*]

She begins by recognizing the privilege her maternal family had: of being able to support people who were forced to leave their homes and start lives elsewhere. At the time of Partition, they lived in a small flat in Delhi's Daryaganj market area, then known as Faiz Bazar. The family consisted of Rabeya's grandparents, dimma and dadu; a granduncle; her great-grandfather, who was settled in Meerut but

---

[*] Rabeya's mother Bharati Sen's testimony of yet another event of this nature from the same time period appears in Chapter 9, 'Hope'.

was visiting; her uncle, who was six years old at the time; and her mother, who was two. In the flat below theirs lived a Muslim family whose one son, Khaled, was friends with Rabeya's uncle as they were both the same age. The father was a gentleman, and the mother was known to all as Begum sahiba. When communal riots struck the area, they were faced with the difficult decision of whether or not to leave India for Pakistan. They would often confer with Rabeya's family, and wanted to cross over to the west side of Faiz Bazar (present-day Netaji Subhash Marg) where they had friends, but it was considered risky to move around.

Finally, the family decided it was best to migrate to Pakistan, but because of the volume of cross-border movement, there was a considerable waiting period to procure tickets. The father needed to leave for a few days to make arrangements, and in the meantime, worried about where his wife and children would stay, turned to his upstairs neighbour, whom he both trusted and respected. Rabeya's family offered to shelter them in their home, no matter how long it took. And so Begum sahiba and her three children, one still an infant, moved into their flat during the curfew hours of the night. Rabeya's uncle and Khaled understood the gravity of the situation and remained quiet. When the infant cried, the sound carried, and other neighbours were told that it was Rabeya's mother who was crying. The Muslim family were given the back room with the largest bed, and the huge glass-paned windows of the room were covered with dark cloth.

During this time, a particularly dangerous incident occurred that could have exposed the hidden family. One of the squares in a park nearby was used every evening by the newly formed Rashtriya Swayamsevak Sangh (RSS) youth group to hold its meetings, hoist the national flag and do exercises. After that, during the curfew hours, volunteers would patrol the streets. There must have been some suspicion about their home, for one day some of the boys came knocking. Rabeya's granduncle – a burly, tall motorcyclist who had trekked to Gangtok – opened the door and asked them what they wanted. In response, the boys boldly claimed that they knew the family was sheltering Muslims and needed to give them up. They insisted on searching the house, but her granduncle in turn insisted that they all go to the Faiz Bazar police station to register the complaint first. It was a well-known fact that in early September 1947 Sardar Vallabhbhai Patel had stationed himself in the area[1] to maintain order and safeguard residents, famously having said that he would 'not tolerate Delhi becoming another Lahore'[2] with regards to violence and rioting. The RSS youth slithered away, leaving the two families in peace, and the very next day the Muslim family left for Pakistan, accompanied up to a safe distance by Rabeya's grandfather and granduncle.

There is a warmth to her story, an indestructible sense of humanity that Partition was unable to break. Inspired by the courage of both families, I ask her, 'Did they reach Pakistan safely?'

'Sadly, the families lost touch after that,' she responds and then on a more hopeful note adds, 'but then, some time in the mid-1980s, while my uncle was at a conference in Bombay, he happened to meet Khaled! Neither knew what had happened to the other, and it was sheer coincidence that this conference brought them together again. They just happened to start conversing, and in doing so they both realized who the other was!'

Rabeya is a policy director for a small social justice NGO in south-central LA working with Black, indigenous and immigrant communities. Her work involves immigrant rights, and racial, gender and environmental justice. When we speak, it is at the tail end of President Donald Trump's administration, and I ask her whether despite being physically far away from South Asia and generationally distanced from Partition, she ever thinks about it in relation to the present day.

Her response is humbling and one deftly shaped by her empathetic upbringing. 'While working with issues of immigrant experiences and forces of displacement, it's hard to ignore the evident patterns that emerge. How, regardless of whatever border we speak of, systems can be abusive and perpetuate further trauma and displacement, particularly towards already vulnerable populations. Stories of

Partition, and my family's in particular, always reminds me of the power we have – individually and collectively – to recognize the humanity in one another. How, though it may seem like the most obvious and natural thing, we *do* have to make an effort to accept love and reject communalism. We have to fight for peace, inclusivity, amity. These are the values my family has inculcated in me. Never again, I tell myself, thinking of all that has come to define this event, can we let such violence and trauma happen. Never again, for the pain associated with it is so deep that it can affect future generations as well.'

SUCH TALES OF friendship and kindness are not at all unusual. In fact, they are scattered throughout the landscape of Partition. But to seek them out requires a shift in perspective, for when one is attuned to look out for stories of kinship rather than brutality, the violence of Partition becomes fundamentally inexplicable. Neighbour against neighbour, friend against friend, and caught amidst the frenzy are citizens of an undivided India who find it difficult to grasp the concept of a divided land – who, at great risk, maintain a semblance of humanity and camaraderie. Every such act of kindness, thus, is a significant one, no matter how big or small, and *cannot* be diminished by the brutality of the time.

Umair Khan has grown up listening to the story about Hindu neighbours who were once dear to his grandfather in their ancestral village Paniala in tehsil Paharpur of district Dera Ismail Khan, Khyber Pakhtunkhwa province in Pakistan. Umair was born in 1987 in Peshawar, where he still lives. Every Eid the family would visit Paniala and there he would sleep on a jute *charpai* different from any he had ever seen before.

'It was taller and had beautifully strong legs painted with intricate motifs. The shape almost resembled a snake charmer's flute, long and rounded at the end. I think it was some time in my early teenage years that I heard this was the *charpai* that our Hindu neighbours had left with my grandfather in 1947.'

My paternal grandmother, too, migrated from D.I. Khan to Delhi, and so this interview is of uniquely personal interest to me. 'Did you understand the meaning of Partition, then, as a teenager? Had you heard stories of what had happened in D.I. Khan?'

'Well, I studied it in school but didn't know anything about the sheer horrors. Back then, I probably never asked about the *charpai*, or why the family had left it, or what had happened to them. But now, when I go to my village, I am constantly thinking about it, and how difficult it must have been for people to leave their homes, their lands. To flee so suddenly with young children or women, or ailing parents and grandparents. I can't even imagine it and I feel very sad when I think about it now.'

I ask him to tell me more about the *charpai*, and in turn he tells me that there are other objects too that the family left in their possession. The story Umair has heard from his elders is that at the time of Partition, Muslims and Hindus used to live in harmony in their village. His grandmother tells him that most of the wealthy population were Hindus, and at Partition the strongest influence in the Paniala area was of the Congress party.[3] But when the Partition line was suddenly announced, all the Hindu families found themselves not only on the wrong side of the border but also in a province extraordinarily far away from safety. Some fled in haste and others succumbed to violence, while some, like their neighbours, took refuge with friends they trusted.

'The Hindu family, consisting of two men and three women, spent the night in our house before migrating to India the very next day. They were well off and owned many shops and animals. My grandfather, Khan Mir Khan, was a zamindar and assured the family that they would be safe with us that night. My phupho, Misab bibi, who is eighty-five years old now and would have been a teenager during Partition, still remembers them well. She said that they ate nothing all night, because they were very sad to have to leave their home behind. When they set off for India the next day, indebted to my grandfather who kept his promise of safety, they left behind two jute *charpais*, a large safe, a teapot and some perishable food like tea and sugar. My phupho even recalls the green colour of the teapot!'

Then Umair proceeds to tell me that there is more to the story of these objects. It is not just that personal objects were left in the possession of a friend, it is also that these objects were the last remaining traces of a friendship. And that fact was sacred to Umair's grandfather.

'In the years following Partition, there used to be announcements made in the village that whoever had anything in their homes once belonging to a Hindu would be arrested.'

I crinkle my eyebrows, not quite understanding how, other than an obviously religious artefact like a prayer book or an idol, does an ordinary object become Hindu or Muslim. I ask Umair what he means.

'Well, my phupho said that after the migration of Hindus from the village, large parts of their properties remained. This included houses and shops and everything inside. The government decided that all of this material would be auctioned off, probably as a source of revenue for the government. Or there may have been another plan for resettlement of property. The two *charpais* were inconspicuous, as was the teapot. But it was the safe that my grandfather was worried about – it is emerald green in colour, quite large, and placed horizontally on the ground, resembling a storage freezer, actually. At first, my grandfather buried the safe in the ground, but then he decided to give it up to the government.'

'But you talk about it as if it is still there in the home...'

'Oh yes, it very much is. My grandfather couldn't part with it indefinitely, especially since it had been entrusted to him in a moment of parting. And so, at the auction, he promptly bought it back! My phupho remembers that many such items – abandoned houses, even – were sold at this auction for prices as low as five or ten rupees.'

'Are the stories of Partition talked about frequently in your family?'

'They are discussed openly but not frequently. My grandfather had many Hindu friends at one time. At festivals and weddings, they would send across both salty and sweet rice to each other's houses. They would buy all their vegetables and fruits from Hindu shops. The more you speak about the days of Partition, the more my phupho reveals how sad my grandfather truly was when his friends were forced to leave the homes and lands where they were born and where they had lived their whole life. These objects still remind us of them,' he maintains. 'They may have left in 1947, but their memories certainly haven't faded.'

WHEN TWENTY-TWO-YEAR-OLD GARIMA Kumar speaks to her maternal grandmother, Shanta Devi, born in 1932, it is about a clandestine escape to the camps with the help of their Muslim neighbours. Born in Noorpur Thal, Sargodha zila, Shanta Devi's family had moved to a village in Lyallpur (present-day Faisalabad) five or six years before Partition. Her neighbourhood had a Muslim majority, and after the announcement of Partition the Hindu and Sikh families began moving out in large caravans, bullock carts loaded to full capacity with their belongings. '*Paidal chal ke o' Hindustan vich aaye si*,' she tells Garima in Punjabi that these people migrated to India on foot.

Garima narrates the story of how, for about a month, her grandmother and her two younger brothers, Ramesh and Atam, used to stand on the terrace and watch these caravans pass. When her mother brought up the subject of their family migrating as well, her father fervently opposed it, saying that whether they lived or died, they would remain where their land was, even though it was now Pakistan. Soon, even the Muslims of their neighbourhood assured the family, swearing on the Quran, that they would do everything in their power to protect them.

'A few days later, however, a gang, whom my grandmother called *junglis*, hooligans, showed up at her uncle's house. Her uncle owed them money. Hearing this news, her father immediately gathered them all and, running across the terraces of multiple houses, they arrived at the village headman's house asking for shelter. When I asked my grandmother if they were Muslim too, she said yes, and it made me reflect on the fact that perhaps the very event that had birthed unprecedented violence had also birthed a unique sense of brotherhood. Apparently, the family hid behind piles of utensils that night.

'But meanwhile, from my grandmother's uncle's house, the gang abducted her cousin, Shanti, who was about the same age. When her mother tried to stop them, her hand was slit in response, and the gang tried to carry the young off on their horses. But they could not get too far from the house, for the brother of the village headman, a man named Talyawand, helped release Shanti by threatening to kill the gang. My grandmother remembers how he firmly said that her cousin "was not a Hindu's daughter but his own". These were all their daughters – *dheeyan* – and they would protect them. He ordered them to leave the girl at once and so Shanti was released.'

'How did the family finally flee?'

'In the predawn hours of the very next day, in an attempt to ensure Shanti's and Shanta's safety, Talyawand and the village schoolmaster rode them on a bicycle each while Shanti's elder brother, Trilok, accompanied them on a third bicycle. Both girls wore burqas, and Trilok tied a *pagri* on his head. They rode for about six kilometres until they caught a *tanga* to their grandparents' house and to safety.'

But the eventual journey to India was long and arduous, and Garima is extremely particular about mentioning each detail. 'From their village in Lyallpur, they moved to the camps where families of migrating Hindus and Sikhs were nestled close to each other in tents. From there, they were taken to yet another camp on the grounds of a college in Lahore, where my grandmother remembers breaking tables and chairs for firewood, and overturned ghee canisters being used as makeshift *tawas* to cook rotis. From Lahore, they boarded buses across the border, first to Amritsar – where they stayed for a night or two – and then to Jalandhar. My grandmother tells me that the city was entirely lit up for Dussehra celebrations, which means that they must have arrived some time in October 1947. In Jalandhar, her father began trading in *khaand*, sugar, as a means to survive. In 1950, her mother passed away of an illness, unable to see the family rebuild all that they'd lost in the move from Pakistan to India. Eventually, they settled in Saharanpur in Uttar Pradesh. And when my grandmother got married in 1954, she moved to Delhi, finally making a permanent home.'

I carefully note down each stop in my notebook. But as the list continues to grow, I feel overwhelmed and bring up this fact with Garima.

Agreeing with me, she says sadly, 'I felt it too, and then I had so many questions. Place after place after place. Another village, another city, another camp. *What is home then*, I would wonder as my grandmother narrated her journey. Where do you belong when your very belongingness has been challenged in this way? Did she ever think about home during this migration? Did she have the time to? Perhaps home was the land of one's birth. Or perhaps it was the land of one's survival. Or perhaps home would be everything in whatever the future held, everything in becoming.'[4]

With these final words, yet again I am reminded of the fact that even stories of safe migrations are not exempt from melancholy. Even memories of interfaith harmony and brotherhood are coloured with pain.

KARNAL-BASED NAGMA NASSA tells me that in 1947 her maternal grandmother, Basant Kaur, twelve years old at the time, migrated from Lalamusa, now in Pakistan, via train. All she was carrying was a small box of her essentials and a hand-knitted shawl, which was confiscated by officials during their journey. The family first arrived at Attari, welcomed by chants of '*Bharat mata ki jai!*', after which they were sent to the Kurukshetra refugee camp, where they lived for a month. Finally, her father found work in the railways in Gaya, Bihar. Nagma was raised by her grandmother, and the pair often spoke about her childhood in Pakistan.

'It was during one of these conversations that my nani revealed to me that I was named after her Muslim neighbour in Lalamusa, a girl she used to play with as a child and whom she had to leave behind at Partition. Nagma – she named me after her friend.'

Ali Samoo, who lives in Karachi, relays a similar story of friendship. 'I faintly remember my grandmother, Bibi Aaminat Soomro, telling me about her Hindu friend, Maari. Perhaps I'm not pronouncing the name right, but my grandmother was quite old when she recalled this story. But she told me how Maari's father made these little clay dolls and that they played with them in the streets of Hala in Sindh. Once Maari's family migrated to India, all my grandmother was left with were these dolls, which she couldn't play with for much longer, for she got married very soon after Partition. She was only thirteen, still a child. After marriage, she was unable to make any new friends, and it was in some ways the end of her childhood. But from the little that she remembered of life before Partition, Maari's memory was the brightest.'

WHAT THESE STORIES really reveal are the voids left behind by friends: Muslims, Sikhs and Hindus studying at schools together, living in neighbourhoods together, celebrating festivals together, blending into one another's families like water. Over the years, I have recorded stories of Hindus and Sikhs waking up with their Muslim friends for sehri and waiting for the evening's Iftar meal with them. I have heard stories about children of all religions flying kites on Basant or singing the songs of Dulla Bhatti on Lohri, bound together by their Punjabiyat rather than separated by their religion. I have listened in lament to stories of how entire syncretic *mohallas* would be lit up for Diwali or Dussehra. I know that a lot of this culture was fractured by Partition. But today, even though so many years have passed, I still find myself thinking about that first Eid or Diwali or Dussehra or Basant after Partition, that the same people must have celebrated without the friend who had now migrated, who had now become the other, whose void probably still remains.

IN 2005, THE Mumbai-based multidisciplinary artist Nina Sabnani[*] created an eight-minute-long animation film titled *Mukand and Riaz*,[5] based on the fragmented memories of her father, Mukand, who remembers and misses Riaz, his childhood friend from Karachi. In November 2017, I had a chance to watch this brilliant film and interact with Nina at the Winter School in Oral History at the Srishti Institute of Art, Bengaluru, where we were both presenting our works.

In her presentation, Nina calls *Mukand and Riaz* a story of two caps. The animation, which uses fabrics and material that were familiar to her father, follows the two boys around the port city of Karachi during the days of Independence and Partition. Mukand wears a cricket cap, which Riaz adores and tries hard to get but it is Mukand's prized possession. They are shown riding bicycles and drinking cool summer drinks together. Then one day, Karachi is in unrest as Partition riots engulf it. Mukand's Hindu family decides they must leave for India at once and begin packing their belongings. At that moment, Riaz arrives at their house armed with kurtas and Jinnah caps to disguise the family as Muslims. Reluctant, Mukand is made to wear a sombre black Jinnah cap over his bright red cricket cap. Riaz drives them to the Karachi harbour, where the family boards the *S.S. Shirala* to Bombay. They had no words to express their gratitude, for young Riaz had saved their lives. The deck of the ship is crowded with refugees, as is the port. Amidst the mayhem, Mukand looks out at Riaz and then he remembers: he takes off his bright red cap and flings it down towards his friend, who catches it. Both Mukand and Riaz wave at each other until neither the port nor the ship can be seen any longer.

---

* A more comprehensive narrative on Nina Sabnani's family history appears in Chapter 17, 'No Man's Land'.

When we speak about the process of making the film, Nina tells me that it was only when her father was in his seventies that he decided to finally begin talking about what had happened during Partition. He had been living in Dubai for nearly twenty-five years and was quite at peace with being a world citizen when he dove eloquently into the memories of his childhood spent in Karachi with his friend Riaz. As she talks about this delayed remembrance, I turn to the notes I took during her presentation in 2017, when she had said, 'Not everything needs to be told, not everything needs to be seen.' Perhaps until it is time – I add an addendum to the phrase.

'Initially the film was called Moti and Riaz,' Nina admits, using her father's pet name, 'but very quickly he said not to call him Moti in the film because he wanted Riaz to know it was him. "How will he find me?" he had asked. After Partition, they never met one another, and so part of the effort was also to reunite lost friends.'

The longest section of the film comes at the very end, when the two boys are waving at each other. It continues on, the view from the sea and from the port, until the boys can no longer see one another. Nina tells me that this was one of the most powerful images for her, emblematic of the pain of Partition and the severance of many such friendships. 'My father waved at himself in the film when he saw it for the first time,' she says. 'It was a closure of some sort for him – a goodbye to himself and his childhood.'

I think about this story for a while, how Mukand and Riaz parted over water, where the border is impossible to determine. I think about how enmeshed society once used to be, and how the creation of fortified national identities has not only limited the scope of such friendships but made them near impossible. I tell Nina that the first time I ever met a Pakistani in the flesh was when I went to college in Canada in 2007. She tells me that she too made her first Pakistani friend in the 1990s, when she was studying in the US, a borderless space for South Asians.

'His name was Shoaib, and before I met him, of course, I had Pakistani friends who were married to Indians in Bombay and so integrated into the family. But Shoaib was from Lahore and was a *muhajir*, his family had migrated from India to Pakistan during Partition, and they too had faced problems in being accepted in Pakistan – not very different from us Sindhis in India.'

She pauses for a few seconds and then, ever the virtual artist, paints a scene for me. 'Think of it like this: you've just gotten on a train and the moment you get inside a compartment, no one will make room for you, and they take forever to allow you to feel comfortable being there; everyone is pushing this way or that way to occupy seats. This is what it felt like, both in India after Partition and also in America. When I met Shoaib, we were trying to talk to some Americans, and they weren't able to understand what we were trying to say, but Shoaib would always just get it. He understood me. And I said to him, "Shoaib, why are our countries fighting? You and I understand each other perfectly!" He would tell me stories about how when he left for America, his grandmother used to tell him not to fall in love with an American, because he would never be able to speak his language of love, Urdu, with them. How would he ever tell them, *"Tum mere jigar ka tukda ho?"* How would he say you are a piece of my heart?' Nina laughs.

Then, catching her breath, she resumes, 'We would go to museums together, play *ghazals* and listen to Bollywood songs. It was so comfortable and it felt like there was absolutely no border.'

'Why does this always happen,' I ask her, 'why does it happen that the minute we leave our territory we become less territorial about it? Particularly with Indians and Pakistanis who meet outside the subcontinent ... it's like the weight of the border suddenly disappears.'

She thinks about this for a few seconds and then replies definitively, 'Because it's all about politics. This line, this border between us, is all about politics. It has nothing to do with individuals. As people, we are the same, on this side and that. *You know that.* And when we meet in a borderless space, we can meet as individuals who come from the same land with the same experiences.'

∽

IF PARTITION RESULTED in the end of friendships, it also gave birth to extraordinary circumstances in which friendships, against all odds, were maintained.

When I meet Raj Suneja[6] in Delhi, she recalls the Lahore of undivided India. '4 Fane Road was our address, close to the Punjab high court, where my father, Amolak Ram Kapur, practised.' Fane Road, prominent due to the many lawyers who inhabited it, was named after General Sir Henry Fane, once commander-in-chief of the Indian Army. She says the *kothis* on the street were few but large, and tries to recall the owners from memory. 'Bakshi Tek Chand, Bishan Narayan, Grover sahib, the Suris, the Sonis.' Unable to remember any more names, she says, 'It was quite a close-knit community, where families respected one another regardless of religion.' Fane Road was also home to the small legal chamber of none other than the late author Khushwant Singh.

I ask her whether she still thinks about Fane Road. Suneja smiles and says in Punjabi, '*Iss umar pe toh kayi cheezein bhool jaati hai, lekin bachpan da Lahore kadi nahi bhoolta, o' shehr di baat hi kuch aur si.* Age makes the past hazy, but memories of the Lahore of my childhood never leave me.' She speaks fondly about the public park on Fane Road, the *akhara*, their beautifully manicured garden, the two cars, cows and *tanga*. She notes with pride that theirs was the first home on the street to get a Godrej refrigerator.

But the highlight of 4 Fane Road was undoubtedly Amolak Ram Kapur's grand library, with hundreds of books collected over the years. Suneja opens her arms as wide as she can to show me the vastness of the book collection. And then she reveals that the family had to leave it all behind when they migrated to Delhi during the summer of 1947, hoping the move would be merely temporary – for a week or two at most. They had fled in haste, acting in response to rumours of ghastly violence against women in Lahore, carrying minimum belongings and clothing.

During the early days in Delhi, they relied on the goodness of friends and other refugees. Partition had not yet happened, but Kapur's eldest son, K.K. Kapur, a well-known film distributor, had an office space in Lahore and proposed to exchange it for a Muslim friend's property in Delhi. And so it came to be that the family occupied 9 Rajpur Road, Civil Lines, in Delhi. Suneja remembers walking along Connaught Place, seeing many of her father's old friends and acquaintances selling their wares on the roadside. At home, food was sparse and relatives from across the border flocked to the small property, making it feel no less than a refugee camp. But whatever the circumstances, their doors would always remain open to all.

As the date for Partition approached, the family would listen to bulletins on the radio and read the newspaper, fearing with every passing day that their home and life in Lahore would soon become a thing of the past. As the summer of 1947 came to a close, Kapur reached out to an old friend with a sincere request. It is the mention of this very communication that first catches my interest.

In his memoir, *Neither a Hawk Nor a Dove*, Khurshid Mahmud Kasuri, a Pakistani politician who has served as the country's foreign minister, also alludes to 4 Fane Road, Lahore,[7] writing from the perspective of his family. In the summer of 1947, the Kasuris were vacationing in Murree, an idyllic hill station in Rawalpindi. Young Khurshid recalls eagerly waiting for the pastry-wallah when his father told the family they had to pack up and return to Lahore immediately. Khurshid, having just turned six, writes about being very angry at one 'Amolak Ram Kapur, whoever he may be'[8] for having cut short his summer vacation. Later, he found out that Kapur was not only a noted Hindu criminal lawyer and his father's close friend but had also rung up to ask whether the Kasuris could occupy his abandoned house on Fane Road, as he feared looters and thieves might enter the grand premises.

When Partition was declared, Kapur realized that his temporary absence would certainly be permanent, and the Kasuris began to pack the Kapur family's belongings. Boxes upon boxes were fitted in a truck and sent across the new border to an old friend. With tears in her eyes, Suneja recalls the contents of the boxes: 'Not only had they sent across my father's vast legal library and his complete and enviable collection of the works of Shakespeare, but the boxes even included all of our warm clothes.' Winter was arriving, and because the Kapurs had left in haste and had no means to buy new winter clothes, the Kasuris had made sure they would not freeze. It was a gesture of absolute kindness and consideration.

'Then, from the boxes, yet another treasure emerged.' Suneja opens an old, dusty file and offers it to me. A photocopy of old pages written in longhand, beginning from Sunday, 13 September 1914. This was Amolak Ram Kapur's personal journal that he had begun as a fourteen-year-old boy in 1914. It too had been packed carefully and sent across to its rightful owner.

'I think Partition broke him – physically, emotionally, even professionally. It was a few months before the East Punjab high court was established in Shimla and we could return to normalcy. Eventually, my father was appointed president of the Bar Association of the Punjab and Haryana High Court. But even in those first few years of beginning again, we tried not to hold any malice for all that had happened. Lahore had now long been left behind. But if we had lost our homes, then so had the people on the other side; and if we had been witness to communal violence, then so had they. The pain of Partition is shared amongst the people of India and Pakistan, and though we constantly remember the madness and bloodshed, we often forget or ignore the courageous acts of kindness and friendship that also occurred.

'My father was so touched upon receiving the boxes of our belongings that he wrote a letter of gratitude to his friend Mian Mahmud Ali Kasuri,' she says. In his memoir, Khurshid Mahmud Kasuri recalls his father reading the letter out loud to the family. '*Aap kay liyee dil se dua nikaltee hai*, I pray for you from the bottom of my heart,'⁹ read the contents of the note. It was truly a friendship that survived the divide and has sustained for generations.

✍

WHILE SOME PRE-PARTITION friendships survived despite there being a border between them, post-Partition friendships, too, were fostered because of the similar circumstances that refugees went through. In January 2016, a second cousin on my father's side got married in Delhi. A morning wedding at the gurudwara was followed by lunch in a hotel reception hall. My family was seated at one of the tables when a petite woman came and occupied the seat next to my grandmother, asking if she recognized her. My grandmother studied her for a moment before breaking into a broad smile. The two women embraced one another, giggling like children.

Apparently, they had lived close to one another in Kingsway Camp. They sat holding hands for a long time and spoke about the past, about their mothers, about camp life, about how if there was no food in one house, they would just walk over to the other's. The woman's daughters – now middle-aged women themselves – came over and touched my grandmother's feet, repeatedly telling her how stories of the camp had populated their childhoods too. I watched the two old women, dressed in their finest salwar-kameez, cardigans and shawls, grey hair secured tightly in buns at the back of their heads, and became acutely aware that I was witnessing something quite beautiful – a friendship that had blossomed during exceptional circumstances. And though my grandmother hardly ever brings up this topic on her own, should it ever be discussed, she never fails to underscore the significance of relationships forged by the crucial post-Independence years.

In the interviews with my father and his siblings in an earlier chapter, there is a mention of Swaran Lata or bhuaji, whom my grandparents met at the camp. She became my grandfather's adoptive sister, but so close was the bond that for the longest time I didn't even know that she wasn't a blood relative! Swaran Lata Kapoor was born in 1925 in Lahore and migrated to Delhi via Shimla just before Partition. Her family[10] lived in a haveli in Matia Mahal in the old city, and she volunteered her days at Kingsway Camp. Not only was she instrumental in my grandparents' relationship but she loved my father and aunts like her own children, and also gave me my name.

There is a photograph from the camp that my grandmother once found in her things. The image is small, smaller even than my palm. It is torn and discoloured but remains an integral part of history. No one knows who took the photograph or how it survived. But in it one can see my grandmother, Bhag, in the middle, flanked by her youngest sister, Dharam, on the right and Swaran Lata on the left. My grandmother is holding a baby, maybe one of her elder sister's children. They look very young, Dharam masi no older than a schoolchild, so it may have been taken in the early years at the camp, 1948 or '49. In the background are open barracks, with women shrouded in white gathered outside them. But what is extraordinary about this photograph is that they are smiling. There is a buoyancy, a lightness that is incongruous with my understanding of the difficulties of camp life, and if one were to replace the background, the three young women could really be standing anywhere.

When I ask my grandmother why they are smiling, her reply fascinates me. 'No one used to take photographs in those days, so maybe that's why we were happy. Or … maybe it's because Swaran Lata was with us, and we were together.' This is probably indicative of the depth of their friendship, one they maintained throughout their lives until bhuaji's death in 1994. While my grandparents were still living in the camp, my grandfather was offered a temporary position at the Salwan School[11] in Rajendra Nagar to teach math, English and Hindi. Swaran Lata helped him overcome his hesitation about teaching Hindi by first giving him lessons that he could further give to his students, and even offered to correct the exam papers for him. Then, when my grandfather bought the Khan Market bookshop, she was the first person to offer funds to buy materials and stock.

My grandmother doesn't remember how exactly they met or what happened to her family that led them to prematurely migrate from Lahore, but she asserts that if it wasn't for bhuaji, her children would not have grown up the way they did. She was a teacher at a school in Chandni Chowk, and after my grandparents moved out of the camp and into their own flat in Netaji Nagar, she would take an autorickshaw every single day to their home to look after the children. Both parents were working, so she would help with homework, take the children on holidays, and spend weekends with the family. All major financial decisions were taken collaboratively by her and my grandparents.

'She sacrificed a lot for me,' my grandmother remembers with deep sadness, 'ever since the camp days. She was my best friend, my sister, my advisor, my confidante. *Ek kisam se, bache toh maine paida kiye, lekin paley usne.* I may have birthed my children, but Swaran raised them.'

LASTLY, AND PERHAPS most evocatively, there are the accounts about the memories of long-lost friendships that are conjured and cultivated by those who have not witnessed them. Whether it is finding a photograph of a grandparent with a friend in a city across the border at a time when there was no border, or discovering a tattered letter written shortly after Partition, promising to remain in touch – these are tangible evidence of friendships lost and broken which allow second and third generations to believe in a syncretic, undivided land. But there are also many intangibles, including the envisioning of friendships that were never spoken about. For Jalandhar-born Arjunvir Singh, it is the latter.

'I must have only been a child when I noticed that my grandfather, Devinder Singh, never read the Hindi newspaper,' he tells me. Arjun is a student at the National Institute of Design, Ahmedabad. He is one half of The Khes Project, striving to document stories around the craft tradition of *khes*, an ornate piece of textile traditionally woven with cotton in Punjab.

'When I asked him about it, he very matter-of-factly told me that he couldn't read Hindi. And I found that so hard to believe because at home we spoke Hindi. And my grandparents lived in Solan, where everyone around them spoke Hindi, so how could it be that he couldn't read it? I was very young, and only when I told him, "Dadu, I will teach you how to write in Hindi" did he tell me that his entire education had been in Urdu; that the only languages he knew how to read and write were Urdu, Punjabi and English. *That* is when Partition came up. He told me about how his Sikh family had migrated from Hafizabad in present-day Pakistan to Amritsar in India when he was seventeen years old. They came in a train and the journey was relatively safe, but so much was lost. One such thing was the language, Urdu.'

I ask him whether they actually went through with the lessons. They could have been mutually beneficial – a Hindi lesson in exchange for an Urdu one! Arjun laughs, but there is deep regret in his voice. He tells me that he wishes he had done that, for there are so many things he never asked about that time. This regret for the unknown is in part what drove Arjun to begin The Khes Project, for though his conversations revolve around textiles and village weavers who produce them, at times they extend into the landscape of undivided Punjab.

'Why is there regret?' I ask.

'Aanchal, when you ask me this question, the only thing that comes to mind is a line that Anne Frank once wrote in her journal – "Regret is stronger than gratitude." We do not value the present. I think I always start appreciating moments when they are gone, when it is too late.'

'I think that's quite common among people...'

'When I realized that I should have asked more, I'd already lost the chance.'

'If you could ask your grandfather one thing, what would it be?'

Arjun immediately brightens up. 'I would definitely want to ask him about his friends.'

'How come?'

'Well, the first thing that comes to my mind when I think of Partition is lost friendships. What if tomorrow there is another Partition, what if my friends are separated from me? In fact, when debates for the Citizenship Amendment Act (CAA)[12] were ongoing,

I would think about Partition repeatedly. It felt so current. You see, I never had any Muslim friends growing up, not a single one. Until I went to college and made very deep friendships that I can't imagine losing. Amidst the CAA protests, I remember discussing this with my friends, because I couldn't help but wonder if people who'd lived through Partition had *also* thought of these things. Did they think they'd be separated from their friends? Did they think they would have to migrate to another country, a new country, and leave all their loved ones behind? What if tomorrow, because of some law created on the basis of religion, or some line drawn due to politics, *I* am not allowed to speak with *my* Muslim friends?'

He takes a breath, deep and sharp.

I cannot take my gaze off him and watch as he struggles with the idea. This clearly affects him viscerally, and I am struck by the ways in which Partition, though an event of the past, remains an event of the present. Its memory transcends generations, affecting people in unique ways, overt or latent, demonstrating how the wounds of Partition remain fresh and raw no matter how many decades old they may be.

'This is why I would have asked my grandfather if he had any Muslim friends that he had to leave behind in Hafizabad,' Arjun continues. 'I would have asked whether he missed them, whether they tried to keep in touch. I would have wanted to know what kind of effect Partition had on friendships. Once when I was speaking with my grandaunt, Satinder Kaur, she told me about her friend Razia. They were maybe thirteen years old in 1947. Razia lived nearby, five or seven houses away, and they studied in the same Khalsa school of Hafizabad. She didn't remember anything else except her name and the fact that there was no hatred between them. The entire time we spoke about Razia, my grandaunt had a big smile on her face.'

I too have a smile on mine.

'Partition,' he says slowly, 'it ruptured relationships. The friendships my grandfather and grandaunt could have retained to this day became memories and stories of the past. It's always bothered me – why people fight over religion, how they can kill one another over religion. I know it may be naïve to think about, because I have no answer and that makes me feel helpless ... but after reading and listening to people talk about the days of Partition, it is clear what the conclusion of such fights is. It is deep, unforgettable loss. The greatest thing I have learnt from Partition is to not tolerate religious intolerance, because I know what it has done to my family and so many others. It devastated an entire way of life, a community, a syncretic culture.'

8
Grief

B EFORE I WAS A writer, I was a printmaker. For the eight combined years of my bachelor's and master's in fine arts in Canada, Gutenberg was a household name in my vocabulary, as were materials like copper, limestone, wood, linoleum, and silk screens. I painstakingly made Gampi *washi*, bound and sewed books, hand-set lead type, painted with acid on copper and zinc plates, engraved blocks of wood, and practised extraordinary techniques of aquatint, mezzotint, chine-collé, and photogravure.

It was in the second year of art school, during a lecture on the 'History of Printing and Printmaking', that I first encountered Zarina Hashmi and her suite of monochrome woodblock prints. From amidst the Dürers and Hokusais, Goyas and Toulouse-Lautrecs, the name Zarina stood out, sonorous. At first, I didn't know whether she was Indian, Pakistani or Bangladeshi, but it hardly mattered, for in a class where I may have been the only student of South Asian descent, she sounded *mine*. Like me, she too had held engraving tools and wooden blocks, she too had descended the depths of ink and paper, she too was in a place far away from *home*, reproducing its longing in visual form. Projected before us, on a screen the size of the wall, was her evocative woodcut *Dividing Line* (2001), and it left me mesmerized.

Within the curriculum, it was quietly nestled in the section on Relief Printing – a woodcut on handmade Indian paper, depicting the border drawn during Partition. The lecture dissected the technique of engraving and the artistic choices of the incisions, the texture of wood grain, even the density of black ink. But it didn't elaborate on the significance of the image itself, nor the psychological imprint this 'dividing line' had left on those – like Zarina – who had witnessed its creation in 1947. I remember immediately feeling a deep sense of ownership over the historical context of the image and, for the duration that it was projected on screen, kept trying to figure out which part of the Radcliffe Line it depicted – east or west, Kashmir or Punjab, Sindh or Bangladesh. *Dividing Line* may have been my first introduction to the visual manifestation of Partition, but it would be several years before my own research on the subject began. And yet I can't forget the sorrow it instilled in my heart, for I left the classroom a changed person.

Today, two decades have passed since this line was first engraved in wood, over a decade since I first encountered it, and about a month since Zarina left this world. As I revisit *Dividing Line*, it is not as a young art student but as a historian of Partition, in order to understand why it imbued me with grief.

Zarina, who preferred to be addressed only by her first name, was born in Aligarh in 1937 and was ten years old when Partition happened. In the decade that followed, for safety her father sent the family to Karachi in the newly formed Pakistan. The experience of fleeing to a refugee camp and seeing bodies left in the road stayed with her.[1] It was this trauma that remained central to her work, manifesting through themes of exile and homelessness in several pieces. She travelled and lived across the world, settling eventually in New York after the death of her parents and husband. In her seminal series *Home Is a Foreign Place*, thirty-six woodcuts represent particular memories of home, inscribed with phrases in Urdu, the mother tongue in decline. In an interview with The Metropolitan Museum of Art, Zarina once said:

> I have had people come to my show and start to cry. I always ask them why, and usually they say 'that is our story also.'

A lot of them were people who were exiles from their own country: Holocaust survivors, or people who had the desire to return home.[2]

From her entire oeuvre, it is *Dividing Line* which has become crucial to my understanding of the grief of Partition. A thick black line cuts across a cream-coloured page in a jagged, undulating formation. Its abstract appearance is indicative of a boundary, yet there is nothing to elaborate which side is which, no religious or national signifiers. Both sides appear the same, equally fragmented, equally minimalist, equally devoid of vibrancy, yet equally propelling themselves inwards towards the force of the border – the deep and darkened wrinkle on the page. In the negative space surrounding the line, some incisions made are shallower than the others, allowing bits of black to settle onto them as the roller has inked the woodblock, transferring onto the final print like dots or cuts: pixelated mesh-like textures that could be homes or villages, barren land or dense populations. The line recurs in yet another woodcut from the same year, titled *Atlas of My World IV,* where 'a snaky black demarcation runs beyond the borders of the map of South Asia, rupturing it',[3] spilling out of the frame of the print. India and Pakistan are labelled in Urdu, the mother tongue.

In retrospectively trying to understand why *Dividing Line* affected me so, I consider the haunting quality of the image, the fact that it portrays Partition in its most minimalist, most un-human manifestation. There is nothing on the page – no people, no voices, no crowds or caravans, none of the commonplace bloodshed or violence. There are only abrasions. This border is made of sharp abrasions, the terrain around it equally searing. The line is pierced into the land, it is carved into the wood, *it is gouged.* Muscle memory reminds me of what it felt like to lay one's hand on a block of birch wood and carve through it. My fingers remember the strength with which the chisel is grasped and how it moves to make every incision into a resisting wood block. *Did the Boundary Commission feel resistance from the land?*

There is something methodical and intentional about carving through a plate of metal or wood as a printmaker. There is a purpose to every gouge, for once a line is laid, it cannot be un-laid, undone. But Zarina's careful and intentional carving of the line on wood is almost contradictory in nature to the hasty act of actually drawing the Radcliffe Line in 1947. What is impossible to forget is that it took only five weeks to partition a subcontinent, and the rapidity of that historic act lends a ghostly vibration to the print. Despite there being a softness, an antiquated nostalgia, despite the paper being the dusty colour of Indian sand, this is an image of an incision, of division, of rupture. I feel the sharpened edges of the burins and gravers used to carve the wood block, of the barbed wire fences laid along either side of no man's land. *Dividing Line* is nothing if not a testament to shared subcontinental pain, made to grieve a land partitioned, a home left on the other side.

THE STORIES IN this chapter are hinged on second-hand grief, collected from the children and grandchild of those who witnessed the days of Partition. In my recording and writing, these testimonies have gained yet another degree of separation; however, little of their poignancy has diminished. In several instances, there is an effort to nurture grief, to descend into it; not to mitigate or uncomplicate it, but to accept it as is, even adopt it as a legitimate generational record of emotion.

Three different types of grief are expressed in the following conversations – first, for the homeland left behind; second, for family that succumbed to the violence of Partition; and third, over the possibility of the unknown, the knowledge that the murky corridors of personal history may always hold more, and that history may one day repeat itself.

'MY PARENTS DIED when I was really young,' the poet Fatimah Asghar, who was born in the US in the late '80s, tells me, 'and because my father's family doesn't live in America, a lot of my knowledge about Partition comes from my mother's side. She and her siblings were from Kashmir, and while migrating to Gujranwala in Pakistan during Partition, they witnessed moments of intense violence. They came either on trains or buses, it's convoluted. But when the violence began, my grandfather decided that the family had to leave immediately. The story I've heard from my uncle, who was probably the youngest at the time, is that his mother told him to pack, and he remembered thinking about the things he really wanted to carry, and then just filling a suitcase with toys, his most prized possessions.' She smiles sadly.

'Did they manage to migrate across to Pakistan safely?' I ask.

'They narrowly escaped being killed, because the people who were attacking the trains or buses were my grandfather's students. They saw him in the caravan of people and helped him and his family. When my uncle told me this story, it was, well, it came out in a rush, tumbling out of his mouth, and I was kind of surprised to hear it. I didn't even know about Partition, I didn't know that such a thing had happened, and that my family could have died in it. He was simply narrating this memory he had of a time that he had once lived through, of being young, and the entire family so close to ... being slaughtered.'

Her voice is calm, but she pauses to take a breath before continuing.

'One of his strongest memories – perhaps his clearest, earliest memory – is when my grandfather's former student saved them by putting the family on a different bus or train. Once they were safely on board, they drove past an empty field or lot full of Muslim corpses. He remembers seeing all these dead bodies from the bus. Not only surviving the very harrowing moment, but also seeing the moment of death for all of these people trying to get to safety...'

She takes another breath.

'He tells me that everybody was so afraid after what they saw happening, knowing that it could have been them. Then disembarking in this field and running through the trees, holding my mother's hand, and running because he was afraid but not really knowing where he was going. Just being deposited to a place that was supposed to be safe and then having to walk in fear to the place you wanted to reach, but not knowing where that place was.'

There is a rhythm to her narration, a poetic beat, an enunciation that makes a historic violence feel palpable. Simply listening makes my heart beat faster, makes the skin on my face tighten.

'Once they arrived in Gujranwala, my grandfather actually returned to Kashmir a few times to try to get the extended relations out and, each time, the family worried because they didn't know if he would come back. There was a real fear, because not only did Kashmir go through Partition, but the first Kashmir war began almost immediately after. And since '47 Kashmir has been a constant battleground for both Pakistan and India. But this is the story of my family leaving Kashmir, and it left an indelible mark on my mother's family. They all remember it, have vivid memories of it, particularly because they were never able to return.'

Fatimah now talks with her hands, moving them in a gesture alluding to migration. 'Never during their departure from Kashmir did it dawn on anyone that they were going away forever. No one thought it was definite. There was a moment of violence, but they were certain it would pass and they would return. So, within everyone, there exists this feeling of severance from Kashmir – *that is where we grew up*. Eventually, they moved to Lahore.'

A short passage of silence cuts through the conversation until Fatimah clears her throat.

'I'm an orphan, I was raised by so many people I consider family who are not related by blood. An uncle who raised me was also born before Partition, somewhere on the Indian side of the border, and told me just a few weeks ago that in the first ten years of his life after Partition, he lived in nine different homes. He said that not having an ancestral home was akin to being a burden. You're always looking for where *home* could be, and what could be *home*. I think it really resonated with me because, being orphans, my sisters and I never had an ancestral home either, the home of our parents – we were always guests everywhere, with so many people taking care of us.' Her tone now becomes sombre. 'Not actually having a place to return *back to* is a really deep suffering, to feel unrooted and ungrounded in that way. I think this was one of the reasons why Partition began to capture my attention, because it felt resonant and familiar.'

'Fatimah, when were these stories first told to you?'

'One of my mother's brothers began properly telling me about Partition when I was eighteen or nineteen years old. But I think I'd always known fragments of our history because, in America, race is so much about how you're treated and how you grow up learning your place in the world, and people would often ask us where we were from. We'd ask my uncle and he would say we were from Pakistan *and* we were from Kashmir. But when speaking to people outside, we would always just say Pakistani, because at the time no one knew where Kashmir even was...'

'We are compelled to distil our own identity,' I observe sadly.

'Yes, exactly, and it came to a point where though I knew my family was from both these places, I knew nothing beyond that. So, when my uncle told me the story of their migration, everything suddenly fell into place. There was a moment when I said, "Oh, so you were displaced." And this is also what becomes important about our story – to know what we were *before* we were displaced. When he spoke about migrating to America in the '60s, he recalled the bombs that fell during the war between Pakistan and India, and being able to tell how close they were just by the sounds, and knowing that he had to leave, once again. And he came to America voluntarily, for school. But that's not the whole story – part of it is war, instability. That is another kind of displacement, isn't it? Though it's a different kind than being made a refugee, it's different than the refugee*ing* of Partition.'

The refugeeing of Partition, I make a note.

'He came to America and my mother went to the UK before joining him here. She lived in America only for a few years before she had me and my sisters, and then she died. She was probably here for less than a decade, and that too at the end of her life.'

'And the fact that she migrated from India to Pakistan means that Partition is separated from you by only a single generation,' I remark.

Fatimah nods, her gaze now meeting mine. 'Despite the decades, it's still so close. For some people it's their grandparents' generation, and they have distance from it, so they don't think it affects their present as much. But, for me, my mother literally went from being Kashmiri and a colonial British subject to being Pakistani to being someone who lives in the UK, someone with British papers, and then to being American – all in the span of a single lifetime. I didn't grow up with stories of either of my parents. I don't know much about my mother's life beyond what nationality or location she was in, at any given time. So many cities and countries and identities, precipitated by a single dividing line. And so when my uncle told me the story of their migration during Partition, I really needed to understand all the details: how did they leave, why did they leave, what did they leave behind, what was the violence surrounding it all?'

There is an extraordinary attentiveness to the untangling of family history as she goes on to tell me that her uncle's stories led her to read, and eventually to write, about Partition.

'Soon I began to notice all the things that could have been a direct result of displacement. The odd fighting, or how the family never threw anything out. There were certain things so linked to a very specific kind of unspoken trauma. And also, because I would live with different family members, I would see similar behaviours manifested within all the different people who had lived through this Partition.'

'You mentioned earlier how the feeling of a violent separation, of being uprooted, felt resonant…'

'Of not having an ancestral home, not having a place to go back to because of being orphaned, and the kind of displacement that comes from that – in a very different way from Partition – but yes, Partition became this obsession, not because of the history associated to it, but because it was mirroring things that I felt. And I'm not equating how I feel to how people felt in 1947 – those feelings and lived realities are not the same, by any means. All I'm saying is that there were things that my family desired about the deep dream and need and want to have *home* that I felt in my heart as well.'

Her voice is somehow simultaneously assertive, yet tender yet harrowing, folded into a tone of grief.

'When you have been in a place for a long time – I don't know how far back my family history in Kashmir goes – but the feeling of when you are in a place that is your home, and then that place is suddenly taken from you, and there is no possibility of your returning to it ... I think that was the hardest thing to come to terms with. Those borders of Partition, when they came up, meant that people lost their entire community. Some died and some fled, but it was a feeling of complete dissolution of community, of culture, of art. Home being a memory is so...' She exhales so sonorously that I feel the hair on my forearm rise up. '...it's so real and alive in my family. The journey of leaving Kashmir and never being able to return has shaped so much in their lives, and I think it's a deep source of pain.'

Each night put Kashmir in your dreams, Agha Shahid Ali wrote.[4]

It is not only nostalgia or grief over the loss of an erstwhile home but also the politics of the subcontinent that emerged after Partition that concerns Fatimah. 'A lot of countries, India and Pakistan included, use religious terminology to justify power. *Justify it.* Religion was used as a way to speak about separation, give legitimacy to the need for Partition. But the real reason was not religion, it was power. These countries were built off the need and hunger for power, and then they became antagonistic.'

'In a way that it becomes hard to imagine them once being one,' I add.

'They are so hateful to one another, they've become almost like antonyms,' she scoffs.

In silence, I place my pen down on the table. Zarina's *Dividing Line* feels threaded into our conversation. *Are Fatimah and I like antonyms*, I wonder. A Muslim family migrates westward and a

Hindu family eastward, both in haste, both cradling loss and longing for what has been left behind, what may never be seen again. *Are they antonyms?*

I first read Fatimah's debut collection of poetry, *If They Come for Us*, with tears in my eyes, surprised at just how affected I was, how deeply and precisely it cut into me. I felt it to be a memoir both of the past and the future, at whose heart was the moment of the subcontinent's division, the reason that she and I would never be antonyms. Her words felt relatable, they embraced me, for notwithstanding the present-day subcontinental politics, they constructed a history that belonged to us both, that neither could be severed from. Two sides of a border, two halves of a whole.

Fatimah writes in one of her poems titled 'Partition':

1993: summer, in New York City.
I am four, sitting in a patch of grass
by Pathmark.
an aunt teaches me how to tell
an edible flower
from a poisonous one.
just in case, I hear her say, *just in case*.[5]

Twenty years later, 2013, it is winter in New Delhi and I am twenty-three, sitting in my grandmother's room when she reveals a small folding knife given to her in Dera Ismail Khan, to keep on her person at all times during the months of Partition. *Just in case.*

'These countries and lands are so complicated,' Fatimah continues, 'they have such long, entwined, complex histories that I don't know the whole scale of. Having grown up in America, I will always be a bit removed, have an outsider's opinion, for I don't know it as intimately as people who live in Pakistan and India do. But, on a governmental or global level, Pakistan has become synonymous with being Muslim, and repressing religious and ethnic minorities, and now with the BJP government, India has become synonymous with Hindutva ideology, and is supressing Muslim and Dalit, Bahujan and

Adivasi people. In both these countries, this suppression is leading to systemic oppression and murder.'

She exhales loudly, closing her eyes for several seconds.

'And when you think back to Partition,' I ask in a quiet voice, 'what does it make you feel?'

She ponders over this. 'Incredible sadness. Yeah, it feels like a constantly bleeding … thing. And there are so many different veins of it – what it took to survive, the number of people who didn't survive, the guilt that may have accompanied survival. The people who did horrible, unspeakable things during that time as well; the way that sits on their souls and their lineages. I think there is an unimaginable grief caused by Partition, and it is a wound that still remains.

'In the West, Partition is not taught to us in schools. When people discuss the history of decolonization in the subcontinent, they speak of Gandhi and how his non-violent movement resulted in Independence. That's what people here know, for the most part, and there is an erasure of what actually led to Independence. When I first found out what Partition was, I just couldn't believe it. How could that be the *actual* history of the creation of two independent nations when we were taught that they were created non-violently? And this is why my fixation with Partition is very important – because I'm trying to make that which has been rendered invisible visible again.'

'You've never been to Kashmir.' I want to ask this as a question, but it ends up sounding more like a statement.

Fatimah smiles sadly. 'No, and I don't actually think I'll be able to go in my lifetime. The only papers I have are the ones that show my Pakistani lineage, and so it becomes difficult not only to travel to India but near impossible to visit Kashmir on the Indian-administered side. And even if it becomes possible to go some day, I don't have family there that I know of, so it would be as a stranger. It would be going with no family roots … But even that, even just to walk on the land, would be such a powerful thing for me.'

'BAAJI – THAT'S what I called my maternal grandmother,' Bhavneet Kaur recalls when we speak. A social anthropologist by training, she currently teaches at O.P. Jindal University in Sonipat, Haryana. 'I was in college and only just beginning to become conscious of the experiences of Partition when she passed away. But throughout my childhood, there was never time dedicated to the stories of what happened to her in 1947, and any discussions were most likely triggered by an incident. Everything I will tell you today is an oral memory that has been passed down to me from my mother, so it might have flaws or gaps and may not be chronological.'

I understand this sentiment and gesture for Bhavneet to begin.

'It was either in August 1947 or a few months before when the violence in Rawalpindi escalated. My maternal grandparents – baaji and dharji – had a son, who was under two years old. One day, my baaji's brother came to the house and took the boy to meet his grandparents, who lived in another part of the city, and around that time was when the violence escalated. As it spread across Rawalpindi, with great difficulty, dharji went to fetch their son and found the entire house of his in-laws completely charred. A police officer patrolling the area asked him to leave, as there were still mobs loitering around. But dharji pleaded with him to know what had happened to the house, to his wife's family, to his son. The officer reported that mobs had repeatedly banged on the front door...'

Bhavneet suddenly pauses and looks at me. 'Now, all of this information is oral, so I don't know who the mobs were. But from what my mother has told me, there were five people in that house – my baaji's parents, her brother and sister-in-law, and baaji's son. Using kerosene, they self-immolated, burnt themselves alive, out of fear of being looted or murdered or raped. They killed themselves before the mob could break in.'

She concludes by taking deep, purposeful breaths, like a swimmer who has just finished a lap and come up for air.

'What happened next?' I ask in a soft voice.

'Dharji broke down, right there, in front of the police officer and refused to go back. It must have been gut-wrenching for him to see the burnt house and not be able to do anything even when his two-year-old son's remains were inside. When he returned to my grandmother and told her what had happened, she fainted as it was too much to bear. As they decided on their next steps and how to leave – because it became clear they couldn't remain in Pindi for much longer – a Muslim neighbour offered for them to stay with him as it would be safer.'

'A Muslim neighbour?' I confirm.

'Yes, he was a Muslim army officer, was resourceful, and knew that his home won't be searched by the mobs, which was probably why he offered shelter to my grandparents. They would be safe there. The couple stayed with him for nearly twenty-five days before leaving for India. Anytime *kaale chane*, black chickpeas, were made at home, my baaji would tell this story. See, when they were in hiding for those twenty-five days, all the provision stores were closed and there was probably a curfew, and not much food in the house. So they were given dried *kaale chane* several times a day to eat. It is rich in iron, which helped them survive.

'Then when the situation calmed down a little, they took a train from Rawalpindi to Delhi. Once in India, they realized that the 509 army base workshop – where my grandfather was employed in Rawalpindi – had a branch in Agra. There, they lived in a refugee camp near the railway station for many months, and only once my grandfather's post was transferred from Pindi to the Agra office was he allotted accommodation. The salary was meagre, maybe Rs 150 at the start, but the couple made do. Baaji lived in shock for a while, unable to overcome all the losses – of her son, of her entire family, of her home. The only kin who remained alive was her other elder brother, who was in the army and away from Rawalpindi at the time.

'My grandparents had six children, and later constructed a beautiful, simple home in Shahganj, Agra. I remember this home so well – four or five rooms and a big courtyard with a huge guava tree. The fruit was never the ordinary white but pink from the inside. I just have such beautiful memories of that home.' Bhavneet smiles. 'When my grandfather died, the house was sold and baaji came to live with us, which was how I managed to listen to some of her stories more closely.'

'Do you think your baaji and dharji spoke to one another about Partition?'

'Yes, I think they would have. For the few years that followed Partition, it was just the two of them. Moving from Pakistan to India, settling into a camp, then a small flat and then into a bigger house. Incrementally putting their lives back together little by little. There was so much shared loss, that I hope some form of catharsis happened between them.'

Bhavneet sighs and looks at me.

'I am thirty-four years old, and only now do I think I can imagine part of their loss, part of their grief. I can't fully understand it, of course. But when I was younger and baaji was living with us, I don't think I was aware of how violent a history she had endured and embodied. She was always just baaji, just a grandmother, you know? I think about this now, how she would have processed the pain. My mother tells me that when she was younger, my grandmother would sometimes talk about the eldest son who died, she would say, "*Aaj tumhara sabse bada bhai bhi hota*," and things like that, but I've never heard this. When I found out, I asked her, and she said she didn't want to speak about it. It seemed like a grief she didn't want to address or confront ... or share.'

'But were there any behaviours or habits that you attributed to her having survived Partition?' I ask.

'What made her pain singular to me was a conversation I had with her and my mother while in college, and it left me disturbed. She thought that during Partition, only Muslims killed Sikhs, that it was one-sided violence and there was no other reality to it. This really stunned me, because I was aware this was not the truth, and it made me angry. I confronted both my mother and grandmother but it seemed that this was their world view, very compactly and neatly bifurcating the victims and the perpetrators of Partition. For them it was unbelievable that Sikhs could indulge in this kind of violence.

At home, there was a one-dimensional understanding of the violence of Partition.'

'Do you think her pain made her believe only her version of the truth?' I ask.

'Yes,' Bhavneet agrees. 'Yes, baaji's experiences of loss and the trauma must have legitimized this singular understanding of truth. The things is, they probably also didn't know what was happening outside their neighbourhood; they probably didn't interact with many Muslim families either. Their own grief itself must have been all-consuming. And then there is a larger agenda to portray Muslims as the villains of the time – forcing Sikh and Hindu families out of West Punjab – so it helps to not think of them as victims as well. This was one of the initial memories of understanding Partition and, of course, countering it. I was very aware that this was not the truth, and though my family didn't have any explicit hatred for Muslims, there did exist this lopsided interpretation of reality. Eventually, I ended up writing my master's thesis on the mediated Muslim identity, and in my acknowledgments, I wrote about how the experiences and perceptions of my own family became a trigger for me to understand how Muslim-ness was constructed in postcolonial and post-Partition India. I would say that the discussions on Partition within our home really determined my own sociological interests.'

Her tone becomes gentler now. 'Now I can understand where this lopsided interpretation comes from. Losing her entire family, seeing only Sikh or Hindu victims around her – in Rawalpindi, in the camps in India, could have made her feel the way she did. She wasn't capable of hate, and nor was she vitriolic; maybe because though her loss was drawn on the lines of communalism and nationalism, her refuge and survival in a Muslim household in Rawalpindi during the riots was a story that defied the overwhelming narrative of communal hatred.'

Things passed down as inflexible truths emerge from a specific context, and sometimes that context is insurmountable grief. A particular version of what happened, of what was taken, of what no longer remained, of what could never again be touched, be cradled, be sung to, be kissed and hugged and loved. She would have dreamt a future for their firstborn, would have imagined him as a teenager, as an adult. I often think of Partition as a composite of many losses, and this was Bhavneet's baaji's.

'Do you think Partition has impacted your aunts and uncles in any way?' I ask her now.

'How do I answer that?' She smiles.

'You don't have to.'

'No, it's just an interesting question. They were all born in India. But, unfortunately, we don't have many conversations around Partition. Even when we are together and remember baaji, there's no conversation about the past, about this lost brother, about what my grandparents must have lived through as a couple – a very young couple who had to completely re-establish themselves in a new country, a new city with no relatives or support system, at a time when the entire subcontinent had been fractured in half. We just don't talk about these things. I once approached my uncle to ask him about Rawalpindi, but he just brushed the topic away by saying things like, "*Ab un baton main kya rakha hai...*"' She pauses to think about this. 'Maybe in their own isolated moments, they remember that this happened, but it never reaches the level of a discussion within the family. Or maybe I haven't tried enough.'

'I'm still thinking about her grief...' My words take shape very slowly. 'It must have been overwhelming to confront, let alone talk about it. I can't stop thinking about this – how do you, years after your child has passed, introduce his memory to your other children?'

Bhavneet is quiet and her eyes downcast, but she is nodding.

'They all know about it, they are all familiar with it. I spoke with my mother on the phone some days ago, in preparation for this conversation, and told her that I was going to speak about baaji, that I'd always wanted to speak about her experience. And it was a very simple conversation, where we were both remembering the past, which we don't do very often, and I ended up feeling such a deep emotional connection. I felt like if I were there with her, I would have seen tears in her eyes, because I too had tears in mine. But, ultimately, we both fell silent and I didn't know what to say to her, how to go further back into the past, so we just ended up saying our goodbyes, "*Chalo aap dhyaan rakhna apna*," and hung up.'

She exhales deeply.

'In the field of sociology, there are two kinds of time – one is chronological, the time of ordinary life experiences; and the second is durational, a duration of experiencing or remembering the atrocity that can neither be transcended nor generalized.[6] In that moment, the past freezes and you cannot free yourself of these memories. I felt this with my mother during that phone call, when we broke the normalcy of not speaking about baaji's grief. In those moments when she spoke about the chickpeas as a means of their survival when they were in hiding in Rawalpindi and the refugee camp in Agra, I sensed the pain in my mother's voice and a shared lingering silence that could not transcend what happened seventy-three years ago. My mother tells me that even when baaji remembered her son, she never admitted any pain or grief over it. They struggled a lot financially, with my grandfather being the only earning member and them having six children; money was always scarce. It was only when my mother, the second youngest child, was five or six years old that they were able to build this bigger house with the guava tree. But in that initial decade or so after their migration, the financial burden may have simply swallowed any manifestation of grief.'

'Hmm,' I say, capping and uncapping my pen several times, making sharp clicking sounds.

'What are you thinking?' she asks.

'...about how verbal language barely does justice to emotional experiences,' I say in a faraway tone. 'I wonder if the conversation with your mother would have been different in person. Touch is integral, the physical presence is comfort. Even if no words were exchanged, I can imagine you'd have wanted to hold her hand, or...'

Bhavneet smiles. 'She would have seen me cry and I would have seen her cry, which she doesn't do very often. This was one of those silences where she was remembering baaji, and though I felt like the silence held so much, I could not fully embrace it, could not interrogate it. I didn't have the words, nor did my mother and, for that matter, perhaps nor did my grandmother. She never spoke about what happened, maybe because there were no words to quantify her grief.'

'There is no single dialect of grief, so maybe her language was not words,' I offer quietly.

As the evening light fades into dusk, Bhavneet rests her face on her palms.

I continue, 'The events of 1947 remain some of the most historic, most violent in the world, but the way in which they are normalized or gain a national narrative – celebrated as freedom rather than loss, as Independence rather than Partition – doesn't confront the personal trauma that families lived through. For so long, survivors didn't talk about it; maybe they didn't *know* how to talk about it.'

Sitting up straighter now, Bhavneet adds, 'Our grandparents may not have had the language to talk about what they witnessed at Partition, but subsequent generations hardly asked about the past either. Now too much is lost, my grandmother is gone. I can't get any more information. I can't ask her, "What did you feel the first night you were sleeping in a refugee camp?" I can't ask her these questions, I can't have tangible access to her emotions and, in this way, parts of my past will always remain inaccessible. But I believe that intergenerational grief is powerful enough that it allows you to empathize with your ancestors' predicament even though you have not lived through it. Merely learning of my grandmother fainting after she heard about the death of her son is a second-hand memory that causes me anguish. This memory wasn't even told to me by her, but simply transmitted down the generations. Through it, I have become imprinted with her grief.'

SEVERAL YEARS AGO, while I was archiving the stories of love lost and found at the time of Partition, Sadia Malik wrote me these lines – 'One huge turn in my grandmother's life changed the entire course – towards a more challenging one.' For some reason, I never pursued the project further,* and we lost touch. But once this book begins to take shape, I revisit the conversation, and we exchange a series of emails where she recounts the story of her paternal grandmother, her dadi, Enayat Begum.

Despite its brevity, the correspondence leaves an incision in my heart, for it chronicles an infinite grief for a future that could have been. Sadia was born in 1977 and is a lecturer of international relations at the Lahore School of Economics, Pakistan. Her family's history of Partition begins when the lanky teenager, Enayat, migrates across the newly drawn border between India and Pakistan. Sadia knows no specifics about the dates or route her grandmother took but has heard that the arduous journey seemed even longer due to the relentless monsoon rain unleashed in the backdrop of a communal conflict.

> The young Enayat was travelling from tehsil Bhatinda, in a group comprising the families of three brothers, which included her in-laws, parents, husband and cousins. The journey was made easier by the presence of their extended *khandan* and perhaps bearable with her husband as a co-traveller. I could never ask my dadi what her dreams were in the new country she was moving towards. [But] safe to assume, she was going to build a blissful life ... with the bond cemented further by the shared transition the young couple were enduring.
>
> The three families with hundreds of others boarded a train from Jullundur to Lahore. I wonder which train it was and exactly when, but she could never remember dates. I read somewhere that on 4th November 1947 'four single trains left Jullundur City for Lahore with 3,900, 4,000, 3,800 and 4,200, Muslim refugees, total 15,900.'7 Maybe she was in those but she had never mentioned any specific details, so I am not certain. The train she had been travelling in came under attack – a regular Partition occurrence as it was not the first attack on

---

a train to or from Lahore, nor was it the last – but for her, the life she had known and imagined vanished forever.

All my life whenever anything would cause my dadi any level of consternation, she would hark back to those terrorizing minutes when her family was wiped out in front of her eyes. Tears would trickle down her lined face as she would say, *'Minnu nai pulda, meray maa pyo shaheed hoy si,* I cannot forget how my parents were slain.' She arrived into Pakistan an orphan, her dream buried under those bodies full of blood, that also included her husband's. As she would find out, the life she was to begin would not compensate for the trauma she had endured [nor] the blissful union she had become accustomed to.

At first, I am struck by the acuteness of Sadia's words, the distillation of her grandmother's particular colloquial of pain. As I read on, I discover that upon reaching Lahore, Enayat Begum and her surviving family members made their way to village Raipur near Okara district to join close relatives. The journey was steered by her widower cousin Iqbal, a policeman, posted to Pakistan from his village Awan in the Zira tehsil of Firozpur district. The economic conditions and devastated fabric of the family helped present Iqbal as an eligible choice to the newly widowed Enayat.

The fact that my grandparents experienced the collective trauma of massacre and loss began to distress their relationship. This post-conflict marriage hence proved difficult and their outer worlds, like their inner worlds, would remain apart. As a distant couple with feuding egos, their three children came with the gap of six years each, witnesses to their mother's mounting trauma and father's unceasing temper.

In *A Grief Observed*, C.S. Lewis writes that 'the death of a beloved is an amputation'. In Sadia's story, it becomes clear how grief after another's death can sometimes persist for longer than their life itself. Because Enayat Begum's grief was connected to both familial and marital love – in the past she had shared with her parents, in the future she would have celebrated with her young husband – it is not impossible to imagine a mourning period that became boundless. That could have extended for days, weeks, months, years and even decades, until perhaps all she may have been grieving for was the memory of what was lost on a train amidst a brutal vivisection. Maybe it was the infiniteness that allowed the emotion to extend beyond Enayat's generation and eventually be bequeathed to Sadia. Maybe this was the encompassing power of grief. I write to ask whether her grandmother ever openly spoke about what happened during Partition, and she responds:

> My dada passed away while I was still a schoolgoing teenager in Karachi, and thereafter my dadi came to live with us. As her tears would flow, she would mention the bloodbath and how her mother's fingers were chopped off, but could never utter *his* name, not even after she had become a grandmother.

It is only during the course of our email exchange that Sadia makes the shocking discovery that the person who had always been projected as her grandmother's fiancé during the tumultuous journey to Pakistan had, in fact, been her husband. When she tells me this, I think about the concept of *iddat,* the mourning period after the husband's death, and wonder how soon she was married again, whether she grieved at all. Briefly, I reflect on the difference between the death of a fiancé and the death of a husband – is death not death, after all – but quickly retract this thought, for it is not death that remains the painful remnant but the memory of a shared life that once was, however short-lived. The uncovering of this fact has allowed Sadia to better understand her grandmother's trauma.

> She not only transitioned from widow to a wife – again – but also became a mother to my paternal step-aunt Rasheedah, who remained close to her till her last moments. But I am curious and appalled that my dadi's loss remained shrouded

in secret. All this time that she cried in front of us, was she, in essence, grieving for her husband and the blissful memory of a marriage not tarnished by trauma? Growing up, I could never understand what her grief meant, and why her mourning proved lifelong. But living amidst patriarchy and maintaining the (im)perfect interpretation of family history meant that 'her secret' would forever remain unuttered. I find it disturbing how much we are lied to about our own histories – personal, social or national.

I never expected her tears to have left a lasting imprint but each time I now hear or read about the carnage at Partition, I am reminded of her. I gravitate towards the stories of 1947, and this attempt to document hers is to redeem her in memory. She took the pain to the grave, having lived a life of unhealed trauma with courage, despite being offered a life with more prestige but less happiness by a well-meaning cousin who perhaps grappled with his own PTSD in the new state.

And then, almost unexpectedly, she adds a poignant addendum:

I wonder if I have been too harsh on my grandfather, whose trauma has remained unaddressed in our correspondence.

Sadia's narration is emblematic of the generational trauma of Partition, both in its delayed discovery but also the depth of despair it has brought her. She tells me how her father speaks about the uncles he never got to meet, who could never cross into Pakistan – 'Mairay mamu,' he calls them. She tells me how her paternal aunt once gave her the DVD of her favourite movie, Pinjar, a story written by Amrita Pritam depicting Puro, a woman who loses everything in 1947, causing Sadia to wonder how much of Puro's predicament her aunt saw reflected in her own mother. At the end of our correspondence, we return to the consequence of Partition which binds the youth of the subcontinent to each other – that of never being able to return to the land of our ancestry.

I live and work in Lahore, teaching at a university that is barely a twenty-minute drive from the India–Pakistan border, yet I cannot imagine crossing over. Amritsar is closer than the capital of Pakistan, yet I wonder how long it will be before my wish to see the Golden Temple is fulfilled. Will I ever visit my friends, Sushma Luthra in Delhi and Sameer Khan in Pune? Walk to the Dargah at Ajmer, shop for the perfect sari or pose in front of the Taj Mahal? With India being the only country denying me a visa, places like Bhatinda and Jalandhar seems as distant for me as they remained for my dadi, Enayat Begum.

'I WAS PROBABLY in my early thirties when I found out that both my paternal grandparents had been orphaned very young, my grandfather at the age of five,' Nishant recalls. 'It was only then, when he was already in his nineties, that we began a series of conversations, lasting several years, anytime I visited him in our village in Shamli district on the border of Haryana and Uttar Pradesh. His memories were never chronological, they were sporadic and sometimes even contradictory, but they revealed his association to Partition.'

Nishant and I were first introduced while standing in line for tea at the Seagull Foundation for the Arts' 'History for Peace'* annual conference in Kolkata in 2018. There, he mentioned that his grandfather may have been involved in the perpetration of some form of violence during Partition, but the details were vague and scattered. His grandfather was ailing, a patient of Alzheimer's, and for several months after we tried to arrange a meeting. But when in October 2019 he passed away, older than a century, Nishant and I began an altogether different conversation on the collection of second-hand memory and the accumulation of an unexpected form of grief.

---

* A network of educators and members of civil society in the subcontinent, the 'History for Peace' project serves as a platform for discussion, debate and the exchange of ideas pertaining to the teaching and learning of history for peace and understanding.

'Our interaction began later in life because, firstly, I was never so fond of visiting the village – there was no electricity, life was still rural, and holidays were far more comfortably spent in Dehradun with my maternal grandparents. Secondly, for as long as I can remember, everyone had been afraid of my paternal grandfather, and only towards the end of his life did this change. He became softer, his memory began to fade and he would divulge more than he ever had. I had always heard of him being this iron-willed, hot-headed man in his youth. He was very proud of the fact that he was the first graduate from his village, paying for his own graduation after his children were born. After middle school, he worked for some time in Lahore during World War II as a clerk, then did his final years of schooling in Ghaziabad, and graduation in Agra after Independence.'

'But he never spoke about Partition or the time before or after?' I ask.

'Never until I began seriously asking,' Nishant shrugs. 'But there is an interesting titbit from the late '90s, when my father, who was in the Indian Air Force, was to be posted in Pakistan as the Air Attaché, and the posting was eventually cancelled. The entire family jokes that this cancellation was because of me, because I was so anti-Pakistan as a child.'

I raise my eyebrows.

'I had a map of Pakistan that I used to aim at with darts! For the longest time, they were the enemy. As a child, there was no nuanced understanding of what had happened in 1947, and then, being from a military family, the sense of otherness was heightened even more.'

Now returning to the conversations with his grandfather, he says, 'They were limited, as I said, to whenever I would visit the farm. We'd talk while walking along the fields and orchards – he grew mangoes. He would simply mention things in passing, you know? Revealing random bits of information. For instance, he told me that right after graduation, the first thing he purchased was a revolver, and this connected to another distant memory my father had told me about how my grandfather was once in jail ... which connected to a third memory my grandfather had mentioned about how if you went to jail as a graduate, you were entitled to a separate room with a ceiling fan. These simultaneous conversations about guns and jails then became lodged in my brain and led me to believe that he may have shot or hurt someone, which was why he was imprisoned. He would always call me *vakeel sahib* because I'm a lawyer, and tried to direct every discussion towards criminal law, even though that isn't the law I practise.' Nishant pauses and takes an exasperated breath. 'I'm sorry, I know that I'm not streamlining my thoughts, but this is how the conversations were as well – one half of a memory would lead to another half, decades before or after, and then that would connect to something else. Bear in mind that in the years we were speaking, his memory was also slowly fading...'

But Nishant's fumbling through inherited memory doesn't bother me in the least. 'You're trying to make sense of a life that is not yours, in a time that you did not live in. You have to be kind to yourself, because there will always be things you won't know, threads you won't be able to tie or events that won't chronologically add up.'

'That's exactly what I thought when these bits of stories began to emerge. I realized that I didn't know *anything* about my grandfather – if he was a farmer, why did he receive a pension? What kind of studies did he do? How was he orphaned? I began to ask, and gradually he began to tell. I learnt that as a child he had travelled to Calcutta and come third in a kabaddi competition, winning three rupees!' Nishant laughs. 'He once mentioned that on his deathbed his father had told him that he was sorry only six acres of land had remained for him to inherit. For a child of five years, this is an extremely poignant thing to remember with the clarity that he did. And then, of course, there was Partition.'

I inch forward with renewed focus.

'We were always led to believe that we had no connection to Partition. I remember asking my maternal grandmother, who was fifteen years old in 1947, if she had any personal memories of the time. She would just shake her head and describe the masses of refugees who had arrived in Dehradun with nothing.'

'So, when did you find out your Partition connection?' I ask, thinking about our conversation in Kolkata.

'Well, it was not so much a Partition connection as a story that took place during that time,' he says. 'I should preface by saying that we are not a religious family. We never felt we had a Hindu identity except for the fact that we have Hindu names, and if you ask me to write my religion on a form, I will write Hinduism. But I did always feel like my grandfather had this ... I would say undercurrent of animosity towards Muslims. It was never expressed, but you could feel it. And I used to dismiss it or attribute it to being part of a larger, post-Babri Masjid atmosphere in the country. We were in Allahabad when Babri happened in 1992, and as children witnessed some of the violence with our own eyes. I was personally very disturbed by the events, where identity suddenly became so important. Each morning in class, as we said our prayers to the Hindu goddess Saraswati, I would wonder what the two Muslim boys in the class were thinking. So that is one point. And the other, highly divergent extreme is the fact that my grandfather has always given the contract for his farm to a Muslim family. Three generations of that family have worked on our land.

'Now, in 2013, there were violent riots between Hindus and Muslims in Muzaffarnagar that spilled into Shamli as well. And I remember asking my grandfather whether anything happened on our farm, because it was run by Muslims. And he said that someone did try to come in and steal all the produce, thinking that it was a Muslim-owned farm, which led my grandfather to take out his gun and chase the miscreants out. This led to a deeper discussion about the riots between communities, where I asked him why people fight with one another over religion.

'He said that sometimes people get scared and don't completely realize what is happening, don't realize what they are doing. And this is the thought that remained with me – that people don't realize what's happening. It was then that he began telling me the story of, well, it could be a year or even months leading up to Partition – he was completing his schooling in Ghaziabad at the time. So he is sitting with a group of boys from his kabaddi team, along with their coach, eating samosas and drinking chai near the Shahdara station in Delhi, when a Sikh man approaches them and says, "What is the point of being strong, able-bodied Hindu boys if you can't see what is happening around you?" A boy gets up and says, "What do you mean? We are as strong as anyone else!" and the Sikh man then says, "Well, people are being killed across the country, and you boys aren't doing anything." He turns their attention towards three shops owned by Muslims and says, "They are selling their wares openly as if nothing has happened." So, all of these young boys along with their coach apparently went and ... well, this is where the story gets hazy because my grandfather never wants to mention what really happened, what they did. He always evaded...' Nishant's voice recedes, leaving the sentence incomplete.

'What did he say happened?' I ask softly, cutting through the quiet.

'That they went and ransacked all the shops. I believe that this was before Independence, because things hadn't reached the height of frenzy yet, the awareness of the riots wasn't there, and someone had to coax them into violence. Anyway, the way he concluded the story was that they went and attacked a Muslim-owned shoe-shop and, by the end, they each had two or three new pairs of shoes. I can't say why, but I assume they killed the owner as well. Then, through the evening, they continued to ransack as many Muslim shops as they could find. Listening to this story always put me in a very problematic position, because I knew vaguely about the gun story that had landed my grandfather in jail as an adult, but then to learn of this thing he had done at such a young age. It just...' He heaves a deep sigh.

'My grandfather never told this story to his children,' Nishant says and looks up at me.

'Well, it is often easier to speak to grandchildren. Not to mention that you were *there*, you were listening, and maybe it was at a time when he was ready to talk ... or reveal.'

'He tried, he tried to tell me about his life and build a relationship – even though it was towards the end, when he had become quite subdued and willing to adjust.'

'And he was unwell,' I add softly.

'He had Alzheimer's and cancer but, at the end, what killed him was a paralytic stroke. But some days were good and some were very bad. He had never been this sort of open person with us his whole life. He had been harsh, and then to have him adopt a role of such vulnerability was what I found most strange. Sometimes he would return to his pre-Partition memories, and talk about how the people on the other side were not how we thought them to be.'

'Oh.'

'I know a lot of the things I'm saying are contradictory to the things I've said earlier, but he was a complicated person. He had anger in him, but part of me believes that there was also remorse. You remember how as a child I used to be anti-Pakistan? Well, I had very romantic illusions of war as well, and probably told my grandfather about my soldier games, where I had dioramas showing India and Pakistan at war – you know, battle scenes and everything. Anyway, the thing I so distinctly remember him telling me was that I should not judge people on the basis of their religion. I should judge them on their actions. And that didn't make any sense to me because, like I told you, I often felt like he had an undercurrent of dislike for Muslims, and yet he always said – do not judge people on the basis of religion. My grandfather was complicated, and his behaviour was defined by his many experiences, not all of them positive.

'One time, when I was in college, I got into a fight and was suspended for over two weeks. I thought my father would be really mad at me, but the only thing he said was, "It's all in the genes, my friend." And when I asked what that meant, he repeated the story about the gun and jail, and how my grandfather had shot somebody, and how there was apparently a knife fight as well, and...' Nishant struggles to find the words. 'I don't lose my temper any more, but when I was young I certainly would. Maybe, deep inside, we all have the ability to be fighters, rioters, given the cause. And communal violence is not only physical but also mental; it can even be an inflammatory tweet. So, I know this is a very roundabout way to arrive at a conclusion, but sometimes I feel that temper is a hereditary disposition – the ability to do something *because* of it.'

I can feel my composure crumble as he says this.

'It made me feel a bit empty about my existence, which is why I value my education tremendously. The exposure, the rational thought process, the knowledge of what is right or wrong, lawful or unlawful. And, to that extent, I can empathize with my grandfather for being somebody who suffered because of his orphan background. The fact that he took such pride in being the first person from his village to obtain a degree makes me believe that he truly considered education as essential – education that he did not have as a child or even a young adult. And, in that sense, if I return to Partition, I feel like we are fed falsities that only Hindus and Sikhs were driven out of Pakistan, but my own family is an example of how this side committed equal sin. Towards the end of his life, my grandfather would talk often about the end, and about purgatory.'

'Purgatory?' I ask. 'The period between life and death?'

'Correct, the suffering or temporary punishment that one endures because of their actions. Was he telling me this to caution me, to make sure I avoid purgatory? Or was he saying that *he would remain* in purgatory? I don't know.' He shrugs his shoulders.

I think about a grandfather forging a relationship in his twilight years with his grandson – ready to speak to someone who was ready to listen, about a past that may have otherwise remained unknown. Aware of the courage it must take to voice, even to think, some of the things that have been said throughout this conversation, I pose Nishant a final question.

'Has knowing your grandfather's stories around Partition made the event feel personal?'

'Well, his stories have certainly informed my understanding of Partition, and I think what I feel is a kind of grief. It is not direct or personal, because we were not harmed in any way, but that doesn't mean that grief doesn't exist, that it isn't present.'

9

Hope

～

'STRANGELY ENOUGH, THE HARSHNESS and cruelty of the time is not uppermost in my recollections,' Bharati Sen tells me, 'even though remembering such injustices is essential to keep history from being repeated.'

'What memories come to mind, then?' I ask.

'Stories of courage and resilience in the face of loss and destruction, of building new lives and, most of all, lending a helping hand. I hold on to the stories of hope.'

Her answer is rare yet remarkable, for one of the most difficult things to locate within the landscape of Partition is hope. It emerges in conversations few and far between, but almost never as a primary character. But since the process of partitioning a subcontinent was anything but one-dimensional, its resulting experiences cannot be either. Thus, if stories of violence and trauma prevail, then stories of hope and resilience must exist somewhere within the spectrum as well.

Bharati Sen was born in 1945 in Delhi's Daryaganj market area, then known as Faiz Bazar. Both sides of her family were originally from Dhaka in East Bengal and in 1914 her paternal grandfather was posted to Delhi, but his children studied across Shimla, Delhi and Calcutta. In 1939, Bharati's parents, Aruna Sen and Dr Subodh Chandra Sengupta, married, and at the time of Partition the family lived in a flat surrounding a beautiful park, at the centre of which stood a mosque with an old mullah as its caretaker.

Bharati now lives in Scottsdale, Arizona, but it was in 2018 that she made her maiden trip to the Partition Museum in Amritsar. Born and raised in Delhi, Partition is a lived reality for her, even though she was merely two years old when it happened. The stories of 1947 – of pain, struggle, love, friendship and new beginnings – accompanied her upbringing and became deeply etched in her mind. But she wasn't consciously aware of this until she began recounting these memories to her daughters.*

It was on the ground floor of the Partition Museum that Bharati spent the most amount of time – in the room that housed personal objects carried by refugees across the border. She kept imagining how they would have once been used in someone's home, gathered at a moment's notice and carried to a strange land, a little bit of their own life and history. Bharati walked through the display of heirlooms and artefacts, almost building an unspoken connection with their owners. But it was once she climbed the stairs to the exhibits on the first floor that a tent in the centre of the room, accompanied by a large photograph on the wall, caught her attention. It was a black and white image of an open ground with many such tents and people walking around them.

'I couldn't take my eyes off it. I stood transfixed, thinking to myself, "I know this place. *I know it*. I have been there." And the memories came streaming, as did the tears.'

The photograph that moved her so was of Kingsway Camp, the largest camp for Partition refugees in the capital. It has now all but been swallowed by urbanization and the North Campus of Delhi University, but in the years following Partition it was a busy network of tents and barracks. It was a place of both tragedy and hope, where people were forced to shed their old lives and adopt new ones on foreign soil. It was also the place where five-year-old Bharati

---

* Bharati's daughter, Rabeya Sen, recounts a second-hand memory from the days of Partition in Chapter 7, 'Friendship'.

would accompany her mother. When I ask what took them there, the narration she embarks upon is partly what she remembers from her childhood and partly what she has heard from her family.

'In those days, there was a popular general provision store in Daryaganj, owned and run by two Sikh gentlemen. The space as I recall was a garage to the adjacent house. It was named Lyallpur Store, and most likely Lyallpur was where the two Sikh gentlemen were from. They were very kind and popularly referred to as Bade Sardarji and Chhote Sardarji, simply by each one's physical stature! The store was one of my favourites, as the two Sardarjis would always give me some candy!

'My mother told me later that one day they sent another Sikh gentleman to talk to my parents about a Bengali woman with two daughters who was a refugee at Kingsway Camp. Her husband and son had been killed as they were fleeing during Partition. Both daughters were of schoolgoing age, and the woman was grief-stricken, with a bleak future. This gentleman was also a camp resident and helped the authorities with refugee resettlement and rehabilitation. He asked if my mother and her Bengali friends could talk to the lady, encourage her or help her. That is when my mother and two of her friends began going to Kingsway Camp and I was her little "camp-follower"!

'The first thing was to ensure that the two daughters attended school. I can't imagine this to have been an easy task for the mother – letting her daughters out of sight even to go to school, given the horrendous familial losses she had suffered. But she finally agreed. My mother met other residents of the camp, the lady's neighbours, and it was as though these kind people – who had themselves suffered enormously, and many had not a penny to their name – had almost adopted her.

'The Sikh gentleman who had come to talk to my parents would tell her, "Mataji, you cook so well, please start making Bengali sweets and snacks. We will bring you the necessary provisions." My mother and her friends would in turn help her find Bengali customers, and in those days, when there was just one Bengali sweet shop in the entire city, her supply was no match for the demand. And thus began a wonderful enterprise and friendship. She started making Bengali *vadis*,* or *bori*, as pronounced in Bengali, and they sold like hot cakes!

'For the children, she would bring sweets like *chandrapuli*, a coconut *sandesh*, and *labangalatika*, a flaky, deep-fried, sugar syrup-coated pastry filled with *kheer*. If my mother ever wanted to pay for the sweets, she would hear no end of it. As her business grew, she came to be known as Delhi's Bengali community's Mishti Didi, but to us she always remained Bori Mashima or Bori Aunty, as she'd begun by making *boris*.'

As Bharati concludes by recalling the day the lady's eldest daughter received her first pay, her tone is one of pure joy and pride. 'She invited my mother, her two friends and me to the camp tent for lunch. It was a hot summer day, and we saw a small table fan whirring in a corner. When her elder daughter had passed her matriculation, my father had made her take shorthand typewriting lessons. She now had a job and, with her first pay, she had bought the table fan! It was only then that they invited us for lunch so that we would be comfortable while we ate. What a happy feast it was, and what a wonderful day!'

This story is like balm to my hopeful heart, not just due to the fact that a five-year-old Bharati was privy to such an empowering experience but that this is the tale of so many women who crossed the border without the support of the menfolk of their family. My own great-grandmother, Lajvanti Gulyani, a widow with four children to feed, educate and settle, became both mother and father, simultaneously working and tending to the home, in a land and culture that couldn't have been more different from the one she had left behind in the Frontier Province. My paternal grandmother, Bhag, tells me that she and her elder sister had no choice *but* to work, for the household depended on their cumulative incomes.

---

* *Vadi* or *bori* is a form of dried lentil dumplings.

Interestingly enough, despite the predicament the Gulyani family found themselves in, my grandmother maintains that Partition gave rise to the possibility of a better future in Delhi than what they would have ever had in D.I. Khan. She often narrates how the women of the house used to stay behind *purdah*, but the custom was abandoned, along with the restrictions that accompanied it, once they migrated to Delhi. She acknowledges that though the years following Partition were fraught with uncertainty and difficulty, they were also the years of abundant opportunity and hope – of being able to contribute to the family's savings, of becoming self-sufficient, independent women.

Since my grandmother's family too lived in Kingsway Camp at the same time, I share a photograph from their days there with Bharati as it connects us in a serendipitous kind of way, removed by decades.

Upon receiving it, she writes to me saying, 'John Guare's play *Six Degrees of Separation*[1] fascinated me when I first read it. But only now, so many years later, do I truly understand the connections that run through us all. What I do in my cocoon affects the whole social fabric.'

After listening to her story about how a single act of kindness provided another person with hope at a time when hope seemed altogether unimaginable, I'm inclined to agree.

'NOT ALL INHERITANCES from Partition are traumatic,' Harsh Vardhan Sahni asserts at one point in our two-hour conversation. At first, I'm taken aback, not only by the words but also the incredible lightness of his voice that's difficult to obtain while speaking about Partition. But the longer I reflect on the statement, the more I understand how for so many families, in hindsight, the rupture of division and migration was eclipsed by the future they were able to eventually secure in independent nations. Of course, no story of Partition is devoid of loss, but through our conversation Harsh maintains that rather than the dispersion of trauma, it is the celebration of being able to rebuild life that has been passed down the generations of his family.

'I will begin from the oldest ancestors I know about,' he tells me, referring to the family tree he has compiled. Harsh was born in 1986, and during our interview he takes me through the three generations that precede him. 'My paternal great-grandfather, Shri Hari Ram, also known as Shahji, hailed from the village of Ghariyala,' he now pronounces the word in Punjabi, 'or maybe it is Karyala, in present-day Pakistan. He was a rich man, a moneylender, a zamindar. My grandfather, Charandas Sahni, was the youngest son from his first marriage; the two had a rift over the ethics of the moneylending business and my grandfather decided to start afresh and have nothing to do with his father's enormous wealth.

'He married my grandmother, Vidyawati, who was from Sialkot. Her father, Desraj Abrol, had constructed a fabulous *kothi* with mirrors and glass called Sheesh Mahal, which I've been longing to locate for the last several years to see if it still stands. After renouncing his father's work and wealth, my grandfather joined his sister's husband in supplying sports goods from Sialkot to various places, including Delhi. It was on one of these visits, just before Partition, that with a borrowed pen he gave the exam at the polytechnic in Kashmere Gate and secured a job as a clerk there. This later became the Delhi College of Engineering.[2] He was also provided government housing in Timarpur – my father actually still remembers the address of the house, 118 C, but now it's all demolished.' Harsh smiles sadly.

'This family tree...' I gesture to his notes.

'Yes, as I was making it, I found myself wishing I'd asked more questions while my elders were still alive,' he says and begins to tell me about its compilation. As the details of names, dates of birth, cities and migration routes tumble out, this document connects the members of the Sahni-Abrol family from a once-undivided to divided India.

'So, when Partition was announced, your grandparents were already in India?' I ask.

'My grandfather was in Delhi, but my grandmother was still in Ghariyala, across the border. They had three children before Partition, and she crossed over with them and the rest of the family. From what I've heard, she carried a *sandookadi* full of gold ornaments, but I don't know where it is any longer. The family didn't keep the gold as my grandfather didn't want anything to do with his father's wealth; he gave it away in his siblings' and nieces' weddings. But no one knows where the *sandookadi* is either; we didn't hold on to anything out of nostalgia, to be honest...'

'I've actually been thinking about how when it comes to Partition, we fall into nostalgia almost naturally, like it's a pre-established, expected state of being,' I muse, slowly working through my thoughts. 'But experiences from that time are so complex that even longing can be viewed more critically.'

Harsh nods. 'Yes, definitely. The things I heard about were less about the wealth or the zamindari or even the longing for a life left behind, and more to do with starting afresh. I've heard that my grandfather was a very morally upright person, influenced by the Arya Samaj, and it reflected in the fact that out of ethical differences, he refused to be a part of the family wealth. In the early years in India, they were by no means financially well off, but they all took pride in being able to rebuild from the ground up. My grandfather already had a footing in India before 1947, and when the Lal Bahadur Shastri National Academy of Administration was set up in Mussoorie in 1959, he moved there and worked as an accounts officer until his retirement.'

'Is that the context in which you first understood Partition? As a new life, a fresh start?' I ask.

'Well, that and other things. My family still lives in Mussoorie, so I shuffle between here and Delhi for work. But I went to school in Mussoorie, where most of my classmates were Garhwali, and they would always speak about their ancestral villages. It was just a thing – *everyone* had a village, a native place. But I didn't have one and I would just say that I was from Mussoorie, because it was all I knew. Then in 2010, when I was at Oxford, someone asked me my nationality, and I asked him whether it was that hard to guess. He said that I could either be Indian or Pakistani, but he didn't want to offend. I suppose...' he says and his voice trails off. 'I suppose it took me by surprise that someone thought I would be offended at being identified as Pakistani.'

'And why is that?' I ask.

'Because I certainly took pride in where we came from, and *what* we came from – my cultural roots are in Pakistani Punjab. Part of my family's life was spent in what is now Pakistan and part of it in India, which means that part of my history is there and part of it here...'

He pauses for a few seconds to think and then says, 'I'll give you another example. When I am introduced to someone, if they ask where I'm from, I'll say Delhi because I live there, but then they'll ask, where are you *really* from, and I'll begin to explain that my family lives in Mussoorie, and then they'll make observations or speculations about my being Pahadi or Garhwali, and so on, and none of them are representative of who I am. So, I simply began saying Pakistan. Because the question "Where are you really from?" is so complicated, and if you want an accurate answer, it will lead to present-day Pakistan. My family is originally from West Punjab, which is in Pakistan, and that is my identity, my historical truth.'

'And one that you are proud of,' I add with a smile.

He laughs. 'I am definitely proud of it. I want people to engage with my whole identity. And as a third generation, I do, of course, want to see where my family comes from. But more than an inheritance of tragedy, there is a recognition of hope and resilience when it comes to Partition and rebuilding life from scratch in India.'

'But there is no sense of loss? Or trauma?' I ask, even though I think I already know the answer.

'Well, my father's family may have had misgivings about giving up their wealth, but in my generation, we are fine. I also understand that as a community Punjabi Khatris prospered enormously post Partition. So, I don't necessarily feel deprived of anything. I know that terrible things happened at the time of Partition, but also that we were not affected by the worst of it. And the truth is, though I am a bearer of this complicated heritage, it is not dramatic, just as not all inheritances are traumatic. Mine is a celebration,' Harsh says with finality.

⁊

IN 2018, THE comedian Amit Tandon and I speak about a comic series he is working on around the theme of Partition. It is a format completely unimaginable to me, to view an event of tragedy through the lens of light-hearted comedy. But on listening to the idea, I realize that Amit – much like the other interviewees of this chapter – consciously chooses to focus on hope rather than despair. His vignettes are born from the stories of common people rebuilding their lives in a new nation and the idiosyncrasies around that. We speak again once the idea of a generational book begins to take concrete shape in my mind, this time about his family's migration to India in 1947.

'I was quite young the first time I remember hearing the word Partition, maybe seven or eight years old,' Amit tells me. He was born in 1975 in Patiala and now lives in Mumbai. 'Every time my parents would meet someone new, particularly within the Punjabi community, the first discussion was always on where they were from: "*Tussi pichho se kithe ke ho?*" – where are you from way back, from behind, from before. It was like an ice-breaker question almost.' He laughs. 'And the other very clear memory I have is of receiving a letter written in Urdu from my paternal grandfather while I was growing up in Chandigarh. He would only write in Urdu, and every fortnight, without fail, a letter arrived in the language that no one else in the house knew how to read. And so, my mother had to walk across the road to the neighbours' house and have the elderly gentleman who lived there read it out to her! That was our routine. So, even as a child, there was an awareness of having migrated from the other side. But I've always looked at Partition as a story of hope, where people were able to rebuild their lives even after having lost everything.'

'What kind of stories were you told?' I'm curious.

'Well, I often heard from my paternal grandmother about how my father was born on the way to India. She would recall how the trains were crammed with people, and one barely had space to breathe, let alone sit anywhere. It was raining incessantly, and my father's grandfather took off his turban and swaddled my infant father in the turban cloth. But the baby would get thirsty from time to time, and so he would hold a corner of the turban cloth outside the window until it was soaked in rainwater and then squeeze the liquid into my father's mouth. These were the kinds of stories she told,' he says casually. 'They got off at the train station, and so many corpses had littered the ground that they had to be careful where to step next.'

I draw a breath in. 'Amit, when did you realize that your father was born on the journey to India?'

'*Shuru se hi pata tha*, I think I always just knew it.'

'But simply knowing about it and realizing the gravity of what it means are two different things.'

'Right,' he exhales. 'That would come much later ... maybe as late as my thirties, actually, when I understood what it would have meant for the family to have carried a newborn across at the time. It was difficult enough to take care of oneself...'

I nod gravely. 'And when you heard this story as a child, what did you think it meant?'

His tone now becomes brighter. 'It was just a fun story. In fact, every single story from my childhood was connected to Partition in some way and always told in a light-hearted way. Migrating across the border, moving from place to place, then coming to Delhi, being allocated a plot and a shop on Janpath. Partition would always find its way into conversations...'

'So where did your family migrate from?'

'My paternal side came from outside of Lahore to Amritsar, then to Panipat, and were eventually allotted lands near Patiala. There is a story they tell about this migration, when they were briefly allotted a home in Panipat which had been recently abandoned by a Muslim family that had fled to Pakistan. And I say recently because they had left everything in the house just the way it was. It was full of things

– clothes, furniture, a kitchen stocked with grains, dals, masalas, everything – a whole life just left behind. Now, my great-grandfather was a very religious man, a staunch Hindu, and he believed in prayer and meditation. So, the family settled into the house and upon realizing that it used to belong to a Muslim family, he insisted that they would not use a single thing. They would not take a grain from the pantry to even feed my father, the newborn child.'

I gasp, but he merely smiles. 'Another story I've heard is how my grandaunt was a widow – her husband had died either because of Partition riots or just before, I don't know exactly. But she decided to go back to Pakistan after Partition to retrieve the money and other items she had probably buried or left behind in haste. She made the journey back all by herself.'

'Oh, wow,' I exclaim, wide-eyed. 'That's incredible.'

'Yes, but the impact of these stories is dawning on me only now as I get older. My mother's family also migrated to Delhi and stayed in the Kingsway refugee camp. But they were able to move out of the camp rather quickly because my maternal grandfather was an engineer who worked in agricultural reforms for the government, and was given a new posting.'

'Amit, these stories are painful and traumatic, but you narrate them with…' I struggle to find the appropriate words. 'I don't know if I'm asking this in the right way, but is it because of your work as a comedian that you gravitate to lightness or satire or even dark humour about this time rather than anguish or horror? Or is that just how the stories were told to you?'

'Aanchal, there may be no right way to ask these questions.' He smiles softly, and I immediately feel at ease. 'I acknowledge that Partition is a serious subject, but it is also a vast subject that deserves to be understood through different perspectives, including humour. Now, I know that looking at Partition through the lens of humour is a difficult thing to do, and one must be careful not to offend,' he clarifies. 'But to be honest, I look at the positive side of life. I always have. And the way stories of Partition were told to me was never through loss or suffering. I'll give you an example –

my maternal family lived in the camp and they often recalled the inhuman conditions there: common latrines, no cleanliness, long lines for ration, the horrible stories people told of what they'd seen on the way. But at the same time, they would mention how every evening the entire extended family would gather. Relatives they had probably seen only thrice a year until then were now with them every day. A sense of community was also rebuilt and fostered this way in the camp. So, I just try to look at each story from a more positive angle – what was gained rather than what was lost.'

'I find that extraordinary,' I say sincerely.

'What is really extraordinary is that so many people who were displaced were able to rebuild their lives despite the devastation that Partition brought ... my family, your family. There is a unique resilience to be found within people who survived Partition. Why should we not celebrate their perseverance, hard work, commitment? Why should we not consider hope as a possible response?' Amit is speaking with his hands and his heart; there is a zeal in his voice. 'The fact that, despite everything, my family was able to settle down, open a shop, feed and educate their children, even save for the future, is a very positive story.'

'You mentioned that your father was born on the journey to India.' I pick up an earlier thread and Amit nods. 'It must have been defining in some way. Have you ever asked him about it?'

'Not really, he doesn't ever talk about the actual moment of Partition, but often recalls his school days in Amritsar and Patiala.'

'I suppose it would've been narrated to him like a story as well when he got older.'

'Yes,' he agrees. 'But all said and done, I would love to see where my family comes from, though I don't know whether it will be possible in our lifetimes. When I began doing comedy nearly a decade ago, I realized just how many of my viewers were from Pakistan. Anytime I perform in the UK, US or Dubai, so many people in the audience are Pakistani. There is obviously a natural connection between us, we understand one another. But I don't know when we'll be able to travel to each other's countries freely and without suspicion. So, if I can dissolve the distance between us for even a brief period, through comedy or laughter, then what could be more beautiful?'

A wide smile appears on my face and I nod enthusiastically. 'I have to admit, it's unusual to meet someone who is touched by the tragedy of Partition but not fixated on it.'

'Well, there is too much to still learn about it,' he responds. 'I refer back to the Holocaust, because there's been such a strong movement to document every single aspect of what happened – positive or negative – from a multitude of perspectives. Maybe we haven't been able to do this with Partition because only a fraction of undivided India was affected by it. But a larger ground still needs to be covered.'

'And it won't be long before there aren't any eyewitnesses left,' I add softly.

'I keep thinking,' Amit now says in a tone unusually sombre for him, 'about that kitchen fully stocked with food in Panipat, and my father who would have been only days old and hungry. A fully stocked kitchen that went untouched because it belonged to the other, to a Muslim.' He exhales deeply. 'Can you imagine that? That is what Partition did, and I just don't want to focus *only* on that aspect. I'm tired of hatred and division being the only perspective we discuss and pass down in our families. I want to remember what makes us better. I don't know how much my children know about Partition, perhaps not enough. But I wish that one day they will want to listen to these stories and, like me, inherit hope above all else.'

'CHEECHA BHAKNA,* THE native village on my paternal side, was cut in half by the border during Partition,' Harleen Singh Sandhu tells me. The 1995-born social historian is originally from Delhi but is based currently in Toronto, Canada, and has for years been archiving the social history of women in colonial Punjab through his project The Lost Heer.[3] Our conversation meanders around both family and

---

* In Punjab, the word *cheecha* translates to 'small'.

colonial history, and how his scholarly interests are ultimately the result of their intersection. It also affirms that almost no story about Partition simply begins and ends in 1947, starting long before and extending long after.

'My ancestors had been living on the tract of land known as the Sarhali Kalan belt for nearly six hundred years,' Harleen says, providing some background. 'According to local lore, the first Sandhu settlements were established by a person named Jaggo Sandhu, and his tribe were originally animists, practising the Jatt folk religion. By the time of the fifth Guru, many became Sikhs due to their proximity to the Golden Temple. Around the eighteenth century, the Sandhus converted to Sikhism en masse, as many joined the local *misls* fighting off Afghan invaders. Baba Naudh Singh, an elder from my village, Bhakna, actually died fighting the army of Ahmad Shah Abdali. Now, when the Partition line was drawn, it not only cut through Punjab but also the Sandhu homeland – half the villages, numbering up to twenty-two, fell in India, and the other half in Pakistan, now distributed between the Tarn Taran (then Amritsar) and Lahore districts.'

'My god,' I exclaim.

He nods knowingly and then embarks on a long and fascinating tale. Barely interrupting his narration, I listen intently to the account of his ancestors' syncretic lifestyle and outlook, which have trickled down the generations to him.

'My great-grandfather, Mehr Singh, was born in 1878,' Harleen reads from his notes, 'but left Cheecha Bhakna as a young man of twenty due to land disputes within the family. He settled in Amritsar and began working at a *kiryane ki dukaan*, a local grocery store, as an assistant. In 1906, as a twenty-eight-year-old, he joins the British Indian Army as part of the 23rd Cavalry, the Punjab Frontier Force, during which time he's stationed at the Mian Mir Cantonment just outside Lahore city.

'In 1914, World War I breaks out, and by the start of 1915 a large number of people involved in the Ghadar Movement[4] return to India and begin establishing contacts within army cantonments in major cities with the intention of rallying the Indian sepoy. Unfortunately, my great-grandfather's regiment was to take part in this mutiny but their plans were ultimately thwarted and they were all arrested. A long trial took place and many of the men were awarded the death sentence, some given life imprisonment in the jail on the Andaman islands, and the rest – including my great-grandfather – were acquitted and, as punishment, shipped across to fight in Mesopotamia, one of the harshest theatres of the war.[5]

'On the way back home from Baghdad, he fought in the Third Anglo-Afghan War in 1919, and once back in India he resigned from the army and returned to Amritsar. Right by the Golden Temple, there was a marketplace called Papad Bazar, where he started a shop of *papads* and *vadis*. Then after a couple of years, he shut shop and moved to Lahore, where he settled in Wachowali in the Walled City and began a very primitive type of banking business.'

Harleen suddenly looks up at me and says, 'What I forgot to mention is that Mehr Singh had gotten married in his childhood, but his wife passed away. So, he got married again, this time to a Gorkha woman from Nepal – my great-grandmother – whose name was Rani Thapa. My grandfather, Labh Singh, was born in 1932, and one year later they moved from Wachowali to the new township of Model Town. My great-grandfather was financially comfortable, but because he had almost lost all contact with his family and their ancestral wealth, he was a completely self-made man.'

He now puts down his notes and takes a deep breath. I am impressed by the plethora of details and Harleen's seasoned storytelling. Having closely followed his work since we first met in 2017 at the Gardiner Museum in Toronto, I was aware that he often strove to archive the most minute details of his historical protagonists, and should have known that he implemented the same methodology to his family archive.

'I know the story has been winding so far, but I promise we are inching closer to Partition,' he chuckles.

'All right, so when my grandfather was four or five years old, his mother passed away. My great-grandfather had remarried late,

so he was a middle-aged father to a very young child. The story I
have heard is that he used to have a Muslim housekeeper, an old
woman who cooked, cleaned, washed the clothes, and lived in the
outhouse with her grandson, Hamid. Now, the neighbours in Model
Town made a hue and cry about this, because at the time it was
considered unacceptable for a Muslim to be cooking in a Hindu or
Sikh household. But my great-grandfather didn't really care for all
this talk, and I think this was because of his upbringing in the village
– Sandhus are Sikhs, Muslims and Hindus, and there were quite a
lot of intercommunity marriages as well. So, he not only continued
to employ the woman but also raised her grandson. Hamid was
educated by him, he was trained to drive a *tonga*, he took care of
the stables.

'Then, just before World War II, his grandmother passed away
from smallpox and Hamid became an orphan. As the war broke,
my great-grandfather encouraged Hamid to enlist in the army.
Hamid left, survived the war, and returned to Lahore, naturally, as
a more experienced man. The banking business was still thriving in
Wachowali, and he began working with my great-grandfather, and
also continued to drive the *tonga*. So now, in the summer of 1947,
either May or June, riots have begun in the Walled City, but they
haven't yet reached Model Town. My great-grandfather is keen to
leave as soon as possible, and he makes his way to Wachowali to
wrap up accounts and retrieve his papers. Accompanying him is
Hamid, who is unfortunately killed in an attack that same day. This
incident really breaks my great-grandfather, because he virtually
raised Hamid as his own son. It just ... it impacted him very, very
deeply.'

I feel a sadness creep up to my heart, as if Hamid were someone
known to me. Though his life and death make a very short
appearance in this long story, I am convinced of the void he left in
Mehr Singh's life.

'What happened next?' I ask in a small voice.

'Well, my grandfather is sent to Amritsar, where his paternal
aunt lives, and my great-grandfather remains in Lahore to save his

property and other things. But by September 1947, things begin getting unbearable and the city unlivable, and so he also leaves, and the father–son duo eventually migrate to Delhi. There, they stay at Kingsway Camp for a while and are then allotted a home in Wazirpur in north Delhi.'

'It's just the two of them, father and son?'

Harleen nods. 'It's just the two of them now. Incidentally, when they arrived in Delhi, my great-grandfather began driving a *tonga* to make ends meet. He did this for less than a year, but the one detail that really touched my heart is that he named his horse Hamid. I found this very beautiful.' He smiles to himself before continuing, 'Father and son continued to live in Wazirpur for the next fifteen years, after which they moved to the newly developed suburb of Tilak Nagar in the '60s.'

Harleen finally folds his notes and, keeping them aside, now looks up at me.

'How do you know all this detailed family history?' I ask, genuinely curious.

'My grandmother used to tell me a lot of stories. I learnt that my great-grandfather was a World War I veteran and, during the centenary, I wanted to discover everything about his life. I reconnected with his extended family, found military records, and then his refugee card from Partition helped with dates and other details. But I've actually learnt a lot from the many meticulous documents that he used to keep. He left accounts, journals, letters. For instance, I own a letter written by him where he announces the birth of his son – my grandfather – and it is written in Landa script, of which Gurmukhi is now seen as a successor. But he was incredibly detailed in the descriptions of the house he lived in, the colour it was painted, what had been cooked at home at that point, what the weather was. It really is a treasure.'

Harleen's particularity for details appears a hereditary disposition, and the historian in me is almost envious of the rich family archive at his disposal. Now steering the conversation towards the present day,

I ask, 'I know that you have been to Pakistan, but did you manage to visit any ancestral sites?'

He smiles. 'The first time my family visited was in 2004, on a pilgrimage to see the sacred sites of Sikh history. But at the time I didn't know the deep connections my family had to Pakistan, and so it was, in some ways, a missed opportunity. We then made a second trip in 2008, which was more focused on ancestral history. In hindsight, though, I was quite afraid to travel across that first time...'

'Because of the media?' I wonder out loud.

'The media hysteria in India around Pakistan definitely did not help,' he agrees. 'But it was also 9/11, the 2001 Parliament attack in Delhi, the resounding conversations on terrorism, the issue of Kashmir, it was everything together. A week before we were to leave – the day our visa arrived, in fact – I locked myself in my room and insisted that I wouldn't go. You just build an image in your mind, flooded with everything you've heard on TV and read in the newspaper, even if you don't understand what it means or represents. Then, all of a sudden, you are going to Pakistan and telling your friends in school about it, and...' His voice trails off and he breathes in. 'Anyway, I think we were all a bit nervous, which was natural. But that first trip to Pakistan completely changed our opinions about everything,' he says with a wide smile. 'It was Baisakhi, and my mother really wanted to see Nankana Sahib, and so we ended up joining this huge *jatha* of pilgrims. We were lucky to have visited then, because many Sikh sites were still untouched and in pristine condition. So, I have incredibly fond memories of that first trip.'

'Did you walk across the border?'

'We took the Samjhauta Express,' he says, referring to the train service started in 1976 between Old Delhi in India and Lahore Junction in Pakistan via Attari and Wagah. In both Hindi and Urdu, the word *samjhauta* means agreement or accord, and in the spirit of bettering relations, the train was named such post the Shimla Agreement of 1972. But over the years the train service too has been compelled to follow the undulating and often difficult relationship between the two countries. The very first break in its service was in

January 2002, following the December 2001 Parliament attack in Delhi. The service resumed again in January 2004, merely months before Harleen and his family would have travelled on the train. Then, in December 2007, after the assassination of Benazir Bhutto, the service was suspended as a preventative measure, and twice again in 2019 – the final time in August, following the revocation of the special status given to Kashmir under Article 370 of the Indian Constitution, leaving 117 passengers stranded at Wagah. Along with the Samjhauta Express, the service of the Thar Express, which ran between Jodhpur in India and Karachi in Pakistan, was also discontinued.

'So, tell me about your trip,' I say to Harleen, living vicariously.

'Well, one of the most unforgettable experiences was the day we went to Gurudwara Panja Sahib in Hasan Abdal, Attock. It is a highly revered site because Guru Nanak's handprint is believed to have been imprinted on a boulder at the gurudwara. But Hasan Abdal is literally on the frontier of Punjab, and they did not have proper hotels in the region at the time, so we ended up staying in an old Khalsa high school. It was incredible, because all of a sudden the teachers and everyone who worked there became our hosts. We were welcomed with the local *dhol* and traditional music, with garlands around our necks and such a warm, loving ambience. We actually slept in the classrooms, where they had laid out *charpais* for us. The entire trip was so memorable.'

'Once you returned, did you feel a disparity between what the media was saying, or what you were learning at school, vis-à-vis what you had just witnessed first-hand?'

'I think the whole idea of how Pakistan had been portrayed was so removed from reality. It was like a fictional world. No country is without its shortcomings, I realize that, but our experience there was nothing like what I had expected it to be.'

'Is that one of the reasons you chose to begin research on a time before Partition?'

'I think it goes beyond just that … this is about my identity. I was schooled at St Francis de Sales, Janakpuri, which is a Malayali-dominated school in Delhi. When we had summer holidays, I remember how all my friends used to go back to their villages in south India. And when somebody asked me whether I'd be going to my village, I thought to myself, well, my maternal grandparents live in Delhi, my paternal grandparents live in Delhi, most of my extended family also lives in Delhi within a fifteen-minute radius of each other, where shall I go? Where is my village?'

This question, again and again and again.

'And I was not the only one, so many of my friends – Malhotras, Kapoors, Khannas, Minochas, all Punjabi Khatris – had the same story. They all had relatives in or around Delhi, but not much further, and certainly nowhere close to a two-day train journey to Trivandrum or Madras. So that question just took root in my brain. Where is our village, why don't we have a village? I would have been ten or twelve years old when I began asking my paternal grandmother about where we came from. And this became my first interaction with an elder who had seen Partition. The more we spoke, the more questions I had, and the more I wanted to preserve these parts of me, parts of my culture. I wanted to delve into history, understand the social history of pre-Partition Punjab – you know, collect personal stories, songs, poetry so that I could get to know a part of me *through* that.'

'I understand that,' I say, proud to share this feeling he describes.

'I know you do.' He smiles widely at me. 'And I know you will also understand when I say that for me one of the deepest connections to an undivided India is through the city of Lahore. Three of my four grandparents were from outside Lahore, but it's a city where they each spent considerable time. Listening to stories of the Walled City, of Mall Road, talking about the *parandi* that my grandmother bought from Anarkali Bazar and carried across the border ... it began a fascination with Lahore. And then, visiting the city, that first glimpse of Lahore railway station – the turrets, the fort-like structure – there's a romance to that image. My first memory of Lahore city is driving past a bridge on a foggy morning and looking out at the resplendent domes of the Badshahi mosque in the distance. Despite how young

I was in 2004, there was already a certain magic, a nostalgia, a familiarity attached to the city.

'The second thing that inspired me to learn about colonial Punjab, in particular, was the Pothwari folk songs my grandmother used to sing. She was a beautiful singer, and it was only when she passed away in 2009 that I realized what a custodian of culture she'd been. I then began speaking to her sister, who is still alive and in her nineties. I would call her and tell her that I wanted to learn their dialect, because I could not bear to see it disappear. Anytime I spoke to her, I could hear my grandmother – and the songs she used to sing – in her. I began connecting with people who lived in the Pothwar region of north-eastern Pakistan and realized what a wonderful place she'd been made to leave behind in 1947. How the music she played, the songs she sang, all reflected the topography of that region.'

'That's beautiful,' I say, tears forming in my eyes.

He smiles. 'It inspired me to look at the microhistories of rural Punjab, of women's lives.'

'The Lost Heer Project,' I deduce.

'Yes, the project actually began as an effort to document the folk songs sung by women. But as the research grew, I realized there was a considerable lack of women-centric narratives, particularly of the ordinary woman, in colonial history. If she is ever mentioned, it is as the daughter of so-and-so, or the wife of so-and-so; she's in the background, omitted even from family trees and genealogy charts that focus only on male members. There was such lack of representation that I knew I needed to do something. So, The Lost Heer documents the voices of women from colonial Punjab from 1849 to 1947 through storytelling, oral history, family anecdotes, archives, photographs and postcards, the popular literature of *qissas*, songs and poetry. But very often these are written in local languages like Gurmukhi or Urdu and so I began translating these as well, to make them accessible to anyone who may not speak that language. In any case, the farther we have moved from Partition, the more languages and dialects we have lost. I'm just trying to preserve as much as I can in the only way I know how.'

'The way you talk about your work – foraging, collecting, collating, detailing – it reminds me a lot of your great-grandfather!' I chuckle.

'I think so too,' Harleen says. 'He used to collect a lot of manuscripts and books – old books, new books. We know for a fact that he had a library called Kitaab Khana in his house, and whenever he would visit smaller villages or towns, he would pick up local lithographs or books of local poetry and *qissas*. After Partition, he continued to lament the loss of this great library in his Lahore home.'

Harleen's unique archive is an endowment for future generations and fills my heart with immense hope that even the minutiae of the past shall not disappear. It chronicles the pioneering participation of women in the fields of politics and education, music, drama and film, literature and travel in colonial India. Each of the protagonists is a role model, both for her time and in her enduring legacy – like Hardevi Roshan Lal, who was not only the first Punjabi woman to start her own magazine, *Bharat Bhagini*, but also the first to write a travelogue, *London ki Yatra*. Or the visionary Bibi Harnam Kaur, a teenage girl who ran the first Sikh girls' school, Sikh Kanya Mahavidyalaya, in Ferozepur in the early twentieth century. Despite being from a generation of women not allowed to leave their homes, she went from house to house – face uncovered – to convince parents to send their daughters to school.

He records stories of the earliest 'purdah party' in Lahore's Shalimar Garden, where the city's elite women belonging to 'purdah clubs' could host women-only parties, for both Indian and British women, whom they would otherwise not be able to socialize with due to purdah restrictions.[6] Using both found and archival photographs, he writes about how with the opening of the Lady Hardinge College Dispensary for women in Delhi in 1921, many female graduates from Punjab University could now study medicine.[7] The Lost Heer Project is a repository of painstaking and passionate research, one that remains elegantly untethered by the boundaries of religion, ethnicity, current citizenship or borders. At its heart is an undivided India, and picking up this thread I ask Harleen my final question.

'I'm curious, does anyone else in your family keep active ties to the other side in the way that you do?'

'Actually,' he begins, 'I learnt recently that we have family who remained in Pakistan during Partition. My grandmother's maternal grandmother and uncle stayed back and converted to Islam and probably have their own family there now. I wasn't shocked to learn this, because so many families were divided at Partition, but I'm very curious to know what they'd be like. No one has tried to look for them yet...'

'Would you want to?' I ask, aware of how this quiet detail allows the legacy of Partition to persist.

'Yes, of course. With a little effort, I hope I'll be able to find them. They are family, after all.'

ACTIVE CONVERSATION AMONG the various generations of a family is the simplest way to preserve the past – a way to ensure that things are not erased from memory, no matter how painful they may be to inherit. In the last several years – gaining particular impetus from the seventieth anniversary of Partition in 2017 – there have been renewed efforts by the third and fourth generations to archive and record family stories of the Great Divide. This is no easy task, to be the memory keeper, but it does often make one a proud bearer of their history. In this section, I speak with Yusra Rasool, who was born in 2002 in Sheikhupura, Pakistan, on her role as an accidental memory keeper.

'I spent most of my childhood abroad in Tanzania, East Africa, and never really got to speak to my grandparents – my paternal side passed away before I turned three, and my maternal grandfather died even before my mother grew up. So, the only person left behind was my maternal grandmother, whom we lovingly called ammi. We visited Pakistan twice a year on holiday, but at that young age we never asked ammi anything serious, and nor did she tell us. Then she passed away, so ... I never grew up in an environment of storytelling as others may have.'

Her voice betrays an obvious sadness, and I ask her how, if there was no one left, did she begin to gather family stories of Partition.

'I was only eleven when we moved back to Pakistan in 2013. At the time, many things needed to be relearned and remembered, many relations needed to be revived. Visiting our paternal village of Sheikhupura, which is an hour's drive from our home in Lahore, became a routine so that we could reconnect to our roots. It took a few years for me to realize that my grandfather's younger brother, Muhammad Hanif, whom everyone lovingly calls chachaji, was the only elder left in our family whom I could engage with, and even consider a friend. We only saw each other when I visited the village, but for the very first time since ammi, I felt the presence of a grandparent. And now that I was a bit older and more mature, I knew that I needed to make the most of this situation. I began to see a reflection of my own grandfather in chachaji. And though I could have hardly expected it, very soon, every conversation became about his life before Partition.'

'Do you remember how the conversations would begin?' I ask.

'I remember everything,' she asserts. 'I had just turned seventeen and we were at the village for Eid. It was while discussing our family tree that the topic of Partition surfaced. I always knew that my grandfather's family was from India but wasn't aware of any details. But that night, something triggered chachaji, who was born in 1928 in Undivided India, to narrate as many stories as he could. In fact, as far as I remember, we ended up so deep into the subject that he stayed up an hour or so past his bedtime. I think my initial reaction was a lot of simultaneous emotions: shock, because of the nature of the stories; laughter, because he wouldn't let anyone interrupt our conversation as he didn't want to break the momentum; and, of course, there was surprise at how deeply he was invested in the subject, to be able to engage with it for hours. Neither did he tire of narrating, nor did the stories finish. It may seem like a small thing for someone to stay up hours past their bedtime, but chachaji woke up for the Fajr prayer every single morning, so you knew that the discussion was important.'

After a while, she adds, 'This just became our routine on every subsequent trip – talking about Partition. Inevitably, ever car ride back to Lahore would be spent pondering over what I'd heard and wondering what I could do with the information that had been dumped on me.'

'Dumped?' I ask, having never heard that word in any conversation. 'Why do you say that?'

'I use that word carefully, after much consideration. I don't know how to explain it, except that I was still quite young; this was a lot of very intense information to receive. To be honest, in the beginning, it was so overwhelming that it felt like a load.'

I am struck by her answer and find myself relating to it more than I would like to admit. As an oral historian of Partition, one's role includes being the bearer of so many people's sadness and tragedies, memories and histories. But week after week, month after month, year after year, now nearing a decade, the testimonies have piled up. Whenever I have felt buried under the lives of others, I actively remind myself that to be able to listen to people's innermost fears and dreams is a privilege accorded only to those they may trust. And I am merely listening to the story, whereas they are living with its memory every day. As a result, every so often, I find myself brushing the heaviness aside, shaking it off, ignoring rather than confronting it, never quite able to admit that it feels like a load in the way that Yusra just has.

Taking a deep breath, I ask her now, 'Can you tell me about your family's migration in '47?'

'Chachaji's family belonged to Sujanpur, Punjab, not far from Jammu and Kashmir. He tells me that they migrated to Pakistan in the same way that the majority did – walking, or piling themselves on to crowded trains and bullock carts. They stopped a lot on the way, depending on the circumstances of the route, and they would take shelter in different places. One story my chachaji narrated was about how, when migrating, they had heard that Sikhs were killing everyone they found out was Muslim, so out of fear the elders decided to hide somewhere till things settled down. Luckily, they met a havildar at the train station who happened to also be Sikh but promised to keep them safe until things got better. He took the *entire* family to his house and let them stay the night. He kept them safe. A Sikh,' she repeats, 'he sheltered and fed my family. The same people that were out there killing us were also the ones protecting us.'

I smile, full of hope.

'It must have been so difficult to leave entire lives and childhoods behind and migrate to a completely new place. But imagine growing up and never being able to freely recount your childhood memories with anyone. This is what I fear most, which is why I became eager to know everything I could about my family.'

Yusra goes on to tell me that as she heard story after story, it dawned on her that though she may never be able to understand or fully grasp the horrors of what the family had witnessed, the conversation could not remain one-sided. And so began her research. The more she read, the more specific her questions became, making their storytelling sessions more detailed and surreal in nature. Soon, she began reading her material out to her granduncle.

'One day, I read out a chapter from Gulzar sahib's *Footprints on Zero Line*.[8] The story was in both English and Hindi, but since I couldn't read the Hindi, I narrated it to chachaji by translating the English into Urdu as best as I could. The story was called 'Crossing the Ravi' and was about a Sikh couple migrating from India to Pakistan, and how a haphazard decision made them lose both their children. That day, I saw chachaji cry for the first time. He tried to contain his tears but I saw them roll down his face. Never before, however horrific the memories he was relaying, had I seen him tear up – not when he told me about passing by a river and seeing hundreds of dead bodies covered in blood, not when he talked about how trains were looted in front of his eyes, not when he talked about having to leave his childhood home forever. Nothing made him cry like that story did. It amazed me how the supposed hatred between

Sikhs, Muslims and Hindus had led to this Partition, yet once again humanity had won over hatred and a devoted Muslim man felt an ache in his heart when he heard of a suffering Sikh family.'

Weeks later, as I read through this story, horror grips every bone in my body and I feel tears pricking my eyes. A pair of newborn twins, a hasty migration, and the butchered landscape of Partition haunt me.

'When chachaji was fourteen years old,' Yusra recounts another memory, 'he had a dream where he saw a river filled with blood and dead bodies. He got scared and told his father, my great-grandfather, about it but he just comforted his son and told him not to tell anyone else. This was in 1942, five years before Partition. When Partition was a certainty, bloodshed too became inevitable, and on the night of their migration, chachaji tells me, it felt like he was reliving his dream. He saw the exact same scenario play out in real life. Bloodshed, rivers full of dead bodies and so much more...'

I can understand now how these stories have overwhelmed her, for even in their second-hand retelling they are deeply vivid in the images they evoke. Turning our conversation towards the act of memory collection, I ask Yusra whether her chachaji ever speaks to anyone else in the family about Partition.

Brightly, she says, 'Since chachaji lives in a joint family with his sons and grandchildren, they've all just kind of spent their life huddled around his *charpai*, listening to his stories, so I'm definitely not the only person he has spoken to about Partition. However, I think I might be that one person he enjoys talking to the most, because the conversation is mutual; I listen and question and discuss, both what he tells me and what I've read on the subject.

'Where chachaji may differ from other people of his generation is in the fact that he doesn't believe in silencing these stories. He believes that they need to be passed down, no matter how difficult they may be to talk about or listen to. In our family, he's the last of his generation, so he knows that if he doesn't share his stories with us, they'll be lost once he's no longer around. I think that scares him.

He wants us to stay connected to our roots and remember where we're really from.'

'Despite being born on either side of the border, you and I feel the same pain, the same loss,' I observe. 'So, this can only mean that if we allow ourselves to look beyond the fortified identities of Indian or Pakistani, of Hindu or Muslim or Sikh, then there is only deep human learning to be found within these stories: that an event like Partition should never be repeated.'

'I think that's it,' she agrees. 'I've never experienced Partition or anything like it, but I've always questioned why it was necessary. And if it was necessary, then how come it left both sides with so much pain? Some things will never make sense to me but the things that do – the human aspects, the Sikh havildar, for instance – make me want to stay close to this subject for as long as I can. Partition should serve as a lesson, and I'm just playing my part in making sure that the memory of what life was like before this division remains.'

Ending on a hopeful note, Yusra alludes to the 'Generation Z' she belongs to. 'I think I would be extremely furious if I saw my generation trying to forget Partition. It can't be forgotten, nor should it be. I have faith in my generation.'

HAVING HOPED FOR long to speak in person but restricted by borders and visas, Anoosha Hameed, another member of Gen Z born in 2002, and I eventually settle for a video call. She has been keen for me to speak to her paternal grandfather, Sheikh Abdul Hameed, who was born and raised in Varpal village, district Amritsar, until he migrated to Pakistan at the age of six during Partition. Calling from Gujranwala, she tells me that she always felt like so much history had been created before she was born, but it was only through her grandfather's stories that she actually understood it.

'Varpal was mostly Sikhs and Muslims; we did not know many Hindus,' Hameed sahib recalls. 'In 1947, amidst the confusion of travelling from one city to another, I was separated from my parents.

They were left behind in Amritsar district, while I made my way to Tarn Taran with my uncle. From that moment on, for about two years, I didn't know where my family was, or whether they were even alive. My youngest sister had been born just two months before, and my other sister was four years old; I was six. In the trains, on the platforms, all we saw were cut-up dead bodies. The village we arrived at in Tarn Taran was blanketed in curfew during the days of Partition, and once the official line was announced, all the Muslim families were escorted to the border in a *kaafila*.'

'How many people were in the *kaafila*?' I interrupt him gently.

'Perhaps three hundred, at least,' he gauges. 'Making our way to the border at Kasur in what was now officially Pakistan, we walked through fields and never on the main road, until the locals told us that there were men hiding in fields, waiting to kill Muslim refugees.' He now snakes his hand in the air, creating a pathway. 'We then walked only on the road up to Kasur, in the heat and in the rain. So much rain, so much flooding. I had a single kurta-pajama, and only one pair of *juttis*.'

Anoosha, who has been quietly listening to her grandfather, now says, 'He was reunited with his family two years later, at a cousin's wedding in Faisalabad.'

With a smile, I ask Hameed sahib whether he remembers how he felt at that moment.

'*Ek ajeeb kisam ki khushi, jo hazm hi nahi ho rahi thi*, a strange and unbelievable happiness,' he recalls.

Now picking up on an altogether different thread, inspired by this cross-border conversation we are able to have, he brings up the examples of the USSR and East/West Germany. '*Mulk toot te bhi hain, mulk judte bhi hain*, countries break apart and they get back together. But the world has learnt from World War II, and Europe is now largely peaceful. Their borders are open, citizens can freely travel between countries.' He now clears his throat and asks me a question. 'Having witnessed the horrors of Partition as a child, having been separated from my family for years, if *I* can hold no ill will against anyone, then why can't India and Pakistan exist as friendly nations? Has enough time not passed to still be living in hatred?'

There is no answer to this question, and I think he knows it too. Wordlessly, I look at him through the computer screen.

'If those who lost home and land, family and friends to a single political decision can look towards peace rather than hatred, then what is stopping subsequent generations, who never witnessed this Partition, to extend the hand of hope? If we have to coexist as neighbours, then why not choose peace?'

I want to tell them that this is the crux of my work and that of so many other scholars. That out of conversation can be born empathy, and out of that perhaps even friendship. But it is not so easy, for we exist within the confines of politics and state.

But picking up on my thoughts, Hameed sahib now says with zeal, 'Justice is essential for common people, but so are the leaders who can provide that justice. I distinctly recall Vajpayee sahib's 1999 trip to Pakistan, and how he became the first Indian leader to visit Minar-e-Pakistan,[9] where the historic Lahore Resolution was passed in 1940.'

Beena Sarwar, the journalist, film-maker and Pakistan editor of the initiative 'Aman ki Asha',[10] writes:

> For Vajpayee to initiate a visit in homage to this spot speaks of his trademark humility ... It stemmed from his sincerity in building peace, but was also a consummate political move, in keeping with his great statesmanship ... Although Vajpayee's constituency was [the] Hindutva right wing, he was a realist. He had not only the moral courage but also the humility to be able to rise above his own ideology for the sake of the larger cause: peace between India and Pakistan, peace in the region.[11]

'Vajpayee sahib was a man of hope, a man with vision,' Hameed sahib states with conviction, though there is also deep sadness in his voice. 'Despite the staggeringly large number of people who died during Partition, we have not learnt any lessons from it. If Vajpayee sahib's leadership had remained, or more politicians thought like him on both sides of the border, the relationship between India and Pakistan would look quite different from what it is today.'

'What do we gain from war, anyway?' Anoosha now asks. 'Why don't we learn from tragedy?'

Her questions are simple, perhaps even naïve, but they are pertinent.

'What I learnt in school and what I heard at home were polar opposite views,' she continues. 'In our textbooks, there is hatred, but in my grandfather's memories there is only love, or at least a hope for love.'

Now going through my notes, I say, 'Hameed sahib, Anoosha tells me that you have visited India several times since Partition. Did you go home?'

Home, a word that can sometimes mean a land now far away, separated by a border.

His face breaks into a wide smile. 'The last time I went back to my village was in 2006. Have you ever been to Varpal?' I shake my head and so he continues, 'It had become a *pakka shehr* by then and so much had changed, but the boundary wall of my home still stood. I met my uncle's class fellows, spoke with many older people who were alive at Partition, and made some new friendships too. Now nearly fifteen years have passed, and after speaking to you, I feel as though I have gone back home again. I can see the village, the sky, the trees ... *sab aankhon ke saamne aa gaya.*'

My heart swells with happiness as I hear this.

'Tell me, *beta,* if Pakistanis and Indians can evoke this sense of familiarity within one another – if a young Indian girl who has never been to Varpal can remind an old Pakistani man of its every lane and field by the sheer virtue of being Indian – then why should we exist in conflict rather than peace? Our borders are not just joined, they are conjoined.'

He then brings his palms together, as if one.

10
Identity

'WITHOUT [THE RIVER INDUS,] Sindh would have been entirely desert,' wrote Roger Pearce in his memoir as an Indian Civil Service officer in the region from 1938 to 1948.[1] It is the stories of this mighty river and the land it nourishes that the fashion designer Karan Torani, who was born in Delhi in 1993, grew up listening to – the very same stories that his paternal grandmother, who was merely months old when she migrated from Thatta in Sindh to Bhuj in Gujarat via boat and further north to Delhi, had probably been told in her childhood. Stories of a 'vanished homeland'[2] across the border.

I first meet Karan when he invites me to his design studio in Shahpur Jat in south Delhi to talk about Partition, a topic that I have deposited into literary work and he into sartorial. Only a few months ago, his eponymous label, *Torani*, entered the luxury fashion market, and though I admit I know little about the Indian fashion industry, I am intrigued. So, on a hot summer evening, I find myself seated in a small office on the ground floor that holds a clothes rack against one wall and pinboards mounted across the rest.

On the boards are photographs of traditional hand-operated Ferris wheels by the beach, and of children wearing Sindhi *topis*. There are various samples of running embroidery, vintage postcards sent at Eid, spindles with pink, yellow and white threads, and a collection of metallic coins and tassels. There are swatches of rose-coloured chintz and desert-coloured silk pinned to the board and, placing my finger inside a mounted embroidery hoop, I graze the sequined pattern of a fish – the same fish shape that can be found in the traditional Jalani leather *juttis* in Sindh and Bhuj. This mood board for the most recent collection, Gulabi Mela, demonstrates how inextricably the landscape of Karan's ancestors is woven into his brand: mythology, history and memory translating into iconography, pattern and drape.

'Each collection inevitably derives elements from Sindh,' he says. 'Growing up in Delhi, I could never speak about the culture I came from because it wasn't the dominant Punjabi culture of the city. After Partition, Hindu Sindhis found themselves dispersed across the world, with no connection to their lands that remained in Pakistan. And within my age group, Sindhis were either unknown or seen as caricatures. So, somehow the Sindhi identity that we celebrated at home, or the language we spoke with such pride, never found a place in public discourse. I was always made to feel like our story was not special, but of course *I knew* that it was.'

Part ethnography, part nostalgia, Karan embarks on the history of his people. 'The indigenous tribes of Sindh were either fishermen or river folk, or worked with their animals in the desert. Their lives were tied to their land, often leaving them at the mercy of the great Indus river, which made them adaptable people. They migrated and travelled extensively, and were in turn influenced by other cultures, like those of Punjab or Kashmir. But one of the most beautiful elements of Sindh is that the communities were identified by land and not religion.[3] This is something my dadi often repeats: that you could be a Hindu or a Muslim or a Sikh, but above all you were Sindhi. Hindu Sindhis are followers of Jhulelal, the sea god, who is regarded to be an incarnation of the deity Varuna, but the Hinduism practised in Sindh is influenced deeply by Sikhism, Sufism and Islam.[4] Naturally, this confluence settled into the clothing of the region as well.

'Traditionally, their garments were loose robes, like a *choga*, which can be considered a Sindhi version of a Kashmiri *pehran*. The Sindhi *cholo* is reminiscent of the *angrakha kurta*, tied at the front, and can extend down to the knees. There were *lehenga-cholis*, still worn in various parts of Sindh and Gujarat, or the *ghaghra*, a heavier version of the *lehenga*, with a backless *choli*. There were *abha kurtas* with beautiful, large yokes embellished with tribal coins or beaten mirrors, and *chokdi salwars* similar to the Punjabi Patiala *salwar*. And, of course, there is the Sindhi *topi*, often handwoven, mirrored and embroidered, and the *koti*, which is a sleeveless jacket. These are some traditional elements I've celebrated in my collections.'

As a writer of pre-Partition material history, I find this foray into historical garments an elegant way to 'wear' one's ancestral identity. I think about the pleasure I take in draping even a machine-made Punjabi *phulkari dupatta*, or wearing my nani's peacock bracelet that her father bought in the 1930s in Lahore, or weaving a *parandi* into my hair during a family wedding. The very act of depositing history into textile or accessory – even objects that aren't heirlooms, yet are created with the same intention – makes them precious items. When I look through Karan's collection, this is the sentiment I find, and am curious to know how he first learnt of the landscape his family left behind.

He smiles warmly. 'In the same way that many of us did – through stories. As a child, I would sleep in my dadi's room, and all the bedtime stories she would tell were from Thatta. They were not well off to begin with but, once in Delhi, the family became extremely poor and her father sold fruit from a stall in Lajpat Nagar. The two-storey house they lived in was the same one I grew up in as well. Then, after I graduated university, long before I set up a brand or a business, I spent months in Kutch – perhaps the geographic and linguistic terrain closest to Sindh in India – learning mirror-work and *rabari* embroidery from the artisans there.

'But the imagery, colours and sentiment behind each piece are either born out of my dadi's stories of Thatta or from my mother, who belongs to a Sindhi family of Bhopal. For instance, in Sindh, my dadi's father and grandfather were fisherfolk and, alongside fish, they would collect drinkable freshwater in earthen pots, *matkas*. This was the only water drunk at home – ten *matkas* filled at a time.

Once empty, the family would wait for one of the menfolk to refill them. This image of ten *matkas* finds a place in Gulabi Mela, which is a romantic ode to the fairs that took place across Sindh during the Cheti Chand festival in the spring, marking the Sindhi New Year.'

I note how the symbol of water – the river Indus or Sindhu in particular – also secures prominence in *Torani*'s visual landscape. From the choice of gossamer fabrics to the undulating wave-like pleats of *ghaghras*, she is ever present. Born from the mighty Himalayas, deified in the Rig Veda, raising ancient civilizations, she nurtures the land of Sindh and finds a place in the memories of those who once fled it.

As I make this observation to Karan, he concurs almost immediately.

'She is ever present,' he says, 'a natural extension of my Sindhi identity.'

'YOU COULD SAY that my father has always donned a dual identity,' the Brooklyn-based artist Sheba Remy Kharbanda says thoughtfully. 'On the one hand, he is very invested in the Republic of India and served in the Indian Police Service (IPS) his entire life. He never even moved to join us in London, where the rest of the family lived and I was born in 1978. But on the other hand, he continues to identify as an Afghani Sikh and holds that heritage close. And I think I just took this duality for granted my entire childhood. But it was only in 2005, some time after he had retired from the police force and I was doing some documentary film work, that he began to share details of what these identities really meant to him.'

Sheba's father, Amrik Singh, was born in 1938 in Landi Kotal, which now falls in the Khyber Pakhtunkhwa (then the North-West Frontier) Province of Pakistan, at the western edge of the Khyber Pass into Afghanistan. His family lived between Kabul and Peshawar. In November 2014, using the interviews she had conducted with her father, Sheba created an installation called *Five Rivers: A Portrait of*

Partition, which illustrated the intimate complexities of 'home' and was on display at the India Habitat Centre in Delhi.[5] Staged inside a traditional Indian wedding tent, a cycloramic screening married a video interview of Singh, flanked by images of the landscapes he grew up in: lush rivers, scenic valleys and desolate mountain ranges. In the interview, Singh admits that any memories of Kabul have been passed down to him by his parents and elder sister, but Peshawar he recalls clearly. The family were traders and their immediate circle mostly comprised Muslim Pathans.

Smiling, she says, 'Most of my father's stories mentioned this sort of conviviality, of the glory days of undivided India, how even his father's turban would be tied in the Peshawari way with a very distinct pleated fan-like *turra*, how they only spoke in Pashto. Partition became the seminal and inexplicable event that drove them out of the region that all of their previous generations had inhabited.

'My father was nine years old when they left before the actual date of Partition, taking only their personal possessions. They left the keys of their home and business premises with a co-worker, as they were sure they would return. They took a train to a Punjab, where they stayed at a refugee camp for a while. But, unaccustomed to the heat of the plains, they made their way further upwards, to present-day Himachal Pradesh, and settled in Shimla, which is where he still lives and where his parents died. But, mind you,' she adds, 'they never imagined they'd be leaving the Frontier for good.'

In the video installation, Amrik Singh speaks about how much of their wealth was left behind. Sheba reiterates that there was only so much they could regain in India, and her father being the eldest son had to look for a government job, which would provide financial security. Despite not being entirely inclined towards it, he passed the civil services exam and was recruited into the IPS.

'While you were interviewing your father, did you discover things you didn't expect?' I ask her.

She smiles. 'Of course. I always knew the skeleton, but I discovered the nuances, the details. I learnt just how much he was holding on to his Afghani Sikh identity on an emotional level. And just the sheer power of memory – though so many years had passed, he was still in Kabul, still in Peshawar; in his heart, in his mind, he could be transported back instantly. Through those conversations, I began to understand how immense that experience of belonging to the Frontier had been, and how important it was for him to retain that identity and merge it with his Indianness.'

Returning to a small detail from earlier on, I say, 'Sheba, you mentioned that you were born in London, yet your father never moved there to join the family...'

She nods. 'That's right. I'll talk about my mother's story later on, but she had been in the UK since the 1960s and loved London. But my father loved India. So, to be honest, it didn't make sense when I was growing up, but it makes complete sense now because of their personalities. And as radical and unconventional as it was, I'm happy that they were able to do what they needed to,' she smiles, 'because women don't normally get to make these choices. But returning to my father, he's not so much a nationalist as ... well, his mixed identity cannot be understood anywhere else but there.'

'But in India, you mean?'

'Yes, in a post-Independence India,' Sheba clarifies. 'His nationality was Indian, but his ethnicity was very specifically Afghani Sikh, and at that time he didn't have trouble blending the two. Their confluence felt natural. But it was during the time I was interviewing him that he started to question whether these two identities were even compatible any more. The politics of the world, of the subcontinent, had changed so drastically over the past few decades, and a sense of finality had begun to take shape. He realized that he would likely never see the places of his childhood again. His identity, as a Sikh and a former IPS officer, made it both unsafe and also politically complicated for him to return to the Frontier. The region has changed and anyone he might have known has likely passed on or been forced to leave. So, the Peshawar and Kabul that he had nurtured in his imagination – the fruit trees, the mountain air, the culture, all that he'd been holding on to – was...' she shrugs.

'It was the imagined landscape of the past,' I whisper, 'which didn't match up to the present.'

'Precisely,' she says sadly. 'And as he was recollecting, there emerged a definitive sense of an ending.' There is a short pause as Sheba looks around the room pensively. 'Partition very naturally took centre stage in these conversations. For me, it became a threshold moment, not just as a line drawn on paper or drawn in the land, but a line drawn through bodies. I understand it as a split that we are still living with. And yes, people like me, in the diaspora, are living with more splits because we are even further away from the partitioned lands. But somehow that split has been easier to navigate than the other split.'

'You mean the split of Partition is still not easy to navigate?'

'*I* feel that way,' she reflects, 'since both my families held on to their pre-Partition identities to some extent. You know, growing up in the UK, navigating being Indian Punjabi yet being influenced so deeply by the Frontier and its culture, and then growing up alongside Pakistani Punjabis ... it was a strange and complicated feeling. And people would always want to classify us: "Are you Indian? Are you Pakistani?" But my mother, she's such a worldly person. She would tell us as children that we were only Punjabi and the Punjab we belonged to was borderless.'

'That's ... extraordinary,' I say with awe.

Sheba nods. 'It's interesting, because she was born in India in 1950, but in a family whose soul was inextricably linked to the other side of the border.'

And with that, Sheba embarks on the tale of her maternal family's migration.

'It is from my mother that I've inherited these stories, particularly of her mother, Vidwant Kaur, whom I call biji. She died in 1970, and I was born eight years later, but I've always been able to see her in spirit. She was born in the 1920s to a mother who died in childbirth and a father who soon remarried and left her to be raised by her grandmother. A part of her early life was spent in Burma, and she was married to my grandfather, who was originally from the North-West Frontier Province but had factories in Karachi. Biji was an artist, a homeopath, a musician, a deeply creative woman who was never really allowed to practise her art. But all of the grandchildren on this side of the family have inherited some form of her creativity.

'Anyway, at the time of Partition, the couple was living in Lahore with their three children. They migrated to Ludhiana, because other family members had already moved there. My grandfather was allotted a house but – and I'm sure you've heard many stories like this – the bodies of the former occupants were still in it. Strewn in the house. Their belongings were still in it too. My great-grandfather immediately refused to live there.'

'Wait, w-what do you mean the bodies were still … there?' I ask, fumbling over my sentence.

Sheba stares at me, speaking without saying anything.

'I've never heard a story like this,' I manage to release the words very slowly.

'Never?'

'Never.'

'Well, it was from one day to the next, I suppose. The family were in the house the day before. Alive, they were alive. And then the next day, they were … they had been … and their things were still in there. But my grandparents just couldn't start a new life there and rented a place instead of accepting this one, which had been given in a claim.'

It takes me a few minutes to return to my notes and, clearing my throat, I ask, 'Did they regain a sense of belonging once in India?'

'Well, my mother, who was born in and spent the first twelve years of her life in Ludhiana city, feels Indian. But I have to wonder whether it's because she's been in the UK for so long now that she needs an anchor that is familiar. I don't think her parents ever felt like they belonged to an independent India, which is probably why they didn't last very long there. They were always harking back to a pre-Partition India where they could move around unrestricted. The way I've come to think about this is that moving to India, being ejected from their part of Punjab, was the death knell for them, and they could never settle. When I write about my grandparents' story, I use the expression "they couldn't settle".

'If I wanted to paint a picture, it would be of a boat which is never anchored. They migrated in 1947 and my grandfather left in the late '50s for Latin America to do business but ended up working in Chile as a farm hand. He thought he could settle the family in the Americas but soon realized how lawless it was and ended up in the UK. After a few years, he decided that that was where he was going to raise his children, because...' Sheba sighs, 'they could never really find a foothold in India. So, in 1962, the family moved to London and became British citizens, keeping their sojourn as Indians very brief.'

'And how do you identify?' I wonder.

'Well, my cousins – all but one – and I were born in London, and we feel like Londoners, and that identity is maybe a little different from just being British because London is like a microcosm of the world, in a way. And I thank my grandfather every time I land on London soil because it *makes sense*. But it didn't make sense to my grandmother. She died only eight years after arriving in England, and my mother – being the poetic person that she is – would say that biji died of a broken heart. I don't think the move was good for my grandmother. It was very, very hard. It felt like everything, just every last possible thing, had been taken away from her. But, for my aunts and my mother, it was like being freed. My mother, especially, grew to become incredibly independent and resilient. She taught me that *I was of the world*.' Sheba pauses and gestures to herself. 'Personally, I say I'm subcontinental. Having grown up with Pakistanis, Afghanis, Nepalis and Bangladeshis, I have a kinship with the entire region. But I do feel like I am carrying my family's memories ... they don't let me go.'

In 2005, Sheba made an eleven-minute documentary short called *The Vilayati Tarti/Foreign Land Project*[6] which chronicled 'the story of women, mostly Punjabi women, who, in the decades following the Partition of India, left for England in search of work and found themselves in Southall, a town in the outer suburbs of West London' that eventually came to be known as Little Punjab or Little India. It opens with the landscape of desolate fields and sunrises and sunsets in the easily recognizable plains of Punjab. A ballad plays in the background and a woman's voice narrates a monologue in Punjabi. The captions at the bottom of the screen read: 'The Punjab of five rivers / You have thrown us across the seven seas / Gladly we lived in your soil, barely we survived day and night / We are neither here, nor there / We left the sun-warmed soil / We have fallen on land that remains forever cold.'

The film is based on audio and video interviews and having watched it long before I speak to Sheba, I'd always assumed that one of the women in it was her grandmother. But the night before our conversation, my eye catches the description where Sheba writes that the project is 'inspired by my maternal grandmother who lived and died in Southall'. With this in mind, I ask her, 'Do you think you may have wanted to speak to your biji about her life?'

'Biji was a remarkable woman, but she never got to tell her own story,' Sheba acknowledges. 'The women I spoke to, who migrated probably at the same time she did, didn't necessarily always want to speak about Partition. There was so much reluctance to approach the subject that it made me realize maybe she wouldn't have wanted to either. But what made *Foreign Land* possible was the interview I did with my father; how he just sat in front of the camera and talked. Similarly, I let these women talk, free-form, whatever they wanted to share. They would tell me how when they first arrived in the UK, they couldn't get masalas, or how cold it was...' Sheba chuckles.

I nod, smiling widely. 'My nana, who migrated to Canada in the late '50s, says the same thing about masalas. There were no desi stores in those days, so whenever he or any of his friends would visit their families in India, they would return to Canada with one suitcase full of only dals and masalas!'

Still smiling, Sheba continues, 'Through our conversation, I'd explain to these women that my generation was trying to understand Partition, and then they would – as an offering, almost – excavate the memories. In their words, I found reflections of what could have been biji's story...'

I sit back in my seat, smiling. There is sincerity and tenderness in Sheba's words.

'If we don't tell our stories, they get clammed up and they can manifest,' she says. 'Scientists are now discovering what all can exist in our DNA, and it's remarkable. There is illness that lives in our DNA, there is trauma that lives in our DNA. But I'm not a scientist, so all I can offer is humanity, empathy. It's that function of storytelling, which is so innate that it connects us to one another as a form of catharsis.'

'Our identities exist in the stories we pass down,' I note, meeting her gaze.

TO LEARN ABOUT identity forged and negotiated by the multiple migrations triggered by Partition, I speak with Tahara Anderson, who was born in 1976 in New York, and her father, Dr Mohammad Ashraf Hasan, who was three years old when his family migrated from India to Pakistan in 1947 and then to America in 1976. Hasan sahib's father lost his father at the age of fourteen and had to begin working. Highly intelligent, he taught himself to read and write and, by the time Hasan sahib was born, ran a successful hosiery business in Ludhiana. The family comprised the couple and three children, of which my interviewee was the middle child, with two sisters.

'When Partition was announced, we had to leave behind *everything*,' he emphasizes, 'our business, our home, and we left with just a few rupees in our pocket. There were threats to our life – "You are Muslim, you need to go to Pakistan. Go away!" we were told – and we took these threats seriously, because it was in this way that my mother's brother-in-law was arrested on false charges. Someone had placed guns in his house and the police came and arrested him. So, we and my aunt's family made our way to the train station of Ludhiana, but there was hardly any room inside the compartment. We packed ourselves into the crowd, and my father sat on the roof of the train.'

Hasan sahib speaks in a mixture of Urdu and English, but mostly English so that Tahara understands. She watches him as he reaches his arm above his head, gesturing to the roof of the packed train.

'Do you remember the journey?' I ask him.

'I don't remember anything,' he says, clicking his tongue. 'I am only telling you what has been passed down to me. My father used to hear rumours about entire trains full of people being slaughtered – I'm sure you know the stories – and these remained at the back of his mind. Our train had left Ludhiana and was making its way towards Lahore when it suddenly stopped in the middle of a field. From both sides of the track, men with swords and knives, guns and other weapons ran towards the compartments, wanting to kill everyone – all the Muslims going to Pakistan. Sitting on the roof, my father witnessed this terrifying scene unfold and said his last prayer. But, thankfully, two soldiers who were stationed inside the train forced the driver to begin the engine again and we survived.

'On reaching Lahore, we were taken to a refugee camp. My mother was originally from a place deeper inside Pakistan called Gojra, about 70 miles from Lahore. Every morning, my father would leave the camp, he had no shoes or anything, and walk to the railway station to stand on the platform where the train from Gojra arrived. He was looking for a familiar face, anyone from my mother's family … you see, no one had telephones in those days. One day, he met a man from Gojra and asked him to deliver a message to the family about where we were. The very next day, my mother's brother found us and took us to Gojra with him. That is where I grew up.'

Tahara leans in and whispers something in her father's ear and he nods.

'My younger sister was just a year old at the time,' he recalls. 'She had gastroenteritis, was dehydrated throughout the journey, and people said to my mother, "Discard her. *Discard*. Leave her here, she won't survive the migration." But my mother simply refused,' he chuckles. 'She's still alive and well, my sister!'

'Hasan sahib, when you were young and living in Pakistan, were stories of Partition told?'

'Well, my father would always speak about his home…'

'What did he say?'

'It was longing. He longed for Ludhiana. The place where he grew up and had lived most of his life. He compared life in Pakistan with what had been left behind. But he was not longing for India or anything like that, only Ludhiana. You understand the difference, right? And I never shared this longing. I always thought that Partition was the right thing to do. It was the right thing. I always say to my children,' he adds, gesturing to Tahara, 'that had I been in India, had we not come to Pakistan, I'd never have become a doctor. Migrating to Pakistan gave me an equal opportunity to succeed. In the country that was mine, I could go on to do whatever I wanted. I feel this deeply.'

'You mean, it may not have been the case if you were still living in India?' I ask to confirm.

'Yes, as a Muslim, it would not have been the case,' he says, nodding purposefully. 'Having read history and watched how the present has unfolded for Muslims and other minorities in India, I think that the demand for a separate state, for Pakistan, was the right thing to do. I am one of the beneficiaries of that decision, and I take pride in my Pakistani identity.'

Making a note of his words, I now turn to Tahara, who has grown up as a first-generation American. 'When was the first time you heard the word Partition?'

'Funnily enough,' she begins, 'my father would tell us stories of his life in Pakistan, but never about Partition. Then in the late '90s or early 2000s, I read a book called *A Fine Balance* by Rohinton Mistry and it talked about ethnic violence and refugee camps. Now, I grew up in New York with a Pakistani father and a Brooklyn-born American–Italian mother, and my brothers and I were really one of a kind. I would try to seek out things from my father, but I didn't know how to begin. So, I would reach for books, even if they weren't by Pakistanis. After I'd read a little, I decided to broach the subject with my father again, and only then did he tell me about Partition. I was … well, I was amazed that I was in my mid twenties and hadn't known that such a thing had happened in his life. My father has so much knowledge, but he doesn't always share it easily; one has to draw it out.' She pauses. 'He likes to tell me how they'd catch bees as children and try to fight them. I've heard that story many, many times. But Partition, *that* took a long time to emerge.'

'Why do you think that was?'

She shrugs. 'I don't know...'

'I can tell you that,' Hasan sahib cuts in. 'I thought they weren't interested. They were American kids!'

Tahara turns towards her father. 'I can't speak for my brothers, but being biracial and visibly different from people around you, I am constantly trying to figure out who I am. And there may always be questions that I won't have answers to. When I was in Pakistan last, my father showed me the monument erected at the place where Muhammad Ali Jinnah declared that there will be a Pakistan.'

'Minar-e-Pakistan, at Iqbal Park, in 1940,' I say.

She nods. 'Exactly. I want to be able to tell *my* sons these stories. I want them to know this part of their history, this monumental event that made their family Pakistani and gave my father the opportunities to pursue a better life.'

'I thank my lucky stars that we moved to Pakistan,' Hasan sahib repeats, 'for a better future.'

Agreeing with her father, Tahara tells me, 'My boys, they're only nine and twelve, but I hope that they eventually reach that path of discovery, just as I did. It's amazing the memories your brain can hold on to. I was in Pakistan as a child, and then again nineteen years later, and I remembered the smells – of the city, of my grandmother. When I'd flown back to America on my last visit, I felt like I was leaving behind a part of me "home" in Pakistan, and those memories stay with you. I want my sons to know that feeling.'

'And Ludhiana? Do you want to go to where your grandfather belonged?' I ask.

She smiles. 'I will go everywhere. My father may no longer have associations to India, but it is still a part of his history, which means it is a part of mine. The first time I watched something about Partition which wasn't a historical documentary was an episode[7] of *Doctor Who*. She's a Time Lord, who in this particular episode travels back to the moment of India's Partition along with her companions. One of them, Yasmin, witnesses her grandmother's tragic past as a Muslim woman whose brief marriage to a Hindu man is ruptured by the violence of Partition, making that relationship a secret that she never speaks of to anyone ever again. By going back in time with Doctor Who, Yasmin sees this event with her own eyes, and yet she's left with so many questions that she can never ask her grandmother in real time. I found myself thinking about my father and how, when he is sadly gone, I will no longer have that primary source of information. I also wondered how many stories there were like Yasmin's grandmother's – a future that could not be because of the division between Muslims and Hindus.'

'THE PARTITION IN the east wasn't just one partition but several – not only between various religious but also ethnic groups – whose consequences have unfolded slowly over time,' Samrat Choudhury explains. A novelist and journalist, he has been introduced to me by another mutual writer friend, Janice Pariat. 'The first was the separation of Burma from British India in 1937, which partitioned the Mizos, Nagas, some Manipuri communities, and the tribes of Arunachal Pradesh between two administrations, damaging both relations between people as well as trade.[8] The second was the 1947 partition of Bengal and Assam on the basis of religion following the drawing of the Radcliffe Line. The third was the separation of Bangladesh from Pakistan in 1971, which also affected north-east India and West Bengal.'

Ever the scholar, Samrat is careful and methodical in constructing the political context for his family's migration post the partition of British India. 'But there were other complications in the east as well, for almost till the end, till May 1947, there was a very strong movement for a united and independent Bengal, to avoid Partition.

H.S. Suhrawardy, the then premier of the province and leader of the Muslim League, along with Subhas Chandra Bose's brother Sarat Bose, appealed to people to set aside religious differences to retain an undivided Bengal.[9] The Bengali Dalit leader Jogen Mandal threw in his lot with M.A. Jinnah and became the first Law Minister of Pakistan, so his supporters also stayed back in East Pakistan in 1947. These are just some stories of Partition which got subsequently buried. Largely buried, not completely.

'And when we speak of Partition in the north-east, the border of India and what is now Bangladesh is a very long one, 4,100 kilometres long.' He snakes his palms. 'Only two small sections of it are with Assam, one where the Brahmaputra curves around the Garo Hills of Meghalaya, and another further east where a portion of the Barak Valley of Assam near Tripura borders Bangladesh. I think that's broadly the structure of it.'

It doesn't surprise me that the geography of the region is imprinted in his mind, for Samrat has spent the past several years navigating and writing about the lands that touch the braided Brahmaputra.[10]

'And your family,' I ask, 'where are they originally from?'

'My maternal side is from Mymensingh and my paternal side from Sylhet, which was once a part of Assam. My mother was born in 1950, but my father was actually born in 1942, and his parents passed away very soon after their migration to India at the time of Partition. In July 1947, a referendum took place in Sylhet, a Muslim-majority Bengali-speaking district of Assam, which in turn was a Hindu-majority province dominated by Assamese speakers. The referendum was to decide whether Sylhet would remain in Assam, and become a part of India, or leave Assam to join Pakistan. It was unique, because Partition was on the basis of Hindu- and Muslim-majority provinces, not districts, and there were no other district-level referendums of this kind, not even in Bengal or Punjab. It happened because of the complications of local politics in Assam, where there was a rivalry between Assamese and Bengali leaders, in addition to that between Hindu and Muslim leaders. After a close and hotly contested vote, ultimately Sylhet was given to Pakistan – except for a part of the Karimganj subdivision in the Sylheti-dominated Barak Valley. The referendum result led to a massive influx of Hindu Sylhetis into various parts of the Indian north-east,[11] but trouble had already started before this. So, I'm not exactly sure when the family fled – my father is a bit vague about these things...' Samrat sighs, 'but the gist of the story is that they came shortly after Partition. My father's eldest brother was much older and was already working in the Garo Hills in a place called Baghmara in Meghalaya.'

'Which borders present-day Bangladesh,' I confirm.

'That's right, it was basically the nearest place they could migrate to, where they had close family. My father was really young, five years old, so I haven't heard any stories from him beyond those about growing up in Baghmara, and how despite living in India he continued to go to school in East Pakistan.'

I raise my eyebrows, and Samrat smiles. 'Even though the border had been drawn, it hadn't hardened. Even now it isn't as hard as, say, the western border with Pakistan; it remains porous, but back then it was even more so, allowing for casual movement.[12] The stories my father tells are about how he used to walk across the border to the nearby missionary school every day, and how they swam in the beautiful Simsang river in Baghmara, which is called Someshwari in Bangladesh.'

'Is it easy to go back and forth?' I ask.

He shakes his head. 'Not any more, no. You need passports and visas. But there was a time in 2003 when I had breakfast in Shillong, where I was born, and lunch in Sylhet, where my father was born. He has never gone back, though. It's just across the border, and I've asked him many times, but he doesn't want to. My mother would like to visit Mymensingh, but my father carries bitterness about Partition.'

'In what way?'

'Well, he lost his parents soon after and blames it on the fact that they lost everything and came across with pretty much nothing, and then his father had a stroke and passed away without proper medical attention. His mother didn't survive the trauma either, so my father grew up an orphan. He blames it on Partition, what it did to the family – physically and emotionally. That's where the bitterness stems from. But he never used to talk about it. It pops out sometimes nowadays, because of the current Hindu–Muslim politics, and things like NRC and CAA.

'The only person who spoke about it was my maternal grandmother. There were things she'd say that I wouldn't understand as a child. She always talked about the *desher bari*. That's the word she used, *desher bari*, which translates to "the home in the country". Slowly, I realized that all her stories were of nostalgia. This great, great nostalgia! About how wonderful everything was and how beautiful their life used to be, with fields of rice, paddy and sugarcane, and ponds full of fish. How lush and green the landscape was. The stories I got were of a...' he pauses and smiles warmly, 'a rural utopia. A utopia that they'd been forcibly driven out of. But, to be honest, I didn't bother about it too much, I didn't really try to find out more.'

When I ask why, Samrat leads me to the political landscape of north-east India, where he was born in 1975, drawing a line from Partition to the present day.

'Why did the National Register of Citizens, which came to national and public light just a few years ago, start in Assam and nowhere else?' he asks me. 'For that, we need to go back to Partition. As I mentioned earlier, after the controversial and unique referendum that separated Sylhet from India in 1947, Bengali-speaking Hindu Sylhetis came pouring across the border into Assam. This created discomfort within Assam, in politics and government, about the large refugee population that ultimately settled there. The NRC was specifically attempted for Assam state for the first time in 1951 to draw up a list of citizens and close the doors on future illegal migration into the state, particularly from East Pakistan.[13] At that time, it was mainly Hindus who were migrating from there to here. That NRC didn't really work, but the anxiety about the influx of refugees remained and in subsequent years led to riots against Bengalis who had migrated from what became East Pakistan. The movement was initially called Bongal Kheda, which means "Drive out the Bengalis". When riots broke out, my father was in college in Jorhat, Assam, and he had to flee for his life.'

In *The Economic Weekly*, a piece from 30 July 1960 titled 'Bongal Kheda Again', comparing these riots in Brahmaputra Valley in Assam with the 1946 Direct Action Day riots in Calcutta, clarifies,

> Outside Assam, an Assamese is one who lives in Assam, whatever may be his mother tongue. In Assam, however, Assamiyas or Assamese are those who speak Assamiya ... The non-Assamese are those natives of Assam ... whose mother tongue is not Assamiya or Assamese. They include the Bengalis of Cachar and Goalpara, the Hindi-speaking tea plantation labourers and the hill people like the Khasis of Shillong. Besides these ... there are many Bengalis, mostly from East Bengal, who have settled in all the important towns of the Brahmaputra Valley. Some are displaced persons from East Bengal.[14]

The piece further illuminates that that the word *Bongal* is used not only to refer to a Bengali alone, but 'embraces all outsiders'. The Bongal Kheda movement, 'sponsored by Assamese job seekers', sought to drive out 'non-Assamese competitors'. During these riots that occurred in towns like Guwahati, Tezpur, Jorhat, Nowgong, Dibrugarh and so on, the violence included assault and stabbing, burning of homes and looting of property, and extended even to students, drawing out people like Samrat's father from the Agricultural College of Jorhat, where he was studying.

Part scholar, part storyteller, he continues, 'My father fled to Shillong and restarted his education at St. Anthony's College and then stayed on, found a job, got married, and that is where I was born. It was also a place where many Bengalis migrated after Partition, because Shillong was the capital of undivided Assam including Sylhet and, for six brief years from 1905 to 1911, the capital of undivided Assam and East Bengal. It was the summer capital and Dhaka the winter one. There were Bengali-speaking families who had associations to Shillong much before Partition, when it was a cosmopolitan place. But post Partition, the imagination of the place began to narrow, and it too gradually became more exclusionary and came to be seen as a homeland of the indigenous Khasi, Jaintia and Garo tribes. We never owned a house there, because we are non-tribal and aren't allowed to buy land.

'Anyway, throughout the 1960s and '70s, these riots became more and more organized and the Bongal Kheda movement transformed into the Bideshi Kheda movement, which meant "Drive out the foreigners", and this eventually intensified into the Assam Agitation over a quite legitimate issue of Bangladeshi migrants having their names in the Assam electoral rolls. Unfortunately, it took the form of ethnic cleansing and, from 1979 to 1985, spread throughout north-east India, with the attacking mobs simply labelling all Bengalis as Bangladeshis. It set in motion a series of cataclysmic events which reached their peak during the 1983 Nellie massacre, where, in a single night, a mob killed about 2,000 Bengali Muslims they suspected were illegal immigrants.'

'When you say illegal immigrants...' I begin.

'Well, the catch-all term is now Bangladeshi. Basically, everybody who had origins in East Bengal or East Pakistan retrospectively became Bangladeshi, even though Bangladesh didn't exist until 1971.' He exhales and draws a pause in his narration. When Samrat resumes, his tone is more personal. 'When I said that I never bothered to ask much about Partition, it was because when I was growing up, in the '80s and '90s, there was immediate danger to our lives because of these multiple insurgencies and ethnic conflicts across the region. There were frequent riots in Shillong between Khasis and Bengalis – basically, the local tribals and people like me, people who were seen as not belonging there – aimed at driving us out. So, we had more immediate problems than thinking about Partition, because whenever there was trouble, the moment you stepped out of your home, you didn't know if you would come back at all, you know? Or come back in one piece. These were our immediate realities.' He smiles sadly.

'Do you think all this reminded your father of Partition?'

'Well, in some ways, it felt like the ghost of Partition. The sum total of everything had taught him – and us – to keep our heads down. I remember, in my childhood, my father was always afraid that something terrible was going to happen. There was a deep anxiety that lived on in him. It had continued from 1947 till 1971, when another exodus of Hindus from what now became Bangladesh occurred, and it has persisted. Throughout the years, many Bengali families have left Shillong. These were people who had faced Partition directly because they were old enough at the time, or people born into families that had been displaced. In this way, they were displaced for a second time, an internal displacement. So, there was always fear...

'I think I must have been about twelve years old when one day I was walking to the library to return some books. Two boys, probably a few years older than me, confronted me on the street, asking if I was Bengali. Even though I knew the right thing to say was no, the answer took too long to come out of my mouth, and by then they'd already punched me in the face. I never told anyone about this at home. My Bengali identity just became something I learnt to avoid from childhood.'

'So, the subject of Partition never came up?' I ask and then correct myself, 'intentionally, I mean?'

'I didn't know anything about where my family's roots lay until just a few years ago,' he admits. 'I had heard my father speak Sylheti with his friends and learnt also to find it funny. It was downmarket, a language of gauche people.[15] I never bothered to learn Bengali history, because my immediate realities were about the experiences of being a Dhkar, which is the Khasi word for an outsider, and is still used today. So, the idea was always to pass your school exams, get the best marks you can and leave Shillong. That's what everyone was *supposed* to do. That's what I did. I went to study engineering in Gujarat, then worked in Delhi and Bombay and Bangalore.

'In 2005, while I was working as the books page editor of the *Hindustan Times* newspaper, I, along with a few other people, was invited for a meeting with the new cultural attaché from the French embassy. One of the people present there was the writer–publisher

Urvashi Butalia, who brought up Partition at some point and I jumped in and said, "Partition! Well, that's history. It's over. Our generation, we don't care about it!"' he laughs. 'And then in 2016, I started travelling to Assam because I was writing a book on the Brahmaputra river and valley, and slowly began realizing that it's not over. The problems, the issues, the differences between various groups of people and the feeling of being an outsider, *it's not over*.'

I'm watching Samrat in stunned silence when he laughs and asks me what the matter is.

'I suppose I'm just a bit surprised to hear ... well, I'm surprised at your belated realization, because to a third person, to me, who is listening to your story, the tremors from Partition seem ever present.'

'Right,' he laughs. 'Right, of course. I think I'd also been away for a while and so I was looking at the region with fresh eyes. So, there I was, shuffling back and forth between Shillong and Assam, and then I was faced with a question which I've had to face ever since I was born. The question is: *why are you here?* That's the question which I would either be asked or inevitably be made to feel. "Why are you people here? You are not tribal. You are not Assamese. You are bloody Bengalis. Why are you people here?" And that became a question that I needed to answer ... for myself.'

I nod, underlining these words so many times in my notebook that I almost tear through the page.

'Anywhere I went, anywhere I lived, I always said I was from Shillong. But the truth is that I was always an outsider in Shillong.'

There is deep sadness in the way that Samrat says this.

'So, I began digging into the region's history,' he continues, 'and very soon after, the NRC issue came up in the news again, which only compelled me to want to know more. It was then that I co-founded the *Partition Studies Quarterly*, which is an academic journal.[16] There were three of us from Shillong, living in different cities, who began to discuss how there was practically no accessible documentation of what happened across the northeast during Partition and thereafter. There is so much written about Punjab, but so little on the east. So, the journal began purely as a task of documentation.'

'Why do you think that is?' I ask him the question that is most often posed to me. 'That there hasn't been enough storytelling about Bengal and Assam the way there has been about Punjab?'

He thinks about this. 'In the west, it was a single split, and then it was done. It was devastatingly violent, but it ultimately settled and the border was fortified and accepted. In the east, the divisions and subsequent migrations happened incrementally, little by little, year after year, for a long time. Everyone has suffered – Hindus, Muslims, tribals – everyone has been, in the story of Partition, both a perpetrator as well as a victim. Everybody has suffered and everybody is still suffering, but they don't know why they are suffering. So, my engagement with Partition is to help people, including myself, understand what happened. To not remain bitter about it, but to at least understand what happened, and then to move on from it.

'I think a lot about truth and reconciliation. But you can't get to reconciliation without some measure of truth, and I think that that needs to happen, the storytelling needs to happen. In the case of the north-east, people didn't think about it. *I* didn't think about it until just a few years ago. We didn't think about the after-effects of Partition ourselves, and our communities continued to suffer because of historical wounds. Obviously, other people are not going to think about it if we don't think about it ourselves.'

In a small voice, he now adds, 'I'm fighting for the north-east but I've never truly belonged. And then last year, we eventually left. The entire family packed up and left Shillong for Calcutta.'

In an equally small voice, I ask, 'How come?'

'Because you figure that you'll *never* belong and there will always be efforts to drive you out. And it might be okay because you have friends and an entire life set up there, but it is the very system of the region that's driving you out.' He pauses and sighs. 'Do you know what I mean?'

Slowly, I shake my head. 'I don't.'

He shrugs.

Ultimately, I return to the topic we had begun with. 'Why did your father never want to go back?'

'To Sylhet? He's bitter, I think he doesn't want to see other people living where their family used to live – in their home or on their land. For a long time, he was bitter about the fact that it was Muslims who drove them out.'

I nod. 'And your mother?'

'She really wants to go and visit Mymensingh, where her ancestors come from. She's drawn by curiosity and wants to see the place she's heard so much about, probably because the loss is not so direct. She was born in 1950 and didn't experience Partition directly.'

'When you went to Sylhet for the first time, what was it like, what did you feel?'

'I've been to Bangladesh thrice now, so I'm trying to recall the first time,' he laughs. 'It was in 2003, and I remember it feeling familiar, but strange. I had been in Shillong, which was different from mainland India. I had been in Gujarat, which was mainland India, a very Hindu mainland India, but this was the first time I was in a place which was visibly Islamic and I saw it on the street, so though it felt a bit unusual, it was still familiar.'

As we conclude, I ask Samrat whether Partition remains an emotional topic for him.

'I suppose I am very practical about these things, so the part which I am bothered by and occasionally upset about is how we are still living the after-effects of Partition. My identity has been forged by it, even though I haven't lived through it and wasn't born any time close to it. I get angry about the fact that it's not over. It's been three generations – my grandparents suffered, my parents suffered, I have suffered growing up, and it's still going on. I've hit middle age and I know that one more generation will likely be impacted and defined by the after-effects of these multiple partitions and separations and segregations and differences. Why doesn't it stop? When will it stop? This is where I get emotional.'

THE SECTIONS OF this chapter have explored the notion of identity – either formed, erased or persecuted – as a consequence of Partition.

Its prolonged effects can span several generations, continuing to remain just as visceral and uncertain as in the previous interview. But what becomes equally apparent is the awareness of being either a majority or minority – ethnic, linguistic, cultural, religious – and where that identity fits into the structure of the nation state. In the tumult of Partition, a Hindu became synonymous with the Indian identity, and a Muslim with the Pakistani one, despite both countries consisting of minority populations of the other.[17] Notwithstanding the presence of groups like Sikhs, Christians, Jains, Parsis, Ahmadis, Buddhists, Bahais and others in both countries, the final section of this chapter looks specifically at the Muslim identity in India and the Hindu identity in Pakistan. For, in a region where the largest minority in one country is the majority in its immediately neighbouring one, this remains a topical discussion, inevitably bound to aspects of belonging and loyalty.

THE WRITER ZEBA Talkhani was born in 1991 into a Muslim family in south India. She grew up in Saudi Arabia, where her parents still live, went to college in India and Germany, and now lives in London with her husband. Though her family did not witness Partition directly, there is much to speak about.

'It wasn't ever directly discussed with me, but I was very aware of being a minority,' she states matter-of-factly. 'While I was growing up, my paternal grandfather, born in the 1930s, was an active politician in the ruling Congress party of Karnataka, and even his job title, Chairman of the Minority Committee, made me aware of our place. Along with that, just seeing what was perceived as default Indian culture: the puja, the festivals, the gods and goddesses, how people outside of India knew of Diwali but not so much about Eid. To realize that this is part of my culture but it is not my culture was very difficult to come to terms with. As a child, I really wanted to take part in all these things, I was enamoured by temples, but was told it wasn't what *we* did. I was made to understand that this is what Indians do, but also this is not what I can do.'

'What about growing up in Saudi Arabia, what was the perception there?' I ask.

'Like with most people outside of India, Hindu culture is considered Indian culture in Saudi Arabia. But I also grew up with many Pakistanis, and their understanding of how many Muslims live in India is maybe how I think of Hindus in Pakistan. How I used to think about Pakistan being fully Muslim, not realizing that there are various minority populations – Hindu, Christian, Sikh and others – that exist there. I'd never thought about it before,' she admits, 'but I was innately aware of being a minority, and especially once I moved to India in 2008.'

I look up from my notebook at Zeba. We both have dark hair and are wearing glasses, our skin colour is the same, she has on a shirt that reminds me of something I own. If we were ever in the same school or university, there'd be nothing stopping me from befriending her. But in my imagination, we are in a place where religion is not one's primary identifier. Though I constitute part of the majority in India, something that strikes me as I look at Zeba now – notwithstanding the deeply reductive nature of this observation – is that without any obviously discernible religious elements, say, a burqa, hijab, bindi, sindoor, mangalsutra, it is difficult to tell apart a Muslim from a Hindu, her from me, without getting to know us or our names.

I recall being in Pakistan in 2014 and not being seen any differently than local women until a stranger found out I was Indian. It was a manicurist at a salon in Lahore who asked me where I was from – Karachi or Islamabad, she guessed, as my accent was a bit different. I casually said 'Delhi' and she dropped my fingers mid-filing and studied my face. Then she looked around the salon, and with wide eyes, voice barely louder than a whisper, she asked me, '*Baaji, tussi Bharat se ho?*' I remember immediately receding, for the word 'Bharat' was not one I associated with, though at the time I wouldn't have been able to explain my reaction. Since then, the writings of Aatish Taseer have helped give words to this feeling that,

...beneath the topsoil of this modern country, a mere seven decades old, lies an older reality, embodied in the word *Bharat*, which can evoke the idea of India as the holy land, specifically of the Hindus. *India* and *Bharat* – these two words for the same place represent a central tension within the nation ... India is a land; Bharat is a people – the Hindus.[18]

I told the manicurist that I was visiting from India and in turn expected either a barrage of complicated questions or suspicion. But instead, all she did was look me up and down with deep curiosity and ask me why I was dressed exactly like her, in a shalwar kurta. Where was my sari, my bindi? Who could wear sindoor? Where were the heavy jewels she'd always seen Indian women wear on television soaps? How did I speak Urdu like her, and could I say something in Hindi? How much did potatoes cost in Delhi? Did I eat meat? She had assumed that I was Hindu, but that assumption was more a deduction, associating 'Hindu' with 'Bharat'. Part of me wondered whether her questions would have felt different had I been an Indian Muslim, or an Indian Sikh, Indian Jain, Indian Christian or Indian anything else. But her curiosity was far more rudimentary, stemming from the fact that she had no idea what an Indian woman looked like, and was not prepared to encounter someone exactly like her.

With this incident in mind, I ask Zeba how the awareness of being a minority was augmented once in India, and she smiles. 'For all intents and purposes, I looked like everybody else and I was never made to feel unwelcome, but there are things outside of your control. For instance, during my time there, there were attacks in southern Karnataka by right-wing parties,[19] and though it wasn't against Muslims, everyone was worried for me. It was the middle of term and I chose to leave the campus to go stay with my grandparents who lived in a nearby town, and ended up missing a few days of class. This is not an exceptional experience, I know, and I was unharmed, but I was forced to be cautious. Because in a small university campus town, you do stand out with a Muslim name, and everyone knows who you are.' She exhales and then adds, 'It was very difficult to forget that I was Muslim.'

In her debut book, *My Past Is a Foreign Country,* reflecting on the rising nature of communal incidents in her home state of Karnataka in the last decade, Zeba writes:

> Every violent incident is viewed politically, and the mainstream reaction differs depending on the victim's religion or caste. As a minority, this made me feel unsafe and unwelcome in my own country. On the cusp of adulthood and as a citizen of India, I was not sure how to come to terms with this insecurity. It seemed my reaction was to distance myself from any public connection to my faith.[20]

She tells me that when her father came from Jeddah to visit her in Manipal, he observed how seamlessly she'd folded herself into her surroundings. 'I couldn't tell if he was joking or not, but as he was leaving, he just said to me, "You look like you could be anyone, Hindu or Muslim," and I don't know what he was feeling when he said it, but I knew that I had made a very conscious effort to dress like everyone else.'

I nod and now bring up the subject of research. 'Zeba, your family were not affected by Partition, they remained in India. But do they at all speak about the event?'

Adjusting her glasses, she says, 'I feel strange admitting this to someone like you who collects stories of the past, but I think my family is just not the kind that talks about the past beyond our lived experiences. I don't know how my grandfather feels. He was alive during Partition and has always been politically active in trying to make life easier for the minority community. But we don't speak about the past in a political way. And I don't know if that's because we are displaced, since our history, as I understand it, only goes back to my great-grandfather, and I don't know where he moved from but it's clear that he has moved from somewhere. Our village in Karnataka is called Talkhani, and it's where we get our last name from. In doing some research, I've found a place called Talkhani in Afghanistan, and I wonder whether there's a connection there. But I can't say why these stories haven't been passed down; were they painful, were they just lost in migration or displacement? The subject of Partition is somewhat like that – there is silence around it, and I don't know if we were affected at all because we remained in India as Muslims...' She shrugs her shoulders.

'And for you, personally?' I ask, since her tone betrays a deep mediation on the subject.

'I feel like Partition does affect me,' Zeba admits. 'During the most recent Delhi riots in 2020, a Pakistani friend posted on Instagram a quote which said something like Indian Muslims will never be free because they chose to stay in India. And it really hurt when I read that, and the entire discourse about people like my family who chose to remain in India at Partition and ... how they – *we* – made the wrong choice.'

'You mention in your book how allegiance is constantly questioned.' I open to a page that I've flagged and read aloud. 'Politicians questioned Indian Muslims' "dual loyalty" and demanded proof of their faithfulness to their birth country. Being Muslim felt at loggerheads with being Indian.'[21]

Palm resting on her cheek, she nods. 'I am always an Indian first and am patriotic in a way that people sometimes make fun of. The national anthem makes me feel very emotional, and I'm quite moved by my Indian identity. It's the first identity I have, and so it hurts whenever it's questioned, because I think to myself, "Well, who gets to decide how I feel?" In Saudi Arabia, I went to an Indian school where we were taught about the struggle for Indian Independence, and it was something I deeply identified with while I was studying: the fact that we wanted a secular, free nation where everyone could be themselves. I felt like Indians of that generation – irrespective of religion – lived through a shared experience of fighting for their freedom, and yet, seventy-odd years later, some Indians still don't have it. It upsets me that we come from people who fought so hard for our freedom and some of them are still not free.'

'I do find it interesting that you feel so strongly about an event that has not impacted you personally,' I note, 'neither in terms of geography, being a south Indian, nor in terms of displacement.'

'Yes, and this is what I struggle with sometimes – am I centring myself into something that is not mine to feel or discuss? Why do I think about this, why am I feeling like this? Sometimes I feel like it's not my thing to talk about because I wasn't ... I mean, there are people like you and your family, who were directly displaced and still feel that loss and pain.' She sighs. 'I know how devastating Partition was for the entire subcontinent, but in particular those who lost their homes, family members, lands, a sense of belonging ... so I do wonder if speaking about it as a person who has no known, tangible connection to it minimizes its significance.'

'I don't think so at all,' I say sincerely.

Zeba looks at me for a few seconds, her face taut. As she exhales, her features soften. 'I understand my privilege as someone who has grown up and lives outside of India, and because it no longer impacts my every day, there is room to ask questions or make observations from a distance. But I've never articulated or shared or asked my family about this; to be honest, I'm scared I might unearth their pain. It is a very peculiar kind of pain – to feel a deep love for your country and not know if the country returns that love. I always found it extraordinary that we expect unrequited love from humans, but we never put that kind of expectation on a country or a home. We simply assume it belongs to us, as we belong to it.'

Zeba's words find particular resonance as I read the historian Gyanendra Pandey's essay, 'Can a Muslim Be an Indian?', where he states, 'Partition produced a plethora of ideas on the question of what would constitute an adequate proof of loyalty to India on the part of the Indian Muslim.'[22] Something that Zeba too had alluded to. In the same vein, the essay analyses an editorial published by *Vartman*, a Kanpur-based Hindi daily in October 1947, which asks *who* the country of India belongs to, and then states a list of religious groups in response – 'Buddhists and Jains, Sikhs, Christians, Anglo-Indians and Parsis'[23] – explaining how each claims India as their native land. The contentious status of Muslims is not mentioned, but Hindus, though also explicitly unmentioned, are simply understood as *belonging*, implying, Pandey writes:

> They are the nation, the 'we' who demand cooperation from the minorities, the 'us' that the Muslims have to learn to live with. Like the land, the trees, the rivers and mountains, these invisible Hindus are the nation's natural condition ... Their culture is the nation's culture, their history its history. This needs no stating. [24]

This question of where religious identity and national identity intersect – as a consequence of Partition – is raised in several interviews throughout this book, but prominently so when I speak with M,* who belongs to a Hindu family from Mithi, a desert town in Tharpakar, Sindh province, Pakistan, and one of the few regions of the country where Muslims do not form the majority.

'During Partition, my ancestors decided to remain in Pakistan since there wasn't much awareness about the political situation. All they knew was what they heard on the radio, that a new country was being formed, but nothing more. So, they chose to stay where they were,' M tells me. 'Mithi is about five hours from Karachi, but barely an hour's drive from the Indian borders of Gujarat and Rajasthan. At Partition, the area didn't witness any riots or violence the way the bigger cities in Punjab or Sindh did; Mithi was simply a desert with even fewer inhabitants than it has now. To date, both Hindus and Muslims live there together quite peacefully – Muslims do not slaughter cows out of respect for Hindus, and Hindus do not openly eat during Ramadan. The festivals of Diwali, Eid and Holi are celebrated by everyone. There is barely any crime or incidents of religious intolerance.'[25]

---

* Initials have been used to retain anonymity, as per the individual's request.

I'd never heard of Mithi before, but the town sounds like an idyllic oasis of Hindu–Muslim unity, as sweet as its name. It feels reminiscent of the stories of an unfractured life in undivided India. At the risk of redundancy, I confirm with M that both sides of his family remained in Pakistan as Hindus.

He nods. 'But both sides are Hindu, and there was no movement to India at Partition.'

'But … how come?' The question spills out, and immediately I cringe at its directness and assumption.

As I apologize, M laughs. 'It's all right, but I'm afraid the answer is not so exciting. It was simply because they were well established, at respectable positions in their work, and this was where their ancestral lands lay. To be honest, I never found it strange, because no one ever had a conversation about Partition, or being a Pakistani Hindu, at home. I was born in Pakistan in 1994, but that same year we left for Dubai, where I still live. Naturally, then, I was raised in a multicultural society. But my cousins who lived in Pakistan through the '80s and '90s and have been brought up predominantly around Muslims must have thought about this. Teachers would tell them to start reading the Quran, most of my cousins know how to recite verses as well, but our family has always been devout Hindus.'

'So, it was never an issue of identity for you … as a Hindu Pakistani?'

'My first identity is of a Pakistani, and I'm proud of it. Everything else is secondary.' He then pauses. 'But, if I'm honest, maybe I'm a proud Pakistani because I've been away from Pakistan for so long. Being in Dubai, raised with Indians and Pakistanis and Arabs, it's difficult to retain a concrete identity. I suppose I clung on to the Pakistani aspects as tightly as I could, whereas my family back home has witnessed persecution, discrimination and suspicion simply for being Hindus in an Islamic nation, and they may not feel as proud of their nationality as I do.

'We moved from Mithi to Karachi in 1969 or '70 but kept our ancestral home in the village. Until then, things were fine, things were good. Then General Zia came to power and the constitutional amendments by him Islamized the country. There was not only sectarian violence or social stigma against minorities but also ethnic violence between communities like Sindhis and Muhajirs.[26] During this time, we were the only Hindus in our neighbourhood of Karachi, and because of continual outbursts of anti-Hindu sentiments, we had to move back to the village several times for months at a stretch.

'In '89, when the violence became too unbearable, my family decided to move to India – parents, grandfather, uncles, cousins. Quite a few family members went over to see if they could live there. But after six months, it became clear that they were unwelcome, because people found out they were Pakistani Hindus and were prejudiced against them. My family came back, but some relatives remained in India and are there to this date. Once back in Pakistan, the family began making connections at a governmental level, and little by little life became better and safer. This was the situation when I was born in 1994, before my parents left with me for Dubai. But one thing you have to understand is that minorities are still persecuted in Pakistan.

'My cousins tell me that there was a time when children would come and throw stones or garbage into our house. But after the family began rising in status, gaining connections and influence, all this stopped. We began to accumulate respect. But I understand my privilege, and that other people born into minority communities in Pakistan may not feel this way.'

I nod. 'Tell me about your parents' marriage. Since both families are Hindu Pakistanis, did they know one another beforehand?'

'Yes, we marry within the community. There are Pakistani Hindus who marry Christians, and Pakistani Hindus who marry Muslims, but we only marry Hindus. In fact, my wife is also a Pakistani Hindu.'

My pen abruptly stops mid-sentence and I scan the page of my notes. Since the beginning of our conversation, I have been writing 'Hindu Pakistani' whereas M has been careful to say 'Pakistani Hindu'. The distinction between the two is significant and important to acknowledge. I've never used the term 'Muslim Indian', always putting the Indian before, so the fact that I was writing 'Hindu

Pakistani' without thought unsettles me. When I bring this up with M, he repeats that being Pakistani is his primary identity, everything else is secondary. In return, I tell him a story from my maiden trip to Pakistan in 2014.

'In Lahore, I'd been introduced to a Hindu gentleman from a family like yours that had stayed back in Pakistan at Partition. On the phone, he insisted that we meet at the Krishna temple. I'd much rather we met in the comfort of his home, with his family – as with everyone I'd been interviewing – but he was keen on showing the sacred site to me as a place that belonged to us both due to our common religious identity.

'I went prepared with questions, similar to the ones I am asking you now, about *why* his family remained in Pakistan. Until then, every interview I had done in Pakistan had been with women and men who had either chosen to migrate there during Partition or had no choice but to flee from India as a result of violence and riots. But this family had chosen to remain as Hindus in a metropolitan city like Lahore, and no one had made an attempt to leave thereafter either. He had grown up in the city, married, had children, grandchildren, and throughout our conversation stressed on how good life had been for them as Hindus in Pakistan, how happy he was to raise his family on the same land as his ancestors. And while I respected that sentiment, I'm embarrassed to admit that I almost expected him to narrate some incident of oppression against the community.'

M's face is unchanged, but he is listening to me intently.

'You follow the news, you read about things – for example, I'd read that the demolition of the Babri Masjid in India in 1992 resulted in the subsequent destruction of over a hundred Hindu temples in Pakistan, how angry mobs had entered Hindu homes and destroyed property and businesses ... not to mention physical attacks or reports of conversion. I know that media in both countries can often be biased and things can be blown out of proportion or further fuelled by communal fire, but...' I pause to take a deep breath in. 'I've never told this story to anyone, nor written about it anywhere. Years have passed, and I've thought about it so many times, but I still don't think I have the appropriate vocabulary to talk about it. Each time, I consider another aspect of the story, and find myself *un*learning, and *re*learning, dissecting my own preconceived notions. But back then, I didn't know how to make sense of what was being said. I don't think I gave the interaction enough respect or consideration.'

'Why not?' M asks now.

I shrug. 'As a twenty-four-year old, I made an unfair judgement against my interviewee because I felt as though he hadn't been completely honest. I thought that his life as a minority in Pakistan couldn't have been as peaceful as he'd made it out to be. But it's far more complicated than that, isn't it? It has taken me years to realize that there were some things he just couldn't tell me, or didn't want to tell me, or didn't want on record. Maybe he didn't want to say them out loud, or maybe there was simply nothing *to* say. But it's taken me a while to appreciate that some things must be left unsaid, even though they may be understood.'

M smiles knowingly. '*That*, I can understand.'

I look down at the ground, still thinking about the temple in Lahore; my fingers are tingling, my heart is racing from finally putting in words a story that I may never do justice to in full.

After a while, I finally ask, 'Do you ever think about Partition? About that decision to remain?'

'It doesn't matter to me,' he says without missing a beat. 'But sometimes I do think about my relatives who moved to India in the years after Partition and were not accepted there. Looking back, had I been alive then and witnessed the violence myself, I may have felt differently. But right now, given whatever I know and my lived experience, I'm happy we chose to stay in Pakistan. Despite being raised in Dubai, whenever I return to Pakistan, I feel like I'm home. It is my land. Wherever else I've lived in the world, London or Sydney, I feel a much stronger connection to the Pakistani community rather than the Indian one. My Hindu religion has never been a barrier for my Pakistani friends, whereas I do feel like my Pakistani identity is an issue for Indians even when we share the same religion. While in London, I was looking for a place to stay and found a flat owned by an Indian family. They asked for my name and documentation and were happy that I was Hindu, but the minute they saw my passport and realized that I'm Pakistani, they rejected the application. No Pakistanis allowed, they said.' He shrugs. 'Fair enough.'

As I listen to M, what I earlier expected would be quite a complicated understanding of identity actually seems fairly simple. All forms of identification are merely constructions of society and community for humans to feel a sense of belonging to some place. In submitting ourselves to a nationality, a religion, an ethnicity, we form our allegiances. With M, the hierarchy of allegiance begins with his nationality as a Pakistani and descends thereon.

He clears his throat and says to me, 'Look, what has happened has happened. I have to make the best of my family's decision to stay back in Pakistan. But I'd rather ... I'd rather my children are born without that burden. I'm a proud Pakistani, whatever my religion may be. And one last thing about minorities: as I said at the start, minorities will always be persecuted, but I've never personally felt this way. I have always felt special belonging to that 1 per cent of Pakistan's population. We are the special people of this country. You write this in your book, because I don't think enough people have met a Pakistani Hindu or know that we even exist. I will be the first to acknowledge the privilege I have, and also the fact that there are many, many people who continue to be persecuted to this day or are seen with suspicion simply because they are minorities in this country. But I want to hope for a better future. There is a reason why our Pakistani flag holds two colours: the green represents the Muslim majority and the white the minorities. *We* are the white in our flag.'

11
Legacy

❦

AT THE CORNER OF Shah Almi Road and Rang Mahal Chowk in Lahore, a sole building, half-burnt, still stands bearing the words, 'Gobind Ram Kahan Chand, Estd 1805, Hindustan Commercial Bank'. The story goes that Gobind Ram, trader of achar, chutneys and sherbets, owned a shop on the ground floor of this building, and was also amongst the partners of this branch of the bank, which had been newly constructed at the time.[1] As perfumers and flavourists, Gobind Ram and company were best known for their khuss sherbet.

On 14 August 1947, his family was forced to flee across the border on the last night train to Delhi, after their shops and factories had been set ablaze. Among them was twenty-two-year-old Kharaiti Lal Bhatia. Son of Kahan Chand, grandson of Gobind Ram, he was one of the heirs to their fragrant empire. Amidst the Partition riots, the family could carry little across, but Kharaiti Lal made sure to bring the journals and vials of his perfume compositions. In Delhi, they started from scratch, making mostly sherbets from their new home in Daryaganj and later Chandni Chowk. But the young perfumer continued to experiment, creating oils and ittars, perfumes and aldehydes, even shaving creams and moisturizers.

Over seven decades have passed when I meet his granddaughter, Pallavi Bhatia, in Delhi. We sit in her office, accompanied by ornate, antique flacons, large glass vials that hold ingredients, and musty journals. Every inch of the small room is soon suffused with the scent of perfume as we open bottle after bottle, gingerly smelling the aged contents. Pallavi was born in the early 1990s and only a toddler when Kharaiti Lal Bhatia passed away, but while speaking about the family's pre-Partition perfumed legacy, she holds a cut-glass bottle up to the light.

'My family discussed Partition quite openly. It was told like a story, but I don't think I realized the gravity of what it truly meant. My grandmother would recall how houses and monuments had been blackened during the Second World War and then, merely a few years later, how they were forced to hide inside their homes from the rioters during Partition. If children screamed or cried, they were gagged. She told these stories so casually, so matter-of-factly, that though I listened to them, I never quite understood the meaning of this Partition. But even to a child, these fragments of memory were terrifying.'

I nod sadly and pick up a companion vial to the one she holds in her hand. It is rectangular in shape, with perforations across its surface that give the bottle a chic, modern look. I have never seen anything like it before, and my fingers graze the layer of dust and fuzz that coats its body.

'Here,' Pallavi says to me, uncorking a bottle that holds a dark, viscous liquid. She hands me the globular glass cork, whose inside is covered with the liquid, and I bring it up to my nose. As the fragrance is released in the air, she inhales deeply and concentrates. 'This has menthol, *nagarmotha* … My grandfather loved working with these ingredients … *kewra,* patchouli. Their khuss was particularly well-known. In fact, in the serial *Buniyad*,[2] set in Lahore during Partition, there is a mention of the khuss sherbet from Gobind Ram Kahan Chand! Nobody did khuss the way we did; it is usually green, but ours was a deep, luscious brown.'

'Did you always want to be a perfumer and continue the work of your forefathers?' I ask her.

'I suppose, if Partition had not happened, we would have prospered in an undivided India,' she begins thoughtfully, 'but all six shops that my family owned across Lahore were burnt down during the riots. After the shop in Hindustan Commercial Bank was set ablaze, we were told that for the next three months a dense sweetness hung in the air, as a reminder of what no longer was. A trail of fragrant beauty and communal terror combined. It's a miracle that the building still stands.

'The only place where my grandfather truly felt comfortable was his lab on Lawrence Road; this is where I, too, am most comfortable now. I was in my mid-twenties when I came across seven journals on perfumery that he had kept over the years, some dating back to well before Partition. I became fixated with the formulas, even though I did not understand them. I think it was the fact that these journals had survived events as catastrophic as Partition and migration, and it was because of the esoteric formulas within them, that the family was able to rebuild even part of their fragrant empire in independent India. It's what actually inspired me to learn perfumery.'

She hands me one of the journals from the table. The spine cracks as I open it, and so I flip through gently. There are places where the ink has bled through to the other side. Notes and cards have been tucked in the spine, wisps of paper fall out as I turn the aged pages.

Monday, 27 December 1955, the date on a page reads. Lavender, ylang, geranium, musk, benzoin, a touch of natural rose form an initial list of ingredients for a perfume called 'Fancy Boquette'. On another page, the ingredient list for 'Fantasia' is far more chemical in nature, consisting of hydroxycintronellal and beta-ionone. There are pages of crossed-out formulas in English, Hindi and Urdu, and numbers, worked and reworked over the years. The dates range from the early 1940s to several decades later.

'There is a perfume called "Himalayan Bouquet" that my grandfather started composing in 1942,' Pallavi says as she searches through the journals. 'Until 1946, he was still perfecting the formula, but it remained unfinished. Then he picked it up again in 1962, in Delhi, and finally completed it to his satisfaction. He worked on it for twenty long years. And this was my first introduction to perfumery, the fact that it was not unusual for perfumers to work on the same formulas for decades. It is both an obsession and a labour of love.'

Pallavi tells me that the foundation of every perfume under her brand, Olfa Originals, is always in her grandfather's notes – menthol, rose, oud, *nagarmotha*, lemongrass, *mitti* ittar, jasmine – tweaked to the modern palate. It was not the fragrances that connected her to his work, but the formulas, the handwriting, a legacy that has persisted for generations.

'Do you feel any connection to Lahore?' I ask her as we begin to wrap up our interview.

She sighs dreamily, 'I wish I could see where my grandfather's perfumery used to be, where he learnt his alchemy, and fell in love with the essence of flowers and leaves. I wish I could go to Lahore and stand before the building that still bears my ancestors' names. Like so many people, I wish I could see where my legacy began, long before a line was drawn in the land.'

I leave her office that afternoon, covered in fragrance, both her grandfather's and hers – an amalgamation of old and new, classic and modern. Kharaiti Lal Bhatia never lived to see his granddaughter become a perfumer, yet he became her greatest teacher. In some sense, through the bequeathment of formulas and the objects he once used, the legacy remains unbroken.

HOW DOES THE legacy of a 'distant and incomprehensible past'[3] manifest within subsequent generations? Does Partition remain an inheritance that eclipses the lives of families that went through it; do they continue to bear its invisible weight – sometimes publicly, as in the case of Pallavi Bhatia, but other times more privately, even unknowingly? Is it carried over through their businesses and occupations, within titles and adopted names, in attitudes and political views, or simply through family histories?

IN THE MONTHS approaching the end of my fieldwork for this book, I receive an email from Mohan Katyal, who was born in 2002 in Delhi. He has just finished reading *Remnants* and tells me that his paternal grandparents migrated from what became Pakistan. His grandfather, Jagdish C. Katyal, was fourteen years old at the time, and his grandmother, Darshna Katyal, was merely ten months old. The email starts with the beginning of his understanding of Partition, when at the age of thirteen he accompanied his grandfather to watch the Hindi film *Bhaag Milkha Bhaag*. He had seen the movie already but went anyway, and about that second viewing, he writes:

> That was the first time I saw my grandfather cry; the tears were just pouring down his face. Now that I think about it, it may have been the only time he actually saw something that looked like his home. Upon seeing him cry, I too began crying. [But] why did he cry? This is a very sad question, and perhaps the simplest answer is that the movie was just too relatable, and, therefore, too unbearable. I can only imagine what it must feel like to see the worst possible reality that your family had endured be represented on-screen.

Mohan further writes that he may not have understood why his grandfather was weeping at the time, but once he unearthed the story of what the family had endured during Partition, tears seemed like the only response to the accuracy of the suffering depicted in the film. I ask him about the year 1947, and for the next few days we exchange emails that span six generations of his family.

> My family comes from a village called Chandana, in District Jhang–Maghiana, Punjab. They were landowners and had been living there for generations. My grandfather – who migrated when he was in Class 5 – has told me that his elders actually used to praise the British on their governance and law enforcement. Hindus and Muslims lived in separate communities, but there was mutual respect. Now, I don't know

how relevant the stories of Partition are to the world, but they remain relevant to me. My parents respect the past but are not as interested in it as I am. Meanwhile, my grandparents cannot understand why I take an active interest in this time but I feel like it is my responsibility to preserve their stories and struggles.

He goes up the generations, telling me the story of his great-great-great-grandfather, Jeevan Das Katyal, who was described to him as a tall, heavily built man with hazel eyes. He had two daughters and two sons, both of whom he sadly outlived. The first enrolled – much against the father's wishes – in the British Indian Army to fight during the First World War and never returned. The second, Mohan's great-great-grandfather, Jawala Das Katyal, a hakim – he studied Ayurveda from a Muslim hakim, who was eventually forced to stop teaching a Hindu because of tensions between the communities – died of natural causes. Mohan writes that in 1947 the family patriarch Jeevan was over one hundred years old:

> ... he used to always wear a solid silver bracelet around his arm. When rumours of Partition arrived and people began to flee from Jhang, the old man refused to leave his ancestral home where he was born. My great-grandfather and his brothers thought that the riots and violence were just a temporary thing and after a few months they'll be able to return. So, in September 1947, they melted all the gold and silver that they had into bricks, and collected all their money and gave it to a neighbouring Muslim family for safekeeping. They also asked them to look after the old man, Jeevan. They'd heard stories of people getting looted along the way, and chose not to take their valuables with them. But they never returned to Jhang.

This is the story of so many families who refused to believe the bitter permanence of Partition, leaving their homes, wealth and lands behind, with the hope of one day returning. I wonder about what happened to the old man, Jeevan, and Mohan tells me that each time he spoke with his grandfather about Partition, the stories of Jeevan inevitably crept into their conversation. When he grew old, he chose to move out of the main house and into an outhouse with his cow, hookah and other possessions. He was a healthy and independent man, but just very old. Unfortunately, he did not survive the days of Partition.

> In 1948, when my great-grandfather, his brothers and their families were living in the Kurukshetra refugee camp in India, their Muslim neighbours travelled from Jhang to find them and tell them that Jeevan had passed. My grandfather was there and remembers listening to the story. The silver band that Jeevan used to wear was brutally taken from him by rioters, injuring his arm, and the man bled to death ... When my family heard the news of Jeevan's demise, they must have felt terrible and must have blamed themselves too – especially after hearing how he died; I mean, the sheer inhumanity of it all. My grandfather thinks that it was a mistake to not bring him along, and I agree, but a part of me also feels proud that he stayed. Taking into account all the tales I've heard about Jeevan and his life, I don't think he would have even believed the fact that his Punjab was now divided between two countries, and the part in which he was born and raised, where his forefathers had lived for generations, was not his any more and he had to leave. The mental pain could have only been surpassed by the physical pain of death.

I ask him about what happened to the family after, and he tells me that, from the Kurukshetra refugee camp, the Government of India began resettling refugees who had come from Jhang in Rohtak, which is now in Haryana. They were allotted some land in India for the land they had left behind in the newly formed Pakistan, and the Katyal family received 20 or 30 acres in lieu of the 500 acres in Jhang. Eventually, Mohan's grandfather joined the Indian Air Force.

During his time there, he travelled to St Petersburg, USSR, for some official work in October 1964. On the way back, they stopped for refuelling in Lahore. While their paperwork was being checked by the Pakistani officer, he asked my grandfather to step aside from the line and follow him. He invited him to his office, treated him with a lot of respect and offered him a cup of tea. Then he began asking about his family – where were they from? Which village they used to live in? My grandfather later found out that when the officer was young, he had a friend named Krishan Katyal from the same village my family was from, and my grandfather also happened to have a cousin with the same name, and he turned out to be the same person! He even suggested that my grandfather never go back to India and settle in Lahore, which, of course, my grandfather kindly refused, but the old friends started exchanging letters because of that chance meeting.

It is only after a bit of back and forth that I notice Mohan's full name and am able to grasp just how strongly the legacy of his pre-partitioned homelands resides in him. Some things, some places became so intrinsic to us that we embroider them into our being, making them proud, visible parts of our identity. *Mohan Jhangi Harjai Katyal*, he signs off.

The word Jhangi means a person from Jhang, and Harjai is the maiden name of my paternal grandmother, derived from the town Haripur in district Hazara (or Hajaara) in Pakistan, where her family originated generations ago. On my eighteenth birthday, I handed in my application to the Gazette of India, adding the two names to mine, making it official. It was the best birthday gift I ever gave myself, to honour my family, the places they come from, to celebrate my roots.

∽

IN LATE 2020, historian Narayani Basu and I meet for lunch to discuss her book *V.P. Menon: The Unsung Architect of Modern India*,[4] published earlier that year. Not only is her book the first comprehensive biography of a school dropout who eventually rose to become India's highest, and arguably finest, civil servant by the time of Independence, but it is also the story of her great-grandfather.

'I come from a family that doesn't really believe in eulogizing,' she begins. 'And so it was with VP as well. I didn't even know that I was related to him until my early twenties. Everyone in my household is a passionate non-fiction reader, and we often talk about the books we read. Inevitably, VP's name kept popping up, and I would discuss him with my parents in relation to bigger events around Independence. It was only then that my mother announced, as if it were the most natural thing, that he was my great-grandfather!'

'And ... then?' I ask.

'Well, I was shocked. He was my mother's paternal grandfather and it just aroused a lot of curiosity in me. It's one thing to have repeatedly read a name in a book, and it's a whole other thing to be suddenly told that that name is, in fact, an intimate relation.'

The dedication in Narayani's book makes the relation even more immediate. 'For Precious' reads the inscription, alluding to the nickname that VP gave to his daughter-in-law and Narayani's maternal grandmother, Premilla Sahgal.

Narayani goes on to tell me that Vappala Pangunni Menon, or VP, as she calls him, was born in 1893 in Madras and is most often confused with V.K. Krishna Menon, India's defence minister. Unlike the latter Menon, VP had been languishing on the sidelines of history for over seven decades, and yet 'his importance to the Government of India, at a time when India stood on the verge of independence, remains unparalleled'.[5] VP served as reforms commissioner to India's last three viceroys – Linlithgow, Wavell and Mountbatten – and in 1937 he added women to the Indian electoral rolls. His hands drafted the final plan to divide British India, he was home minister Sardar Vallabhbhai Patel's right-hand man, and together they integrated 565 princely states into the Indian union.[6]

'That is a ... difficult inheritance,' I say.

She breathes deeply. 'It is, it's very much a difficult inheritance. People of that generation, who witnessed the years of Independence and Partition, did not really talk on their own. I actually think that the less they talked about things, the greater an impact those things may have had on them. *Now* we've almost overturned in that regard. But in those days, if there was trauma or grief, or even rage or shock at what was happening around you ... well, you didn't generally speak about it. My grandmother, for instance, was Punjabi and was in Shimla at the time of Partition. I'm sure that even though she was safe, and did not personally have to migrate across to India, she would have witnessed the caravans of refugees arriving in Shimla or fleeing from there. It would have certainly left an impression.

'But an additional layer of silence existed in VP's case, for he was a public figure,[7] and very much had to self-surveil when it came to the official narrative. He toured most of north India right after Partition. But if you read his reports[8] on the integration of states or of the violence he witnessed, his language is almost clinical. He writes about facts and numbers, but never the depth of horror or massacre.'

I now introduce the primary source of Narayani's book. 'You've employed a unique method of oral history in your book – listening and responding to the tapes of VP's interview with the economist Harry Hodson in 1965. Did it feel like you were forging a belated relationship with an ancestor, returning to the days of independence *with* him?'

She laughs. 'In a way, yes. To be honest, it's been difficult to think of him as an ancestor because he had such a public personality. But it *was* indescribable to listen to him narrating how events unfolded, in his own words. In 2016, quite serendipitously, I received a grant to travel to London to look at Hodson's papers[9] and listen to the tapes he recorded with VP. I had no publishing deal in hand, no book project in mind. I was simply curious about this person who happened to be a part of my family...' Her voice trails off. She now dons the historian's hat. 'Henry Vincent "Harry" Hodson was a civil servant who first met VP during wartime in Shimla in 1941 while they were both working in the Reforms Office. They became good friends, probably the best of friends, personally and professionally.[10] In 1965, one year before VP passed away, he gave his final interview to Hodson, who stayed in VP's home, "Shelter", in Bangalore for about six months while researching his own book, *The Great Divide*.[11] By then, VP was in his early seventies. He was quite unwell and his breath rattled in his lungs,[12] but to listen to his voice was such a gift. I genuinely don't have the words to describe how it felt.'

My pen is tearing across the page of my notebook, taking note of this simultaneously historian–subject/ great-granddaughter–great-grandfather relationship that begins with listening to these tapes.

'The recordings were the first things I heard when I embarked on this project; they were my first piece of research. At first, I was almost taken aback by his voice, because the Malayali accent was so thick. I think I expected something more ... anglicized. But anyway, I often played the recordings twice or thrice to understand him. He had a lisp. He had a tendency to shout when he was excited or angry. It was like the words were practically falling out of his mouth. He was speaking really fast because sometimes Hodson would ask him things about certain moments that he obviously still remembered clearly and couldn't wait to talk about. So, there was this urgency in his voice.' Narayani pauses for a few seconds before adding, 'I think what I heard was somebody who was finally free to tell the truth. It was important to him. He told Hodson about these moments from his life because he wanted the record set straight at some point. And I feel like *that* is my legacy from my great-grandfather, from the time of Partition and Independence. A legacy of truth, without sanitization, without eulogizing.'

'What do you mean?'

'The recordings are vast in the time period they cover and the people they introduce. For instance, VP talks about Nehru and Mountbatten, about the first time he encountered Jinnah in 1925, and then later on in 1946, and how within a span of twenty years Jinnah was a completely changed man.[13] He speaks about elections, reforms, princely states, even the drawing of the Partition line. But then, as I mentioned earlier, there are moments in these tapes that differ remarkably from the official records VP left, and this is where my interest truly lay – the oral history, the memory.

'In the months following Partition, he travelled across Punjab, surveying the aftermath of division. In October 1947, he went to Bahawalpur, and his official report of that trip, which is housed in the National Archives of India, is sterile, careful, trying not to push an already precarious situation even further. He is diplomatic about what he writes, like the government has things under control and so on. But in the recordings, he talks freely about how he saw the "streets littered so thickly with bloodied, decaying dead bodies that he found it difficult to breathe, let alone walk".[14] Photographs were taken. He had to take official photographs, and he says that when his daughter, Meenakshi, saw them, she told him that he needed to destroy them immediately because she would never be able to sleep at night otherwise. He did destroy them, but he says on the recording that he knew "that this was an India where no one knew where to go".'

In the few seconds of quiet that follows, I think about what it feels like to find something unexpectedly – an object, a document – of an ancestor I never had the chance to know. And how that small artefact makes me feel: connected. Here, Narayani has not only inherited a public legacy but has also had a chance to engage with her ancestor in this highly unusual, decades-removed sort of way. I wonder what my great-grandparents would have had to say if they were given a chance to recall and record their experiences of Partition. I wonder how I would have felt listening to them, decades on.

'Did *you* feel anything while listening?' I ask Narayani.

'Well, at the beginning, I found the research immensely boring. He was talking about drafting clauses ... I couldn't comprehend anything. It was only when I began to correlate records with recordings, files with transcripts from different archives, that I began to grasp the sheer scope of the work he was involved in. Even when he was a typist – that's how he began his career. He was the principal typist of the Montagu-Chelmsford Report, for instance. The more I studied the political events he'd been present at or privy to, the more I realized that there was another layer to the Independence movement that one doesn't immediately consider.'

I raise my eyebrows.

'Well, you don't like to think of the Independence movement as paperwork,' she chuckles. 'Our perception of that time is of leaders making grand speeches, cities drenched in blood, people sacrificing themselves for the freedom of the country. It's not exactly exciting to think of Independence or any colossal moment in a country's history as paperwork in duplicate and triplicate, or the shortage of personnel so people are working overtime, or the doubling up of different committee heads.'

'Yes,' I admit, 'I suppose I never thought about it like that.'

She shrugs, smiling. 'This was my task: how to make Independence and Partition – which have been written about by so many people before me, including yourself, and will be written about by so many after us – interesting, when seen through the eyes of a bureaucrat.'

'And is it still relevant to talk about Partition, to write about it?'

'It is a festering wound,' she says thoughtfully. 'Even for someone like me who considers my personal legacy – despite this public legacy of VP – one of detachment. I am removed from the event of Partition. I have the privilege of speaking decades on, after the event. But like I mentioned earlier, my grandmother wasn't someone who spoke of trauma or traumatic events easily. And to that extent, the depths of the horrors that they may have heard or witnessed, how many friends they may have lost or seen distant relatives harmed – I don't know those depths. We never discussed it, really. Silence or privacy was usually the way it was. In hindsight, I'm a bit sad about this, both that I never asked and that it wasn't spoken of – because there are so many memories that are lost and so much we could have built from there that we haven't been able to. But as far as I know, my family was safe, and they did not witness the violence first-hand. And yet, there is something that lingers, persists, and I can feel it. It is both the politics we practise and the relationships we keep with our neighbours. We are not granted the luxury of forgetting Partition.'

I nod in agreement. 'And do you think that through the writing of this book you learnt to accept VP as a great-grandfather, and not just a name that appeared in texts?'

'Well,' Narayani begins and then pauses. 'I think I just felt really proud of him. Of what he had accomplished in his own personal capacity – to have come from nowhere and been nobody, to not have had formal education, and then gradually rise to the position of one of the highest civil servants in the country by 1947. Yes, of course, he was my great-grandfather and that is a bond of blood, a legacy. But more than that, I emerged inspired by the man he was, full of complexity and honesty, imperfections and diligence. He was inspiring,' she beams.

✐

A FEW DAYS later, the novelist Karan Mahajan and I speak via video call. Morning has just broken in Providence, Rhode Island, where he currently lives, and night is setting in Delhi, where I am. Though we have been friends for years, the topic of Partition has only recently begun to enter our conversations.

'I think any conscious knowledge of Partition first arrived in the form of lament,' he says. 'It was through the most common narrative of Hindus and Muslims being brothers and then torn apart by division, or through films like Deepa Mehta's *Earth* – those are what come to my mind. But there's no distinct memory of my family ever discussing Partition, it was never a big part of my childhood...'

'I find that surprising,' I exclaim, thinking of his great-grandfather as Karan continues.

'The word "Lahore" was very important, though, and my parents were both born right around Partition – my father in 1946 and mother in 1947. So, I have this image in my head of their being carried across the border as infants.'

'So, both sides of your family were impacted by Partition?' I confirm.

'Yes, and neither side really speaks about it. It's definitely a subject shrouded in silence. My paternal great-grandfather, Mehr Chand Mahajan, retired as the third Chief Justice of independent India.'[15]

While a judge in undivided India, he was also elected to the Lahore High Court in 1943, was a member of the Royal Indian Navy Mutiny Commission in 1946, and served on Sir Cyril Radcliffe's Punjab Boundary Commission as the Hindu judge in 1947.[16]

'In my mind, of course, I always ascribed a lot of influence to his being on the boundary commission, but now, having researched it as an adult, I know just how little power the judges on the commission had. I never met my great-grandfather – he passed away before I was born – but there is a lot of family lore around him.'

'What kind of lore?' I ask.

'About his excellence as a judge. And his role in the inclusion of Gurdaspur into the Indian union during Partition because it was an important passage for goods and communication in Kashmir. But again, these are things that I am still learning about and researching on my own,' Karan states.

Justice Mehr Chand Mahajan, who was appointed the Prime Minister of Jammu and Kashmir under Maharaja Hari Singh in 1947-48, has left future generations with an extensively detailed account from the days of Independence, Partition, the announcement of the boundary awards and the consequences in his memoir, *Looking Back*.[17] I imagine Karan learning about his ancestor belatedly through this text.

'Belonging to a family with such a political legacy,' I ask, 'when did you first understand the implications of Partition?'

He says, 'I still don't think I quite understand the implications of what it meant for my own family. I know that everyone came across the border suddenly, but the actual losses – the money, goods and lands lost – have never really been discussed. My maternal side migrated, via Amritsar and Dalhousie, to Delhi, where my grandfather, Dr Dharm Pal, was a teacher and was supporting a large family. But it was very hard to make ends meet. He taught at a camp college while they lived in crowded accommodation near Old

Delhi. He then got a job with the Indian government as a historian–researcher and, after a posting in Shimla, received accommodation right by Khan Market, in a government colony called Bharati Nagar, then known as Maan Nagar.[18] My father's family also came to Delhi, where they lived in government quarters before moving to Friends Colony in 1954. But I have to say that my understanding of Partition has been shaped by literature rather than my family's experiences, mostly because they weren't directly passed down.'

I am intrigued, for in each of Karan's own novels there is a shadow of Partition, serving either as context or collective memory, which I assumed had been inspired by his own history.

'I've been most clearly informed by Yashpal's *This Is Not That Dawn*,'[19] Karan admits. The novel was originally written in Hindi as *Jhootha Sach* and published in two instalments, in 1958 and 1960. 'I consider it a masterpiece of Partition literature, but it didn't appear in English until 2010, when it was translated by Yashpal's son, Anand.[20] It is one of the greatest novels about India, spanning some 1,100 pages, and paints an extremely detailed picture of mohalla-life in Lahore, showing spaces where Hindus and Muslims and Sikhs were mixing in college life or daily life, while at the same time highlighting the segregation in the city.

'I grew up in the '80s and '90s in Friends Colony, a part of south Delhi that borders Jamia Nagar, a Muslim area, and got a profound sense of the divisions between Hindus and Muslims. And what I keep trying to turn over in my head – which I'm sure you do as well – is how we are brought up with this myth of a syncretic past, where Partition becomes *the* moment when everything is ripped apart. I'm interested to see how much truth there is to that picture. Sometimes, the vastness of numbers and statistics of the violence during Partition serve as a distraction from the truth of the situation. It's a big rupture that obscures all the micro relationships that may have existed before. I'm not a historian, but I am curious to learn more about it.'

'It does always find its way into your work,' I note. 'Either subliminally or consciously, traces of Partition linger in both *Family Planning* and *The Association of Small Bombs*. You fold the event into your characters, their attitudes, their memories. It provides a lot of the context to the book...'

'Yeah,' he agrees, 'I am interested in it because my own life has played out as a series of migrations. My parents migrated to the States in the '70s and then made the unusual journey *back* to India in the '80s, when I was two years old. Meanwhile, my grandparents had a forced migration from what became Pakistan in '47, and then there is my own voluntary migration to the States. I'm interested to know if these many migrations give rise to similar feelings. When you know that everyone before you has gone through a similar kind of loss or displacement, does it salve your wounds?'

I nod, so he continues.

'I don't know whether it's the silence around Partition in my family that restricts entry into the memory of that time...' he says, pausing for a few seconds, '...but there is a sort of self-hypnosis that occurs while writing fiction that allows my subconscious to delve into terrains that I may not have access to otherwise. For instance, when I'm talking to you right now, I have my analytical brain on and I'm trying to explain my points of entry into the subject of Partition. But try as I might to reason it, I do believe that it's an innate part of so many of us who are children and grandchildren of post-Partition refugees.

'Additionally, in my own family, there is a romanticization of Lahore as this Edenic, irretrievable place from which we have fallen. I've never been there, and I don't know when I will get to go or *if* I will get to go. But I wonder if the life my family recreated in their adopted city after Partition was a copy of the life they'd left behind, a recreation of Lahore in Delhi, as far as was possible. I also often think about my parents being the first generation of Punjabi refugees to freely explore and discover Delhi. They had a more passionate relationship with the city than their middle-aged parents, who'd been broken by Partition, whose behaviours and lifestyle had been impacted by Partition, who had lost their motherland and gained a nation. There's just so much there for a novelist to unpack.' Karan chuckles.

His observations are fascinating and ones that I have not considered before. They remind me of the introduction to the English translation of Yashpal's epic, where the critic Harish Trivedi writes:

> The first volume of the novel is titled 'Vatan aur Desh', *vatan* being the land where one is born or one's motherland, while *desh* is the nation. It is the forcible split and unnatural dichotomy caused by Partition between these two normally synonymous terms that lies at the heart of the novel.[21]

'If you *are* thinking with your analytical brain and not your novelist brain at the moment,' I begin, 'what is the dominant emotion when you think of Partition?'

'That it was completely needless,' Karan is quick to respond, 'that so many of the horrors of Partition – rapes, murders, all forms of savagery – could have been avoided merely by the British caring as much about *people* as they did about infrastructure. One of the most interesting things when you begin researching Partition is how so many of Radcliffe's decisions were built around great achievements in the field of infrastructure, like the canal and irrigation system. How do we draw a line so these great systems of the colonies are preserved? But he's not really thinking about what's going to happen to the people, their livelihoods, their fates after the line is drawn. This is one aspect of the needless slaughter.

'And the second aspect is the sheer chaos that erupts when the borders are finally announced. For so long, people didn't know what Partition meant, and they didn't know whether there would be "soft" borders or not, which cities or villages would fall on which side, and so the confusion, the inhumanity, the violence. I-I...' His voice trails off, and he exhales. 'I'm sorry, I'm sorry, I'm just talking in circles now.'

I smile. 'Don't be sorry. Almost every person I've spoken to in the last few years – whether they were alive during Partition or have inherited its stories – feels this confusion. And especially with our generation, I think it's so difficult for us to fully imagine the days of Partition because we are constantly sewing together fragments of history we have read or watched, or memories we've been told by our families. It's a bit difficult to not talk in circles if your information is fuelled by your imagination of what *could have happened* in those days.'

'Right, yeah,' Karan says. 'So I would say, what actually comes to mind is just confusion. I feel intense confusion, or an image of chaos, when I think of Partition, which I'm fortunate to have never experienced in my own life: an extreme disruption.'

'But Justice Mehr Chand Mahajan's legacy is not the first thing you think about?' I ask.

'Well, I personally never knew him, so all I have are the outlines of history to remember him by ... like anybody else. Of course, I'm fascinated to have an ancestor who was so close to moments of political change, and I've read his memoir, which I find really interesting. I would have obviously loved to have been there to see what his actual day-to-day was like, what he felt about the historic era he lived through.'

I admire how Karan never allows his genealogy to colour his understanding of Independence or Partition, rather inspiring him to learn more about that time. As our conversation draws to a close, he returns to Yashpal's *Jhootha Sach*.

'Do you know what really struck me about the novel? Particularly in relation to my own writing?'

'The kaleidoscopic representation of a pre-partitioned Lahore?' I offer, the words tumbling out quickly.

'Yes, absolutely.' He smiles enthusiastically. 'But it was not just the incredible richness of detail and recreation of Partition, written merely ten years after the event. There was something about the rhythm of the book, the attitudes, the language. It went straight to the core of my own ways of seeing and being that had been inherited from a culture I'd never been able to put a name to before: the culture of an undivided Punjab. This may be a minor realization, but it made me so aware of all the intangibles that had been carried across during Partition – ways of being, living, interacting – that still remain and are inherited by subsequent generations, despite families having acclimatized to their adopted cities post migration. I suppose, what I'm trying to say is that...' Karan pauses to frame his final thoughts, '...your influences may be in the places where you are not looking, because those places are now inaccessible.'

IT IS WITH the discovery of a refugee registration certificate that Sanjana Chopra, born in 1996, and I begin to speak about Partition. In a piece written for the Museum of Material Memory,* entitled 'Train to India',[22] Sanjana and her sister, Ria, collaboratively write about the certificate. It is dated November 1947, when their great-grandfather, Mangal Sain Chopra, whom they call bauji, registered himself at the Paharganj desk of the Ministry of Relief and Rehabilitation, five months after arriving in the capital city of Delhi. This formal document became the family's first identification of belonging to a new land – of having officially left behind their home in what was now Pakistan and settling in India.

Mangal Sain Chopra was born in 1904 and grew up in the village of Chak Maluk, Chakwal tehsil, district Jhelum. He got a job with the railways after his matriculation, moving to Multan where he worked at the divisional superintendent's office. He married Kaushalya Devi in 1946, after which the couple moved to Rawalpindi, which was the last place where they lived in undivided India. Sanjana recalls how stories about their great-grandfather had been told ever since they were children. 'I have this very strong memory of being in Grade 4 or 5 when Partition was first introduced in our history textbook. But by then, I was already aware of how it had shaped my family, so I raised my hand in class and told my teacher that we had migrated to India in 1947, leaving everything on the other side.'

---

* The Museum of Material Memory is a digital repository of material culture of the Indian subcontinent, tracing family history and social ethnography through heirlooms, collectibles and objects of antiquity.

'What did the teacher say, and the rest of the students?' I ask, impressed.

'The next day, many of my classmates told me they'd gone home and asked their families about Partition as well.'

I smile widely at the thought of Sanjana being a story collector even at the age of eleven, and ask whether anyone else in her family, apart from her and Ria, takes an interest in these stories. Brightly, she tells me that it was actually her father who began asking his grandfather, bauji, questions about Partition. She suggests that maybe like the stories themselves, this habit of asking questions, too, has been passed down. I am intrigued by this legacy of curiosity, which can often skip generations, but, in this case, has graced every member of the Chopra family.

'When bauji passed, my father was still only thirty-four years old. Throughout his twenties, he would ask him about why they came to India, and, most importantly, why he never joined the freedom movement. Everyone around bauji would have been fighting for independence and freedom *from* the British, and yet he was working *for* the British in the railways. They spoke about this topic extensively, and I think the conversation was mutually engaging – because not only was my father asking all these questions, but bauji, in his old age, was available to answer them. He had a lot of stories to tell, mostly around the sacrifices that people of his generation had made by moving to another country to give their children a safer life. It influenced my father a lot, and he realized that whatever he did in life had to make the family proud in some way, in order to honour the sacrifice. Bauji's stories were then passed down to my sister and me.'

'And what kind of impact did the stories have on you?'

She responds with the question, 'Do you remember when Google Earth was launched?'

'I do,' I reply curiously.

Sanjana beams. 'The first thing our grandfather did was search for Chak Maluk. He spent the next few days looking at every mohalla he had visited as a child, every field he played in, and every city they visited in the summer holidays. Both of bauji's offices – in Multan and in Rawalpindi – are still divisional offices of the Pakistan Railways. When our grandfather showed them to Ria and me, it seemed almost incredible that bauji had spent so many of his years in these distant places. He had walked in these corridors, signed papers in these rooms, shared chai with his colleagues in these very lawns.[23] These stories were our legacy.'

'It must have been so moving for your grandfather to be able to see an image of his birthplace, or point on a map and say, "Look, this is where I'm from."' I raise my finger and point to an imaginary map. 'You may not be able to go back there, but you can touch it on a map, you can look at its landscape through a computer. It's obviously not the same, but it's one step closer...'

'Exactly, and my sister and I weren't looking at it through the lens of loss. I don't think that's what our inheritance has been. It is not loss, but of being able to trace our history to a particular land, to a particular culture.' She pauses before she adds, 'You know, nearly seventy-five years have passed since Partition, but I don't know how much we've learnt from it. Our collective legacy is not yet one of tolerance or reconciliation or harmony.'

As I gesture for her to continue, our conversation takes a suddenly serious, less nostalgic turn.

'Partition remains relevant to our society, particularly because of the discourse around religion in India today. Has Partition not shaped long-lasting perceptions about religion?' she asks me.

Several instances come to mind – personal, public, political.

'In my family, there's been a lot of unlearning in terms of religious intolerance – we are mindful about fostering a legacy of tolerance and harmonious living, in society and within the family. But while Partition was a sociopolitical event, the intolerance, the lack of trust and disharmony that was a consequence of it, is still evident in the world around us. After Partition, many families may have achieved upward financial and social mobility, but I don't think we've learnt to resolve any of the differences that caused Partition. And not only have we *not* resolved those differences at a societal level, but we have also *not* learnt to live together *within* our own communities and families.'

'What do you mean?' I ask.

'Our ancestors witnessed an incredibly painful period of history, undertaking great personal risks, and the only hope that kept most of them going was that this would ensure a "better" life for themselves and their children. Did this "better" only mean financially better, or something more? Our communities were torn apart in 1947, but did we learn to value the relationships that accompanied this betterment? Essentially, seven decades later, where do we stand? Have we learnt anything at all? The conceptualization of the "other" shifts from context to context – sometimes it's other communities, other times it's anyone who is different from you and gets alienated all the same.

'I've been lucky that much of my perception has been shaped by my father, who has a way of contextualizing stories, even the most violent stories of Partition. He reminds me of the other side, and how one can never determine "who killed more" or "who suffered more" because, well, *everyone* suffered in their own way. But this narrative, however reductive, is still being wielded in society today. Not to mention, there were so many intangible and invisible losses that occurred at Partition...'

'Many of which are only now being unearthed and understood, so many decades later,' I add.

'There is much we still need to learn,' she says, nodding gravely. 'But this quantification of suffering and trauma is dangerous, because it only takes away from that learning.'

'WHAT CAN'T BE cured must be endured,' wrote Salman Rushdie in *Midnight's Children*, and it is exactly this condition about which I speak with Arpita, born in 1992, and her father, Pranab Akhanda, born in 1956 – the rejection of a divided Hindustan by their ancestor, Asim Akhanda, who was born in Srikail, Comilla district (in present-day Bangladesh), in 1925.

'My father came from Comilla in East Bengal to Calcutta in West Bengal in 1941 to go study in Santiniketan. But he ultimately ended up joining the freedom movement under the leadership of Prafulla Chandra Ray, who is regarded as the father of chemical science in India. My father was introduced to him through his maternal cousin, Paresh Chandra Acharya, who was Ray's disciple in Kolkata,' Pranab tells me. 'Partition has been a frequent topic of discussion in our home ever since my childhood.'

'In fact,' Arpita adds, 'my grandmother was from Barisal (also in present-day Bangladesh and erstwhile East Bengal), so both sides of Baba's family have been impacted by Partition.'

Arpita, like her grandfather, is at Santiniketan at the moment, a practising artist with bachelor's and master's degrees in fine arts from Kala Bhavana, Visva Bharati University. Meanwhile, her father is at their home in Cuttack, Odisha. I join the video call from Delhi, watching the duo talk about the days of Partition as much with me as amongst themselves – adding, debating, confirming and reminiscing. Sometimes, Arpita translates into Bengali for her father; other times, he speaks in English and Hindi. As I ask them what kind of stories they have heard about the time, the inspiring legacy of Asim Akhanda and his undying belief in an undivided India begin to emerge.

'In 1943, when there was bombing and famine in Calcutta, my father returned to his village in East Bengal,' Pranab narrates. 'Then from there, he travelled to Benares with his guru, Swami Swarupananda Paramhansa Dev, to practise karma yoga, living in the ashram till 1950. But in 1946, when riots ravaged Noakhali, he rushed back home to Srikail, for the last time, to bring his second brother and mother to Benares with him. It was during this time that their eldest brother migrated to Tripura, but in the chaos of the riots and the violence that ensued, the family lost touch with him.'

'My grandfather was very disheartened by the idea of a possible Partition,' Arpita says. 'He was attached to the freedom struggle, believed in independence from British rule, but did not endorse the idea of a divided Hindustan. He did not agree to freedom on *those* terms.'

Pranab picks up the story. 'In 1946, while he was on his way back to Comilla, he stopped in Calcutta. This was around the same time that the Indian National Army (INA) trials of Colonel Prem Sahgal, Colonel Gurbaksh Singh Dhillon and Major General Shah Nawaz Khan were going on at the Red Fort in Delhi, and there was a simultaneous movement of support for their release in Calcutta. These were momentous times.' His voice grows sombre. 'But they carried their fair share of tragedy. It was here that my father's friend, Ramesh Banerjee, was shot down by the police.'

'I think this is one story that was very close to my grandfather.' Arpita's tone echoes her father's. 'Whenever he spoke about this protest, he would describe how they were standing side by side when the bullet flew by his ear and shot his friend. There was no ambulance in sight, and he quickly dragged him to a water tank to get him some water before he lost his life.' She inhales deeply. 'This incident was close to his heart, because he would often bring it up.'

'Do you think it continued to impact him?' I ask.

'Ramesh was a very close friend of my father's,' Pranab says, 'and they had undergone many struggles together when my father was actively involved in the freedom movement. They were very close. But, you see, my father narrated these stories throughout his life. It was not only this incident that impacted him but also the decision to bisect the nation. He never accepted Partition, and the day it was announced...' He smiles and gestures to his daughter to complete the story.

'The act he performed on the day that Partition was announced is very interesting. He took the clothes he wore while protesting against the British and immersed them in the river Ganga, as if to say that he did not accept a freedom granted at *this* cost. That Hindustan was divided was a deep regret he lived with for the rest of his life. As you may know, in Hinduism we have this idea of *tarpana*, to give away, to offer. This was a kind of offering, or rather a gesture of relinquishment.

'In 2015, as the Independence Day drew closer, as a visual artist, I kept thinking how our bodies carried the idea of freedom within them, how it was represented as a performative gesture. In a group discussion with friends, we thought about recreating various performances at the moment of Independence – the first, a very public kind with Jawaharlal Nehru hoisting the flag at midnight, and then with Mahatma Gandhi fasting in Calcutta in order to pacify the unrestful masses. But after my father shared this story of my grandfather's offering, his *tarpana*, I kept thinking about the act of political performance that I carry within my body, and to commemorate the gestures of my ancestor, I performed a similar act in a river. Repeating the past this way was an act of revisiting what had been forgotten, and these stories have now become the core of my art practice. It was a very emotional connection between two generations.'

'And symbolic as well,' I note.

'Tell me,' Pranab now asks, more rhetorically than anything else, 'what was the use of this Partition? What good has come of it? Nothing is done, no? Only some lakhs of people have migrated from one side to the other, there is agony, suffering, violence, bloodshed, anger, hate, everything bad. No gains, only loss everywhere.'

'So, you think things would have been better had Partition not happened?' I ask.

'Obviously!' he replies in an instant. 'India would have been in a much better position today. Powerful, developed and diverse. My father believed in that kind of a nation. One Hindustan for all.'

There is pride in his voice as he recalls his father and the ideals he stood for. I smile softly and nod in response. It is a utopian thought, and though I can't disagree with him, I do ask, 'But what do you say to those who gained nationhood – Pakistan, Bangladesh?'

'Yes, they have their own country today; we cannot debate that and nor should we. What is done is done. But just imagine how commanding a country we would have been had we stayed united? Today, we have so many micro divisions, even within our own country, based on caste, class, religion...' He clicks his tongue. 'We are more divided than we were before.'

'And how do you feel about this?' I ask Arpita.

'The same,' she maintains. 'Before visiting our village I may have thought differently, reasoned through Partition. But on 1 January 2018, I travelled with Baba to Srikail, seventy-two years after my grandfather had left it. We stood at the same place where he had taken the last photograph of his village. We spoke to the people, listened to the stories from the days of Partition and understood that no one wanted to leave their homes from this side or that. It was then that I began wondering – as my father and grandfather had for decades – what the point of Partition was.'

Pranab agrees. 'Nobody wanted it, only the British and the politicians. And politicians knew nothing about common people. It was common people who suffered, who died, who starved, who lost family, home, land, wealth. Common people.' He gestures to the three of us as he says this.

'And it is common people who are still paying the price for division,' Arpita chimes in. 'So many families were divided on both sides of the border, or simply separated from one another in the confusion. People migrated to different places out of fear and persecution. My own grandfather's eldest brother – the one who went to Tripura and lost touch – was reunited with him twenty-five years after Partition!'

'What?' I ask, aghast. 'Twenty-five years later?'

'From 1946, after the Noakhali riots, to 1971, the two brothers did not meet,' Pranab tells me. 'Each thought the other had died. How could people keep in touch in those days? It was so confusing, so much chaos, migration, violence. In 1956, my father moved to Cuttack and made it his base. A few years later, through some connections, he discovered that his eldest brother was in Tripura and had written him a letter, which was sent to my father, and they began corresponding. Then, in 1968, their mother passed away in Cuttack but the eldest brother couldn't see her. In 1971, he finally travelled to Cuttack and the brothers were reunited. I saw it in front of my eyes – long-lost siblings, holding each other, crying for hours.'

'After twenty-five years, 1946 to 1971,' Arpita reiterates. 'This should demonstrate the sheer madness that Partition created. Maybe this is one of the reasons why there's so much remorse around Partition in our family – the fact that we lost twenty-five years of togetherness that we're never going to get back. You know, in our family, we sing a song written by our guru Swami Swarupananda Paramhansa Dev, called *"Khanda aajike Akhanda"*, which means let the ones divided unite today. My grandfather has taught us all to pray for this, not just for ourselves but for the entire universe.'

'*Poora duniya ke liye,*' Pranab repeats. 'To pray for peace and unity of the whole world.' He then says something to Arpita in Bengali, bringing his hand to his heart, and she nods attentively.

She clears her throat and turns her attention towards me. She is smiling widely.

'Our legacy is embedded within our last name, Akhanda, which in Bengali, like in Hindi, means something that is unbreakable, which cannot be divided, fragmented, or broken into pieces.' Quietly, she adds, 'Like the dream of an undivided, unpartitioned India.'

12

Loss

❦

SITTING IN WHAT SHE calls The Lahore Room in her central Delhi bungalow, Sumohini Bhagat (née Tek Chand), daughter of the late Justice (Dr) Bakshi Tek Chand, tells me that even though her father was an advisor to Sir Cyril Radcliffe's Punjab Boundary Commission, the family left Lahore unprepared and unwilling. They simply did not believe that Partition could become a reality and, once it did, that it would remain permanent. Migrating to Dalhousie as a temporary arrangement, they soon had to accept the fact that 'Lahore was now lost forever'.[1]

When we meet in 2016, almost seventy years have passed since Partition and, reflecting on the sudden assimilation the family underwent, Sumohini Bhagat says, 'Looking back, I think we were able to overcome the tragedy of Partition solely because of our parents. I am the youngest of seven sisters, and I can't remember anyone in our family lamenting the loss of our house or lands, saying, "*Yeh reh gaya, Partition ho gaya, zindagi khatam ho gayi.*" No, that was never allowed to happen. Our parents told us to look forward, not dwell in the past and to take Partition in our stride as something normal … which it really wasn't.' She looks around The Lahore Room and sighs.

The room we sit in contains all the objects that the family managed to carry with them across the border: paintings, artefacts, documents, even furniture. On the entrance wall, to the left, are two marble plaques from No. 6 Fane Road, Lahore, bearing the words 'Bakshi Tek Chand' on one and 'Shanti Bhawan' on the other, in Hindi, English and Urdu. Decades after Partition, the grand house was being demolished, and its new inhabitants travelled to Delhi, where the Justice's family now lived, and delivered the two plaques to their rightful owners.[2]

There is an exceptional energy here, and I carry this thought with me long after I leave: Lahore was lost but The Lahore Room remained. It was something that could be put together, cultivated, so that a part of home may be retained, as if it were transplanted to another city in another country. In a strange way, the existence of this room both compensated for what had been left behind but also remained a resolute reminder of that loss. Within the four walls, there lived a shadow of the Lahore on the other side.

Inspired by this interview, I begin to collect memories of the losses caused by Partition, and very quickly arrive at the conclusion that the passing of years has not made these losses easier to bear.

AS A MEMBER of the Fakir family from his paternal grandmother's side, Farhan Ahmed Shah spends his days immersed in the preservation of history and culture. My first introduction to him is through the Fakir Khana Museum,[3] located near Bhati Gate in Lahore's Walled City, presently run by the sixth generation of his family. Tracing their connections to the Sikh Empire, three of the family's ancestors, Fakir Nooruddin, Fakir Azizuddin, and Fakir Imamuddin,[4] were ministers in the court of Maharaja Ranjit Singh. Over time, they accumulated extraordinary artefacts, including many bestowed by the maharaja himself, that can be found within the walls of this family home-cum-museum, opened in 1901.

Farhan was born in 1980 in Lahore, and our conversation meanders around the profound relationship he shares with his city. In a piece entitled *Legends of Lahore*, he once wrote:

...at its heart, Lahore is a survivor ... It has seen ages of war and devastation, as well as periods of cultural, intellectual, musical, literary and humanistic evolution. It remains a city of vivid differences and haunting nuances; where bustling bazaars, frenzied streets, fading elegance and assorted architecture merge into a history that is both dramatic and fascinating. For those who know how to listen, every place in Lahore – from the most monumental structure to the most ordinary street – has a story to tell.[5]

'Our generation is slowly losing all ties to the history of an undivided India,' he says to me over the phone one evening. 'All the people who knew my grandparents are in their twilight years, and once that generation is gone, our link to a syncretic past will be ruptured. But this history is part of what enriches the culture of my city, and I have an interest in keeping it alive.'

'But your family did not witness any displacement during Partition?' I ask.

I can hear him smile even over the phone, across the miles that separate our twin cities. 'One doesn't need to have felt displacement to feel the loss of a shared culture caused by Partition,' he says. 'My ancestors have always been from present-day Pakistan. But I feel a resonance with a pre-Partition Lahore, which was drastically changed by the drawing of this line.'

'How so?'

'For instance, if I ever chance upon an old building on Mall Road, or when I'm in the walled city and see a pre-Partition structure, *main usko dekhta hi rehta hoon*, I just keep staring at it. In my head, I'm trying to replay the life of that era. I'm trying to transport myself back to that time. The lived history of a city is what fascinates me, and Lahore is peppered with the remnants of a multicultural, multi-religious life before Partition. How did people live, what were their habits, how did they coexist in these old lanes, in these homes that still betray traces of their identities? The homes that still have Hindu names or symbols on the outside facades, or a church that exists on the fringes of a busy marketplace, the traces of Devanagari and Gurmukhi. I have a lot of affection for that time before Partition when Lahore was the hub of syncretic culture.' Farhan's voice is full of joy. 'I think about how someone must have been going to a gurudwara, someone else had a *tilak* on their forehead, there was the sound of the *azaan*, or a mixed group of students riding their bicycles to Government College. I become consumed by these thoughts, and the reason I can entertain them for so long is that I've never been able to come to any conclusion. I have conjured up this image in my head of a beautiful era, but...' His voice trails off.

'What kind of conclusion are you hoping to find?' I ask.

'The exactitude of those times. *Waqt kaisa tha, log kaise the, unki zubaan kaisi thi, unke dinn kaise the.* These are mundane things to think about, but they consume me. And sometimes I think I may never want to reach any conclusion because I'm afraid of defiling the romance I have created in my head about that era.'

'It's ungraspable,' I nod, 'the imagined landscape of the past.'

'The imagined landscape, yes,' he repeats. Farhan then descends into the moment of the subcontinent's rupture, speaking slowly, working through his thoughts, knowing well that Partition is what separated my family from his city.

'Partition is very complicated, *you* know that. It is possible to have many thoughts about it, and to have those many thoughts contradict one another as well. While on one hand, yes, I feel this incredible romance towards the past – and I accept that there was camaraderie, festivals celebrated collectively, there was amity, or at least respect, between Hindus, Muslims and Sikhs – but then there were also everyday incidents of othering, like the division of water and utensils. There was a latent nationalism, which came alive to make Partition possible.

'Of course, I do mourn the fact that, with Partition, an entire epoch of cultural diversity was lost, and I am physically reminded of this each time I see a house with a Muslim name engraved on its façade standing alongside a house with a Hindu name engraved on its façade. It makes me very sad that this culture was unable to survive, and that in itself is a charming, rather utopian, thought. But at the same time, I will say that there were problems between communities, and those problems percolated over time...'

There comes a natural pause in the conversation as he gathers his thoughts.

Sometimes when Farhan and I speak as friends, I almost forget that he is in Lahore and I am in Delhi and there is a border between us. I forget that he is Pakistani and I am Indian, that he observes Independence Day on 14 August and I the day after. I forget that I am half an hour ahead in time zone. I forget because it's easy to forget. I forget because when it rains in his city, it rains in mine too. Sometimes while we are speaking, I genuinely forget that we are now separate peoples. But inevitably, one is reminded.

'Contrary to popular belief,' he begins, carefully drawing together both research and observation, 'I don't think it was people like Jinnah or Nehru or Patel who affected Partition; it was too huge a phenomenon to be impacted by a handful of people within a specific time frame. My view is that it was the people who caused Partition, that Partition was a forgone conclusion. It became an inevitability the moment the British took reins of our land. It was the first time that Muslims or Hindus resorted to political group formation based on cultural identities in order to protect their community's interests from the (perceived) threats of the other. There were no Muslim Leagues or Hindu Mahasabhas, any Two Nation Theory or Hindutva ideology before the Raj. Partition was merely a culmination of decades of distrust that brewed between communities over time, courtesy the British. It was made possible by the masses, and people like Jinnah or Nehru were just leaders the masses chose to lead them.'

Farhan's voice now carries both the past and the future. 'I speak as a proud Pakistani, for even though Partition resulted in so many losses, it also gave birth to two distinct national identities that have evolved significantly over the last several decades. To be one again is no longer possible. But perhaps the only way this loss can be overcome is through conversations and friendships, through empathy and curiosity about the other side, by gently trying to remake cultural ties.'

❦

SEVERAL YEARS AGO, Amrita Singh, a doctoral scholar and assistant professor, invited me to speak to her students at Kamala Nehru College, Delhi University, about my research on Partition. After the lecture, over a cup of tea, she mentioned to me that her family was originally from Montgomery (now Sahiwal) but her grandparents studied and married in Lahore, and her grandfather's first job was in the city. In 1947, they migrated to Delhi, but the stories of Partition were so commonplace in her childhood that she always understood 'home' to be a place beyond the border.

A few years after our meeting at the university, when I begin to write this book, we exchange emails on the subject. Amrita doesn't write much, but even in the brevity of her words, a Lahore-shaped hole begins to appear, unable to be filled by any other adopted home.

Partition evokes a sense of longing in me, a second-hand nostalgia, and sometimes hurt and anger too. But most resonant is the loss of homeland. The places that my family once inhabited are inaccessible to me. In 1995, when I was ten years old, we visited the Attari–Wagah border. I remember how my father had pointed to the long road between and beyond the gates that connected Amritsar and Lahore, and said that one day we'll drive through and visit 'home'. Each time I visit the border areas, I'm reminded of his words and despair that it's unlikely to happen in either of our lifetimes.

If Lahore continues to capture the imaginations of those who migrated to India, those in Pakistan long for Amritsar, merely an hour away. Lahore and Amritsar share a unique, umbilical relationship, which is not only difficult but rather impossible to rupture by the mere exercise of drawing a line between the two. For instance, if the beating heart of Amritsar is the Golden Temple, Sri Harmandir Sahib, then one must also remember that the foundation stone of that very gurudwara was said to have been laid by Lahore's Sufi saint, Mian Mir, at the invitation of the fifth Sikh Guru, Arjan Dev. Bound by the overarching notion of Punjabiyat, the residents of the two cities cannot deny the 'the persisting continuities of long traditions, sustained habitations ... and cultural geographies...'[6]

In a 2015 travel piece titled 'From Lahore to Amritsar', Fatima Bhutto writes:

> Tonight, I packed my bags for a journey I have made over and over again in my mind. Two countries, two cities, partitioned by history and imagined distance, 68 years ago, over two days in August. I don't have a favourite number or anything, but two seems to show up an awful lot as I plan to cross the border between Pakistan and India, stepping from Lahore over to Amritsar. Two. But how do you journey across one Punjab? Is it travel if you constantly feel like you're at home?[7]

For Dr Ali Usman Qasmi, associate professor at the Lahore Institute of Management Sciences (LUMS), the word Amritsar has been embedded in the collective memory of his family and feels like second nature. Both his parents were born in Amritsar before Partition, though they were infants when their families migrated to Pakistan.

'I have known it as a place of origin or belonging. My father's mother always lamented that it did not rain as much or as beautifully in Wazirabad, where they finally settled, as it did in Amritsar! She even missed the city's rainfall, and nothing else was even half as good.' Ali smiles when he says this.

Smiling widely in response, I ask him, 'What other stories were you told?'

'Well, my paternal family was able to assimilate into Pakistani society and benefitted a lot from their migration to this side. When it comes to Amritsar, their memories are always full of love and a very strong sense of nostalgia. But my maternal family was completely destroyed by Partition; they were never able to recover from the losses, not only economic but also emotional. There is a deep sense of displacement associated with their migration that was never overcome.'

'And what side do you find yourself associating more with?' I ask, keeping in mind Ali's own scholarship[8] on Partition and its related subjects. In 2018, he along with the historian Pallavi Raghavan[9] jointly taught a course titled 'Beyond India and Pakistan: Changing the Foundations of South Asian History', as a collaboration between LUMS and the O.P. Jindal Law School in Sonipat, India. Every Friday, the students 'met' on Skype, physically separated by hundreds of miles and a tense political border, to discuss everything from the Indus Valley Civilization to Sayyad Ahmad Khan, and were divided into mixed groups for projects that were completed using Skype, WhatsApp, email and other forms of social media.[10]

'Perhaps it is because of my work,' he begins, 'but I do tend to gravitate towards my mother's side and the intergenerational trauma that they don't really want to discuss. Now, there are only three women left in the family that remember Amritsar – my mother and her two sisters. Everyone else has passed away. But the loss they carry within them is palpable – and almost haunting.'

'Why do you say haunting?'

'Because you can imagine what once *used to be*, a shadow of a life – the large family, the successful businesses, the status in society. And it all sort of falls apart because of the colossal impact of Partition. My mother was born in 1946 and was only one year old at the time. She has spent her whole life in Pakistan, and years have passed now – decades, even – but that sense of displacement is still so profoundly felt.' Ali pauses for a few seconds before juxtaposing the two sides of his family.

'Meanwhile, what I find interesting is that despite being so pro-Pakistan, my father insists that he is very much Amritsari as well; for him, those two identities can exist simultaneously. He takes a lot of pride in being from a community of Kashmiris that settled in Amritsar in the nineteenth century,[11] and that this community also included figures like Saadat Hasan Manto and A. Hameed, Rustam-i-Hind Gama Pehalwan and Sufi Tabassum. Amritsar makes up a lot of the heart of my father's personality, and this is the great contradiction. How does one categorize this emotion?' He looks at me curiously, but it is clear that the question is rhetorical. One can be many things at the same time, and those many things can rebut one another, even at their core.

'Do you know when I truly feel the impact of Partition, the loss?' he asks me now.

Quietly, I shake my head.

He sighs. 'Even as I'm thinking this, I feel *something* – whenever I fill out a visa form and have to put in the birthplace of my parents, I write down Amritsar, and I feel that connection. I am always confused whether to follow it up with British India, or Undivided India, or just India, but the connection is undeniable. And the more I think about it ... well, we didn't have the *muhajir* experience, we are not a divided family, no one remained on that side, and yet the connection to Amritsar is visceral. I can feel it, even though I was born in Pakistan. It is an invisible attachment, something that I have not lived but lost.'

I smile. 'But not every loss can be seen.'

'Exactly.' Ali's voice now carries a shade of warmth. 'It is only felt.'

'The visa form, the way you speak about Amritsar with ownership and conviction...' I begin.

'Yes, because no matter what, no one can take this away from me. *Yeh toh likhna padega*: "Born in Amritsar." It belongs to my grandparents and parents ... and, through memory, to me,' Ali says with pride.

And as he says this, I remember a passage from Kavita Panjabi's poignant essay titled 'A Unique Grace', where she writes that though 'the sense of homeland left behind forever remains as a powerful memory of loss, handed down from generation to generation', human beings have the ability to rebuild and remake their homes. They are resilient, and as they find new habitats and acclimatize, the loss of an erstwhile home is gradually folded into the past, becoming memory. Panjabi asks why so many of us, then, have 'carefully nurtured this sense of loss across generations, for far from being our own experience, [it] is but a memory borrowed from our parents and grandparents'.[12]

∽

'ALL OF PUNJAB is burning,' the Urdu satirist and columnist Fikr Taunsvi wrote in his journal in the days following the announcement of the Partition line. For nearly four months, he diligently recorded the metamorphosis of an undivided land into two divided, bloodied halves.

> Everyone was shocked. But everyone was silent. I was neither shocked nor silent. I was busy creating my routine. I had grown used to hearing everything: today, in such and such town, so many Hindu–Sikhs had been gunned down; at that station, 2,000 Muslims were put under the sword; today, in such-and-such district, young women were denuded and paraded naked on the streets of free India; a train arrived empty today except for only two injured people, it had lighted itself of the cargo of the corpses on the way. Only this much? Tell me some bigger news. Tell me that today there is not a single human left in the Punjab![13]

'A massive exercise in human misery' was how the American photographer Margaret Bourke-White described the movement of refugees across the newly formed border. Recording the evidence of human loss on both sides, one night she chanced upon an encampment of refugees who had survived not only the man-made disaster of violence but also the natural disaster of the flooding of the river Beas. She spoke with a man called Rasik, who had fled from Jullundur, where he and his brothers once owned a 10-acre orange grove. He was digging a grave by the side of the road for his eight-year-old son who had died that afternoon. Rasik had been carrying the child's body the entire day until he had a chance to bury it with dignity and recite a prayer, as any father would wish to do.[14]

By 1948, as the great migration drew to a close, between 12 and 15 million people had been uprooted, and between 1 and 2 million were dead – this was the human cost of Partition, the insurmountable loss. Keeping these vast numbers in mind, the two conversations in this section are from district Mirpur (in present-day Pakistan-administered Kashmir) and speak to the loss of family members during Partition.

'WHEN I WAS young, my paternal grandmother, Chanchal, would tell stories about living in the rehabilitation colony of Lajpat Nagar in New Delhi,' Nivedita Bobal begins our conversation this way. She was born in 1999, over fifty years after Partition. 'And almost every story was about the widows who had been allotted plots. All four of my grandparents came from across the border to India – from Multan, Peshawar, Chak Hamid and Mirpur – but it is my grandmother's story that has shaped my understanding of 1947. The first time I learned of what this Partition was and what it had done to her family was when I was in Grade 7.'

'That's still quite young,' I note.

'It was, yes. My grandmother was born in 1943, so she was only four years old at the time of Partition. There are things she remembered, but most of it, the really traumatic parts, had been … maybe forgotten is not the right word, but supressed. They were very hard on her mind. So, my grandmother began exchanging emails with her elder cousin, Vishwanath, who had migrated to Canada. He was ten or eleven years older than her and remembered every single detail of what had happened to the family in Mirpur, and how they had fled. When we began receiving his emails, I read them but didn't quite understand. They just remained on the periphery of my mind. But a few years later, I revisited them and…' Nivedita closes her eyes and shudders, '…the sheer horror of those days hasn't left me since.'

I say nothing, and she takes a few seconds for herself.

'My grandmother, her siblings and mother were in captivity for quite some time after Partition...'

'At Alibeg?' The words tumble out of my mouth involuntarily. Stories of the violence at Mirpur, the imprisonment of Hindu and Sikh refugees at the Alibeg gurudwara, and their retrieval by the International Red Cross in 1948 have cropped up consistently over the years of my research.[15] Sometimes, I wish I didn't come across as many stories from the region as I do, for the sheer brutality endured by the families never fails to send shivers down my spine.

'They were at Alibeg, yes,' Nivedita confirms, looking through the notes she has made. 'My grandmother didn't remember the name of the camp, but her cousin wrote it in the email, which is how I know. Shall I ... shall I just tell you what I know from the beginning?'

'If you want to,' I say softly and bring out my notebook, 'then I am listening.'

'My grandmother was the youngest of three siblings. Her sister, Sudarshana, was five years older than her, and brother, Sudesh, was three years older. They were born in Mirpur city, and my grandmother tells me that it falls in Pakistan-occupied Kashmir right now. My great-grandfather and his brothers lived with their families in a big haveli. They had Muslim help, and relations were friendly. Everyone lived in peace. It was November 1947 when their home was surrounded by tribal forces called Kabailis, who began firing. No one understood what was happening or where to go, and they fled, scrambling in all directions. My grandmother's father had made sure that all the children wore heavy, red-coloured plush coats because it was snowing outside. My grandmother actually also had a younger sibling, who was barely two months old at the time. He...' Nivedita stops to exhale loudly, overwhelmed.

'Are you all right?' I ask.

'Yes, I'm fine. It's just ... when you read about the numbers displaced at Partition, they don't have the same impact. But when you read the human stories *behind* those numbers ... now that is difficult, and that is what I am affected by. My grandmother's two-month-old brother died in a stampede in the Alibeg camp. He was stepped on and died immediately. How is that fair, how is that humanity? I have heard of people burying their children alive because they could no longer carry them on the long journey to India, or couldn't protect them from violence along the way. Can you imagine arriving at that kind of decision, having no other alternative? That death by the hands of one's own family is preferable to whatever torture one may be put through at the hands of rioters. *These* were the very real consequences of Partition: that there were family members we lost, and many we will never even know about. My grandmother had this cousin, Ladli; he was so small and he just disappeared during the riots. There was no trace of him. My father tried to search for him years later on Google, but they didn't even remember his real name. Aanchal, the pet name Ladli – it means beloved...'

She bites her lips in sadness and I am overcome by the maturity with which she has been collecting all of these painful family stories.

'What you were saying earlier about the statistics of Partition...' I speak with my arms outstretched to both sides, 'they are so vast – a million killed, 15 million displaced – that all the nuances of a human life are lost. When I learnt about Partition at school, I was not made to feel like it was *my* history; it was taught as any other event of the past, completely removed from the present day. Learning about it didn't inspire me to go home and ask about it. But then, the moment you do discover that your family was impacted by it, this grand subcontinental loss suddenly becomes so intimate and personal; decades collapse immediately. The history of Partition is a people's history ... of families like yours and mine. We should be teaching children about common people who were affected, and their stories.'

Nivedita nods passionately. 'All we were told to do at school was regurgitate facts so we could pass exams and write essays. We weren't encouraged to understand it, let alone internalize it. All I knew about 15 August was that it was Independence Day, not that it was married to the tragedy of Partition. Why was I told to memorize the name Maximilien Robespierre[16] in school, even though he had nothing to do with India's history and everything to do with the French Revolution, but I needed to do my own research to discover the name

Cyril Radcliffe, even though the history of independent India begins with his map-making?' Her voice is frenzied, and I agree with every word she says, for I have felt this too.

'Tell me what happened to your grandmother once they were taken to the camp...' I propose.

'She told me that all the children were made to wear these plush red coats with the names and addresses of their father and grandfather sewn inside them for identification purposes. And the family dealt in gold, so each of their pockets was filled with nuggets of gold along with dried fruit. The Kabailis took them to the Alibeg camp and then separated the men from the women and children, who were all kept somewhere underground. My grandmother's brother, Sudesh, was left outside by accident and he fell down in the snow. Someone brought him in – his red coat was easily identifiable – but he had turned completely blue. You know, in all of these stories, my grandmother never mentioned her father. Not once. It was always her mother and siblings. But after reading the letters from Vishwanath uncle, I learnt that her father, Bansi Lal, had died helping his sister retrieve a bullet from her arm right after the Kabailis had surrounded them. No one saw him again after that. In the letters, Vishwanath uncle wrote that my great-grandfather had a robust personality, and he knew how to play the harmonium. But what broke my heart was to read that my grandmother looked exactly like her father, that her face was an exact copy of his.'

Nivedita is visibly emotional, yet she perseveres.

'There are fragments of stories I know ... how my great-grandmother gave birth to another child in the Alibeg camp. I have heard of how all the women collected firewood to make a fire to kill themselves, but never did. An aunt's husband had a shawl embroidered with gold coins that he lathered with ash and mud to protect it from being stolen. These were the coins that helped them restart their life once they arrived in India. I have to admit, it is all a bit overwhelming when you hear it together,' she comments, and I nod in agreement.

'Vishwanath uncle wrote about how my grandmother and her family stayed in the Alibeg camp for six months before they were retrieved by the army* and brought in trucks to Chakrata. Here, they stayed in abandoned English bungalows for some time. Chakrata, now in the Dehra Dun district, was once a cantonment town of the British Indian Army. Then, my grandmother's grandfather brought them to Goraya, in Jalandhar, and it was Vishwanath uncle who eventually brought them all to Delhi. You know, he wrote about the entire experience of surviving the massacre at Mirpur in instalments. He could never write the whole thing all at once, and each time he ended an email, he would say that his eyes had become hazy, or his head felt heavy, or he was losing concentration. It still impacted him, even to think about it...'

'I suppose there are things you cannot forget, even if you want to,' I say.

She nods slowly, folding her notes and keeping them aside. 'I think about all that my grandmother has survived, and how she has emerged stronger because of it. She grew up with no father, and her elder brother, who was only three years older than her, became a father figure. Their strength inspires me, because I don't know how they overcame the magnitude of that loss.'

'At home, do you often speak about Partition?'

'Not the time of,' she says thoughtfully, 'but the before and after, certainly. I have distance from it, so I've been able to make some sense of what happened. I have read books, gone through archives and watched films to gain knowledge of that time. But I fear,' she says gravely, 'I fear that living through Partition was more traumatic than we will ever be able to imagine.'

BETWEEN 1948 AND 1956, a central recovery operation was carried out by the Government of India, 'which sought to recover those

---

* Though the family was of the view that the Indian Army had rescued them, survivors of the Alibeg camp were rescued by members of the International Committee of the Red Cross (ICRC) in March 1948.

women who had been abducted and forcibly converted during the upheaval, and restore them to their respective families and countries where they rightfully belonged'.[17] In 1949, the Abducted Persons (Recovery and Restoration) Act was passed, and during the course of operations, some 30,000 women were recovered: 22,000 Muslim women from India and 8,000 Hindu and Sikh women from Pakistan.[18] Along with the governments of both countries, the International Committee of the Red Cross (ICRC) was also instrumental in setting up active operations to trace women and children who had remained on either side and reunite them with their families. It is on this subject of the recovery of Hindu and Sikh women from the small town of Islamgarh (formerly Ikalgarh) in District Mirpur that Dr Bilal Ahmed Ghous, who was born in 1993, and I speak.

'It was perhaps a year ago that a cousin from Scotland wrote and told me the story of Nazeer, her grandmother and my grandaunt. She said that Nazeer bibi's daughter, Khaksar, now a sixty-eight-year-old resident of the UK, was trying to find her mother. The two had had no contact since Nazeer bibi was taken away all those decades ago. So, I began asking around in Islamgarh, interviewing elders who were alive at Partition, and the story that emerged turned out to be completely different from anything I could have imagined. It was, in fact, the opposite!'

'What happened to Nazeer bibi?' I ask. I am fairly well versed with the consequences of Partition on Hindu and Sikh families that once inhabited the area and were forced to flee. But Bilal hails from a Muslim family of Mirpur, and I am curious to know about the stories he has heard.

'When Partition was announced in 1947, people thought that Mirpur was a safe place, because it fell under the princely state of Kashmir, ruled by the Dogra king Hari Singh. As a result, Hindus and Sikhs from Punjab began migrating to Kashmir. But I have heard from my elders that when the tribal forces entered the city, they first warned Muslim families of the impending attack so that they could make preparations to leave. My grandfather was very young at the time, but he remembers how his family further warned their Hindu and Sikh neighbours to leave as well. There were deep friendships that existed back then. Even the town itself, Mirpur, was founded nearly six hundred years ago by two saints, Hazrat Ali Mira Shah Ghazi, a Muslim, and Gosain Budh Puri, a Hindu. From the name of one was taken "Mir" and from the other was taken "Pur" to make Mirpur, a symbol of interfaith unity.[19] But the families didn't listen, and chose to remain, and so the Muslim families vacated their homes temporarily.'

'I have also heard from older interviewees that the city proper was inhabited by Hindus and Sikhs and the periphery areas were mostly Muslim,' I say.

'It was laid out exactly this way,' Bilal confirms. 'But as soon as the Muslim population left, I am told that Hindus and Sikhs began looting their shops and lands.'

I've never heard this detail before and am tempted to interrupt him for clarification. But then I stop and remind myself that all I've heard till now are the stories of Mirpuris who migrated to India. Naturally, then, the stories told by Mirpuris who became Pakistani may illuminate a different perspective of the same event. I say nothing and continue to listen.

'Meanwhile, the tribal forces and army regulars bombarded the gates of the city in November 1947. And when the Muslims of Mirpur returned to find their properties looted and damaged, they too participated in the violence in retaliation. The massacre it eventually resulted in is astonishing. I was reading about this: how homes were razed to the ground, and tens of thousands of people were brutally murdered and their women abducted and carried into the interiors of Pakistan, sold in the villages of Punjab. I have heard from my elders that another factor fuelling this communal fire was the trains that arrived from India, laden with dead bodies, which angered the population further. Amidst all this, Hindus and Sikhs began fleeing, walking towards India, but many were killed on the way, their bodies littering the long roads and jungles, and their blood turning the waters of rivers red.'

Bilal now raises two fingers and says, 'I want to talk about the Hindu and Sikh women that were left behind in Mirpur, particularly two that became members of my family. The first was a lady named I,[*] who was around sixteen years old in 1947 and was soon married off in the next village and now lives in the UK with her family. And the second was my grandaunt, Nazeer bibi, who was much younger at the time, maybe eleven, and everyone in the house used to call her Munni.'

He takes a deep breath before he admits, 'Now, I don't know how they became part of our family – whether they were adopted after their own families died in the massacre, whether they were saved or … I cannot say. All I can tell you is what I have been able to gather.'

I am struck by Bilal's honesty and candour, particularly on a subject that remains sensitive and personal, even with the passing of decades. I gesture for him to continue.

'Nazeer bibi was not from Mirpur. Her father worked as a legal writer, commonly known as a munshi, in the courts here, but she had travelled either from Hoshiarpur or Akhnoor, because these two cities keep coming up in conversations. After Partition, she lived with our family for three years before she was married to my grandfather's brother, Afsar.[**] No one remembers what her name was before, but once she came to us, she was renamed Nazeer.

While this was happening, the influential families of Kashmir, like Chaudhary Ghulam Abbas's,[20] whose members were stranded on the Indian side, appealed to the governments of both countries, and I am told that a one-for-one policy was created. In this way, the repatriation of citizens began. I have read how, in 1948, the ICRC liberated around 16,000 Hindu and Sikh prisoners from the Alibeg Camp.[21] But Nazeer did not leave in 1948, not even when the police began going house to house, looking for girls who had been left behind. Nazeer was young, it would have been difficult to distinguish Hindu from Muslim. Maybe she was made to hide inside.

---

[*] Initials have been used to maintain anonymity on the individual's request.
[**] He also migrated to the UK in the 1960s.

'Now, in 1953, Nazeer bibi gave birth to her daughter, Khaksar, and a year after that she went into severe depression. She had assimilated into her marital home but could not forget the circumstances that had brought her there. She desired so strongly to leave that she herself contacted the local authorities for help. Two of the family members, one of whom was a soldier in the maharaja's army, helped her in this matter. They told her that when the police came looking, she should tap her legs so that they would know that she was the intended person they were searching for. They did not want to openly go against the family but wanted to help her.

'I believe she was finally recovered by the Red Cross and the police, who took her to the local Daak Bangla. Are you familiar with that term? It is basically a government rest house and was being used as a temporary shelter for all those who would be sent to India. The family did try to stop her from leaving, they did. But when Nazeer bibi was taken from the house, her husband, Afsar, who was a teacher, was posted far away and was not there to stop her. I am told that they did love one another and continued to exchange letters even once she was taken to the Daak Bangla.'

'Did he not come home to try to convince her to stay?' I ask.

'Many people tried,' Bilal responds sadly. 'From what I've learnt, he did visit, but also promised that he'd help her find her family, so he didn't stop her. She had to stay at the Daak Bangla for a few months until they collected enough people from the area to send across together. Every day, my grandmother would bring Khaksar, who was still an infant, so that Nazeer bibi could feed her, and then she'd bring the child back home. She tried very hard to persuade Nazeer bibi not to leave: she had a child to take care of and a husband who loved her. But she would lament and ask how she could remain in a place where her entire family had been slaughtered. She could no longer bear it, and I think that loss only continued to grow as the days passed.'

As Nazeer's story unfolds, I wonder how she would have felt seeing her daughter every day, holding her, feeding her, and knowing that after a certain point she no longer would be able to.

'It would have been a complicated decision to make,' Bilal says when I bring this up, 'and I can't say what was going on in her head at the time. But it was only when I learnt that she had exchanged letters with her husband that I realized it had been her choice to leave. I always thought that she was forcibly taken, *lekin woh apni marzi se gayi thi*. We think that she left via Sialkot and was taken to a camp in Rajouri and then further into India. The only way we know this is there was another woman with her in the Daak Bangla who was recently tracked down by her relatives in Pakistan. They are from a nearby village and they told us that this woman remembered Nazeer bibi being with her in Rajouri. She told us that they actually stayed together in the camps for months, waiting for family members to come and get them. While the parents of this woman came and fetched her, Nazeer bibi was still stranded there, waiting for her grandparents to come from either Akhnoor or Hoshiarpur. After that, no one knows what happened to her...' he concludes with a heavy exhale.

After a few seconds, he adds, 'I have found out these things in bits and pieces, and since then I have been trying to look for Nazeer bibi, hoping that she is still alive. Maybe telling you this story is another way to try to find her. And it's quite strange, but even though I never knew her, I have inherited her loss. I feel it for my cousin and her mother, Khaksar, who was made to grow up without a mother and has found no closure.'

I wonder whether Khaksar, having known her mother for only a year, has ever conjured an image of what she may be like now, what her *home* – India – may be like. I wonder whether she ever dreams about her, whether she feels a phantom touch every now and then, whether she hopes that one day Nazeer would reach out. The intimacy of this thought is enough to crumple my heart.

'There are things from the days of Partition that I am still discovering,' Bilal admits, breaking me away from my thoughts. 'The history of a once-composite Mirpur has been wiped out. Even the memory of that history has disappeared. The massacre of thousands of people – no one speaks about it, even I was shocked to learn of it.

And how the old Mirpur city has sunk under the water of Mangla Dam, as though it simply could not bear the weight of all that it had endured, as though the heaviness of the past has submerged it,' he scoffs. 'I suppose, then, that there is a certain price you have to pay for how history has unravelled, certain losses you have to bear.'

⁕

ON A PLEASANT January evening in 2018, I am introduced to Kalyani Ray Chowdhury, or Titta, as her grandchildren, Amitesh and Agneesh Ray, call her. The four of us are seated in the living room of Titta's Kolkata home, joined by the writer Karuna Ezara Parikh, Amitesh's partner. My conversation with Titta spans her birth in Chittagong in 1929, childhood in Mymensingh, and the months prior to Partition, when her family was vacationing in the city of Patna. Unable to travel back home to Mymensingh due to rising communal and political turmoil, they found themselves living as refugees in Calcutta in West Bengal while their home remained abandoned across the newly formed border in East Pakistan.

While speaking about the sudden loss of everything that constitutes a home, Titta tells us that the family left everything as it was in the Mymensingh house. Then she gestures to the room we are sitting in. 'Now, imagine … imagine leaving *all* of this, your whole life, going on holiday and then realizing that you could never return to your motherland. You could never see anything again, and everything that once belonged to you was lost forever. It was a strange reality to understand and accept. I had left all my toys, my Japanese dolls, my storybooks. Who would own them now? My sister used to play the sitar, and I still remember exactly where it sat when we left. All our beautiful furniture made in Burma teak, so shiny and glossy, we left behind. Beds and tables and chairs made of original Indian rosewood, *sheesham*, we left behind. My father could not go back to his job at the hospital, we could not go back to school … I remember all of this now, but nothing could have been done then. Life had to begin from the beginning again. In Calcutta, we stayed in a friend's house for a few weeks before moving to a cousin's apartment in Bhagalpur in Bihar and then finally, a few weeks after that, we came back to Calcutta to stay with another relative who had also moved here. But even there, the furniture we bought was cheap and of poor quality. Not good.' She shakes her head disapprovingly.

'Was that because you couldn't afford it?' I ask naively.

'Where would we put the furniture?' she asks in return. 'The land was not ours, nor did the house belong to us. We were living in borrowed space, trying not to be a burden. Do you know what that feels like?'

Her words cause a tightness in my heart. A house with 'stuff' was a house that was lived in and inhabited, but in Calcutta, Titta's family had no physical space to call their own at all. So, the desire for ownership continued to linger, as did the simultaneous sense of loss for everything that had been left behind.[22]

A SIMILAR SENTIMENT is evoked in the following conversation, where Ragini Kashyap's paternal grandmother would always tell her about the loss of stature that accompanied Partition.

Born in the late 1980s, Ragini is based out of Mumbai. In 2018, she started the Third Culture Cooks supper club with a menu featuring dishes birthed during Partition. She asserts that the word 'Partition' has been such an integral part of her life that she cannot remember a time after she was ten or eleven when she did not know about the family's migration. Three of her four grandparents – her dadi, Swadesh 'Guddi' Kashyap; her dada, Ravinder Nath Kashyap; and nana, Colonel R.C. Kapur[23] – were displaced from Lahore in 1947.

'It was my dadi's story that shaped my understanding of the event, probably because she was the most vocal about it. Anytime we sat down with her, she would regale us with stories about her childhood. For her family, Partition was really a fall from grace, and they lost everything. So somewhere subconsciously, it was very important for her to tell her grandchildren that there was *more*. We came from *more*. That idea has always been very important to her.'

'And she blames Partition,' I mean this as a question but it ends up sounding more like a statement.

'Absolutely, one hundred per cent,' Ragini is quick to answer. 'The social strata of the family changed significantly – they went from being upper class before Partition to definitively middle class after it. My dadi grew up in Lahore in a large flat on Mall Road, and all the stories she tells are of an opulent lifestyle: her father sitting at the head of the table at dinner, the children being raised with very proper, western manners. And they were a business family, and so once the business was lost, there wasn't much else.' She thinks for a few seconds and says, 'While I do think there was a certain romanticization of the past, of things being grander, there is no denying the serious material losses that they endured.'

Ragini was born in India but moved shortly after to Oman, where she lived until 1989, and then in Qatar until 2004, after which she moved to Canada. Having grown up away from the subcontinent, she gravitates to anything that brings her closer to 'home'. But, for her, home is not only found on the Indian side, where her family lives, but also on the Pakistani side, where they came from. And this sense of a lost home is what she tries to gather and understand.

'Since three of your grandparents came from Lahore, do you find yourself connecting to the city?' I ask.

She smiles warmly. 'When I hear my grandparents' stories, or when I read about Lahore, I feel so certain that if I ever went there, I will say with pride that *my* people were from here. With no right to really say it in my lifetime, I do feel as though my home was taken away. There is just an unexplainable proxy loss.'

'Why do you say unexplainable?' I'm intrigued.

'I-I...' she begins to elaborate and then laughs. 'You see, I genuinely don't think I have the words. How do you claim a time that *you* were not born in, or a land that *you* have not physically lived on? And yet, it feels like *you* have been transplanted from there to somewhere else. As if the natural culture has been eroded.' She is speaking as much with her words as with her hands, body and, most poignantly, her heart.

'In my family, Partition is told as a story of loss; that has always been the overwhelming theme. Less about the freedom that was gained and more about the losses that were incurred. With my dadi, it is definitely more material, more tangible – the loss of lifestyle, of stature, of business and home. And with my dada, who is more reserved and had to be asked very pointed questions for him to return to a time before Partition, there is some of this material loss as well – the family owned a textile store on Mall Road and lost a massive amount of wealth even before Partition because they chose to support the Swadeshi movement. They had previously supplied many of the British administration's uniforms, and basically burnt the entire non-Indian inventory during the movement. As Partition drew closer, they paid out their workers and left without very much for India. His immediate family was also spread out before Partition – some in Gujranwala, some in Shimla, some in Lahore, and so eventually they all found their way to Delhi.'

I nod, noting all these details down.

'Sometimes, it is the loss of *what-could-have-been* that can consume you,' she admits.

'What do you mean?'

'Well, my best friend from Doha, Maryam, and I recently discovered that we would have probably still been best friends had Partition not happened.' There is a sudden buoyancy in Ragini's voice now. 'A connection that predates our existence! Apparently, our grandfathers were at the same college at the same time and we didn't know this until now. And not only that, they also lived on Mall Road. And it dawned on us that had we not been divided, we may have just grown up right next to one another and gone to the same school and still been friends!'

My heart swells at the beauty of that thought, and then, ever the realistic, the words escape my lips, 'But you may not have even been born had Partition not happened.'

'Ah, yes,' she chuckles. '*Everything* returns to Partition. It is both the end and the beginning of things.'

'This is true,' I concur. 'Tell me about yours and Maryam's ancestors.'

'Well, we've been friends since the age of eleven or twelve, and our families have connected on so many levels, and we've spoken about our grandparents, but probably never in as much depth as recently. We always knew there was the Lahore connection, and that her nani came to Lahore from Myanmar, and my nani's family came to Delhi from Myanmar. So, we had had these surface conversations, but it was only when I actually interviewed her nana[24] that we discovered all the intersections that could have been. Her nanaji, Mian Tariq Mustafa, was born and raised in Lahore, and his elder brother was at Government College at the same time as my dadaji. I don't know if they knew each other, but this connection was so serendipitous.

'What is also interesting is the dichotomy of their experiences – both how they lived through Partition and how they dealt with its memory. Mian Tariq Mustafa's elder brother was enlisted during Partition as someone who was handed a gun and put on duty as a watchman for the trucks coming from India into Pakistan. But he never really recovered from that experience, from everything he saw and everything he had to do. Meanwhile, my dadaji, a young man of the same age, actually went through Partition, his family was actually displaced, but it was a far less violent experience for him. Whereas this other young gentleman whose family had not at all been affected by Partition suffered the invisible consequences of it. It remained imprinted in his memory. It also goes to show that the trauma of Partition does not exist only in the stories of migration but in all stories of that time.'

I nod sadly.

Ragini now sighs. 'I know that there is a romanticization for the cities left behind on the other side. So many of us imagine what it would be like to walk on the soil of our ancestors. I certainly do with Lahore. This belated sense of loss for something so close, yet so far away is…'

'Unexplainable?' I offer her own word.

'Exactly. In the early 2000s, Government College had a reunion for their alumni, and they procured visas for everyone in India who wanted to go. Both my dada-dadi went back and it was a brilliant experience for them, but it was so emotional for me, even vicariously. *They were going home!* Everyone thought it was nice, but I couldn't get over the fact that they were going *home*, back to a place that was ordinarily so unreachable. Anyway, as part of the alumni reunion, they had an exchange programme with a family from Lahore which took them in as visitors and showed them the city. And then a few years later, that family came and stayed with my grandparents in Delhi, and it felt like our relatives were visiting. My dadi always talks about the heart of Lahore, the heart of Lahoris, and how it's something you don't experience anywhere else. Lahore Lahore *aye*. And now this Lahore is on the other side, separated by a line, yet closer than any other place in terms of culture and language and a sense of familiarity. *This* is the loss I mean.'

13
Love

∽

'I AM MEANDERING A BIT from the days of Partition, but you might find this interesting,' Professor D.P. Sengupta warns me as we sit in his office at the National Institute of Advanced Studies in Bengaluru in 2016. He leans back in his office chair and I inch my recorder closer to him. 'It is a memory that belongs to my brother. A memory of affection, or maybe just a comfortable habit.'

I am intrigued.

'My elder brother, Sunil, was very good-looking in his youth. We were born in Barisal, in present-day Bangladesh, but migrated to Calcutta during Partition, when I was in Grade 6. Across the road from our house in Barisal lived a Muslim family that had a son and a daughter. The son's name was Jehangir, and he was a friend of my brother's. His sister was always behind purdah and they hardly ever spoke, but she had a soft spot for him. I don't think my brother knew, though. Anyway, the house was very old, and the family had huge geese that used to run after us as children. Now, many years after Partition, my brother went back to visit Barisal and went to the house where we used to live. He found the house across the street was older and frailer looking, but it was still there, and so were the geese! Out of plain childishness, or nostalgia, he yelled out, "Jehangir, are you there?" And you wouldn't believe what happened next.'

I raise my eyebrows and cup my face with my palms in anticipation.

'From inside the house came a female voice, "Sunil da, *na*? Is it not Sunil da?"' It was Jehangir's sister.

I gasp and Professor Sengupta nods enthusiastically. Goosebumps have erupted across my arms.

'I was absolutely thunderstruck when my brother told me about it. After so many years, this woman, who was likely now in her fifties, still remembered his voice. *His voice*, imagine that. So many years later, perhaps out of habit or affection, she remembered his voice. These are the things that are still embedded in my memory. These are the things that even a Partition line could not obliterate – the depth of human emotion, the memory of a beloved. No line can erase that.'

Later, when I am in the taxi back to my hotel, I think about this memory again. I shut the insufferably slow Bengaluru traffic out of my mind, close my eyes and try to remember someone's voice from my childhood – a neighbour, a friend, someone I have not heard in years – but I cannot. Voices change, naturally, and yet, even decades later, Jehangir's sister remembered Sunil. As Professor Sengupta rightly said, Partition may have drawn a line across the land, but it could not always reproduce that line in people's hearts. Tenderness could not be erased by politics or the passage of time. It remained resolute, if this story was any evidence.

I wonder why I have not heard more stories like this during the course of my research. Why is this anecdote a sidebar, a 'meandering'? Why have the events of Independence and the subsequent Partition been so concretely immortalized through the images of politics and violence? Surely, there is ample space in the vast emotional landscape of Partition for stories of tenderness and love to survive, if only in memory? I make a note to search for stories of love to shine a light in the darkness of Partition.

∽

'THEIRS IS A love story my cousins and I grew up with,' Proma Huq tells me about her grandparents. 'I can't remember when I first heard it, but it's something my grandmother narrated to us often. In retrospect, it's interesting that the setting or focus of this story is not so much Partition, but rather the strength of their love in the face of religious differences – not the larger storm brewing around them.'

Mustafa Anwar was born in Jessore in present-day Bangladesh in 1917. A commercial pilot by profession,[1] he met Susmita Roy, born in 1926 in Calcutta, some time in 1946. It was at a dinner party hosted by her parents that twenty-seven-year-old Mustafa captivated the guests with his musical skills. Susmita, then a bookish nineteen-year-old, was upset about not having enough time to finish reading as she had to help prepare dinner for this 'unknown Muslim guest'. Her parents, lovers of music and poetry, had met him at another friend's home and invited him to a singing *jolsha* at theirs.

'The specific Bengali word my grandmother used to describe how she felt about their first meeting was "*birokto*", annoyed!' Proma says, and I laugh.

Still smiling widely, I ask her about how they got to know one another finally. Proma's grandfather, her nana, passed away decades before she was born, so all her memories of him have been bequeathed by her grandmother, whom she calls dida.

'She described their courtship as getting to know each other better over more such dinner parties at their home, or through badminton games with her four younger siblings on the front lawn of her house in Dum Dum. They were seldom alone together but exchanged clandestine notes. In one such note, she wrote, "Not all affairs of the heart must end in marriage." When she told us this, she said she thought herself quite mature in the response, but apparently he was very upset ... She saw no future for the two of them. But her parents were so impressed by nana that they ultimately supported the union. And so they were married on 24 April 1947.'

'And was his family equally supportive?'

Proma first shows me a lovely sepia photograph of the couple – Susmita sitting regally, draped in a dark-coloured silk sari with a long garland of flowers around her neck, and Mustafa seated to her right, dressed in a white dhoti-kurta. She then delves into her family history to explain why nana's father was initially resistant to the match, and though dida's parents may have approved, the extended family on that side, too, was quite against the marriage.

'Nana was the eldest son of a renowned Bangladeshi poet, Golam Mustafa, who, during Partition, supported the creation of Pakistan. This is perhaps one of the reasons for his resistance to my grandparents' interfaith, potentially cross-border marriage, which he did not attend nor accept. The wedding was small and held in Calcutta, and though he did not come, nana's siblings did. But after meeting dida, it is said that my great-grandfather warmed up to her and the resistance died down rather quickly.

'On the other hand, dida's mother was a bit of a romantic, I think, as she supported the marriage wholeheartedly. The repercussions were greater within her extended family, though. From what I know, dida's maternal great-grandfather was a famous historian, Dr Ramdas Sen, who was a zamindar in Murshidabad and a polyglot – a scholar of Sanskrit, Prakrit, English, French and Bengali.' Proma deviates from the topic but her knowledge of family history leaves me in awe. I listen as she relays the stories of four generations with relative ease.

'So, Dr Ramdas Sen was supposedly the first Bengali to obtain a PhD in Europe in the 1800s and had met Victor Hugo in Paris, who autographed a set of books for him, now the property of the National Library in Calcutta. There's a reason I bring this up in the same vein as nana's father, to whom his religion was of utmost importance. Dida came from a very proud Hindu family that valued its heritage and education. An interfaith marriage, particularly to a Muslim during Partition, was especially unpalatable for them.

'There is also a Bollywood-esque twist to this story, with dida's maternal uncles rushing to stop the wedding the morning they registered it in her parents' home. She said that just as they were signing the wedding register, her uncles were climbing up the three flights of stairs to their home, and upon reaching and learning that the marriage had already taken place, they disowned her. They never reconciled, so there isn't much family in India we are in contact with. Dida's father, my great-grandfather, lost his job as an advocate at the

Calcutta High Court. His colleagues allegedly gave him a lot of grief about allowing his daughter to marry a Muslim, and he was forced to resign. He later became a professor of history, which sadly meant a drop in the family income as well.'

Proma lives in Washington now, and her family in Bangladesh. But I am curious about where her grandparents finally settled. They had married in April 1947 and Partition happened barely four months later, putting her home town in India and his in East Pakistan.

'I had actually assumed they'd moved to Dhaka after they got married, but I just learnt that they remained in Calcutta and lived in Park Circus. At the dawn of Indian commercial aviation in 1946, nana – or Captain Anwar, as he was known – was part of Mistry Airways and one of the first Muslim pilots. Post Partition, he joined Air India as a commercial pilot and, after the airline was nationalized, became a "VIP pilot", commissioned to fly foreign dignitaries like Zhou Enlai, the first premier of China, upon invitation by Nehru. But by the time of his death in 1959,[2] he lived with dida and their two young children in Karachi, where he'd been posted for his new job with Pakistan International Airlines. I believe he switched jobs as he faced increasing resistance working in India due to his religion.'

I think about a young Hindu woman moving to Pakistan with her Muslim husband in the decade following Partition, as if it were the most natural thing to do, almost resisting the creation of the man-made border. Professor Sengupta's words resound in my ears and I remind myself that there *is* love so deep and true that even a thing as concrete as a Partition line cannot obliterate it. For Susmita and Mustafa, an undivided India was the background of their love, and so it would always remain.

'You mention that your grandfather passed away in 1959...'

The response is coloured with sadness. 'Yes, he died in a plane crash, actually. It was so tragic; they were married for only twelve years. She risked so much only to be widowed at thirty-two, and then had to figure out a way to provide for her two children.'

'After his death, did she consider moving back in with her family in Calcutta?"

'She must have considered it but felt that her children should grow up in their father's community and so she chose to live in Dhaka with nana's family, who welcomed her. Her own siblings were strewn across the globe by then, so I think she wanted her children to be around their paternal cousins. And all five of nana's siblings had a great relationship with dida until she passed away in 2019, at the age of ninety-two.'

'Did she retain her Hindu identity?' I ask.

'Yes, she never converted during their marriage – nana had never asked her to, despite his father's requests – but after his passing, she raised their children as Muslim. She then also adopted Muslim religious practices, like learning *duas*, and ensuring that her children finish reading the Quran. Dida once told me a story about when she first realized her children perhaps saw her as "other", separate from them. When my mother, aged five, asked her, "*Ma, tomader biye ki bhabe hoe*?" Ma, how do you all get married? "You all?" dida had replied, puzzled. "Yes, you know, *your* people."'

She goes on to tell me how her uncle, who was ten years old and at a boarding school in Chittagong, wrote to his mother about fasting for Ramzan. In a separate instance, as a teacher, she witnessed her own students fasting, and fasted in solidarity with them. The children spent time in Calcutta with their maternal grandparents, where they celebrated Durga Puja and ate special meals of West Bengali delicacies. And while growing up in Bangladesh, they were offered an abundance of nostalgia for Calcutta, their mother's first love – the bustling streets, memories of Flury's bakery, the colours, the festivals. In truth, the children were raised with the ethos of East and West Bengal.

Proma's grandmother's legacy is luminous and inspiring by all accounts. 'Thirty-five days after nana's death,' she recounts, 'dida sat for an entrance exam at Dhaka University, where she obtained a master's in education – the very first batch of the programme! – and began teaching to support her children, working her way up to becoming principal. During the 1971 Bangladesh Liberation War, she accepted an offer to go to Harvard on a research fellowship. So, the pride that I feel is more towards her resilience as a single mother and a minority in Muslim-majority Bangladesh.'

I agree wholeheartedly and then return to the beginning of our conversation.

'How do you feel when you think about Partition, in the context of your grandparents' marriage, but also as someone with a direct legacy from both East and West Bengal?'

'I feel curiosity and awe. My grandparents created a haven of unity and love at a time when the entire subcontinent was being divided. But I also marvel at the strength and resilience of millions who packed up their lives, uprooted and pushed towards an unknown. This curiosity also stems from the fact that Bangladeshi collective memory doesn't seem to dwell on Partition as much[3] … as if the '71 liberation was the singular point of our beginning. Currently, our Bengali-vs-Bangladeshi identity seems to be in flux; it is evolving in tandem with the influences that permeate our present while building on the traumas of Partition, the '71 war and our collective past. There is almost a minimization of Partition here – one of the reasons I have so many gaps in my knowledge of it.'

Contemplatively, she adds, 'The sentiment is contrasted by the twin Independence Days of our neighbours and former countrymen in India and Pakistan, while it seems that Bangladeshis – as K. Anis Ahmed poignantly writes – "tend to gloss over its brutality as a pathology of the moment; it is but an echo of the distant past".[4]

BORN IN THE shadows of Partition is another story of love, one from my own family that I hardly knew any details of growing up. It was only when I began seriously speaking to members of my family about the bookshop which my paternal grandfather had set up in Delhi in 1953 that the story of how he met my grandmother resurfaced in our conversations, buoyant and integral. Before that, I thought that they had had an arranged marriage, when, in fact, the relationship had been lobbied for with a quiet passion and a singular determination.

Talking to my grandmother about how exactly she met my grandfather takes time. We sit in her room each evening, under a fluorescent tube light, with my grandmother sipping a cup of hot, milky coffee and me, sitting beside her, scribbling down notes. At first, she is quite matter-of-fact about it – 'We met at the camp' – but eventually, with each conversation, she divulges more and more, and ultimately enough for me to imagine the blossoming of young love. Our first conversation begins with the facts: she wants to make sure I understand the landscape of Kingsway Camp, where she lived from 1948 until her marriage in 1955. Kingsway, estimated to have accommodated over 30,000 refugees, was the biggest camp in the city. Spread around the old British barracks of north Delhi, it was divided into four lines for incoming refugees – Hudson, Reeds, Outram and Edward – where housing was provided on the basis of need.[5] My grandmother's family lived in Hudson Line, and my grandfather's in Reeds.

In our next conversation, she speaks about employment. I try to interrupt, to remind her that I am interested in her love story, but she tells me that everything is connected. This, too, the rebuilding of livelihood in a newly independent India, is important, for only when they were able to stand on their feet again was the prospect of settling down with another person even considered. That evening, I learn that for the entirety of 1948, my grandmother was enrolled in a sewing course on Curzon Road, so she could learn a practical skill.[6] When she returned to the camp, she began volunteering at the social service department,[7] which was where she met my grandfather for the first time. Upon hearing this, I intervene again, but she wants the particulars of her employment noted – it was a big deal, for part of the household ran on her salary – and, embarrassed at my impatience, I settle back into my notebook.

In 1949, she was transferred to work at the Faridabad refugee camp, and by 1951 my grandmother had a stable job at the Ministry of Rehabilitation while all her sisters and mother worked as well. Meanwhile, my grandfather worked odd jobs, from selling coal at train stations to fountain pens in Chandni Chowk, to teaching temporarily at the Salwan school. In 1953, he was able to open a bookshop called Bahrisons in Khan Market, on a plot of land he managed to raise enough money to buy.

'*Ab poocho jo poochna hai*, ask me what else you'd like to know,' my grandmother finally concedes.

'So, you were both volunteering in the social service department,' I state, and she nods. 'Do you remember when you first spoke?'

'At first, I think we only saw each other – our eyes met but we didn't speak. *Pehli baar dekha toh nazar mil gayi*,' she laughs. 'All this was new for us, we were young.' She was sixteen years old and he was twenty. The person who was instrumental in introducing them was Swaran Lata, my grandfather's adoptive sister, also a volunteer at the camp though she did not live there.

The next day, she tells me that her younger sister, Dharam, too, met her husband in the camp. It is during this time that my mother discovers a box of old photographs in the house. From the many tattered envelopes in the box, I retrieve a set of four tiny photographs, measuring six by six inches, of what appears to be a wedding ceremony. Excitedly, I show them to my grandmother and she confirms that these are from Dharam's Anand Karaj, the Sikh wedding ceremony, which took place in a tent set up behind my grandmother's sister's flat in Rajinder Nagar, Delhi. Her sister, whom we all call masiji, can be seen standing with her husband to be, her face completely covered in purdah. In two photos, they are seen walking around the holy Guru Granth Sahib. I marvel at the discovery, and, caressing the aged prints with my finger, ask my grandmother to tell me more about her and my grandfather's courtship.

Over the last few evenings, she has gotten used to these storytelling sessions about the past. Part of me thinks she even looks forward to them, provided that the remembrance is on her terms. These days, because we are speaking about my grandfather, she has come alive again in many ways. There is a childlike radiance to her as she recollects the years of their courtship – a simultaneous eagerness to talk about him while retaining the boundary that is required when speaking of such intimacies with family. Her eyes light up when she mentions his name, or sometimes refers to him more formally as Bahri sahib, always inevitably finding their way to his portrait on the wall.

'In the camp, we hardly ever visited each other's barracks. But one day, I heard that Balraj-ji was quite unwell and so I borrowed a girl's bicycle and went to see him at lunchtime. His family stayed in two connecting barracks – one where the parents lived with the younger children and the second where Balraj-ji and his elder brother, Davinder bhai sahib, lived. So I went to see him, just to make sure he was all right.' She chuckles and adds, 'I doubt my mother even knew!'

'Did she approve of him?' I ask.

'I wrote a letter to my mother telling her about your grandfather. *Mooh se nahi bol sakti thi yeh sab*, I could never have admitted this to her face to face, so I wrote telling her that I liked someone, and if I were to marry then it would be to him, otherwise I would stay unmarried forever. My elder sister, Shakuntala, and younger sister, Dharam, were both already married by then, so I was the only one remaining. "If I cannot marry him," I wrote to my mother, "then I will stay with you."'

'And what did she say?'

'She said, "*Woh humare udhar ke nahi hain.*" They were not from our side, from the Frontier, and she didn't know the family.'

'Even though you had both survived Partition and were both living in the same camp? There was a ... a commonality to your experiences.' But as soon as I say this, I remember how she had earlier dismissed my suggestion that couples who both lived through Partition would speak to each other about it, could understand each other better, could accept even the silences. To her, the common experience of Partition did not matter in their relationship, except that it brought them to the same volunteer programme at the same camp in the same city.

'After Partition, many families sought out people who had migrated either from the same village or city across the border, or those who were already known to them, to marry their sons and daughters to.* In our case, *apni-apni mitti thi*, we had migrated from completely separate corners. We were from D.I. Khan in the Frontier, they were from Malakwal in Punjab. But I told her that all this didn't matter to me, and if I must get married, then it will be him. I told her to go speak to his family, and, of course, Swaran Lata accompanied her and even encouraged the match. It was because of her that both mothers agreed, in fact. She was our *bicholi*, our intermediary … our matchmaker!' she laughs.

She recalls another memory from before their betrothal, when my grandfather had just set up the bookshop in 1953 – a tender, far more private memory affirming that sometimes even unthinkable circumstances in life such as Partition give birth to the most sacred of unions.

'Sometimes we would meet in the camp after work. But it was not like the couples of today, not so direct, not so candid. That was a courtship where we spoke far more with our eyes than with words. We would just look at each other from afar – no movies, no dinners, *uska zamana hi nahi tha*, that was not the norm. But every night, without fail, after shutting the bookshop, he would stop at India Gate and buy flowers for my hair on his way back to the camp. He would present me with a jasmine *gajra* and I would sleep with it tied in my hair, and in the morning my hair would be fragrant. It may have been a small gesture but it was full of warmth and devotion. Now that is love, isn't it? Yes, that is love,' she declares adoringly, turning to his portrait.

Bhag Gulyani and Balraj Bahri Malhotra were married in 1955 and remained together for sixty long years, until he passed away in February 2016.

---

* This is evident in many of the stories told throughout this book, as well as in the case of my own maternal grandparents, whose families were known to one another in pre-Partition Lahore.

WHILE ON FIELDWORK for *Remnants*, I hear a story from a Lahore-based architect named Noor Qadir about how both sets of his grandparents migrated from Jalandhar to Multan during Partition and continued to feel deeply for the land they had left behind. His maternal grandfather, in particular, did something quite extraordinary to preserve ties with his homeland:

> Pirzada Abd-e-Saeed Pakistani – who had believed so fervently in the creation of Pakistan that he added the suffix to his name – very ceremoniously renounced it after Partition, replacing it with another. Unable to comprehend that his beloved home town wouldn't be part of the new country, he became Pirzada Abd-e-Saeed Jullunduri, carrying his identity, synonymous with Jullundur, with him across the border.[8]

But what else is interesting about our conversation is the fact that Noor's parents' *rishta* had been fixed because of their common pre-Partition origins. After the book is published, I keep in touch with Noor's mother, Tayyaba Pirzada; we speak mostly about Partition and her father, with the occasional Eid–Diwali wishes. Around the time when I begin writing this book, she sends me a message that Noor is getting married and his fiancée *also* happens to be from Jalandhar. 'Aleena's grandfather, like Noor's, is from Jullundur,' she writes. 'This introduction was enough to melt my heart.'

Like her, I too am moved by how the connection to soil cannot be diminished even though one remains on the other side of an impenetrable line. In fact, as in this case, it gets deeper with generations. Perhaps, Aleena and Noor's Jalandhari love story is mere coincidence, or maybe, as I would like to believe, it is fate. Whatever it is, it begins a conversation when Ms Pirzada tells me about the relationships in her family and their intrinsically deep connection to an undivided land.

'As I age,' her message reads, 'I realize day by day our connection with *mitti*, soil. I may never get a chance to visit Jalandhar, or the Indian side of Punjab, where my ancestors lived and breathed its air, no matter how much I try. But I am certain that one part of my heart still beats there. This love and longing passed down the generations is too strong ... and these feelings aren't diminished by borders or time.'

'It breaks my heart to read your words,' I write back. 'But in many ways, the relations your family has made in Pakistan have kept Jalandhar alive for you.'

She agrees and goes on to mention that once he migrated to Pakistan, her father only supported businesses with the name 'Jullundur' in them, set up by those who had migrated from his city. Auto part shops, grocery stores, even the butcher! Such was the lure of land. When I ask her about how her marriage to the architect Abdul Qadir was fixed, she writes, 'I clearly remember that it was done purely because my husband's family and my father were friends and neighbours in Jullundur. But what is truly incredible – and this should tell you about my father's sheer faith in his fellow Jullunduris – is that my elder sister's *rishta* was *also* done into a family from there. My brother-in-law was working in Saudi Arabia at the time – this was 1984 – and the wedding was fixed without even meeting him, purely on the basis of the kinship that came with being from Jullundur before Partition!'

Ms Pirzada lovingly invites me to Aleena's and Noor's wedding, but because of visa restrictions I know I may not be able to attend. I wonder about how the love for Jalandhar is passed down the generations of her family, how it finds them, how it seeks out their partners even, and invites them to forever be one with the Jalandhari soil. I keep thinking about *mitti* and how Ms Pirzada longs for it. I promise myself that the next time I travel to Pakistan, I will carry a fistful of soil from Jalandhar for her. If she is unable to visit the land of her ancestors, then I will bring a small part of that land to her.

THIS MULTIGENERATIONAL JALANDHARI story brings another to mind, told to me by thirty-four-year-old Harsh Vardhan Sahni,[*]

---

[*] The complete story of Harsh Vardhan Sahni's family can be found in Chapter 9, 'Hope'.

based in Mussoorie, whose family migrated from Sialkot. When we speak, his younger sister has recently gotten married to a man with a similar Punjabi background. Harsh tells me that at the wedding the groom's maternal grandfather, now ninety-two years old, addressed both families. Paraphrasing his speech, he relays it from memory: '"History may have brought us together so many times, without us even realizing it," nanaji said. "Both families were once in Pakistan but we never met. Both families came to India around Partition but we met never met. Both family members studied in the same school in Timarpur in north Delhi, got medicines from the same CGHS dispensary, and we never met. I got my appointment letter from ONGC, Dehradun, in 1959 while your family moved to the Dehradun–Mussoorie area. Still we didn't meet. I kept getting transferred around till I was posted back in Dehradun in 1984. God knew our case is pending for a long time, so he has intervened and joined our families today with Mitali and Nitin's union.'

Harsh lets his voice trail off and a melancholic smile plays on his face. 'You know, he talked about it as if it were predestined, and that was really moving. He is a man of few words, but he drew that line from before Partition to the present day, talked about how we find our way back to one another. Regardless of partitions and migrations, we find our way back ... that's who we are as a people.'

'IT WAS DURING the time I was an undergraduate student at Dhaka University in 1999 that my father wrote me a letter in response to one that I had written him. My letter was about heartbreak, but his was about love.' Dr Anisur Rahman, who is speaking to me from Chittagong, smiles into the camera. 'Or rather, unrequited love,' he adds.

'What did the letters say?' I'm curious about this epistolary relationship between the father and son.

'Basically, I'd written...' He pauses and looks at me sheepishly. 'Well, I'd broken up with my girlfriend at the time and she had gotten married to someone else, and I was feeling terrible, so I wrote to him about it. And in response, he told me a story about Partition.'

I inch closer to the screen, as if inching closer to the story.

Anisur begins his story from the moment the land was divided. 'At the time of Partition, my father, Sirajul Islam, used to live in a village called Dohokula, which currently falls in the Kushtia district of Bangladesh. He had a Hindu friend whose father was a zamindar in Kumarkhali. The zamindar never liked their friendship, probably because my father was Muslim and came from a lower class. But that friend also had a relative called Aarati, and as a young boy, my father fell in love with her. He would have been in Grade 10 at the time...' Anisur tells the story slowly, thinking about the details. 'When Partition happened, they left East Bengal for India. There was no contact between them for a long, long time. And then out of the blue, in 1975, my father received a letter from Murshidabad in India, and it was from her – Aarati.'

I softly gasp, bringing my palm up to my mouth.

'She wrote to him something along the lines that her father had died, and she had acquired considerable property and wealth, and...' he pauses to remember and then continues, 'she said that she wouldn't wait for his reply, she just wanted him to join her in Murshidabad. As soon as possible.'

'But...' I calculate, 'twenty-eight years had passed.'

'Yes, and that was most interesting. She had waited all that time for him. Even though they had parted as children – in their teen years – she had waited. Anyway, by the time the letter arrived, my father was married with three children, my siblings. He'd also lost his father, so there were a lot of responsibilities and expectations of him, and it was very difficult. Given everything, he decided not to go, not to see her again, and I don't think he ever told anyone about this. That is, until the time when he wrote to me.'

I am thinking of the right words to say, but there is an ocean of crashing waves inside me. If merely listening to the story has affected me this way, I try to imagine how Anisur feels, or how his father may have felt. A few seconds pass in silence before Anisur cuts through it.

'Initially, I was not feeling very good. I-I did not talk to him about this, or bring up the letter.'

'Because it was uncomfortable?'

'Yes, it was uncomfortable, so I did not reply or ask anything. But about ten years later, my father suddenly died of a heart attack while I was in JNU for my MPhil. And then, during my PhD, I was reading a lot of Partition stories in my courses, and this letter came to mind. So I returned to it, and after reading it again I felt like I wanted to find her. I wanted to talk to her, see if she was still alive. I started talking with people from India, friends from Kolkata, asking if they recognized the address. But they didn't, so then I reached out to the local people from her birthplace. Her family still has schools and colleges in their name, and they had their land transferred. In their paperwork, I found that they had shifted to Krishnanagar, not Murshidabad. But my father was very clear that the letter came from Murshidabad, so I'm not sure which one is right. He recalled it from memory, though…'

'What do you mean? Did he not keep the letter?'

'I don't think so, no. But basically, when he wrote to me, it was to console me, to tell me that things will be okay, that life will work out despite all odds. Then he told me that heartbreak was something he had survived as well, and Aarati's name came up. He narrated this story, that he had this kind of relationship, and he could have left his family, he could have been reunited with her, and she was ready to accept him. He wrote down her complete address from memory … and now I wish I had asked him more. If I'd asked, my father could have told me.'

I say nothing.

'My intention is to know about my father's childhood, to know their story, how they met, how they were made to separate, her story of Partition. I want to know what my father was like at that time.'

'Were you very close to him?'

'I was, yes. I shared many things with him, but I did not pay attention to this letter, I did not think it was an interesting story. Rather…' His voice trails off. 'I was feeling uneasy about asking him anything. But I think he was ready to share, and would have loved to share, had I asked, had we spoken.'

'I think we find it difficult to see our parents just as people,' I say.

'Hmm,' he agrees.

I do not quite understand this ground we are treading. I clear my throat and, when I speak, my voice is small. 'Do you think ... he missed her?'

'Yes, I think so, otherwise why suddenly – after twenty-four years of receiving the letter – would he recall the incident? That means that inside his mind he may have nurtured the thought of her, of their story. That made me more interested in her. He had a very good relationship with my mother, but he held on to this part of his life and did not forget it.'

'I suppose it means we can love many people, in different ways ...'

'Maybe, yes. But this was his first love, and it was a forbidden love. She was from another religion; she was the daughter of the local zamindar.'

'Yes, true. So, do you think that he wanted to see her? When she sent the letter, I mean.'

Anisur's reply is thoughtful but emerges after several seconds of quiet. 'I think so. He had something in mind. If he were encouraged to find her, I think he would have ... But a sense of duty and responsibility prevailed, and he never looked for her, and probably never talked about this.'

There is a sombreness to this conversation, and despite it being about love, it ends up being more about the loss of love – unrequited love, love divided by a border, love interrupted by Partition.

Before we end our video call, I nervously ask Anisur whether he may consider showing me the letter his father wrote to him in 1999, or at least the parts relevant to Partition. A few weeks later, a six-page scanned document arrives in my inbox.

On the last day of 2020, my friend Sayantan Ghosh and I meet in a café in Delhi's Green Park to read the document. I cannot read or understand Bengali, and Sayantan has always been kind enough to translate bits of text for me over the years. The ink of this letter has bled on to the back of pages, making the words difficult to decipher. Sayantan first reads to himself, scrolling up and down the page, zooming in and out, repeating strings of words under his breath. I keep peering at the letter, though I understand nothing.

'The letter is dated 9 May 1999 and begins like a regular letter from father to son,' Sayantan says. 'This is how my father would speak to me – read a book, remain active, exercise and everything will be all right. Maybe it's just a Bengali thing,' he jokes and then starts to translate.

I hope and pray that you will turn into a diamond, the letter reads, and we both chuckle at the sweetness of the thought. *Every morning or evening or before you go to sleep, read a book for five to ten minutes ... Breathe in with your mouth, exhale from your nose. Say in your heart that you are receiving the power of life, while exhaling and inhaling. All the pollution from your body is leaving ... think and feel in your heart that from within you have become completely calm.*

Build a house in your heart, and when you stand in the balcony of that house, you can see a beautiful lake. It's surrounded by trees and flowers, and you can always hear the sounds of birds. Tell yourself that you will be confident, independent, and strong. Eventually, the peace of your mind will return, all the pain and sadness in your heart will go away – if you continue to do what I told you, for two or three weeks.

Looking up from the screen, Sayantan asks me the context of the letter and, when I tell him, he comments, 'Ah, he is sending his son strength to overcome the heartbreak. It now makes sense. So, on the next page, he has written that he was already aware of the separation but didn't think that he needed to say anything about it to his son ... And then he writes, *But now that you've written me this letter, I can tell you that your father also fell into the same trap!*'

I sit upright in my chair.

But now when I look back and think about it, I think it was all foolishness. A stupidity ...

'Falling in love, you mean?' I interrupt.

'Yes, I suppose, because he writes, *Yes, from fondness comes love, that's true. But a love you won't be able to nurture – there is no point in holding back that love, or holding on to it.* The page ends here, and from the next page begins the story of Aarati.'

Page number five of the letter bears her exact address, as recounted by Anisur's father. Sayantan spends several minutes reading the text and then paraphrases what she must have written to him. *I'm waiting for you, hoping that you will come. I'll continue to wait for you all my life. You don't have to respond to this letter, but I hope to see you in person some day.* He pauses and scans the page again, and then remarks, 'It's quite cinematic, the whole thing. But what is interesting about the way this letter is written is that there are many words that we – in West Bengal – would not use in our vocabulary. Words used here, like *yaad*, the Urdu word for remembrance, or the word *nani*. There are also old Bengali words that we don't use any more, that I may have used while I was in school. Anyway, he goes on to say that he had to pay a price, but he doesn't mean a literal price, it is a symbolic one, something larger...'

As Sayantan is reading the letter to himself, fingers tracing the handwritten words onscreen, I am looking over the notes I have taken during my conversation with Anisur. I could ask him to translate this letter for me, but I wonder whether he would want to revisit it. These precious pages he has shared are treasure enough, and I am grateful to be temporarily invited in to such an intimate and amorous piece of personal history.

This way, translating it with Sayantan, we both learn and discover as we go along. There is a collaborative effort in understanding the pain and longing of a man none of us know, and with that understanding there is a responsibility to take care of those emotions. Sayantan translates with great care and delicacy, but also with great curiosity, for this is written in a dialect close to the one that his grandfather, who also migrated from East Bengal in his twenties, spoke. If this is personal for me – part of my research, of my need to understand the ways in which Partition impacted the lives and loves of people – then it is personal for him too. It is a way to speak in a dialect that he hasn't spoken in since the passing of his grandfather in 2001.

When he tells me this, I am taken aback. 'You never mentioned you had Partition history!'

'You never asked,' he smiles. 'My maternal grandfather came from a village in Faridpur in present-day Bangladesh. He arrived in Calcutta with his four sisters and ageing mother, who passed away shortly after. He had to think constantly about how to make a living; he had no money, no house. The only thing he did have was an education. He had studied. That was his only skill and advantage, so he began teaching. He was a very matter-of-fact man, but his memory I trusted.'

'Did he speak to you about Partition?'

'Yes, he talked about it, but never lamented. My grandmother would often get emotional thinking about all that had been lost, or how their lives had changed virtually overnight, but my grandfather would always just say, "So what, everyone else's did too! Losing something during Partition was not special or extraordinary." I'm sure he felt the pain as well, but this was his approach to life. I think as long as my grandfather was alive, I was very close to the event of Partition. I was very aware of it. And also because of the language. He spoke in a tongue which no one else in our house used. *This*, the language of this letter. Nobody in our house spoke in Bangal[9] except for him, and because I spent considerable time with him as a child, I am able to read so much of this letter…'

I sit back in wonderment, for one story of Partition almost always leads to another.

Sayantan returns to the letter. 'These are some beautiful passages,' he begins to read aloud in Bengali, repeating some words, stressing on others. 'Wow,' he finally whispers before translating the entire section without interruptions.

Giving someone love is easy, but receiving it is difficult. If you receive love, then to protect it is even harder. That's why I'll build a bridge and then break it down. And then I'll start looking for another bridge to build. That's why one must not feel sad about the history of a human life … there is no point in lamenting about a human being's personal history.

My pen races across the page and Sayantan pauses, waiting for me to catch up. I tell him to continue, since I am quite used to taking notes while people speak, and do not want to interrupt his train of thought or the flow of the letter. 'All right, so this next passage here is about a guardian. He writes: *My guardianship may have been snatched away but it isn't lost, though.* And then this is written in English: *I have no hope, I have no life.* There are words here I can't read. But this is a very intimate letter, a fragile patchwork almost. It is confessional and inward and…' His voice trails off.

The letter is indeed confessional but it is not apologetic. It is vulnerable but not defensive. It is poetic and prophetic and profound and full of longing and deep loss and, by the end, we can both feel it – an overwhelming sense of intrusion.

'How does the letter end?' I ask.

We have spoken a lot … and now you must sit in the house in your heart and talk to your heart when you can. Everything will be all right. The important thing is that we are all alive and well. May God protect you, keep you happy and safe. Tomar abba.

With that, he turns the computer screen towards me, sits back in his chair and sighs.

'It's heartbreaking – both the love story and the letter,' I say.

'Hmm, it is sad … but what can be done?'

I repeat his words, 'It is sad but what can be done. I think that encapsulates what so many people feel about Partition. That so much was lost but there was no sense of closure, no definitive ending. Just sudden rupture. Stories like Sirajul's and Aarati's left unfinished…'

'But maybe Anisur will find her,' Sayantan suggests.

'I hope so, I really do,' I agree with a smile.

WHERE THERE IS love, there is also the boundary of love, and the definition of who is allowed to be loved and who is forbidden. For

G,* the most internalized consequences of Partition were felt three and a half decades after the event had taken place.

'In 1947, my dadi was a new bride, forced to flee from Multan to Delhi. They came from a fairly well-off background, but, of course, that wealth was lost or left behind at Partition. During their migration to India, her mother-in-law passed away, and my grandfather decided to stay back mid-journey and cremate his mother, promising to meet his new bride in one of the refugee camps in Delhi. Against all odds, they managed to find one another and were ultimately allotted a flat in one of the new refugee colonies of the city. This is where I was also born and raised. My grandparents had five children – two sons and three daughters – and eventually one of the daughters got married to a Muslim and my grandparents disowned her.' G tells me this by way of introduction. 'I never knew my grandfather but I grew up with my grandmother, and to think that she had such a strong dislike for a single community makes me feel ashamed...'

I ask her how it happened, how her aunt left.

'I should say that despite the difficulties that my grandparents faced in starting a life completely from scratch, they made sure their children were all well-educated and ended up with excellent jobs. Most of them worked in government offices, this aunt of mine as well, which is where she met her partner. I believe she brought him home and told her parents that they'd like to get married, and they asked her to make a choice – them or him. So, she packed up her things, which most likely comprised her educational certificates and qualifications, and walked out. I think this must have happened in 1980.'

'You were born nine years after that, so how did you first come to know about this?'

'I learnt of my aunt's existence from my neighbour, believe it or not! Her grandmother had told her about it, and she told me, and then I asked her grandmother more questions. Only after that did I tell my elder brother, and together we asked our mother about it.

---

* Initials have been used to maintain anonymity on the individual's request.

But to date, my father does not know that we know. I think I would have been eighteen years old, in my first year of college, when I found about my aunt.

'You know, my brother and I spent most of our days with our grandmother because both our parents worked, and the two of us fought a lot. We used to drive our grandmother up the wall, and in her most distressed moments she would say to us, "*Maine chaar bachche pale hain, aur woh bhi mujhe itna pareshaan nahi karte the!*" I have raised four children in this home, and even they didn't trouble me this much! Even in those moments of despair or anger, not once did she let slip that she has five children. She would always say four. So, just imagine the kind of...' There is a long pause before G speaks again. '...the kind of hate she felt towards what her daughter had done. She had completely omitted her, both from her memory and vocabulary. It was a form of conscious erasure.'

'Did you ever ask her about it after you found out?'

She shakes her head. 'Never. My brother – who is older by a few years – told me that this was a topic never to be discussed, that I did not realize how sensitive it was. It had happened in the past, and no matter how hurtful it felt to have this kept from us, we were not to bring it up.'

'How did you feel, though?'

This question seems impossibly small the moment it exits my mouth, and I wonder what single feeling could encompass the enormity of this discovery. Quietly, I watch her confront a loss much older than her – a loss she did not know she would one day inherit.

'There were different stages – first, I was furious. Then, I hated them for doing this, keeping her a secret from us. Then I got really sad that, you know, your own flesh and blood is gone because of something that's just been created by us humans – religion...'

Her voices fades into contemplation, and she extracts an old memory from her teenage years. 'Around the time that I first found out, we were taking things out of storage. I was looking through some books and I casually flipped through one, only to find her name inscribed in it. And it was just such a natural reaction – all of us were sitting together and I picked up this book and I read out the name. I didn't really think about what I was doing, but my father, who was sitting opposite me, was so startled that he demanded I hand over the book. I think it was a Wren & Martin grammar book or something, and he just looked through it and then gave it back.

'Then there were other things I began to learn about her – after she had left the house, she would still visit her elder sister at her work, maybe to speak to her, and one day my eldest aunt's husband caught them. Caught is the word because they were both reprimanded and she was categorically told to stay away from her sister and her family. Since then, nobody knows where she is. She did not even come to her father's funeral.'

There is a lump in my throat as I suggest, 'Maybe she didn't know...'

G smiles softly. 'Yes, maybe.'

'Do you ever think about her?'

'Often. And whenever I do, I feel quite sad, because no one should have to go through something like this, being cut off from one's parents and siblings. I'm guessing my aunt wanted to remain in touch with her sister but her husband wouldn't let her, and at that time women did not have much agency. So, maybe she couldn't take a stand, and there were no cell phones or internet or email. So, she just ... disappeared.'

'But do you hold Partition responsible for this?'

'Partly, yes, of course. If Partition hadn't happened, then maybe my grandmother wouldn't have been so cruel towards a community. Nobody deserves it, neither Hindus nor Muslims. And no one should be paying a price for what someone else experienced decades ago. But the more I think about it, the more I am convinced that events as painful as Partition can leave scars and wounds that can form concrete personality traits which may then get amplified as the years pass. For my grandmother, it was whom you could fraternize with, whom you could employ, whom you could love – that became irrefutably well-defined. It was us or them.'

'I'm curious, how did your great-grandmother die on the journey to India? Was it during riots?'

'She wasn't killed, as far as I know…' She pauses, thinking about it. 'But maybe, well, it could have been because many people were on both sides. Maybe that happened and we were never told. I can't say, but it's such a traumatic thing to think about, let alone tell it to a small child. So, I'm just speculating. But what I *do* know is that my grandparents suffered greatly. They both came from affluent families in an undivided India and, once in Delhi, my grandfather had to begin working in a small shop for someone else. There was such a loss of status and grace and wealth, and then raising the children. I think the sheer difficulty of rebuilding a life from nothing was what left a bad taste in their mouth. My grandmother's life turned upside down virtually overnight. She never got to celebrate being a young bride, probably never wore the finery in her trousseau. All those joys were snatched away from her because of a partition line, and she blamed Muslims for it.'

I can see how talking about this makes G both sad and frustrated. I want to comfort her, but more than anything I want to just listen, because I don't know how many people she can speak to about this.

'All this division, this decades-long hate towards people who were once ours, people who also lost so much at Partition, is one of the reasons my aunt was made to leave. You know, I'm hoping she's still around, I'm hoping that I haven't completely missed the opportunity to know her and her family. I cannot believe that in all these years not once did my grandmother falter and say that she had *five* children instead of four. Not once. So, imagine the amount of hatred she had for her daughter.'

'Maybe it was not hatred,' I offer finally. 'Maybe it was just hurt. Maybe she was hurt that her daughter didn't pick *her*, didn't pick *them*.'

'Maybe it's both in equal parts, but I can't separate the two. I can't imagine my life without my son. I can't imagine it. I agree that if I had four or five children, it may not be the same as having just one and feeling the loss of that child, but still…' She sighs deeply two or three times before saying, 'I'm sure she must have struggled with the decision too. I'm only thinking about it now, trying to put myself in her shoes. It sounds like a film, the way I was told about the choice my aunt had to make – *either us or them.* But I'm sure she must have tried to convince them; they must have had a series of conversations or meetings. This is my assumption, or my hope. And eventually she must have decided that she wanted to marry him and then they must have asked her to choose ... Even so, it's still shocking and disheartening.

'There is something that I really want to do – I want to track her down, I want to see her. Maybe not even tell her who I am. I just want to know where she is, maybe stalk her on social media.' She laughs but there are tears welling up in her eyes. 'I can do that.'

My heart sinks. 'I'm sorry to have upset you this way.'

'You haven't. It's just...' she sniffles, 'you haven't. We've been discussing this for over an hour now, but it's just something so personal and so delicate and ... so close to my heart. That poor woman, imagine, if I were asked to leave the house, how would I feel? Maybe I would hate my family initially? But then as the years would pass, I'd surely miss them. Though I'm certain her husband is a good man because, clearly, she never felt the need to come back.'

I notice how she does not say home, just *back.*

'I'm assuming that she's happily married and felt complete with her better half. She felt content, she didn't feel the need to come back to us, to the people who had disowned her. Or maybe she's no longer here in the city or the country – maybe they moved away?'

As I listen to her, part of me wonders whether her grandmother ever thought about her daughter after she had left home, ever thought about reaching out or finding her, ever wondered if she had had children, ever hoped that the high wall erected by deep-seated bitterness could, one day, dissolve on its own. I wonder if she ever thought of her own partition line, for she too had separated herself from love.

14
Memory

❦

FOR AS LONG AS I can remember, my paternal grandmother has kept a small white envelope bearing the words 'S.N. DAS STUDIO' inside the plastic box that holds her medicines. Sometimes she lays its contents out on the bed for me, almost ritualistically. Inside the envelope is treasured history, photos of her family members, taken either before Partition or in the years immediately after.[1] Nearly every person in these photographs is now deceased, but accompanying this ritual are stories – about the studio where these were shot, the days of the camp, the romance with my grandfather, or the rebuilding of life in India.

On a winter afternoon in early 2021, along with this envelope she hands me a plastic sleeve with some folded pieces of paper inside. It has been eight years now that we have been speaking about Partition and I have never seen this. Very carefully, I peel the plastic away to find three certificates from Panjab University, dated 1954 and 1956 and sent from Solan in present-day Himachal Pradesh: one is a birth certificate and the other two academic. She tells me that during Partition, even the university of Punjab, originally based in Lahore, was divided between India and Pakistan, the Indian one eventually distinguishing itself with the new spelling of Panjab. After 1947, there was no campus for nearly a decade, though the administrative office was at Solan and the teaching departments functioned in several cities like Jalandhar, Amritsar, Hoshiarpur and Delhi. In 1956, the university finally found a permanent home in Chandigarh, where it still stands today.

Of the two academic certificates, one is a duplicate, classified as 'SESSION 1947'. I assume that it is of the matriculation exam she gave in the spring of '47, just before Partition. The second certificate is of an honours degree she received in Hindi after taking the modern Indian languages exam in November 1954, one year before she got married.

'You never told us that you went to university!' I exclaim upon reading the certificate. 'I always thought you had to begin working as soon as you arrived in Delhi.'

'Evening classes, after work,'[2] she tells me, smiling.

I spend some time with the certificates, holding them up to the light, studying their fragile pages. They have been folded for so long that the creases have found homes in the paper, refusing to smoothen out. The edges are dog-eared, the surfaces are worn and musty, and yet the red in the embossed emblem of the university crest is vibrant still. These are the first documents of my grandmother's life in an independent India that I have ever seen and I am amazed that she still has them. Very carefully, I slip them back in their plastic case and hand them back to her.

Shaking her head, she says, '*Abhi kuch purani yaadein baaki hai*, there are still some old memories left.' She places the sleeve back into my hands. '*Woh sab bhi tum saath rakh lo*, you can keep those safe as well.'

That night, I think about the accumulation of memory as the sedimentary layers of the ocean: shell, coral, algal debris collecting year after year, forming layer upon layer. Having spent much of my early career in a studio as a printmaker, the only parallel that comes to mind is of limestone, which is used in traditional lithography. Each time an image is etched onto and printed off of the surface of a limestone rock, it needs to be ground down to blankness with fine sand and a levigator in order for the stone to be ready for a new image. In this way, the limestone becomes slimmer and slimmer each time an image is printed from it, as if it has parted with some of its body weight, its mass, its memory.

Similarly, each time I speak with my grandmother about the days of Partition, I descend deeper into her memory. I begin to know her as a teenager, understand more about how she would have felt, what she would have lost and what she would have gained. I remain struck, though, by how every time we speak on this subject, there is always something new added, something more, something deeper that has been retrieved. And I think to myself, *how can there always be more?* Is the inherent nature of memory to be cavernous? It is never chronological, often sporadic, a latticework of images, requiring gentle nudges and cues for remembrance, but always offers more.

But, in the same way that we have to work on a limestone, remaining very careful not to destroy its original, beautiful, sedimentary chemistry, I have to remain quite patient in our conversations, for not everything is offered at once. Eventually, she parts with bits of her former self and we descend the layers of memory as each question and subsequent answer finds its way closer to the heart of the experience. What is required the most, of course, is time.

I think about the first time her story was told to me, and how many more details have been added since to the same journey. How many times my grandmother has become a fifteen-year-old girl again; how many times she has stood on the platform wanting to go back to Pakistan on 16 August 1947 with her mother, because of their predicament in India, despite corpses littering train compartments; how many times I have asked her to enter Kingsway Camp for the first time, describe their barrack, list the details of her employment. How many times she has revisited the memory of a home left on the other side. How many times she has felt the same pain, the same sadness, the same loss in renewed ways. And how many times *I* have felt a shade of that loss.

I have often considered whether her memories of Partition have somehow transferred to me. Whether, through the tenor of her voice or the frailty of her touch, through the details she provides and the silences she recedes into, I can feel part of what she feels. Obviously, I cannot feel with the same acuteness or accuracy, but some form of transference has allowed this memory to be shared and perceived deeply across generations. Marianne Hirsch, while writing of the second generation or postmemory of the Holocaust, touches on the close proximity to tragedy:

> Second-generation fiction, art, memoir, and testimony are shaped by the attempt to represent the long-term effects of living in close proximity to the pain, depression, and dissociation of persons who have witnessed and survived massive historical trauma ... Loss of family, home, of a sense of belonging and safety in the world 'bleed' from one generation to the next.[3]

In this way, as my grandmother shares her memories, she bequeaths the images to the next generation – 'bleeds' them, in Hirsch's terms. Thus, the intimate way in which I, and many others, receive and feel the consequences of Partition is evidence of the fact that the memory of trauma does not end at the generation that witnessed it. It *can* be passed down, sometimes purposefully, but most times subliminally and in quiet, unspoken and even unintentional ways.

But there is another, more delicate and complicated aspect to consider here. Though this transference – whatever shape it may take – results in the preservation of memory by subsequent generations, what happens to the first generation *after* memory is recalled? And I have to admit that because so many of the interviewees I speak with often readily agree to their testimonies being recorded – on their terms – I have always assumed that memory is ready to be exhumed. But a passing comment from my grandmother one day makes me reconsider this assumption.

We have been speaking for an hour maybe when I propose a thought: 'Do you think it would have been beneficial if there had been oral historians to speak to people after Partition? Maybe in

the camps, to ask you how you felt, to talk about loss … to listen?'
I realize that my question arises from a contemporary and rather
privileged place of people wanting to speak to others about how they
feel. But still, I am curious.

'We were only children, what could we have known about feeling
loss? Yes, our mother would have certainly felt overwhelmed by it – a
single mother all alone in a new country – though she never talked
about it. *Shayad jo dukh humari ma ko mehsoos hua, uske baare
mein humne kabhi socha hi nahi.*'

'Well, do you think she may have liked to speak to someone, if
she could have?'

'If someone had asked, perhaps she would have spoken,' she
speculates.

'Do you think it may have made her heart a bit lighter?'

'Maybe.' She thinks about this for a few seconds and then, as if
speaking from experience, she says, 'Maybe it would have become
lighter, or maybe it would have gotten heavier. When someone
asks about such deep pain or loss, whatever is buried comes to the
surface; it is exhumed. Then it remains on the mind for long after the
conversation is over. The person continues to think about it, *zehen
mein rehta hai*, and it can consume them…' Her voice trails off.

'So…' my voice is now a whisper, 'is that what happens when I
ask you about Partition?'

'That is what happens,' she confirms, tiny tears forming in her
eyes.

'Sh-should I not?' I'm taken aback by her response, so I pause and
clear my throat. 'Would you rather I not ask anything else?'

'No,' she says and then there is a long silence. Finally, she shakes
her head from side to side. 'No, no. I'm not saying that you shouldn't
ask. You *should* ask, you should ask because no one has asked this
way. You should know what happened at the time. But remembering
is difficult, and wanting to remember is harder, perhaps harder than
wanting to forget, even. You see, my mother felt sadness not only
for Partition or leaving D.I. Khan but also because my brother died
immediately after. It was barely a few months that we had been in

Delhi when Madan Mohan was killed in an accident when a truck rammed into his bicycle. He would have been eighty-eight years old today had he been alive.' She sighs.

'So, onto the loss of home and land was added the loss of a child. My mother had longed for a son, and Madan was born after four daughters. Our father passed away when we were young, so he would have been our support, the only male member of the family. For a while after his death, she stopped eating or even going to work. Just remained in our barrack in the camp. But she never opened up about anything, not even to us. Maybe your asking me questions has made me wish that I'd asked her at the time, unburdened her heart, as you say. But everyone in the camp was suffering in some way, everyone had to begin their lives again. There was no time to sit and cry over what had been lost or discuss how one felt. And there was no one like you going around with a recorder or a notebook, collecting people's memories.' A small smile appears on her face as she gestures to our set-up, but I immediately feel tears pricking my eyes. 'So, neither did we talk to anyone, and nor did our mother,' she concludes.

'THERE ARE PLACES in memory you do not wish to go with others,'[4] writes Edmund de Waal in *The Hare with Amber Eyes*. In the 1960s, his grandmother, Elizabeth, an advocate for letter writing, burnt hundreds of letters and notes she had received from her grandmother, Evelina. Several decades later, when Edmund learns of this fact, he deduces that she may have burnt them not because she didn't think anyone would be interested but because the correspondence was private and belonged to them alone.

> There is something about that burning of all those letters that gives me pause: why should everything be made clear and brought into the light? Why keep things, archive your intimacies? Why not let thirty years of conversation go spiralling in ash...? Just because you have it does not mean

you have to pass it on. Losing things can sometimes gain you a space in which to live.[5]

Is it better, then, I wonder, to not ask about Partition, in order to prevent the burden of traumatic memory from being resurrected? Is Partition always a private wound? And just because it's there, does it mean that it needs to be passed down? I think about the well of silence that Partition memory has resided in for so long, all the conscious forgetting, and how much that could have been preserved has already been lost. Anything I may say is derived from the selfish act of wanting to retain history and memory. However, neither law nor archive nor historian can ultimately prevent forgetting.[6] It has taken years for my grandmother to open up in the way that she has about her memories of Partition, allowing us into them, and even then there remain things she would rather not recall. She maintains the view that during the process of Partition, she never thought subsequent generations would be touched by what had happened, what they had witnessed and survived. Part of that time will always remain unremembered. And it is here that I have to remind myself of the many layers that protect memory, and that to remember is not so simple and cannot always be willed.

THE HINDI WRITER Krisha Sobti, born in Gujrat, present-day Pakistan, had once said that Partition was difficult to forget but dangerous to remember.[7] On the fragile boundary of remembering and forgetting can be found the stories of Partition. In September 2018, while on field research in Jammu, I record an interview which for me now encapsulates the process of wilful forgetting. One evening, Sumedha Mahajan – who has helped set up this interview – and I are invited to tea by the family of a gentleman who had migrated in November 1947 from Mirpur district in what is now Pakistan-administered Kashmir. Sumedha's grandparents too are from Mirpur, as also distant acquaintances of this family.

We are taken to a brightly painted room, where a young man gives us some background information about his father, whom we will soon meet. Sumedha exchanges pleasantries about her family, and I talk about the work I will be doing in Jammu. After we finish our tea, he leads us to an inner room, where an elderly, balding man is sitting on the bed. Behind him, on the ochre yellow wall, is a calendar featuring Hindu gods. As he shifts around to get more comfortable, I get a fleeting glimpse of some Urdu text tattooed on his right forearm and the symbol of Om on his outer palm, between the thumb and forefinger.

Everyone around us is smiling, his family is delighted that a scholar has come to speak about his experiences of the journey from Mirpur to Jammu. He must have conceded as well, since he greets us when we enter the room, but then he retreats into silence. His eyes are wide open, but they are fixed on the ground, staring at nothing and no one. Everyone else's eyes are fixed on Sumedha and me and, clearing my throat, I ask about where he was born and when. He answers each question, but his gaze never meets mine.

'And what was it like?' I ask him.

'Mirpur? *Bohot badiya,* it was good. It was a place where everyone was happy until they weren't. It was a good place,' he replies.

'Do you remember it?'

He nods. '*Watan toh watan hota hai*, it's my birthplace after all.'

'What do you remember about it?

'Well, it is in Pakistan now, drowning under the water of the Mangla dam, but when the water level recedes, I have heard that our old city rises to the top.'[8] This is the longest sentence he has spoken, and his arms limply create a bridge, a dam, before us. Then, just as quickly, he brings them down and folds them back in his lap.

His family members remind him of the anecdotes he has told over the years. Everyone starts talking at once, remembering bits of memory, fragments of family lore, something that someone has once said but was never verified. Son, daughter-in-law, other family members are sitting around us, even the children are playing with their toys, peeking in from behind curtains, grabbing a biscuit and nibbling on it. Sumedha and I listen as best we can; we are both taking notes but it becomes difficult to discern one voice from another.

They tell us about how his mother's brother-in-law couldn't walk and remained locked inside a room when the family left in November 1947; they couldn't go back for him. They tell us how his sister-in-law's neck was hacked with an axe, a *kulhari*. They speak of the Alibeg concentration camp, where his friends were held, and how young girls of the family were picked up and carried away by people known as Kabailis. They cradle their arms before their bodies as they tell us about a fourteen-day-old baby wrapped in a shawl and brought to India over a journey of three days with nothing to eat or drink.

After a while, there is only noise; there are too many voices but not the one that truly matters. Seated on the bed, the elderly gentleman is swaying very softly from front to back, his bulging eyes still fixed on the ground. The family members coax him to remember, but he doesn't. They speak louder, for he cannot hear well. I look at Sumedha and breathe in sharply. I don't know what to note down any more. This is her first time accompanying me on an interview, and she doesn't quite understand either. We look at the family members talking animatedly amongst themselves – and the gentleman quiet amidst it all. My heart is breaking with guilt for what I can only assume is going through his mind. He doesn't divulge any sadness, but he doesn't discount it either.

Over the voices of the others, his son finally says, '*Mirpur di koi gall sunao na*, tell us something about your home.' He speaks in Pothwari, which has all but disappeared from modern conversation. It sounds like Punjabi, and I can catch some words, but it is much brisker, and his intonations make the language sound more musical than when I have heard it before.

His wife leans in closer to her father-in-law and repeats, to make sure he can hear, '*Mirpur di gall?*'

The gentleman shakes his head from left to right and returns his empty gaze to the ground.

'*Koi changi si gall?* Something good, a good memory. *Achchi yaadaan vi sunao,*' she prompts.

'*Koi takki di gall, kedi takki thi ghar de kol,* tell us about a street close to your home,' his son says again. But his father says nothing about Mirpur. He just keeps swaying softly from front to back, repeating, 'Everything was very good, people were happy with one another. *Sab kuch theek tha.*'

There are no other words he offers, for sometimes forgetting is as important as remembering.

THE MEMORY OF Partition is complex by all accounts – studied seven decades on, it is a canvas left with many blank spaces. Purposefully forgetting to remember, consciously remembering to forget. Sometimes 'I cannot remember' can also mean 'I don't want to remember'. And in returning to the notion of transference, I deduce that no matter how nuanced a memory we may collect from another, no matter how close it may *feel* to us, no matter how deeply it may inform our understanding of the past, it will never truly be ours, for we have not experienced it.

In this sense, the conversations in this chapter are born from the understanding that received memory of Partition is distinct from eyewitness recall, because it will always be mediated by unavoidable distance. Those who preserve the memories of their ancestors and others are not trying to emulate any feeling, but to create new engagements with the same memory. 'How can we best carry their stories forward, without appropriating them, without unduly calling attention to ourselves, and without, in turn, having our own stories displaced by them?' Every generation *feels* differently, and within that generation there will be further distinctions among groups. The purpose of conversations with subsequent generations on the memory of Partition – its remembering and forgetting – is purely to understand how memory is disseminated, discovered and reclaimed.

THROUGH THE TWO third-generational accounts in this section, I touch on both the evocation as well as erosion of suppressed Partition memory due to the condition of mental illness: in particular, dementia. In *The Generation of Postmemory*, Hirsch writes that 'the role of dementia is to hold the parent or grandparent with the disorder in a transitional space, as if we were witness to the very moment of memory becoming postmemory'.[10] Dementia is defined as the steady deterioration of memories over a period of time,[11] and involves losing the accurate perception of time and memory function. Those suffering from the condition sometimes have impairments in short-term memory but are able to recall remote memory with relative ease.[12] In the following conversations with Surangana Makin and Kinshu Dang, the remembrance of Partition by their respective grandparent is either aided or hindered by the condition of dementia.

'I MUST HAVE been in middle school when we first read about Partition,' Surangana, who was born in 1995, tells me. 'And when you really think about it, 1947 isn't that far back in our history, and so as I was learning about it, I convinced myself that my grandparents must have definitely been around when it happened. So, armed with this information, I went to them one day and simply asked, "Were you there when it happened? Did you see Partition?"'

She pauses and chuckles. 'It was very confrontational, but I was young, couldn't have known any better. Children are so unafraid to ask the questions that as we grow older we find ourselves tiptoeing around.'

Several years before this interview, I had the opportunity to speak with Surangana's maternal grandparents, both of whom had migrated from Multan – her nana by train to Lucknow and her nani by flight to Indore via Delhi. Her nani was quick to dismiss the subject, quite unimpressed that I spent my days absorbed in stories of an undivided India, but my conversation with her nana, Om Prakash Khanna, took time, for he was visibly still affected by the events of 1947. One of twelve siblings, he was sixteen years old when Partition was announced. He was sent early on to Lucknow, where his eldest sister's marital home was. Their parents followed eventually.[13] Many of my questions were met with silence that afternoon, and I only later understood that I was asking him to venture into memories that he may have long entombed. Partition was too much to bear for his father, Malik Tikaya Ram Khanna, and he died soon after, so there was not only the loss of home to overcome but also that of family. It was these silences that had made me feel like an intruder – urging him to revisit unspoken years, to excavate chambers that had been consciously cemented shut. So, I am curious about the stories he told Surangana, if any.

'Well, what did your grandparents say?' I ask.

'We were eating lunch and the question obviously took them both by surprise. My nana was evidently taken aback, but he just gave a casual smile of sorts and continued eating. My nani, very conveniently, changed the topic. I let it go for a couple minutes, but it was his smile, it hinted at something more, so I continued to pester him. "*Aap wahan the, the kya aap, the kya?*" It was almost as if Partition was a physical place and I was asking him whether he was there, whether he'd been there, whether he'd seen it. We'd never spoken about it at home, not once. But I kept persisting until he finally conceded and said, "*Haan main tha, theek hai*? I was there," and then went on to suggest we play carrom because I'd brought my carrom board along. And that was when I *really* knew that there was more, because though my grandfather was great at carrom, he hardly ever wanted to play or teach me the tricks of the game.'

We both laugh, and Surangana continues, 'I literally locked myself in a room with my grandfather until he told me more about his journey to India. Those first few conversations were quite formal and sparse. He told me that his family had witnessed the riots and had migrated – like millions of others – during Partition, and that's how it began. I think it was summertime, actually, and I was staying with them for the holidays, which is how we could manage to get many hours together. But we only spoke when my grandmother was not around.'

She looks down at her notes and then says, 'The time he talked about Partition the most, though, was when he was diagnosed with dementia – when his memory physically began to break down and he had less control over it. In his last years, he was immersed in a pre-Partition life; it was difficult to extract him from it.' She clicks her tongue and sighs, 'Of course, I hate the circumstances in which he really began talking openly – it was difficult for him as well as his family – but a by-product of the illness was that it allowed him to return to a past that he hadn't really confronted in depth.'

'His recent years began to erode away…' I begin.

'Not only that, but time became non-linear and malleable, as if his mind was able to stretch back into the past and return to the present quite deftly. I remember, often on days when we talked about his childhood, he would address me as "Raj" or "Krishna", who were his sisters, or my nani as "bhabhi", which is what he called his mother. He would very naturally gravitate to the past. Particularly when we were alone and no one else could change the subject, he would remember very nuanced moments both from before Partition as well as immediately after. Sometimes, he would imagine he was speaking to someone who once lived in his lane in Multan. I absolutely hated the confused look on his face when I'd ask him who he was talking about, or to have my question met with silence.'

I ask her how his recollections made her feel, and thinking about it she remarks, 'It was mere curiosity that allowed me to speak with my grandfather about a pivotal moment of his life. Sometimes I think that if I hadn't been as bold or confrontational as a teenager, the story may never have emerged. It would have remained buried, particularly since one half – my grandmother – consciously strove to evade the subject, even though her family didn't experience loss in the way my grandfather's did. But I can't tell you the number of times I wished I could have helped my grandfather climb out of that bottomless pit of confusion and return to present reality, away from Partition. Dementia is possibly the harshest and most torturous illness I have known so far.'

IN AN EMAIL exchange, Kinshu Dang, born in 1993, writes to tell me how her grandfather, Desh Raj Dang, now has dementia, but she is glad that she asked him about his life while he remembered everything. Born in 1934 in village Choodi, Chak 147, Lyallpur city (now Faisalabad), he is the eldest of five siblings, brought up in a joint family set-up with his father's siblings and their families. During the riots in 1947, they migrated to Delhi via Ludhiana, the Kurukshetra camp and Kunjpura. I write back to ask when she first began speaking with him, and if, as he got older, he chose to reveal more to her than he had to others in his youth. In response, she writes:

> It is so interesting when you write that memory reveals more to us as we grow older and how in our fading years we recede, almost always, back to childhood. I see this happening with my grandfather. After undergoing a blood clot removal surgery in 2011, his health has been on a decline. But these were also the years when I asked him the most questions. As a teen, I was told that we come from a refugee family but I never knew the details. I started asking questions when I went to college. The questions were mostly prompted by discussions in the classroom. Last year, he was diagnosed with dementia, but the signs had been there for a while. All he now utters are some songs and slogans, fifty per cent of which have a nationalist undertone. For example, he keeps saying, 'Hindustan jeet gya, Pakistan haar gya,' or 'Hindustan zindabad, Pakistan murdabad.' Sometimes he sings 'Saare jahan se accha Hindustan humara,' or 'Jana Gana Mana'. This reminds me of Toba Tek Singh and his gibberish. My cousin and I were wondering if these were signs of PTSD...

But apart from lingering trauma, other unexpected vignettes also remain lodged in the crevasses of memory. Kinshu writes about a film her grandfather watched in his village, which is in fact the first thing that comes to her mind when we begin our correspondence.

The screening was arranged by the British administration for a film named *Bhookha Desh Bachana Hai*, We Must Save [Our] Starving Country. What I find intriguing is how wide the reach of the British propaganda was. Even the means were creative. I wish I could ask him more about this now, but he won't be able to answer. I think this anecdote has remained with me because everything else about their Partition story seemed pretty standard. I have never seen my grandfather ever watch a movie, not even at home on a TV. So, this idea of a young Desh Raj watching probably his first ever movie was fascinating.

On reading this, I wonder whether Kinshu is now the keeper of her grandfather's memories, whether she is holding on to things *for him* because he no longer can. Whether they are both equally moved by the event and consequences of Partition in their own ways, whether their reasons for forgetting and remembering are equally valid. Her final response speaks to how the ineluctable silence of an entire generation post Partition contributed greatly to voids in personal and familial history across the subcontinent. Yet it makes sure to end on a hopeful note:

I'm told that in Pakistan my grandfather's father owned a desi medicines shop. But as a thirteen-year-old who migrated to Delhi, my grandfather did everything possible to make ends meet, and I feel he never really had the time to process any trauma. He was too busy setting up a business, getting his four sisters married, making sure his children were well settled. The quality of their life on this side of the border drastically improved over a generation, and they managed to climb the social ladder significantly. Learning this has helped me appreciate how hard they must have worked to give my generation a great education and comfortable upbringing. But once all that was done, my grandfather began to slip into depression. Then the blood clot, and finally dementia. Seventy years later, he now seems to be confronting 1947.

Contrastingly, in me, Partition has always generated a feeling of curiosity. I want to know more, and ever since college I have left no opportunity to either record my family's history or contribute to the scholarship of oral history. But despite my enormous interest in the subject, [what] bothers yet amazes me is that my grandparents have never expressed any desire to visit their home town in Pakistan. Ever. The most common trope in Bollywood or even Partition literature is this nostalgia for the lost homeland. I would always feel left out of the mainstream nostalgia narrative when my grandparents would say, '*Ab kya karna wahan jaakar, sab kuch toh yahaan hai*,' what is the need to go back, our whole life is here now. But one of my dream projects is to visit my grandfather's village in Pakistan and locate his house. To see where my ancestors come from.

At the risk of repeating myself, when I read her words, I think again about how difficult it truly is to do this – cross the border, set foot on the other side – as if it's some forbidden land. How many generations will it take for the shadow of Partition to no longer linger, to be able to lay claim to a complete history and walk on the soil of our ancestors with both ease and dignity.

A UNIQUE QUALITY I have noted about the experiences of Partition is that the same memory can be remembered differently by different members of the same family. Furthermore, as generations remember *together*, Partition testimony gains a new life and acquires yet another layer of depth.[14] When I speak with Priyanka Sabarwal, born in the 1980s in Delhi, she tells me that anytime she spoke to her maternal grandfather or his brothers about their journey during Partition, they would each tell it slightly differently. As a result, she would emerge with versions of the same event.

'There were seven Thapar siblings in total,' Priyanka counts out loud, thoughtfully, trying to remember each one. 'Of the three sisters, one was married in Bombay and died before I was born, another worked with Gandhiji and also passed away early, the third, Santosh, migrated with the family. Of the brothers, the eldest, Satyendar Kumar, worked in the Life Insurance Corporation (LIC), India, and was eight or nine years older than my grandfather. The second brother, Jitender Bhushan, was a singer and a devoted fan of K.L. Saigal's. When Saigal came to perform at Minto Park in Lahore in 1937,[15] the family went to his concert and he decided that he would join his troupe and left. No one knew where he went or how to find him after that. The third brother, Satpal Bhushan, stayed back in Lahore after Partition to take the Urdu exam for his bachelor's degree. He retired as air commodore in the Indian Air Force and participated in wars that, in his own words, he wasn't sure he believed in. And then was my grandfather, Bharat Bhushan, the youngest, who also worked for LIC. Today, none of the brothers are alive.'

'Do you know how they migrated, or where they came to in India?' I ask.

'They moved just a few weeks before actual Independence, I believe. They travelled from Lahore to Ajmer, to Agra, Mathura, and then to Delhi. Of these cities, my grandfather lived the longest in Delhi. He knew the city like the back of his hand, but he never spoke about it in the same way that he talked about the Lahore of his childhood – where he used to have his lassi or halwa-puri, or how they would go to the river. Strangely enough, he rarely ever mentioned Partition. Those stories were always told by his middle brother.'

She brings her hand to her chin and remembers, 'I was in school when the bus service from Delhi to Lahore began, and I would ask my grandfather, "Do you want to go? I will take you," and he would always agree because he did want to revisit Lahore, but then he would recede and worry about whether it would be the same any more, and how he'd confront all the changes involved in coming to a home that was now a different country. When I think back to the way he talked about it, Lahore was the one home he had. I have never heard him talk about anywhere else like that, not even the house he lived in once in India.'

She pauses and her voice softens as she repeats, 'He never called it home.'

'But he never talked about how they migrated or the days of Partition?' I ask.

Priyanka shakes her head. 'And these are the things that make me wonder about where I come from; maybe his memory just didn't allow him to venture into those days, and so a lot of my knowledge about that time came from books. But his middle brother did tell stories about Partition – and very vivid ones. One that has stayed with me, and which I partly eavesdropped on as a child, was something that happened to their eldest brother, the LIC officer. He was already married and working at that time, and would travel in trains, even during the riots all through the summer of '47 and well into Partition.

'So, some time after the family had already migrated, he was on a train where everyone in his compartment was massacred, but somehow he survived. I don't know how, I've heard different versions of how it happened, but he was really disturbed after it. It impacted him tremendously. He was in therapy and would get these epileptic fits towards the end of his life. I was only in middle school, but I still remember them vividly. Everyone just assumed it was epilepsy, but actually...' There is a sudden, very deep tone of sadness that enters her voice. '...actually, it was dementia where he was forgetting everything except that horrendous night. Those riots were the only memory that remained with him till the end of his life.'

I say nothing, only look at her in devastation.

'At the time,' she continues, 'I used to think to myself how is it that someone can forget an entire life and remember just a single night, in a way that it becomes the entire memory of life.' She exhales deeply.

'That is really the question, though,' I remark. 'How are the memories of trauma so powerful that they embed themselves within us and become almost representative of our lives...'

She nods. 'Completely, yes. And I found it really strange how all three brothers went through it really differently. The oldest one

– it became a part of his subconscious being; the middle one dealt with it by telling all these stories again and again to all of us; and my grandfather was ... well, he would talk about everything *but* Partition.'

'Maybe they all *chose* to remember it differently,' I suggest. 'Memory is a fragile thing. On the one hand, it can consume us, but on the other hand, we can wilfully suppress it.'

Priyanka nods again. 'Yes, for the eldest brother, I think he understood the reality of what was going to happen with the announcement of Partition. He was old enough. The second brother, who had stayed back to give his college exams, had some level of denial about accepting that life was going to change forever, and so drastically. He really thought that they would return. And then, my grandfather, who was only a teenager. But I think it was the sheer contrast of memory that really struck me. Listening to this bloody, gory, traumatizing story of the train ... it was so deep, it sat so deep in me, and I couldn't understand how someone would be able to overcome that kind of experience. And then, in complete opposition were the memories of my grandfather, which were warm and delightful, and did not betray any fear or violence of any sort. They were full of real happiness for his Lahore days.'

In our earlier interaction, Priyanka had mentioned that she writes fiction inspired by Partition. When I ask her whether her stories emerge from family experiences, she smiles. 'A large part of my writing and storytelling came from my grandfather. I grew up being very close to him, and so most nights I would sleep only after he told me a story, and inevitably every story was about Lahore. His words would paint pictures of that era, of his childhood, of the friends he had.'

Her smile becomes incrementally smaller. 'Through these storytelling sessions, there was a sense of becoming deeply acquainted with a place one had never been to, a place that was once home and now inaccessible. What I have really inherited from Partition is the unanswerability of memory – the acceptance that there are many things I know about my grandfather's life in Lahore but there are still so many questions I will never have answers to because we cannot return to that time. It's like a quest, you know – you can't give up, but you also may not find out. I just have to keep exploring on my own, particularly now that my grandfather has passed.'

'Do you ever feel a sense of belonging,' I ask, 'to the other side?'

'When I was in college in the States, people used to ask, "Where are you from?" and I would say India. But at the back of my mind was always the fact that my origin, the origin of my ancestors, the birthplaces on the passports of both my grandparents are cities no longer in India. That they aren't places we can visit freely, not like a remote part of our own country. Their, *our* origins now lie in another country altogether, which is right beside India but so...'

'...unreachable,' I finish her sentence.

'Yes, within reach but unreachable. Lahore will always remain important for me, as it was for my grandfather. It was not only his home, but because his mother had died when he was merely six years old, Lahore was the only place where he ever knew her. It was important to him, because whatever stories he told about her, whatever memory he carried of her, was from there.'

'It is fascinating how memory becomes the source of our history sometimes,' I remark.

'Both in its remembering and its forgetting,' Priyanka adds.

'I DON'T THINK I ever heard the word Partition in school,' Kavita Puri tells me when we speak. 'I don't think I ever heard it in my house either. But the odd thing is, when I think of the word Partition now, I only hear my dad say it in a kind of heavy Indian accent.'

Kavita was born in the 1970s in Kent and works as a journalist for the BBC in London. For nearly a decade, she has been recording stories of British South Asians, trying to understand the migration flows to post-war Britain and how the history of Empire is inextricably linked to the modern history of South Asia. The first time we meet is after her debut book, *Partition Voices*, has just gone to press, and my debut book, *Remnants*, has been out for a year. Ever since that first meeting, our relationship has not only been anchored by the stories of Partition but also by a deep understanding of the oral history process.

'In my absolute subconscious,' she continues, placing a hand over her heart, 'Partition begins with my father. I don't think of the mass migration, or the sheer numbers of people, or even the violence. I think of the ... small things, the individual, the personal losses; what it did to the single human being; the kind of consequences it had on the lives of people. And that's probably because of what I observed in my own house, even though I didn't know what it was.'

'Growing up in the UK, so far away from South Asia, when did you first understand Partition?'

'Understanding means a number of things to me – one is the statistics of the event, learning about the magnitude of it in a disassociated way and quite late in life as it was never taught in school. But understanding its impact on people's lives happened probably when I began working on my BBC Radio 4 series *Three Pounds in My Pocket* in 2013. It looks at the people who came to this country from the Indian subcontinent from the 1950s onwards, and I couldn't understand why so many of them kept talking about Partition. I would ask them about Britain and they kept returning to Partition, and I just couldn't comprehend why that was. I'll never forget this one woman I spoke with in Birmingham, whose husband was a bus driver and she had come over from a village in Punjab in Pakistan. And she told me how excited she was to migrate to Britain, not because she would meet English people – she expected that, coming to England – but because she wanted to meet Hindu people! She had heard that there were many Hindus in Birmingham. Her village used to have a significant population of Hindus before Partition, and then it didn't, and she had to migrate to Britain to be able to meet them again.[16] These kinds of things kept coming up...

'That's when I realized that something much bigger was waiting to be exhumed, and I began doing deep research on Partition a few years ago. As I interviewed people about what they had experienced in 1947, and as I witnessed the rawness of their traumas first-hand, I began to slowly understand Partition. What it had done to people, what it continues to do to people, and what it was doing to subsequent generations.'

I pick up a copy of *Partition Voices* and leaf through. It was published in 2019, two years after the BBC radio series commemorated the seventieth anniversary of Partition.[17] *For my father and my girls*, the dedication reads, threading three generations – the past, present and the future – together. The last and final chapter of her book is titled 'My Father'. Ravi Datt Puri was born in 1935 in Lahore and was twelve years old at the time of Partition, when his family migrated to Moga in India.

'When did you begin speaking to him?' I ask.

'My parents lived in America for a few years. On my father's seventieth birthday, we were on a holiday in New Hampshire when I interviewed him about his life. My mum was sitting in the room with us and it was a really beautiful morning. He was a very open, gregarious man – talked about everything. But when I arrived at the topic of Partition, he clammed up, as he always did. This other time, I had to read out something at the funeral of one of his friends – they had both gone through Partition and I wanted to mention that in the eulogy. But my father told me to take it out. I asked him why but he just insisted I take it out, and so I realized that it was a taboo subject.

'But I also knew that I had to understand what exactly it was he couldn't talk about. I spoke to his friends, even his family, but they weren't very helpful. Then, when the radio programme *Partition Voices* actually went out, he asked me why I hadn't interviewed him for it. And I said it was because he wouldn't speak to me! I think by then he had heard so many people talk about it, watched programmes on television, and was encouraged by the testimonies of others. He felt that he could open up because others were too. He talked to me quite seriously and in depth, I would say, between September and October 2017 ... and then he died in November.'

'Do you think that...' I begin hesitantly.

'Yes,' she cuts me off. 'Yes. I do. I know what you're going to ask, and the answer is yes. Did he tell me because he knew he was dying? Yes, I think so.'

I watch her compose her thoughts.

'I think he knew that he was dying, but I also think he knew that I was listening. And he told me the story as if to say that I should never let this happen to me or my children, that I should never judge or treat people differently on the basis of their religion. When the riots intensified in the summer of 1947, the family migrated to my maternal grandparents' home in Moga, Ferozepur. Two days after Partition, they got word that Moga had become a part of India. The family had made arrangements to move further had it been awarded to Pakistan.'

She sighs. 'Honestly, no matter how intimately we spoke, I think there are still things he didn't tell me. The pauses, the silences, the hesitations. They all meant something. I remember him saying that after Partition happened, there was a Muslim family that lived at the end of their road in Moga, and they were slaughtered by a group of Sikhs. The girls of the family were very beautiful, and he implied that they were raped but he never said the words. He just stopped talking suddenly. So, though there was more to be said, he told me whatever he could allow himself to say.

'I interviewed him after I'd interviewed several other people, and so I knew about the violence and the bloodletting, and expected that. But it was the small details that I could have never anticipated – like the fact that they saved their cow in Lahore. After they migrated to Moga, they made arrangements for their cow to follow, because – in my father's words – they loved it and didn't want it to be killed. The cow travelled by train in a wagon car by itself.[18] These were the details that were so surprising they stayed with me. In the midst of utter chaos, they chose to save the cow they loved,' she smiles.

Ravi Datt Puri completed high school, did his BA in Delhi and worked for Pfizer, and in 1959 migrated to the UK. He had applied and been accepted into a graduate traineeship programme in Middlesbrough at Dorman Long – the engineering company that made the Sydney Harbour Bridge and London's Lambeth Bridge.[19] In this way, Kavita becomes connected to present-day Pakistan, India and Britain equally. When I ask her about this, she agrees that like her father, she too feels a profound connection to Lahore.

'I've been thinking about this a lot, and what I feel is a physical pull to the land. I was once on a panel at the Adelaide Festival with Sanam Maher, the Pakistani journalist,[20] and though we had never met before, when I saw her, I wanted to hug her. Even though she is from Karachi and not Lahore, she is from the place my father came from, where he always wanted to go back but never could. I feel like it's already a part of me. In my head, there is no border, it's completely undivided. I would be in a place that is connected to me, and so whether that place is called Pakistan or not is completely irrelevant; it is so deeply a part of me.'

A warmth spreads across her face. 'When my book came out, it was difficult to get it in Pakistan, and I asked a friend of mine who was going there to just put the book somewhere, even if it was just under a bench in a park, because then it would be touching the earth and somehow, a part of my father would have returned. I never understood why my father came to Britain, you know. It was so cold and so difficult to make a new life in a foreign land, where you may or may not be accepted, and you were alone and couldn't call your family often because it was so expensive. And I thought, *why would someone do that?* But it was only after we spoke that I realized the worst had already happened, home had already been taken away from him. After Partition, India was a place that he lived in, but it was never really home in the same way as Lahore.'

'Why do you think it took your father seventy years to talk about what had happened?'

'I think he remembered everything, because when he spoke, it was always with such clarity. He remembered every murder or atrocity he witnessed at that time; he described it in such vivid detail as if he were a twelve-year-old boy again. So, the memories had obviously stayed with him over the years, they had never gone away. But he always said he never wanted to burden us, which is interesting because I think even if you don't talk about it, subsequent generations know that there is something there, they can feel it, and it is heavy. Even silences are telling. So, it passes down anyhow. But he didn't want to burden us consciously and have us grow up with bad feelings against people of the other religions.[21] He worried that if he told us this story of division, we might grow up with prejudice, because he had seen the logical conclusion of that – I think that was his rationale. But also remember, Aanchal, when you move to another country, you can actually distance yourself, and you can say that was my past and this is now my present, and you can attempt a fresh start.'

Her palm wipes the table in front of her, as if cleaning the slate.

'And has Partition shaped you?' I ask, even though I already know the answer.

'I think, even beginning with *Three Pounds*, it has shaped me completely. It shapes the way I see people, even on the street. Now, any time I see a British South Asian, I think: *What is your story? Where did it start from? Why did you come here?* I see people differently. I see their reservations differently. I see that life is heavy and complex. And once you start looking for these stories, you find them all around you.

'But I've also learnt that if people want to keep their silence, you have to respect that. Just like talking is a choice, silence too is a choice. And this silence pervades the British South Asian community for a number of reasons. Practically, they were just trying to make a new life, there was no time to look back to the past. And often in those early days, they were dealing with an environment that was hostile to their presence. But also, there wasn't a public space to share or lament, and no one was asking these questions. And when we finally did, a lot of people spoke, but some didn't, and we have to respect that. It is strange because this learning goes against my instincts as a journalist, where one keeps pushing, keeps searching for answers. But here it wasn't possible, because these conversations were so fragile and I would feel protective of them. You cannot push; you must respect the boundary of memory.'

'Forgetting is a conscious choice, just as remembering is,' I say.

'Exactly.' She takes a deep breath and exhales.

'Do you think Partition is still relevant? Does it belong to you?' I wonder.

'Yes,' she says immediately. 'It is mine ... and sometimes I wish it wasn't, because of the heaviness. But it very much belongs to me and will to future generations. Partition has left such a deep and invisible impact on the lives of people that even through inherited memory you can feel its presence. We can't let it go because it's threaded into our lives – my life, *your* life. Just because something happened a long time ago doesn't mean it's relegated to history. There is trauma, still, which can be passed down, even in silence. There is a universality about Partition as there is with the Holocaust, or the Rwandan genocide, or with the countries of former Yugoslavia – the universal lesson of what humans are capable of doing to one another. And it never starts with mass killings or ethnic cleansing; it starts in the small acts, the othering, the words we use, and it can escalate very quickly. The violence around Partition is just one horrific reminder of what can happen if we choose division instead of inclusion.'

'And what about in Britain?'

'Particularly in Britain, I think, where we don't learn about Empire or how Empire ended – with Partition – at school. People don't really understand why my father and those who look like him came here, people don't have that knowledge. The history is so entwined and yet its knowledge is absent. Empire and Partition explain contemporary Britain, who we are today, why *we*, South Asians, are here.

'My father became a refugee at the age of twelve and, you know, he was just the generation before me. I could touch him, I could touch that history. It was very real and visceral. And so, if he could be uprooted in his lifetime even though they were happy and had a good life, what's to say that that couldn't be me too at some point. And so, deep, deep down, I do have this feeling that maybe things could turn again, and I'm very vigilant of it, perhaps even hypersensitive because it happened to my father.

'But when you are second generation in an adopted land, as I am in Britain, you always wonder how far you are accepted...' Her voice trails off. 'So, you have to fight for your place here, because you have nowhere to go back home to. What is my home? I was born in Britain. I could go to India, but that's not really home. I could go to Lahore, but that's not home either. This, here, is home. And yet, even at home, we ask ourselves: to what extent are we accepted? It is very complicated and, in some ways, all connected to migrations that happened after Partition. So, yes, conversations about Partition are relevant still.'

Nearly two hours have passed since we began talking. Kavita now brings her palms over her face and massages her eyes. There are tears but she hasn't let them fall once. Our conversation has touched the farthest corners of history and heart. There is a heaviness to the space we are sharing, a density we both are well acquainted with. But here, at the end, the formality of the interview gives way to a conversation between two oral historians, from two different generations, in two different geographies, with different reasons to preserve memory of the same historical event. A conversation between two friends.

'I don't think of myself, ever,' she finally confesses. 'While doing interviews with others, or even with my father, it was never about me: what it was doing to me, how listening to these testimonies was changing me. It's so hard for people to say the words out loud, to talk about Partition. It's so difficult for them to utter what happened, and how they felt, that you – the interviewer – hardly matter.'

I nod. 'You are merely listening to the story of what happened, while they have not only lived the reality but carried forth its memory.'

She agrees and says, 'You know, my father died so soon after I interviewed him. When I listened to the recording again – and I usually don't listen back, but I had to for the book – I could hear how his voice sounded different, like he had already left this world. It was completely unbearable.'

For the first time, then, she breaks down.

Tears sting my eyes too and I cradle my face in my palms. I know this feeling.

'My paternal grandfather died while I was writing *Remnants*, just a few years after I'd interviewed him. He was a bookseller his whole life, yet he never saw me become a writer. But listening to his recordings posthumously was so haunting. I remember, as I wrote the chapter on him, I kept talking to his photograph. It felt a bit mad, but in truth I was very angry at him for having gone so suddenly…'

Kavita chuckles through her tears.

'…and without notice. I know it's childish but I was sad, because I knew there was so much in him that I had never asked about. Even though he had opened up, like your father, there was so much silence he had maintained. Now he's gone and I still have so many questions, and no one can answer them. I felt anger but also so much pain.'

'Well, at least you recorded his story,' she comforts me. 'And in this way, the memory of Partition will remain in your family, as in mine. I will pass it down to my girls, and I hope they will pass it down to their children. It is not about whether Partition is too painful to hold on to. It is about remembering what happened, and continuing to remember, so we can make sure such a thing never happens again.'

15

Material Memory

‿℘

To COMMEMORATE THE SEVENTIETH anniversary of Indian and Pakistani independence and the subsequent Partition, the BBC's 'Museum of Lost Objects'* podcast explored the 'artefacts and landmarks that were caught up in the events around 1947'. The series was presented by Kanishk Tharoor, an Indian, whose grandmother, Saroj Mukherji, was a teenager in Calcutta at the time of Independence, and it was produced by Maryam Maruf, a Pakistani, whose father, Maruf Khwaja, was just shy of nine years when he migrated from Delhi to Karachi. The Partition of India would not only be a division of people and land, skies and rivers, but also objects like mechanical equipment, furniture and books. Independent India, for the most part, had the machinery in place, but Pakistan was to set up a new capital at Karachi, and for that it would require the everyday paraphernalia for the running of a nation. Tharoor details how a special council was set up to oversee an almost forensic separation of the assets of India:

A batch of sixty ducks that had been ordered the year before Partition from England had to be appropriately divided. An

---

* The 'Museum of Lost Objects' traces the histories of antiquities and landmarks that have now been destroyed or looted in Iraq and Syria, India and Pakistan (BBC, UK).

371

elephant called Joymony, that was the property of the Forest department, caused a bureaucratic saga when it was given to East Pakistan, but its mahout, its driver, chose to stay in India. Then, there are lists of objects allocated to either country that are almost farcical in their precision. For instance, to Pakistan, from the Ministry of External Affairs in Delhi, went 21 typewriters, 31 pen stands, 125 paper cabinets, 16 easy chairs, 31 officers' tables and 20 benches. To put it mildly, this was an incredibly fraught process and not always effectively executed.[1]

Freedom at Midnight dubs this division as 'the most complex divorce in history', wherein, alongside the division of monetary assets, government offices across India began counting their tables, chairs, brooms, typewriters, mirrors, hat-pegs, bookshelves, clocks, fans, bicycles, inkstands, musical instruments and staff cars, among other things. Arguments broke out over the division of these petty material goods, 'bargaining an inkpot against a water jar'. The Encyclopaedia Britannica was divided up, with alternate volumes given to each country; dictionaries were ripped in half – A to K going to one country and L to Z to the other. Indians refused to share the only press that printed currency in the subcontinent with their future neighbours, and as a result Pakistan 'had to manufacture a provisional currency for their new state by stamping huge piles of Indian rupee notes with a rubber stamp marked "Pakistan"'.[2]

But the anniversary episode of the 'Museum of Lost Objects' discusses at length a treasure so precious that neither country would possess it whole. This was the 4,500-year-old jade necklace from Mohenjo-Daro. Tharoor describes the artefact as a long necklace strung together on a thick gold wire with gold beads, semi-precious stones – jade, jasper and agate – and seven pendants, capped with gold, hanging in the middle. After Partition, the site of the Indus Valley Civilization, from where this necklace was excavated, fell in Pakistan. However, given the shared archaeological heritage of the region, India felt that it too had a right over the objects of the time.

And so began an exercise in dividing antiquity, with negotiations continuing for two years, on relics including the jade necklace.

Historian Vazira Fazila-Yacoobali Zamindar describes how this process was trying to 'divide what was essentially, and arguably, indivisible', for the ancient history and culture of the region could not be untangled into simply Pakistani or Indian, and 'any exercise to do so obviously requires leaps of imagination, political force, as well as destructive force'.[3] In the end, however, the necklace *was* cut up to make two new necklaces, piece by piece, stone by stone, one half given to Pakistan and the other to India, devoid of any and all wholeness. Historian Sudeshna Guha adds that not only was the necklace divided but 'every bit of duplicate or twin object',[4] like a beaker, a bangle, or a brooch, was partitioned. Sadly, in the exhibits of neither country is there any recognition of the fact that these objects were halved and separated from their pair.[5]

But, naturally, if the impact of this brutal dissection remains on people and land, then objects too hold its memory. Their surfaces, no matter how inanimate, absorb the narrative of division and migration. They remain mute spectators to history. The bisection of official assets between India and Pakistan is painstakingly recorded in historical archive, but it is the objects of common people – personal, intimate, often mundane things carried across borders in 1947 – that I have spent the early years of my career documenting. Objects, both public and private in nature, that tell stories of family, love, loss, yearning, displacement and even violence. Objects left on shelves or stored at the back of cupboards for years, quietly carrying memories of the *other side*.

My first book, *Remnants*, defines 'material memory' as 'the ability of an object or a possession to retain memory and act as stimulus for recollection'.[6] It considers the object a primary character around which the past is arranged. But the inherent misfortune of mundane objects, unlike those preserved in museums and private collections, is that they are often underappreciated. Due to their everyday nature, it is rare to find them valued for their age, rarity, technical virtuosity, beauty, or even their serendipitous survival.[7]

'IT WAS WHEN we found this in 2019 that a lot of stories from the days of Partition emerged.' Anas Khan, born in 1994, shows me a palm-sized ochre-brown piece of card with the words 'Curfew Pass (general)' written on it. 'My father and I were searching for some documents and we came across an old bag full of papers, mostly in Urdu and Farsi, dating back to 1901, 1903 ... this curfew pass was in that bag.'

'Dated the 30th of August '47,' I read.

'Yes, it was merely fifteen days after Independence that this curfew pass was issued to my great-grandfather, Mohammed Umar, in Delhi,' Anas says as I study the document. The pass has a deep crease running down the middle, where it was, no doubt, folded in half to be pocketed. The paper itself is discoloured, with water blotches across it, but the printed text is brilliantly legible still:

(For non-official only)
The holder of this pass, Mr. Mohd. Umar, is permitted to be out during the period of the Curfew order issued by the District Magistrate, Delhi, on 28-8-47 and as subsequently renewed or amended.

It is signed in the bottom right corner by the district magistrate of Delhi, and in the top left is a round stamp, all but faded. The handwritten name Mohd. Umar is also nearly washed out now. Right above the name is another stamp, of which only the first two words, 'INDIAN NEWS', are discernible. This curfew pass may have also been issued to journalists, as the word 'Press' is printed in the left corner.

'How come this curfew pass was issued?' I ask.

'The pass was issued so that my great-grandfather could continue going to work even under curfew. There was widespread violence for weeks after Partition, which is why a strict curfew was imposed.[8] My family has been in Old Delhi for nearly 200 years; they were called Motiwale, dealing in the business of pearls, *moti*. But my great-grandfather, Mr Umar, owned a workshop in Civil Lines, where he would repair all kinds of modes of transport like *tongas*, cycles, even cars. Actually, my father didn't know much about the curfew pass, so I asked his elder brother, who has kept alive the family business. I had heard fragments of it before, but his chronological narration put things into perspective. I will tell you what happened to the family's living conditions during the days of Partition, which should give some context to what the city of Delhi was like at the time.'

I nod, notebook in hand, and Anas begins.

'My great-grandfather and his two brothers lived together with their respective families in a big haveli in Teliwada, Sadar Bazaar; their parents had passed. The area was Hindu-dominated and, with the announcement of Independence, they chose to leave it temporarily. The neighbours had already warned them that if there was violence or rioting, they may not be able to protect them. So, as precaution, they went to Ballimaran to stay with relatives, but the situation was no better there. From there they moved yet again, this time to an abandoned property in Nawabganj, Azad Market, where they thought they could safely camp out for two or three months.'

'Abandoned property...' I interrupt, 'abandoned by Muslims who had left for Pakistan?'

'Yes,' he says, considering the irony, 'a property abandoned by Muslims who chose to leave, and occupied by Muslims who chose to stay. But the reason they went to Nawabganj was actually the highly intricate channel of lanes that went deep into the neighbourhood. Another reason was that the railway line was quite close by, just in case one needed to flee. They meant to stay for only a few months but ended up being in that house for nearly seven months, and then for three years after they had no permanent home.'

'What do you mean? They were from Delhi itself.'

'Partition did not only displace those who crossed borders. Everyone was affected in some way or the other. My family left Nawabganj to go back to Ballimaran because things had not quietened down yet in Teliwada. From there they moved to Azad Market and then found out that their actual home in Teliwada had been allotted by the government to a family that had migrated from Pakistan. The government simply assumed that because it was unoccupied, it was evacuee property. And thus began a long-drawn-out court case while the family remained in Azad Market.'

'Is that where you live now?'

Anas laughs. 'Believe it or not, we moved back to Ballimaran after that. There was *a lot* of moving around! Eventually, an ancestral haveli, which still stands, was re-established in Ballimaran, and in the mid-2000s my family moved to Civil Lines.'

'Your great-grandfather's workshop was also in Civil Lines – was that why the curfew pass was required?' I return to the object.

'Yes, to be able to continue to get to work, Mr Umar had this pass made. And what is really quite beautiful is that at the back' – he turns it over, showing me four lines of handwritten Arabic text in nearly faded blue ink – 'there is a *dua*, a prayer written to protect the person who is venturing out. It reads, "*Ya hal-lal-mushkilaat, ya dafi-al-baliyat, ya qadih-al-hajaat, ya mujeeb-ad-dawat,*" which translates to, "O Changer of Difficulties to Easiness! O Averter of Calamities! O Fulfiller of Needs! O Responder of Supplications!" The last line reads, "*Har namaz baad 104 martaba, alaw, aakhir 11 11 martaba, Durood Sharif,*" which is an instruction on how and when to recite the *dua* – 104 times after every namaz, and, before and after the *dua*, the Durood Sharif is to be recited eleven times respectively.'

'Wow,' I whisper.

'I have heard of an incident from my grandmother: one day, while going from Azad Market to Civil Lines, Mr Umar was attacked. There was a route that went through the jungle towards the railway lines and there was often a lot of violence in that area. So, while he was passing through the area, someone attacked him from behind, and all he had to defend himself was a small walking stick, a *chhari*-like object called a *gupti*. It could be unscrewed, in the same way that a pen is uncapped almost, and inside the stick was a small knife or spike used to defend oneself. So, the story goes that he was being attacked and this *gupti* was all he had, but in the meantime, he was saved by a General Shah Nawaz Khan.'[9]

'The same one from the Indian National Army?' I ask, eyebrows knitted together.

'Well, that's the story my grandmother tells – that he was passing by with a group of people and saved my great-grandfather. I have tried to do some research to find out whether General Shah Nawaz Khan was, in fact, in Delhi at the time or not, but she asserts that it was *a* Shah Nawaz Khan. Coincidentally, it was around then that I also found his grave,[10] which lies between Jama Masjid and the Red Fort, alongside that of none other than Maulana Abul Kalam Azad.'

'Anas, I hope you don't mind me asking, but what were the factors that led your family to decide to stay?'

'This is an almost perfect segue into that, actually,' he smiles. 'They stayed mostly because they had long-established businesses here, family history, family graves. But my great-grandfather was also an ardent admirer of Abul Kalam Azad and heard his speech at Jama Masjid after Partition, which quite strongly impacted his decision to stay in India.'

In March 1940, while Muhammad Ali Jinnah delivered his presidential speech to the All India Muslim League at its Lahore session, stating that 'Hindus and Muslims belonged to two different religious philosophies, social customs and literature', Maulana Abul Kalam Azad addressed the Indian National Congress as its president at the Ramgarh session with the following words:

Eleven hundred years of common history have enriched India with our common achievements. Our languages, our poetry, our literature, our culture, our art, our dress, our manners and customs, the innumerable happenings of our daily life, everything bears the stamp of our joint endeavour ... The thousand years of our joint life have moulded us into a common nationality. Whether we like it or not, we have now become an Indian nation, united and indivisible. No fantasy or artificial scheming to separate and divide can break this unity.

In October 1947, after the Partition line had been drawn, Azad addressed his fellow Muslims from the steps of Shahjahan's grand mosque in Old Delhi, appealing to citizens like Anas's great-grandfather to remain on a land that had raised generations of their families:

> Where are you going and why? Raise your eyes. The minarets of Jama Masjid want to ask you a question. Where have you lost the glorious pages from your chronicles? Was it only yesterday that on the banks of the Jamuna your caravans performed *wazu*? Today, you are afraid of living here. Remember, Delhi has been nurtured with your blood. Brothers, create a basic change in yourselves. Today, your fear is misplaced as your jubilation was yesterday.

'Not everyone stayed, though,' Anas tells me now. 'My great-grandfather Mohammed Umar was the second sibling, and his younger brother chose to go to Pakistan. If I think about it, the story of the three brothers is quite heartbreaking. The eldest, Mohammed Yaseen, was an officer in railway management at the time of Partition and actually died in the riots, which really impacted the family. His photo hung in the New Delhi railway station until the 1980s, along with those of other officers who had died at the time. We don't know much about what happened; his body was lost and so there is no grave. But I was told that a letter was sent home to inform the family that a male member had died in the riots, and that the authorities were trying to locate the body. So, naturally, this incident caused a lot of fear. But the youngest brother, Mohammed Yunus, chose to migrate to Lahore, and once he left, no one heard from him or his family ever again. We don't know if they travelled further into Pakistan ... or if they reached at all.'

'Are you saying that you don't know what happened to him?'

Anas shakes his head. 'No. I am the fourth generation that has heard this story, and, of course, we are so connected by technology now that it's almost impossible to fathom the fact that at the time there was just no way to locate someone without an address or a phone number. It was near impossible to keep track of those on the other side, particularly since the family in Delhi moved so much in the first three years. How would my great-grandfather have looked for his brother, who would he have asked, where would he have written?'

A sadness creeps into his voice, and when he speaks again, his tone remains reflective. 'This curfew pass is certainly the reason why so many of these stories have emerged to the surface again. But I think what affects me the most when I think about Partition is the feeling of separation. It's something that no one wants to discuss any more, because it's so painful. The separation from family, from country, from *home*. That was the hardest thing for me to imagine, to have a home and yet be separated from it out of fear. To be hiding in alleyways and abandoned properties, and for how long? It really saddened me to learn that in the days of Partition, one was not home even in one's own home.'

'Not home in one's own country,' I add. 'To have to fight to remain in one's own country.'

'In one's own country,' he repeats pensively. 'To live like refugees in a city where one has hundreds of years of family history … can you imagine that? You know, during the CAA protests in 2019, so many people kept saying that it felt like another Partition.'

It pains me that I have heard this statement more than once.

Returning to the curfew pass now, Anas smiles sadly. 'I suppose *this* is a tangible reminder of the days when we chose to stay; how, despite all the hardships and setbacks, we remained.'

ONE AFTERNOON OVER video call, I speak with Mujtaba Hussain, a lawyer, born in 1971 in Srinagar, India, and Saba Qizilbash,[11] an artist, born in 1977 in Lahore, Pakistan, who now live in Dubai with their two children.

'Both our families have been impacted by Partition in different ways,' Saba begins. 'My maternal grandfather, Wajid Ali Khan, or Aghajan, was born in Dalhousie and embarked on a very long and difficult journey to Lahore. Mujtaba's granduncle and his wife migrated from India to Pakistan and settled in Mirpur. In that sense, the family was divided, and the border remains a painful memory.'

'To be honest,' Mujtaba adds, 'I heard about Partition from my mother on several occasions growing up. The topic emerged quite naturally when we were just sitting by ourselves and talking – these stories of relatives she had not seen in thirty or forty years.'

'It was in 2000 that Mujtaba was finally able to travel to Mirpur for the first time,' Saba says brightly, 'and there was a lot of excitement on his mother's side. They come from a very big family – they are very clannish, very loving. And so when Baba – they call him that – was to come, the entire Mirpuri side of the family prepared a big celebration. For his mother, it was an enormous deal that their representative, her only son, was travelling across the border to meet the family that had been separated for decades.'

'Once I was there,' Mujtaba reflects, 'I thought about the stories my mother had told me and the love and longing with which she spoke about her relations in Pakistan. Now I was able to situate her stories in a context – I was able to associate names to faces, intangible memories to tangible places. Things became more real, and I saw no difference between us and them. We were family.'

One year later, in May 2001, the pair met in San Francisco.

Saba was a twenty-four-year-old student who, after a four-month-long artist residency in Oregon, had arrived in the city to experience the Bay Area's art scene before starting graduate school at the Rhode Island School of Design. Mujtaba was a thirty-year-old lawyer attending a fellowship in environment law at Stanford and Golden Gate universities.

Mujtaba recalls the day. 'Sometimes, when you have a real connection with someone, even an unspoken one, life just suddenly pauses, and you gather so much courage that it surpasses any rational thought that may possibly exist in your mind at that time. All I was thinking when I saw her that day was that God had brought me there, in that moment, to *her*.'

'Divine intervention?' Saba teases him.

He smiles. 'You can call it that. But I think it happens to everyone, not only with romantic partners but also friends. You feel a sudden unexplainable connection.'

I now turn to Saba. 'Do you remember that day?'

She laughs and embarks on her version. 'All too well! We met quite randomly on a bus. I was sitting with my head leaning against the window when he boarded the bus, and I saw him look at me but didn't make much of it…'

'I love how his narration is so serious and spiritual and yours is the Bollywood version!' I laugh.

Nodding happily, she continues, 'Absolutely! So, we got off the bus at the same stop, and I was waiting to take another bus. It was a very windy day; I remember my hair flying all over my face. He approached me and very formally introduced himself, "My name is Syed Mujtaba Hussain" – he always introduces his full name with the lineage – but he only had a few minutes before my bus arrived. So, he pulled out his ID card and told me that he was a lawyer from Srinagar and asked whether I would accompany him to the Black and White Ball, which has been an annual ball in the Bay Area since 1956.'

'Okay, in hindsight, it *was* very abrupt,' Mujtaba admits sheepishly.

'It was!' Saba turns to him. '*It was*! Now what is interesting is that the only thing I picked up from his introduction was not the Black and White Ball, or the fact that he was a lawyer, but that he came from Srinagar!'

I raise my eyebrows.

'This was because my grandfather spent his youth in Srinagar, and I will get to that story in a little while. But in that moment I thought of Aghajan and all the ghosts of my long-dead ancestors standing behind me, encouraging me, telling me to give this gentleman from Srinagar a chance. What he refers to as divine intervention was for me multiple layers of history and memory colliding.'

I am struck by how, in all this time that we have been speaking, the word Partition has not been uttered even once. The fact that Saba and Mujtaba, who hail from either side of the Radcliffe Line, have been able to erase its presence from between them in an almost enviable way gives me hope that a human relation will always be stronger than a man-made line.

'Now, for me to go back to Pakistan,' Saba continues, 'and tell my mother that I had met a man – a Syed, a lawyer, but an Indian, and that too from the disputed territory of Kashmir – would have been impossible. The sheer idea of the two passports side by side made the Line of Control feel very real, graspable. Of course, *now* years have passed, and when we place our passports next to one another, they speak to the strength of our relationship rather than the weakness of division…'

Mujtaba smiles to himself as he hears this. On the other side of the video call, I feel my heart expanding at the power that an undivided land can possess if we allow it to.

'…but, when we met, it was impossible for me to take this relationship forward,' Saba concludes. When I ask why, she says that she was not willing to take the risk and was apprehensive about exactly that which has now become her strength – the fact that they came from either side of the border. When I ask Mujtaba whether this ever factored into his pursuit of her, he shrugs.

'Not even for a moment. At the end of the day, I just realized that both India and Pakistan are creations of a political force, because the people are the same on either side. You can draw a line but you can't eradicate centuries of shared culture. I see no difference. Look at us – I am married to a Pakistani, she is married to an Indian – can you see the difference?'

I shake my head, for what he says is apparent from their relationship.

'Saba, did your grandfather's flight from India during Partition also play into your apprehensions?'

'Of course, that was one aspect, but what was more alarming was that after we spoke a few times, I would ask Mujtaba about his future plans, and every answer he gave included me. Meanwhile, I didn't know what I would be doing in the future, so when I began grad school in Providence in the autumn of 2001, the conversation sort of fizzled out. Until 9/11 happened.

'Mujtaba was in Delhi working at a law firm and I was in Providence, and he phoned me to ask whether I was okay, whether I was anywhere near New York City when the Twin Towers fell. He was concerned, and I was scared and disoriented. Then, a few days later, I got a phone call from Lahore saying that my mother had been diagnosed with cancer, and it was all too much to bear. So, I decided to defer graduate school and return to Pakistan to take care of her. She was a single mother, and I was her only daughter. She needed me. That was when I told Mujtaba that I was returning to Pakistan and he actually helped me through the process.'

'The 11 September attacks brought a change in everyone's lives, especially South Asian Muslim students in America – I wanted to make sure she was okay,' Mujtaba says, and then, with a smile, adds, 'but it did also give me an opportunity to begin the conversation again.'

'When we met in San Francisco,' Saba adds, 'I had given him my business card, which had my home phone number in Lahore. And so, while I was in the air, flying from America to Pakistan, Mujtaba had already phoned and spoken to my mother. Even before I'd landed!'

I gasp. 'Wh-what?'

The couple laugh at my reaction, and Saba continues, 'Yes. He actually called my home and my mother picked up – it was the landline – and he basically introduced himself and said that he'd like permission to call upon her daughter.'

'Very old-fashioned,' I note.

'So here I am, just landed in Lahore, and my entire family – mother, grandfather, brother – have come to the airport to receive me. They were worried about the flight, especially since it was the very same day that the US began bombing Afghanistan, and there was just so much fear. We drove home and my mother said nothing to me about Mujtaba, nor did I. I had figured that we'd spend the next year or so talking over email, getting to know each other. The very next day, I hit the ground running with ultrasounds and biopsies, and we were on our way to the diagnostic centre in the car when my mother mentions Mujtaba. She asks who he is, and I truthfully tell her that I've met him for maybe ten minutes in my entire life. And then she says that he called and asked for permission to court you. I was so taken aback! But sure enough, two hours later, he phoned the house to ask how I was and how my flight was and how my mother was feeling. He would always speak to her, you know, and was always very open – even with her – about his intentions with me. He did things the old-fashioned but proper way.'

'Well,' Mujtaba smiles, 'I believe everything needs to be done the proper way. But on a lighter note, at the time, I was working at a small law firm in Delhi and my salary was only Rs 30,000, of which I would spend Rs 28,000 on calls to Lahore!'

By December 2001, Mujtaba wanted to travel to Lahore to officially propose to Saba. But yet again, they were betrayed by the politics of the region, for on 13 December 2001 the Indian Parliament was attacked and all routes between India and Pakistan were to close by the end of the month. By means impressive, desperate and incomparable, coaxing officers of the Pakistan High Commission with his story of love, Mujtaba managed to get a Pakistani visa for the last three days of the year and travelled by plane and bus for twenty hours instead of what would have otherwise been a mere forty-minute flight between Delhi and Lahore. When he finally arrived at 5 a.m. the next day, Saba and her family were waiting for him. He had arrived too late for the hotel stay he had booked, and so, in a rather unconventional gesture, the suitor from Srinagar was taken to their home. Saba's mother immediately went into the kitchen and cooked him an omelette.

'I remember how cold it was,' Saba says. 'December in Lahore is as cold as it is in Delhi, and the homes in neither city are made for the season. So, we were all sitting in front of the heater, and I was looking at Mujtaba in awe. I thought to myself, "Who is this guy who's come out of the fog?"' She chuckles.

'And what did your grandfather say, Saba?'

'Well, Aghajan lived not far away and had a habit of coming to our home every single evening to check on my mother's health – she was his undisputed favourite! But for those three days that Mujtaba was in Lahore, I told my cousin to make sure Aghajan didn't come home ... mostly because I didn't know what I was going to say to Mujtaba yet.'

'In any case, we spent the days in police reporting and then I took the flight back to Delhi,' Mujtaba completes.

'What? You've forgotten everything!' Saba exclaims. 'We went to Laxmi Chowk and around the walled city, we took him to kebab places, and yes of course we had to report to the police station, as all Indians while visiting Pakistan and all Pakistanis while visiting India have to do, but we managed to do quite a lot. We would sit around the fire at home talking about Mujtaba's upbringing, his relatives ... Before he left, we went out for dinner and he presented me with this beautiful shawl his mother had sent. Then, on the last day, he turned to my mother and said, "*Mujhe apna beta bana lain*," make me your son-in-law!'

'I haven't forgotten any of it,' Mujtaba says sincerely. 'You know, each time I would tell my mother about Saba, she would ask – how will you make it work, the visa, the travel, India and Pakistan, how will you manage? And I remember saying to her that there will never be an occasion where this will be a difficulty for us. I will make sure of that, and this was the same promise I made to Saba's family. This chequebook she will speak about later, there is a significance to it. That chequebook from her grandfather was a symbol of acceptance.'

I take a deep breath as our story inches closer to the object that ties this story together.

Saba now says, 'But it is also really important to remember what was happening between our countries at that moment, between late 2001 and early 2002, because it played a huge role in whether we could accept Mujtaba's proposal at all. The embassies in both countries shut down temporarily and there was a lot of hostility stemming from India after the Parliament attack. Newspaper, TV, even the radio would constantly discuss the relations between India and Pakistan. My mother worried that if I accepted the proposal, she may never be able to see me again. So, the politics of the time was playing out within our homes as well.'

'And your grandfather?' I ask, thinking about the chequebook. 'Did he ever find out that Mujtaba had visited?'

'Oh, yes. When he left, my mother told Aghajan about him, and he got so emotional. There were tears in his eyes as he told my mother, "*Mujhe mila toh diya hota*. You should have introduced me, he had come from Srinagar. I would have met him with pleasure, *itne shauq se milte. Mujhe mila toh diya hota*." I was completely stunned by his reaction; in fact, my whole family was taken aback. And I immediately felt bad that I hadn't introduced them, because Mujtaba would have helped Aghajan go back down memory lane and relive his days in Srinagar, the city he loved so much. I felt really bad that I kept him from Aghajan.'

For the next few months, both families navigated the hurdles of politics, passports and visas until, finally, the proposal was accepted and a date was set for a monsoon wedding in 2002. Mujtaba and his parents came to Lahore for the wedding, and his mother was reunited with her Mirpuri family. Everyone in Saba's neighbourhood was impressed that the *baraat*, the wedding procession, had come all the way from Srinagar. But, most importantly, Saba received the greatest gift of all from her Aghajan.

In *The Hare with Amber Eyes*, Edmund de Waal writes of beloved bequeathments:

How objects are handed on is all about story-telling. I am giving you this because I love you. Or because it was given to me. Because I bought it from somewhere special. Because you will care for it. Because it will complicate your life. Because it will make someone else envious. There is no easy story in legacy. What is remembered and what is forgotten? There can be a chain of forgetting, the rubbing away of previous ownership as much as the slow accretion of stories.[12]

In 2001, when Saba and her mother had introduced Aghajan to the possibility of a cross-border marriage, he had been overcome with emotion. The next day when he came by, he brought along a gift. His consent and emotions surrounding the proposal were folded and tucked into his shirt pocket, from where he pulled out an ageing document and handed it to his granddaughter: a chequebook faded to a manila colour, with bright pink text printed upon it that read, 'IMPERIAL BANK OF INDIA, SRINAGAR, KASHMIR'. The emblem of the bank was delicate and floral, within which was printed the year of establishment, 1921.

Recalling the moment now, Saba says, 'I couldn't contain myself as I ran my hands over the print. Imperial Bank of India, Srinagar, Kashmir. The last set of cheques were dated October to November 1947. That was the quickest display of trust from a man who usually took a lifetime to accept outsiders.'

'What happened to him in 1947, Saba?' I ask now.

'Wajid Ali Khan, or Aghajan, as I called him, was born in 1923 in Dalhousie, and at the time of Partition he was based in Srinagar, where he ran a successful business as an optician. As the Pakistan movement began to gain momentum, he participated actively in local politics in support of the Muslim League. But as the border was drawn, mayhem unfolded, and Aghajan's immediate and extended family began to make their way across to Lahore. But those in Kashmir – him included – were confident that it would become part of Pakistan, given the Muslim majority of the princely state, and so they remained. Four months later, roughly around November, as he sat at a tea stall, an old acquaintance spotted him and reported him to the authorities for his participation in League activities and strong pro-Pakistan views. I remember Aghajan telling me that one of his acts of resistance had been to hoist a hand-stitched Pakistani flag at a government building in Srinagar.'

She pauses for a few seconds before continuing, 'Aghajan spent the next ten months in a New Delhi jail. Many years later, he would recall the terrible conditions political prisoners were kept in, and chuckle at his own description of the thick, cakey dal that was served in place of meals. Immediately after his release, he bought an air ticket and flew over to Lahore. But for those many months when he was unaccounted for, the elders in the family were fraught with worry.'

'So, this chequebook is like an emblem,' I say softly. 'He was giving you his ... well, I don't want to say permission, but he was giving you the last remnant of *his* Srinagar. As if he was saying, "Here, Srinagar can now be yours."'

Saba sighs and nods. 'You know, I hold on to the chequebook like a medal of honour. I continue to tell the story of how it came into my possession and the significance of its last cheque entry from November 1947. More than merely an old object or document, it is a connection between my memories and my grandfather's, between his Srinagar and ours.

'Unfortunately, he passed away only a few months after our wedding. Our *walima* was a spontaneous event in Srinagar, two years after our wedding.[13] It was also the last trip we took as a family, for my mother passed away two years later. But after the customary *walima wazwan* was served and the last guests left, my mother, brothers and I became tourists. We drove around Dal Lake and saw the valley through Aghajan's eyes. We shopped in Suffering Moses, one of the oldest businesses on Polo View, and tried to imagine him sitting there, sipping golden *kehwa*. It somehow felt like life had come full circle, because of *us*.' She gestures lovingly to Mujtaba. 'Because of our relationship, his persuasiveness. Otherwise, my mother had never thought she would be able to visit Aghajan's Kashmir in person.'

THERE ARE INTRIGUING cases of buried objects retrieved after Partition, either by family members who have returned to their native places, or those who have now come to occupy the property. Just as these objects are passed down the generations, so are the stories and circumstances of their burial and exhumation.

Tanjima Kar Sekh, born in 1988, shows me an exquisite piece of heirloom jewellery – a gold bracelet that survived the 1946 Noakhali riots[14] that took place in the Chittagong division of East Bengal (present day-Bangladesh) one year before Indian Independence. The bracelet is stunning, and the evidence of the handcraft makes it even more valuable. Its radius measures 6.5 cm, and it is surrounded by a wreath of gold foliage, the insides of each flower fitted with brilliant stones of emerald, ruby and pearls. Tanjima's grandfather, Bhabendu Bikas Majumder, one of ten siblings, was born in a family of zamindars from Panchgaon, Noakhali. The original bearer of these ornate bracelets was his mother, Snehalata Majumder.

'It was 10 October 1946, the day of Kojagori Lakshmi Pujai,' Tanjima narrates, 'when a Muslim woman informed the Majumders about a probable attack during the evening prayer the same day. Despite this warning, the puja was organized, as my family probably could not fathom the violence awaiting them. But in the evening – just as they'd been warned – gangs of Muslim men entered the household, plundering, killing the *kanchas* who guarded the doors, and taking the gold idol of goddess Lakshmi. It felt like an ultimatum to the Hindus of the district to flee.'

Tanjima tells me that the family soon escaped to Dashani in Khulna, hoping to stay there as long as the unrest continued. But driven by the fear that had gripped the household, Snehalata Majumder had thrown all her jewellery in the lake behind the house. When the riots finally subsided, the family returned to Noakhali and began living in an abandoned, unoccupied house. However, in a gesture of good faith, their old neighbours retrieved a large amount of their possessions and jewellery and kept them safe for the Majumder family, which is how the pair of gold bracelets was reunited with Snehalata.

Even after Partition, the family continued to live in what became East Pakistan, though they no longer enjoyed the same wealth or status. In 1948, Tanjima's granduncle migrated to India, followed in 1949 by her grandfather. The pair lived in a slum called Dilwaruddin Basti (near Picnic Garden, Calcutta) and survived on meagre earnings until both brothers found employment at the Chittaranjan Locomotive Works.

Tanjima shows me a faded, speckled sepia photograph of her great-grandmother, Snehalata. 'This pair of bracelets was passed down by my great-grandmother to my grandmother at her marriage, who presented one bracelet to me on my wedding day. I had never met my great-grandmother in person, but when I wore the jewellery that once belonged to her, I was overwhelmed. The story of the survival of this inanimate object is synchronized with the lives of my family members, who managed to rebuild everything after the crisis that Partition had brought upon them. That is what makes this bracelet extraordinary and valuable, the fact that it has endured the times, borne witness to history.'

NARRATING A SIMILAR instance of original owners being reunited with their long-buried pre-Partition treasures is Arslan Athar,* whose maternal family migrated from Dasua village in present-day Hoshiarpur, India, to present-day Faisalabad, Pakistan, naming their adopted village Dasuha, after the one that had been left behind.

'Because they were able to come across unaffected, Partition is not really discussed,' he says, 'but there are stories about the close relationships between Muslim and Sikh families.'

'What kind of stories?'

'One that's told repeatedly within the family is about when my mother's grandfather was on his deathbed and two Sikhs arrived at the house, some time in the late '60s or early '70s. The men would speak to no one but him, even though he was almost gone. No one

---

* The remainder of Arslan Athar's testimony appears in Chapter 5, 'Family'.

knew why they had come, but my mother's grandfather, feeble as he was, met them. They handed him a single piece of paper and he told the family to allow them into the *sehen*, which is like an *aangan*, a courtyard in the middle of the haveli. Many questions were asked, but the old man answered none. A while later, the family learnt that the Sikh men had dug up the *sehen* to excavate a large amount of gold and jewels and all sorts of wealth.'

I gasp. 'Had it all been buried at the time of Partition?'

Arslan nods. 'Apparently, right after Partition, when my great-grandfather was searching for a home in Pakistan, he came across a Sikh gentleman who was migrating to India but hoped he may return one day, and he buried his treasure in the courtyard of his house. He essentially gave my great-grandfather the home, with the promise that if one day – no matter how many years later – his relatives came to collect the wealth, all they would have to do was show the piece of paper that had been signed by the Sikh gentleman. And this was how my great-grandfather would know that they were the original owners of the wealth. I suppose he never told any of his family members, for fear of greed or theft. He kept the wealth a secret for nearly two and a half decades until the rightful owners came and collected it.'

THIS STORY OF discovering hidden wealth inside the floors or walls of a pre-Partition home is by no means unusual, for many refugees buried their treasures with the hopes of one day returning. But sadly, in most cases the treasures remain buried to date, and these stories of hidden boxes and wrapped-up jewels make their way down the branches of family trees in the form of mythical keepsakes. Priyanka Sabarwal,* whose family migrated from Gawalmandi in Lahore to India, tells me about how her granduncle, Satpal Bhushan, stayed back after Partition in order to take the Urdu exam for his bachelor's degree.

---

* The remainder of Priyanka Sabarwal's testimony appears in Chapter 14, 'Memory'.

'It always fascinated me that while a large part of the population of Lahore was engaged in the fight over "Hindu" and "Muslim" homelands, a young Hindu college student wanted to brave the violence and stay back in what was now a new Islamic country to take his Urdu exam!' Priyanka says, smiling widely.

'You mentioned that he left behind a box,' I say.

'Of all of my grandfather's brothers, he told the most stories about Lahore. I think he never expected the family to *not* return, and this box was something he had had since childhood. Growing up in a house with four brothers, three sisters and numerous cousins and an open door for neighbours, he told me that all important things had to be protected and kept "personally",' she giggles as she says this, 'so this was his box of important things!'

I ask if he remembered what all was in it, and Priyanka replies immediately with a list.

'He had the razor his father gave him for his first shave. He lost his mother fairly young, and her gold earrings were kept in this box. He mentioned a bottle cap but did not clarify what its significance was. There was a love letter he wrote to a girl he liked in college ... but never sent, I assume. He did say that it included a Ghalib couplet, though. There was a ticket stub – from a music show or movie, I'm not sure. A pen he won as an award at school, along with some coins he "earned". When he was leaving Lahore, he wasn't sure if it was safe to take this box with him, so he buried it near a tree in the backyard of their house...'

'I wonder if it still remains, or if someone else found it.' I smile at the thought of someone one day digging the earth under a tree in their backyard in Lahore, only to discover a box of pre-Partition remnants – ordinary yet extraordinary treasures of a young man's life.

THE FINAL SECTION of this chapter explores objects and heirlooms discovered long after their original bearers have passed.

On 1 October 1910, twenty-year-old Texas-born J. Waskom Pickett set out via steamship from New York City to British India to assume leadership of the Methodist congregation founded by a missionary and theologian, E. Stanley. Three months later, in Lucknow, Pickett was ordained into the ministry as an elder of the Methodist Church. While in India, he met Ruth Robinson, the daughter of Elizabeth Fisher Robinson and John Wesley Robinson, a Methodist bishop, at the Lal Bagh church. Born and raised in Lucknow, Ruth had attended school in Nainital, and the Isabella Thoburn College in Lucknow, following which she travelled to America for university at Northwestern. In her own words, Ruth writes:

> ...before coming to the States, I'd met my fate in India, where a fascinating, new and very young missionary had arrived as the pastor for our church. Romance blossomed, and when I did come to America to complete my college course, it was as an engaged girl! Marriage in Evanston, after graduation, took us back to India in 1916, and from there on, I was a missionary wife ... [in] a place called Arrah.[15]

Over a century after her great-grandparents settled in Arrah (present-day Bihar) as a married couple, I speak with Meg Sagan, born in 1978 in Wisconsin, about the legacy that binds several generations of her family to the Indian subcontinent and, specifically, to the days of Partition.

'It was during a Thanksgiving party that my aunt first showed us a trunk of old items belonging to my great-grandparents. The entire family was together and she thought it would be fun to look through it all. But what I found most interesting was seeing my aunt, who had not been present at those moments in India, articulate their memory to others through these aged family documents. My grandmother, Margaret, and her siblings – Elizabeth, Miriam and Doug – were all born and raised in India, and she often spoke about how coming to America for university was a culture shock!' Meg laughs.

The trunk contained old photographs, letters and notes. There were books written by and about J. Waskom Pickett. There was an official state invitation addressed to 'Bishop and Mrs J.W. Pickett' for the 1967 Republic Day dinner at Rashtrapati Bhawan. There was a table plan for lunch on Thursday, 14 November 1957, where Bishop J. Waskom Pickett is seated in close proximality to both the prime minister and the president, between Abid Ali, Union deputy minister for labour, and Bakshi Ghulam Mohammad, prime minister of Jammu and Kashmir. Notable attendees at this lunch, hosted likely to celebrate Prime Minister Jawaharlal Nehru's sixty-eighth birthday, were Indira Gandhi, Morarji Desai, Lal Bahadur Shastri and Shah Nawaz Khan, among others.

As Meg and I peruse these documents, she tells me about how she has always felt connected to both her grandmother and great-grandmother's life stories. 'My full name is Margaret Ruth Sagan, so I carry both of their names. They were both born in India. Margaret left at age seventeen, in 1944, during the Second World War to go to college in America, and would continue here for the rest of her life. Ruth left in 1956, when she would have been sixty-one years old. At the time, her husband, J. Waskom, told a church gathering, "We are not going home, but we are leaving home and going to America."[16] This perhaps rightly encapsulates the feeling that often emerges in family correspondences.

'Margaret spoke freely about her formative years in India – trekking in the hills of Uttarakhand and attending boarding school. I remember stories she told me as a teenager of her own teenage years in Bombay: babysitting for the future conductor Zubin Mehta and taking violin lessons from his father, Mehli Mehta. She would also talk with emotion about some of the national leaders at India's Independence; American political leaders were rarely discussed in such vivid terms. Her father was an admirer and supporter of Nehru, whom he knew well. Jinnah's role in the creation of Pakistan was discussed. He interacted with Mahatma Gandhi. My grandmother told me about Dr Ambedkar as a champion of civil rights and a key author of the Indian Constitution. I later learned how her father had participated in informal discussions – on conceiving an India open to all religions – with the Constituent Assembly members who wrote Article 25[17] on religious freedom. Eventually, I came to see that my great-grandparents had a very specific, more or less Nehruvian political alignment.'[18]

'And Partition,' I ask, 'was that ever spoken about?'

'Sometimes.' Meg thinks about this. 'My grandmother wasn't in India at the time, but she must have spoken about these months with her parents because she'd tell us how families had to leave their homes and how my great-grandparents set up medical relief and schools during the upheaval. But it was when I found Ruth's notecards in my aunt's trunk that I truly got to understand her own perspective on the time.'

'What did the notes say?'

'Well, they are historic documents in their own right. She writes in detail about the country she was born in and the church she served. There are parts where she speaks about helping a woman give birth in a village when she herself was pregnant. Her husband was obviously a prominent figure in the church, but this was her perspective; it was more personal. She had a voice, and these notes showed that she cared very much about the land and its people. Ruth and Waskom could both speak Hindi, which my grandmother called Hindustani.

'From 1945 to '56, the couple lived in Delhi, on the grounds of the Christ Methodist Church near present-day Tis Hazari. Waskom served as president of the National Christian Council (NCC) and the head of the medical council of the Methodist Church of India. When Partition violence broke out, he was appointed to the United Council for Relief and Welfare, an umbrella organization led by Lady Edwina Mountbatten, to coordinate the efforts of fourteen volunteer relief agencies. He also worked closely with the health minister, Rajkumari Amrit Kaur, on sourcing and distributing medicines for the large Muslim refugee camps at Humayun's Tomb and Purana Qila. Over 250 Christian refugees – perhaps those who had been displaced in the turmoil or migrated from Pakistan to India – took shelter on the church grounds in the days following Partition.'[19]

The notecards are a set of thirteen, written by Ruth Robinson Pickett for a lecture she delivered on 11 December 1973 about her life in India. Each one is numbered at the top. They are handwritten in blue ink and held together by a silver paperclip and, despite the passing of decades, remain completely legible. As I comb through them, what I find most fascinating are the accounts of relief and medical aid provided by her and her husband to refugees during the days of Partition:

Streets were filled with corpses which couldn't be disposed of. The stench in hot, steamy September was terrible, inescapable. The smell of fear a reality. Curfew was clamped on the city. Our mission homes became refuges. Hundreds of Christian refugees were driven from their home. For many nights, we sheltered women and children within our house, their men sleeping on the verandas as best they could, taking turns as guards ... Government, with Mr Nehru at their head, opened enormous refugee camps in walled areas, to where Moslems could flee and be protected by military force ... Mr Nehru trusted all authority over to the Christians, and Lady Mountbatten formed various groups who could serve. My husband opened medical and food centres in the name of the National Christian Council, calling on Methodists to help. This they did valiantly. Food and water had to be provided somehow, medical supplies, trenches dug for sanitation, and grounds ... for burials ... The smell of gangrene was part of the atmosphere. A little girl had her buttock sliced and hanging down, a woman with a sword cut under her arm so deep it could let a hand in, a child with her heel shattered by bullets ... I tell you truly – events of each day were past belief.[20]

Ruth continues to write that their street was jammed with huts and temporary homes set up by refugees. Women would wait in line morning and evening to fill water from a single faucet, and often tempers would wear thin. Added to their worries were their children, now displaced from the educational system, who had no access to any school or books. Ruth finally asked the women whether they would like a school started for their children, and the response was an immediate 'Oh yes, *han ji!*' and thus was born The Pickett Garage School:

> I found a young Christian woman, with children of her own, who would be happy to conduct a little school in our garage for Rs 30 a month salary. She had some teacher training, but the real purpose of this school was to preserve some order for a few hours a day ... But classes went on for eight years, and some 200 children at least had part of their idle time turned to good use.

In the years after Partition, the Picketts often corresponded with their children.[21] Meg shares a letter with me dated Friday, 22 February 1951, written by their youngest son, Doug, who was returning from New York via Genoa and Alexandria to see his parents, who lived in Delhi, en route to Khatauli, where he would teach at a junior high school. Doug was stopped at the port of Karachi, now in Pakistan, before travelling on and alighting in Bombay – which elucidates how Partition had limited the routes he could take:

> It seems a shame that the rivalry between the two countries necessitates the trip to Bombay. I can't see all the *dik** about the border ... Picking up the Indian music on the radio makes home seem so close![22]

When I ask Meg whether she has developed a relationship to this historic time in the subcontinent's history *through* these letters and notes, she maintains that the relation to India is both strong and

---

* '*Dik*' (دق) in this letter may refer to an abbreviated form of the word '*diqqat*' (دقت), which is spelt loosely here as '*dikkat*', meaning trouble or inconvenience. Doug was a fluent Urdu speaker his whole life and it is not unimaginable that he, like many of us do in the subcontinent to date, peppered his English with words and phrases from Urdu.

undeniable. Her knowledge of her great-grandparents' roles during this time is mediated by the letters and books she has read and the photographs they left behind. Her relationship to the subcontinent is also rooted in an emotional connection and the sense that we all have to cultivate ties if they are to grow over time. Among other things, the connection to physical land remains, for her great-great-grandmother is buried in Delhi and her great-great-grandfather in Nainital.[23]

Concluding the topic of Partition, she says, 'The very word is associated with suffering to me, with mass migration, dispossession, lives lost too soon. I wonder what it was like to be a Christian woman who grew up and lived in cosmopolitan areas with large Muslim and Hindu populations, and to see new borders drawn up to create two countries with different religious majorities. Her notes seem to indicate that she thought the political boundaries themselves caused a polarization that wasn't necessarily there before. I can't imagine how it must have felt for people to have a border suddenly imposed. But I sometimes wonder about my great-grandmother Ruth's belief that Partition was unnecessary, that a united India that encompassed Pakistan and Bangladesh was possible. Would this have really worked in the long term?'

'IN THE THIRTY years that my parents had lived in Delhi,' Sam Dalrymple tells me, gesturing to the artist Olivia Fraser and the historian William Dalrymple, seated at either end of our lunch table at their Chhatarpur home, 'granda* had never once come out to visit. Mum's family and even dad's childhood nanny had come out, but not granda. But it was only when he died that we understood why.'

On 26 December 2018, Sir Hew Fleetwood Hamilton-Dalrymple passed away, and the entire family travelled to North Berwick, a tiny seaside village outside Edinburgh, where he lived. The night before

---

* Grandfather or grandpa is known as 'granda' in Scotland and Northern England.

his funeral, as they were sorting through his belongings, Sam came across a scrapbook that dated all the way back to 1947, to the very days of Partition, and this began an exercise in piecing together what had happened over seventy years ago for the then young captain to never again set foot on the subcontinent.

'There are photographs of monuments around Delhi and Agra. He's at the Qutub Minar, which is ten minutes away from our home,' Sam exclaims. 'There are seating plans where he's at the same table as Mountbatten, Nehru and Jinnah. And I was shocked to find them, because he'd never actively spoken about that time, or shown any interest in India. But there he was, at the heart of history.'

I turn to William. 'Did you know about your father's association to India?'

'We knew that he was here during World War II and through Independence and Partition, but that was the extent. In fact, I tried to interview him about it, but like the visit to Delhi, he kept putting it off. You see, this was never my period, I'd mostly always written about medieval or Mughal India.[24] And then, as it so often happens,' he admits sadly, 'your parents become background, they are the wallpaper of your life. It was only when he passed away and Sammy found this scrapbook that we started to understand why he'd been so reticent.'

That spring afternoon, sitting on the patio by the radiant mandarin tree, I learn of the Dalrymple family's association with India and their unique, long-unspoken connection to Partition.

Sir Hew Fleetwood Hamilton-Dalrymple was born in North Berwick in 1926. At the age of eighteen, in 1944, he graduated from the Royal Military Academy Sandhurst with the Sword of Honour and was commissioned as an officer in the Grenadier Guards. He was appointed as aide-de-camp (ADC) to Sir Frank Messervy, in charge of the Northern Command in India at the time, and served in the subcontinent until Partition, retiring in 1962 as a major.

To create a timeline of his father's association with India, William begins with the City of Palaces, the eighteenth-century capital of British India: 'I have only learnt of this in the last few years, but like many Scottish families trying to make ends meet at the time, generations of my family were born, lived and died in Calcutta. Stair Dalrymple was the earliest ancestor; he died in 1756 and his name can still be found on the memorial in St John's Church. Several generations were born in Calcutta thereafter, as recent as my great-grandfather, Walter.[25] My father was born and raised in Scotland, and I don't know how much of this past he knew, but by the tail end of the war, he too was stationed in India.'

Sam, who was born in London in 1997, is a Partition scholar and co-founder of Project Dastaan,* working with the generation that lived through the divide. He now shows me documents and photographs from the scrapbook, where each item has been pasted on an individual page with accompanying captions.

'It seems an odd juxtaposition,' I observe, 'for your granda to have created this archive with such care and intimacy, preserving a paper trail of these significant moments he was present at, and yet never...' I cannot finish the sentence, but I don't need to, because Sam nods knowingly.

'Yes, he held on to this in silence. But he was very particular about things, though,' he smiles, 'the kind of person who had you sign a visitor's book when you left his house. So, this was probably ... out of habit.'

As we move chronologically through the set, we first locate his grandfather in New Delhi.

He is invited to dinner to commemorate Their Excellencies' silver wedding at the Viceroy House (now Rashtrapati Bhawan) on Friday, 18 July 1947, at 8.30 p.m. At the top of the page is the King's Crown, embossed in gold. The centrefold of the invite reveals the dinner plan, where the viceroy and his wife are seated opposite one another in the middle of a long table. Seated next to him is Pandit Jawaharlal Nehru, and next to her, Mr Jinnah. Among others, the guest list includes Sir Cyril Radcliffe, Mrs Indira Nehru Gandhi, H.H. the Maharaja of Patiala, Miss Jinnah, Mr and Begum Liaquat Ali Khan,

---

* Read more about Project Dastaan in Chapter 20, 'Returning'.

Dr Rajendra Prasad, Mrs Sarojini Naidu, Sardar Vallabhbhai Patel, Lieutenant General Sir Frank Messervy, and, of course, Captain Hamilton-Dalrymple.

I gasp when I locate his name at the table, near the entrance of the room.

'I had the same reaction as you,' Sam laughs, 'except with the knowledge that this is my granda!'

'So, this is one month before Independence,' William notes. 'In the run-up, Messervy, who after Partition is appointed the first commander-in-chief of the Pakistan Army, is shuffling back and forth between Delhi and Rawalpindi, and so we see that my father, his ADC, has access to these moments of history. A seat at the table, so to speak.'

The second document Sam shows me brings us to the days of Independence. It is an invitation from the Quaid-e-Azam, Muhammad Ali Jinnah, and his sister, Miss Fatima Jinnah, requesting the pleasure of Captain Hamilton-Dalrymple's company at a reception on Wednesday, 13 August 1947, at 10 p.m., to meet Viceroy and Viscountess Mountbatten of Burma. Above, in handwriting, are the words 'Karachi Independence Day, August 15th, 1947'. The dress is uniform for essential services, short coat or equivalent Indian dress for civilians and an evening dress or equivalent Indian dress for ladies.

'He is present at the flag hoisting for Independence Day in Pakistan,' Sam notes and, referring to the next document, says, 'and then just days later, on 16 August 1947, is invited to a dinner party in Rawalpindi to bid farewell to the officers leaving for the Union of India.' With independence comes a change of insignia; an invitation with ornately deckled edges, on behalf of the Officers of Rawalpindi Garrison, now bears the brilliant green Pakistani flag. Flanking the flag are the words 'PAKISTAN ZINDABAD'.

'Dad was based in Rawalpindi after Partition,' William says. Then with a chuckle he adds, 'In fact, when I was to interview General Musharraf at his residence, he very casually mentioned that Command House at the cantonment in Pindi was once his home. I was going to his home!'

I look at him wide-eyed.

'See, he never talked in one long, uninterrupted way about India. It was always these accidental anecdotes, little stories about how he put his Hindu staff on trains to India during Partition, but never once mentioning the horror of those days. I mean, there's a small section in the scrapbook where he's still in Pindi and his sister, Gene, who was his best friend, dies of polio and he writes about Darling Gene more than he ever mentions Partition.'

Sam continues from where his father has left off, 'I suppose it makes you wonder what he saw, whether he lost friends or colleagues, how much it affected him, and if he suppressed it all or not. He was no older than I was when I found the scrapbook, so was he already resilient to war and death?' He pauses and takes a deep breath.

'I'm trying to put it in the right words, but for the longest time I had assumed that my family had lived in rural Scotland and that my parents were the ones to come out and settle here in 1989. Even when I began working with Project Dastaan, Partition remained a detached event. I was deeply invested but didn't have a personal connection, like so many of my colleagues did, whose families were displaced to either side. And then to find these invitations to dinner parties, seating charts, official correspondences from the very moment of the subcontinent's division suddenly made the event so personal. I wish that he had spoken to us more about this period of his life.'

'Did you feel a sense of regret when you found the scrapbook?' I ask in a small voice.

'Absolutely,' William says.

'Unequivocally,' Sam echoes and then directs my attention to a page of roughly passport-sized photographs. At the top are the handwritten words 'Odd Indian & Pakistani photographs'. There are a few of the Taj Mahal – the entrance gate and the west face of the monument; there are two of a nondescript residence and one of the staff at Viceroy House. And then there are two photos at the Qutub complex in Delhi.

Pointing to them, he says, 'Now *these* are overwhelming. Right now, I could walk to Qutub Minar from my home and stand at the same spot that he'd once stood at. It was always sad that my father never got a proper interview, but it was another thing altogether to find these photographs. It's quite affecting to visually see him here, so close, barely a mile away, rather than just hear that he was once in Delhi. It's surreal.'

'While writing *City of Djinns*, I was working at the Nehru Memorial Library at Teen Murti Bhavan,' William recalls, 'and he just mentioned in passing that he had lived there as well. Before it became the prime minister's residence, it was home to the commander-in-chief of the British Army, who happened to be dad's superior, Frank Messervy. Comments like these didn't figure much in his conversations, but I've made a lot of sense of them since then.'

'So, when Partition happens, he is in Rawalpindi?' I confirm. 'And then?'

'Then he applies for leave and goes to Kashmir.' Sam searches for the next document in the timeline.

'It takes him ... and this was the *one* story he loved to tell,' William says, leaning forward on the table, 'that it took him two hours to get to Kashmir and six months to get back!' he laughs.

Sam explains, 'So here we have it. He had befriended Captain Scott, who'd gone out to India in 1940 as part of the Indian Civil Service and joined the viceroy's office as his assistant private secretary in 1946. He held the post until Independence, which he witnessed in Delhi.'[26]

On the official letterhead of the commander-in-chief of the Pakistan Army, based in Rawalpindi, a notice addressed to Captain Scott and Captain Hamilton-Dalrymple, on 16 October 1947, reads:

> The above officers have the permission of the Commander-in-Chief, Pakistan Army, General Sir Frank W. MESSERVY, KCSI, KBE, CB, DSO, to proceed to SRINAGAR, KASHMIR, in the Commander-in-Chief's vehicle BA No. 608282 on the 17th October 1947.

'So granda drives from Pindi to Srinagar and Captain Scott comes up from Delhi, and I believe this was a shooting trip, because he has a permit dated up to 20 October,' Sam reads out loud, 'to shoot an ibex, an antelope, a gazelle and a brown bear. But it says so on the permit that he doesn't manage to shoot the bear. He was also allowed to shoot one markhor, four gorals, and there's a photo of him shooting some ducks. There's also a photo of him on a cupboard-looking boat, floating across a river. But while they are up there, the invasions begin across Kashmir and he's stranded in Srinagar.'

William now picks up the story. 'I remember having this conversation with him once because in 1984, thirty-seven years later, I was stranded in Srinagar due to Operation Blue Star, and at the time he said to me something like, "I've been stuck there before; there are worse places to be stranded in." So now the journey back takes him a few months because he jumps on a plane heading to Delhi, from where someone puts him on a sleeper train to Bombay which takes forever, and from there he gets a flying boat to Karachi...'

'...And it's in Pakistan that he learns of Gandhi's assassination,' Sam completes, offering me the final document – a *Pakistan Times* newspaper from Saturday, 31 January 1948. The front-page headline reads, 'MAHATMA GANDHI ASSASSINATED: Fatally shot on way to prayer meeting. Moving scenes at Birla House: crowd seize assailant.' In the left-hand column, a photograph of Gandhi is captioned, 'Irreparable loss to India, says Quaid-e-Azam,' and on the right, 'Light has gone out of our lives, says Nehru.'

I look at the father–son duo now as they both lean back in their seats. Mid-morning has turned to afternoon. Lunch has given way to coffee. Olivia has long retreated to her studio. Even Fudgie the dog, who was wandering aimlessly at the edge of the farm, has now settled at the foot of the stairs. I look through the pages of notes I have taken – the discovery of an ancestor's life through two generations of a family.

I clear my throat now. 'Is this the first time you've had a conversation of this sort?'

'Well, the closest we ever got before this was the night before the funeral. We've slowly started piecing things together since, and today was probably the first effort to create a loose timeline. But the more I write on Partition, the more personal it feels and the more questions I have,' Sam says, having recently embarked on writing his own manuscript on Partition.

William admits that apart from briefly writing on Partition in *City of Djinns*, he has not touched the subject as it has never been his time period, and then reflectively adds, 'I have to say, though, that my father was always a very hands-on parent. He would regularly – unnecessarily regularly – come to see my siblings and me at uni, and it's a bit sad that he never came out here, to see our life in Delhi, because he would have loved it very much.'

'Do you really think he saw something at Partition that didn't allow him to return?'

'We say that to each other; we assume that's why.'

'And also that he continually refused to talk about it when it was brought up,' Sam clarifies. 'Partition, specifically.'

'When I was researching *From the Holy Mountain*, I found that the generation who lived through the Armenian genocide would never talk about it. And it was only a generation later that any form of remembrance began. It's often a generation that has to pass before...' William's voice trails off as he thinks. 'The first time an occasion arose for me to start asking questions about Empire was when Attenborough's *Gandhi* came out, and then *Jewel in the Crown* the year after that, which we saw as a family. They'd just shown two or three episodes before I'd first flown out to India in '84. I remember those conversations, and my father talking about the Raj in a way that I'd never heard him do before. There'd always been a fair degree of collective amnesia, and then suddenly these films paved the way for conversations about figures like Jinnah and Nehru and Liaquat Ali Khan. Then, too, he didn't touch on Independence or Partition but spoke about these men with great familiarity.'

Sam, who has been listening to his father, now says, 'The more I think about it, the more I have a sense of having missed it all.

You know? I missed getting the answers, having the conversations, knowing my history.'

I wonder if this has to do with the fact that Project Dastaan is hinged on detailed interviews with eyewitnesses about the days of Partition and their unfractured life before it. When I bring this up, he smiles sadly. 'That's definitely part of it. My siblings and I were raised in India, and I travel to Pakistan for research, so the animosity created by Partition saddens me. And the fact that I am helping to preserve other people's histories while I don't know enough of my own is, well, ironic. But by extension, as my father mentioned, there's so much silence around Empire in Britain, which is only now being addressed, that most people don't associate Empire with something close to family. I acknowledge that granda may not have felt the magnitude of Partition the same way that Indians or Pakistanis did, but it must have had an impact on him. I would have loved to know about that, not even as a scholar, just as a grandson. Though this scrapbook helps to build the landscape of his days, it will never replace the experience of actually talking to him, listening to the stories in his words, even returning to those places with him.'

Sam's voice now feels deeper, sadder. 'A whole year has passed since I first found the scrapbook, and over this period, Dastaan has actually given me perspective on granda's life and the choices he made. For thirty years, he had the opportunity to come to India to visit his son. And he chose not to. I don't think he wanted to come back and confront whatever it was that he saw here. Don't get me wrong, it would have been wonderful had he shared his memories. But there should be no obligation to speak, and I am slowly learning to respect his silence.'

16
Migration

༄

'IT WAS A TUESDAY,' Shweta Notaney tells me of her paternal grandmother's migration. 'She remembers the ship they boarded and the storm during the journey. She remembers her home in Karachi and the port of Bombay.'

'But does she remember the migration with any sadness or loss?' I ask.

'Neither. She sounded sort of indifferent to Partition, remembering it like any other life experience.'

Shweta is a graphic designer, born in Delhi in 1998. The stories of her grandparents' migration from Sindh during or after Partition are not discussed at length in the family, but there are snippets she has collected over the years. She briefly mentions her maternal side – where her grandmother was too young to remember anything, and her grandfather was eleven when his family migrated by train from Bhan, Sayedabad, to Mathura in India and ultimately settled in Vrindavan – and the remainder of our conversation is focused on her paternal side.

'My grandmother Nirmala's family did not migrate from Karachi when Partition was announced. Her father was in government service and her brother had been a freedom fighter. But on 6 January 1948, they left their residence on Burns Road[1] and fled via ship to Bombay, because their house was suddenly looted by the neighbours. It happened very quickly: her father was not home when the looting happened, her sister was left behind, and all she kept repeating to me was how her mother wore seven gold bangles in each hand that were all taken, and the food supplies were destroyed.'

'Her sister was left behind?'

'She was abducted, in a way,' Shweta confirms. 'There was a childless couple in the neighbourhood who had grown affectionate towards her. They took her with the promise of returning her in a few days, but never did. When the looting began, the family had no time to search for her and she was left behind. My grandmother doesn't even remember when they were reunited in India, but says that many years later her father saw the couple at a railway station and approached them. They had raised the girl as their own and were now marrying her off. My grandmother's family even attended the wedding and kept in touch after. But the single moment of their migration from Pakistan changed their lives in such unforeseen ways.'

'You mentioned that your grandmother is indifferent to Partition. What do you mean?'

'I identify as a Hindu Sindhi,' she asserts, 'but no one in the family really seems to take an interest in the subject, apart from me. While I was at the Indraprastha College for Women, we were meant to interview a family member who had witnessed a traumatic event during their lifetime, and that was when I first spoke to my grandmother about Partition. Before that, it hadn't ever been mentioned and, personally, I think it's because they never considered it a major event in their lives.'

This is an unusual perspective on Partition, and I am intrigued. I have several questions, but before I can ask them, Shweta offers to tell me about her grandfather's story and the multiple reverse-migrations that took place in his family.

'My grandfather, Sunderlal, was from Larkana, and passed away before I could learn anything about Partition or Sindh from him, and so anything I know has been told to me by his brother. My grandfather had a BSc degree in agriculture from Sakrand Agriculture College in Nawabshah. In 1947, his family migrated to Jodhpur in Rajasthan, but they didn't like the place, and as Sindh had seen virtually no violence during the months of Partition – the violence would come much later in the year and spill into 1948 – they decided to return to Sindh.

'My grandparents' families knew one another, so, some years later, Sunderlal's mother travelled from Sindh to Delhi to ask for Nirmala's hand in marriage for her son. In 1958, the two were married in Delhi, and several family members from my grandfather's side travelled from Pakistan to India to attend the wedding. Meanwhile, due to Sunderlal's father's government job, the family moved from Larkana to Mirpurkhas, which was where, six months later, Nirmala joined her new husband.'

'One decade after she had migrated to India because of Partition, your grandmother migrated back to Pakistan as a new bride?' I ask and Shweta nods.

'And the family continued to live as Hindu Sindhis in Mirpurkhas?' Shweta nods again.

'I know their story challenges the conventional migration patterns we have come to understand as a result of Partition, but it should tell you just how complex and drawn-out the exodus truly was. Till today, Hindu families exist in Sindh.[2] Anyway, because I was curious as well, I asked my grandmother whether she noticed any changes after she went back to Sindh, and she simply replied that the number of Muslims living in the area had increased. But from 1967 onwards, the family began to migrate to India in phases. My grandparents made the journey in 1968, though they visited Sindh thrice after that – 1985, 1987, 1992.'

'What eventually led to their migration to India?'

'I asked my grandmother that as well, and she said, "It was not our land, and we had to come to India some day." But when I asked my grandfather's brother, he said, "*Koi apni marzi se thodi aata hai? Sab majboori mei aate hai.*" Though he alluded to the fact that they had no choice, he said nothing more.'[3]

She pauses for a moment. 'I'm told that things were difficult for the family in India. My grandfather faced discrimination at the workplace because all he held were Pakistani degrees. Recruiters would not give him work. His brother tells me that he was often treated as the "other", and my grandmother also seemed quite upset about the fact that it took him a long time to find work. But they made sure that all their children graduated from good colleges in India. Sometimes, I can't help but wonder if they would have lived a more comfortable life had they remained in Pakistan. They have no regrets, though.' She shrugs. 'Another interesting thing I've noticed is that my grandmother does not directly blame Muslims for what happened in Sindh during Partition. She asserts that violence first broke out in India and, as a ripple effect, arrived in Sindh. She considers Muslims as others but feels no hatred towards them. It is the second generation, I believe, that carries this hate.'

'Why would you say that?' I ask, and then quickly add, 'And has Partition or have these many migrations had an impact on your life as the third generation?'

Shweta answers these questions slowly and separately. From the unperturbed tone of her voice, it is evident that this is a subject she ponders over frequently.

'I feel that even though I was not born when Partition happened, it has shaped the life I am living today. The fact that I am here, in India, telling a story of multiple migrations back and forth across the border, depends so much on fate and the decisions that my ancestors took. Partition may have happened in 1947 but its effects were physically felt by my family for decades after. Personally, it is the loss of Sindh, the inaccessibility of it, which consumes me. Whenever my friends go to visit their villages in Punjab or Haryana, I can't help but think about how separated I am from my ancestral land – a place where my grandparents lived not so long ago, and yet I don't know if I will ever be able to walk on Sindhi soil.'

Unlike the partitioning of the provinces of Punjab and Bengal, the entire landmass of Sindh remained in Pakistan, causing the Hindu Sindhi population not only to migrate to India but also disperse across the world, becoming a people with no accessible roots back to homeland.

'In the Sindhi language, the word *dhar* means separation, and Partition literally separated us from our land, which meant that everything tethered to it – language, food, culture – also eventually followed. My grandparents could read, write and speak in Sindhi. While my mother can speak it, I only understand it, and recognize that after my generation this language may ultimately die. That's a scary thought,' she sighs. 'With the exodus, so much was lost, and I would never want anyone, irrespective of their religion, to go through the same thing.'

Further elaborating on the generational consequences, Shweta says, 'Recently, my father and I had an argument with a relative on the political scenario of the subcontinent, and the latter rebuked us by saying, "Since your family crossed over so late, you have sympathies for the enemy country, Pakistan." Just because my family crossed over the border twenty years after his doesn't make us any less Indian. But this is what I meant by the fact that subsequent generations carry more hate than those who actually lived through Partition.'

'Do you think it's because those who witnessed Partition also witnessed a largely syncretic society before it? In several interviews I've conducted with Sindhis over the years, I've been told that the Sindhi identity was far more important to people than their religious identities, Hindu *or* Muslim.'[4]

Shweta nods. 'Yes, perhaps. But I personally feel that Partition did not just carry displaced refugees from one side of the border to another. In some cases, it brought with itself a heavy baggage of hatred, and since then this hatred has been passed down from one generation to the next like an heirloom.'

With the coming of independence to India, the world had the chance to watch a most rare event in the history of nations: the birth of twins. It was a birth accompanied by strife and suffering, but I consider myself fortunate to have witnessed and been able to document the historic early days of these two nations: India and Pakistan.

With these words, the American photographer Margaret Bourke-White's report begins in *Halfway to Freedom*. In April 1946, she arrived in India in her early forties to photograph Mahatma Gandhi for *LIFE* magazine at his ashram in Poona, only to find that in order to photograph him at the spinning wheel, she too would have to learn to spin. After a rushed and awkward lesson and instructions on how to be in the presence of the Mahatma, she was led to a dark hut, illuminated only by a single beam of sunlight, scarcely able to compose her frame. As her gaze became accustomed to the shadows, she saw the figure of the Mahatma, long, wiry legs, a bald head and round spectacles. He sat in complete silence beside the spinning wheel she had heard so much about. Pulling it closer, he 'started to spin, beautifully, rhythmically, and with a fine, nimble hand'.[5] The result is an iconic monochrome image of the Mahatma, flooded mostly in shadow, gaze lowered towards the newspapers in his hand and, beside him, the spinning wheel or the charkha, the symbol of India's struggle for Independence.

The following year, she returned to India, this time to witness – as she writes – the birth of twin nations. Bourke-White was one of the few photographers[6] to capture the horror and scale of the mass migration that took place between India and Pakistan. From 2013 to 2017, as I researched and wrote *Remnants*, interviewing women and men who had made the journey across to either side of the border, I found myself relying on her images as companion to their testimonies. My interviewees would speak in hushed voices and angry tones, with animated gestures and dense silences, about the memories that refused to leave them, and Bourke-White's monochrome record of the days became my point of reference. Photographs of long caravans of cattle and carts, of parents carrying young children, of children carrying old parents, of terror-stricken refugees crawling across barren land, in heat and dust and rain, amidst hunger and exhaustion. A flash flood. A dog picking at a corpse. A young, bewildered boy at a refugee camp. A landscape of tents. A cholera hospital. Sher Shah's mosque giving sanctuary to refugees.

In the autumn of 1947, she had arrived in the plains of Punjab on assignment for *LIFE* magazine to photograph the massive exchanges of population – Hindus and Sikhs migrating to India, and Muslims to Pakistan. I walked with her as she had walked with them, capturing the price that people had paid for freedom:

> Babies were born along the way. People died along the way. Some died of cholera, some from the attacks of hostile religious communities. But many of them simply dropped out of line from sheer weariness and sat by the roadside to wait patiently for death. Sometimes I saw children pulling at the arms and hands of parents or grandparents, unable to comprehend that those arms would never be able to carry them again[7] … What had been merely arbitrarily drawn areas on a map began emptying and refilling with human beings – neatly separated into so-called 'opposite' religious communities – as children's crayons fill in an outline map in geography class.[8]

The sheer scale of migration was phenomenal. The Indian civil servant V.P. Menon wrote they were of 'truly Himalayan proportions'.[9] Both Urvashi Butalia and Yasmin Khan record that about 12 million people migrated between the two countries;[10] others peg the figure at upwards of 15 million.[11] Studying the migration patterns over two decades, Haimanti Roy writes that 'between 1946 and 1965, nearly 9 million Hindus and Sikhs moved into India and approximately 5 million Muslims moved to both parts of Pakistan'.[12]

In October 2013, during my very first interview for *Remnants*, my maternal granduncle, Yash Pal Vij, had made an interesting observation connected to their migration. Belonging to a Hindu Punjabi family originally from Lahore, having arrived in Delhi via Amritsar before Partition, he had claimed that the owners of all the stores around theirs in Chandni Chowk were 'anti-Punjabi' and spared no chance in telling his family that their jewellery store would not survive. He made the distinction that these store owners were Hindustani-speaking Hindus, as opposed to the Vij family, who were Punjabi-speaking Hindus:

> They were averse to anyone who was not from here, anyone who posed a threat to their business. This behaviour prevailed for *years* before the Partition too. At that time, there were not so many Punjabis in Delhi. It was like when you make roti, you add a pinch of salt to the dough ... the Punjabis living and working in Delhi were like that pinch of salt in dough.[13]

But all this changed after Partition, when the influx of refugees from West Punjab into Delhi transformed the very fabric of the capital city, giving it a predominantly Punjabi character.[14] Picking up this thread, my paternal grandfather, a refugee from Malakwal, West Punjab, had often maintained that though his religious identity in India was aligned with the Hindu majority, it was not always enough for them to be easily assimilated into the new landscape. Often, the labels 'refugee' or '*sharnarthi*' (meaning 'he who has gained refuge') accompanied them in India – to the extent that Khan Market, named after Khan Abdul Jabbar Khan, set up in 1951 as an economic opportunity for those who had come from across the border, and where my grandfather opened his first bookshop, came to be known as a 'refugee market'. While working in the refugee camps in Delhi, Begum Anis Kidwai also contemplated the nature of these terms, calling the word *sharnarthi* 'a special gift of the times', claiming that for days they could not even pronounce the 'fat, unwieldy word' properly.[15] In Pakistan, the term *muhajir*, immigrant, 'has largely become an important source of identity for Urdu-speaking Partition-related migrants and their descendants from the United Provinces living particularly in Karachi.'[16]

ONE OF DELHI'S greatest chroniclers, Ahmed Ali – whose masterpiece *Twilight in Delhi* was first published merely seven years before

Partition by Virginia and Leonard Woolf's[17] Hogarth Press – could never imagine that he would be exiled to Pakistan after Partition. Here, the word exile becomes crucial, for this was not a migration by choice. 'In this world of shadows nothing ever remains the same,' Ali wrote from Karachi in the Introduction to the 1993 paperback edition, and thus described the process that separated him from his beloved city:

> I was in China on foreign service, sent by the British Government of India as British Council Visiting Professor to the National Central University of China in Nanking, when the subcontinent was divided into two, Bharat (now India) and Pakistan ... I was prohibited by the overnight-turned-Hindu Indian authorities in 1948 to come back to India, and for no other reason than because I was a Muslim. As their Ambassador in China ... told me, 'It's a question of Hindu and Muslim.' ... [It was] the loss not only of home and whatever I possessed, but also my birthright, when I had no hatred of any caste or creed in my heart.[18]

The suffering of this forced migration was further augmented by the fact that when a local edition of *Twilight in Delhi* was brought out in 1966, the book was not allowed to cross the frontiers of India and reach its author in Pakistan. When it was suggested that a televised version be presented from Karachi, the local station manager refused on the grounds that it was set in the 'forbidden city across the border'.[19] As I read about the restrictions on literature and film in Ali's Introduction, it saddens me to think of how these have continued to date to a large extent. I find myself wondering whether this book, which chronicles, along with Indians, the lives of so many Pakistanis and Bangladeshis, will ever find its way to their bookshelves.

It was while writing *City of Djinns* that the historian William Dalrymple read *Twilight in Delhi* and travelled to Karachi for an audience with the elusive Ahmed Ali. During his bitter recollections, the novelist admitted that after Partition he found himself stranded in China, and once his salary at Nanking stopped, he travelled to Hong Kong, from where some friends put him on an amphibious plane to Karachi.

'Where else could I have gone if I couldn't go back to Delhi?' he asks rhetorically. 'I never opted for Pakistan ... The civilization I belong to – the civilization of Delhi – came into being through the mingling of two different cultures, Hindu and Muslim. That civilization flourished for one thousand years, undisturbed, until certain people denied that that great mingling had taken place.'

'In that case can't you go back to Delhi?' Dalrymple asks. 'Couldn't you reapply for citizenship?'

In the tongue of many who have lost their homeland, Ali replies, 'Now no country is my country.'

He ends the conversation by recounting an incident from when he was returning from Australia and due to a mechanical fault the plane was diverted to Delhi. He refused to exit the aircraft and set foot on his erstwhile homeland. The novelist says to the historian, 'How could I? How could I revisit that which was once mine and ... now no longer mine?'[20]

IT IS THE memory of one partition eclipsed by another, and the staggered migrations caused as a result of these events, that the New York-based mental health educator and therapist Israa Nasir and I speak about.

'The first time I heard the word partition was in the context of what had happened in 1971 in Bangladesh,' Israa recalls. 'I was born in 1987 in Karachi but grew up in Saudi Arabia and went to a Bengali school, where there would be a full celebration around 16 December, which was when the war ended and the Pakistani army surrendered, leading to the birth of Bangladesh. But I am Pakistani, and so there was a strange dissonance to being part of these celebrations, because they were essentially villainizing Pakistanis,' she laughs awkwardly.

'But, yeah, that was the first time I heard the word partition. As a child, the concept of India and Pakistan wasn't as important as that of Pakistan and Bangladesh. It was only when I grew older that I learnt of the Partition that had occurred in 1947.'[21]

'Were you aware of 1971 because your family had witnessed it?' I ask and she nods.

'The lives of three generations of my family have played out in a series of migrations – first across the subcontinent, and then across the world. They migrated as Muslims from British India to East Pakistan at Independence, then with the creation of Bangladesh they fled to Pakistan as Urdu-speaking Muslims, and then further to Saudi Arabia for economic opportunities and eventually to Canada.'

'Did either of your parents witness the first migration in 1947?'

She shakes her head. 'No, but both families migrated to Dhaka then – my father is from Calcutta and my mother is from Faizabad, just outside of Lucknow. My parents were born in Dhaka city in the '50s, and though my mother does not have a strong affiliation to it, my father has held on to that identity very strongly. For instance, when we were younger, each time we visited Pakistan in the summertime, my father would first spend a week in Dhaka and then join us in Karachi.'

Here, Israa introduces me to the concept of 'Sunday stories', a time when she and her siblings would talk to their parents about their childhoods and histories. It was through these weekly storytelling sessions that memories of Partition first emerged. 'I know more about my father's family than my mother's, and I think that's because of the way people identify with their trauma. On my father's side, everyone speaks about what happened at Partition; they enjoy reminiscing about the past. But in my mother's family, '71 dominates the narrative, maybe because of how traumatic their experiences were during the war.

'My dadi, dada and my father's eldest brother, who was four or five years old, along with my dadi's sister and her husband left Calcutta on a chartered plane to Dhaka. They were in the film business, distributing reels to cinemas, and led a fairly comfortable life. But for this flight, they dressed up as Hindus – my dada in a dhoti, my dadi wearing a bindi and sindoor. The Orient Airways flight held a total of twenty-two passengers. They had already boarded the plane when someone from the authorities came and asked them to get down because they wanted to recheck their papers, and –'

'How come they disguised themselves as Hindus?' I gently interrupt her.

'They thought they'd be murdered otherwise. That's what my uncle had said, what he'd been scared of. But they managed to fly to Dhaka and an acquaintance then arranged an overnight stay in a haveli with a group of strangers. The next day, a Hindu man was getting rid of his double-storeyed house and leaving for Calcutta, so my grandfather and his younger brother purchased it. My family lived there for almost a month before moving to their own home on Urdu Road, and the other relatives remained in that house.'

'Your uncle was only a child – do you know if this experience impacted him in any way?'

'It certainly disrupted his ability to obtain an education,' she says after some thought. 'When they reached the other side, they literally had to begin from scratch. They'd carried some money and jewellery, which helped to rebuild life. My uncle went to school till Grade 10, and then, because of the family's financial struggles, he began working. I've heard him say over and over again how he had to sacrifice his education so that his younger siblings could get one. You see, the ramifications of their migration to East Pakistan were not just immediate or short-term but long-lasting and multigenerational, and they demanded unique sacrifices from everybody. I've heard my uncle talk about 1947 only twice, maybe. I don't think he saw any value in talking about it, because nothing good came of it. But I don't know, maybe this is just a projection of mine,' she says sadly.

'Have you spoken to him about it ever?'

'Once in Pakistan, when we were all sitting together and watching a Bollywood film that must have touched on the topic. I was younger, in Grade 10 or so, and I just asked him what had happened on the day they fled. That was it, no context or nuance or sensitivity at all. I was young and uninhibited,' she laughs.

I smile in return. 'And what did he tell you?'

'Just a single incident. He told me that they had one almirah at home – you know the steel ones that are a fixture in every South Asian house? So, he remembers the family opening it and throwing whatever they could into a *chadar* and tying it up and leaving.' She pauses for a moment. 'But he didn't offer any more details, and I don't remember us speaking about it ever again.'

'And what about your father? Do you think that 1947 impacted him?'

'Deeply,' Israa says, her voice full of feeling. 'He may not have lived through 1947, but the family's dislocation from Calcutta and the multiple migrations that followed as a result didn't allow him to have a concrete understanding of home. He never considered Pakistan his home because he left for Saudi so soon after moving there. He feels affection towards Bangladesh, but it's a place that's caused him tremendous pain. Despite being born there, he feels like a visitor each time and talks about this a lot. When I was thirteen years old, he took us to Calcutta because he wanted us to see *where we were from*.'

'Where you were from?' I confirm.

'He wanted us to see where we were *originally* from. Those were his exact words. He must have pulled, like, a billion strings to get the whole family visas to go there, because it meant so much to him. But he often refers to himself as a nomad. In one of the Sunday stories, he said ... he used the Urdu word for it,' she laughs, trying to remember.

'*Banjara*?' I offer.

'That's the word!' She snaps her fingers. '*Banjara*, someone who has no permanent home, a nomad.'

'And what about you?' I ask her. 'Do you ever think about these migrations?'

'Well, they impact me through my parents' lives,' she begins slowly and thoughtfully. 'How the consequences of their histories have trickled into parenting styles and daily habits. But it manifests differently for both my parents, which is really what I wanted to speak to you about.'

I meet her gaze and gesture for her to continue.

'For my father, constant migration has moulded the idea of what a comfortable and safe home, a safe family should look like. In that sense, there is compensation or perhaps overcompensation for the times that were difficult. For instance, we never have only one packet of sugar at home, we'll always have three or four. Whenever one gets over, it will be immediately replaced, so you never run out. The concept of *wanting* something and not being able to have it really drove my father's parenting style. He made sure that his children never experienced any *want*. This habit was a direct result of the displacement of 1947, of having to start from nothing, remake an entire life, only to go through the displacement all over again after 1971, and then having to begin once more.

'And my father makes mention of this, how he never wants his children to feel like any opportunity was taken away from them. He missed his medical school entrance examination because of a riot in Dhaka, and one of his biggest regrets in life is that he wasn't able to pursue medicine. This really drove him, and he carries it in his conscience: wanting to provide his family with everything he may have been deprived of.'

She takes a breath before continuing, 'Language also remains an important thing. Before Partition, the family was living in Calcutta and so my father and his relatives all speak proper Bangla. I understand it fully, so if you were to drop me anywhere in Dhaka, I'd be able to find my way around,' she chuckles. 'So, Partition comes up quite casually on my father's side. My dadi would often reminisce about their home in Calcutta – the courtyard, the trees, the building. It's been rented out as an apartment complex now, but it still stands. Calcutta just has an immediate pull for the family; it is talked about with nostalgia and longing.'

'I find it incredible, actually, that your father took you to Calcutta to show you the family's origin, and there remains a sense of intimacy towards it, and yet he's never lived there himself. Do *you* feel any connection to Calcutta?'

'Not at all,' Israa is quick to answer. 'I was thirteen when I visited, but even if I reflect on it now, I don't feel a connection. But I think my father feels it so strongly because his family was there for a long time. Besides, anything after Calcutta was temporary – East Pakistan was temporary, Bangladesh was temporary, Pakistan was temporary, Saudi Arabia was temporary. And now, in Toronto, my parents are immigrants. I think this is why my father feels that his roots lie in Calcutta. But he doesn't identify as Indian, I want to make that clear. He separates India and Calcutta, which is odd.' She ends her statement like a question.

'It's more common than you think,' I smile.

Everything after Calcutta was temporary, I underline these words in my notebook. There are places in the world that can be considered home, even though one has personally never lived there, simply based on the fact that, ancestrally, it has been home.

'Now that I'm thinking back,' Israa smiles widely, 'I can see how important these trips were for my father – to Calcutta and to Dhaka, where we'd walk all the lanes he'd walked as a child, ate all the street food he ate. It was pure nostalgia. But returning to the notion of home, I feel like we add on a layer from every place we live or take refuge in. When I got married, my brother made a speech where he alluded to the nomadic nature of our family, how we have migrated to many places and at each stop we have picked up people and history – ending with how I'd eventually folded my husband into our family as well. But he started the speech from Calcutta, switching between English and Urdu, which captured the duality of our lives.'

'Does your mother's side retain that same connection to Faizabad?' I ask.

'All I know,' Israa admits, 'is that they came to Dhaka in 1947. I don't know anything about their migration from Faizabad, and I think saying it out loud this way makes me feel quite sad because now my nani has passed, and though we were close when she was alive, I never asked her about this. The only thing I do know about her pre-

Partition life is that she used to work at a hand-rolled cigarette shop – she actually rolled cigarettes for work – those slim ones, *beedis*. I think Partition caused a lot of poverty for the family, and when they migrated to Dhaka, my nana started a bicycle repair shop. But their financial situation was so dire that they would make *atta* out of the leftover husk from wheat grain and eat those rotis to survive. My father tells me that living through Partition was quite traumatic for my nana, and he carried that trauma and anxiety throughout his life. Some of this has trickled down to my mother and her sisters.'

'How come they migrated to East Pakistan rather than West?' I ask. 'On your father's side, Calcutta is closer to the eastern border, but to have taken this route from Faizabad...'

'When I asked my parents, they both said that route was considered more dangerous. My father had relatives in Dhaka, but my mother's side went eastward because the route was safer than West Pakistan.'

Israa goes suddenly quiet, as if mulling over a thought, and then slowly repeats, 'West. Pakistan. West Pakistan. That sounds ... odd on my tongue. I've never said it.'

I look at her in silence, thinking about how the many partitions of the subcontinent meted out unique terminologies to each of the nations involved.

'Anyway, the migration from Faizabad to Dhaka in 1947 is almost wholly obscured by 1971. That dominates the narrative of displacement in both memory and conversation,' Israa notes. 'On the night of their displacement, the area my family lived in was attacked by an angry mob, from what I understand. It was my grandparents and their three daughters. All my mother remembers, very distinctly, is grabbing the boxes of powdered milk because she had two little sisters. They threw them into a *chadar* – not unlike my uncle's experience in 1947 – and then my nana threw that bundle over his head and they left. My nani had once told me how, over the years, she had accumulated a lot of silver jewellery, and on that night she tied it all into a dupatta and hid it in a corner of the house she thought would remain unchecked by the mob.'

'Who were the mob?'

'They were the freedom fighters,' is all she says.

In 1971, Israa's family were Urdu-speaking Muslims in East Pakistan, at a time when Bengali nationalism was at its peak.

'And just like that, they fled their home. By the time my mother looked back, the house was on fire, and by the time they reached the end of the lane, the entire row of houses had been set ablaze. They were never able to return home; that was that. With their belongings on their back, they arrived at the Geneva Camp[22] but never ended up living there. They stayed with friends before finding another house. East Pakistan became Bangladesh, but the family didn't leave for years after. In fact, my parents got married in Dhaka and left for Pakistan only in 1982.'

'So, it was a prolonged displacement, from 1947 till well after 1971,' I observe.

'A staggered migration,' Israa adds, 'broken up strategically – first, two of my mother's sisters were sent, then two others, and so on. I asked my parents, "Why wait so long, or why move at all?" They had married in Dhaka, so they could have just settled there. And they told me that they wanted to migrate to Pakistan once they were fairly sure that they would be successful there, because they had often heard stories about discrimination against *muhajirs* or Urdu-speaking refugees. Meanwhile, they knew they could not live in Bangladesh for long because of the animosity towards the Urdu speakers who had stayed. It became hard to find work and they didn't feel safe – especially my mother, who had worked ever since she'd been a teenager. From her experience, Urdu-speaking women were viewed as a commodity, and the kidnappings and rapes persisted long after the war. Being from a family of sisters, this also became an important factor for why they wished to leave.

'Now, in 1971, the Concern team from Ireland arrived in Bangladesh to provide aid when my mother was in a refugee group.[23] But she spoke English, so instead of being the recipient of that support, she was offered work as a translator. She was taught to use the typewriter, trained in shorthand and secretarial work, which essentially lifted her out of poverty and disability. Concern was training women in skills like teaching or embroidery or micro-entrepreneurship so they could earn an income, and my mother became a manager for the programme because she was multilingual.

'She must have been just fifteen or sixteen, because she would go to Concern after school on rickshaw and on the way she would eat a banana and a roti. That's the story she tells: "*Main rickshaw mein kela-roti khati thi*!" She took the opportunity because they needed the money, and my mother contributed to the household income this way. To date, she remains a very motivated person, and this experience built her perseverance and foundation. From Concern, she applied to the United Nations Developmental Programme (UNDP) for a secretarial position and eventually rose through the ranks and worked in the Saudi Arabia office once we moved there.

'During the years she was working with the UN in Bangladesh, she recalls feeling a very deep sense of "difference" – to the point where she actually told her boss that she'd feel more comfortable with a chaperone bringing her back and forth. She talks a lot about feeling a lack of physical safety being an Urdu-speaking woman, but this fear must have settled in women from both sides at the time,' she acknowledges.

Looking through my notes, I now return to the beginning of our conversation, clarifying the family's many migrations. 'So, both sides fled from India to East Pakistan in 1947 and then, with the creation of Bangladesh in 1971, they stayed on in Dhaka and migrated to Karachi, Pakistan, in 1982, soon after which your father moved to Saudi Arabia, where you grew up, and then as a family immigrated to Canada in 2001.'

'That's correct,' Israa nods, 'and I should mention that the kind of nostalgia that my father fosters for the past is not found in my mother. She doesn't believe in these "bookish things", as she calls them, "*kitaabi baatein*" or indulging in reminiscences.'

'Why do you think that is – the difference in your parents?'

'With my mother, it's the trauma of witnessing trauma that has impacted her life and even her parenting. The conception of safety and fear is something she struggles with. She is a fearful mother, and there is anxiety which is a direct result of her family's experiences. Living in the diaspora, these traits may be common to many South Asian immigrant parents, but my parents also come from Partition-displaced homes, and they've carried their many displacements like shadows.'

'Where is home, then?' I ask, keeping the question deliberately vague.

'Calcutta may remain a place of rootedness for my father, his origin. But, for my mother, I would say that she feels most accepted in Canada; of all the places where she's lived, she feels most integrated there. She feels respected.'

Breaking into a smile, Israa now tells me a love story. 'My mother, Tahzeeb, must have been fifteen years old when my father, Nasiruddin, who is a few years older, was her English and chemistry tutor. He and his friends were giving free group classes to any Urdu-speaking person so that their education would not be impacted by the war. This was particularly true for many young women who were being married off at an early age and denied education due to fear and political circumstances. That's when they first met. And then a few years later, when they were both working at the UNDP in Bangladesh, with women living in the Geneva Camp, they were *reintroduced*,' she smiles. 'But I think it was the mutual experience and memory of Partition that brought them together.'

'The *second-hand* memory of Partition, you mean?' I confirm, since neither had been born in 1947.

She shakes her head. 'No, they both lived through Partition.'

'The Partition of 1947? But how can that –' I stop myself abruptly.

'The Partition of 1971,' she replies, unperturbed.

I'm confused, but it hits me only after a few seconds.

'You are Pakistani,' I say with measured words, 'and I am Indian.' Israa nods, following until now.

'So, naturally 1971 is *also* a partition for you.'

In the Preface to her book *1971*, the Pakistani oral historian Anam Zakaria details some of the terms she grew up associating with the birth of Bangladesh – 'Saqoot-e-Dhaka', the Fall of Dhaka, and the 'dismemberment of Pakistan'. In the Pakistani collective imagination, she writes that '1971 represents a loss, the break-up of a nation, the "second Partition" of the subcontinent'.[24]

Suddenly, I find myself replaying our entire conversation in my mind.

'Well, what do *you* call 1971, if not Partition?' Israa interrupts my thoughts.

After a few seconds, I say, 'The third India–Pakistan war.'

'Oh.'

A cautious silence grows between us – the kind that feels opaque and palpable, that exists as its own organism. It is the ghostly shell of a once-undivided India, bifurcated and further trifurcated. There is nervous laughter before we both accept the identities that history has dealt us. Pakistan views 1971 through the lens of loss and Partition. For Bangladesh it marks the realization of Bengali nationalism, it is triumph and liberation. For India, it is the third India–Pakistan war and a continuation of the rivalry between the two countries.[25]

Perhaps this is why all we end up collecting are fragments – often conflicting and contradictory – of the same story.

PARTITION DID NOT just precipitate a series of migrations within the newly formed countries of the Indian subcontinent, but also outward migrations to other parts of the world, particularly to the UK and North America. While documenting the Partition generation in Britain, the journalist Kavita Puri writes about the unprecedented scale of migration after the Second World War and its link to Partition. 'The areas of India and Pakistan which were most disturbed by Partition were major contributors to the emigrant flow to Britain.' In *Partition Voices*, she discusses how South Asian migration seriously started in the 1950s and was connected to 'post-war labour shortages in the mills, factories, foundries, and public services', thus explaining the presence of so many groups of South Asians scattered in cities across Britain.[26]

Emigration to North America had begun during colonial rule but the numbers were insignificant. According to a report by the Migration Policy Institute, between 1820 and 1900, only 700 people migrated from India to the United States, rising over the next thirty years to 8,700, most of whom were Punjabi Sikhs working in agriculture in California.

In 1904, Canada, still a part of the British Empire, recorded a population of only 100 Indians. In the three years that followed, this number rose to 5,000 'before a restrictive immigration policy required whoever landed in Canada to make a continuous journey from the country of one's citizenship. Since no steamships travelled directly from India to Canada, Indian immigrants were intentionally excluded.'[27] With the Independence of British India in 1947, the Canadian government removed the continuous-passage regulation but replaced it in 1951 with an annual immigration quota for the countries of the subcontinent – 150 for India, 100 for Pakistan and 50 for Ceylon. At that time, Canada recorded 2,148 South Asians, expanding to 6,774 by 1961 and 67,925 by 1971.[28]

'I think living in the diaspora is kind of like living in the shadow of Partition,' the artist and poet Jagdeep Singh Raina says as he speaks to me over video call from Guelph, Canada. His gaze is faraway, looking outside the window into the darkness that floods his street. It is afternoon in Delhi, which means that the day has not yet broken where he is.

'Partition is one of the reasons why families immigrated across the world and chose to rebuild their lives in new lands, away...' he pauses, trying to find the words.

'Away from the past?' I offer.

He nods, bringing his hand up to his chin. 'The fact that we lost so many family members to the violence of Partition, and that we were forced to abandon homes and lands, definitely triggered the realization that Kashmir was no longer a safe place for us. For me, living in the diaspora feels like a direct result, because Partition didn't just destroy community and identity but also led to the creation of so many kinds of hybrid identities formed in other parts of the world.'

Jagdeep's family migrated from Jammu and Kashmir to Canada in the 1960s, and he was born in Guelph three decades later. He holds an MFA in painting from the Rhode Island School of Design and currently teaches at the School of Fine Art and Music at the University of Guelph. His interdisciplinary practice – which spans drawing, textile and poetry – engages with historical memory and patterns of migration, and has in the last several years begun to incorporate the remnants of Partition, focusing on the ecological and environmental consequences that it left on the once-entwined, now-divided landscapes of Punjab and Kashmir.

'I think about Kashmir,' he admits, 'which makes me think about the dislocation *from* Kashmir because of Partition. Through the stories of my family, I keep imagining it as this beautiful, flourishing place and what it must have been like before Partition, what my paternal village Chakothi in Muzaffarabad must have been like, what my maternal home in Baramulla must have looked like. I think about the mountains and the trade and the spice routes and the travellers that passed through between Kashmir and Punjab.'

Jagdeep tells me that it is only in the last seven or eight years that he has begun seriously thinking about Partition. He hardly ever heard the word until his late twenties, when he was finishing his undergraduate degree at Western University in London, Ontario. There he read books like *The Other Side of Silence* and *Ice Candy Man* – one a work of non-fiction by Urvashi Butalia and the other a novel by Bapsi Sidhwa, both dealing with the subject of Partition – until his interests became more specific and localized to Kashmir.

'Both sides of my family are Kashmiri Sikhs,' he says. 'My dada, dadi and nani are from the Muzaffarabad area – my dada's and nani's mothers were sisters – and my nana is from Baramulla. In October 1947, Muzaffarabad was attacked by tribal forces and my dada fled to Srinagar, and from there made his way to a refugee camp at Nagrota in Jammu. I never had the chance to speak to him about

Partition, but in a video that my uncle recorded, he describes how there were '*aag ke shole*', or fire embers, everywhere, and that entire villages were massacred, including his family. I learnt that his house is now a school, but Chakothi itself is so close to the border that it still frequently witnesses violence, and its inhabitants are tired of living in constant fear of war.

'These stupid borders,' Jagdeep scoffs, shaking his head from side to side, 'I think a lot about this Line of Control running through Jammu and Kashmir, separating it into India and Pakistan.[29] I think about the scale of loss at Partition, and how we continue to live in the shadows of distrust and trauma. There's *so much* unspoken trauma in my family from that time – I discovered that my dadi's grandmother jumped into the Chenab river, my nani's sister was abducted, her father was murdered...'

As the list continues to grow, relative after relative, he never once meets my eye, still looking out of the window. Then, moving on to his maternal side, he says, 'The Balis were a prominent family from Baramulla, and I learnt a lot about the extended family through Andrew Whitehead's book, *A Mission in Kashmir*, where he interviews them.'

The world is very small, I tell Jagdeep, as my paternal grandmother's sister is married into this family.

'My mother's siblings were born before Partition,' he continues, 'and there are memories that I have collected from them. As the tribal forces swept through the villages, killing Sikhs and Hindus, looting their homes, her family fled to Srinagar on foot with a large group. On the journey, they lost their grandfather, a cousin was abducted, and an uncle was shot by his own Muslim servant. Eventually, they arrived at a refugee camp in Srinagar, and then moved in with relatives. In April 1948, over six months later, they found the courage to return to Baramulla, to discover their home damaged and looted – it had been used as the tribal headquarters in the area – and one of their dogs shot dead, with the bullet still lodged in the front door of the house. It remained there, affixed, for many years. But there are shades to every story, for they had a Muslim servant, Shabana, who continued to keep an eye on their home from a distance and told them what had happened during the time they were away. It was in the 1960s that my uncle first came to Canada, followed by his siblings and their families, deciding that Kashmir was no longer safe. My mother was the youngest, she migrated as a teenager, and, in June 1984, went back to marry my father in Kashmir and they settled down in Canada.'

The shadow begins to lift from his face as the room becomes bathed in a pink light. The sun is rising on his side of the world as dusk is flooding mine. Behind Jagdeep, in the corner, I see part of a *phulkari* textile embroidered in deep gold and orange – a recurring emblem in his work.

'No one in your family really spoke about what had happened at Partition?' I confirm.

'Not until I asked,' he clarifies. 'In fact, just a few months ago, I was taking a walk with my mother and we were talking about how individualistic North American or Canadian culture can be. Don't get me wrong, I feel very privileged to be born here, but sometimes I think that growing up in Canada disconnected me from my roots. As we walked, she told me that had Partition not happened, they may have still been living in Baramulla, which is something my father often says about Chakothi. When I hear them say these things, I feel really upset over what could have been.

'Anyway, that day, for the very first time, my mother recounted a story that *her* elder sister had told her when she was a child. My aunt was sixteen at the time of Partition, and her best friends were these two Sikh girls who were abducted; they just disappeared amidst the violence. My mother wished she'd asked more questions at the time, because my aunt died in the '80s. When I hear these stories, I just feel a deep-rooted sense of sadness and rage.'

'Because of how traumatic the past has been?'

'*That*, of course, but also how migrating to another place, to a foreign country, forces you to silence so much of that past – forget and move on almost – rather than confront or talk about it. Canada really forced them to move on with their lives. It accelerated the need to create new experiences, because they had to learn a new language, find jobs, go to school, acclimatize to a different and faster world.'

'Incidentally, my maternal grandfather also immigrated to Guelph in the late '50s, though it was not motivated by Partition,' I tell him. 'But I always wondered whether in the diaspora one would have had to interact with the same people that one had been separated from in the subcontinent due to Partition.'

Jagdeep starts to nod, smiling. 'My mother felt like this growing up in the '70s, and I thought it was beautiful. All of a sudden, you're not a Sikh or a Hindu or a Muslim, you're just a brown person, and you're friends with other brown people. Geography, religion, borders did dissolve and you learnt to stick together, because there was so much racism all around you anyway. It became almost like pre-Partition,' he chuckles, 'like one beautiful subcontinental landmass. But gradually over time as the diaspora grew, these communities grew, and distinctions began to appear. Punjabis began socializing with other Punjabis, and Gujaratis with other Gujaratis, and Sindhis with other Sindhis, and so on.'

I nod and then return to an earlier topic. 'This border between India and Pakistan, between Kashmir and Kashmir, you said you think about it a lot...'

He nods. 'I think about it a lot because of the distance I have from it ... from it all, from my own history. As the generations before me laid down roots in new lands, they became more and more disconnected from Kashmir, and this grows with every passing generation. From just my parents' generation to mine, so much has been lost – land, languages. Kashmir is drifting farther and farther away, becoming harder and harder to hold on to, and I don't know what will happen to the generation after me, but I want to preserve as much of my history as I can.'

In December 2019, Jagdeep became an artist-in-residence at the Mariam Dawood School of Visual Arts and Design in Lahore. He tells me that often when he walked through the galleries of the Lahore Museum, Pakistanis would come up and tell him how wonderful it was to see him there, shake his hand, talk in Punjabi. A turbaned

Sikh, he became not only aware of his status as a minority in Pakistan but also how warmly people welcomed him to the city that his ancestors would have once frequented.

'I felt an immediate kinship with Lahore, and kept thinking about how if I'd grown up in Chakothi or Muzaffarabad, it would have been *the* big city I'd have visited. I had an uncle who lived there before Partition, so we would have had family there as well. I thought about how it was once the Paris of the East, with artists and writers who made the city their muse. While I was in Pakistan, my father called me and it was the first time that he was very chatty on the phone, telling me stories about Chakothi in a very excited voice – I think maybe because he had wanted to be there as well. In fact, my entire family was very obsessed with my being there. But the highlight of the trip was the Kashmir Gate,' Jagdeep sighs.

'The Kashmiri Darwaza?' I ask, smiling. Of the thirteen original 'gates' to the walled city of Lahore, some, like the Delhi and Kashmiri Gate, were named after the cities they faced.

He nods enthusiastically. 'I felt this obsession with the gate, I returned to it again and again; it had an absolute pull over me. It was hypnotic to consider that had I kept walking on the path through that gate, it would have eventually led me to Kashmir, to my grandfather's village. To Chakothi. The more I thought about this, the more it dawned on me how liquid these cities once were – Srinagar, Lahore, Delhi, entire parts of Kashmir and Punjab – so connected, so entwined. People would have once travelled freely between the provinces, beyond regimes, kingdoms, states, borders, without passports or visas, and this porosity of land was both beautiful and … now, heartbreaking. It pains me how definitive these borders have become when compared to how liquid, how malleable the cultures of these great cities once were.'

In the poem 'Everything I Wish You Had Told Me', Jagdeep writes:

On Sunday I went to the Kashmir Gate
I thought of mother who says Kashmir Katham Hogeya

Kashmir is over. But this death isn't new.
This death happened long before partition.
And long after the Punjabi Bloodshed stained us.
And long after Amrita painted three women, and Amrita
screamed to Waris.[30]

'What happened when you returned from Lahore?' I ask. 'Was your family curious about your trip?'

'Not just that but the stories that emerged thereafter!' he laughs. 'When I came home, we had a get-together with uncles, aunts, cousins, and everyone just kept asking me questions about what it was like being in Pakistan and what Pakistani people were like, and I was a bit taken aback by that.'

'How come? What were you expecting?'

'Well, I wasn't expecting anything, but they had all once lived on that side of the border, so I don't know, I didn't think,' Jagdeep shrugs.

'A lot *has* changed since 1947,' I say with a small smile.

'Yes, indeed, both on the physical land and in the psychological understanding of it.' He mirrors my smile. 'But my dadi was most thrilled that I had gone to Lahore, because it was a city that held importance for her husband, my dadaji. The trip also began a conversation with my aunts, related to us by marriage, who told me that their grandfather had also lived through the violence in Kashmir. I just remember sitting there listening and being completely blown away by the depth of pain and trauma that still lived inside them. Seventy years later, there was still pain, there was still...' Unable to finish his sentence, Jagdeep looks away. When he returns to this thought, he is composed. 'The fact that I had travelled back, *returned*, made them reflect on all that had been left behind, and I think that actively asking my family questions has helped them come to terms with some of it.'

The day has now completely broken in Guelph, and the room is painted in bright sunshine. Jagdeep studies my face for a few seconds before asking, 'Don't you feel sad when you think about Partition? You write about it every day.'

Hardly anyone asks me this question, and it catches me off guard.

'I feel very sad,' I say, but the word seems so inadequate.

'And a sense of bafflement,' he adds.

'Without any healing or closure.'

'Not to sound cynical, but I don't think there will ever be any closure.'

I give a half laugh, but really I want to cry.

'When I came back from Lahore, so many stories resurfaced, stories that had been buried or forgotten or unspoken. Of those, there was one that both shocked and broke me. After Partition, when my paternal grandfather was dividing time between Srinagar and Jammu, he heard news of a distant cousin who had been abducted during the violence. She now lived in Pakistan, had a family there, but she would come to the border and wait to see if anyone appeared on the other side.'

'W-what border was this?'

'Jammu–Sialkot. My grandfather went to meet her once.'

A single, well-landscaped road runs through the border post. The Indian tricolour is painted on one side and a Pakistani star and crescent moon on the other. Identical trees fill the landscape beyond.

'He stood in India and she in Pakistan, and they just waved at one another. They were family, separated by a border, a line, a road.'

17
No Man's Land

Ɋ

IN LATE 2017, I attended a lecture at the United Service Institution in Delhi, on the role of the Jullundur Brigade[1] in the Great War, for a novel I was plotting at the time. As people found their seats, a distinguished-looking Sikh gentleman with a neat white beard, a forest green turban and a red pocket-square began to introduce the speakers. He was Pushpinder Singh Chopra, a military historian who wrote extensively on the Indian Air Force and the history of aviation in India,[2] and the editor of two magazines, *Nishaan* and *Vayu*.[3]

After the hour-long lecture, speakers and attendees gathered in the outdoor courtyard for tea, and I realized – much to my surprise – that not only was I decades younger than everyone else but I was also the only woman. Needless to say, others noticed this as well. It was then that Mr Chopra walked up to me and with a smile asked what my interest in the Great War was. 'Nothing,' I told him meekly, 'nothing more than curiosity yet, anyway.' The plot of my novel had not even fully come together, and it seemed futile to present a vague elevator pitch, so, instead, I said, 'I mostly write on Partition, actually.' At this, he smiled, told me that he was born in Murree and was five years old in 1947, and then proceeded to narrate the story of the establishment of the most infamous border post between India and Pakistan.

But before I relay the story that was told to me, I want to lay emphasis on the terminology that will guide us through this chapter.

A border is a line that divides two countries. A borderland is the territory near the border.* And, finally, no man's land is the area between the borders of two countries which is not controlled by either side.

The Attari–Wagah[4] border has come to represent an iconic and emotionally charged physical space for both Indians and Pakistanis. Thousands of spectators visit it each day to witness the dramatic, synchronized goose-stepping of troops to the backdrop of the flag-lowering ceremony at sunset, which first began in 1959. Today, both sides have large iron gates that are opened each morning and closed each evening, but it was only as recently as 1986 that solid barbed wire fences were first erected. In fact, on 17 August 1947, when the Radcliffe Line was announced, there was no border here. Major General Mohinder Singh Chopra, then a brigadier, and father of Pushpinder Singh Chopra, was tasked with setting up this post – demarcating the once-undivided territory into a border, a borderland and no man's land.

'Two months after Partition, my father was sent to Amritsar to take control of the brigade that would patrol along the Grand Trunk Road. But first he had to establish the border, because until then *koi border hi nahi siga*,' Mr Chopra says, bewildered. 'The line had been drawn on paper but there was no demarcation of where it was on the land.'

'I don't understand,' I say, equally bewildered. 'Were there no coordinates, or...'

'On paper, it simply ran through open fields and villages. There was no river or hill or any feature that was assigned to this side or that. But traumatized refugees continued to migrate east- and westwards, so it became imperative to define the border – where India ended and Pakistan began.'

Brigadier Chopra's appointment was no random choice, for he was born in Amritsar in 1907 and 'the army believed he would be

---

* The stories of borders and borderlands are discussed in Chapter 3, 'Borderlands'.

particularly sensitive to the situation there'.[5] He was also a highly decorated officer who had graduated from the Royal Military Academy Sandhurst in 1928, served in the Persia and Iraq Force and in Burma during the Second World War, and in July 1947 had overseen the security during the referendum in Sylhet,[6] which eventually became a part of East Pakistan.

Mr Chopra describes how, on 8 October 1947, his father took over the 123 Brigade of what was called the EP (East Punjab) area. Incidentally, his counterpart in Lahore was Brigadier Nazir Ahmad, who had served with him before Partition in the 13th Royal Frontier Force Rifles of the British Indian Army. 'Two months ago, they had been part of not just the same army but also the same regiment, and now here they were, citizens of two countries at war with one another.' He pauses for a moment. 'So, he proposed that they meet on the Grand Trunk Road, the only road which passed between the two countries. They fixed a point between Wagah in Pakistan and Attari in India, where the border would fall. On 11 October, they traced that border in chalk, *chune naal lakeer kaati*.' His hands draw an invisible border. 'Then, taking two whitewashed drums, they wrote "INDIA" on one and "PAKISTAN" on the other, and that became the new international border.'

'What did it look like at that time?' I ask.

He chuckles, 'That was it.'

In his journal inherited by his son, Major General Chopra details the sparse set-up:

> Some tents were pitched on either side, two sentry boxes painted in the national colours of each country, and a swing gate to regulate the refugee traffic was erected. Two flag masts were also put up on either side and a brass plate commemorating the historic event was installed.[7]

A few years have passed since Mr Chopra narrated this story to me, but sometimes I think about how odd it would have been for the two officers – friends, no less – to begin the process of demarcation.

I do not know what this would have looked like, but I imagine them standing across from one another on a barren land, every man's land, their fists full of powdered chalk, and laying down a line where there was none before. Did a line in chalk reverberate – feel as pronounced, hold the heaviness of its history – the way today's border does? By the end of the process, I imagine they must have retreated from that freshly drawn line until they were both standing on two sides of a border, in no man's land.

IN A PRELIMINARY conversation for what would eventually be recorded by the Partition Museum, Amritsar, as a more formal interview, I meet Padam Rosha at his home in Delhi in 2015. If the demarcation of the official border had separated friends, sending Mohinder Singh Chopra and Nazir Ahmad to their respective sides, then, in his official capacity as a police officer, Padam Rosha made use of the rare potential offered by no man's land to bring people together. To momentarily exist in a state that was stateless, neither here nor there, neither this side nor that.

Padam Rosha was born in 1923 in Ambala and was a twenty-four-year-old PhD student at Government College, Lahore, in 1947, when he fled to Jalandhar during Partition. But Lahore city remained ever-present in his mind, and he speaks about it as if speaking of an old friend. 'When I'm not doing anything, I close my eyes and find myself wandering down the streets of Anarkali with four *annas* worth of *chilgozas* in my pocket, going to have a cold glass of lassi,' he reminisces during our conversation.

In July 1947, he took the All India Services examination and was selected for the Punjab cadre of the Indian Police Service. By 1948, he had become an officer in independent India and a part of the team that set up the Border Security Force. Then, as a young superintendent at the Wagah border, he had the opportunity to organize a meeting between two iconic singers: Lata Mangeshkar of India and Noor Jehan of Pakistan.

Born as Allah Rakhi Wasai into a Punjabi Muslim family of Kasur, Noor Jehan was discovered and trained by the legendary music composer Ghulam Ahmed Chishti before she made her mark in cinema. Meanwhile, Lata too was beginning to draw attention in the world of Indian cinema. Their paths crossed briefly in the film *Badi Maa* in 1945. With Partition, Noor Jehan migrated to Pakistan, but the two songbirds continued to keep in touch and had great admiration for one another.

In the winter of 1951, Rosha received a phone call from Lata Mangeshkar, who had travelled to Amritsar and wanted to meet him. 'Naturally, I was very flattered,' he recalls in the recorded interview for the Partition Museum.[8] 'She came to my office in the barracks, which were rough and still mud-plastered, and said that she had spoken with Noor Jehan in Lahore and requested me to set up a meeting. In those days, there wasn't even a proper demarcation or boundary pillar as we have today. But a wise man had left about 50–60 yards of space between the two gates, which became a no man's land of sorts. So, the very next day I arranged for some carpets and chairs to be set up on one side of the road in the no man's land (between Amritsar and Lahore). From Lahore came a burqa-clad Noor Jehan with her husband, Shaukat Rizvi,* and they brought with them utensils full of biryanis, kormas, kebabs and other foods.' Padam Rosha remembers sitting and talking with them for an hour to an hour and a half. '*Ghente, ded-ghente baad*, I came back and left them alone. The two ladies talked until the evening and only got up once the gates had to be shut.'[9]

But this is not the only extraordinary incident that the no man's land has been witness to. In the video for The Partition Museum, Rosha also recounts how around the same time, he was contacted by Agha Muzaffar, the then transport secretary of Jammu and Kashmir, whose sister was to be married to a young man from Pakistan. Though the bride had got a visa for Lahore, neither family could go to

---

* Shaukat Rizvi was originally from Azamgarh, United Provinces, British India.

the other's country for the ceremony due to strict travel restrictions. So, Agha Muzaffar requested Rosha to allow them to solemnize the wedding in the no man's land. Thus, in a narrow stretch between India and Pakistan, a colourful wedding celebration took place, a union of two families – one Indian and the other Pakistani – a *pardah* was set up and a *nikah* read, a feast was shared and gifts exchanged, and at the end the bride crossed over into Pakistan with her in-laws.[10]

∾

IN 2018, WHEN I was invited to the Karachi Literature Festival, I decided to walk across the Attari–Wagah border to feel perhaps a fraction of what people must have felt when they migrated at the time of Partition. I wanted to be very conscious of my steps as I crossed the few-inches-wide painted white line that separated me from the land of my ancestors – the same line that had been drawn in chalk on 11 October 1947. But it was over this very line that the formal procedures relating to visa and luggage checks were conducted, and so the ceremonial nature of my first self-important step in Pakistan was reduced to merely another step in a land that looked no different from the one I had just left behind.[11]

On the way back to India, however, I walked through the iron gate of Pakistan towards an identical one on the Indian side, suitcase in tow. Lahore behind me, Amritsar ahead. After my documents were checked, I made sure to pause, take my time, and even requested the Pakistani Ranger to indulge me for a few seconds as I 'performed' my feelings of duality. Maybe they thought it was childish as they watched me place one foot on either side, with the border falling exactly in the middle. Maybe others had done this before me, but in that moment, it felt exclusively mine. This swift action was one of the most privileged moments of my life, and the enormity of the gesture has not diminished even now. I took a photograph on my phone – the composition is hasty, but the sentiment is singular and incomparable.

For the briefest of moments, I stood in no man's land.

∾

THE IMAGE OF no man's land is most prominently captured in popular imagination through Saadat Hasan Manto's short story 'Toba Tek Singh', published in 1955. In the essay 'The Partitioning of Madness', Anirudh Kala and Alok Sarin write about how after Partition, apart from the transfer of refugees, abducted populations and prisoners, there was the case of patients with mental illnesses admitted to hospitals on either side of the border. It was in the archives of the Nehru Memorial Museum and Library, Delhi, that the pair discovered hospital reports from both the British Empire and the newly independent India. And with this 'came the epiphanic realization [that Toba Tek Singh] was actually based on historical facts'.[12]

On 31 July 1947, the last viceroy of India, Lord Louis Mountbatten, wrote is his diary:

> One of the few institutions that will not be partitioned immediately is the Punjab Mental Hospital. It will continue to be shared for some years. Some Hindu inmates of the asylum have protested against being left in Pakistan. They have been assured that their fears are imaginary.[13]

In Manto's story, a few years after Partition,[14] as the 'partitioning of madness' was underway, an old Sikh patient, confined to the Lahore Mental Hospital for fifteen years, learns that he is to be transferred to India while his village would now fall in Pakistan. His real name is Bishan Singh but everybody calls him Toba Tek Singh, after his village. On a cold winter evening, he and other patients are put on a bus headed towards Wagah and the dividing line between Pakistan and India. In what becomes quite the operation in maintaining decorum, the patients are transferred one by one. But when it comes to Bishan Singh, he simply refuses. When officials try to push him across the line to India, he does not move, while constantly speaking gibberish. Devastated, he stands in no man's land, announcing *it* to now be the village of Toba Tek Singh. No further attempts are made to push him across and there he continues to stand, in the middle, as the night wears on. Just before sunrise, refusing to belong to either side, he collapses on the ground:

> ...behind the barbed wire, on one side, lay India and behind more barbed wire, on the other side, lay Pakistan. In between, on a bit of earth, which had no name, lay Toba Tek Singh.[15]

When speaking about the physical no man's land between India, Pakistan and Bangladesh, it becomes important to acknowledge the minuscule fraction of the present-day population that will ever have the chance to step on it, let alone cross over it. Hence, the most common signs of 'no man's land-ness' appears in our mental spaces – the ways in which we think about borders and nationalities while being cognizant of our family histories of Partition. Several people who witnessed Partition have performed shades of Toba Tek Singh's final act through the feelings of confusion or bafflement surrounding their migration, or in wanting to retain the homeland that they were forcibly made to flee.

The following sections of this chapter explore the ideological notion of no man's land – constructed with both physical and temporal distance from the actual event of Partition – within interviewees of subsequent generations. Included are stories of families who remain suspended between the two sides or those who feel like they belong to neither, renouncing ownership and giving meaning to the term 'world citizen', and stories of how elements as invisible as radio air waves can serve as no man's land.

THE BRITISH-PAKISTANI ACTOR, writer and musician Riz Ahmed's latest album, *The Long Goodbye*, exemplifies the feeling of being stranded in no man's land between a home departed and a home adopted, not least because of the track 'Toba Tek Singh', inspired by Manto's short story. Ahmed, born in 1982 in London to Pakistani parents, is a grandchild of Partition – his maternal grandfather migrated across the border from India to Pakistan during Partition, and then further across the oceans to Britain in the late '70s.

The astoundingly visceral album is prompted by the build-up to Brexit, and not only borrows the vocabulary of Partition but applies its distinct sense of departure and betrayal to the present day, to Ahmed's own feelings of rejection by the country he was born in, and 'the pain it has caused for anyone seen as not sufficiently British'.[16] The politics of the past and present generations, albeit different in context, coalesce in the album as reflections of one another. In a live-streamed performance of *The Long Goodbye* at the Great American Music Hall, San Francisco, Ahmed repeats his grandfather's enduring words, carried across geographies, gaining significance as they accumulate newer identities like layers of new skin: *What am I doing here? Do I belong here? Did I make a mistake coming here?*

In a spoken word piece, he narrates how in 1947 his grandfather finds himself standing on a railway platform in northern India, unsure of whether he wants to get on a train heading westwards to Pakistan. First, because many of the trains travelling between the two countries are ghost trains full of massacred people, and, second, for the simple reason that India has been his family's home for centuries. And though he is told that he no longer belongs there, he does not care. 'He wants to dig his heels in. Make a home in no man's land, if he has to.' In the end, chased by mobs, he and his family have no choice but to cross the border and become Pakistani.

Ahmed's grandfather was a poet, but towards the end of his life he no longer understood the point of words. That, coupled with Alzheimer's disease, would render him confused about 'whether it was 1947 India or 1971 Pakistan or post 9/11 England'. Each of those places, similar in their perpetuation of his othering, Ahmed reveals, 'asked him the same questions: *What are you doing here? Do you belong here? Did you make a mistake in coming here?*' The last question ends up being his grandfather's final words to him.[17]

No man's land-ness is carried throughout *The Long Goodbye* in the form of intergenerational trauma stemming at Partition and manifesting through the years right up to the present day, as if having quietly occupied the body and descended its generations – a longing for a home that is made to no longer feel like home.

✍

'*EK TARAF HINDUSTAN*,' Azim sahib says, gesturing to one side, '*doosri taraf Pakistan*,' he adds, gesturing to the other, '*aur hum, ek kashti mein, un dono mulkon ke beech*.' He now brings both palms together to create the hull of a boat, a *kashti*, and suspends it mid-air.

At first, I cannot be sure whether he is speaking literally or figuratively. But when I look beside him, the expression on his son Hamza's face is solemn, as if to say: *this is how it happened, this is how my father fled from India to Pakistan*. It is this metaphor of the boat suspended between two banks that comes to define our conversation, as it has Azim sahib's life.

Abdul Azim was born in 1957 in Chinatown, Calcutta, ten years after Partition. He speaks to me now from Karachi, where he has lived since 1971. He is excited to talk to someone from India and immediately asks me, '*Apni ki Bangla bolen*?' To which I nervously reply, '*Ektu*, just a little bit.' Hamza explains to him that my ancestry comes from the Punjabi side, and to me that his father still speaks perfect Bengali. I am grateful to him for setting up this call, as conversations that include multiple generations of a family often reveal the unique and sometimes differing generational perspectives on Partition.

Hamza, born in 1995 in Karachi, begins our interview with his grandparents' story. 'I spent a significant part of my childhood with my grandmother, Sahleha, witnessing her memory fade with Alzheimer's disease. She was a Bengali Brahmin from Calcutta who fell in love with my grandfather, Abdul Rashid, an Arab trader and a seaman, and converted to Islam. They had different personalities but they were happy. It was only towards the end of her life, when the past and present became difficult to untangle, that she acknowledged it to be a controversial marriage. It had soured relations with her family, who were not in favour of the interfaith relationship.'

Making a note, I ask whether during Partition the couple remained in Calcutta.

'Oh yes,' Azim sahib now answers. 'At Partition, only my father's sister was married in Dhaka but everyone else stayed on. There was no violence around us, so there was no need to migrate. When I was born, Calcutta was lush and green, like a jungle with hardly any development. The people were wonderful: Hindu, Muslim, Chinese, all friends. We would go to the theatre and the circus; it was a good life. But danger came during the riots of 1964, *hungama hua, maar-kaat hui, dange-fasaad hue*, life became very difficult for us and we fled.'

'Are you sure you mean 1964 and not 1946?' I wonder if he is confusedly referring to the Great Calcutta Killings that took place in August 1946, but he shakes his head passionately.

'*Unnees sau chaunsath*,' he confirms so that I make no mistake, '1964.'

A BBC headline from 13 January 1964 reads 'Riots in Calcutta leave more than 100 dead'.[18] On reading the report further, I learn that this was the first incident of religious violence in the city since 1950, erupting due to the disappearance of a precious relic – believed to be a strand from the beard of Prophet Muhammad – from Hazratbal shrine in Srinagar. Anti-Hindu riots and violence broke out across East Pakistan, leading thousands of Hindus to arrive in India as refugees. The events further sparked attacks against Muslims in the rural areas of West Bengal, the violence then making its way to the cities. The report indicates that in Calcutta, along with the 100 people killed, over 7,000 were arrested and 438 injured. A twenty-four-hour curfew was extended to five areas of the city following arson attacks and the looting and destruction of Muslim property. By the end, over 70,000 Muslims fled their homes in the city and 55,000 were recorded to have been sleeping in the open, under police protection.[19]

In *The Shadow Lines*, Amitav Ghosh writes of this time:

It is evident from the newspapers that once the riots started, 'responsible opinion' in both India and East Pakistan reacted with an identical sense of horror and outrage ... [But] by the end of January 1964 the riots had faded away from the pages of newspapers, disappeared from the collective imagination of 'responsible opinion', vanished, without leaving a trace in the histories and bookshelves. They had dropped out of memory into a crater of a volcano of silence.[20]

While this may serve to indicate why the riots were not common knowledge, I wanted to know what exactly had happened to Azim sahib at the time. When I ask, the first thing he makes clear is that the migration of 1964 made his family Pakistani, while his mother's family remained in Calcutta, as Indians, where they live even now. Both he and Hamza have visited the family twice.

'I was young, only seven years old when we fled to Pakistan, so even if there was danger, how much can a child discern? There was a curfew in Calcutta, this I remember. We didn't have a phone, but a telegram came from my father's sister, who was married to a trader in Dhaka, asking us to come there. Walid sahib was travelling, but he somehow arranged for a broker to help my mother and all the children cross over, and he'd join us in East Pakistan. So, under the cover of darkness, in a boat, we and several other refugees travelled from Calcutta to Saat Khera at the border of East Pakistan, then to Jessore and, finally, to Dhaka.'

'To your aunt's home?'

He shakes his head. 'No, we hoped they'd give us shelter but we ended up at the Mirpur camp in Dhaka, where the kind of life we endured was unimaginable. In Calcutta, my father was a successful trader and we'd been well off, but in Dhaka the situation was different. We began our lives from scratch, the relatives we had relied on did not help, and in the camp we shared a tent with three other families. All the people around us had come from India at the same time. The environment was dirty and unsanitary and difficult to live in. It is how you imagine a camp to be, how they show it in films – one time you may get food and the next time you may not. Eventually, we rented a flat in Noakhali and found whatever work we could. The next year, the 1965 war between Pakistan and India happened, but our lives continued in the same way. Then, six years later, I had only just passed my matriculation exam when there was yet another war. At its end, East Pakistan was dissolved, Bangladesh was created, and the Urdu-speaking Muslims there had to flee yet again.'

Now Hamza says, 'I have heard stories about this time from my grandmother. She would tell me how so many of their friends and acquaintances were killed right before their eyes. Burnt alive sometimes, picked up and jailed, beaten, butchered, murdered. He will tell you.' He gestures to his father, but Azim sahib does not want to revisit the violence and is quiet for a few seconds. He need not say anything, though, for archives, reports and other interviews of the time have allowed me, to a certain extent, to imagine the scenes he would have witnessed. When he speaks again, it is to narrate the story of yet another boat, another journey, another migration.

'1971, *unnees sau ikahattar*. At 4 p.m. on 7 June our tickets were confirmed and we left at 11 a.m. the very next day. Everything was left behind in Dhaka except a single trunk full of belongings that we carried. My eldest sister was married in Dhaka, so she stayed behind. Another sister and brother were adopted by my aunt as she had no children of her own, so they were left behind. Only my parents, two siblings and I boarded a ship named *SHAMS* that dropped us in Karachi on 14 June.'

I am astonished that he remembers the details, and when I ask why, he replies without missing a beat, 'Because I have lived these moments. I have lived through war and fear and sorrow and hunger and poverty. I can still feel it under my skin, the fright and haste with which we fled. *Sab kuch chhod diya, sirf apni zindagi bachai.* We only escaped with our lives. I have lost many homes but I cannot forget their memories. I am telling you these things so you write about them, so there remains a record of what happened to the people' – with his forefinger, he gestures to my notebook – 'in their own words.'

'My grandmother said,' Hamza adds, 'that the agony of a life should always be written about. She insisted on remembering these stories, because though these moments brought her sadness, they were also moments that she had survived,' he sighs. 'Imagine, she left her whole family behind in India and migrated to East Pakistan, and then just years later she and my grandfather had to leave some of their children behind and migrate further to Pakistan. My father left behind his siblings. Now I keep thinking how it must feel to be separated from family permanently. When my aunt was dying in Bangladesh, my father could not get a visa to see her. Wars, borders, visa restrictions now prevent family, *siblings*, from meeting one another.

'I spent so much time with my grandmother that I feel her pain, her courage – *khandaan se jung, taksim ki jung, mulk ki jung, zinda rehne ke jung*, she survived the conflict with her family, the struggle during Partition, the war for nationhood, and simply to stay alive. At the end of her life, because of visa restrictions, she couldn't go back to see her family in Calcutta and that remained her deepest regret. On her deathbed, she would sing the ghazals of Jagjit Singh, listening to "*Woh Kaagaz Ki Kashti*" again and again, and everyone in my family could relate to her pain.'

As the boat, the *kashti*, is evoked yet again as a symbol, I begin to treat it as an heirloom passing down the generations of this family.

'She would weep while telling me stories about being a three-year-old in Calcutta. The lanes, the houses, her family, her friends. Due to her condition, her memory sort of became trapped in the period before Partition – before any riots or suffering or migrations.'

Azim sahib reaches out to hold his son's hand and, looking at me, says, '*Ek mulk se doosre mulk jana asaan nahi hota*, it is not easy to migrate from one country to another. More often than not, you remain suspended between places, making homes without ever making homes.'

'But you did make Pakistan your home eventually,' I say, 'Karachi became home.'

'Yes, we all worked very hard to start our life again in Pakistan. We sold anything we could to earn money, to eat. We suffered through poverty and learnt that one should never be ashamed to do any kind of work to support one's family. Eventually, I began work at a printing press, which is very labour-intensive.'

'My father suffered a lot because of the *muhajir* identity associated with refugees in Pakistan,' Hamza tells me. 'There was always discrimination, or issues with his passport or other documentation. Each time they would apply for any new identification in Pakistan, questions would be raised about their journey to Karachi, their time in East Pakistan and India, and all their papers would be scrutinized. My grandmother used to tell me that during the war, they had no time to collect papers because they were busy trying to save their lives. *Hum kaagaz nahi samet te the, hum jaan samet te the*, she used to say. Even when I applied for my first passport, the authorities asked about my grandparents' documents from East Pakistan. To claim identity remains difficult.'

'Well, what is your identity?' I ask them both.

'I am Muslim,' Azim sahib states simply, 'that's all, *bass*.'

Hamza chuckles, 'And to think that all the sadness in their life began due to communal sentiments. It was religion that made people believe that they couldn't live together. All over the world, where there is religion, there is difference. If only we fought for humanity the same way that we fight for religion.'

'And how do you identify?' I ask him.

'When I think about identity, I think many times before saying anything. *Apni pehchaan dilaane mein bhi sochna padta hai.* Do I derive my identity from my ancestors?' He looks at his father. 'Who *I* am is a part of who *he* is, and that is a part of who his parents were. This is my legacy, and I take enormous pride in calling myself a Calcuttan Bengali. I don't like the term *muhajir*; I don't want to be known as that. My family may have crossed many borders to arrive in Karachi but they will always remain Calcuttan Bengalis, and that is the identity I am proud to don.'

Azim sahib is looking at me, listening to us, and wiping the tears from his eyes.

Being in his presence reminds me of the years of interviews I conducted with witnesses of Partition. They would often speak without speaking, making it clear that some things could not be repeated or exhumed but only understood in their unspoken-ness. As I look at him, I find myself apologizing for bringing up a painful past.

He tells me that these are not tears of sadness. '*Aapne udaas nahi kiya, yeh baatein toh mere dil ke paas hi baithi rehti hain.* But sometimes, when I think back to those days, I feel scared. Then there is also the question of age – when we are young, we are able to endure more, struggle through more. But now, at this age, I feel anxious when I think about my childhood and everything we went through. *Allah Ta'ala woh din kisi ko na dikhae jo maine dekhe hain.* May God never bestow the days I have seen upon anyone; this is my only wish. People who talk about war and dominance with pride have not seen war. It is only destruction – of lives, homes, history and land. Common people's destruction, people like you and me. But I tell Hamza about this, I tell him all that I have endured and survived.'

Hamza nods. 'Survival is the most important lesson I have learnt from my family.'

Azim sahib now looks at me with renewed purpose. 'But you must write this in your book, *yeh zaroor likhna – ke hum na iss ghat ke hain, na uss ghat. Abhi tak hum kashti mein ghoom hi rahe hain.* We are from nowhere, belonging neither to this side nor to that, still adrift on the boat. Place to place, adopting the nationality of where our boat docks. *Jahan gaye, wahin pahan le li.*'

'There's no sense of true belonging,' Hamza echoes. 'He is stuck in no man's land.'

'AS A CHILD, I didn't like being Sindhi because everyone made fun of us,' the multidisciplinary artist Nina Sabnani, who was born in Ahmedabad in 1956, admits.* 'Growing up in Gujarat, there was a phrase I would hear often that terrified me: "If you come across a

---

* A short except from this interview, which focuses on the animated film *Mukand and Riaz* (2005), can be found in Chapter 7, 'Friendship'.

snake and a Sindhi, you should first deal with the Sindhi and then the snake." Can you imagine hearing this as a child? It both petrified and embarrassed me to a point where I never revealed my Sindhi identity to anyone.'

'You were born in the decade following Partition,' I note. 'Do you think the influx of refugees into the state had anything to do with this stigma?'

'Absolutely, that was one of the main reasons. Post Partition, refugees all over the country became competition to local businesses, whether they were Punjabis who came to Delhi or Sindhis who came to Gujarat. The added stigma here was that Hindu Sindhis migrated to India but Sindh remained in Pakistan. We had no land of our own, and someone without their own land or territory cannot be trusted – they are like nomads. It didn't matter whether I disclosed my identity or not, because my last name gave it away. So I hardly had any friends as a child because of the stigma attached to this identity.'

Nina tells me that she understood early on that both sides of her family had migrated from Sindh, and that Sindh was not a part of India. 'When I was five or six years old, we were living in the Gujarati town of Bharuch, by the river Narmada, and I went to a missionary school that children of all backgrounds and religions attended – Christians, Muslims, Hindus, even Burmese refugees. But the one common subject they all talked about was their native place. Even the *tonga-wallah*, Ibrahim chacha, who would take me to school and bring me home each day on his horse carriage, had a native place, a village, a *gaon*. So, early on, this difference set in – that we didn't have a native place, we didn't have a state.

'At school, everyone would ask me, "What is your native place?" And when I would say that I don't know my native place, they would tell me to ask my father *his* native place. My father would tell me that he used to be from Karachi, but after Partition he became from "here". So, what was my native place? It was the place where I was born. When I went back to school and told everyone that my native place is where I was born, they asked, "Were your parents born there?" No. "Were your siblings born there?" No. "Was your grandmother born there?" No. "So this cannot be your native place." They were not convinced. Once again, I asked my father, and he said Jaipur is where my grandmother lived and I used to live there with her for a while, so Jaipur could be my native place. Armed with this information, I went back to school and told my classmates that my native place was Jaipur. And they said that a native place couldn't be such a big city, so "*Kaunsa gaon hai tumhara*? What is the name of your village?" Then I just gave up on the whole thing. In a sense, that was the moment when I became a recluse and just enjoyed the company of my Enid Blyton books, which couldn't ask me stupid questions about my native place.' Nina exhales and reaches for her glass of water.

'Did your father think it was strange that you were asking such questions as a six-year-old?' I ask.

'He knew something was bothering me because I would tell him, "Look, so-and-so has a native place and so-and-so has gone to their village," but we didn't talk about this subject again for a long time after that.' She pauses to collect her thoughts.

'When I went to college in Baroda, I saw students from Bengal or Kerala or even Gujarat comfortably talking to one another in their mother tongues. But anytime two Sindhi students met, they preferred to speak in English or Hindi, and I found this distinction very peculiar. There were stereotypes attached to being Sindhi – flashy clothes, lots of jewellery. I was teased for my surname ... but never for my food. And that became a way to claim identity, even if one didn't have a native place,' she smiles.

'Sindhi *kadhi, saag, dal pakwan...*' I begin to list the dishes I know.

'Sindhi *mawa*, the milk cake,' Nina adds. 'Food became a means to start accepting myself, because my friends showed an interest in eating our food. Sindhi food was *ours*.' She holds her palm over her heart. 'After Partition, Sindhis migrated all over the world, which made us a people who adapted easily, who acclimatized to different places. We wore what everyone else wore, we spoke the languages of the cities we lived in, we folded ourselves into the everyday. But food, that was something we retained, we carried, we passed down. Sindhi food was *ours*.

'In college, I had a lovely teacher, Nasreen Mohamedi, who said that because her best friend was Sindhi, she considered herself half-Sindhi. And all of a sudden, I felt...' – she searches for the right word – 'I felt acknowledged. I was no longer embarrassed to speak my language. In fact, I even became interested in reading and writing Sindhi, and asked my father to teach me. He would say, "What will you do with the language? You won't be able to communicate with anyone but your parents and grandparents!" It was then that I asked whether it bothered him that we didn't have a state. That all of Sindh remained in Pakistan after Partition. That we, as Sindhis, were stateless.'

'What did he say?' I ask softly.

'He said that Gandhiji had called us world citizens. That we shouldn't allow ourselves to feel stateless, because he had called us world citizens.'

I gesture for her to go on.

'For a long time, I struggled to belong. But today, I have accepted it, because I think this association to land is too tenuous. It creates its own set of problems in people who are tied to their land. At least we are free of those problems.'

'But do you not think this means that so much has been lost?'

'Of course. For us, everything physical was lost – language, culture, home – because it was tied to land. Sindh was just a name on the map of a country I could never visit. But if I left it at that and found my own boundless territory as a world citizen, my land became the land of inherited memory. And that is a "space" that you can claim, create or even invent.'

If there is one thing that the acceptance of being stateless has infused into Nina's work as an artist, it is empathy. Using that as context, I now ask, 'In 2005, you made a film called *Mukand and Riaz* about your father's journey from Karachi to Bombay by ship, and the friendships he left behind. Have you ever made anything about your mother's journey?'

'For a long time, I focused only on my father's story, because he was more willing to talk about it. It's only in the last two years that I've interviewed and written about my mother significantly, because she finally spoke about what happened. But she never wants to go back to Sindh, never wants to return to Pakistan. Even as the second generation to live outside our homeland, I feel Partition to have been an enormous rupture. But, for her, there was deep, personal trauma attached to the larger, collective trauma. She was born in 1933 in Sukkur, and at the age of six she was adopted by her eldest uncle and aunt, whom she became very fond of. But at the age of thirteen and a week before the family migrated to India during Partition, she was "returned" to her biological parents, much to her confusion.[21]

'This loss of the couple whom she considered her parents is closely associated with that sudden and hasty departure from Sukkur. In the middle of the night, they drove to Jacobabad, from where at dawn, under a red and pink and orange sky, they flew to Ahmedabad in India. My mother had never been on a plane before that. From there, they took a train to Udaipur, travelled further to Jodhpur and, finally, settled in Jaipur. She remembers arriving and feeling very unwelcome – they were called *sharnarthis* and they spoke only Sindhi.'

'In India, would Kutchi be closest to the Sindhi language?'

'Kutch is the one place that has made me very conscious of my Sindhi identity,' Nina smiles. 'For some time, I worked with the artisans of Kutch, documenting their traditional art forms in a film called *Tanko Bole Chhe*, or The Stitches Speak. It was in the Banni district of Kutch that I could speak to people in Sindhi – or Kutchi-Sindhi, as they call it[22] – and for the first time feel any sort of community. I made another trip with my mother and it was as if the place just triggered memories in her. For so long she hadn't wanted to talk about Sindh, but here she told me it was the closest that we would ever get to *being in Sindh*. Kutch became the place where I began to inherit the memories of a homeland, and I find myself returning to it again and again, like a pilgrimage.'

While reading Rita Kothari's *Memories and Movements*, a fleeting sentence catches my eye:

Believe me, if I were to take you to any of the villages in rural Sindh, it would be exactly like Banni.[23]

Looking at Nina, I say, 'There is a sense of rootlessness in your words.'

'I cannot help that, it is natural,' she replies quietly, her palm resting on her chin. 'I recently wrote a paper titled "Roots in the Sky",[24] using the metaphor of the banyan tree, whose roots hang in the air. Because when there is no land for the roots to grow out of … when your land is … I mean, you are the outcome of a fractured history.'

'A fractured history,' I repeat.

She nods. 'And you have to make peace with that, otherwise you will always be upset with the outcome that history has dealt you. This is why Partition remains relevant to so many people – because there is no closure from that history. Until we have processed what it did to us as communities and nations, there will never be closure. And I return to roots because that is what continues to concern me. When you go to inner Rajasthan, for example, and you ask someone their name, they can rattle off seven generations, because that's the importance people from the subcontinent give to genealogy. But for those of us whose genealogies have been fractured by Partition…' She now meets my gaze as someone who shares this concern, this inaccessibility to family archives left on the other side. 'My father could not tell me the names of any of our ancestors past his grandfathers'. We don't have any documents, any physical history.

'And as far as Sindhis go,' she concludes, 'because there is no sense of territory to which identity may be tethered, memory becomes the only place where some form of anchoring is possible. These borders may disappear, new borders may be laid, but my memory will remain my certainty. As world citizens, we hold on to the invisible threads of memory.'

✑

IT WAS AFTER an interview in Lahore's Misri Shah that I first heard about the cross-border reading of letters on the radio. As I was leaving, my interviewee – who had migrated from Ludhiana to Lahore during Partition – had stood outside his home, his kurta fluttering in the warm September wind, his left hand waving goodbye. He used neither WhatsApp nor email, so I promised that I would write him a letter from Delhi to keep in touch. Laughing to reveal his missing teeth, he told me that he may never even receive it, for the transport of both goods and correspondence across the India–Pakistan border was sparse at the time.

'*Pehle zamane mein toh hum aapka khat radio pe hi sun lete,*' he had said, alluding to the fact that in the olden days he would have been able to hear my letter being read out on the radio. Though his response confused me, I did not think to ask him what he meant. But the comment remained at the back of my mind until years later when I came across a discoloured sheet of paper bearing a printed programme of the All India Radio (AIR) Urdu Service and realized that, at one point, letters from India used to be broadcast to listeners in West Pakistan, and vice versa.

Through the work of historian Isabel Huacuja Alonso, I learn that in the aftermath of the 1965 India–Pakistan war, the space of air waves began to function as an extraordinary no man's land. As negotiations for peace between the two warring nations proceeded at Tashkent, a thirty-minute radio service was inaugurated with the aim of providing updates on the political and diplomatic developments to both Indian and Pakistani listeners. However, what began as a brief news service had, by the end of 1966, blossomed into daily programming of nine hours, focusing mostly on entertainment. 'The AIR Urdu Service technically formed part of All India Radio's Exterior Service Division ... dedicated to broadcasting abroad, [and] received funding to broadcast to West Pakistan as one of India's foreign policy initiatives.'[25]

As I am introduced to the programme *Awaaz De Kahaan Hai*, hosted by Abdul Jabbar, my interviewee's fleeting comment suddenly makes sense. For thirty minutes – at first, once a week on Friday evenings, and, when the programme gained popularity, on Sunday evenings as well – Jabbar played songs from pre-Partition films and read out letters sent to him by Indians and Pakistanis. Born in a generation nurtured by technology, I admit I find it hard to imagine a time when contact was literally impossible. However, after nearly a decade of recording oral history interviews on both sides of the Radcliffe Line, I find Abdul Jabbar's efforts to be an elegant means to 'sustain aural ties across the increasingly impassable border'.[26] Often in Pakistan, when someone learnt that I had come from India, they would want to know about the cities and villages they grew up in, or whether I could help them track down childhood friends or neighbours. Similarly, in India, when someone learnt of my access to Pakistanis, they would approach me with similar requests. Despite the concreteness of the border, the firm establishment of nationality and the fighting of four wars, there remains – even seven and a half decades later – an innate and palpable desire to know about the other side.

The title of the programme, *Awaaz De Kahaan Hai*, can roughly be translated as 'Call out to me; where are you?' and is derived from one of Noor Jehan's most famous songs, '*Awaaz de kahaan hai, duniya meri jawaan hai*', roughly meaning 'Where are you, my world is still young', from the 1946 film *Anmol Ghari*. The title, chosen for its pre-Partition sentimentality, may also allude – in this context – to seeking out a voice perhaps in the far distance, perhaps even across a border. Transmitted from western India, the AIR Urdu Service could be heard across West Pakistan and throughout north India, up to the states of Uttar Pradesh and Bihar. But it is not surprising to learn that the programmes were most popular among the Punjabi and *muhajir* communities, those which had been most impacted by Partition on the western border – like the gentleman from Misri Shah.

With restrictions on travel and communication in the wake of the war, the radio became a way of remaining in touch, so to speak, with family, friends and even strangers. Listeners would write letters to the host, asking him to either play a beloved song and narrate a memory associated with it, or simply read out their letter on air.

These requests would be sent out through transmissions, flooding out of thousands of radio sets on the other side, to people who may, at times, be inspired to respond through that very same medium. Abdul Jabbar was particular to play only pre-Partition songs, sometimes going to great lengths to obtain their records, in order to preserve the essence of an undivided land.

A listener once wrote in asking about the mango orchards in the village where he was born in India, and a few months later a response was read out confirming that not only were the mango orchards still there but the fruit was just as delicious as it was before Partition.[27] For those who had carried memories of places with them, places that they were never able to see or return to after Partition, the exchange on this programme also became a way of retaining some form of ownership or memory of an erstwhile home.

It is in this sense that I consider *Awaaz De Kahaan Hai* an intimate and aural extension of the no man's land between India and Pakistan. Often, in the last few years, I have imagined sound waves floating across one sky and reaching another, and in the process never once touching any ground, surpassing all conventional formalities of passport, visa and inquiry, in order to restore a memory from someone else's past. Sometimes I wonder whether such a programme will ever be possible again, because I do not know if my letter ever reached Misri Shah.

18
Pain

꩜

'**P**ARTITION WAS A BEDTIME story,' Sumedha Mahajan* says. 'I was only four or five years old when my nana, Krishan Lal Gupta, began narrating how he left his home in Mirpur and fled to India, and this continued till the end of his life. Each time he told this story, something new was added and another layer would unfold.'

'That's quite a young age to have been made aware about Partition,' I remark.

She smiles. 'It never began with the violence or horror, which paints almost every Mirpuri story.'

I meet Sumedha in the autumn of 2018, when she is twenty-three years old, and she invites me to spend some time in Jammu to listen to the stories of Hindus and Sikhs who had, in the months following Partition, fled the areas of Kashmir that now fall across the border – Mirpur, Kotli, Dadyal, Muzzafarabad, Bhimber. The accounts of these areas can only be described as unspeakable and as such have remained largely undocumented in official archives. In a very short span of time, together we record stories of violence, abduction, rape, murder, immolation, sacrifice, starvation, separation, flight, migration, poverty, rehabilitation and reunion – sometimes all in the same family. We listen to un-confrontable memories that are often being uttered for the very first time. I take pages of notes and hours'

---

* Sumedha is also mentioned in Chapter 14, 'Memory'.

worth of audio recordings that I cannot bear to listen to again or transcribe until a whole year later. The stories of the region swallow me into their sorrow.

But in the time that Sumedha and I spend together in Jammu, I deduce that even in its second-handedness, the pain of Partition is visceral and deeply rooted. I feel it in the way that she not just interacts with our interviewees but also accepts their histories as hers. This pain is not a wound that one can touch, or an abrasion that eventually heals, but is imprinted in memory. This memory can be dulled with time but can never quite be forgotten, and is certainly passed down even through silence.

'The way my nana told stories,' Sumedha continues, 'made me envision Mirpur. It was so vivid – like reading a book. I could imagine his house, and his father and grandfather, who used to deal in gold and jewellery. And as I grew older, the stories inched closer to Partition. I would have been in Grade 9 or 10 when I first learnt about what happened to them. My great-grandfather had given my nana some money, maybe Rs 500, a very large sum at the time, and told him to keep it safe. "*Ise sambhal ke rakhna,*" I clearly remember him saying. Merely days later, the massacres in Mirpur happened and his father was slaughtered right before his eyes.'

She takes me back to the days of Partition, narrating how in August 1947 Mirpur district was peaceful, as it fell under the erstwhile princely state of Jammu and Kashmir, controlled by the Dogra king Maharaja Hari Singh. The population of Hindus and Sikhs in the district amounted to about 20 per cent, but it surged after refugees from west Punjab began fleeing to the state, seeking shelter. However, it was only after the state's accession to India that violence in Mirpur began, around 25 November 1947,[1] when tribal forces, known locally as Kabailis, occupied the area. They murdered thousands of Hindus and Sikhs at sight and the remainder were marched to and imprisoned in a concentration camp set up at the Alibeg gurudwara.[2]

'I think that single memory of my nana's father being slaughtered in front of him was enough to tell me how violent it truly was.[3]

Women were being raped and abducted in plain sight. His mother and sister fled with another group, and his sister tried to jump in a well to save herself, but it was already so full of bodies that she had to climb back out,' she exhales. 'My nana and his two younger brothers were separated from everyone, and one of the brothers was quite sick. Someone told him to just leave the brother behind and carry on, save himself. Each time he told this story, I could sense the desperation in his voice – how could he leave a brother behind? And so he carried him on his back the entire way until they found shelter. They were eventually reunited with their mother and sister at a refugee camp and then sought refuge at a relative's house in Jammu.[4] They were then reunited with their eldest brother, who became akin to a father figure.[*] There was much respect amongst the siblings, and they remained close until the end.'

'All four of your grandparents come from Mirpur,' I remark. 'Have the stories from the region formed your understanding of Partition?'

'Though my nani is from Mirpur, her father was in the army – he passed away in an accident – and they were already posted on the Indian side when Partition happened. My dada and dadi, whom you have met, have their own stories of the exodus.' As she speaks, I can feel the melancholy fill the empty space between us. 'Sometimes I think that because all of my grandparents have shared a very similar past, I have accumulated four times the pain. With my paternal grandparents, I think it was very clear ever since I was young that this was a memory that wasn't meant to be opened up or discussed at length. To be honest, it was only when you spoke with them that I learnt in detail about the things that had happened. And it was after that that the conversations began at home.'

During our interview, her dada, Sant Kumar Gupta, who was seven years old in 1947, spoke with exceptional clarity about the events of 25 November. Around 11 a.m., he and his brother had been

---

[*] The story of this brother is narrated by Sumedha's mother, Seema Gupta, in Chapter 21, 'Separation and Reunion'.

soaking the winter sun on the roof of their three-storeyed home when they heard screams from below, telling them to run, that the Kabailis had arrived. Barefoot and in the clothes they had on, without picking up anything from their home, they dodged the raining bullets and ran to a camp on the outskirts of the main city and remained sheltered there until the day had set. But the firing began as soon as they tried to run again. So, along with some 600 other people, they crawled on the cold, wet winter ground until they reached an abandoned village where they were finally able to find some kernels of corn and satiate their hunger.

On the second day of their journey, Sumedha's great-grandfather, who had been holding his youngest child for forty-eight hours straight, set the crying infant down on the ground and walked away. Many people left their children behind, placing large stones on their chests so they could not move, even burying them alive. So, the father, momentarily devoid of energy and reason, walked away from his child. But thankfully his eldest son managed to find the child and carried him all the way till Jhangar, a village that now falls on the Line of Control in Nowshera, Jammu. Sant Kumar Gupta spoke about their rehabilitation in Jammu and how unwelcome the residents had made Mirpuri Kashmiris feel in those early years. They were shown no respect, and the only people who helped them were other Mirpuris who had already established themselves in Jammu. '*Humare apne log*,' he said – our own people.

Upon learning that I would be coming to interview them, Sumedha's dadi, Kuntal Gupta, told her that she did not think she could speak about Mirpur. She did not have the words. And so, that afternoon she mostly insisted that what was done was done, '*ab khatam ho gayi baat*,' that there was no need to relive the horrors. Instead, she spoke about claims and compensations post migration, and how many rooms the house they were eventually allotted had. But, between themselves, the couple had talked about 1947, for though she did not wish to speak about it herself, she listened as her husband narrated on her behalf, nodding gently now and then, gaze downcast. He told us that after the attack in Mirpur, her mother was taken to a camp somewhere deep inside Pakistan and only returned to India in a population exchange in 1948. Her grandmother was taken to the Alibeg concentration camp and retrieved by the International Committee of the Red Cross six months later. The only remark Kuntal Gupta made that day was that for the remainder of their lives, neither her mother nor her grandmother talked about what had happened to them in those months.

When we met her elder brother, Krishan Kumar Gupta, a few days later, he filled in the gaps in his sister's story. At Partition, he was twelve years old and she was seven. He showed us a scrapbook he kept about Mirpur – photographs and newspaper clippings he had collected over the years, memories from his childhood he had written down. Recalling how they had run from roof to roof, trying to hide from the firing, he told us that a bullet nearly shot off his right ear. 'Now that you are asking me about it,' he said to Sumedha and me, 'I feel that my soul wants to cry.' I wondered then how Sumedha would have felt listening to her grandmother's history in this way, for each time her granduncle spoke, he looked directly at her.

He recalled how their father, an advocate, and two uncles were hacked to death with an axe, and how because he and his sister were the only ones alive, he did not let go of her arm for the entirety of their three-day march from Mirpur to Jhangar. He described in detail how they had worn the same clothes and had neither eaten nor drunk anything during the journey. And all the while as he walked, he kept count of the number of family members they had lost in a single day. Seven. 'You tell me who I can blame for what happened,' he said to us, the pain emanating from both his voice as well as his gestures as he held his scrapbook to his heart. He wanted to remember the good part, but all he remembered was this.

At the end of our conversation he told us that he had written out his last will, and when he died he wanted no tears or Hindu rituals, just a celebration of his life from undivided India until then. Then, trailing his hand as if to show the tributary of a winding river, he said, 'But most of all, I want my ashes to be submerged in the Chenab river at Akhnoor, from where they will flow westward, back to Mirpur, across this border to the place where I was born.'

These are the conversations that have bound Sumedha to the geography of Mirpur, and me to her over the years. Since then, she has been recording the stories of other Mirpuri families in Jammu. I ask her about how these stories have influenced her life.

'It was my nana's stories that initially shaped me,' she admits. 'The power of his words and the resilience of his actions – that even after everything is finished, even when you have nothing, not even family, you must find the courage to go on and make something of your life. I used to feel very helpless that I couldn't do anything to lessen their pain. I began feeling this particularly after he died in 2018 – just months before you and I met, actually. He passed away on 28 January, and on 3 February, what would have been his birthday, we immersed his ashes in the Chenab river so that life could come full circle and they could find their way back to Mirpur.'

'Like your dadi's brother,' I remark.

'Yes, despite whatever horrors they endured, they do feel like a part of them still belongs there,' she agrees. 'After my nana died, I realized the impact that his stories had had on me. Because he was no longer there, I felt a greater responsibility towards them. I wanted to create awareness about what happened in Mirpur, particularly so that the younger generations of Mirpuri families understand the sacrifices made for us to be where we are today.

'To be completely honest, I don't think I can ever understand the loss or pain that any of my grandparents felt. And so, all I can do is try to empathize, because some things will always remain inaccessible to me. For instance, with my dadi, there is so much she has never said, and yet I understand just how painful it is to even evoke the past in memory, let alone utter the words out loud.'

'There is so much to say about Partition, yet there are so few words.' I smile sadly.

'But not all things need to be said, some only need to be felt.' Sumedha smiles in response.

⁓

ON THE SAME trip, a passing comment from one of my eyewitness interviewees leads me to the events that occurred in Jammu in September 1947. But rather than refugees migrating *to* Jammu, it is the opposite journey that he reports. A teenage scout at the time of Partition, he tells me how he had been asked to peacefully patrol the Kathua border as lakhs of Muslims fled westwards to Pakistan from Jammu. When his son retorts that he has never heard of a Muslim majority in the city, his father recalls how the violence after Partition turned the district from a 'Mohammedan majority to a minority'.

When I return to Delhi, I read more on the subject. In the 1941 census of India, Jammu province is shown to be 61.19 per cent Muslim, 37.19 per cent Hindu and 1.41 per cent Sikh.[5] But as the word 'massacre' begins to appear over and over in my research, I realize that, much like Mirpur, the carnage in Jammu too has been forgotten in public discourse, but not in individual people's memories. Christopher Snedden, the Australian political scientist and author of several books on the region, writes that 'the massacre appears to have slipped through the cracks of subcontinental history, overshadowed by the communal slaughter in neighbouring Punjab around the same time'.[6] Ian Stephens, the journalist and editor of *The Statesman* newspaper from 1942 to 1951, writes in *Pakistan*:

> ...in the Jammu province ... within a period of about eleven weeks starting in August, systematic savageries, similar to those already launched in East Punjab and in Patiala and Kapurthala, practically eliminated the entire Muslim element in the population, amounting to 500,000 people. About 200,000 just disappeared, remaining untraceable, having presumably been butchered, or died from epidemics. The rest fled destitute to West Punjab.[7]

Several months later, I speak with Maira Qadir, born in 1978 and raised in Dubai. Both sides of her family migrated from Jammu to Jhelum in the months following Partition. One evening after work, she sets up a video call so that her mother, Noshina Rohi, born in the mid-1950s, can tell me of the memories she has inherited of this migration.

'My paternal grandfather used to work for the maharaja,' Noshina begins from the earliest stories of her family's position in Jammu. 'He was educated, could speak English and worked as the motor mechanic for the royal household. Sometimes when the maharaja would go to Jhelum to hunt, my grandfather would accompany him and became familiar with the lands.

'The family lived in a predominantly Hindu area and my grandmother tells me that theirs was one of the few Muslim houses. The mohalla was called Darbargarh, Raje di Mandi, and was in the heart of the old walled city, overlooking the Tawi river. It used to be across one of the gates of the Mubarak Mandi palace, the old residence of the maharaja. So, when news of Partition riots arrived in the area, my tayaji, my father's elder brother, who was twenty-two years old at the time, was told by his Hindu friends that they should make provisions to leave Jammu. Of course, they did not want to, *koi nahi chahta apni zameen chhod ke jana*, and so they stayed on as long as they could. My father-in-law, who was thirty years old, is my father's second cousin, and lived in proximity to them. The entire extended family was forced to leave once the situation became unliveable.[8]

'At the time, trains and buses were organized by the state to take refugees to Pakistan,[9] but there was no guarantee that the people would reach their destination safely. I was often told by my elders that when these vehicles returned to Jammu, they would have to be hosed down with water, and even after that the interior would remain painted in the light pink residue of blood.'

Upon hearing this detail, Maira, who is quietly listening, closes her eyes and shudders.

Breathing deeply, her mother continues, 'Naturally, people were very worried because it was becoming difficult to remain in Jammu. Every day the family would receive news of fresh violence against Muslims, how complete mohallas had been slaughtered.[10] So, the elders decided that each bus sent across to Pakistan would be guarded by a young, able-bodied man. He would drop the refugees across the border and return for the next lot, confirming that people had reached safely. My father-in-law tells me that both he and my taya did this duty. But soon *they* started to be targeted.'

Here, I interrupt, 'Targeted by whom?'

'Hindu, Sikh – at the time we didn't know who ... but my father-in-law was certain that they wouldn't be spared. They were making trips back and forth, making sure people got to the other side safely. With dread, he would think, "*Ab yeh nahi chhodenge hume*, now they will not leave us." So, on one of the trips, he decided to stay back in Pakistan and tried to convince my taya to stay too. Holding on to his arm, he told him not to leave, that it didn't feel safe. But my taya was fearless, he had dismantled a gun and tied it to his leg. My father-in-law asked how he would assemble it in time to protect himself, but my taya told him, "Bhai-jaan, you go on, I'll get the next batch of people and meet you on the other side." But he never did.' Noshina looks away sadly. 'That was the last time anyone saw him.'

'Ammi, tell her how he looked, tell her what you were told about him,' Maira prompts her mother.

Noshina smiles. '*Humne toh kabhi nahi dekha Shareef taya ko*, I have never seen him, but when my son was born, I couldn't tell whom he looked like. He was extremely fair and had blonde hair. My father-in-law took one look at him and said that he looked exactly like my uncle Shareef.'

I lean back in my chair and sigh. 'How did you feel when you heard that?'

There is a long silence before she speaks again.

'It felt surreal to feel his presence in that way, in *some* way, but the loss...' Her voice trails off and she is overcome with emotion. She tries to find the words but cannot. And so Maira intervenes, 'Whenever the family speaks about Shareef taya, it is still very emotional. Neither my mother nor I have ever met him, but somehow we understand and relate to the pain of losing him.'

'Maira, when did you first hear these stories?'

'I've been lucky to know both my mother's father and her grandmother in my lifetime,' she smiles. 'I would have been ten years old, maybe, when I heard about Jammu, sitting on a *charpai* on the roof with my nana. *Yeh sab unki zubani suna hai maine*, I have heard all these stories from him. He would tell me about how brave and honest his elder brother was, how everyone trusted him, and how all the jewels and valuables had been given to him for safekeeping. Everyone thought that whether or not they reached, Shareef would reach the other side.

'For eight to ten years, my nana and his mother were certain that Shareef taya would return. They would hear stories of people showing up years after Partition, finding their way back to their families somehow. They had hope. But then something happened, and they stopped waiting, accepting that he would never return. My great-grandmother had a dream one night where she saw her son, Shareef, floating in a river, and she took it as a sign. He had now passed on to the other side; there was no use hoping, *ab ummeed karna bekaar tha.*'

Maira takes off her glasses and wipes them clean. Her mother's face has turned pink from sadness. I look at them as they hold one another.

'We still feel for the suffering our family has endured,' Noshina says quietly. 'How they had to leave everything behind so suddenly, flee from Jammu to Pakistan, lose family...'

'Actually, the deepest is the pain for the family that Partition took away, the family that we never got to meet,' Maira adds. 'And ours is not the only family that endured this, it happened to so many people in so many unthinkable ways. Ammi tells me about her aunt whose daughter was very young at the time, an infant, and how she was constantly worried that Sikhs would abduct the baby. She was migrating in a big group, and she found out that a couple in that group had drowned their baby in the Tawi river because of this fear of abduction. Imagine that.' She sighs deeply and then continues, 'I have been born and raised in Dubai, I never lived in Pakistan and I have never been to India, but there is a pain I feel for what *could have been*. And now when I see the situation in Jammu and Kashmir on both sides of the border, you can trace all that sadness, all that violence, all the unrest directly back to Partition. The situation is not the same as in Punjab or Bengal, where things did eventually normalize. But in Jammu and Kashmir, the tremors of Partition are being felt even today.'

I nod and, looking at my research notes, ask, 'Due to Jammu's proximity to Sialkot, it is recorded that many Hindus and Sikhs migrated to Jammu and Muslims to Sialkot.[11] Is that where your family went as well?'

Maira confirms this with her mother. 'Once in Pakistan, they first stayed in a camp, either Suchetgarh or Dalowaali, near the Sialkot border for two or three months. Then they stayed in Sialkot city with relatives in Kashmiri mohalla, and then moved to Jhelum, as Ammi's grandfather knew the area well. Approximately ninety *marlas** of land was allotted to them in Darapur village, but they chose to continue living in Jhelum city.'

Noshina adds to the story, 'In Jammu, my father was in his first year at Prince of Wales College, which became Gandhi Memorial College after Partition, but he had to begin work once he came to Pakistan. He was employed by the claims department, but chose never to put a claim for his own property left on the other side. That is how certain he was that they would return to Jammu, or Jammu would somehow become a part of Pakistan. "*Humne idhar hamesha thodi na rehna hai,*" he would say, claiming that they wouldn't remain in Jhelum forever. It was only a few years later, when they were living in a very run-down house, that they conceded to the fact that Partition was permanent, and Jammu had been left behind. They were eventually allotted a house on Railway Road, Jhelum.'

She now looks at me. '*Hindu aur Sikho ke saath bhi aisa hi hua hoga, na?* Hindus and Sikhs who had to leave their homes in Pakistan and thought that they would eventually go back … but never could.'

---

* The *marla* is a traditional unit of area that is used in India, Pakistan and Bangladesh. Under the British Raj, it was exactly one-160th of an acre.

I nod wordlessly, for not one of my grandparents could ever go back to their home towns.

'My nana was alive until 2018,' Maira says, 'and he remembered everything about Jammu – every road, every mohalla, every bazaar. He could see the city in front of his eyes. Now, as the third generation, I'm still connecting all the dots, but the connection to land is certainly there.'

'Do you feel a sense of belonging to Jammu?' I ask them both.

'Whatever my elders felt, I feel the same,' Noshina says. 'Jammu was their homeland, they had been born and buried there and longed for it deeply after Partition. This is how I feel too – there is familiarity with a city that I have never been to.'

Maira nods. 'Both my nana and father have now passed, but while they were alive, they always said that they would want to visit Jammu if they could. "*Kabhi border pe halaat achhe hue toh ek baar wapas zaroor jaake dekhenge.*"'

Noshina sniffles. '*Ab bas*. Thinking about Partition makes me sad.'

'But Ammi, it's okay to be sad,' Maira tells her, 'otherwise we won't remember. We must keep this hurt alive, so we can make sure no one ever feels it again. And hurt doesn't see Muslim or Hindu, Indian or Pakistani, it feels the same to everyone whose families witnessed Partition.'

'I'M QUITE AMAZED at how much I already want to tell you,' Prarna Mansukhani admits when we first speak. 'Never has anyone ever asked me about Partition, especially someone my own age, just wanting to listen. In South Asian cultures – particularly within immigrant families like mine – we so rarely focus on the individual. With regards to Partition, I've had to dig for information, even within the family, and it's taken a while to come to terms with the frustration of not having the tools to understand my own history. So, I don't know how much of what I say will be useful to you. I did not live through Partition after all.'

'All the more reason why we must try to understand how and why it affects you,' I offer.

Prarna sips her tea and then places the cup on the counter. She takes a deep breath and then begins, 'It feels like each time I open a door, three hundred more doors appear, and I'm shocked to learn how little we've been told about our history. I am 100 per cent Sindhi; both sets of my grandparents came from Sindh – Karachi and Hyderabad – to Bombay during Partition. When my father emigrated to the States in the late '70s, it was only a matter of years before he brought his parents over as well. I live in New York City at the moment but I was born in Chicago and grew up with my paternal grandparents in the same house. My grandfather passed away when I was seven or eight, but my grandmother, whom we called bhabhi, was alive until I was seventeen. She was like a second mother to me.

'The knowledge that I was Sindhi was instilled in me from a very young age. We were part of a big Indian community in Chicago, and at the community events, everyone would say what they were – Punjabi, Bengali, Gujarati – and I would unquestionably say that I was Sindhi.'

'At that age,' I ask her, 'were you aware that there were Pakistani Sindhis as well?'

She smiles sadly. 'I never knew that until I was an adult, actually. But I did begin asking my grandmother questions from a very young age. I must have been six or seven years old when I met a Native American person in school, and she impressed upon me the importance of understanding our grandparents' stories. Immediately, I began engaging with my grandmother about her life, and the first thing she spoke about was Partition. I don't remember what I would have asked, but growing up with my grandmother was the most special experience – it makes me emotional just thinking about it and her life.'

'How do you mean?'

'I think it was the starkness between her and the way she was living – the clothes, the language, even the food – which was in contrast to the outside world. I grew up in a predominantly white neighbourhood, where people were mostly from the Midwest. So, I was constantly computing the differences between my home life and outside life, code-switching, maintaining two different personalities. I think, for many immigrants, it is difficult to enmesh both parts of yourself – the land you have left and the land you have adopted – and there are two very distinct extremes of either owning all of your differences with pride or erasing them altogether. But it is complicated, and in navigating all of this our own history was not addressed growing up at all.'

'So, you would speak to your grandmother not only about the world she had left behind but also a world before that – a pre-Partition world,' I remark.

'Exactly, yes. She would speak in Sindhi and I would answer in English, and we would mostly understand one another,' Prarna laughs. 'My first memory of our conversations is that her family was on the docks, waiting. They had roots in Hyderabad but at some point had moved to Karachi. My grandmother was in her twenties and was the eldest of ten siblings – the youngest was probably three or four. Their mother had passed away, so she had assumed a maternal role and was very much the caretaker of all the children. I remember her telling me that they had to leave very suddenly and with little planning, and found themselves on the docks in Karachi trying to take a boat or a ship to Bombay, but there were none. So, they had to wait for three or four nights – they basically lived and slept on the docks.

'But then one night, one of her teenage sisters got her period for the first time. The family had carried bed sheets; I think they'd carried very few things and bed sheets were among them. And she remembered ripping up the bed sheets and creating cloth pads for her sister, right on the docks.'

I am struck by this nuanced recollection and I wonder what a young Prarna would have made of it.

'Honestly, I think it was exhilarating to see a different side of my grandmother. I think that there is always a bit of shame tied to the first-generation immigrant experience, mostly because there is so much sacrifice attached to it. And the way that sacrifice is represented is that it was done in order to give *you* a better life. As a result, I was always aware of these sacrifices and nervous that I may not be able to live up to them. But then, at the same time, I loved listening to these stories of my grandmother from when she was this other, younger person. This woman who had seen so much in her lifetime. She talked a lot but hardly about herself, so these conversations between us, where she was reflecting on the past, became even more precious.'

Prarna's tone becomes suddenly serious. 'I learnt really young that you have to keep asking questions and only then may you find something beautiful.'

'Did your parents ever speak about Partition?'

'Almost never. They were both born in the decade after Partition, and there was a lot of shutting down of the subject. My mother is so resistant to the fact that Partition could have caused any pain in the family; it's almost like a denial of its impact. But even my grandmother would only talk about it when I'd ask her.' Prarna uses her words very carefully here, as if she has already thought in depth about how she feels and has tried to untangle her way through it. She is particular to not generalize the consequences of Partition but speaks about her own unique bequeathment. 'There were two things – one was how there were almost no words to describe the experience of uprootedness, but even as a child I was aware of how poignant it was. So, the dissonance between the significance of the experience versus how much it was being spoken about was very evident. I learnt to characterize that as definitive of trauma. The second thing was that either because I am a creative person or a deep feeler, I could sense, almost viscerally, how much was still unresolved. I could feel it in my body, like a physical pain.

'And then' – she moves her hands as if descending a flight of stairs – 'the way the memory of Partition translated for my parents' generation was through hatred. My father was part of the RSS growing up – and this is something that I am still learning to grapple with – and he went to the camps and developed a very strong

Hindu national identity. He was angry but didn't have the tools to understand or address that anger.'

'What was he angry about?'

'His family came to Bombay from Hyderabad in Sindh and they lost everything they had. A home, wealth, even career. My grandfather decided to become a tradesperson and was employed as a mechanic for Indian Airlines. But the family struggled financially for many, many years. He grew up in a joint family that lived in a one-bedroom home on the campus housing of the airport. I realize that this is such a typical story, I'm sure you hear it a lot,' she interrupts herself, but I encourage her to continue.

'Every night the family would eat dinner, clean up the surface of the table, lay down a blanket, and my father would literally sleep on the kitchen table, which served as a makeshift bed, until he was a teenager. So, he has a lot of anger about his family's situation. I think he feels some sense of victimhood about that, and anger towards Pakistan and Pakistani people for, I guess, putting their family in that situation. It really breaks my heart that one can feel so much belated anger for a group of people who also may have similarly lost their land and home. But this is also quite typical of a lot of Hindu Sindhis, because the entirety of their land remained in Pakistan. So, we were suddenly people *without* a homeland, without *any* connection to *any* land.'

'And when you lose the connection to your land, everything associated with it is also slowly lost,' I echo the thought that many other interviewees have stressed on.

'Right,' she agrees, her eyes wide, 'and this concept of being disenfranchised from one's land did not settle in me until very recently. My entire family, both grandparents and all of our extended relatives, are Sindhi, and they are always moving forward, wanting to achieve more, trying to stabilize their lives. No one is looking back, maybe because it's too painful. The severance from your land, or the inability to return to a place that was once yours, has driven the community to constantly look ahead. I never understood this until recently.'

My pen races across the page, trying to note down everything she is saying, for these post-Partition behaviours can be seen in the displaced population throughout the subcontinent. The story of Partition is too often thrust into the comfort of longing for a home left behind, but the spectrum of emotions manifested consequentially was vast and included – as in the case of Prarna's parents – both anger and denial.

I now clear my throat. 'You mentioned earlier that you're still trying to grapple with your father's past in the RSS. Is that something you want to talk about?'

She thinks about this for a few seconds and then says, 'I have difficulty explaining it to people who don't necessarily understand its history or context, and only know of the RSS through its present iteration. But at the same time, *I* too am trying to understand more every single day. It is a huge part of my father's identity, there is so much pride when he speaks about it. When I began asking questions at home, I was always looking for more than just the mantras of moving forward or accumulating wealth or stability, and the only other stories he told were of his days in the RSS. In his childhood, his father sent him to the Sangha Shiksha Varga camps, where he did levels one to three,[12] and I got the impression that it was a way to build a Hindu identity as a Sindhi person. They wanted to rebuild community in independent India, and so both of my grandfathers were also members.

'It's been a very difficult journey to understand the history of my family, because while I'm uncovering the pain, I also see the resilience, and have compassion for people like my grandfathers or my father. I have such a deep connection to my father. But on the other hand, even though he is no longer actively involved with the RSS, I cannot help but think about the evolution of the organization and the things associated with it today. And I don't want to speak for my family, but the impression I got was that it provided some sense of belonging or identity at the time. So, it's not quite as black or white, and there's a lot of complexity. And, well … we weren't there at the time.' Her voice is quiet.

I nod my head slowly. 'Of course,' I say, acutely aware of being let into a very intimate part of her life.

'You see, even though my father did not witness Partition, he has a sense that something was taken from him,' she says thoughtfully. 'No one in my family thinks Partition was a good thing. I remember my grandmother used to maintain how their neighbours were Muslims, and their friends were Muslims, and they all lived as one people. Another piece to their story was that before they even made it to the docks, it became very unsafe for them to remain in their home, and so they stayed with their Muslim neighbours, who were like their family friends. My grandmother remembers wearing her neighbour's burqa, because there were police raids where they'd come inside and check all the homes.'

After a few seconds, she adds, 'My grandparents never carried any hate or anger; all they spoke about was how much they had to be grateful for. I attribute anger to the second generation.'

'And what about you, as the third generation?' I ask, curious.

'I have been trying to put this into words recently, and I think what I feel is a kind of pain. But I'm trying to say this the right way...'

She picks up her cup of tea once again and sips from it pensively.

Speaking from experience, I say, 'There may not be a right way to say it, though. We want to give words to this feeling and we want those words to be precise and complete so that others don't misunderstand our inherited emotions. But, unfortunately, we may never get there – the feelings towards an incomprehensible event like Partition *are not* and *cannot* be one dimensional. And they may also change depending on the stories you hear. So, there may not be a right way to say how you feel.'

She laughs sadly, cupping her face with her palms. 'Yes, that's true. Let me try then. So, while I was growing up, 100 per cent of my family's focus was on education and career – do well in school, go to college, go to graduate school, get married, make money, have a career in the sciences or engineering. Those were the only things anyone cared about, talked about, elevated or celebrated. But there was a whole other side to life that had been silenced. I know that I never experienced Partition like my grandparents, or faced the postcolonial fallout like my parents. I didn't have the personal experience of running away from something or towards something, but I found myself caught up in the momentum of everybody else running. And that was very painful because I felt like I could never really show up in my full humanity – if you only confront part of your life, part of your history, then it only allows for a part of your humanity to be expressed or explored. And the pain I feel is of not being able to show up as a full person.

'But it wasn't until I was an adult, in the last few years, that I was really able to piece together my history and see why this running is occurring. They are running *away* from the pain. And though I cannot feel the same pain they are feeling, what is passed down to me is a different kind of pain – of silence, of hidden history. It is in the undercurrent of everything. We are told not to question anything, not to dig up old wounds. But how else will we learn if not by asking questions; there are so few sources documenting individual experiences from Partition.' She exhales deeply, as if deflated. Her tone is now part frustrated, part helpless. 'Do you know that I only recently learnt the etymology of the word Hindustan, and how it's derived from the word Sindh, or Sindhu, meaning river?'[13]

I nod in response.

'Sometimes I talk to my husband about Partition' – she gestures to the room where he is – 'but it didn't impact his family. They come from a small village near Hyderabad in Telangana, and he has a sense of rootedness there. His paternal family had been farming on the same land, decreed to them by a king, for over 500 years. He sometimes says that he sees his village in his mind's eye before he wakes up in the morning, and has a deep connection with that land. I always feel so envious of him, because I can't even go back to where I'm from.'

'Where *are* you from?' I ask.

'Well, I grew up in Chicago...' she begins and then pauses. 'Wait, do you mean like a broader question?' She draws her hands apart, as if holding an invisible globe between them.

I shrug.

'My parents grew up in Bombay...' she continues.

'Has there ever been a time when you told someone that you are from Sindh?' I ask with a smile.

She laughs. 'I'm definitely building the confidence towards that, but with my friends I do always emphasize that I'm 100 per cent Sindhi.'

'But is saying you're Sindhi the same thing as saying you're from Sindh?' I ask, my smile broadening.

She is taken aback, part surprised, part amused, and mirrors my smile. 'You're right!'

'Sindhi is an identity that can be cultivated anywhere in the world; Sindh is one place on a map...'

'And you can't ever feel close to a land unless you wholly embrace it,' Prarna completes my thought.

As I begin to pack away my notebook and recorder, Prarna tells me that some day she wants to take a trip with her husband to visit the two Hyderabads – the first in Pakistan, where her family comes from, and the second in India, where his does. Because of the complicated visa process, she is unsure whether she will ever get to stand on the land where her ancestors once stood, but this will not stop her from trying.

Contemplatively, then, she leaves me with these words: 'Sindh is all but lost to us now. Its landscape, language, culture and craft all feel so removed. Yet somehow, even though I've never seen it and I don't know if I will, there is still a sense of longing for it and belonging to it, because I've needed the past in order to understand the present and move forward into the future.'[14]

'MY NANA'S SISTER was married on the train to India, to a man the family had met just then,' Suhail Nayyar, who was born in 1989, recalls one of his maternal grandfather's stories he has heard since childhood.

'What do you mean?' I'm confused.

'The family migrated before Partition officially happened. On the same train, there was a gentleman whose wife had died and he was already a father of two. My nana was a teenager at the time, and though the entire family was travelling together, they were worried – because of all the stories of rape and abduction they'd heard – about how they'd protect the women. So, the parents spoke to this gentleman and got their daughter married to him on the train to India.'

My mouth falls open. 'Did you ever meet this grandaunt?'

'No, I never met her,' he chuckles, 'I've only heard the story. Ah, then there is another one … On 13 April 1981, my nana and nani took a pilgrimage to Nankana Sahib gurudwara in Pakistan, and upon their return, my nana's mother asked him whether he'd been able to go back to the *aangan* of their house in Peshawar and dig up the gold they'd buried there before they left! Apparently, our family had left the house in possession of their Muslim neighbours. But my nana reported that not only were the neighbours long gone but so was the house and, quite likely, the gold!'

Suhail lives in Mumbai and has acted in films like *Udta Punjab* and, more recently, *Hotel Mumbai*, joining the short list of Indian actors working in Hollywood productions. Naturally, then, the world of film meanders through our conversation. I cannot remember the first time we met – it was probably years ago – but I know this is the first serious, recorded conversation we are having about his family's experience during Partition. Delhi, where the both of us were born, and Lahore, where both of our ancestors come from, are twin cities, and in this way Suhail and I are tethered to the same landscape and the longing for it.

'When I was six or seven years old, my dadi would tell me about how my great-grandfather, Lala Chunni Lal Nayyar, used to own a *tonga* and was the president of the shopkeepers' association in Gawalmandi, Lahore. They lived in Laxman Galli, Shabadan Mali Chowk, and it was the second house on the left side.' Using his hands, Suhail creates an invisible map leading to the house.

'Is the building still standing?' I try to remember the streets of Gawalmandi.

'Not any more; my friends in Lahore tried to look for it. My grandfather's brother lived in Ludhiana, and when I learnt that he was slowly losing his memory, I told my cousin to ask him the address of their home. He immediately told him, as if he'd never forgotten!'

Suhail has never been to Lahore, but the familiarity with which he addresses the Garden City across the border both charms and intrigues me.

'Talking about Lahore enlivens something inside me,' he reveals. 'Even now, as I'm saying the word, I can feel an energy associated with it. But I used to be quite patriotic growing up, to be honest, because the news and all the films that released when we were children reinforced a certain idea of nationalism – that to be Indian is to be against Pakistan. Films like *Border*,[15] for instance. These made the message of Pakistan as the enemy quite clear and also showed how India always put forth the hand of friendship first, how we always had the bigger heart, *humara dil zyada bada hai*. Now this wasn't always wrong, but it wasn't the full picture either.'

He pauses for a minute, and then says, 'I think the very first time that Pakistan was humanized in any Indian film, where Pakistanis were shown as people just like us, was *Raazi*,[16] and that released in 2018, over seventy years after Partition! When the media in both India and Pakistan change the way they depict the other side, societies' perception will also change. I am certain of it.'

'Isn't that a bit idealistic?'

'Definitely,' he laughs, 'but only idealistic people can change the world, only they understand that the world is capable of better. If you aren't trying to change the world, then you accept the world as it is.'

'That's true,' I agree. 'So, is Partition a topic of conversation in your home?'

He shakes his head. 'Now there is no member of my family left who carries the first-hand experience of Partition, and I was the only one who'd initiate these conversations with my grandparents. As I grew older, I learnt how the story of Indian and Pakistani independence is entangled with the story of Partition' – Suhail places his hand on his heart – 'the partition of *my* Punjab. The more I read about it, the more this cultural separation pained me. Partition did not just affect land and population but also the idea of Punjabiyat[17] – language, song, food, music, a shared cultural identity – that was ruptured in 1947.'

'I feel that loss as well,' I admit softly.

'*Everyone* feels it, Aanchal, at least everyone I know whose families have been displaced by Partition,' he responds. 'For the longest time, my mother couldn't understand why I was so fascinated with the other side. She would keep telling me – we are Indian, they are Pakistanis, we are now separate and there's no need to hark back to the past. But then she began watching Pakistani dramas, and in them she heard the same words her nani used to use, the same phrases, and she just broke down. She kept trying to imagine what it would have been like had Partition not happened. Maybe we'd still be living in Lahore, we'd still be one, and how politics is single-handedly responsible for this division. The minute there is awareness that the culture is the same, the people are the same, their habits are the same, then there is acknowledgment of the many losses caused by Partition.'

Suhail now takes me back to when he first understood the culture as a shared entity: 'When I was younger, I would notice extremes when it came to cultural identity – either through radicalized expression or complete ignorance. As I tried to understand my own Punjabi identity, what I found was an amalgamation of so many cultures and customs. From all the invaders that passed through Punjab, to the civilizations that the land has seen, it was the texture and richness of that syncretic, enmeshed way of life that was lost at Partition. It just pains me how much cultural loss we have borne.'

'How do you explain feeling such loss for a time you haven't even seen?' I ask, for I can almost sense it emanating, reflecting, reaching outwards, like an invisible web.

'I suppose...' His voice trails off until he has collected his thoughts. 'I suppose sometimes you feel something profound about a place without understanding why or being able to explain how. Once, while I was at the Attari border, I saw the milestone for Lahore, and I was so moved merely looking at that word. You are connected to some places by soil, *mitti ka rishta*, and that's what it's like with Lahore. I may not have the words to explain this feeling, but perhaps I can try through music...'

I break into a wide grin. 'Tell me more.'

He leans in and his voice becomes immediately softer. 'The realm of art *cannot* be divided by any man-made border. There are those whose works resonate as much with me as they do with anyone on the other side – be it the poems of Bulleh Shah, the words of Ali Sethi, or Nusrat Fateh Ali Khan sahib ... for me, *his* is the voice of God.' As he says this, he raises his palms up to the heavens. 'Art does not have a nationality or a citizenship, it cannot be wielded by frontiers or documents.' But Suhail is not the first person to deem this border invalid in the face of culture, and he certainly will not be the last. In conversation with Professor Alok Bhalla, the Hindi writer Krishna Sobti had once noted:

> When politics, religion and humanism are transmitted in literature, human faith is transformed. I feel in my inner recesses a certain richness that is part of our common heritage. Guru Nanak, Baba Farid, Amir Khusro, Bulleh Shah, Waris Shah and Shah Latif – can we divide this whole lot of poets into theirs and ours? No doubt we divided the territory – but tradition, music, art and literature are not like geographical areas, they continue to remain undivided and are indivisible.[18]

'And I also want to tell you about an incident that's happened to me twice now, in exactly the same way. The first time, in 2013, as a student at the Film and Television Institute of India (FTII), Pune, I was doing an acting exercise where we had to perform any activity to music. I chose to fold a sheet against the background score of Piyush Mishra's "*Husna*". Aanchal, I can't explain what I was feeling, but throughout that entire exercise I was weeping inconsolably. I felt such strong emotions ... Have you heard that song?'

I take a deep breath. The first time I heard '*Husna*' is imprinted in my memory. Originally written as a poem by the Indian actor Piyush Mishra, and produced for Coke Studio India by the composer Hitesh Sonik, whose family bears a history of Partition, the song is nothing short of extraordinary. The rendition is simple, Indian percussion with an acoustic guitar, but every single note is impregnated with the grief of separation. With the very first word that Mishra sings – 'Lahore' – I felt a deep incision in my heart. Goosebumps erupted across my arms, and I remember pausing the track immediately, unprepared. Such was the solemn comfort in his voice that, when juxtaposed against the words, it was almost haunting:

> *Lahore ke uss pehle jile ke do pargana mein pahunche,*
> *Resham gali ke duje kuche ke chauthe makaan mein pahunche,*
> *Aur kehte hain jisko dooja mulk uss Pakistan mein pahunche,*
> *Likhta hoon khat main Hindustan se pehloo-e-husna mein pahunche.*[19]

Composed as a love letter from Javed, who is in India, to his beloved Husna, now in Pakistan, written in the years following Partition, the writer confesses to how much he misses her, but also asks her what life is like in Pakistan without him and after this separation – of land, of hearts. He writes that he feels like he is walking through Lahore's first district, on Resham street, in Pakistan, which they call a different country now.

In an interview, Hitesh Sonik said that he was spellbound when he first came across the poem, for he never imagined there could ever be a romantic aspect to the horrors of Partition. He admits that his father's stories of being a seven-year-old at the time of Partition had never left him, and their impact on him was perhaps at its peak when they were working on '*Husna*': 'I was at home, looking for home.'[20]

Sonik's words also encapsulate how I felt upon that first listening, for as Mishra took us down the lanes of Lahore, I kept thinking about the time I had set out in Shah Almi, in the walled city of Lahore – just weeks before this song released, in fact – also looking for my grandmother's home. As I listened to the ballad, I had tried my best to not move, breathe as quietly as I could, resisting the urge to pause and pace myself, for I feared missing out on even a single nuance.

As I think about the song now, and how visceral a reaction the very sound of the word 'Lahore' prompted in my body – as precisely as Suhail described it – I wonder whether people in Pakistan and Bangladesh react similarly to the names of Indian cities left behind by their ancestors. Do the words Delhi and Bombay, Shimla, Gurdaspur, Calcutta and Lucknow evoke a similarly magnetic energy?

I am lost in this thought as Suhail's voice brings me back. 'As I was folding the sheet and listening to Mishra's voice, I felt such strong emotions. I felt like *my* land had been taken from me, *my* Punjab had been brutally divided, *I* had been displaced. It was supposed to be an acting exercise but it became a completely out-of-body experience. The song became a trigger. I was folding and concentrating on the lyrics, and before I knew it, I was crying. There was this deep, deep longing … this excruciating pain for a place left behind. I felt it in my body.

'Then the same thing happened in an autorickshaw in 2015. I was listening to *"Husna"*, and this time I was consciously thinking about the words, about what we gained from Partition, what we lost at Partition, how many beloved people were sacrificed on either side because of religion, and what lay across the border. Mishra asks, *"Patte kya jhadte hain Pakistan mein waise jaise jhadte yahan? Hota ujala kya waisa hi hai jaise hota Hindustan mein*? Do the leaves fall from trees in Pakistan too, as they do here? Does dawn break the same way as in Hindustan? *Aur rota hai raaton mein Pakistan kya waise hi jaise Hindustan, o' Husna*? Does Pakistan also cry like Hindustan at night?"'

These are questions that have been asked time and time again by those who long for the other side.

'Do you know that I grew up in a neighbourhood called Gujranwala Town?'

With a sad smile, I list other similar neighbourhoods in Delhi, counting them on my fingers. 'Gujranwala Town, Derawal Nagar,

Multani Dhanda, Kohat Enclave, Mianwali Nagar, all named after cities left behind in Pakistan and bearing the remnants of life carried across.'

We are an hour into our conversation. I return now to his work and ask, 'Suhail, have you ever worked on a film project with anyone from Pakistan?'

'Not yet, but I really want to, and of course I also want to visit Pakistan, just to see the land, meet the people. Anytime I have met Pakistanis anywhere in the world, they have felt like my own. During the cricket world cup, I met up with some Pakistani friends in London and we were watching the match together. When India lost to England, they teased me in the same way that my cousins do, that my family does. There was an immediate familiarity because we are one, from the same land. So how can I ever think that they are from a *dushman mulk*, an enemy state?'

'Do you think about this often, these ongoing similarities, this historic separation?'

He nods his head slowly. 'And each time I do, *mujhe apna baanta hua watan hi yaad aata hai*, I think of my divided land, my divided Punjab. Here again, I want to return to music – there was a Punjabi folk song, *"Ki Banu Duniya Da"*,* originally sung by the Pakistani singer Sarwar Gulshan and then later made popular by Gurdas Maan in India. It was further popularized with added lyrics from Gurdas Maan, for a Coke Studio rendition performed with Diljit Dosanjh. Midway through this new version, there is a line, *"Wagah de border te, raah puchdi Lahore'an de"* – at the border, I look for the path that once led to Lahore. This line always breaks my heart.'

I know the song well, and together we softly hum another verse:

Saanu sauda ni pugda, Saanu sauda ni pugda,
Raavi toh Chenab puchda, Raavi toh Chenab puchda
Ki haal ae Sutlej da.[21]

---

* This loosely translates to: 'What is to become of our world?'

The hair on the back of my neck stand up. This deal – Partition – is not profitable, it has cost us deeply, the verse begins. Then, as Ravi and Chenab, two of the five rivers of undivided Punjab, ask after their sibling, Sutlej, the song evokes the tragedy of how even nature was divided as these rivers now flow through both Pakistan and India.

By now, both Suhail and I feel wrung out by this conversation. It has lasted long and dug deep. It has meandered through music and film, language and poetry, forming the now ghostly boundaries of an undivided Punjab. Finally, I ask him what his hope for the future is.

'Any form of unification is not possible, I know this. But I do hope for peace and cordial relations between the countries. The division of culturally similar people on the basis of religion is something I don't think I will ever understand. But I do know that those who hate the other side have not felt the pain of Partition.'

That night, Suhail sends me a poem he has written, one that encompasses the syncretism he longs for:

Ishq mein Khuda, ishq mein Ram,
Khuda hi ishq, ishq hi Ram,
Ab kaho ishq ko Khuda kahun
Ya Khuda ko kahu Ram.

19
Regret

∽

O F THE MANY STORIES about Partition that I have heard from the second and third generations, almost all begin with some form of absence. Either the absence of knowledge, or the absence of an ancestor who may have been able to provide knowledge. But what is extraordinary about this absence is that we are tethered to the past by it. Even in its invisibility, in the lack of detail or clarity, its hinges are strong enough to link generations. My introspections, too, began with absence – the absence of knowledge about the journeys of my grandparents or even the names of the cities they had migrated from. But never once did I feel the regret of not knowing until I was made aware of it. And once I was aware, all I saw was a dark chasm of the past, yearning to be populated with information and memory.

Similarly, while recording the stories of others, particularly second and third generations who no longer have tangible links to the past, I am often overwhelmed by the incompleteness of personal history. As humans, we are the sum total of our pasts, and yet so many of the pasts I try to write about are fraught with blank spaces. For far too long Partition has been cloaked in silence, and due to that being the dominant narrative, many children and grandchildren have not inherited its stories.

As a result, several of these generational interviews do recede into reticence – where sometimes half-remembered facts are produced, other times promises of asking elders and returning with more information are made, but most resonant is a sense of regret. Many speak about not knowing enough merely because they had not asked when they could have, and now 'it's too late'. Their parents, grandparents, grandaunts or uncles have now passed, and with them have disappeared the experiences of Partition. Without this fountainhead of memory, it becomes difficult to piece together personal history – some of which remains on a land inaccessible due to an international border. There is a distinctly discernible tone in these interviews of time running out, of not knowing where you are from or not knowing where to begin looking.

AFTER READING *REMNANTS*, the 1965-born financial analyst and author Anirudha Dutta[1] speaks to me about how he knows very little of his father's family's migration from East to West Bengal during Partition: 'There have been stories, but unfortunately I never paid much attention to them. What I know is that my grandfather was a postmaster in the village of Kaliganj. They moved after my father, Amal Chandra Dutta, passed his Class 10 examinations, travelling on foot for a few days. They had stuffed coins and some valuables inside their socks and clothes; much of the jewellery and other valuables were put inside the well in their house with the hope that one day they would go back. They never did. When they crossed over, they stayed in a refugee camp in Shantipur village, and then moved to Bansdroni, Calcutta, where they were allotted some land. My grandfather fell ill immediately after coming to Calcutta and passed away soon thereafter. Eventually, my father enlisted in the army as a jawan (non-commissioned officer) and was inducted into the Corps of Electronics and Mechanical Engineers (EME). The enormous regret is that I didn't ask him much about his life before the army, and now that he has passed away, I am realizing what I have missed.'

When I ask why these conversations on Partition never happened in the household, his response is contemplative. 'While I was younger and living at home, I didn't ask my parents any questions. An army life also meant that my father was posted away from the family for many years. When I grew up and moved out for college, I suppose I got consumed by life, the headiness of youth. Plus, this was the period when communication was not easy when you were away from home. As a lower-middle-income household, we didn't have a telephone. In fact, I didn't have one even when I started my career! It was such a different India. I suppose, regret sometimes comes with age, with more knowledge and maturity.'

What he does mention is that he wishes he could have asked more about his parents' childhoods, their India, for it would have helped him better understand where he came from. In the email, he attaches a six-page letter that his father had once handwritten to his niece, who used to live in Sweden and is now in the United States, and had asked her grandfather to tell her about his life. The letter is brief, for it attempts to compress over eight decades into six pages.

'Obviously it lacks in detail but there is a mention of his village, his birth, the freedom struggle and then Independence. He writes about how my mother's family is also from Mymensingh district, now in Bangladesh, but she's never been there, because her father always worked in West Bengal,' Anirudha tells me. 'I once actually did ask my father about this time, and he said he didn't remember much. But reading this letter again made me wish that he was still around, so I could get a chance to fill the gaps in my knowledge. I would have persisted in asking him about his journey during Partition. I would've wanted to know what he thought and what he heard and how he felt at the time.'

WHAT HAPPENS, I wonder, after first-hand testimony is no longer available? When only half stories are inherited, or fragments of memory are passed down, is regret the most natural consequence? And can that regret itself be a means for the collection of a different kind of memory – populated by external sources like books, archives, letters, photographs, films, testimonials from similar geographies – one that is no longer dependent on familial informants?

༄

FOR THE MOST part, the stories of my grandparents' lives during Partition are known to me, except for my maternal grandmother's. Her experiences were, for a long time, completely unknown as she passed away in 1988, two years before I was born. When I began recording the histories of my paternal grandparents, who came from North-West Frontier Province (now Khyber Pakhtunkhwa province) and district Gujrat in Punjab, and my maternal grandfather, whose family had moved to Delhi years before Partition, I felt an incompleteness that could not be helped. My nani, Amrit Bery, was from Lahore and had migrated to India during the Partition riots. I longed to know not just what she saw in 1947 but also what life in Lahore before Partition had been like. She was my direct link to Delhi's twin city across the border.

When I ask my mother, Rajni, about what nani's journey during Partition was like, she says she does not know. 'I only became interested in my mother's life years after I became a mother.' There is a tinge of remorse in her voice but she doesn't say much else.

'When was the first time someone in the family spoke about Partition?'

'It may have been with the rubies in Toronto, and that too was a passing reference,' she smiles.

I should explain.

In 1958, after obtaining a bachelor's degree from the Pusa Institute, Delhi, my maternal grandfather, Vishwa Nath Vij, applied for postgraduate studies at the Ontario Agricultural College in Guelph, Canada. His family was originally from Choona Mandi in Lahore but had migrated to East Punjab years before Partition, settling in Amritsar, where he was born in 1936, and eventually moving to Delhi. During Partition, they lived at Mori Gate in Delhi's old city and witnessed communal horrors in their neighbourhood. In accepting the offer in Guelph, my grandfather became the first person in his family to travel internationally. After his postgraduate studies, he pursued a master's degree in 1960 at the University of Toronto while also playing varsity football. Thereafter, he took courses at Ryerson, playing football for them too. All this while, he picked up jobs on the side to support himself. A few years ago, my aunt presented me with a collection of photographs from his early years in Canada. The backs of most prints bore long, detailed notes in Hindi, and were presumably sent to his parents.

Vishwa Nath Vij returned to Delhi towards the end of 1963 and was married to Amrit Bery in April 1964. The families knew each other from their Lahore days, which is why the alliance was made in the first place. At the time, my grandfather was working as a production manager at the Beecham Group, a British pharmaceutical company, and my grandmother was working as a stenographer for Pfizer on Asaf Ali Road. After the wedding, my grandfather returned to Canada and my grandmother followed him in June 1964. My aunt Mona was born in 1965 and my mother in 1968. Eventually, my grandparents sponsored their families' move to Canada, and my grandfather's youngest brother, the popular radio and television broadcaster Prithvi 'Lali' Vij,[2] joined them, as did my grandmother's siblings, Jiwan Vohra and Surinder Bery. 'Rubies' – which my mother is referring to – was her misunderstanding, as a child, of the word 'rupees' that came up in discussions about money, a topic the family sometimes spoke on when they met.

My mother tries to recall the days of the early '70s. 'When the family got together, they would certainly speak about India, but I suspect they would touch on the past as well … maybe Partition. That's where I must have heard the word for the first time.'

'But how come you began to think of nani's life after you became a mother?'

'Well, I would sometimes think about how they came to India or what her childhood in Lahore had been like. I don't think they had much difficulty during the journey, but I didn't really ask anyone about it. She wasn't around any more, so, in a sense, it was too late…' she says in a small voice.

'Do you regret not asking?'

'I don't,' she says and pauses. 'It never crossed our minds. We were oblivious because we'd never experienced something like that ourselves. And then, growing up in Canada, there was so much else to consider that this got buried under.'

The interesting thing about the Vij–Bery family is that, for the most part, Partition is not discussed on either side. This is not to mitigate the horrors that the Vij family may have witnessed in Delhi, or the displacement that the Bery family felt while migrating from Lahore, but simply because, at the end, both families were relatively safe. They were privileged enough to find their footing in an independent India and did not struggle in the same way that my paternal family, or so many others, did. The most prominent story told in the Vij household is of Jallianwala Bagh and how my great-grandfather, Chunni Lal Vij, then twenty-one years old, was present at the time of the firing and escaped by using his dhoti to scale the wall of the maidan. Partition, thus, became a word uttered in the house only after I began asking about it.

It is important to note that in 1973, my grandmother was involved in a terrible car accident in Toronto that left her immobilized until the end of her life in 1988. My grandfather then adopted the primary role in raising their girls, aided by other family members. If there are gaps in my mother's memory about her mother's past, perhaps this is one of the reasons. Not only were they living as immigrants in a distant land, but they were also affected by a great personal tragedy. Maybe my mother would have asked her mother questions if she could have. Regret, I suppose then, is inevitable and applicable to so many aspects of her and her sister's lives, though to my knowledge they have never been consumed by it. The girls spoke no Hindi until their adolescent years, and any interest in history – personal or otherwise – would have arisen much later, only when they moved back to India.

So, a part of me wanted to make sure that my generation – siblings and cousins – and those who come after us knew where we are from. Or maybe I did not want my mother or her sister to one day wonder about their family's history and have no one to ask. In that sense, any collection of memory about my grandmother's life would be to not only eradicate the regret that I may one day have, but it would also be to return parts of her to her daughters – a pre-emptive measure for future regret, almost. And in speaking to my grandmother's elder sister, Jiwan, the one who would ultimately provide the most information, I also realized that she had not spoken about Lahore or Partition ever since they had left in 1947. And this became the third incentive – to reinstate a sense of belonging over a city long left behind.

My grandaunt Jiwan still lives in Toronto with her family. The first time I went to visit Lahore in 2014, these were the details she shared with me. 'Your nani was born in 1939 in the Machhi Hatta bazaar area of Shah Almi Gate and was the fourth of seven siblings. We both went to Sacred Heart school in Anarkali, across which was the first branch of Punjab National Bank that our grandfather had actively taken part in setting up.'

Armed with these details on my maiden trip, I found my way to Sacred Heart Convent in the old city of Lahore. It was a weekend and there were no students. With great difficultly, I convinced the security guard at the gate that I had travelled from very far away and this was the sole detail that I knew about my grandmother's life before Partition. He gave me a few minutes to walk around and take some photographs of the brick-coloured buildings with beautifully arched corridors. I promptly sent across the photos to Toronto, much to my grandaunt's delight!

When I see her next, we speak about what happened in 1947. She begins by telling me and her eldest daughter, Vibha, who has joined us, that in March, when there were riots in Lahore, as a ten-year-old she found herself stranded in a bank by herself. One of the employees brought her home that evening, but soon after the family moved out of their home in Shah Almi and to their grandfather's home close to Sacred Heart, which they deemed safer. On 21 June 1947, they watched their entire mohalla of Shah Almi, then a stronghold of Hindus and Sikhs, burn down in a single night – houses, businesses, residents and all.

'My father, Narain Das Bery, had already decided that we would be leaving Lahore, at least temporarily, and so my parents, their five children – of whom I was now the eldest since the elder two were already married – and our help took the night-long train across Punjab and then travelled by bus for four and a half hours further to the hill station of Shimla. Your nani would have been eight years old at the time, just a child. We stayed in Shimla from July till the end of October, and in our absence, Partition happened and Lahore fell on the Pakistani side. On 1 November 1947, we finally migrated to Delhi.'[3]

I ask her whether the family thought Partition would be permanent, and she replies, 'We could certainly never imagine it. Lahore boasted of such a composite culture before Partition. But in these riots, we lost our home, our land and our extended family.' She tells me how her cousin's husband, who worked for the military accounts, was violently stabbed to death in his train compartment while travelling from one city to another. 'But you cannot stay bitter forever,' she adds reflectively. 'What was done was done, and we had to move past it.'

She now smiles warmly and says, 'I'm sure you already know this, but in 1968 my youngest brother married a Muslim girl, and when my mother found out about it, she was initially quite upset. I suppose it made her recall the time of Partition. But my father accepted the match, and it was my husband, Ved, who told her that if *she* did not welcome the new bride today, then tomorrow others wouldn't either. This rift between communities that had augmented as a result of Partition needed to stop. Hindus, Muslims, Sikhs – Indians or Pakistanis – had all lived together before Partition, and had all lost equally after Partition. It is what brings us together that matters, not what draws us apart.'

That afternoon onwards, I hold her words in my heart, for they speak to a kind of future I want to be able to witness and contribute to. Before my next trip to Pakistan in 2018, I call her up from Delhi and note down as much information as I can about where their house once stood. It may have been razed down, but perhaps some remnant remains still. Once in Lahore, a photographer friend, Kumail Hasan, and I begin to explore the winding, intersecting lanes of the old city.

'The area was called Machhi Hatta,' I tell him, but he has not heard of it, for the names of old areas have also now changed. 'My grandaunt doesn't remember the name of the street but said that there used to be a large wrought iron gate opening into the street they lived on. From the mighty Shah Almi Darwaza, the house was about a kilometre away, a long walk.'

Kumail nods and we begin to walk around the older parts of Shah Almi, but because the area was completely reconstructed after Partition, not many older parts remain.[4] I tell him that she once mentioned an old pond behind the house, *paani wala talab*, and, asking around, we arrive at a lane of older-looking houses. He points to the constructions that have withstood the test of time, their fragile, wooden latticework *jaalis* and ornately carved *jharokha* windows jutting out of the building façade, holding on for dear life. The front doors of several homes are open, and fine bamboo curtains cover the entrances. A few lanes still bear the original Hindu names – *kucha* Kirpa Ram, *kucha* Chabakswaran, *kucha* Hanu Man. The outer walls of some houses are plastered with Urdu posters and little green and white Pakistani flags. As I walk through, I realize that not much of my grandmother's life now remains here. The only thing that remains is the land, the soil, and even that has a new name.

I photograph every four-storeyed house I see, and when Kumail asks why, I say, 'That is one of the details my grandaunt clearly remembered: that they lived in a four-storeyed house on a plot of land that held three buildings. Theirs was in the middle, the tallest one. From the outside, it looked ordinary, small, with a single window facing the road. Near the entrance was a water tap, and the first room was a storeroom of sorts where their father would keep the bicycles, trunks and extra blankets. In the room behind that was a table with a radio and another window, and if you looked out, you could see a small stepwell.'

I am standing in the middle of a narrow lane and speaking to him with my arms, my hands, my body, my heart. My turquoise shawl is flailing in the air as I move from side to side. As I describe to him a house I have never seen, I realize that I have convinced myself that this landscape once existed, even though there is no trace of it anywhere. This is the power of my belief in memory, and yet I have nothing tangible to show for it. My fingers trace the ceramic name plaques that have now replaced the original stone ones at the front of old homes, desperately wishing to somehow, miraculously, stumble upon the plaque of Narain Das Bery, somewhere, *anywhere*, but there is nothing.

What does end up happening, though, is that people who have seen us walking around in circles again and again, residents of the walled city, begin to take notice. '*Aap Bharat se aaye hain*? *Apna ghar dhoondh rahe hain*?' They ask if I have come from India and am searching for my ancestral home. A heavy word, *home*. I feel myself nodding and wonder whether the regret is painted clearly across my face. They ask if I know the house number, lane number, or any landmarks, but I draw a blank. They then remind me that history has not been kind to the neighbourhood. My heart sinks further as I learn that after the fire, smoke had risen from the ashen mohalla for days. And now, in place of the once-dominating Mughal Gate and multi-storeyed houses hang lengths of electrical wires, not unlike in the old city of Delhi.

That afternoon, sitting among a group of Lahoris, as my grandmother's family once would have, I keep thinking about what I had hoped to find there. Did I want to see how they had lived, or what had survived of it? Or merely to walk the lanes that they had wished to return to one day?

I think I needed a sign, something exceptional, something to return to my grandaunt in the same way I would have to the grandmother I never met or knew. *Something from home.* Something that bore witness to the fact that they had once lived there. But it is only much later that I realize that my being there did exactly that. So, maybe what I was really looking for was a sense of second-hand closure, the conclusion to a pre-Partition life.

I do not know anything about how Amrit Bery would have felt as an eight-year-old when she left Lahore. Every piece of information I have about her at that time has been foraged from other people's memories, or collected from archives and books, and put together with great effort, yet it is mere speculation. Of all of my grandparents' birthplaces in present-day Pakistan, I have only been to Lahore, and even there I have found nothing to physically connect me to the land apart from memory. This does not make the land any less mine; it just means what I bequeath further down the generations will also be an invisible heirloom. But at least it will not be a void in memory, and it will possess no shade of regret.

THE MORE I listen to stories from 1947, the more I think about whether regret, in the case of Partition, settles differently within different generations. Does the first generation that lived through the divide regret it happened, or did they welcome the creation of separate states? Perhaps it is impossible to generalize, not to mention how difficult it is to answer and how futile it is to deliberate on such a question now, with the acceptance and fortification of national identities, but I do think about it and sometimes include it in my questionnaire with eyewitnesses. With subsequent generations, though, the feeling of regret is often a consequence of not being able to do anything when so much time has already passed, as in the case of Anirudha Dutta. But keeping in mind my own efforts, sometimes I do wonder whether there is actually a difference between second- and third-generational regret, whether the second generation's is somehow more cavernous, more painful because of the proximity to Partition, and yet its memory has still gone unrecorded, unremembered. But it is difficult to generalize this supposition, as my own parents are perfect examples of its contradiction.

I can say this, though – being from the third generation – that it is, to date, most proactive in the preservation of Partition history. This generation (sometimes extending to the fourth) has been blessed with sufficient distance and time from the event of Partition to be able to view it through an objective lens. On the other hand, this passage of time has also acted as a deterrent to the lucidity of memory and resulted in the fading of cross-border ties. The final section of this chapter is a conversation where, due to a fourth-generational introspection hinged on the shadows of regret, a unique Partition story has been preserved for posterity.

∽

ARYAN D'ROZARIO HAS prepared for our conversation. A big file with several old papers rests in his hands. Though this is the first time we are speaking, I conducted an interview years ago with his aunt's father-in-law, Rajendra Nath Seth, or Uncle Raj as he was called, who passed away in 2019 at the age of ninety-two. He had migrated from Lahore to Delhi via Shimla, but his father, Pran Nath Seth, had decided to remain in Pakistan as a Hindu after Partition. My conversation with Aryan now touches only briefly on the Seth family. Instead, he offers me a wholly unrecorded, unexpected story.

'My grandfather, Ashok Alvin John D'Rozario, was a hoarder,' he laughs, 'and he kept basically every piece of paper, every letter he ever received – no matter how obscure. This is how I found these two letters from our family in Pakistan, the only two letters ever sent and both during peacetime: one in 1984 and the other probably around 1986 or '87, based on the information in the letter.

'In 1946, my grandfather left India for the United States, because his father, Dr Albert Michael D'Rozario, was a diplomat. At the time, Independence seemed imminent and Pandit Nehru and other members of the Congress were sending Indian diplomats abroad in an unofficial capacity to take over the Indian missions around the world – a kind of precursor to embassies, if you will. As a result, my grandfather spent three years growing up in Washington, DC, from 1946 to '49 and that included Partition. The information they received about Partition was through letters and official correspondences that would arrive at the mission in DC. And I don't know whether that shaped his later perception of Partition but he was always of the view – and I remember him saying this very clearly – that Partition was inevitable and that it should have happened because Hindus and Muslims couldn't live together. That was his view.

'Now, because of my great-grandfather's diplomatic career, and he and his family being abroad all the time, they lost touch with family members in the subcontinent. There were only so many letters one could send, and phone calls were still very expensive. They would, of course, reconnect once they returned, but some connections were lost for many, many years, which is what happened with Justice Cornelius.'

Throughout the telling of Aryan's story, I interrupt very little, and only when I need to. It is evident that even though he was born in 1999, over half a century after Partition, he has been holding on to this multigenerational tale for long, and wants it told in the way that it deserves. He is precise about the details – dates, years, postings – but is careful not to speak on behalf of those who are no longer around. He merely puts forth a fair perspective of what could have been felt at the time. To that end, he refers to his notes often, and it becomes apparent that what we are doing through this conversation is a recollection of his collection of memory.

'Before I go any further,' he says, 'I think what is important here, and many people often forget, is that Partition wasn't limited to just Hindus, Muslims and Sikhs. Other religious communities – Parsis, Jains, Jews, Buddhists and Christians, like my family – were also affected and divided between the two countries.

'This is the story of Justice Cornelius, my great-grandfather's cousin, and how he was separated from his family by the Partition line. They were related through Justice Cornelius's mother, who was a D'Rozario before marriage. The first reason my family lost touch with him is that they were living aboard, as I mentioned. And the second is that at the time of Partition, Justice Cornelius chose to stay in Pakistan. And though the D'Rozario family accepted this decision, they could never quite reconcile with it, given their own personal views on Independence.

'It would seem that Justice Cornelius had quite a myopic view of the world. He considered himself a civil servant, and he didn't really care where he was, or whether the passport he held was Pakistani or Indian. He cared very deeply about his job, and for the city of Lahore – it was his adopted home. He spent so many years there that he just couldn't see himself leaving. But that one decision impacted his family greatly because they all cut off communication with him – perhaps not immediately but certainly later on, and for most of his life until he died in 1991, because it was just not sustainable. They were government servants in India, and he was one in Pakistan.'

'Do you mean to say,' I ask him, 'that his entire family remained in India and he was the only person who lived in Pakistan?'

He shows me a black and white photograph of a family of six sitting in their garden. At the bottom, written with a black pen, are the words 'Indore, 1936'. 'This the Cornelius family. The older lady at the bottom in the white sari is the matriarch, Tara Cornelius (née D'Rozario). Her son, the justice, is missing from this picture because he was already in Lahore.'

If Justice Cornelius's decision to remain in Pakistan is a curious one, the background of his family is just as interesting. In an article on Christians during the Partition in Punjab, Dr Yaqoob Khan Bangash, a Chevening Fellow at the Oxford Centre for Islamic Studies, writes that the Justice Alvin Robert Cornelius

…was born in 1903 in Agra to Professor Israel Jacob Cornelius who taught mathematics at Holkar College in the princely state of Indore. His father's ancestors were Hindus and were from the family of Naikor landlords, who served in the military of the Madras Presidency under the East India Company. It was Justice Cornelius's grandfather, Perayya Kait Pillay, who, after having fought during the conquest of Burma by the British in the late nineteenth century, settled in the then central provinces and became a schoolmaster. It was there that he converted to Christianity and adopted the surname 'Cornelius' after a centurion who had converted to Christianity at the time of the Apostles. Justice Cornelius's mother, Tara D'Rozario, was also from a family who had converted from Hinduism, and her father, Michael D'Rozario, was a forest officer in Central India. Thus, from both his parents, his lineage was Hindu. [But] it was the ancestry of his wife, Ione Francis, whom he married in 1931, which connected him to Islam. Both the parents of Ione had come from Muslim ancestry ... converting to Christianity. Thus, while Justice Cornelius was a Christian, he had deep connection and understanding of both Hinduism and Islam in South Asia.[5]

Aryan goes on to list the justice's postings until Partition. 'He was commissioned to the civil service in 1930 and his first posting was to Lahore. He began his judicial career in 1943 at the Lahore High Court, and by 1946 he had been elevated to the bench. Then, in the summer of 1947, he assisted Chief Justice Sir Abdul Rashid in the split of the court. Apart from his love for Lahore, though, the decision to remain in Pakistan was quite a practical one. He knew well that when Partition happened, Indian civil servants would be given the opportunity to choose between India or Pakistan. Since most civil servants at the time were Hindu and would likely go to India, there would be space for those experienced officers who remained in Pakistan to not only find prominent places in the government but also rise up the ranks rather quickly ... which is exactly what happened to him. It was a calculated decision.

'So, after Partition, he was in Lahore and his family was in Indore. He became Pakistani and they remained Indian. His brothers were also in government service – George was the municipal commissioner of Ratlam, and his other brother, Selwyn, was a tax commissioner in Bangalore – and didn't keep in touch with their brother in Pakistan...'

'Do you think they tried, though?' I ask.

'It was difficult, I think, simply because of the politics of how the two countries came into existence – the violence, the suspicion, then there was war and surmounting tensions all the time, and though they may have wanted to, they couldn't risk anything. And it was the same for my grandfather and great-grandfather as well – they loved Cornelius as a cousin but it was too dangerous. So, what they did instead was to meet on neutral land. My great-grandfather spent the early years after Independence in Britain, where he was posted after the United States, and at the time Justice Cornelius was busy creating the Pakistani cricket team. He was the chairperson of the Pakistan Cricket Board from 1949 to '53, and one of his tasks was to introduce the Pakistani team in the global cricket world. And so he would bring the team to London, where they played their matches and he would secretly meet my great-grandfather, his cousin. My grandfather would tell me that London was neutral territory – that as Indians and Pakistanis, they could meet there in peace and dignity, and no one would know or censor the meeting.'

'Isn't that just the greatest irony?' I scoff. 'That Britain becomes a neutral, safe territory for an Indian and a Pakistani to meet after Partition?'

'It does make me angry,' he confesses, 'but it also makes me sad that we have to meet our own so many thousands of miles away even though we live footsteps away from each other.'

'A single step past Attari is a step into Wagah,' I say.

'Exactly. Because of the identities formed due to this Partition line, Justice Cornelius couldn't travel to India much. He came only as a Pakistani government representative and could barely meet his extended family. And I don't think it was because he didn't want to, I think it was simply because he was either told not to or innately knew that he shouldn't. It just wasn't an option, because, in fairness, Justice Cornelius had a very illustrious career, and one wouldn't think that a Catholic like himself would end up becoming the fourth Chief Justice of the Islamic Republic of Pakistan.' He pauses and then looks at me. 'This is a bit of a deviation, but I want to tell you about a small incident from when I was in college.'

I nod eagerly and he continues. 'I once had a professor who was an expert in Islamic affairs, focusing on Islam in North Africa, and his wife was Pakistani. She came from a very illustrious family of Lahore, and when we met, we naturally spoke about Partition. I told her that I had an uncle who stayed back in Pakistan and how he rose to become the chief justice, and she refused to believe it, merely on the grounds that he was Catholic and not Muslim. She said it was impossible, that perhaps I was mistaken, that maybe he was just a judge. Anyway, she went home and looked it up and spoke to her parents, who were just as taken aback. And that small incident just proved one thing that my grandfather had said to me: that in Pakistan everything that happened before Zia-ul-Haq's reign has been contorted to fit a particular narrative, because after him the country changed significantly and markedly. He believed that Justice Cornelius was ignored or rather erased after Zia came to power.

'This is the sad thing about Justice Cornelius's legacy. Maybe the older generation of Pakistanis who served in government will remember him, but ordinary and young citizens have no idea who he is. The fact that he was the only non-Muslim to head the judiciary in Pakistan. That his tenure distinguishes him as the second-longest-serving Chief Justice of Pakistan – under General Ayub Khan, from 1960 to '68 – and the Law Advisor under General Yahya Khan, from 1969 to '71. That even though Pakistan did not have a parliamentary democracy throughout his tenure as chief justice, he still tried to ensure that the courts played their part in the protection and enforcement of fundamental rights in the country.[6] That he was awarded the Hilal-e-Pakistan,[7] the second-highest civilian award in the country. I wish his legacy was better known.'

He sighs deeply and smiles at me. 'Anyway, returning to Partition, Justice Cornelius had two sons – Michael and Peter – both of whom had been at St Joseph's Academy, Dehradun, for five years when Partition happened. In his old age, Michael once wrote to me saying that his saddest memory from 1947 was actually from before Partition happened, when his mother came to fetch him and his brother in Dehradun and they drove to Lahore. He had spent five very happy years at Doon, and suddenly he was snatched away from his friends, from his school and also – because he considered himself Indian – that identity was snatched away from him, and he was taken to this new country of Pakistan. Within a few years, both boys went

to boarding school in the UK and they never came back. They lived
the rest of their lives away from the subcontinent – Michael died
a few years ago in St. Louis, Missouri, and Peter died in England.
Michael had no hesitation in admitting that he was very angry at
what Partition had done to his family. He once even told me that by
the time his father was dying in the late '90s, he regretted his decision
to stay in Pakistan even though he reached the pinnacle of his career.'

'Why do you think he regretted it, despite all the success?'

'He became disillusioned with the country and its treatment of
minorities. When he had decided to stay back in Lahore, certain
promises were made by the Muslim League to protect the interests
of religious minorities in the country – the white in the green flag.
But in one of the letters Justice Cornelius writes to my grandfather...'
His voice trails off and he begins to search for the paper. 'The first
one he sent, well after his retirement. He writes here, "We have had
a referendum, of which the major feature is that the Nation has its
commitment to Islam as it's regiment for government and all else."
Basically, the letter alludes to the fact that in Pakistan there seems to
be a trend of always following the Islamic scriptures and living life
based on the scripture, and only a minority wants democracy.

'The letter is dated 23 December 1984, and in it he also mentions
the assassination of Indira Gandhi. So, when they did write to each
other, it would always be over Christmas. He actually begins the
letter with, "My dear Albert, this letter will reach you long after
Christmas, but it brings you and yours our best wishes for the joys of
the Nativity season and for happiness and success in the New Year.
I have been meaning to write but never got down to it until your
Christmas card arrived a week ago. I see it is dated 1st December.
There must be heavy censoring going on. I hope the censors get
something interesting to read now and then!" There's a bit of dark
comedy, as if he's making a joke by using an exclamation point, but
he was quite serious about the censors.'

'There are only two letters?'

'Only two, but the more you read them, the more you feel the
regret seep through. He writes at one point about how whenever he

writes a letter to my grandfather, he remembers the fields of Madhya Pradesh where he grew up. He remembers the cattle and the farm. He says that he's never seen a piece of farmland since leaving India. And any time he receives letters from my grandfather or his sister or their cousins, he's reminded of all the things they used to do as children.'

'That's heartbreaking,' I whisper, but the words feel weightless compared to the enormity of emotion.

Aryan smiles sadly. 'You know, he never got to say goodbye. Because of his decision to remain in Pakistan, he never got to officially bid his family farewell. He was already in Lahore when Partition happened. He writes in the second letter about receiving word from home: "The day your card came, there was also a letter from Georgie saying that he was very ill with a severe condition of stomach. He has lost weight and strength, and he can only move very slightly. He said the condition developed over ten months, during which he had never written. When he last wrote he was in Ratlam, but now he is in Indore and apparently his youngest daughter, Bulbul, is looking after him. If I had known some months earlier, I could have arranged to visit India with our cricket team ... but now I would need to make an individual effort for a visa, which is very tedious. I will start trying soon."' Aryan sighs and puts down the paper. 'He never could come – I don't know whether he tried to get a visa and was rejected, but he never came.'

'What happened to his brother?'

'Georgie died shortly after, I think.'

There is a thick, solemn sadness around us, and, inhaling sharply, I ask, 'When did he finally retire?'

'He left his post as Law Advisor before the war in 1971. General Yahya Khan had asked him and G.W. Choudhry of East Pakistan to draft a constitution, to which Zulfikar Ali Bhutto objected, saying that he was a *dhimmi*, a non-Muslim, non-believer, so how could he make a constitution for a Muslim state? It had to be reworked,[8] and that really upset Justice Cornelius. I think it's at that point that he realized that whatever he did, however faithfully he served Pakistan, he would always first be identified as Catholic.

'He himself never owned a house in Pakistan and, despite holding such prestigious posts, was quite simple. He lived in government accommodation while he was a judge, but from 1953 until his death in 1991, he and his wife lived in two connecting rooms, No. 1 and 2, at Faletti's Hotel. When his wife died in 1989, after a marriage of fifty-eight years, he moved into a single room at No. 1. He lived for over thirty years at the Faletti's Hotel, was one of their ten life members, and the room is still named after him! He never owned many possessions – drove the same car, a 1953 bottle green Wolseley, till the end of his life – and had few friends – among them, the late human rights lawyer Asma Jahangir and Hamid Khan, who is the vice president of the Tehreek-e-Insaf party and a partner at Cornelius, Lane & Mufti, a law firm.[9] He organized a conference in Justice Cornelius's memory a few years ago, ensuring that his legacy did not die with him. I wish I could have travelled to Lahore to attend the conference, but obviously it was not possible. I mean, we still haven't gone to see his grave in the Christian cemetery on Jail Road.'

'The one behind the gymkhana?' I ask and he nods.

If I close my eyes, I can actually see the intersection of Jail Road and Zafar Ali Road now, I can see the hut-like entrance to the cemetery. Gora Qabristan, or the white graveyard, as it is sometimes known, is one of the oldest Christian cemeteries in Lahore. I can even see my room on the ground floor in the new wing of the Lahore Gymkhana Club. I can see myself walking out of the club; on the left is the resplendent golf course and beyond it is the Christian cemetery. How many times I would have passed it, how many times I would have been within reach. I wish I had known earlier.

'Someone once sent me a picture of his grave and I was very disturbed to see it chipped at the sides. I felt really helpless because normally, in Christian families, we would go and take care of the grave – clean it, put fresh flowers – but no one had been able to do that for Justice Cornelius because no one is left in Pakistan. I don't know whether any of his friends have ever done that for him, if any of them are still alive. But the sheer fact that we can't...'

As he says this, I hope in my heart that those from Lahore who read his story will visit his grave and honour his memory.

'Aanchal, I know this conversation has been story after story, but if you will indulge me, there is one more and you'll love this one because it's tied to Uncle Raj. In the '80s, when Uncle Raj's son, Kabir, proposed to my father's sister, Shaila, and she said yes, one of the things that he wanted to do was take her to see his grandfather, Pran Nath Seth, who was still alive in Lahore, and receive his blessings. They only spent a few days there, but one day his grandfather took them to Faletti's, saying that he wanted them to meet an old friend. At the time, my aunt did not know who Justice Cornelius was.

'So, Pran Nath Seth walks into the room, and he says, "Bobby" – that's what everyone used to call him: Bobby, Bobby Cornelius. So, he says, "Bobby, my grandson and his fiancée have come from India, and I want you to meet them." So, he introduces his grandson as Kabir, and then his soon-to-be daughter-in-law as Shaila D'Rozario, and Justice Cornelius, he just kind of ... well, this is how the story was told to me and so I'm repeating it. He stood there, looked my aunt up and down and asked her name again. "My name is Shaila D'Rozario," she said, and then he asked her father's name and she replied, "Ashok D'Rozario." And then he asked her grandfather's name, and she replied, "Albert D'Rozario." And he just looked at her and said, "You are my niece, I am your uncle." My aunt couldn't believe it because she had never heard of him before. She came back from Pakistan furious that no one had told her we had family there!'

'My god...'

'It's very heartbreaking because Justice Cornelius didn't think he would ever meet anyone from the D'Rozario family. And so, from what I was told, he was very quiet for the remainder of the meeting. They drank tea, he asked a few questions about how her grandfather and everyone was, and that was the reason my aunt believed he was family – because he knew everyone's names. "How is Albert? How is Victor? How is Ivy? How is Mercy?" These were all relatives who lived in Delhi, lived in India – and so my aunt knew them. But he never repeated this incident to his sons; neither Michael nor Peter were ever told that Shaila visited.'

'Tell me, Aryan, how did you find out about Justice Cornelius?' I ask, and then add, 'It's always complicated to have a public inheritance from Partition, but more so one that defies the normative binary of Hindu versus Muslim or Indian versus Pakistani. How old were you when you discovered him?'

'It is complicated, and I'll be very honest – even though I went to a fairly liberal school in Delhi, as children, we didn't like Pakistan because we were made to believe that it wasn't something we should associate with. But funnily enough, I actually found out about Justice Cornelius *because* of a school project some time in 2012. I had to interview someone who had lived through Partition, and I chose my grandfather. We were given a list of questions and one of those was, "Do you know anyone in Pakistan?"'

'Oh!' I exclaim, taken aback. 'That's an oddly direct question.'

'Yes, exactly. I remember many of my peers feeling very uncomfortable asking their family this type of questions, but I did not hesitate. When I asked my grandfather if he knew anyone in Pakistan, he very casually replied that he had an uncle who used to live in Lahore. Then I asked him his name and he told me that he was a judge and, naturally, I googled him and all these pages and tributes came up, of Pakistanis remembering him. We went through them all together, and suddenly my grandfather was going down memory lane and telling me not only about Justice Cornelius but also all the friends he had in Cambridge who now lived in Pakistan.

'After the interview was over, I told him that he should get back in touch with his old friends. I reminded him that Uncle Bobby – Justice Cornelius – was present for his birth in 1936 and his baptism, and they were so close but could never meet because of censorship in the mail or fear due to governments. I didn't want him to have that kind of regret, because now, with technology, people can speak to each other easily. I did a bit of research and actually reconnected him with his friends.'

Aryan has a wide smile on his face as he says this and, reflecting his smile, I ask, 'What did they speak about?'

'Mostly about Justice Cornelius, actually. It was a common topic in the house in those days. My grandfather wanted to ask whether there were any books in Pakistan about him. Eventually, the search led us to a book written by an American professor, Ralph Braibanti. The book is titled...' He shows me a copy.

'*Chief Justice Cornelius of Pakistan: An Analysis with Letters and Speeches*,'[10] I read it out.

'The funny thing is that when he was writing this book, much of the family was against it. Justice Cornelius was a simple man, he would never have wanted to be famous, and so when the book came out, not everyone was pleased about it. But as it happens, now we are actually quite glad that it was written because if it wasn't, his name may be erased from Pakistani history. In Pakistan today – like in other places – they want to remember history in a certain way. But I have thought about this a lot and come to the conclusion that it's not such a bad idea that they remember him, however they want...'

'As long as they do?' I ask.

'As long as they do,' he affirms.

I think about everything we have spent the last two hours discussing, and the meticulous manner in which Aryan has preserved this legacy. 'You seem to be the keeper of your family archive, and also very emotionally involved in it. Does the event of Partition affect you personally?'

He chuckles. 'Yes, I suppose I am the keeper, but it's because I grew up with my grandparents and we bonded over this, over family history. I do preserve whatever I can, keeping files with detailed information, so that the next generation – my children and my brother's children – at least know where they come from, because I think that's important. Not only as Indians but also as Christians. And not because we identify purely on religious terms, but I just want future generations to know that we did our part in terms of building India. Even though the family has been out of civil service for generations, in the early days, we participated in the freedom struggle, we marched with Gandhi ... I don't want future generations to forget, I don't want them to carry the regret of not knowing.'

'I remember watching a film[11] once,' I say, 'where the protagonist is an elderly Jewish lady who has returned to Austria, decades after she fled during the Second World War, to reclaim a painting stolen from her family by the Nazis. She takes the fight for what is rightfully hers all the way to the United States Supreme Court, and I remember her saying in the film, "I have to do what I can to keep these memories alive, because people forget – especially the young." Those lines have always stayed with me.'

'Exactly. This way' – he pats the files – 'everything is remembered.'

He thinks for a moment and then speaks again, 'There is a second motive as well, and that is to preserve both parts of our legacy – Indian and Pakistani. My father, as you know, is an Indian Christian and my mother is Hindu. She comes from a Hindu Punjabi family from Hoshiarpur, and though they were not displaced during Partition, they told nightmarish stories about what they had seen in Hoshiarpur during the riots from 1946–47 – walking down streets that were littered with dead bodies, the incoming trains, the stench of human remains. And I always thought that because they were Punjabi, Partition was their story. It belonged to them. What I knew about my father's side, however, was that they came from Rajasthan and Indore and before that from Goa, and so I never expected us to have a Partition story, and certainly not one this layered or complex. And when I discovered it, I felt ... robbed. I felt that Partition just took away one side of my family, and so I made it a point to get back in touch with each and every one of them who was still around, be it Michael or Peter.[12]

'For most of his life, my grandfather did not mention Justice Cornelius to a single soul – not his friends, his children or even his grandchildren. It was only through my school project that I managed to find out something that I probably wouldn't have otherwise. It was supposed to be a secret, you know, having family in Pakistan.'

'Do you think that he never told anyone because he was never asked about it?'

'That's a good question, and yes, probably to an extent. I know it's complicated to maintain cross-border relations – it was complicated then and it remains so now – but it's the dichotomy. I remember my grandfather sitting with Uncle Raj in the evenings, sipping whiskey and talking about how many Indian men Pakistan is killing at the border, whereas it was the country where his family lived.'

'Both their families, if you think about it. Because of Partition, both your grandfather's uncle and Uncle Raj's father remained in Pakistan.'

Aryan nods. 'Yes, and there was so much regret everywhere because of this line, this divide. My family regretted not being able to see Justice Cornelius anywhere but on neutral territory. Justice Cornelius regretted how Partition had separated him from his entire family. Michael regretted how his father's decision had alienated him from his cousins. My grandfather regretted not keeping in touch with his friends. Even though we continue to live in a divisive world, we need to find a way to keep the connection alive between common Indians and Pakistanis as much as we can, because of our shared history. These age-old chains of regret need to stop before it's too late.'

20
Returning

∽

'WOULD YOU WANT TO go back to see what Sillanwali is like now?' I remember asking Balbir Singh Bir when I first interviewed him while doing fieldwork for *Remnants*. Born in 1938, he had migrated to India as a nine-year-old during Partition, so, naturally, it surprised me when he drew a detailed map of his home town entirely from memory nearly seven decades later. It was complete with the lemon trees he hid behind as a child and where the schoolboys celebrated the victory of the Allied Forces in the Second World War, even though they had no idea what a war looked like or where it was being fought.

After pondering on my question for a few seconds, he had said, '*Mann toh bohot karta hai*, it is my heart's desire to find a way home, though now I have no strength – neither in my heart nor in my body. But memory remains the saving grace. And so I close my eyes and I make the journey back. Every single day I plunge into the heart of my memory. *Har roz*.'[1]

As I write this, a year has passed since his death. In a way, this chapter is an homage to him, for he exemplified how there was more than one way of returning 'home'. And ever since that conversation, I have made it a point to ask every interviewee about returning – whether they would like to go back to where they or their ancestors were once from. The answers almost always surprise me, to an extent – how even within the desire to return, there may be a story of how

512

one can never return; and how even amongst those who have no interest in returning, there may exist a nostalgia for the place that one can no longer return to.

In this vein, I often go back to Georges Perec's freeform essay 'Espèces d'espaces', translated into English as 'Species of Space', where, in the conclusion titled 'Space (Continuation and End)', he writes:

> I would like there to exist places that are stable, unmoving, intangible, untouched and almost untouchable, unchanging, deep-rooted; places that might be points of reference, of departure, of origin: my birthplace, the cradle of my family, the house where I may have been born ... My spaces are fragile: time is going to wear them away, to destroy them. Nothing will any longer resemble what was, my memories will betray me...[2]

While Perec's initial desire for a static, unchanged past as the nucleus of one's identity appeals to me tremendously, it is his exploration of the reality of the past that I most often encounter in my interviews. In them, the pre-Partition landscape exists as an imaginary space – populated entirely by memory, hence, also changed by memory. As Perec states, *time* wears down the past into fragility, but the Partition line further renders it unreachable. In that sense, as illuminated by Balbir Singh Bir, the process of 'returning' cannot be limited to physically travelling across the border, and has no choice but to extend into other realms like the emotional, sensorial and dream states.

FOR NAVEEN FARHAN, the UK-based historian and PhD candidate at Oxford University, the second-hand memory of where her family comes from before Partition is more beautiful than any lived reality. It is through her research on nostalgia within the remembrance of Lucknow that she chooses to return to the undivided landscape.

'Both sides of my family are originally from the United Provinces*
in India and migrated to Pakistan in 1948,' she tells me. 'My father
was born in 1945 and his family came from Aligarh and Agra, though
during Partition they were in Delhi. I believe my paternal grandfather
stayed back to wrap up work and life while the rest of the family
migrated to Pakistan. He lived temporarily at the refugee camp in
Delhi...' Her voice trails as she tries to remember. 'At the Red Fort?
The Delhi Fort? No, that's not right.'

'Was he at the Old Fort? Purana Qila?'[3] I offer.

'Yes,' she smiles. 'But I don't exactly know when he migrated to
Pakistan and a part of me is really irked that I don't know enough,'
she laughs and adds, 'as a historian, I mean.'

'I know what you mean, but for the longest time the people of
the subcontinent have not been record keepers, as those in the West
have. Our history has been mostly oral, and only now are we getting
into the practice of writing down family stories,' I say in a nod to
our conversation.

'That's true,' she agrees. 'But I think it irks me because I have
done work on Partition as well, and sometimes I end up knowing
more about other people's narratives than my own. As a child, in
school you would hear stories from peers about how their families
migrated across, and they were always so sensational. And I
remember thinking – oh, well, my family's story is just kind of boring,
you know?' she smiles, and then, adopting a graver tone, adds, 'Of
course, when you're that young, you don't realize that having a
conventional or even a boring story – as I thought – was a matter
of immense privilege. The fact that your family was able to migrate
safely across...'

I nod sombrely and then ask, 'You mentioned that both sides of
your family came from India?'

'That's right. My mother's side actually did the exact opposite,
where my maternal grandfather came first to Karachi via plane and

---

* The United Provinces of British India were renamed Uttar Pradesh in
  1950, with the adoption of the Indian Constitution.

then made arrangements for the rest of the family to follow in 1948. They are from Lucknow. My grandfather worked for the British Court of Wards, and I always find it fascinating that amidst all the madness and uncertainty of Partition, they had the privilege to safely plan the journey across. My mother is the youngest of five siblings and the only one born in Pakistan. There's this portrait of all of her elder siblings sitting in a studio, posing away, and I'm told that this photo was taken just before their migration. The idea was that just in case something happened, you needed some sort of photo identity of all the children together.'

'Oh wow!' I exclaim.

'So, the family took a train from Lucknow to Delhi,' she continues, 'and from there they travelled to a border near Sindh in India. I'm vague about details because they're vague about details. What I know is that they were to take a train for the last leg of the journey to Pakistan, but the track had been destroyed. So, they eventually crossed into Sindh on camelback and arrived in Karachi.'

What I really want to do is ask her about Lucknow – why she writes about it, whether she was inspired by her family's stories when she began writing, whether she has ever gone 'back'. But before that, I gather some context. 'Growing up, did you always know that your family had migrated from India?'

'In school everyone would ask each other if they were Sindhi or Punjabi. And I remember being really confused about it and asking my parents, "What are we? Are we Punjabi or Sindhi?" They told me that I was from Karachi and so I deduced that if I'm from Karachi, which is in Sindh province, then I must be Sindhi. I went back to school and told everyone that I was Sindhi, and all the Sindhi kids said I wasn't, but I insisted that I was from Karachi. So, they asked me if I spoke Sindhi, and I said I didn't, and...' Her voice dissolves into an awkward laugh.

'Your family would be *muhajir*, then,' I say.

'That's exactly right. And the term I eventually adopted was Urdu-speaking.' She pauses for a few seconds, as if gathering her thoughts. 'You know, the way history is taught in Pakistan is so state-centric, around the national identity of being Pakistani. *Muhajir* families, well, the narrative told to us in Pakistan was that we were oppressed in India, we struggled to achieve a homeland. India was never our home, and eventually through our struggles and destiny we ended up in Pakistan. Meanwhile, within my maternal family, there remained a lot of nostalgia for Lucknow, which is why I became interested in the city and began researching and writing about it. What is confusing, though, is that my family identifies with Lucknow but not with India – do you know what I mean?' she asks me.

'I do. My paternal grandfather always said Qadirabad and Malakwal, but hardly ever said the word Pakistan. My grandaunt always just says Lahore. Their associations remain localized to the cities and villages they were from, not necessarily the national identity that accompanies them.'

A smile now spreads across Naveen's face. 'There are some people, though, who can immediately recognize that we are from Lucknow. "*Aap Lucknow se hain*," they ask us when we're out shopping, "*aap UP wale hain*?" Just based on the way my mother speaks Urdu.'

'Can you give me an example?'

'Well, the words she uses,' she chuckles, 'sometimes I tease her about them. For instance, my mother will call a plate a *tashtari*, which is the proper, rather uncommon, Urdu word for it, while most people in Pakistan call it a plate. We even say plate in Urdu! But she says it's because she speaks "Lucknow-*wali* Urdu"!' Naveen laughs.

'What's really interesting is that she's the only one who *wasn't* born in Lucknow,' I note.

'And yet there's something quite intrinsic about it within her. She has a sense of belonging to a place that she has never been to, which is why it fascinates me even more,' she reflects.

Intrigued by her comment, I ask, 'So, how do you think we create these invisible connections to places we haven't been to and where we may never go?'

Naveen claps her hands together. 'Isn't that the million-dollar question? In fact, it is *the* question of my thesis! The crux of my research. I think the feeling of belonging to a place rests in the memory that's been passed down of that place.'

'Do you think memory is strong enough to create landscapes of the past? Strong enough that you can return to the past *through* them?'

'Isn't that exactly what memory is?' she asks sincerely. 'To facilitate the imagination of a place, a time, a home? When I began working on Lucknow during my undergrad, I interviewed several people whose families had migrated from there during Partition. I spoke to a woman whose story was similar to my mother's – her parents were massive Lucknow nostalgists, but she had never been there. And when she finally visited her ancestral home in Lucknow, she felt like it was haunted. She said that she didn't like it and felt very uncomfortable the entire time she was there. And so I asked her whether she regretted going to Lucknow, and she said yes, because she grew up hearing these fantastical stories, and the reality couldn't have been more different. When she actually saw her ancestral haveli with her own eyes, the beautiful, imagined landscape was shattered.'

I knit my brows together and then, thinking aloud, say, 'Maybe it's natural to commemorate the house of the past as something beautiful and nostalgic? It makes us feel like another kind of reality was possible, because of the people who inhabited the haveli, and the lifestyle they had, and the memories they created there. But perhaps the present reality just doesn't match up to past memory because it's devoid of the people? All she saw was an old house, not a home.'

Naveen sighs. 'Maybe it's also because the stories she heard were from a completely different time period, of a world before Partition, before gentrification and development. So, there may be an incongruence between what she knew and what she saw.'

'Does your mother want to visit Lucknow?' I ask, now curious.

'She's on the fence about it. Whenever I ask her, she says yes, but then she also reminds me that because of relations between Pakistan and India, it may not even be possible any more to return.'

'And what about you? Since all your work is on Lucknow?'

She thinks about this before answering. 'Actually, because I work on Lucknow, I feel like I know everything about its neighbourhoods and streets, and if you ask me, I can probably even draw you a map of the city! There is a sense of familiarity, a sense of belonging to it. But there are two kinds of questions I always get asked – the first is: why do I work on a city in India rather than one in Pakistan? Why do I work on Lucknow, and not, say, Lahore?'

I nod, listening intently.

'And the second is: how come I work on Lucknow but I've never been to Lucknow? Or, am I going to go to Lucknow? Or, why am I not going to Lucknow?' she laughs, and though I smile, I feel like these are valid questions.

'To be honest, for me, it's not that important to actually go to Lucknow. The physical space is somehow less significant than the imagined one, the one in people's minds, the one they carried, the one they've nurtured. They return to it in their memories and I return with them through second-hand memory. A lot of people I've spoken to in Pakistan approach Lucknow with the idea that they have been separated from it. And often times, I feel the same way.'

This I understand.

'The subject of my identification is the memory of Lucknow rather than the physical space of Lucknow,' she states. And then after a few seconds, she adds with a smile, 'But it's not to say that I don't *return* – I return through the memories I've inherited, through the stories I've collected, through my family, through my research, through books. I return to Lucknow in my own way.'

'MY MATERNAL GRANDFATHER comes from a village called Khurshimul in Mymensingh district, present-day Bangladesh,' Ipsa Samaddar tells me. She was born in Kolkata in 2002 but is currently studying at Ashoka University, Sonipat, and it is through her professor Devapriya Roy that we are introduced.

'At the time of Partition, he was attending school in Gouripur, quite far from Khurshimul, and while the region did not face as much violence as other parts of East Bengal at the time, people had certainly already started migrating to West Bengal. His sister had married into a family in Calcutta, several cousins had moved in 1946. But my grandfather didn't leave till 1949. After his matriculation exams in 1947, he returned to Khurshimul to be with his parents, and by 1949 he'd seen enough packed trains and platforms to know that he would have to leave soon. That was when he boarded a train to Calcutta all alone. His parents stayed behind to look after their property and livestock.'

I ask her why they didn't accompany their son. 'My great-grandmother, Mrinalini – quite the matriarch who controlled the finances and the property – was certainly worried about the future, but my great-grandfather, Nalini, on the other hand, was a sort of absent-minded man. He was absolutely stubborn that he would die where he was born. The India–Pakistan conflict was really nonsense to him, and he was sure that he wouldn't be harmed for staying back.'

I cannot comment on how wise the decision to remain was, but there is something to be said about the almost sacred, undying association to one's land.

Ipsa continues, 'Mrinalini decided to take matters into her own hands and little by little began carrying their precious and inherited objects across the border so that the heirlooms remained safe.'

'What did she carry?' I ask, intrigued.

'Some jewellery, but the bulk of it was brass utensils.' She shows me a large tray with ornate patterns engraved on it, two long-handled ladles and a set of boat-shaped spoons called *kosha-kushi*. 'These utensils had been used annually for Durga Puja in their home since 1910. And these were huge utensils; they took up two trunks, so she would end up making several trips between East Pakistan and India. The people they'd employed in their fields would help her carry the goods to the station. But she made the journey alone. She'd only meant to transport these to the other side and return, because there were several property affairs to be settled in Khurshimul.

'Along the railway route, there was a checking point at a border station called Darshana, and usually the guards wouldn't let anyone take goods from East Pakistan to India. But what my great-grandmother would do was take her luggage directly to the officials, show it to them very clearly and declare that the items were for her children in Calcutta. Apparently, they always let her go, and she managed to bring everything across the border. I've actually heard this story numerous times since I was a child!'

'She sounds incredible,' I say with awe. 'For how long did she go back and forth?'

'All her trips were made roughly between 1950 and '56, because after the last trip in 1956, my grandfather stopped her and refused to let her go back. She was terribly sad because there was much work left in Khurshimul, and she had no faith in my great-grandfather to do anything responsibly.'

'Does that mean that he remained there?'

'Exactly. Between 1956 and 1969, my great-grandparents lived on opposite sides of the border, Mrinalini in India, as her son would not let her return, and Nalini in East Pakistan, because he refused to leave his homeland. She protested for quite some time because they had a good amount of land she needed to sell off and twelve cows that she wanted to entrust to someone else in the village. But she knew her son was keeping her in India out of concern. He himself had returned to Khurshimul several times since leaving in 1949.'

'Did he think that Khurshimul had changed in the years after he left?' I ask.

'I remember asking him what Khurshimul seemed like when he returned, and he said it was hauntingly empty. He specifically used the Bengali phrase "*Dhoo-dhoo korchhilo*" and I translate that as hauntingly empty, because it's the same phrase I've heard being used when someone describes walking through an empty field at night. I remember it specifically from some poem by Tagore, when he was talking about travelling through a field at night before being attacked by dacoits. I suppose that wouldn't be entirely inaccurate if we think of the several houses lying empty and theirs being one of the few occupied ones.'

'Did he say it with sadness?'

'He said it in the same way he had narrated the whole story until then – in a wistful tone, but also very matter-of-fact, as if to say nothing could have been done about it.'

Now returning to Mrinalini and Nalini, who lived on either side of the border for thirteen years, Ipsa says, 'My great-grandmother stayed in India, supporting the extended family and helping her son settle down. He had married, bought some land and even secured a job at the Life Insurance Corporation (LIC) of India. But my great-grandfather wasn't so easily convinced; they wrote to him repeatedly and he would just refuse to migrate every single time. It was only in 1969, as East Pakistan progressed towards the liberation war of 1971, that he was compelled to leave. But that is another story in itself.'

'Ipsa, do you think that your grandfather missed his home in Khurshimul?' I wonder if, like so many others, nostalgia colours her grandfather's history too.

'What is interesting is that though he never spoke about his memories of home, they certainly did influence the kind of plot he chose. He made sure that there would be empty land beside the house so that they could plant fruit trees. He wanted to live close to water, because they'd lived by a river in Khurshimul, so he chose a plot with a pond behind it. My mother was born in 1968, and they lived for about four more years after her birth in that house until they moved to a larger one close by that they'd managed to buy. But before they could start drawing the house plan, my great-grandmother selected spots where she would plant coconut and banana trees. So, my mother grew up in an environment that largely resembled their ancestral property in Khurshimul.'

I am so moved by this, for it means that one can 'return' through recreation of landscape as well.

'In some ways,' I say to Ipsa, 'it seems like he carried an unshakeable image of home, which he tried his best to reproduce, not just for himself but I assume also for his mother, who had been cut off from her land by no choice of her own.'

'Yes, absolutely. But I don't know if he consciously thought of those efforts in terms of creating a home in the image of the one left behind – as much as my great-grandmother might have. That was probably the only landscape of home he knew, so it came naturally to him.'

'You mention that your grandfather never spoke about his home. But have you ever tried to directly ask him about Khurshimul?'

'I actually began interviewing him recently for an assignment. During the interview, I was noting his expressions and where he went quiet, and somewhere along the way I understood that that experience has shaped who he is as a person. He came to Calcutta alone in 1949 and didn't want to depend on his cousins to make a living and support his parents – he had a natural sense of responsibility. More than anyone else, I think it was clear to him that things would not go back to how they used to be before Partition, so he never complained and nor did he look back. Though I'm told that any time Hemen Gupta's film *1942*,[4] based on the Quit India Movement, aired on television and the family was watching it, he'd leave the room.

'He minutely keeps track of the finances and is very independent. He made it a point to instil into my mother and her sister that they must get a stable job before anything else. He's also very quiet and bears any suffering, physical or mental, stoically. He prefers to take responsibility of the family affairs as he always has. My mother, in many ways, is exactly like him, and I've wondered sometimes if those experiences leave some sort of genetic imprint, or if life lessons can be passed down as inheritance.'

'I suppose both are possible, and also likely,' I offer.

'Initially, I was hesitant to ask about Khurshimul and my mother had to explain the project to him. After that, he told me everything I wanted to know, maybe because he considered it necessary for my college assignment. But he doesn't speak of it unless he's asked to.'

'And your mother? Have these stories carved their way into her life?'

'My mother certainly was brought up on a diet of stories from "over there", so most of what I'm telling you has been passed down from my great-grandmother to my mother. She grew up much closer to the kind of environment and times that these stories come from. She could envision it all before her eyes, she could "return" there through second-hand memories and stories. The family did a lot of the activities they did back there, like making pickles and baskets and planting trees, and even the traditional Durga Puja. But my mother also always asserted that she'd never seen either her father or her grandmother explicitly express sorrow or regret over those years.' And then she adds, 'However, there was the incident with the cows.'

I ask her to elaborate, and she takes me back to the 1990s, when her mother was still in college.

'My mother would sleep in the same bed as her grandmother, Mrinalini, ever since she was a child. One night, she woke up hearing her crying. She was saying that she'd failed to do anything about the cows.'

'The cows she wanted to leave in the care of her neighbours?' I recall.

'Exactly. When my great-grandfather had finally been convinced to leave East Pakistan in 1969, my great-grandmother had written to him asking him to sell the property and give the cows to someone who would take care of them. But he had to flee very quickly, so he left the cows to graze in their fields. When he reached Calcutta, the first thing my great-grandmother asked him was what he did with the cows. When she found out, she went very quiet and never said anything about it in the decades to come. This is why my mother was surprised that night. She cried at night a few more times afterwards. She was sure that someone had taken and killed them.'

'What was your mother's reaction?' I ask.

'It was while I was doing research for my assignment that my mother told me this story; it kind of tumbled out. She said that she was initially very surprised, because no one at home ever expressed sorrow over the life they'd left behind. And then, gradually, she tried to understand this sorrow, and perhaps felt it very deeply herself as well. My mother had a pet cat, and she would imagine that the attachment would have been similar, because my great-grandmother used to remember each cow by name and cry for them. My mother used this phrase, "*bhetore jano hahakar*", to describe my great-grandmother's state, which can be translated as "there was a tumult of sorrow within her". But she never got around to asking her why the incident with the cows had resurfaced when it did.'

Keeping in mind all the ways in which her family members have returned "home" – through memory and dreams, conversation and inheritance – I ask Ipsa whether she has a desire to physically return to the land that her great-grandmother loved so much. Her answer is both coloured by a nostalgia for the past and a practicality for the present.

'I'm able to put a patchwork image together. For instance, there was a river called Dinga Pota, a tributary of the Dhanu, that ran close by their house. My great-grandmother would tell me how she would see funnels of water during the monsoon, like elephant trunks, rising on the river in the horizon – she'd been talking about tornadoes! But I've never been exposed to a rural way of life, and so – I don't know how to put this – in my head, it seems like a place that exists only in memory. I've always heard from my family that East Bengal was an unbelievably beautiful place, and I've read countless poems about this too. But they've also maintained that much of that beauty was ravaged by war. So, I don't know if their home still exists, or if the course of the river has changed.

'Also, my grandfather has never wanted to return. I feel like he doesn't want to know what it looks like now. He wants to preserve a pristine image of his home in his memory. You see, I've looked up all these names – Gouripur, Mymensingh, Khurshimul – and Google images suggest that much of the scenery is still rural. But perhaps it's just the way my grandfather speaks about it, like something that *was*, that has discouraged me from seeking it out.'

I understand this, for it is a thought nurtured by those who left their homes and hearths behind – that nothing may exist any longer, that all traces of it now live entirely in memory. But Ipsa is careful not to end our conversation on a sorrowful note.

'I know that image of his home is still very dear to my grandfather because of an incident in Kerala. We had rented a houseboat to visit the backwaters of Alleppey. When the houseboat set out, my grandfather suddenly got very excited and began telling our guides what the river in his home town looked like, and how he and his friends would take a boat out and catch fish. Watching him made me feel simultaneously happy and sad. I've had mixed feelings about going to visit Khurshimul, but, who knows, if I can convince my mother to come along, I might go some time in the future.'

I AM NOT the first person in my family to have returned to the other side. Decades before me, my paternal grandmother's cousin, Lakshman Bir, travelled back to his home in Muryali, D.I. Khan, to discover that the grand ancestral haveli had now been converted into a local school and hostel. Then, some time in their middle age, my grandparents too applied for a visa to visit their homelands, and while my grandfather was granted permission to travel to West Punjab, my grandmother's visa to the erstwhile Frontier Province was rejected. Thinking back to that time, she often tells me that they had promised one another they would go back together or not at all. And so it came to be that that home was now, officially and administratively, out of reach. As a result, when she talks about how Lakshman Bir was able to physically return to Muryali, I listen carefully to discern any sadness or envy in her voice. But all I find is a sense of painful acceptance, that now she may only be able to 'return' through YouTube videos or Google Earth.

However, no matter how removed or impersonal technology may appear to be, it has become one of the only means by which those who left their homes and lands behind can 'see' them once again. Often, children and grandchildren also seek out ancestral homelands using hashtags and geotags. In recent years, initiatives like Project

Dastaan[5] have emerged, where attempting to overcome the near impossibility of witnesses being able to travel across the border, volunteers collect details and descriptions of the childhood landscapes they wish to see.

Having been a part of Dastaan's interviews first-hand, I know that the descriptions can range from something as vague as the fields in so-and-so village or the small hill one used to climb as a child, to as detailed as the exact location of a gurudwara, temple or mosque one took refuge in. Then, teams in India, Pakistan and Bangladesh document these landscapes in film and 'reconnect Partition refugees with their childhood home' through virtual reality. In the last few years, they have reunited refugees with their communities, landscapes, long-lost neighbours and friends on the other side. It is an extraordinary, almost futuristic way to return, but every single volunteer of Project Dastaan is connected to the event of Partition in some way, making it a collectively personal endeavour.

DAYS BEFORE THE seventy-third anniversary of Partition, an elaborate video call – spanning India, Pakistan and America – takes place as a result of a story I had recorded while on field research for *Remnants*. Along with documenting Balbir Singh Bir's memories of Sillanwali, I had also interviewed his wife, Gurdeep Kaur, whose Sikh family had migrated from Burewala Mandi, Multan, to Delhi. Part of her testimony that I had shared online reads:

> The only radio of Burewala Mandi, Multan, belonged to the Muslim family across the street. The first time anyone from my family ever listened to a radio, it was to hear about the war. The year was 1942. After that, it became routine. Every night the news was broadcasted at 9 p.m. and everyone from the village would gather around that sole radio – Hindu, Muslim, Sikh, it didn't matter. *Jung di khabar sab nu chahiye di*, everyone followed the war with keen interest. My brother was also born during the 9 p.m. news. The year was 1947 and I was barely six years old, but I remember that I ran across the street

to tell the good news to my father. That night, neighbours of all religions celebrated the news of the birth together. And then, barely forty days later, those very same neighbours were separated by the news of the Partition.

Halfway across the world, in New York City, 1987-born Sanam Zaman Khan reads this excerpt and comments that Burewala Mandi, in present-day Pakistan, happens to be her home town.[6] Balbir Singh and Gurdeep Kaur's son, Jasminder Gulati, who was born in 1970 in Sindri, Bihar, and divides his time between Delhi and Hyderabad, responds to the comment and thus begins a conversation between the two where Sanam asks Jasminder whether his mother still speaks 'Burewala Punjabi', and revealing that her father, Malik Inayat Ullah Khan, is the *numberdar*[7] of Burewala. She proposes to set up a call between the elders. Jasminder, in turn, replies that 'tears are perhaps in order'.

A quick phone call eventually leads to a longer video call with various members of the two families as they discuss what remains of Gurdeep Kaur's ancestral haveli in Burewala. Her family asks questions about the still-standing homes, the gurudwara, the lanes, the bazaars, the skies, the fields, the earth, the smells. Through the eyes of Sanam's parents, a Sikh family originally from Multan and now dispersed across the world 'return' *home*, and in the process find themselves part of a unique cross-border, multireligious, patchwork-like family. It is a privilege to be invited to join this call, and the irony is not lost on me that in a few days, as we approach the seventy-third anniversary of being divided, there are still ways of remaining united, if our hearts so desire.

A few weeks after this call, I speak with Jasminder.

'All I can start with is to say that it was surreal to "go back" this way – the fact that it's even possible through technology, the fact that a place across the border suddenly feels so close, almost within grasp, you know? There's always been a sense of wanting to touch a piece of my parents' history, wanting to return something to them.' He pauses and with a smile continues, 'But I could have never imagined that there was a whole next generation of divided South Asians willing to ... engage with one another.'

I smile, because 'the other side' always seems so inaccessible until it is a mere video call away.

'It had never occurred to me before that I could actively seek out someone of Pakistani origin. And speaking specifically about Sanam now, this connection is not just between her parents and mine – the generation that lived through Partition – but also her and me. That was the most powerful realization.'

'You've always been interested in preserving the stories of Partition,' I comment.

'Yes, but I do have a confession to make – it's only in the last ten years that I became intrigued about my father's story. For most of my life, I've been closer to my mother. And then I found out that my father had lost his mother at the age of five, and, I don't know, perhaps I began making up for lost time, but I started to actively document his history in a very serious way. I was curious about where he came from and how he grew up. In that sense, I've always been fonder of my father's Partition story than my mother's. Years ago, it was *he* who you came to meet and then ended up documenting more of my mother's story. But my father was always the natural storyteller.'

'How so?' I ask, thinking back to our first meeting.

'My mother would tell the same stories repeatedly – so did my father, but he had a repertoire which was larger or rather more intriguing. For instance, a story he told often was how every night after dinner at 9 p.m., he and his friends would play a game where they would search for a specific leaf from a specific tree – mango or guava or lemon, or whatever. It was such an endearing story, and each time he narrated it more details were added, another layer of childhood was offered. Now this story is kind of lodged in my head, and I replay it over and over every night.'

I want to ask Jasminder if this is particularly the case of late, ever since he lost his father. But I don't have the heart to voice this question, and so I merely listen.

'My mother wouldn't give me these childhood stories. And so I just thought that my father had humbler, more grounded, more interesting stories than she did. But maybe I didn't give my mother adequate time, as I'm able to now that...' His voice trails off.

I reflect on what he has said. 'Your father's stories were more connected to where he was from. There was a sense of belonging, of actively remembering the spaces he came from. He would think about the landscape, he would dream about it. He was also older than your mother when Partition happened.'

'Also, the fact that my mother was a young girl who was not allowed so much at that time,' he adds.

'That's exactly what I was going to say. He had access to a more visible history. He spoke of the war and how the railway tracks were ripped out so that their metal could be used in the war effort, how he would go and play even after dinner as the day settled into night. As a young girl, what did she remember – the house, the food, the shawls, the *parandis*, the *naale*, the more intimate aspects of daily life? I guess their ways of storytelling were different. But why I was more fascinated by her stories was because they were, in some sense, the quieter histories of women and ordinarily inaccessible. I found them to be jewels of information, almost.'

Two houses belonging to Jasminder's mother's family still stand in Burewala Mandi today. To demonstrate just how small the world truly is, the house that was once Jasminder's granduncle's is adjacent to Sanam's granduncle's property. Situated on the main road in Multan, the red-brick house surrounded by a lush garden and tall trees was integral to her childhood memories. During the call, her family mentioned how it now belongs to an eminent member of parliament and is the hub of political activities in Multan. The second house is close to the main bazaar and a few minutes' walk from the local gurudwara, which remains intact in all its glory.

'I don't know how to put this in words,' Jasminder begins, 'but the houses were still alive in Burewala, the gurudwara was still alive, *abhi bhi zinda tha, khada tha*. People have come and gone through history, the land itself has changed in name and citizenship, but those buildings have survived. They were still standing and that was surreal to grasp ... I-I'm not able to put what I feel into words,' he says, overwhelmed.

I wait till he gathers his thoughts, looking into the distance, smiling, and then with composure he begins again. 'What I mean is that sometimes you make a connection with a place, and even though you may leave the place, it endures, it continues as it always has. Life is lived around it still, just as it had been when you were there. Maybe there is a certain romanticism at play here, but I feel like places have strong characters; they have life, they see things. Have you ever had that feeling?'

'*All the time,*' I stress. 'I always feel as though even unmoving, inanimate places have life. Their doors, their walls, their hinges, their windows absorb energy and contain memory. I don't know what happens to them while they're waiting, but they wait. Sometimes they wait for people, other times they wait out their fate. You're lucky that your mother's house is still there, and what you will feel when you actually go back there will be incomparable.'

'Exactly.' He nods enthusiastically. 'The house is alive. It has history. It is waiting for someone to come back. Can I write to the house and find out if my mother will ever return there? Can I speak to the house? Can I ask it, *Will you encounter this woman again?*'

I feel my cheeks getting warmer. I have asked these questions before – about my paternal grandmother's home in Muryali now turned into a school, about my maternal grandmother's home in Lahore razed to the ground during riots, about my two grandfathers' homes I know nothing about. I have asked these questions sometimes just to hear them out loud.

'I can imagine these conversations with the house,' I say to Jasminder with a small smile, 'I can imagine you asking, *Will you wait for us? We aren't far, will you endure a little longer?*'

'This waiting to touch a home of the past is another large theme that has remained in my mind after that video call,' he says. 'Placing your hands on the wall, feeling the ground beneath your feet, even seeing the house from a distance may give you the highest sense of peace. I think that is the kind of closure so many people who were separated from their homes at Partition seek – to go back just once, to see it all again with your own eyes. There is a sense of wanting to become one with a place you know is an intrinsic part of you. Mere photographs may never do justice to that feeling.'

Holding on to these words, I write an email to Sanam, curious to know her impetus for reuniting Jasminder's mother with her childhood home virtually. Her response is inspired by her own separation from Burewala since 2018:

> The pain of leaving one's home town and immigration came naturally to me. I felt that we shared the love and longing for the place where we were born and brought up and had to leave. But we each carry that place in us wherever we go. That place becomes a precious part of our memories. We visit it often in our dreams, in our conversations with our loved ones. I felt it my responsibility to connect her with her beloved birthplace of which she talked so lovingly. In her memories, I found a melody of the heart that resonated with my own homesick soul. I found my own way home, the shared place where we belong. It is in this way – in her memories and mine – that Partition remains relevant in the present world.

THE LEGENDARY INDIAN photographer Raghunath Rai Chowdhry, better known as Raghu Rai, was born in 1942 in Jhang, present-day Pakistan. Trained to be a civil engineer but abandoning the profession soon after starting work, he picked up his brother's Agfa Super Sillete film camera in 1965 and accompanied a friend on a shoot to take photographs of children at a local village. But it was a donkey that made Raghu Rai truly want to become a photographer. In an interview with *The Guardian* nearly forty years after the incident, Rai spoke about seeing the donkey foal in a nearby field. He tried to get closer, but when he was about ten feet away, the animal began running and the children burst into laughter. This led him to chase his subject for nearly three hours in order to amuse his audience. When the donkey got tired, Rai photographed the animal up close, head bowed, in the soft evening light against a fading landscape.[8] This first photograph went on to be published in the *Times*, London, as a half-page spread with a byline. And so a photographer was born.

Five decades later, I meet Raghu Rai in his Delhi office, and as we speak about his family's migration from Jhang to India during Partition and the return to his home town thirty years after, I encounter another story about another donkey.

'I don't indulge in nostalgia,' is the first thing he says when I broach the topic, 'but the fact remains that I was five years old at the time of Partition.'

'What happened to your family at the time?'

'We are from Jhang–Maghiana,' he says, pronouncing it in a uniquely lilting Punjabi way, as *Mighyana*, 'and I was just a child when we left. But what I do recall is that from the main bazaar of Jhang there was a lane that cut to the right, and in that lane every house was multi-storeyed. The lane couldn't have been more than 100–150 metres long, and at the end was our house, three or four storeys high. And the good thing about it being the last house was that our back door opened into the next lane. This is the one thing I remember well. In 1947, when the Partition riots began, all our neighbouring houses were set on fire.

'The neighbours knew that our house opened on the back, and they collected there so we could all eventually escape together. It was around midnight when we trickled out into the back lane. Eventually, we made it to a very big refugee camp on the Pakistani side. I had five sisters and three brothers, and along with our parents we stayed in that camp for a few days until we could catch a train to the Indian side.'[9]

'What do you remember the most from that journey?'

'The fires,' he says immediately, 'I remember the fires most vividly. That was the most horrible sight.'

'And you were just five years old – what did you think was going to happen?'

He chuckles, 'Just that we all may die! What else could I have thought? If our house had not opened on the back side, we may have been trapped.'

I return to the refugee camp. 'How did you finally cross over into India?'

'We caught a train. We were packed in like luggage. And that is how we reached Jalandhar.'

I ask if he recalls the month, or even the weather, and with a click of his tongue he dismisses it. 'Oho, what a difficult question! Now there are no elders left for me to even ask. Paul, my elder brother, remembered a lot, he had a phenomenal memory. But I don't remember Partition being discussed at home, or maybe it's because I am not a nostalgic person...' His voice trails off for a few seconds, and then, picking up a disconnectedly connected thread, he says in a rather sombre tone, 'Though, in 1971, when I was working in Bangladesh,[10] photographing refugees in camps, walking across the border, seeing the state they were in, I would think to myself that perhaps this was what we must have looked like as well. This was what the 1947 Partition must have been like. I used to remember our journey, the shorts I was wearing, the train we boarded.' He takes a deep breath and then looks at me, as if returning to the present day.

The sound of traffic from the street below floats into the room through an open window and merges with dim sounds of *bansuri* playing in the next room. Clearing my throat, I now say, 'Avani told me that you've had a chance to return to Jhang.' It was his daughter who had invited me to speak with him.

A wide smile appears on the photographer's face. 'Actually, in 1977, when Vajpayee sahib went to Pakistan as the foreign minister, I was working with the *Sunday* magazine and was asked if I'd like to be part of the accompanying press delegation. Saeed Naqvi went as the correspondent from *The Indian Express*, as did K.K. Katyal from *The Hindu*. Mr Katyal was also from Jhang and had done his graduation from Jhang College. So, we travel to Pakistan and at an official dinner are introduced to President Zia-ul-Haq, who is aware that many of us would be from that side of the border. He asks me where I'm from. "*Aap toh paas se hi honge*," he says, and I tell him that I am from Jhang–Maghiana, as is Mr Katyal, who stands beside me. He asks the two of us whether we would like to visit our birthplace once again, and naturally we say we'd love to. So, the very next morning, Mr Katyal, Saeed – who remains a good friend – and I are taken to Jhang in the presidential car!' he says with a laugh.

'1977 would have been exactly thirty years after you left,' I observe.

'That's right, I was thirty-five years old. Mr Katyal was older than me, so he remembered his neighbourhood and home. He visited his college and met the principal. They began sharing stories, with a side of tea and biscuits. The principal cried, Mr Katyal cried, and it wasn't even as though they knew one another before Partition, but the sheer fact that Mr Katyal had returned *home* was connection enough. Then I was asked about my house, and I said that though I wanted to find it, I didn't remember where it was. The difficult thing in 1977 was that my parents were no more, and there were no mobiles. I tried calling Paul but couldn't get through; he was some sixteen-odd years older and would have remembered. But anyway...'

I now begin to understand what he means by not indulging in nostalgia. His recollections are light and animated, even on matters that remain heavy. He does the voices, the accents, the gestures. Much like his photographs, he invites one into the landscape of his history.

'So, we begin walking the streets of Jhang, and every Pakistani we meet is so affectionate. We don't know the address of my house, but we meet an old woman, a *dai*, a midwife. I tell her it's possible she was present at my birth and she begins to ask about my parents: "*Puttar, kaun si tere pita, kaun si teri mata?*" But she didn't remember them. Then, as we are walking up and down the streets, trying to recognize anything that may look familiar, people begin to gather around, walking with us, talking to us lovingly. In the crowd, there was a small boy...' He reaches out to the shelf behind him, grabs a book titled *Family and Friends*, and opens it to a particular page. '*Yeh dekho*, take a look.'

At the centre of the page is a young Raghu Rai, seated – almost unbelievably – on a donkey! Men with turbans on their heads or chadars wrapped across their bodies, and boys in sweaters surround the photographer in a narrow street in Jhang. Everyone is smiling. Rai himself is laughing and the donkey bears a lovely resemblance to the donkey in the 1965 photograph. A slim, elegant minar can be seen at the back, and traditional brickwork houses with arched windows flank the crowd on either side. The image is striking and jovial, the kind that immediately fills your heart with warmth, an apt depiction of *returning home*. The description, in Rai's own words, reads:

> …the people on the street were so warm and hospitable, they started following me saying, '*Hindu aaya, Hindu aaya.*' As we were walking from street to street looking for a house, one boy with a donkey was following us. He couldn't resist and offered me his donkey as an expression of friendship. 'Bauji, you've been walking around, you must be tired, why don't you sit on my donkey?' 'Sure!' I was thrilled. And Saeed … grabbed it with my camera.

'This is beautiful,' I say, though I can barely speak through my smile.

'It was so sweet, so well-meaning. Just look at the number of people around us, look at their faces. And thank god for Saeed, he had the imagination to capture this photo! It's such a vibrant way for me to remember the day. I never found my home, but that didn't really matter because just returning to Jhang was quite a memorable experience.'

THE STORIES OF returning are shared not only by those who left their home towns in 1947 but also by subsequent generations who have independently travelled to the other side.

'To give you some context,' 1985-born Shreyoshi Saha, a social entrepreneur and founder of ImmerseGo,* tells me, gesturing to her sister, Shiny, 'we are third-generation settlers in Delhi, and our paternal grandfather joined the Royal Air Force well before Partition, leaving behind a wife and three children in Simulia. At the time, the village was in district Bikrampur, East Bengal, but today falls in district Munshiganj of Dhaka division in Bangladesh. He took part in the Second World War but was not deployed overseas. Just to be clear, we never heard any stories from our grandparents about their migration from East Bengal to India at the time of Partition.'

Shiny, who is one year younger than her sister, now adds, 'We never really took an active interest in asking them stories of Partition either.'

Shreyoshi was in the first year of college when their grandfather passed away, followed by their grandmother the next year. She tells me that because of the air force, the family was posted across the country, and so stories of how they reached the airbase in India during Partition were eclipsed by how they ultimately settled in Delhi. But encouraging her sister, she now says, 'Tell her about your trip to Bangladesh.'

Shiny nods. 'Before I get to that, I want to reiterate what my sister said – though we grew up with our grandparents in a joint family, we rarely asked about the past. Our grandfather was quite a reserved person; even after his retirement from the Indian Air Force, many of his work habits remained with him. He kept a schedule for his day. I remember only a single time when I was a child that he spoke about Simulia. He told me that he and his friends would go boat-racing as the village was on the banks of a river, and they would sing songs as they raced – you know, racing songs,' she chuckles. 'But even then, I don't really remember caring so much about this as a child. I didn't

---

* ImmerseGo is an Art Integrated Education Technology platform for institutions, educators and learners, offering programmes and toolkits to aid multidisciplinary, experiential and joyous learning.

pay attention. I guess you assume that the people who are there now will always be there to tell you their stories.'

Shreyoshi, who has been listening to her sister, adds, 'When I look back, I do think it's a bit weird that there wasn't a more active connection built across generations. We never used the medium of storytelling to connect to the past.'

'Well, do you regret that now?' I ask.

'I do.' She thinks about this. 'I certainly wish that we had asked more about their journey to India. But the one thing I do remember distinctly asking my grandmother about was her home – she was originally from Narayanganj, also now in Bangladesh. I'd ask her to describe exactly what it looked like, creating an imaginary landscape in my mind. I suppose I thought that if we can't physically travel back to her homeland, maybe we can do it through her memories. So maybe there was awareness as we grew older, but not really as children,' she says. 'But the real story of our returning begins with my sister.'

'It was in 2014,' Shiny says, 'that I first went to Bangladesh for work – I'm a development professional in the not-for-profit sector. And of course, I wanted to see our ancestral village, but I didn't know how to find my way there. I was travelling with a senior colleague who was also Bengali and wanted to visit his village, but his grandparents had built a school there, so he could trace it back easily. He'd also been in touch with people in Bangladesh through Facebook and had clearly done a lot more planning than I had.

'It made me feel ... well, unprepared. But see, I had three important details that my father had given me. The first was that we were from a village called Simulia; the second that it was in district Bikrampur; and third that it was right by Tarpasha jetty. So, once we were in Bangladesh, we had a free day and my colleague told me to come along with him to his village, and I thought to myself, *Well, why don't I just try to find mine instead?* So, I began asking around within our research organization, and someone happened to locate the village on a map and told me that it now fell in district

Munshiganj. He also put me in touch with someone named Lenin, who was from there and could help.

'I was also told that he had a literary bent of mind; he liked to write. Coincidentally, our day off also happened to be the day that community elections were taking place in Munshiganj, and Lenin was headed there to cast his vote. So, as I was waiting at my guest house in Dhaka, a car drives up and a man steps out and asks me if I'm the guest from India. I assume that this is Lenin but turns out it's not. This man is named Hannan and he is someone from his entourage. He tells me that though Lenin bhai is from Munshiganj, *he* is actually from Simulia and will help me find our home, if it still stands. So, I get into the car and –'

Shiny suddenly pauses, thinks about what she has said, and her face contorts into a strangely alarmed expression. 'Come to think of it, I didn't even have a working phone! I just hopped into a car with two strangers in a foreign country! Imagine that.'

'I actually didn't even think of that,' I admit in a quiet voice.

'Me neither,' she says, still a bit alarmed. 'I think I was just so caught up in the excitement and nervousness of what I may find that I didn't think of all *this*. But anyway, Lenin and I are sitting in the back, and Hannan is in the front with the driver. Now, since he is literarily inclined, Lenin gives me a book or two that he's written and he expects me to read them. I have grown up in Delhi and didn't learn Bangla in school. I can speak it, but I have to admit that I struggle with the reading. With trial and error, I somehow manage, but it takes me half an hour to read, like, four words – most of which was guesswork!' Shiny starts laughing.

'The fact that one doesn't read Bangla is really looked down upon amongst the greater Bengali intelligentsia,' Shreyoshi explains.

'Well, I'm Punjabi and I can't read Gurmukhi or Shahmukhi, and only understand very basic Punjabi.' Though I am embarrassed to say this aloud, it dawns on me that this, too, may be a consequence of Partition. The further we move from an undivided India, from the landscapes where we originally belonged, the more diluted our languages, scripts and customs may become. Untethered to our soil, we acclimatize to our adoptive homes, learn new languages and begin to establish and practise new customs. I cannot forget how my paternal grandparents almost always spoke in Punjabi or fragments of Urdu with each other – for those were the languages they had grown up with – but with me they conversed in English or Hindi. I have heard my parents playfully speak in Punjabi at family events and weddings, but it has never been the language of communication within our home. Maybe because I hardly heard it, I didn't pick it up, and it has ironically now become a language that feels almost unnatural and foreign on my tongue.

'But I haven't heard of Punjabi grandparents looking down on their grandchildren for not being able to speak the language,' Shiny comments with a smile.

'That is true,' I agree, and she returns to her story.

'I pretended to read the book, but the car was moving, so it took even longer than usual, and then I just came clean. As expected, he gave me the what-kind-of-a-Bengali-are-you-if-you-can't-even-read-Tagore-in-the-original look. And I thought to myself that this was going to be one *very long* car journey. We got into a whole discussion on mother tongue and growing up in Delhi...' She waves her hand in dismissal and tells me that eventually they reached Simulia.

'How did it feel to finally be there?' I ask with anticipation.

'I've been asked this question many times before, actually,' she admits. 'Last year alone, I travelled to Bangladesh three or four times, whereas I haven't been to Kolkata in nearly five years. But that first time, it wasn't so much an immediate connection – like, this is where my ancestors are from – as much as it was a kind of strange and comfortable familiarity. It was the countryside, and it just looked very similar to the Bengal countryside in India. It was lush and green and there were water bodies. I didn't feel out of place or like I was in another country; it just felt familiar. But the single thought running through my head was how little a chance we had of actually finding the house.'

'No research,' Shreyoshi reminds me.

'Yep,' Shiny agrees. 'So, Hannan called up one of his contacts who happened to be Hindu and told him about our grandfather and great-grandfather. And this Hindu person pointed him in a general direction because I was able to provide the name of the jetty the house was around. And so we reach this house, this very big, very grand house...'

'You found it?' I ask, eyes wide.

'Yes, and Hannan had planned further than I had because he handed me a plastic jar. He said that I had returned to my roots and it was only fair I took some earth back with me. I had that in mind as well, but clearly I didn't even imagine we would get this far,' she laughs. 'So, I begin filling the jar, but then I suddenly stop and think to myself that it all feels too easy, that I should at least confirm that this is our house. Our grandparents had seven children, three before Partition – our father's eldest sister was seven at the time – and so, standing in front of the house, I phone her. I should mention here that no one in our extended family knew that I was going to Bangladesh, and so she was shocked and kept asking me if I was really there. Now, for someone who had left her home when she was seven years old to suddenly recollect memories, as if on demand...' Her voice trails off.

All the while, Shreyoshi has been listening to her sister with as much investment as perhaps the first time she heard this story. She now says, 'But she told Shiny exactly where to turn, what river body to cross when, and how far *our house* was from that grand house they thought was ours. Our aunt is eighty now, but during that phone call it was like she returned to her seven-year-old self. Her recall was remarkable. It was as if a map of her childhood home had remained imprinted in her mind.'

Shiny smiles and says, 'Meanwhile, another old man, who also happened to be Hindu, walked up to us and Hannan told him that I'd come from Delhi and we were searching for my ancestral home. He asked me my grandfather's name, and I said, "Kanai Lal Saha," and he replied in the Bangal dialect. Do you know the Ghoti–Bangal distinction? The Ghoti dialect is spoken in West Bengal and Bangal in East.' I nod, so she continues, 'Our grandparents spoke it, but I can't, so I didn't follow what he said, but Hannan told him to keep quiet, which naturally only intrigued me further. Eventually Hannan told me that the old man had said something I may take offence to – that my great-grandfather had had two marriages. But I just nodded and told them that his first wife had passed away, which was why he remarried. Anyway, cutting a long story short, because I confirmed that my great-grandfather was married twice, this old man could confirm that we were in front of the wrong house! Just like my aunt had said. And so, obviously, my first instinct was to dump out all the earth from the plastic jar!' As she says this, the two sisters burst into laughter.

'Y-you threw it out?' I ask.

'Well, yeah,' Shiny says as she catches her breath, 'because it wasn't … you see, the house was really very grand, and naturally you begin to imagine the kind of grandeur you come from. One minute you think you've come home, and the next minute you realize you're just taking earth from someone else's yard!'

I am kind of in awe as I watch Shreyoshi and Shiny narrate their story with a lightness that I hardly ever encounter while speaking about Partition. At the same time, the humour and buoyancy in their delivery never seem to take away from the seriousness of personal history.

'Bottom line,' Shiny tells me, 'the original house no longer exists, there's just a small shack in its place.'

'And it's a flood-prone area,' Shreyoshi adds, 'next to the river Padma, so the shack is on stilts. But I don't remember hearing that we lived on a house on stilts.'

'Exactly,' Shiny laughs and picks up the story again. 'So, we get to the location and, obviously comparing it to the grand house, I think to myself, *This is the house we had?* But this was just a caretaker's shack, and so I take the soil from *this* land, *our* land, and fill up my plastic jar. We walk closer to the river and there are shops – also on stilts – and I remember that our family used to own a shop there. The old man, who is still walking with us, shows me the shop that our great-grandfather owned, which has now been divided into four shops! One of them was a *mithai-wallah*, a sweet shop, and the owner gave me a piping hot rosogolla. Then, because it was too hot, he poured water over it, and I'm not even joking, it was the best rosogolla of my life!' She brings her fingers up to her lips and smacks them, blowing a chef's kiss.

'Wait!' Shreyoshi interrupts her. 'Tell her the full story about who the man was. How can you forget? I can't believe *I* remember!' She turns to me and laughs.

What I witness that evening is a fascinating apportioning of memory – where one sibling vicariously lives through the experiences of another who has had the opportunity to return, not once but multiple times. Through the telling and retelling of these experiences, Shreyoshi has memorized the details in a way that they come to her naturally even if Shiny may have forgotten them. Because she was not witness to history, she has made sure to preserve every detail of it, even in its second-handedness. I have only ever witnessed this transference between the generations of a family, but even amongst siblings it is beautiful, for it means that memory can settle deeply in anyone who has the desire to preserve it.

'The person who owned the mithai shop,' Shreyoshi tells me excitedly, 'was actually someone who used to visit our great-grandfather's shop as a child. Each time he came by, our great-grandfather used to give him something to eat, like a sweet or a snack. They were generations apart but they shared a unique bond. So, when he found out who Shiny was, he got so emotional and … then when we heard this in Delhi, *we* all got so emotional because we had apparently just missed eating the best rosogolla on Earth! He had given Shiny two of them to eat together, and … did he also start crying?' She turns to her sister.

'He had tears in his eyes for sure.' Shiny's voice is wistful now. 'It was very overwhelming to meet someone who actually knew our ancestor, had spent time with him. And I have to say that if it wasn't for our aunt, we may have never found the real plot of land. She was our last anchor, in a way.'

'Our father has always wanted to visit Bangladesh,' Shreyoshi says, 'but we never had any tangible connection to the other side, we never knew where or how to begin before Shiny actually went there. Now our resolve to return has strengthened.'

'THE FIRST CONVERSATIONS on Partition may have been about my grandmother's pet elephant, Kusum,' Varun Mallik recalls, and I am immediately intrigued. 'My thamma, Nanda Roy Mallik, filled my childhood with her stories from East Bengal. She was born in 1939 into a zamindari family that lost everything during their migration to India. But I grew up hearing stories of the palanquins used for travel, and seeing large, framed photographs of ornately designed mansions.' He shows me a sepia photograph of an elephant with her mahout. 'That's Kusum, standing by the main steps of their home in Taljanga.'

Varun was born in 1998 and now divides his time between Kolkata and Oxford. In 2014, his family visited Bangladesh to see what had remained of his grandmother's childhood on the other side. This was preceded by many years of storytelling and nostalgia, which inspired them to take her back to the land of her birth.

'The house that my grandmother was born in was built by her great-grandfather, Raj Chandra Roy, probably around the 1850s–60s, and was named after him. She was the second youngest of seven children – five daughters and two sons – and grew up between this ancestral home in Taljanga, a city house in Mymensingh, where her grandfather worked as a lawyer and had easier access to the courts, and a third summerhouse in Kishoreganj. When Partition happened, they didn't immediately migrate to India but certainly worried about the growing violence. There is evidence in the form of letters that my grandmother's mother wrote to her sister-in-law living in Calcutta at the time.[11] My grandmother was one of five sisters and her mother was very concerned because each day they would hear horrific stories of abductions, rapes and violence against women. There was a lot of correspondence within the family during this time, but they remained in East Pakistan until 1948.

'My grandmother's youngest uncle was married on the day Gandhi was assassinated, 30 January 1948. They got news of the death and immediately imagined the worst in terms of rioting and violence. Gandhi's death has historically been known to mark the end of Partition violence, but, for my family, it symbolized that things were never going to be the same again. And that is when they migrated to Calcutta. They came as refugees, but not in the conventional sense – they had a home to live in but carried nothing much apart from items of religious importance like their idols or prayer utensils or jewellery. They thought they'd be able to return in a few months. My grandmother's father also frequently visited Taljanga, as their bank accounts and wealth were very much still there; taxes were being paid there. The government began an exchange programme where property was granted in lieu of what had been left behind, and for the Taljanga home they were offered a cinema hall and a very grand property in India, but my great-grandfather refused it because he was just so certain that the family would eventually return *home*.

'It was in 1951 that he finally accepted the permanence of the border, and everything began to sink in. They had lost all their houses where their children had been born and raised, all the land that had been in the family for generations, the soil where their grandparents had lived. Everything was now lost, and my great-grandfather just spiralled into depression and died in 1955. Four years later, his wife followed, which meant that my grandmother and her siblings, who were all still young, lost both their parents and their homeland within a few years. They had no income of any sort and no property apart from the house they lived in. So, they grew up with the support of their uncles and slowly sold off all the family jewellery to be able to survive.

'My grandmother tells me that it was a difficult upbringing, but it sounds like the need to move on almost eclipsed all the surmounting losses. I think the loss began to gnaw at them only when they had settled down, gotten married, had children of their own. It was only then that they could think back to what had truly happened at Partition.' Varun pauses to consider a thought and then says, 'Though, looking objectively from a distance, I think they started realizing that things were changing the moment the elephant was taken away from them. I think it was a sign for what was to come…'

I crinkle my eyebrows. 'What do you mean?'

'Kusum was a domesticated elephant that belonged to my grandmother's great-grandmother, who was the real matriarch of the family and looked after the finances, lands and property. Her husband passed away in 1914, and she remained a widow until she died in 1941 or '42. Bura ma, she was called by all, great-grandmother. When the Second World War began, Kusum was taken either to Assam or Burma to fell trees for the war effort; all the elephants owned by zamindar families were brought in. But Kusum wasn't used to any labour, so it took a toll on her fairly quickly and she passed away. Bura ma died after she got news of Kusum…' His voice dissolves into silence.

I feel rather silly for how full my heart suddenly becomes. 'I don't know why but the elephant is really affecting me,' I manage to admit.

Varun smiles. 'I think her story affected me deeply as well.[12] As I said, it was one of the first interactions I had about the Taljanga house and my grandmother's life. I think this is also how my generation and my parents' differ in our interactions about the past – I really believed these stories because my grandmother was at an age where she could indulge in them again. Whereas, perhaps, when my parents were growing up, life was still very much about settling down. So maybe grandchildren interact with the past on a different, more intimate level. My brother and I are far more affected by the loss of our grandmother's homeland than our parents. It is central to our upbringing and certainly the reason why I chose history as a discipline for further study. It was also why we knew we had to go back to Bangladesh.'

'Tell me about your trip,' I say, and together we step into the past and across the eastern border.

'It was after I'd done very well in my Grade 10 board exams in 2014 that my parents asked me what I wanted as a present, and I told them I'd like to go to Bangladesh. I'd seen photographs and heard so much about my grandmother's life there, and it was her seventy-fifth birthday that year. I didn't think there could be a better present for both of us than to go and see whether her home was still standing.

'But a bit of backstory. My grandmother went back to Bangladesh in 1984. She was the only one to do so, and this surprised me because every single one of her siblings and cousins constantly spoke about Taljanga but never went back. Anyway, my grandfather was in the civil service and went to Dhaka on an official trip, accompanied by my grandmother. After two days in Dhaka city, they travelled to Mymensingh, where she discovered that her grandfather's house had been taken over by the Bangladeshi government and converted into a college, and then to Kishoreganj, where a maulvi sahib and his family now lived in their summerhouse. She was delighted to see them both, though, and because of her trip, we knew the houses in Mymensingh and Kishoreganj still stood, but nothing about the Taljanga house, which was really the emotional tether for my grandmother, because that's where she was born.

'In October 2014, my grandmother, parents, younger brother and I travelled from Kolkata to Dhaka. Accompanying us in Dhaka was a man called Masoom Mian, the driver-cum-guide for our entire trip. The Mymensingh house was close to a railway track, and we knew this because one of my grandmother's uncles had fallen in love with a woman who lived across the railway tracks and they would see one another from their respective terraces on either side. They eventually married,' Varun chuckles. 'We located the house, which had since been renamed Alamgir Mansur (Minto) Memorial College. A large portion of the estate had been renovated but the main house still served as the administrative block of the college. We even went up to the terrace and saw the railway tracks. An old caretaker with a long white beard recalled how someone – my grandmother – had come to see the building in 1984. He also confirmed that the Taljanga house still stood, since he knew that it was once owned by the same family.

This was a revelation to us. So, we ended up collecting some soil from the land and labelling it, and then returned to the hotel, quite happy!

'On the third day, 27 October, I think, we headed out in search of the Taljanga house. At the time, my grandmother's sister was still alive. She was eighteen years old when Partition happened, so her memory of the house was quite clear. Armed with her directions, as well as an old black-and-white photograph of the house, we began driving. Masoom Mian would often stop and ask people about "*boro bari*", which means big house, and they kept telling us to drive on until we reached the "*jomidar bari*", which is what they called the zamindar's house. But we still didn't know whether it was my grandmother's house. So, we drove until we came across a small river with a bridge that led to a big iron gate that opened to a plot of land, and on our left' – he takes a deep breath – 'there it was – the Taljanga house!'

I gasp. 'You found it!'

He laughs. 'There was a lot of excited squealing: "*Roko, roko, gaadi roko.*" And we all scrambled out of the car. I don't think there was anything more exciting than actually finding the house. So much of it had remained the same, as if time had stood still since their migration, and yet so much had also changed. The house was abandoned and had become dilapidated to the extent that nature had swallowed it. Large creepers had claimed every wall, the staircases were covered in moss, foliage had entwined the grand columns...

'We began walking around, taking pictures, and it was very, very emotional. Even now, just thinking about it is making me emotional. A few people came up to us and asked who we were and my grandmother introduced herself. Meanwhile, students from the school that had been built right across the house made their way to the grounds, and within minutes a hundred people surrounded us: children, adults, teachers, locals, all telling us about how they'd heard of the zamindar family that once lived here, but no one had ever returned to the house. Multiple groups of people began showing us around, and some even came up with their ancestors' photos, saying their father used to work as a cook in this house, or their grandfather took care of the gardens. So, they all had their photos, just as we had ours. It was a really beautiful moment of shared history, all revolving around this historic house.'

Showing me photographs from his trip, Varun tells me that there still exists a plaque on one of the sections that reads '*RAJ CHANDRA HALL, 1914*', which is the year the patriarch passed away. The delicate balcony on the front of the house has caved in and fallen, but on the façade above, completely obfuscated by large trees, the name of the home, '*RAJ CHANDRA BHAWAN, TALJANGA*', remains engraved. There still stands the *thakur dalan*, a three-arched platform, where the annual Durga Puja would have taken place.

'We spent around five hours in and around the house. Most of the family remained on the lower levels and the ground floor, but my brother walked up to the first floor. There were seven small ponds around the house, and we managed to locate all seven, though they had diminished considerably in size. What we didn't know, and perhaps my grandmother didn't remember to tell us, was that there was a family temple right next to the house. It was a Kali temple, and the priest had managed to save one arm of the original idol, which had probably been destroyed during the 1960s or '70s. Subsequent generations of the priest's family had worshipped that remnant of the idol and prayed in my grandmother's family name, "Roy", even though they had never met anyone from the family. But his grandfather had done it, so had his father, which was why this priest, too, had continued the tradition. It was one of the most moving things to learn: that they had worshipped on our behalf for over seventy years. Standing in front of the temple, we called my grandmother's sister, and a lot of tears were shed – of sadness, of joy.'

'Did anyone remember the elephant?' I ask, thinking of Kusum.

'Oh, yes,' Varun laughs, 'many older people did. They showed us where she was kept, where the horses were kept. Then they showed us the memorial that was built where R.C. Roy was cremated; even the school across the house was called Taljanga R.C. Roy High School. We toured the entire village until we reached the municipal office, where the officers basically told my grandmother that they thought we had come to reclaim the property as ours. It was over two or three hundred acres of land, many people lived and worked on it, and they were now suddenly afraid that they would lose it. They kept asserting that this was government property since it had been abandoned at Partition. So, we spent time pacifying everyone and making it very clear that we'd only come to see it and nothing else. There was a sense of belonging to that land, but we also knew that the land was not ours any more. Do you know what I mean?' he asks me now.

'I understand. There may have been emotional ownership over the land and home but no longer a physical one,' I offer and he nods. 'Professor Kavita Panjabi writes about this, about returning to her father's homeland in Sindh and knowing that though it was part of her history, there was no longer any territorial ownership over it. She calls it "a unique grace, of claiming belonging without possession".'[13]

'That's exactly how it felt,' he agrees. 'At the municipal office, we were shown a *daleel*, a document, which had tax records as well as the names of the male family members. It was all very surreal. We were given sweets that my grandmother's mother used to make, and they gave us fruit and coconuts and all kinds of food to take back with us. I think we were just trying to soak in everything before we had to leave, because we didn't know when we'd be able to come back again and whether the house would even be standing. Of course, we took some soil, but my brother also picked up one of the bricks – a very ornately carved one from the balcony – and brought it back to Kolkata. It was … it is …' Varun pauses, trying to gather his words.

'I can't really describe how surreal it felt that we were able to take my grandmother back to the house where she was born, just weeks before her seventy-fifth birthday. But, for her, the fact that we found the house is not as important as the reception she received there, how she was welcomed back with so much love and respect. How so many people wanted to talk to her and hear her stories and tell the stories that they had heard from their ancestors. There is something sacred and unbreakable about that bond, which surpassed any border or the confines of nation-state; it is a bond built around a house, around a land, around a certain time period, around shared culture. The warmth she received is something she's going to cherish for the rest of her life, and she's still in touch with some of these people.'

'It must have been very overwhelming.'

'Incredibly so,' Varun replies, his eyes wide. 'It took weeks to process everything, because when we were there, so much was happening, so many feelings were being felt and evoked all at once. And it was very important for my grandmother to be able to show her children and grandchildren where she came from – the origin of her story and the aristocracy that we'd only ever heard of. There was pride in being able to share that with us.'

'While you were in Bangladesh, did you think of the border, of Partition?' I now ask my final question.

He smiles sadly. 'It's a bit difficult not to consider the futility of the border when you experience such warmth on the other side. When we were in Bangladesh, it felt like the border didn't exist. But once we returned to India, the border felt suddenly ever-present, because it separated us from that land which had felt so immediate just moments ago. The desire to return becomes quickly eclipsed by other things like politics and visa restrictions, which is when the event of Partition still feels relevant.

'But I do want to say this: going to Bangladesh only strengthened the emotional connect that I'd felt to my grandmother's stories. I feel a shade of the loss that she feels; it's obviously not comparable to living through Partition as she did, but I can empathize more with her now. Returning to Taljanga has given her memories and stories a concrete shape for me. I know what she is talking about, I too have walked on the land, smelled the air, touched the bricks, seen the family temple, formed my own bond with the ancestral home. I think that is my legacy of Partition, and it has been forged by the privilege of being able to return.'

21

Separation and Reunion

ON 31 MAY 1935, between 2.33 and 3.40 a.m., an earthquake of magnitude 7.7 on the Richter scale, with its epicentre at Quetta, Baluchistan, resulted in the deaths of 30,000–60,000 people, making it one of the deadliest earthquakes to hit the subcontinent in recent history. 'It is not possible to describe the state of the city. [It is] razed to the ground,' reads the regimental journal for the 1st Battalion of the Queen's Royal Regiment, 'corpses were lying everywhere ... and every available vehicle in Quetta was being used for the transportation of injured.'[1]

This natural disaster was the first time Ritesh Banglani's paternal grandmother, his dadi Rajkumari, then an eight-year-old, was separated from her family. A second separation, merely twelve years later, was due to the man-made disaster of Partition. Much of our conversation is about this dual separation, but Ritesh, who was born in 1977 and is a Bengaluru-based venture capitalist, first establishes some familial background and context.

'Both sets of my grandparents actually migrated from Rohri in Sukkur district, Sindh, to India, and yet the way they recalled their experiences was very different. On my paternal side, my dada and dadi were quite open to speaking about Partition, about their life and home in Sindh and their immediate post-Partition life in India. It was a frequent topic in the family, and their curiosity and longing for the other side was ever present. But we almost never spoke

551

about the violence. They had witnessed it and I had known about it, but it was a very small drop in the ocean of memories they chose to share. On the other hand, my maternal side, my nana and nani, bore this very curious silence towards Partition. You could not get them to speak about it; they would immediately change the subject or dodge it. If ever they did choose to speak about it, it was only about childhood and never the years from their adulthood actually surrounding Partition.'

'That's such an extreme dichotomy,' I note.

Ritesh laughs. 'As a child, I always found this contrast very strange, because one side spoke about Pakistan with such fondness and the other never even mentioned it, as if their life only began in 1950. As I grew older, I figured that it actually had less to do with the witnessing of violence and more to do with how much each side had lost.' He pauses for a moment. 'I know that our conversation is meant to focus on my dadi's stories of separation, but I want to mention how the difference between the two sides of my family eventually impacted the way my parents were raised.'

'Of course,' I say, for the very purpose of this study is to be a generational one.

'During Partition, my nana and nani lost everything, not just material possessions but also family. They lost people, relatives were left behind and never seen again. So, it remained a lot more traumatic for that side, which is why they were, in a way, always trying to hide that trauma. Their silence was very telling, and it definitely left a shadow on the next generation. My mother, born in 1953, knew very little about her parents' lives in Sindh. The fact that Partition was a taboo subject and never openly discussed led her to develop a lot more of a hard-line attitude towards Pakistan, towards Muslims. And I do believe that the bitterness that her own parents held had a huge role to play in her understanding of the difficult subject of identity politics.'

'What about your father?'

'If my maternal side had traumatic memories of Partition, then my paternal side had traumatic memories from *before* Partition, for instance, how the Quetta earthquake changed my dadi's life. But the richness in those stories revealed a fondness and lack of rancour, even though she was the one who was separated from her immediate family. My father, born in 1949, grew up a lot more open in his politics and his attitude towards Partition, Pakistan and Muslims.'

'And what about you?' I ask, descending the generations.

'As far as my generation is concerned, I think to a large extent it was a second-hand reaction. If I may give the analogy of light bouncing between two mirrors, then I was seeing a reflection of a reflection. What I was experiencing through the memories of my parents were not even their memories, and I think that provided crucial distance, because my parents didn't have that benefit of distance. I grew up hearing two conflicting versions of the same story from my parents, and as a teenager wanted to investigate the truth for myself. So, I spent long hours with my dadi, who had never hidden the difficult parts of her story even when I was a child. She was always most open with me, and because of the sheer richness of detail, her story is one I know very well, and it is hinged on a dual separation.'

With that, Ritesh takes me back in time to the Quetta earthquake.

'My dadi, Rajkumari, was eight years old in 1935. It was May, summertime, and due to the heat, she and her sister Duru had insisted on sleeping on the terrace with their father. This childish insistence saved them both, for when the earthquake struck, the rest of the family – her mother, grandparents and two other sisters – were buried alive. Their father was badly injured but managed to pull out her sister, Sursati, from the rubble. He held the barely alive child in his arms while the other two girls walked beside him as they searched for help. My dadi had to relieve herself, but even amidst the chaos, she wanted to find a private spot to do so. When she returned, she couldn't find her family. Dawn was breaking but she had no clue where she was or where their house was. She wandered about, crying constantly, all day.

'Now, her family were Sindhi migrants in Baluchistan, and the only language she knew was Sindhi. I keep thinking about how terrified she would have been, walking through the crowd and the rubble, unable to communicate with anyone. But it is this linguistic difference that eventually saved her. She found a Sindhi family who could understand her, but the problem was they were visiting from Sindh. They searched for several days, but the entire city was destroyed and my dadi was unable to provide enough information about her family. So, they decided to take her to Sindh with them and come back to search later. And just like that, she found a new family. They lived in a large house by the Indus river and had children of their own. But, by all accounts, they loved her, even spoiling her as the youngest of the family.'

'What happened to her sisters, Duru and Sursati? And their father?' I ask, wide-eyed.

'Sursati died the same night, and their father also succumbed to his injuries. Duru was the only family member who made it alive and was raised by relatives. They were reunited at some point, but my grandmother continued to live with her adoptive family in Sindh. Then, at the age of eighteen, in 1945, she married my dada, Nautan.'

As we inch closer to Partition, Ritesh takes a deep breath. 'Something I remember distinctly from our conversations is the fear that had settled into their lives in 1946, more than the actual violence they witnessed in 1947. My dadi was a young woman, just twenty years old, and she remembers being locked up in her house for months out of fear and not being able to trust their neighbours. The actual violence was a bit matter-of-fact, but any time she spoke of this year, it was very nuanced and textured. Now that I think about it, I was young, a teenager, and she may not have wanted to describe the violence in a vivid manner,' he shrugs. 'The most striking element was how afraid she was of rape or of being abducted. This is the detail that has stayed with me.'

'Had she heard of these kinds of stories at the time? Is that why she was afraid?'

'Abduction was one of her biggest fears, and I think she had carried it since Quetta. The other thing she always carried with her was a knife. Imagine how traumatic it must be for someone who's just out of her teens – having to carry a knife even when she's in her own neighbourhood.'

I tell him that this is not the first time I have heard of women having knives and other weapons on their person for self-defence. In fact, long after Partition, many women continued to sleep with knives under their pillows and mattresses.

'This is what she used to tell me as well,' Ritesh says. 'I keep thinking about the level of preparedness in that one year. They would keep jars of oil inside the home. It's a strange detail for a grandmother to tell her grandson, but they kept jars of oil ready so that if a mob came by, they could heat the oil and throw it on those trying to scale the walls. They had converted all their wealth to gold, to be able to flee as soon as there was trouble. This was the level of preparedness in 1946, when there wasn't even a timetable for Independence or announcement of Partition. These details are so telling of the constant and all-consuming fear. They had formed squads in their neighbourhood to protect one another. My dadi would tell me about her brothers, the adoptive brothers, who were older than her and part of these squads that would patrol the streets and give advance warnings in case of a riot. Apparently, mobs would go out looking for people from the other community who had strayed outside their mohallas, and attack and kill them. The one detail that I remember my dada never really getting over was how these mobs were made up of people they knew. People they did business with on a daily basis, or had some social connection with, or were working in the same office. This was what shocked my dada.'

'How did they eventually migrate to India?'

'They actually migrated just before Independence. They came by train, through the Punjab and travelled eastwards directly to Delhi, which is where they experienced the night of Independence. My dada's parents, his sister, my grandparents and their infant child migrated quite safely across to India. They were prepared, but of course they left behind the ancestral house in Rohri. And till his dying day, it was my dada's deep regret that they were not able to sell it, because they genuinely believed that they would come back.'

I smile sadly.

'But there is a positive story in this.' His tone is bright. 'They'd actually left it in the care of their Muslim neighbours. In the mid-1980s, my grandparents visited Pakistan and they went to see the house and found the same Muslim family living in it. They took a lot of solace in the fact that the house was well taken care of and not vandalized or given away to somebody else. So, while my dada regretted not having sold it in time, they were actually really touched and even stayed there as the family's guests for a couple of nights.'

'Had it been changed at all?'

'The elders were still alive, and what I know from my grandmother is that even the paintings and murals of Hindu gods had been retained. She would never tire of saying that even though they were Muslims, they kept everything as is, even the religious aspects of the home. She'd repeat this as if to validate a pre-Partition way of life.'

I now return to the moment of migration. 'You mentioned a second separation?'

'Yes, my dadi was separated from her family for the second time in her life – only this time, it was her adoptive family.'

'My god,' I sigh. 'To live through this not once but twice in a lifetime.'

Ritesh nods his head. 'This was very traumatic for her, but the fact that her family remained in Pakistan was a considered decision taken by her brothers and parents. Her adoptive family was quite well-off; they owned the largest brand of soft drinks – soda, they called it – in Sindh. For them, the downside of leaving it all behind was very large, which was why that side of the family decided not to migrate. Then, towards the end of 1947, when Sindh was up in flames, one of the brothers chose to relinquish his share of the business and migrated across.'

'Was he alone?'

'He was completely by himself. So, my dadi knew that he had left, but there was no way of making sure if he'd gotten through safely or if he was even alive. For about two or three years after Partition, my grandparents didn't have a permanent address in Delhi – they stayed with relatives – so no one from that side could really communicate with them. Even if her brother made it to Delhi, he wouldn't know where to begin looking for her. As a post-Partition ritual, my dada, while trying to figure out their own life, would go from camp to camp looking for his brother-in-law. He would take the train to Madhya Pradesh, because he'd heard that refugees from Rohri had migrated there, or he would go to Bombay ... For three years or so, this was the only topic discussed in the family.'

'Were they reunited?' I ask with hope.

'Eventually, yes, though I don't know the full details. But he made his way to Ujjain and contacted some relatives who knew my grandparents' address.'

'What about the rest of the family?'

'Almost fifty years after Independence, her eldest brother migrated to India. But my dadi never saw her parents again.' After a few seconds, he quietly adds, 'Adoptive or birth.'

I sigh. 'What about her real sister, Duru?'

'They, too, eventually reunited; she had migrated to Bombay.'

If I had any doubt about whether the pain of multiple separations enveloped the joy of reunions, Ritesh clears it right up. 'For anyone else, the twin tragedies of her childhood and youth may have crushed their spirit. But not Rajkumari. Till the day she died, she was one of the most cheerful people I knew. Her new family gave her the nickname Bhagya, which means luck. They could have been talking of her luck in survival, or their own in finding her.'

STORIES OF SEPARATION quite naturally weave themselves into the landscape of Partition memory. However, through the chapters of this book, I have made a distinction between families who found themselves divided between the newly independent nations and those who were unexpectedly separated but eventually reunited. Though the terms are related and often used interchangeably, in this context I interpret the word 'divided' to be a bifurcation or trifurcation of familial identity due to the choices made while migrating or the fortification of borders and travel restrictions over time,[*] and the word 'separated' to allude to periods of weeks, months or sometimes years when family members found themselves estranged in different parts of a country or on either side of the newly formed border due to unexpected circumstances.

While on a research trip to Jammu in 2018, a short anecdote is narrated to me about a man who continued to search for his wife long after the borders had been drawn and cemented. The story is tucked between lunch and dessert, almost whispered around the table, for even seven decades later, its sadness is too much for the family to bear.

'I was a child when I first heard this story,' Seema Gupta, who was born in 1968 to a Jammu-based Mirpuri family, recalls. 'The fact that it remains ingrained in my mind should tell you the degree to which it shaped my understanding of Partition. How it divided not just country but also family. How it separated people, sometimes temporarily, due to the suddenness of the border, and other times permanently' – she pauses – 'due to death.'

Every single member of the generation before Seema's had fled Mirpur, now in Pakistan-administered Kashmir, to India in the months following Partition. But it is her tayaji whose story she narrates that afternoon.

'His name was O.P. Gupta, and he was in his mid-twenties. His wife, Veeranwali – meaning the one who has many brothers – lovingly known as Veer, was eighteen years old. They lived in Lahore and had been married for three years. She'd recently suffered a miscarriage and had decided to spend a few months at her parents' home in Mirpur. It was in this short span of time that Partition happened.'

Listening to the story, I feel my heart tighten at the reason for their separation, for the loss of a child must have completely been engulfed by the loss of home and land, and then, even worse, the loss of one's beloved. Seema tells us that her tayaji never spoke about this parting

---

[*] Such stories can be found in Chapter 5, 'Family'.

or what happened thereafter, but any time the elders discussed the couple's fate, she thought it a tale of fiction, far too painful to be real.

In the winter of 1947, when Mirpur city was attacked by tribal forces, members of their family fled to a camp, where they were all given poisonous pills to consume, should their fate at the hands of the enemy be any worse. Amidst this chaos, Seema's aunt recalls Veer fleeing in another direction with her mother, which was the last time she ever saw her, the last memory anyone from the family had of her. But neither Veer nor her husband could have known that their brief separation would become indefinite.

'Did she consume the poison?' I ask.

Seema shrugs. 'We don't know if she swallowed the poison or if she was killed by the attackers. We only know that tayaji was never reunited with his wife. He was in his twenties, she was just a teenager, and their marriage lasted only three years. But hoping against all hope, he travelled from refugee camp to refugee camp across the country, for many years, likely until the camps existed. He never found her, and he never married again either.'

A BRIEF SEPARATION finds its way into my family history as well. For six months after Partition, my paternal great-grandfather, Daryay Lal Malhotra, was held back in Pakistan to train the new staff at the Mandi Bahauddin bank where he had been the manager. On the day of the family's migration to India, a group of men boarded their train compartment and dragged him off to the platform. Amidst the family's cries and screams, a gentleman known to them – whose son was my grandfather's friend – made the promise that my great-grandfather would safely be sent to India in a few months' time. Daryay Lal agreed, for he could not take the risk of declining, knowing what may happen. To make matters worse, my grandfather's eldest brother, Devinder, was still employed at a bank in Rawalpindi and unable to join the family. The father and son would have to find some way to make it to India eventually.

That day, leaving them behind in what had overnight become Pakistan, my grandfather Balraj, now the acting patriarch, helped his mother and younger siblings back on to the train and journeyed onwards to India. Once settled in a camp in Amritsar, he wrote letters – one to his father, addressed to the bank in Mandi Bahauddin, another to his brother, addressed to the bank in Rawalpindi, and a third to the rest of the family in their native village of Qadirabad. It felt like shooting arrows in the dark, for he did not know whether any would reach, but he had to let them know that the family was waiting in Amritsar. It would be months before he would receive a reply and they would be reunited.[2]

I never had the chance to speak to my great-grandfather or my granduncle about staying back in Pakistan after Partition, but I have often wondered about this separation. In *Chronicle of a Bookshop*, the book that my father wrote about my grandfather's life, there are sections that I return to often. In it, thinking back to the camp in Amritsar, my grandfather narrates how people all around him would talk about who had made it across the border and who had been left behind. Though he mentions rarely partaking in these discussions, I do wonder whether they amplified the dread or fear he must have felt for his father and brother. And despite the tone of the book being quite reserved, there is a single line that gnaws at my heart.

'I could not be certain that my father would ever come back,' he says.[3]

IF THE VERY act of partitioning a land had separated family members who depended on fate to somehow reunite them, there were also some who were deliberately separated from one another because the conditions they found themselves in could not guarantee the survival of all.

In Kolkata I speak to Aparna Bhattacharya, who sets up a meeting with her father-in-law, Saktipada Das, born in 1938 in Narayanganj, Dhaka district, present-day Bangladesh. Das sahib sits by the window, sunshine spilling across his indigo shirt, and relays to me the memories that have shaped his childhood. Sometimes Aparna translates from Bengali, other times Das sahib breaks into a hybrid of English–Bengali–Hindi sentences.

'My earliest memory is of the Bengal famine in 1943. I was five years old and had accompanied my father, who was a lawyer, to collect ration. I didn't understand why there was a famine – we were well-off, so it didn't impact us – but I remember it clearly. Similarly, I remember the day of Independence and the riots following Partition. In an ashram near our home, men were taking up arms, and I saw the weapons, but again couldn't understand what was happening. We remained in East Pakistan until 1948, when Hindus had become such a small minority in our area that we had no choice but to migrate.'

'Do you remember the journey to India?' I ask.

'I was young,' he smiles boyishly, 'but so excited because we were going to a new place. There was a feeling of adventure. Narayanganj was a port, and so we took a steamer to Goalundo Ghat, from where we caught a train to Barrackpore, and further to Calcutta.'[4]

'He still has the refugee certificate from when they first entered India,' Aparna adds. 'His father had practised law at the Dhaka High Court but had great difficulty resuming his practice once in India. The family struggled for a while, and then just as he'd begun to find his bearings at the Alipore court, he died suddenly of smallpox. This was 1949, when my father-in-law was only eleven years old.'

Das sahib shrugs his shoulders. 'There was no treatment for smallpox at the time. I was the second son and had one elder brother and three younger ones. The family was unprepared. My mother became a widow with no means to support us.' Extending his arms to create an imaginary road, he says, 'I walked six kilometres to collect the money for my father's last rites.'

He now rests his hands one atop another in his lap and, through his spectacles, I see his eyes soften.

'Das sahib, do you hold the migration after Partition responsible for what happened to the family?' I ask.

After thinking for a few seconds, he says, 'I never used to feel it was directly responsible, *jo hua theek hua*, because we never questioned our father's decision to come to Calcutta. But it was so soon after our migration that everything changed for the worse. Our whole world turned suddenly upside down … many days we went hungry because there was no food,' he sighs.

Aparna watches him fall silent. When she picks up from where he has left off, her voice is strained. 'These are the stories I have heard ever since my marriage. My father-in-law had to grow up suddenly; he became like an eleven-year-old man. The family was left in unthinkable poverty. The loss caused by Partition was eclipsed by the loss of his father. His eldest brother assumed the role of patriarch and began working. And then' – her voice becomes even smaller and tighter as she reveals the real consequences of this tragedy – 'unable to take care of all her five children, his mother ended up sending him and his two younger brothers to an ashram-like orphanage. She and the youngest child moved in with relatives.'

'F-for how long?' I ask, bewildered.

'They were separated for about eight years. From age eleven to eighteen, my father-in-law hardly saw his mother, but he remains thankful for the fact that he and his siblings were fed and clothed – something that the predicament of the family would not have allowed otherwise.'

'We were given rotis according to our age,' Das sahib adds. 'They were numbered and counted.'

'The number of rotis in the ashram was limited, and everyone was given rotis based on their age,' Aparna explains. 'He and his younger brothers got two each, but they still went to sleep hungry. The younger brother couldn't understand the rationing and used to ask for more food, and so my father-in-law would give one of his own rotis to him.'

I am quiet, but perhaps my face betrays emotion, for Aparna says to me, 'I know it's difficult to imagine it now, leaving your children this way. But they found a sense of happiness in the ashram. Their mother could not provide for them, and the way that life had turned on them, the children could not afford to feel betrayed. In a way, I think they developed a sense of belonging to the place over time, and it has influenced and shaped their character. My father-in-law goes there every year during Durga Puja and also helps out in the kitchen and household work of the ashram. Spending time there gives him solace. But despite all this, whenever the past is discussed at home, you can tell that the impact of that separation was so deep that it has remained.'

Das sahib does not let the pain colour his recollections, but, from time to time, it is discernible. As we conclude, he shows me a rectangular mirror, its frame made of dark-brown wood, the inside edges ornately carved. He carried it to the ashram, a part of his mother's trousseau from East Bengal and still dear to him today.

Later, when I speak with Aparna alone, she admits, 'As someone whose family wasn't affected by Partition, I was amazed that my in-laws still talk about how drastically it changed their everyday lives. They have preserved every single thing carried across, except for the jewellery, which they sold. My husband always returns to the fact that they could have been living a very different life had Partition not happened. He was born in Calcutta forty years after but feels he is part of that struggle to rebuild the wealth and stature they lost. And my father-in-law, though he may not be able to voice it, remains deeply scarred.'

'I can't imagine someone not being,' I respond. 'Does he speak about that time?'

'Even if he didn't, it would've been evident. All those things he was deprived of as a child...' she sighs. 'He is extremely conservative financially. His father was the university topper, and he couldn't finish his education. All these things have left a psychological impact somewhere. He is borderline obsessed with keeping anything that belonged to his parents.'

That evening, long after our conversation has ended, I imagine what it must have felt like to be cut off from everything and everyone familiar at such a young age. Though Das sahib spoke little during our interview, I understand that the memory of separation can be reproduced even in silence – in the tenderness with which he held his mother's mirror up to his face, in the hoarding of heirlooms, in his thriftiness. What you feel, even when left unsaid, can be seen in what you do.

~

OVER THE COURSE of a few years, I listen to a story about the separation of two sisters after Partition, told through two different perspectives by two different people. The first is the sister who was brought to India when the family fled Pakistan in haste. The second story is inherited by the elder daughter of the sister left behind in Pakistan and later retrieved. In these retellings, I become interested not only in the details that naturally overlap but also in the details that differ, for together they are two halves of a single story.

During my childhood, my family had a tenant named Anju Mehta, who lived two floors above us – she was always Anju aunty to me and remains to this day as close as family. But it was well after she moved out and I had grown up that she mentioned the unbelievable circumstances that separated her mother from the rest of her kin in 1947. One afternoon in January 2017, we drive from Delhi to Gurugram to speak to her aunt, Ramesh Kumari Dutta. We sit in the living room, accompanied by her husband, who had also migrated from Chakwal as a ten-year-old.

The day is dim and cold, and my interviewee sits in an armchair, wrapped in a beige-coloured shawl and woollen cap. She speaks very fast, her sentences hardly allowing for pauses. Notebook in hand, my recorder placed beside her, I lean in, afraid of missing even a single detail. She knows why I am there and, without wasting any time, starts at the beginning.

'The only way I know my date of birth is that a letter was sent to my brother, who was fighting in Burma during the Second World War, to tell him that his sisters were born. Calculating from those letters, Anju's mother, Sudesh, known as Deshi, was born in 1940 and I, Ramesh, known as Meshi, was born in 1942. We are from district Bhimber.'

'Mirpur division, now in Pakistan-occupied Kashmir, POK,' her husband clarifies.

'I only have disjointed memories, *sab suni-sunai baat hai*,' she says, 'but I will tell you what I know. It was Karva Chauth, and Partition had already happened.* We would divide our time between the villages of Daura and Bhimber, where we were at the time. It was the middle of the night and Deshi was sleeping in the other room when we heard noises of bullets being fired, *dhar dhar dhar*, like firecrackers. We all ran away from the house as fast as we could. I was only four or five years old and had to be carried but, in the chaos, Deshi got left behind. Someone tried to wake her, but she must have kept sleeping, and only once we'd gotten quite far did we realize that she wasn't with us. But the bullets kept raining and there was no way to go back and retrieve her. People were running in all directions, trying to get to safety. There were some 1,300 of us who fled the village, and our caravan reached Haveli tehsil,[5] where we found shelter in an abandoned structure. Hiding inside, we could hear the terrible sounds of people being killed and bullets being fired outside. Amidst all this, I have a faint memory of a boy coming up to us and saying, "*Ram naam ki goli le lo.*"'

'What was it?' I ask.

'Tablets, he gave us some tablets.'

'Tablets of ... poison?' I ask instinctively, recalling this to be a frequent feature from the time.

'Poison,' confirms her husband, nodding.

'My brother took the pills, broke them into smaller pieces and distributed them amongst the family. He told everyone to just place a piece in their mouths, and' – she clicks her tongue – 'one by one, they all fell to the ground. Some vomited, some reacted in madness with strange side-effects, and some died then and there. It would be many years before I learnt that the pill – *Ram naam ki goli* – must have been cyanide. It was given to us so that we could take our own life and not be at the mercy of the enemy.'

---

* In 1947, the Hindu festival of Karva Chauth fell on 2 November.

'But you survived,' I remark in a small voice.

'I spat it out immediately, it was too bitter. But the others – my mother, my brothers, my cousins – all died. Of the 1,300 people who had collected there, only 600 remained.'

I gasp and look at Anju aunty. But no one says anything; we all wait for her to continue the story. Meshi goes on, unperturbed by my reaction. 'We had heard that outside the enclosure, the mobs were killing, looting, plundering, carrying away women. But I was only five, I couldn't have known what was happening, *bachche ko kya hosh hota hai*. So, all this has been told to me by those who survived.'

In barely a whisper, I ask who all did survive.

'In my family, only four people. My father, my elder sister Soma, who'd been married just six months ago, my sister-in-law, who was pregnant and due any day, and me. At the time, I didn't realize that everyone had died.' She breathes in and continues, 'They were just lying there, all of them. And we had no choice but to leave them there, we couldn't carry the bodies. Keshu died, Joginder died ... *sab khatam*.'

'Do you ever think about that time?' Anju aunty now asks her aunt.

'All that comes to mind is that we were lucky to be alive.' After a pause, she says, 'But I do wish that it had not happened. I wish the mobs had not attacked the village; I wish we were still in Bhimber. Then our family would still be alive, my mother would still be alive. I never had the chance to know what a mother was, and because my father died in 1950, I've spent almost my whole life as an orphan. My relatives used to tell me that we belonged to a very rich family in Bhimber, but I have lived a very, very hard life. Had Partition not happened, we would not have been so helpless or homeless...' She shrugs, as if to say that it was pointless to think about these things now, and continues the story. 'From the abandoned shelter we left one by one, crawling out of a small window – it couldn't have been larger than a *roshan daani*, an opening for some ventilation – that led out to the jungle. And then we walked through forest and mountain, all the way to India. I am told that it took seven days, but I don't remember.'

'Guddi didi, my cousin, was also born along the way,' Anju tells me.

'Oh, yes, she was born as soon as we reached Haveli tehsil, actually, before the family succumbed. My sister-in-law was at full term, as I told you, and she gave birth to a daughter. But we were barely clothed; we'd been woken so suddenly from sleep that someone had fled in their petticoat, someone in a vest. My brother had to remove his pyjamas and give them to my sister-in-law so she could be properly covered while giving birth. When we left Haveli, the baby was with us. On the way, walking through the forest, we saw a small child, maybe six or seven months old, abandoned, wailing. Nobody picked him up, we just continued –'

'But why did no one help?' I interrupt.

She scoffs, 'People were telling my sister-in-law to leave her child in a similar way. They kept saying, "*Yeh tumhe marvayegi, isse yehi par chhod do.*" The baby will get you killed, leave her here. She was so exhausted after giving birth that she couldn't even hold the child. When bullets rain from the sky and the sound of guns follows you, when all you are trying to do is save your life, you cannot think clearly. Nothing makes sense. I don't know why no one helped the crying child.' She looks directly at me. 'I was a child myself, my sister-in-law held my hand throughout, and my sister tied the newborn to her body with a dupatta. In this way, we carried on in our caravan. At one point, I remember, we fell asleep on the side of the road. The journey was long and we were tired, and in my sleep I heard a voice trying to wake us up. It was an old man with a long, white beard, wearing a dhoti. I don't know who he was but he was trying to caution us to continue walking. When we didn't move, he threw a small stone at us, and only then did we wake up.

'On the fourth day of our journey, when my niece was four days old, we finally stopped by the Jhelum river. My sister-in-law very carefully opened the bundle on my sister's back to see whether her baby had survived. If she hadn't, the bundle would have been floated off on the river, but if she had, it would be no less than a miracle. The dupatta was undone and, much to everyone's surprise, we found a cooing baby. She hadn't eaten a single thing nor had a sip of water or milk, was not adequately clothed for the winter month, but had miraculously survived. It was a moment of rare joy. So, we bathed and cleaned her and tied her back in the bundle before continuing along.'

'Where did you enter India from?' I ask.

'Akhnoor,' she confirms, but goes on to list city after city, 'where we stayed for two weeks in a tall, four-storeyed building. I think it was a home that had been abandoned by Muslims fleeing to Pakistan. From there we went to Jammu, and then to Amritsar, where we spent two months. I remember the festival of Lohri, so it must have been January 1948. From Punjab, we wrote a letter to my brother-in-law, who was in Bombay, and he came to pick up my elder sister. She suggested that I come live with her and that was how I found myself in Bombay. From there they got posted to Sangrur, where I studied till Grade 2, and then in 1952 I came to Delhi.'

'You sister Deshi – this entire time, all these years, did you think about where she was?' I ask, their separation weighing on my mind.

She shakes her head. 'At the time, I didn't even know what a brother was, what a sister was. At that age, a child forgets easily, you know...' She smiles sadly. 'Ten months after she was separated from us, my elder brother found her in a camp and retrieved her. But I only met her again in 1952.'

'Do you remember the first time you saw her?'

'Yes, *that* I remember,' she says slowly, both her gaze and tone faraway. 'She was wearing a frock, and her hair was cut short, like a bob. She was so small that she could not climb down the stairs freely and had to hold on to the railing with both hands for support. I remember this image clearly, of her slowly walking down the steps, one by one.'

When I ask if she knows what happened to her sister in those months of separation, she tells me that Deshi had been all alone in the home when a mob of men came to loot it, and one of them took pity on the child and adopted her. But his wife considered the child no less than a servant, ill-treating and beating her, and several months later she was deposited at a camp. Their eldest brother, who was in the army and had contacts in Mirpur district, found her there, but the camp commandant wouldn't just hand over a child to anyone. When he was taken to where she was studying with a group of children, she saw him from the window and ran towards him. And thus they were reunited.'

As the story concludes, she sinks back in her chair. Holding up her palm, signalling the end of our conversation, she says, '*Bass*, that's it. This is our story; this is what happened.' One eye at a time, she wipes the tears that have collected in the crevasses. Then, with flattened palms, she massages her head, heavy with memory. I cannot get myself to utter a single word.

Meshi gets up and adjusts her shawl.

'Chai? Everyone will have chai?' she asks, a question so abrupt it punctures the dismal atmosphere in the room.

We nod in unison and she walks out, still massaging her temples. Then, just a moment later, she comes back and looks directly at me. 'I do not hate Muslims. I do not want you to think I blame them for what happened. I don't blame them for the death of my parents or the separation from my sister. If these things happened on that side with us, they must have happened on this side with them. There's no malice in my heart towards them. It was just the madness of those days, it was circumstance, *haalaat hi aise the, beta*.'

FOR A LONG time I am left wondering about Deshi but cannot muster the courage to ask Anju aunty the details. What must a seven-year-old child, stranded all by herself in a home that was no longer her own, on a land that was no longer her own, have felt? Often, I think about travelling to Jalandhar, where I know Deshi still lives. But three years later, I speak to Anju aunty's elder sister, the 1962-born Pratibha Jain, or Pinky, who is based in Delhi. Over the course of an afternoon, she shares her mother's story with me in a way that its generational consequences become hard to overlook.

'We have been listening to the stories of Partition since childhood, but it was only maybe four or five years ago that I learnt that my mother, Sudesh – Deshi – had been left behind. We must have been discussing the subject and this fact just suddenly emerged. But we'd never heard of it before.'

'How did you feel when you learnt about it?' I ask.

'Weird,' she says immediately, '*ajeeb sa laga*. Yesterday I spoke to my mother about this for the very first time. Just her and me. I wanted to prepare for our conversation today, but all the stories I'd heard had been from someone else – either her elder sister or her sister-in-law. I wanted to hear what had happened to her in her own words, in her own voice. And since yesterday, I am feeling very disturbed, as if the trauma is not hers but mine.' As she says this, she points to herself, and a pained expression grows across her face. 'I can't stop thinking about how difficult my mother's life has been, how hard those months of separation must have been.' She shakes her head.

As they spoke about this for the first time, I wonder if the story emerged without difficulty or hesitation.

'She told it to me easily, because now so much time has passed. My mother has poor memory, and I was worried that she may not remember something that happened so long ago.'

'But this is not just *any* memory,' I say softly, 'it is difficult to forget something like this.'

'She has not forgotten, she cannot forget.' She pauses. 'The family that kept her in Pakistan, ill-treated her, tortured her – she even remembers their faces and ages with clarity.'

As Pinky descends into the story of what happened to her mother in 1947, the same characters begin to make an appearance. But it is the manner of her narration that I find extraordinary. This retelling has distance, by the sheer virtue of being an inherited memory, but, in a strange and unique way, its impact feels as visceral as lived memory, as if it has been transmitted on to Pinky *through* her mother's experience. As I listen to the particular words or phrases she uses, or the way in which her voice tunnels through to the past, I am struck by how immediate Partition feels to someone who has not lived it.

'My mother's family belonged to the area of Pakistan-occupied Kashmir. Division Bhimber, district Mirpur. We have known these words since childhood but only heard them in the news a few years

ago, during the surgical strikes in the area. As far as I know, in the
months following Partition, when their village of Daura had become
very unsafe, they travelled to their elder sister's marital home in
Bhimber. There were very few Punjabi Hindu families in the area, I'm
told; most were Muslim. It was on the night of Karva Chauth that
the riots began in Bhimber. The house they were staying in was at the
foot of a hill and the attackers had placed a machine gun on the hill
above. Bullets rained into the veranda of the house and around it. For
safety, no one left the premises. The entire joint family – grandparents,
parents, siblings, cousins – everyone stayed hidden inside the house.

'But at night, the attacks began on the ground and the entire
family fled from there. At the time, my mother was asleep and
was left behind. No one even thought to check that everyone was
together. There was such panic that all they could do was leave the
house as fast as possible. My masi, Meshi, was so small that, I'm told,
she either had to be carried or held on to someone's hand the entire
time. It was only when the caravan from the village collected in a
shelter a short distance from Bhimber that they realized Deshi wasn't
with them. But the situation had gotten so bad that it was difficult
to return and retrieve her. All the elders of the village decided that it
wasn't worth risking everyone's life for a single child...' She takes a
deep breath. '*Ab jo reh gaya, use rehne do*, they said, leave whoever
has been left behind.'

Pinky's voice now quivers as she says, 'I have only heard this story
now, but my mother lived it. She was only six or seven years old.'

I wonder whether she is now speaking as a daughter or as a
mother herself.

'When my mother awoke, she found the house completely empty.
She looked in all the rooms but couldn't see anyone, so she started
crying. News of the attacks in the area had been floating around for
a while, and she must have thought that ... well, you can imagine
what she must have thought had happened to her family. So she sat
all by herself in the darkness, crying.

'Meanwhile, a mob entered the house and she tells me that they
were Pathans. In those days, they used to warn the villagers by saying

the Pathans have arrived: "*Pathan aa gaye, Pathan aa gaye.*" The men carried knives and swords and they threatened her and asked where all the jewellery and cash in the house was. My mother was scared, this wasn't even her home, and she tried to tell them that. But then she saw one of them carrying a photograph of her elder brother, Keshav – we never even met him but heard that everyone used to call him Keshu. When she saw his photograph, it became clear to her that they'd been looting houses in the surrounding villages and had already been to theirs in Bhimber.'

Now, this is where the story differs slightly from her aunt's telling in the way that her mother became a temporary member of a Muslim family, and the conditions of her retrieval.

'The mob looted the house and then brought my mother to a crowd of people, Hindus and Sikhs, who'd been rounded up from the villages. They had all either been abandoned or left behind. There were many young girls in the group; some were converted to Islam and married off, some were made servants, and others were … well…' Pinky looks at me in a way that I am meant to understand what she means. When I nod, she continues. 'My mother was only a child, so she was sent to work for a Muslim family that comprised a couple and their three children – a young man of twenty years, a girl of eighteen and a young boy, maybe fifteen years old. The months she spent with that family were very traumatic.

'She cleaned the house, washed the dishes but was regularly beaten by the eighteen-year-old girl. The family kept buffaloes and goats, and my mother was told to take care of the animals. When the youngest son would take the cattle to graze out in the open, he would take her along with him. When any goat ran away from the herd, the boy would beat my mother as well. She came from a wealthy family who'd once owned a dried fruit business, and she'd never had to do such menial labour. But for seven or eight months, this was how she survived.'

'How did she escape?' I ask.

'When several months had passed and an administrative government had been formed in Pakistan, the two countries began operations to retrieve all those who had been left behind on either side. Women, children, anyone who had been kept by force, anyone who was being hidden inside homes. That is when the army rescued and retrieved my mother and brought her to a camp in Pakistan. Joo-lee-yana, it was called something like this. From there, she and several other people were brought across the border to a refugee camp in Jammu, where her elder brother, who was in the army, found her. She ran to him at the camp, and he brought her to Amritsar, and then to Rewari and, finally, to Delhi, where she was reunited with Meshi masi.'

She exhales deeply and adds, 'I'm sure you already know the story of how the rest of the family made their way to India – and how many lost their lives on the way.'

I nod quietly and allow the heavy silence to envelop us.

'Have you heard other stories like this?' Pinky asks me. 'This is your work, after all.'

I shake my head from side to side. Even in the sameness of two experiences, there will be differences.

'I have read a lot of books, watched a lot of films on Partition, but never found a story like this,' Pinky says. 'Some of the things endured by people are so unbelievable that they feel like fiction. And when I think about my family's story, I feel...' She looks up at me, unsure of whether to continue.

'What *do* you feel?' I ask.

'I feel a lot of mixed emotions and I don't understand why I'm so attached to this subject, because I have not lived through Partition. In the 1980s, I read Balraj Sahni's book, which he'd written in his mother tongue, Punjabi, called *Mera Pakistani Safarnama*, about his trip back to Pakistan.[6] It took me fifteen days to complete it, one for every day of his journey. Through the pages of the book, I travelled to Pakistan with him, talking to the people he talked to, looking at the sights he saw, riding on buses, walking on his childhood streets, knocking on the door of his ancestral home. I was in a place that I didn't want to come back from, a place that I felt was mine. I picked up the book again recently, but it felt more emotional this time. Maybe it has something to do with growing older, or thinking about this subject in greater depth, but I couldn't read it. I don't think I'll ever be able to return to the book. It just cut too deep,' she admits as small tears begin to trickle down her face.

On 9 October 1962, the actor Balraj Sahni travelled from Delhi to Lahore by train, accepting the invitation of his old friend Dr Nazir Ahmed, then the principal of Sahni's alma mater, Government College Lahore. Once there, he met old friends like the writer Imtiaz Ali Taj, best known for writing the 1922 play *Anarkali*, and the poet Ahmed Rahi, who had migrated to Pakistan from Amritsar.[7] Sahni's book, *Mera Pakistani Safarnama*, is both travelogue and memoir, and reading through it I was often reminded of my own learnings and un-learnings while in Pakistan. Of course, for Sahni, it was also a return 'home', to the land where he was born in 1913. His reflections are cognizant of the imposition of differences due to national identities where there would ordinarily not have been any. Upon crossing the border for the first time after Partition, he writes: '*Ab main Pakistan mein tha, Musalmaano ke desh mein, ek gair mulk mein. Par yeh insaan toh maine pehle bhi dekhe the. Yeh toh mere liye na naye hain, na paraye.*' He was now in Pakistan, in the land of Muslims, in a land different from his own. But he had seen these people before. And so they were neither new to him nor were they strangers.

As Pinky continues to speak through her tears, an aged sadness finds place in our conversation. 'I can't explain why I feel the pain of Partition, but no one at home understands it. An old wound, old trauma, *purani baatein*, they say, and dismiss the subject. I don't know who else to speak to about this.' Then, focusing her attention on me, she says, 'This is why I'm very interested in what you write. You must have heard so many stories … but do people still want to read them? Tell me, do they still want to think and talk about Partition?'

'Some do,' I say after a while.

The truth is that even though this book is a testament to the fact that there are many people who have lived through Partition and many who have inherited stories from that time who still want to think about it and talk about it, there are far more who would rather forget. For them Partition is a bitter truth, a buried memory. There are many who focus on the celebration of Independence rather than the pain of Partition, and I am no one to comment on that choice. But I am curious about why Pinky feels this powerful connection to the event, and whether it is a trait she has inherited from her mother. When I ask, she is quick to reject the idea.

'My mother is not emotional. In fact, sometimes I feel like because I am the first child, all this trauma that she lived through during Partition has been biologically passed down to me. Like, she had buried it deep inside her and it carved its way to me. Is that possible? I feel it with such intensity, far more intensely sometimes than her. Just like my mother was separated from her family, I feel like I was separated from a land that could have been mine.'

As I concentrate on her words, I realize that where there is fragility in her voice, there is also strength in her sentiment, and this becomes my takeaway.

'I have never felt any hatred towards Pakistan or Pakistani people,' Pinky admits. 'Despite everything that happened to my mother's family, it was their home, their land. *Bass ek baar wahan ja paoon, toh hasrat poori ho jaye*, it is my deepest desire to visit Pakistan. Even my father studied in Lahore, and I crave to walk on the land that he walked, to touch the soil, *wahan ki mitti ko chhoona*. I have visualized Lahore – Mochi Darwaza, Anarkali Bazaar, *Ravi ka kinara*, I can see them all before my eyes. And because I cannot physically go there, I travel through television dramas and books. *Karachi toh zubaani yaad hai*,' she smiles, 'I know Karachi by heart. But the average person will not understand this. They will not understand that hate and bitterness are not the way forward.'

Her tears begin to fall again, and using her dupatta she wipes them, slowly and purposefully.

Then looking into my eyes, Pinky confesses, 'Whenever I have gone to Wagah border, I have cried. I have wanted to stand in the middle of no man's land and scream, because the consequences of this border feel so painful. All I see is a partitioned land, and a celebration of that separation.'

22
Silence

∽

THE SILENCE SURROUNDING PARTITION is as old as Partition itself. Over the decades, it has become cavernous and opaque, resolute and well-established. It is a dimension within which exist remembering and forgetting, truth and untruth, trauma and solace, interpretation and misinterpretation. Among the generation of Partition survivors, silence may be practised as a choice, due to the incommunicable nature of past trauma[1] or the immediate need to rebuild lives in nations now partitioned and independent. In both circumstances, however, silence envelops memory, creating a space for forgetting.

But there are cases where that veil is partially lifted to allow for selective forms of remembrance. The most common of these that I have encountered, within my own family as well as in several eyewitness accounts, is when survivors recall with ease a life *before* Partition – a childhood untainted by tragedy, the school, the fields, the mohalla, the neighbours, the bazaar, the languages, the food – nurturing the nostalgia. But everything *after* – the weeks and months surrounding the moment of Partition – is either vague or surrendered to silence, particularly if that 'memory continues to intrude into the present life of the survivor'.[2] Of course, there are always exceptions: those who speak about these moments with both clarity and intention. However, within my family, it has taken years to exhume these details through gentle and continual conversation.

I suppose anyone who writes on the human history of Partition considers the notion of silence, having no choice but to encounter it at some stage. Since the subject of this research is not eyewitness memory but its inheritance, my questions became about how much of the past has been silenced and why, and how much of that silence may have contributed to the creation of bias, prejudice, fear, curiosity, longing, romanticism, misinformation, or even ambivalence within subsequent generations of Partition-affected families. In other words, what shape does silence occupy in its bequeathment?

In the Foreword to Dr Sukeshi Kamra's *Bearing Witness: Partition, Independence, End of the Raj*, her father, Mulk Raj Kamra, to whom the book is dedicated, poignantly writes:

> I feel privileged at this opportunity, given to me by my daughter, to speak. For I am one from the 'silent' generation, 'silent' because no one seemed to care to hear, 'silent' because we were so busy restructuring our destroyed future.[3]

On a spring morning, I have the chance to meet with Dr Kamra in Gurugram just before she returns to Canada, where she has lived and taught for decades. Our conversation touches on many aspects of the active remembering and forgetting of trauma,[4] but what remains with me is the fact that only now, as her father approaches his late nineties, have anecdotes from his childhood in Lyallpur (now Faisalabad) begun to make an appearance. She tells me that though Partition may have been mentioned in her home, it was never monumentalized, and if I return to her father's Foreword, part of me understands why, for the need to 'restructure' superseded the need to lament or commemorate. The other part, however, focuses on how silence existed because 'no one seemed to care to hear'. But now, two decades have passed since Dr Kamra's book was first published, and the endeavour to record eyewitness testimony before it is too late is certainly underway. However, in my experience, it takes tremendous effort to eradicate or even begin to disperse the silence that envelops Partition, mostly because of how entrenched it is. In the introductory essay to the 2013 cross-border anthology *This Side, That Side*, Vishwajyoti Ghosh, the curator of the collection, writes:

> Restoring Partition can never be easy ... one has to look beyond those maps lodged in our nervous systems that make nervous headlines on our televisions. To listen to the subsequent generations and the grandchildren and how they have negotiated maps that never got drawn.[5]

This chapter, thus, investigates the realm of silence as a prominent character as subsequent generations attempt to unearth or claim the past, or – borrowing Ghosh's phraseology – to draw new maps.

'I WAS JUST a child when my grandfather and I had the sole conversation about Partition. Otherwise, it was a subject of silence,' the 1980-born, Pennsylvania-based teacher Maleeha Malik says. 'But I know something about living with silence. My family are Ahmadis, and in 1974 the government of Pakistan constitutionally redefined the status of the Jamaat Ahmadiyya, no longer recognizing it as a Muslim sect.[6] While growing up in Pakistan, I was cautioned never to tell anyone that I was Ahmadi, but so much of this identity is woven into my family's journey during Partition.'

Using this as a starting point, Maleeha travels back in time, piecing together the history of her family's migrations across the cities of Rangoon in Burma, Qadian in India and Dulmial in Pakistan. As she narrates without interruption, I realize that, at times, silence is protection, and other times, silence is erasure. But some people have no choice but to practise both.

'In the late 1800s, the city of Qadian, just outside of Amritsar, emerged as a centre for the Ahmadiyya Muslim community, and remained so until Partition, as it was the birthplace of Mirza Ghulam Ahmad, the founder of the Ahmadiyya movement. As I told you, my maternal grandfather, Muhammad Sadiq Malik, whom I call Nana

Abbu, spoke directly about Partition only once. He had served in the signal corps in Egypt and the Pacific during the Second World War, and married right after. He was probably in his mid-twenties, and my grandmother, Razia Begum, or nani ama to me, was only a few years younger. Both were originally from Dulmial, but shortly after their marriage, in late 1946 or early '47, the couple made the journey to Qadian, where his brother lived. Everyone told them not to go, that there was talk of unrest and rioting throughout the Punjab, but he was adamant to be with his brother. I also don't think he had a stable job after the war, and so he was probably hoping that once he got to Qadian, he'd find permanent work and settle down there. Moreover, being the birthplace of the Jamaat Ahmadiyya, Qadian remained of deep and reverential importance to my grandfather.

'I'm breaking chronology now, but I want to go back a few years into the war to tell you about my grandfather's brother. His name was Captain Abdullah Khan, and he too served in the Second World War in Burma. Around 1942, with the fear of Japanese invasion, he, his wife and three children – all under the age of ten – fled Burma for Qadian. From stories I've heard over the years, I know they left Burma as a large group, like a mass exodus. Some family friends travelled with them. They also had three children, the eldest a teenage girl. This is how nana abu's brother made it back across to India and settled in Qadian.'

She looks up at me and says, 'I can only imagine this journey across during wartime to have been a traumatic one. My mother recently told me that Captain Abdullah Khan's wife, Hajra Bibi, gave birth during this journey and the child died shortly after birth. Their other son, who was a young child at the time, never openly or directly spoke about the things he saw, but towards the end of his life, on his deathbed in 2016, it all returned to him. He said that the violence from Burma to Punjab was something he'd never forgotten or gotten over. He had constant nightmares about it throughout his life. No matter how many years had passed, you could see the impact that migration had left on him.

'Now, in 1946, my grandparents joined them in Qadian and would have barely been there for a few months when riots broke out across Punjab. It was probably March or April 1947. For some reason, the family friends' three children from Burma were also with them, and nana abu and his brother started to plan their migration in a group of six children and four adults. One day, they discovered that some military jeeps were transporting Ahmadis from Qadian to the train station and there was still room for people to join. So, my grandparents and the family friends' children hopped on the jeep and made their way to Amritsar. The rest of the family eventually followed. *This* was the moment nana abu had narrated to me, the only conversation we ever had about it.'

'When was this?' I speak now for the first time.

'It was in the '90s, when a large part of my maternal family had already immigrated to the US and we would go and visit them from Pakistan. I clearly remember sitting in his living room in New Jersey and boldly asking my grandfather whether he remembered anything about this Partition. "*Apko yaad hai uss waqt kya hua tha?*"'

I smile. 'Had you learnt about it in school?'

'I think so. I'd kind of understood that after a lot of violence, one country was split into two new countries. Something historic and important had happened. And someone had told me that nana abu was there, so I thought to myself, "Okay, well, I must ask him about it," because I was an ever-curious child. He had this style of speaking, where if something was emotional, he'd get choked up. When I asked him about Partition, he said something like, "*Oho, main kya bataoon uss waqt ke baare mein,*" that there were no words to speak about that time, but then he proceeded to mention the dead bodies strewn around the town, and how one would open the door to find rivers of blood on the streets. I remember that conversation distinctly.'

'From Qadian they returned to Dulmial?' I ask.

'Yes, so my grandparents and these three children reach Amritsar station and, as soon as they arrive, nana abu witnesses some of the worst violence. From just the photographs and films about the time, I can imagine the confusion and havoc and fear and panic in people trying to get to safety. So, in between all this, he witnesses the murder of a Sikh man – someone shoots him – and that moment stays with nana abu. When he was telling me the story, he kept repeating what a terrible time it was, and how he'd seen this man get killed at Amritsar station – alive one moment and dead the next,' Maleeha says, with wide eyes.

'My grandmother, she was a young bride at the time and had a suitcase full of all these things she'd got as part of her dowry, beautiful things. She'd sent the suitcase across beforehand, because she didn't know if they'd be able to carry luggage or not. But on the jeep she had brought a thermos full of chai, and nana abu just got so angry when he saw it,' she chuckles. 'He said that there wasn't enough place to seat people, and she had got a thermos full of chai with her! I think he threw it away. Nani ama never spoke much about Partition either. But when I asked her about it, she said Hindus and Muslims had lived relatively peacefully with each other in our village, Dulmial. She remembered how at weddings, people would send uncooked rice and lentils to each other's homes. When Captain Abdullah Khan was getting married, his mother said the *baraat* wouldn't leave until her friend Iqbal Kaur, a Sikh, came.'

'Why do you think that was the only conversation you had on Partition? Why was it a subject of silence?'

'Well,' she begins thoughtfully, 'probably for two reasons. One, because of the practicality of life. There just wasn't enough time for him to sit down and tell these stories; one had to carry on. But the second reason was that it was painful. Even when we talked about it, when over four decades had passed, it seemed painful. Nana abu was visibly and viscerally affected by what he remembered. And he didn't really want to open that door to say, "Look, this is what happened, this is the traumatic thing that I had witnessed."'

I nod. 'For many years, my own grandfather never spoke about Partition either. The reason for his silence was that there was nothing to be said that would change the outcome of what had happened.'

'That too,' she agrees, 'that too. You know, the daughter of the family friends who left Burma with my grandfather's brother – she was barely a teenager then and saw so much violence. By the time she reached Qadian, she was already mentally impacted by it. And then to witness communal violence yet again while crossing over from Amritsar to Pakistan' – Maleeha takes a sharp breath – 'she was never the same. It impacted her so drastically, to the point where she had to be taken care of for the rest of her life. She eventually immigrated with her family to the UK but remained mentally unstable.'

'The same trauma can affect different people very differently,' I note.

'That's very true, and if I think about my family's reaction' – she holds out her left hand – 'there is a silence that says we are purposefully not going to talk about something' – and then she holds out her right hand – 'and then there is a silence of practicality. I think my family's was the latter. Their silence was practical and incidental. After Partition, they were allotted a home in Mandi Bahauddin, where my mother was born. From there they moved to a small town called Rabwah, which became the headquarters of the Ahmadiyya community after Partition in Pakistan. It's on the banks of the river Chenab and has now been renamed Chenab Nagar. But at one point, nana abu was working in Karachi and my mother was still living in Rabwah, and they had this physical distance between them. Then when he immigrated to the United States and she was still in Pakistan, the distance only grew. It's so hard to speak about topics that are intimate and personal when you have so much distance to overcome. How do you sit and make the time for these stories?'

'Do you wish he had, though?' I ask.

She smiles warmly. 'Of course, because I have so much faith in people's memories, particularly about a time like Partition. I used to think about all the Ahmadi Muslim families that got divided on both sides of the border, and how if my grandfather hadn't decided to leave that day, we would have been Indian. The impact of one person's decision resulted in a completely different nationality. I think about how our shrines remain in Qadian in India. This Partition – it feels like the ripping apart of limbs. Just the word is powerful enough to conjure the most violent of images, even for those who weren't there. I suppose, if nana abu chose not to speak about it, I have to learn to accept his silence. Right?'

I don't know whether her question is rhetorical or not, but I find myself nodding in response.

IN 2017, I worked for a few months with The 1947 Partition Archive to curate exhibitions commemorating seventy years of Independence and Partition that August. The archive, set up in 2010, is a non-profit oral history organization in Berkeley, California, that collects and preserves accounts of Partition from eyewitnesses living across the world.[7] It was during this work that I first met Ritika Popli, who was born in Delhi in 1992. She was coordinating the exhibits on behalf of the archive and had earlier completed a BA from Indraprastha College and an MA from Jawaharlal Nehru University. Over the course of a few months, we became good friends, our shared interest in Partition always at the core of that friendship. Several years later, as I am working on this book, I reach out to her at Ohio University, where she is currently a doctoral candidate in rhetoric and culture at the School of Communication Studies.

'I've never met my grandfather,' is the first thing she says when we speak. 'He passed away in 1974 and is always referred to as bauji in our house. He worked in the railways as a low-grade engineer and was the only earning member of the family. They were not well-to-do, and Partition only affected their status further. We were Punjabis but lived in Bihar at the time, because most of bauji's work would take him around Bihar and Bengal. What I do know about the day he passed away from pancreatic cancer was that my father had his Grade 11 exam. Bauji's body was placed in the veranda of the house, and my father just crossed it and left. He didn't even look at the body, just took the exam and then came back to cremate him and perform the last rites.'[8]

'How did he do in the exam?' I ask with concern.

'He topped the class, actually. You see, he was the eldest son, and there was a lot of pressure on him to succeed.' Ritika pauses. 'My father would always tell us this story, and it seemed so ominous and morbid that I'd wonder why he was narrating it. Now I think I understand – it's a very middle-class idea where you tell your children: look how we persevered, look how we had to go on, because what else did we have? These traits of perseverance and hard work, particularly in the aftermath of Partition, were all they had to pass on.'

'What happened to your family during Partition?' I ask, eyes still fixed on my notebook. When my question is met with silence, I look up to find Ritika sitting with her chin resting on her palm.

'I don't know,' she admits, shaking her head. 'All I know is that bauji was born in Ahmedpur Sharqia, also known as Ahmedpur East, in the Bahawalpur district of Punjab, Pakistan. Though he and my great-grandmother spoke Seraiki,[9] I'm not sure whether or when they moved to Multan city. So, along with the silence surrounding their migration to India, there is also a blank space on where they lived before Partition.'

I watch her, placing my pen down. 'Does that bother you?'

'Of course. I wish I could ask someone, but there's no one left to ask. After bauji's death, my father and his siblings naturally became closer to their maternal side. But this is what I do know – bauji, his elder brother and wife came with absolutely nothing from Multan and somehow, they reached Delhi. I don't know if Delhi was the first place they came to or if they had lived in other cities before. I don't know if there was violence or difficulty during the journey. A lot of details are missing, so I won't be able to provide a full picture, but once they arrived in Delhi, they lived in the neighbourhood called Andha Mughal in the western part of the city. They saw a house that had a lock on it, which had likely been vacated by a Muslim family, so they broke in. And that's how the house became theirs. That's how it happened.'

'How is Partition viewed in your family then?' I wonder what stories are passed down in silence.

'Economic loss,' she says, 'a struggle to find your bearings – this is what most of the memories are about. My father's mother is also from Pakistan; she came from Lahore. I know her story, but her elder sister's version of it. My grandmother passed away in 2015, but even when she was alive, she hardly ever sat down to tell us stories of Lahore.'

Ritika tells me that her grandmother was always economical with her memory, frugal with the details, but the one story she knows for certain is why they migrated. 'Her father was a low-grade government official. One day, while serving his British sahib tea, he was very casually told that there will be a partition and he should leave Lahore. My grandmother came from a large family of ten siblings and lived in the railway accommodations for Hindu employees, so her father must have immediately started making arrangements. In her stories, there is no mention of any violence or riots. But in her sister's version, their neighbourhood was flanked by two large gates and someone had come in and set fire to the roof of the neighbouring house – "*Aag ke gole phenke the*". The family saw that and left the very next day. But my grandmother never mentioned any of this.'

'I can't help but think of how long you worked for the Partition Archive, and yet your own history –'

'And this bothers me,' she says even before I can finish the sentence. 'As a researcher, I find this very frustrating. But what is strange is that it never bothered me until I began working at the archive. Partition had always been a subject of silence, but that didn't seem like an odd thing. In fact, I'd never even heard the word until later in my school years.' She thinks about this for a few seconds. 'The word I *did* hear was refugee.'

'In what context?'

'In *every* context,' she laughs. 'My grandmother would use the word repeatedly; she fixated on it and the loss of property and land that accompanied it. "*Hum refugee ban gaye, hum refugee log hain, Dilli mein refugee rehte hain*," she would say. My father was in the army, and once, when I was five or six, we were posted in Pune and my grandmother came to visit us there, and that was probably the first time I heard her use the word. I would ask her what it meant, why we were refugees, or what a refugee colony was. So, my understanding of the word "Partition" comes through the word "refugee". Then I read about Partition in school and made the connection that we had been part of it. This was the loss my grandmother kept referring to, this was why they became refugees. And for her, it was always about property – land, colony, neighbourhood, home – these were the dominant words in her vocabulary. She would constantly compare the lack of what they had in independent India with all that they lost in 1947, particularly if she was upset about something...' Her voice trails off.

'But in all other aspects except this, there was a pervasive silence. I have no clue about what happened and why it was never spoken about. I don't know if this history has shame in it – of losing home, of witnessing violence, or worse – I don't know why there was an unwillingness to talk about it. But what was truly frustrating was listening to other people's stories while working with the archive. Interviewing people, listening to them detail the minutiae of their days surrounding Partition ... I mean, *you know* how nuanced those memories can be.' She looks at me.

'The specificity is what really strikes me,' I admit, 'the memories are hardly ever vague.'

'Exactly. So, seventy years later, some people still remembered everything and were willing to speak about it, and I was recording these stories. Yet, I had no idea about how my family had fled or survived.'

I nod sadly. 'I never actually knew that you were part Lahori. I only knew about Multan.'

I think I detect a shade of sadness when she responds. 'It's mostly because I'm trying to latch on to something that I feel is lost.' Immediately, I am reminded of how we began our conversation with the death of her grandfather, the severing of ties to Multan. 'I feel like if I don't tell people about it, or circulate this identity, then who am I and which place do people associate me with? I feel a strong need to hold on to Multan.'

'Can we talk a little more about the word refugee?' I ask, and she nods slowly. 'Why do you think your grandmother held on to the term so tightly?'

Ritika's response is candid, yet heartbreaking. 'I don't think she understood the ways to make her life better. She lost home, land, her husband at a young age; she had to raise three boys on her own. She resigned to a lifetime of anxiety and constant instability, a feeling of being uprooted. She was never at peace, and I'm not saying that Partition was the only reason, but maybe it was the beginning. She lived her entire life that way.'

'Did you ever speak to her about it – any of it?'

'No, and this is something I think about a lot: how we probably never asked the right questions – or *any* questions. I began working with the archive a few months after her death, and only then did I receive an adequate vocabulary for what to ask. Before that, I didn't know where to begin, or even that silence could be addressed. When I interviewed my grandmother's sister, I understood some parts of her story, but it was not in her words, and I regret that. Now I work on the premise that human beings are essentially flawed and they learn to live with their discomfort, mould themselves around it, as my grandmother did. But I don't think we can fully put the blame of silence on the generation who witnessed Partition. That is unfair. No one in my family sat down with my grandmother and directly asked what happened, or wanted to know more about her life before Partition. If anything ever came up, we would say it's in the past and leave it at that.'

'If you could ask her something now, what would it be?'

'Oh, there are just so many things,' Ritika smiles. 'I would ask her what her childhood was like. I'd want to know what she did, whom she played with, who her friends were, what she learnt at school.' She cups her face with her palms and breathes out. 'In my imagination, my grandmother is never happy. So, I'd want her to tell me at least one memory of her life where she was happy, where she was carefree, not tense or worried.'

I lean back with a sigh, crumpling in my chair.

'Maybe many people who lived through Partition became this way,' she speculates, 'but my grandmother was never happy. I want to know her at a happier time, and I know that's only possible if I find a way to go beyond Partition into an undivided India.'

What remains with me from this conversation is the need for a vocabulary of trauma. Despite the abundance of public and written knowledge on Partition over the last seven decades, all we may still receive from our families are hushed details or half memories. Some are luckier than others, though, in that they find a space where a dialogue between generations is possible. But, for the most part, we inherit and bequeath incomplete histories. As children and grandchildren of Partition, we don't know how or what to ask, and, similarly, the survivors of Partition may not know what to say, or how much to say when and if they are asked. As a result, to merely begin the conversation is difficult.

But notwithstanding these fortified and accepted practices of silence, what I keep wondering about is this: if the very creation of independent nations was the result of a violent division, then should we, who carry the event in our histories, not somehow be equipped to speak of its consequences? My fear is that a hundred years will have passed since Partition and we may still be in the same place, finding the right words to penetrate this silence.

FOR THE 1991-BORN, British–Bangladeshi journalist and photographer Adib Chowdhury, there is fear that the gaps he has encountered while seeking out family history may ultimately lead to a form of partial erasure. 'Since so much of our history is handed down orally, all it takes is for one generation to not really be bothered about what happened. And having grown up in Britain, the distance from my homeland also affects this.'

When I enquire whether his family was affected by Partition, his response is tepid.

'There are some things I know about boro nana, my maternal great-grandfather, but they're not well-defined. His name was Muhammad Abdul Huq and he belonged to a Bengali zamindari family from the Sylhet region, but he was a man of education, which was rare at the time, particularly given his landed background. He attended what was then known as the Calcutta Madrasah and has now been renamed as Aliah University, in the Park Circus area of the city.[10] The only certain piece of information I have, which my grandmother showed me, is a medal of academic excellence awarded to him at his graduation in 1915.

'But after this moment, there are vast time gaps. It is said that he got involved in politics and, alongside others, used his academic knowledge to form the intellectual strands of dissent that would eventually overturn British rule. He went back to his village to abolish the system of zamindari on their land in revolt. I've heard stories where British officials threatened to take away all the land, but this coincided with Partition, and so...' Adib stops abruptly and looks at me, a bit helpless. 'This is no use to you, is it?' he laughs. 'I won't be able to tell you any details or dates about, well, anything ... because I don't actually know myself.'

This opacity of family history introduces silence as a prominent character in many conversations.

'Well, let's talk about what you do know,' I propose. 'The medal, which is something tangible. When you saw it, what did you feel?'

'I felt frustrated that no one had told me about this pre-Partition past, and when I began inquiring, the attitude was something along the lines of: "We don't really know much about it, and we don't talk about it, but if you want you can always ask." So, naturally, I ask, and I'm directed towards so-and-so relative, a granduncle or aunt, who further tells me that someone else may know. But I found nothing more, and I just began wondering whether anyone had ever kept a record of this. Are there family records of this time? Who would know about my great-grandfather's years in Calcutta, or of his move back home to what would become East Pakistan, or if there were any other relatives who made the journey from India to Pakistan? Over the years, I've discovered that there's no official or written record of what happened before or during Partition, and the stories have just casually been told by the elders – some of whom have passed away – and this lack of information makes me feel frustrated.'

'Many people, particularly from our generation, share this sentiment,' I say, 'but then I remember how at the time most of the local population wasn't even educated enough, so record-keeping…'

'Of course,' he sighs, 'of course. But this alarms me as well, because when there is no information to pass down, history becomes naturally and incidentally silenced.'

When he says this, I begin to think about how the practice of silence can itself become a hereditary endowment. And when there are no memories to associate with a particular historical moment, perhaps we are forced to imagine what *could have* happened. Laboriously, we construct personal history from the collective history of the time, borrowing and stitching together from similar histories, imagining why an ancestor's experiences could have been rendered mute. Bringing this up with Adib, I ask, 'Why do you think the stories have not been passed down?'

'There's a few different ideas that I've toyed with, actually. And whenever I inquire into it, it just adds more fuel to my theory, for lack of a better word. I reckon – and my father has also dropped little hints to this end – that our relatives witnessed violence in the areas of India where they lived, and were forced to flee across the border. The trauma of being made a refugee is so painful, and this seems to me one of the most plausible explanations as to why there's silence around the issue. The second reason – the more horrible one – is that perhaps they were involved in the violence,' he shrugs. 'I don't know what happened to create silence in my family about Partition, but I do hope it's something more innocent, like they didn't like to ask and they weren't told. And then no one bothered to follow up on it because time passed and life resumed, and it just got lost.'

I nod. 'Do you find that in your family the stories of Bangladesh liberation in 1971 overshadow the stories of Indian and Pakistani Independence in 1947?'

'Undoubtedly,' he agrees. 'Those stories are told with clarity and awareness. In fact, my father was born in East Pakistan and witnessed the creation of Bangladesh. Just recently he showed me his Pakistani passport, which I was both fascinated and shocked to see,' he smiles.

I keep returning to the fact that all of Adib's journalistic work has focused on conflict zones and the chronicling of identities made and unmade by war. For years, he has documented 'the forced migration of the Syrian civil war, reporting from the fringes of conflict, following refugees as they make their way through the Balkans',[11] and the ethnic cleansing of the Rohingyas in 2017 along the Bangladeshi–Burmese border, noting witness statements of the survivors. These efforts have allowed moments of history to be documented, to not be erased or forgotten. And though I fear I may be reading too much into it, I can't help but make the connection to his own life – whether it is, in some way, to prevent a future generation from looking back and encountering silence.

'Is there resonance?' I ask him.

He smiles. '*So much*. You could say that I was driven by the stories of those affected by conflict, including my own family. I studied international relations and one of the first things we were taught is how the nation state is a western construct, which fascinated me enough to learn about how this man-made concept of boundaries, borders and sovereignty affects refugees or migrants or those who find themselves stateless. In our part of the world, this question returns most naturally to Partition and extends from thereon: How were people made refugees? How did it affect their everyday lives? How is it *still* affecting their everyday lives? There is trauma and silence – sometimes personal, other times institutional – that still resonates with much of the population.'

I nod. 'And despite not getting clear answers, do you still ask your family about Partition?'

'Oh, yes. And I know time is running out, and those who were alive then may not be alive for much longer. So, I'm very aware that the conversations are time-sensitive and this only makes me want to dig deeper … But as to whether I'll make any progress or not, I can't say. I'm also very conscious of the fact that I was born and raised in Britain, and the generations after me may need stronger ties to their homeland, to Bangladesh. I wish that I spoke more fluent Bangla – enough to really probe and extract nuanced answers,' he smiles and shrugs. 'So, despite the silence, I want to be able to record *some* history for the future, but…'

An intentional pause is lodged between us.

'You know about this better than anyone,' he resumes, 'how hard it is to find the line between where you're recalling an old trauma and where you're asking about a memory that your ancestor may not wish to bring up, or have any idea about themselves. It is difficult sometimes to determine which silence it is.'

'I WOULD SAY that I felt betrayed,' Jasmin Athwal, born and raised in Birmingham, admits. When we speak, she is in her early twenties. Her father immigrated to Britain in the early 1980s, and her mother, after marriage, in the late 1990s.

'Betrayed?' I repeat.

'I know it's a bit of a strong word, but I feel it adequately sums up the vacuum of South Asian history in our curriculum in Britain[12] as well as the silence around family history at home. I was ignorant about Partition until I took a course at university, because neither had it been discussed in school nor had anyone from my family spent the time to tell me about it. In fact, when I initially asked my mum if anyone she knew had been affected by Partition – we belong to a Sikh family – she said no. But when her mother, my nani, was visiting us, I asked her and she very clearly told me that her parents had migrated from Pakistan to India. I was shocked because this meant that my mum didn't know either.'

'Wow. Do you know where they migrated from?' I ask.

'I don't, I'm sorry.'

'What about whether they came before or during or after Partition?'

Jasmin shakes her head from side to side.

'Hmm … maybe how they crossed the border – train or bus or on foot?'

Again, she says nothing but looks out her window.

With a soft smile, I say, 'Well, that's all right. Tell me, what did your grandmother say about her parents?'

'Nothing apart from the fact that they came to India and were given lands in the Jalandhar region. That's all she knew as well. Look, you've probably already encountered this in your research, but some people just don't want to talk about that time. Maybe it's upsetting, or maybe it's just too far back in the past – I don't know, but nobody wants to talk about Partition. It's hard to describe, but sometimes it feels like the question isn't taken seriously enough,' Jasmin emphasizes.

'I don't like to use the word "missing" because it alludes to an incompleteness,' I begin, 'but, for lack of a better word, do you think that there is a part of you that's missing because you don't know these details?'

'Yes, and that part lies in Pakistan. It's become even more prominent now that I've begun to learn about the extent of the Sikh empire under Maharaja Ranjit Singh and how it spilled over the current international border between India and Pakistan. I mean, the very concept of these two independent nations is relatively new, they are young countries. But I feel like in returning to the Sikh empire, to an undivided land … I don't know, am I just rambling now?' She looks at me, flustered.

'No, please, go on,' I encourage her.

'Well, I'd never thought about it so much before. But "missing" is actually the right word. I feel like some essential part of my history – both as a Sikh and as a British citizen – is missing from my own understanding, because it has been silenced. My connect to

Britain is one generation, but before that everything is a blank, and I can't explain it but I know it leads back to an undivided Punjab. Sometimes, I think about how if I don't know my history, future generations will be even less aware.'

'And there is so much beauty in the heritage of an undivided Punjab; in these Punjabi roots that are common between Indians and Pakistanis; between Sikhs, Hindus and Muslims,' I say with a smile.

A look of longing appears on Jasmin's face. 'Which is why I want to reconnect with it. I understand that my father moved to Britain for a better life, for economic opportunity, but I am now feeling the long-term consequences of the disconnect from my culture. I wish that I had someone to ask because Partition is a looming question. I feel there are so many stories that still need to be heard, but whom do I ask? And what about those who died during the violence – are they just lost in history?' She draws in a sharp breath and then exhales. 'For a long time, I used to send messages to my family in India on Independence Day, but I couldn't get myself to do it this year. I've arrived at my own interpretation of what this day means, how Independence is tied to Partition. I often wonder if someone in my family succumbed to the violence, or if it impacted someone deeply. I don't know, but I don't want to celebrate it.'

'You mentioned that your mother wasn't aware that her grandparents migrated from Pakistan,' I begin.

'Neither that nor the sheer scale of violence or horror … especially with women,' Jasmin says with wide eyes. 'This was the conversation I had with my nani and mum – the plight of women and how they were abused and abducted and abandoned. At times they were returned to their families, but their families didn't always accept them and just sent them away to camps or shelters. Some of the experiences of these women were literally unbelievable, and I felt so disturbed by their suffering. So, I asked my nani and mum, "How did people do that? How could they just disown their daughters or wives or sisters?" and my nani simply said that she understood it. She understood why families did it, and I found that … shocking.'

I nod sadly. 'Do you think there's a deeper reason why the stories of Partition weren't discussed? At times, to remember trauma is to relive it. I wonder if your great-grandparents even told your grandmother about what happened to them or what they saw.'

'I think about this a lot,' she reveals in a small voice. 'What has been rendered unspeakable and why. The reasons are deeper than I know, that's for sure. And I just feel sadness that I'm never going to know. That I'll never fully claim ownership over a part of my history. I feel betrayed by that silence.'

23
The Other

༄

'A S SOMEONE BORN IN 1942, Independence and Partition remain a somewhat hazy but definitive memory,' the senior Pakistani journalist Asif Noorani sahib states.

It is February 2018 and we are seated for breakfast on the deck of the historic Beach Luxury Hotel[1] in Karachi. I have travelled here from Delhi, crossing into Pakistan via the Attari–Wagah border, to release *Remnants* at the Karachi Literature Festival. This time of year is the coldest in Delhi, but in the port city of Karachi the day is sunny and pleasant with a mild breeze. Noorani sahib casually waves his hand over his breakfast plate as he continues his thought. 'But now younger people in their twenties and thirties are not so bothered about Partition. When you speak to the grandchildren of those who migrated, they can at best only recall the names of the towns from where their grandparents came.'

I turn to look at Anam Zakaria, the Pakistani oral historian, researcher and author,[2] who is seated beside me at the table. We are both in the age group he has mentioned and have dedicated most of our careers to documenting and preserving stories of Partition. Anam and I conduct our research in a similar fashion on either side of the Radcliffe Line, but my trips to Pakistan and hers to India are rare, and so any time together is often spent exchanging stories. We listen to Noorani sahib as he continues his recollections.

'Perhaps it was on the eve of Independence that my father took me to see the illuminations on the buildings. We enjoyed the view from the upper storey of a double-decker bus in Bombay!'

Asif Noorani was born in Bombay, in an undivided India, and migrated to Karachi, Pakistan, via ship in 1950. He tells us that another defining moment of his childhood also took place on a bus, while he was travelling with his entire family. Switching between English and Urdu, he recalls, 'Communal riots had just ended in the city, but there was still tension in the air. In those days, *kaafi achhi buses hoti thi*, the buses used to be quite good, and eight passengers were allowed to stand in the lower half of a double-decker. Like my parents, I too was standing when a man in a dhoti offered to share his seat with me. My father told me to go and sit with the distinguished-looking man but, out of fear, I refused. What was worse, I told my parents, "This man is a Hindu, he will kill me." The man smiled benignly and told me in a soft tone, "Murderers are *mawaalis*" – this is the Bombay word for scoundrel,' he informs Anam and me, chuckling, '"they are neither Hindus nor Muslims, they are simply murderers." He seemed so disarming that I agreed to sit between him and his wife. They asked me about my school and the games I enjoyed playing. That changed my entire perception of Hindus.'[3]

I first met Noorani sahib in 2015, when we were both speaking on a panel about Partition at the Kumaon Literature Festival in India. We kept in touch, and he often sent me the pieces he wrote for *Dawn* newspaper, ranging from topics of history and film to music and cricket. From his writings and our interactions, he immediately came across as empathetic and wise, borderless in his actions and an ardent crusader for the need for close contact between Pakistanis and Indians. He became someone I could turn to for advice during my research. So, it makes me quite sad when he ends our conversation that morning by telling us that in the sixties and seventies, and even later, whenever he's written about the need for friendship or the desire to bridge the cultural gap between the two countries, people have dubbed him 'an Indian agent'.[4]

My heart sink even lower when Anam, who has put in ample effort in the last decade to write unbiased histories and forge relations amongst Pakistanis and Indians – working across generations, from grandparents to young students,[5] by means as diverse as oral history interviews and school textbooks – chimes in sadly, '*Main aapke saath hoon*, sir, I am with you. They call me the same thing.'

WHAT I DO not mention to Noorani sahib or Anam that morning is just how many times I have been called Pakistani because of the work I do. Even admitting it here on paper is difficult. On that trip alone, among the people who messaged or commented on my social media updates, the number of Indians who wished to travel to Pakistan one day and those who wished for me to remain there, were equal. For all the people who feel the pain of Partition, there will be an equal number for whom Partition validated a certain bifurcation of history. I have lost count of the times the word 'Pakistani' is used as an insult in India these days – and the ease with which it is said, always denoting otherness or meant to cause hurt, is incredible. And I have to admit that, at first, it did hurt.

But what had I done for anyone to doubt my Indianness this way? I had written about Pakistan with an open and compassionate heart; I had depicted Pakistanis the way they are, which is culturally and linguistically not very different from the way of north Indians; I had longed for the cities of my grandparents' birth; I had made meaningful connections with Pakistanis in the same way I would with anybody one spends a certain amount of time with. Such was my crime, which I suspect was exactly what my fellow scholars were accused of as well.

If there is anything I have learnt during my research – apart from being an active and engaged listener – is that to write about Partition, one needs to embrace *both* sides equally and do justice to the experiences that occurred on *both* sides of the border. Thinking, writing, recreating the days and understanding the consequences of

Partition require us not just to be borderless in our thoughts and perceptions but also impartial and honest in our research. This is easier said than done, of course, for we all are held hostage to some form of bias. Thus, I unlearn and relearn every day, which in turn causes me to make and unmake the other.

∽

GROWING UP IN Delhi in the 1990s, I barely had any interest in Partition, Pakistan or politics, apart from what I learnt in history textbooks. My grandparents never talked about what they had witnessed during their journey to India. The Kargil war was fought when I was nine years old, and I only vaguely remember its coverage. But despite all my indifferences, I knew intrinsically that Pakistanis were perceived as 'the other'. Even the way the word is used in India will catch your attention because it stands out from the rest of your everyday speech. I notice this now, when I am speaking to people and may casually mention how my research has taken me across the border. There is an energy to the word '*Pakistan*' that seems to evoke simultaneous curiosity and discomfort.

I finally had a chance to interact with Pakistanis when I went to university in Canada in 2007. There, far away from my land and language, I sought refuge in hearing familiar words in the study hall or the elevator of my first-year residence, ultimately making friends with several students from across the border. It is embarrassing to admit how shocked I was to learn the similarities between us. But I don't know what I had been expecting, or how this image of the other had subconsciously taken root in my mind.

We looked the same, we spoke the same language, we could correctly pronounce each other's names, we missed the same food, we even swore in the same way. When I was shown photographs of the Badshahi Mosque, I reciprocated with descriptions of the Jama Masjid. In the sub-zero Canadian winters, when they would describe the salty air at Clifton Beach, I would add my memories of Marine Drive. Together, we would dream about the intoxicating smell of rain and the warmth of a subcontinental sun. We would collectively despair at the sweetness of the butter-chicken gravy in Canadian restaurants, and participate in 'desi' festivities at university, regardless of whether it was Diwali, Eid, Holi or Garba nights. I don't remember feeling that their Pakistani identity diminished my Indian one, or hindered my understanding of them, and vice versa. Rather, it was our conjoined subcontinental identity and the comfort accompanying it that we revelled in. Living so far away from home, where we were collectively the other in so many North American eyes, our own perceived otherness of one another seemed to dissolve completely.

AS THE YEARS rolled by, I became interested in writing about Partition and, while working on *Remnants*, travelled to Pakistan for the first time in 2014. Growing up as a Hindu, I was part of the majority in India, but for those few weeks in Pakistan, I became the other. For the most part, people welcomed me quite graciously into their homes, excited that I had come all the way from India to speak with them, but there were moments when my otherness stuck out – like how, for the first two days, I instinctively greeted everyone with a 'namaste', as I would back home, rather than with an 'as-salaam-alaikum'. Or how, during interviews where there were conversations of Hindus perpetrating violence against Muslims during Partition, I would shrink back, acutely aware of my otherness. Sometimes I would nervously ask whether they knew I was Hindu, a comment which would often be met with, '*Arre, par tum toh beti ho*, but you are like a daughter.' Even then, I had thought this to be a complicated notion, but could never quite grasp how to reason through it. Hopefully, as this chapter progresses, I will address it through various conversations with my interviewees. Needless to say, though, my trips to Pakistan and sustained interactions with both Pakistanis and Bangladeshis have taught me to celebrate the similarities and respect the differences between us.

But this is not the case with everyone. It was during one such conversation with a second-generation interviewee in Lahore that I learnt how, because of this ingrained othering, the information passed on about Indians to Pakistanis and vice versa was often more conjecture than actual fact. It created mythical beings out of people across the border, people who were once one.

> Fateeha Saleem narrated a comical incident about the very first meeting with her family, who, during Partition, had remained across the border. 'I had never seen my aunt, my phupho, before, but only heard about her. The first time we went to visit India, I was ten years old and didn't know what to expect ... The only Indian thing I had seen till then was the currency, the banknotes, and on every single one was drawn the Ashoka pillar, with its four lions standing back-to-back. Four heads. So, when we met for the first time, I looked at my phupho's face and then looked to her side and back, and in a very confused tone asked, '*Par aapke baaki sar kahan pe hai,* where are the rest of your heads?' I had never seen an Indian before; how could I have known any better? Nobody in our family had told us that we were the same people; nobody had talked about what life used to be like before we separated.[6]

This small incident encapsulates the tragedy of the Partition legacy so succinctly – that if just the second generation after the division knew so little about those who lived across the border, then generations after them would know even less. Of course, with the advent of social media, people are now able to virtually 'see' life on the other side and even make friends. But, for common Indians and Pakistanis, the only physical space where meeting is possible is a third land – away from both countries, devoid of the burden of the border, free from visa restrictions – where popular media does not inevitably morph and distort the other into an enemy.

Years after I record that story in Lahore, another small incident crystallizes this realization. On 1 June 2020, Asif Farrukhi, the Pakistani writer, teacher, Urdu scholar and co-founder of the Karachi Literature Festival, passes away after a prolonged illness. Asif sahib, who had received the high honour of Tamgha-e-Imtiaz in Pakistan, was the first person to invite me to a literature festival across the border and welcome me into his classroom at Habib University, Karachi, where I presented my work to his students. He refused to let anything encumber the deep friendships he maintained with many Indians, and his passing is a profound loss for Pakistan's literary and cultural landscape. When I tweet about this, of the many responses that I get, there is one from a fellow Indian, asking why I am praising a 'Pakistani' when 'Pakistan is our enemy', which upsets me deeply.

Writing about this incident now, I recall an anecdote from Anam's debut book, *Footprints of Partition*, where she notes how autorickshaws in Lahore would sometimes carry signs that read, '*Bharat se rishta kya? Nafrat ka, intikam ka.*' What is our relationship with India? One of hatred and revenge.[7]

For many Indians and Pakistanis, loving their nation means hating the other, as if they are antonyms of one another. But, in fact, they are twins, mirror images, born from a bloody cleave in one land. When I read anything hinged on this kind of hate, I need to remind myself that the border between our two countries is *man-made*, and hence, the natural landscape is undivided. However, to accept this requires deep and continual personal effort to unlearn any unreasonable, accumulated hate. And so, for the most part, the legacy of Partition remains defined by otherness. Even in the way that we address our neighbour – *the other side* – indicates someone who is different from us, thereby laying the boundaries of our identity as well as theirs.

In a piece that Anam wrote for the seventieth anniversary of Partition, she states:

> Pakistan and India define themselves in opposition to each other, both nations determined to justify that they are better than the other ... 70 years later, [both] are holding on to Partition like an existential imperative; it helps them define national identity, lead antagonistic state policies, and instil patriotism in citizens – patriotism based on the hostility of the other.[8]

As Anam's piece concludes, such ways of perceiving a shared past 'serve as the raison d'être of both nations', giving rise to all forms of casual othering. If the anonymous tweet is evidence of anything, it is that the communalism which transpired during Partition has sadly trickled down the generations – not limited to Partition-displaced families alone – into society today. The question is what can be done about it, and how can we retain our differences and yet engage with civility and kindness with our neighbours?

Keeping this in mind, I read the tweet several times and think about what to reply, if at all. I can refuse to engage in such discourse, rebuke the person who posted the comment, or even report it as a violation. But all I write back is this: '*Nothing good has ever come from hating someone you don't know or understand either. This is the kind of hate that is rooted and propagated through generations. Please try to rise above it.*'

∽

AT THE 2018 History for Peace conference in Kolkata, Naveen Kishore, the managing trustee and publisher of Seagull Books, begins his opening address with the following words:

People are born into their versions of truth. They live them, every day, in the confinement of their solitude. Simple, even troubled truth. Some do it with a degree of magnanimity about other truths, existing, breathing, living what we call our lives, not in a singular manner, plural, regardless of our unpalatable lives. These breaths, these existences maybe ... others are distressed, agitated, angered by the presence of parallel truths in their lives and in the lives of others. Other, always the other, hinting, condoning, pointing at exclusion. There is the truth of us. Therefore, there is the lie of the other. Because this will not match their own frames or ours for that matter, you must arrive, arrive, I say, at an understanding of what works best for you, and ... learn to live with difference.[9]

Having passionately inscribed these words into my notebook, I often return to this phrase – *There is the truth of us. Therefore, there is the lie of the other* – considering it not only in the context of Partition but applying it to our relationships with the world in general. Through this book, I become interested in not just the creation of the other but also the boundary of the other. How we live amongst or in exclusion from those we may consider the other. Stories that explore how otherness is not limited only to those with whom we share a hostile, divided history – that is, our neighbours – but also to those whom we deem different within our own land. A difference that may have arisen at the time of, or even before, Partition, and how it is passed down the generations, fostered and added to over the years. Equally, I become interested in whether any generation of a family interrupts this endowment.

'PARTITION AFFECTED BOTH sides of my family,' Ayushi says. She is a criminal lawyer, born in the mid-1990s in Delhi. It is afternoon, and she narrates how several members of her family perished after Partition, either by their own hands or in the communal violence that ensued, and how these memories have been bitterly passed down to her.

'A distant aunt once told me about her father's family, which was living in Lyallpur (now Faisalabad) at the time. During Partition, his family was preparing to migrate to India but, out of fear, his sister ended up burning herself and her children, who were barely one or two years old, in a large fire. I suppose she thought that it was better to kill yourself than let someone from the other community besmirch your honour.'

I have heard stories like this several times in the course of my research, but this does not make listening to them any easier. Ayushi tells me that at her work she often hears cases of this nature, and so it may not affect her as much as others, but it does not take away from the heinousness of the act.

'My aunt's father managed to save his sister's sons, but she perished then and there. Her grandfather also died during Partition at the hands of a mob.'

I am quiet for a few seconds, almost taken aback by the calmness with which these stories of violence are narrated. 'What are your feelings about Partition, then? Does it affect you at all?'

'Of course, it does, because in my home, this dislike for the other side stems from Partition. They still blame them for all that was lost, for how suddenly they had to leave, for beginning the violence, which led to the deaths of so many family members. And this mentality has been passed down to their children, and further to *their* children. It's become like an heirloom, where they hate a community without even thinking about it twice.'

Hate as an heirloom, I write down the words.

'And do you feel the same way?' I am struck by the directness of my own questioning, but when I look at her, she is at ease, unaffected.

'No, not at all,' she answers without missing a beat. 'When I ask them why they judge a person based on their religion, they hark back to the stories of Partition. But it was the circumstance of those days, *uss samay ke halaat hi aise the*, that led people on both sides to commit acts of madness. I tell them that even if nine out of ten people are bad, I will still not judge the entire religion based on them.'

Hope grows in my heart as she states matter-of-factly, 'The anger of seventy-five years ago cannot determine our relationships in the present or the future. When I asked my father why he hated Pakistanis even though he'd never met one, he cited the lost standard of living after Partition. His grandfather was the diwan of Akalgarh, and everyone knew him in Lahore. *Woh bohot naami the*, and all that wealth and stature was lost when they came to India. When I ask my mother why she feels bitterness even though she has not lived through Partition, she always narrates the incidents she's heard from her mother's youth about the horrible violence they witnessed, just barely escaping with their lives. These are the stories they've been told, and if a child repeatedly hears them from a young age, he too will grow up knowing only this to be the truth. But you cannot live your life according to what has happened to other people in the past. In my opinion, *this* is also how hate gets propagated through generations, without context or understanding of certain events.

During Partition, if Hindus and Sikhs lost their lives on that side, did Muslims not lose their lives here?'

I nod gravely and she concludes, 'I cannot deal with a superiority that's based on religion. I don't subscribe to the rhetoric of hate and I will not pass it down.' She pauses and looks at me. 'When I told my mother that I want to change this mentality, she said to me, "What can a single person do? *Hum akele kya kar sakte hain*?" But I still think ignorance is worse than anything else. It can be bliss for some people, but for others it can be their annihilation.'

Listening to Ayushi is inspiring, and reaffirms that a single person *can* make a difference, for history has often shown us how even the largest of movements have begun with the efforts of just one person.

SEVERAL WEEKS AFTER this conversation, I speak with AJ,[*] whose family has not lived through Partition but has inherited the othering that grew as a consequence of the event. Her parents are from Rajasthan and she has grown up in south India, far away from the frontiers affected by the division of 1947. And yet she begins our conversation with, 'My father has a deep-seated dislike of Muslims. And each time I try to reason with him, try to have this conversation, it almost always ends with one of us crying.'

'Why?' I ask, perplexed.

'Because that is how we express anger,' she admits.

In *Grief Lessons: Four Plays by Euripides*, Anne Carson's Preface titled 'Tragedy: A Curious Art Form', begins with the lines, 'Why does tragedy exist? Because you are full of rage. Why are you full of rage? Because you are full of grief.'

It is this grief that AJ attempts to trace through her father's life. The youngest of five siblings, he was born in the late 1960s in a village in Rajasthan, to a father who seemed more interested in helping the village folk than paying attention to his youngest child. As a result, the boy grew up craving love, which he found in education. He became the only member of his family to study; he was a rank

---

[*] Initials have been used to maintain anonymity on the individual's request.

holder in school and eventually caught the attention of the local RSS leader in the village. For the first time, the young boy felt recognized and appreciated for his talents.

'He was probably only in Grade 5 but was dedicated to the organization. It became his only extracurricular activity. I think...' She takes a breath and continues, 'Because he was the youngest sibling – one of his brothers was nine years older and the other twelve years older, and his sisters needed to take care of housework – he felt quite isolated. They treated him like he didn't exist. So, when he found his place in the RSS, it felt like he mattered. He would tell us about this time constantly when we were children.'

Her face then breaks into a small smile. 'When I was a child, I joined the Scouts and Guides. Even though it's a different sort of organization from the RSS, my father saw a lot of him in me ... But I don't agree with his opinions about Muslims or any other "other".'

I say nothing, so she continues.

'In the city where I live, there are designated areas for different people. Jains live here, Tamils live here, Muslims live here, and so on. As children, we gave shape to God and, in the same way, I felt like I was meant to give shape to the other ... But who is the other? This is the question. Is it someone we don't know, someone who is different from us, someone whose community we may have been told to steer clear of? Then one day, when we meet a person from that community and they change our opinions, we begin to question why they are considered the other: "All Muslims are bad, but you, my friend, are good. Similarly, all Hindus are bad, but because I know you, so you are different." No, because we cannot assign single attributes to entire communities – good or bad...' She pauses, interrupting her train of thought, and then, suddenly flustered, says, 'We are supposed to be talking about Partition, and I'm going off on all kinds of unrelated tangents...'

'But it's all eventually related,' I assure her.

'It is, it is. Partition – how I am connected to an event that neither I nor my family witnessed.' She becomes self-aware, as if she has thought about this topic several times. 'I'm going to say it the way I understand it. Partition speaks to pain and homelessness, a sense of unbelonging. I think the reason I was so drawn to it was how relatable it feels. I am not trying to negate what millions went through, nor am I belittling the enormity of their experiences by comparing them to mine. But when I say it is relatable, what I mean is the experience of not belonging, of feeling uprooted – which at that time meant either fleeing from the land you called home or becoming a minority in that land. Either way, it carried a definitive uncertainty. When I think of Partition, I think of the imposition of someone else's will upon you – where the boundary of who you are, where you can live, who you can live amongst is defined by someone else.

'I was born and raised in south India, but I relate neither to this culture nor the Rajasthani culture of my parents. Am I north Indian or south Indian? Even within my family, I am discriminated against for how educated I am. Ironically, the only place where I felt like I belonged was the one place I was told I never would – when I fell in love with a Muslim man eight years ago.

'No one knows about it, and for the longest time even I doubted whether it would last because the differences between the communities had been instilled into me right from childhood. I know my family did not live through Partition, but Partition augmented these differences, it underscored them. And sometimes I wonder if I'm being silly relating my life to the consequences of Partition, but I feel that pain. I feel the division I have been raised with.'

AJ takes a deep, steadying breath, visibly emotional, part angry, part helpless.

'My father loves me and supports me, but we are ideologically so different, and I keep returning to his childhood. Had he been more accepted at home, had he not been part of the RSS, he would have definitely been a different person. But I think his affiliation with the organization was also about ... well, he continues to agree with it on a subconscious level, because if he doesn't, he thinks it will be a betrayal of what once gave him strength...' She clears her throat before continuing, 'It is extremely difficult to love people who are opposed to each other. I love my family, but I love what they hate too.

'While there remains the narrative of how the creation of Pakistan was inevitable and Muslims are a separate culture and so they have to live separately, this entire narrative gets debunked with every story about being affected by Partition. It's not so black and white, it cannot be. And if it was meant to be, there wouldn't be so much continuing trauma from the event. That Partition brought about such a huge loss is in itself telling of the fact that something that was naturally whole was dismembered and forcibly broken. Its legacy continues to eat into the chances of millions like me in both countries who just want to know each other and meet a part of themselves on the other side.'

I watch her in silence for a few seconds and then shut my notebook. I feel guilty that every conversation I have with someone about Partition eventually leads to a place of deep vulnerability. The present appears a complex, tangled remnant of the past. But a part of me is also astonished to discover how the invisible tremors of 1947 are felt decades later across the expanse of the subcontinent, even by those who are completely removed from the actual event or its direct consequences. I tell AJ that we can continue our conversation another day, but she shakes her head.

'I used to be very insular and religious, you know,' she admits with a soft chuckle, 'but it all faded away when I met people outside of my community, not just Muslims but others too. Life opened up, and I began to gain confidence to ask about things I didn't know, religions or customs I didn't know about, and it dispelled the many myths that I'd been raised with. My partner can recite Hindu *shlokas* from memory that his mother taught him. I was shocked to learn that he knew more about my religion than I did. But the knowledge of Hinduism or Jainism didn't take away from his own identity or dilute his beliefs in any way.' She looks up at me now and says with finality, 'My experiences so far have only shown me how humans rarely belong to a singular space or group.'

⌒

IT IS IN January 2018, after spending the morning exploring the old and abandoned mansions of Hindustan Park in Kolkata, that the writer Karuna Ezara Parikh first tells me a story. It is about an Indian Hindu woman and a Pakistani Muslim man who meet in Wales, far away from the fortified border dividing their two countries. A dancer and a lawyer who find unexpected common ground. *Daya and Aaftab in no man's land.* Right from that first nervous narration, I am enchanted by the story. Two years later, it is published as *The Heart Asks Pleasure First.* And though from the outside it may not seem like a conventional book about Partition, it carries so much of its burden. How we can be shaped by a single moment in history even if we have not lived it, how it can impact our understanding and creation of the other, and, consequently, how that perception can be completely shattered by a chance meeting. In many ways, it becomes a testament to a possible world, for with tenderness it stitches together a subcontinent divided.

When Karuna and I speak a few months after the book is released, she tells me that though no one from her family was physically displaced during Partition, she remembers being very young when she first asked them about it.

'My father's family are from Amreli in Gujarat, and I would ask my grandparents again and again – *What was it like? Gandhi was Gujarati, tell me more about that time* – and there was just deep reluctance to talk about it. But a really strong memory from my childhood is from a family wedding in Amreli when my aunt took the hands of a granduncle and showed them to me. They had these big, deep scar tissues across them, the kind I'd never seen before. I remember her telling me that I could touch them, and when I did, she asked, "Do you know why he has them? The British nailed him to a tree when he was caught planning to set fire to a local British school in protest!"'

As I hear this, I bring my hands up to my mouth in horror.

'Yes, exactly.' She nods. 'On his palms were these huge, shiny marks where the wounds had healed. I was stunned, I couldn't have been older than thirteen, and I remember asking him whether it hurt.

And he, like every jolly old man in India, laughed it off and told me that it hurt very badly, but that he was there now and he was fine. But I just recall this being a very strong memory connecting my family to that time – to the Independence struggle, to Partition. Apart from that, though, they didn't speak about it.'

'How did the event of Partition then make its way into the novel?' I only ask because books relating to Partition more often than not begin as personal endeavours.

'I had many Pakistani friends while in university at Cardiff, and I suppose what I felt was a first-hand experience of the heritage of Partition – or the heritage of hate, let's say, that it carries. They were a group of Pakistani boys who, well, the spectrum was interesting – because on one hand what they were saying was that they couldn't be seen out on the streets of Cardiff with an Indian girl, that their entire community would have a problem with it. It wasn't such a problem for me because I didn't have much of a community there yet. But the irony was that even though they were saying this, their actions spoke of anything but. They were not about hatred or holding on to past trauma, they were almost healing. They would cook for me almost every day, they checked in on me when I fell sick, they took me to the hospital. I stayed in their home when I was unwell. Everything they did was so full of love that I couldn't understand the dichotomy of that relationship.'

I smile as her book comes to life in my mind.

'You know,' she says as she mirrors my smile, 'one of the boys whose character eventually became Wasim in my novel – he didn't speak English and I didn't speak Punjabi, and at the time my Hindi was also terrible. So, I learnt to speak my own language from him. In those years, when I would come home to Delhi on holidays, my friends would ask me why I'm speaking this Urdu-*wali* Hindi, because my speech was peppered with the words my Pakistani friends would use.'

There is a warmth to Karuna's voice, one that can only be born from deep affection or deep absence. 'When I think about it now, it's actually quite beautiful how my relationship with the character who became Wasim progressed, because he genuinely learnt how to speak English more comfortably through me and I learnt to speak my language comfortably through him. It was a wonderful exchange, but the sad thing is that I never saw that group of friends again. We were so close for so many years, and then after university we just lost touch. The years in Cardiff were our liminal spaces, our no man's land, where we had banished the border and we could care for one another in the ways that people would have before Partition. The end of university was, in some ways, the end of my friendships from an undivided land.'

She sighs, 'And for me, this is the tragedy of Partition – that even deep friendships can't really go anywhere, and this imaginary line becomes a real line very fast. I wanted to explore this in the novel, with Daya who comes from India and Aaftab from Pakistan, and the love and pain that appear in their world because of a line.'

As she says this, I recall a section in her novel embodying this thought perfectly. Deftly, she quotes it, 'It was in the lighthouse that Daya had said, "Every time we make love, we're straying across a border." And [Aaftab] had replied, "No, Daya. We're rejoining lands."'[10]

'Of course, I know there's no rejoining of lands now, but...' Her voice trails off. 'You know, one of the other interesting things that one of the boys said to me in Cardiff was that if Pakistan ended tomorrow, there would only be four generations of Pakistanis. He said it casually, but I'd never thought of it like that. And certainly never in the context of Partition. How young a nation it really is, you know, and how fleeting a concept that can be. And then you weigh it against the amount of hatred we, as Indians, have gathered towards it, it just doesn't make sense. So much hatred for a land and a people who were once ours. And it makes me even sadder that in the last ten years of this story being in my head, it remains just as relevant and controversial a topic in our political and historical rhetoric.'

'An Indian and a Pakistani falling in love, you mean?' I ask.

'Yes, that. And then how easily the phrase "go to Pakistan" is used, not just for Indian Muslims but anyone who shows empathy towards Islam or Pakistan. The sheer idea that if you empathize with someone who is considered the other, then you are the enemy.'

My conversations with Noorani sahib and Anam echo in my head, ever clear.

'I think a lot about the ownership of land,' Karuna continues pensively. 'Nobody owns a country, and I think when we begin to dictate who has "rightful" ownership over land, the fine line between patriotism and nationalism is blurred.'

'Often leading to jingoism,' I add.

'Exactly. That's why I always say that a border isn't a noose around a country because this idea is so suffocating and can be so diminishing. My mother is half-Bengali, half-German. My maternal grandmother was a Christian in Germany and she lived through the Second World War; her brothers fought for the German army. She lost them all before they were even twenty; I think one was as young as fourteen. This is another part of my history that I have had to reckon with – that we were on the wrong side of the war. And I have seen this side of my family really, *really* deal with their guilt and their shame. There were immense losses here too – brothers, parents – and my grandmother was raised by her sister. This is the other side of war, that even though she was German and she was Christian, she was still a victim of the war. But I have seen her put aside her self-pity to wholeheartedly accept the fact that her country did so much wrong. I have seen her family and friends reflect on the Holocaust and there is so much shame and apology in their hearts. There is so much reckoning.' She takes a deep breath and a long swig of water. 'But not here in the subcontinent, not with Partition.'

'What do you think the reconciliation between India and Pakistan can look like?' I ask. 'It hasn't happened yet. In fact, the countries that were affected by Partition don't even have a shared understanding or a singular version of the event, because it meant different things to each of those countries. We don't have even a single monument...'

'I can only speak for India, but I don't see us doing that with Partition yet. Neither reflecting nor regretting. So, are we to never heal the wounds from that time? We should take ownership of the legacies of hate that we have spread during Partition and also since – whether it's 1984 or 1992 or 2002 or even the recent riots in Delhi in 2020. These are all echoes of Partition; they don't happen in isolation. And so we must start from within, by looking at ourselves.'

Her suggestions, like mine, are humane ones. 'People may reconcile once they listen to each other's stories. And not just stories of the bloodshed or the trains or piles of corpses, but stories of humanity and friendship and sacrifice. We need to start telling different stories. The ordinary person needs to know that on the other side similar losses were felt, similar heartbreaks were experienced, similar burdens were carried, similar pains were endured, a similar and equally heavy legacy exists. I think until we listen to each other's stories and quieten the noise of *you are at fault*, we won't begin to heal these wounds. We won't unmake the other.'

'But what about people who say Partition is so far back in the past that it cannot affect the present?'

'To them I say: I wish. I truly wish we could say that Partition no longer affects us. I live in the hope of a world where one day Partition truly cannot be felt any longer. But I refuse to believe we are in that place already. I also feel that those who say Partition doesn't affect us are similar to the people who say that caste doesn't exist, and that perspective comes from a place of immense privilege.' She pauses for several seconds and then continues with her thought, 'I don't think you will find a Muslim person in India who at some point has not felt the legacy of Partition. Even in a fleeting way. Similarly, you won't find a Hindu person in Pakistan who hasn't felt it. And I certainly don't think that anyone who has tried to empathize with the other in any way has gone unscathed from the retaliation and force of hatred that follows. You know better than anyone what I mean.'

I nod slowly. 'The other thing I often find difficult to grapple with is how people that were once from the same soil can have so much hatred towards one another. And it's usually not the generation that has witnessed Partition, because they have seen an undivided India. But the subsequent generations, those who have not witnessed

Partition, have somehow largely inherited a legacy of hate rather than empathy. I wonder why that is and how it's disseminated.'

'It's interesting, right?'

'Yes, but I can't explain it. How can you hate someone you've never met? Moreover, how can you hate someone who may have experienced the exact same thing?'

'Here is the thing I find very ironic – you won't find anyone from either of these countries saying, "I hate the British." Hardly ever. And I think to myself, 200 years of oppression, slavery, dividing the country, slicing it up, departing and leaving it in bloodshed and bankruptcy, but we're all dying to go to Covent Garden.' She laughs an exasperated laugh. 'I find this legacy of hate so ironic.'

I smile, but really my heart is breaking because everything she is saying is the truth. 'We believe in the reasons of difference. They are convenient to accept because they portray Partition as a clean cut, a definitive division of land and its people. But the reality is far more complex and quite amalgamated.'

'Yes, which is why I think it's important to tell people's stories, human stories. And this is why I returned to my university days in the novel, because saying you hate Pakistan cannot be the same as saying you hate Pakistanis when you may not even have met one.'

We are both quiet for several minutes, looking at each other. I am thinking about the first time I read Daya and Aaftab's story. I am thinking about the passage where Daya is visiting home for the holidays and is at her friend Milni's house, and General Musharraf appears on the TV screen, a Pakistani flag behind him. Milni's nephew suddenly makes a gun-like hand gesture, a finger gun, and pointing at the TV says, '*Dhishoom*!' before turning around to face Daya, rather pleased, blowing the imaginary smoke off the tip of his finger. When she asks the child why he did that, he promptly replies it is because he hates Pakistan. In that moment, Daya wonders what it means to hate a country. 'Do you hate the word? Do you hate the land?' she thinks this to herself but says nothing. Later, when she tells Milni about the Pakistani boy she has fallen in love with, Milni reminds her of the unspoken rules: that Daya cannot love a Pakistani, and yet Daya thinks, 'But I do.'[11]

'There is one last story I want to tell you,' Karuna's voice cuts into the silence. 'So, my paternal grandfather, Amritlal Vithaldas Parikh, grew up in this town called Amreli in Gujarat, and his neighbour was a man called Akber Ali. Before Partition, the families were very close and my family would always invite them over for Diwali and they would invite us for Eid. They were best friends – my grandfather and Akber Ali bhai, as my father still calls him. But at Partition, his family left for West Pakistan and my grandfather didn't really hear from him after that. Years passed and in 1971, Akber Ali, who was by then doing business in East Pakistan, now Bangladesh – and this is another wound we don't speak about, the second Partition – drove from Dhaka to Calcutta to meet Amritlal, or Ammu bhai. He came in a Toyota, which was very exciting for the family, and he actually gave the car to my grandfather as a gift! My father tells me they sadly had to send it back to Bangladesh soon after, as India didn't allow car imports at the time. Then, years after that, the internet gains popularity, the world becomes more technologically friendly, and so people can reconnect, and my father and Akber Ali's son, Abbas Ali, get in touch.

'Anyway, all these years pass and my father is now living in Delhi in Mandi village, and I'm somewhere between seventeen and twenty years old. Our neighbour is a gentleman named Mr D.G. Singh, who has lived through Partition. Mr Singh is on his way to Pakistan for a business trip, and when he lands in Karachi, he is told by the authorities that he can't enter the country until someone, a Pakistani, vouches for him. He doesn't have a letter of recommendation – I think that's what it's called – and as he's standing in line looking lost, the airport authorities tell him that he will need to get on the next return flight if he cannot find someone to vouch for him.

'So, in line next to him there's a gentleman who overhears the conversation and asks what the problem is. When he hears the explanation, he says that his family came from India during Partition and he will vouch for Mr Singh. So, it all works out and the pair leave the airport together, and as they are parting, the gentleman gives our neighbour his card, and –'

'Please, tell me it is…' I say, my heart racing.

Karuna laughs. 'He tells him to get in touch if he needs anything while in Karachi. So, Mr Singh takes the card and reads the company name. Amreli Steels. He asks why it's called that, and the gentleman says, "My family comes from a small town in India called Amreli." And Mr Singh tells him that he too knows a man from Amreli.'

'I have goosebumps,' I whisper.

'So did I when I first heard the story, and every time since! This gentleman was Abbas Ali, the son of Akber Ali bhai. Can you imagine?'

'I really cannot. What are the odds – and thank god his company was called Amreli Steels!' I laugh.

'Yes! So, in a way, two sets of my family's neighbours from neighbouring countries united. But I truly believe that there is a force greater than us, yearning for these stories to be told – stories of love and friendship to come out. This here is a story of one good turn after another after another after another. For me, it is about love being repaid over generations, almost serendipitously. And these are the stories of Partition that we don't hear – the story of rejoining of hands, of healing, of undoing the image of the other,' she beams.

24

The Quotidian

⁊

PARTITION IS OFTEN DESCRIBED as a wound, but there have been times I've considered it more like a scar, indelible, ever present. While working on *Remnants*, I became interested in the ways in which Partition and its consequences entered people's everyday lives. How they carried it, not only through their conversations with me – which, of course, were centred around the subject – but also in their habits, practices and behaviour patterns that could be attributed to the trauma of witnessing a violent division, displacement and forced migration, and eventual rehabilitation. It is but natural to deduce that any event of such magnitude would leave a physiological imprint upon the body and its daily routine, resulting in specific traits being adopted, inherited and propagated – either out of sheer desperation, mere circumstance or as defence mechanisms.

Several stories throughout this book underline the ways in which the lives of people changed after Partition. Several more contribute to the specific changes in attitude and conduct that can be considered a result of it. Though this is by no means a comprehensive study, the four distinct sections of this chapter attempt to highlight some of the ways in which Partition has continued to seep into the quotidian life, as told through the perspective of second- and third-generation participants.

⁊

THE STORY OF a blood-soaked ledger carried to India on 14 August 1947 begins a conversation with Kanpur-born Harshit Kohli about the annual traditions practised by his grandfather Ved Kohli and his brothers since Partition.

In July 1947, the Kohli family migrated from Wazirabad (now in the Gujranwala district of Pakistan) to Jammu because of the riots, but Ved's father, Tara Chand Kohli, did not believe that Partition would take place, so the family returned to Wazirabad. Barely a month later, on 14 August, they were forced to leave again, and their train was attacked within minutes of leaving the station. Tara Chand Kohli and his wife, Dayawati, got off to pacify the rioters; she was stabbed and he was carried away. Suddenly orphaned, the Kohli siblings remained on the train and somehow reached India, where they found refuge at their cousin's house in Jammu. In total, they were five siblings: one sister, Kanta, and four brothers, among them Benarasi Lal, who was married and had a six-month-old daughter (his wife, Shakuntala, had hidden in the bathroom with her sister-in-law); a middle brother, Sikander Lal, who carried the ledger; eleven-year-old Ved, who hid under the seats of the train and still bears a scar on his forehead from a knife cut he received during the attack; and the youngest brother, Harjinder, only four years old, who passed away two years after Partition.

'My grandfather still has regrets that he wasn't able to perform the last rites of his parents,' Harshit tells me when we meet one spring evening at a café in Delhi.

'Does he ever talk about it?'

'Every 14 August,' he replies without missing a single beat. 'For about fifty years after Partition, the brothers would get together and lament the incident. It was a tradition, almost.'

'And when did you first realize the importance of this date?'

'Quite early on, actually, when the film *Gadar*[1] was released. It showed the riots and train journeys during Partition, and my grandfather would tell me that it was exactly how they had migrated to India. I knew since the age of six or seven that we were not originally from Kanpur, where we now lived – that we were from

Punjab – but it was only after watching this film that the details emerged. My grandfather started documenting his life story around this time, and that is how we children came to know about it. I felt as if the story was out of a film. My first, rather naïve, reaction as a child was that when all this wrong was happening, where was God? Why did God not help the family?' Harshit chuckles.

'Had you seen the bloodied ledger as a child?'

'I have a vague recollection of it. The family was in the agriculture business, so the ledger had records of their debtors and creditors. It was placed in the only bag they had carried, in the hands of the second brother, Sikander Lal. But it does haunt me even today, for it is the only physical remnant left from Wazirabad.' He pauses to think. 'After Partition it was in the possession of my grandfather's eldest brother, Benarasi Lal, but I don't exactly know where it is, now that he has passed. I remember that the blood on the ledger that was once bright red had faded to dull brown spots ... it was from the injuries the family had suffered along the way. They were all injured, and their blood had seeped into the pages. When they reached Sialkot, many RSS workers came to their aid and helped lift the dead bodies out of their train compartment. My family survived mostly because they were able to hide, but I'm told that most of the train succumbed to the attack.'

I draw in a sharp breath. But there is more.

'During the journey the family was in an area where they feared they'd be attacked, and there was a woman, a distant relative, who was about to deliver a baby. She somehow gave birth without shrieking, but they couldn't let the child live,' he exhales, 'because if the child began to scream or cry, the rioters would hear them and they all would be attacked. So they buried the child. Born yet unborn.'

I cover my mouth as I gasp. I want to ask what happened to the mother, how she may have parted with the child she had carried for months inside her. But I haven't the heart, nor the words. Despite the noisy café, the silence on our table feels thick and palpable. Harshit looks at me, helpless.

'He wrote letters,' he finally says. 'Every Independence Day, my grandfather wrote me a letter.'

'What about?' I ask in a small voice.

'Well, as I told you, the brothers would get together on 14 August each year and lament their journey during Partition. It was a recognized day of mourning in our home. They talked about their parents, but sometimes also about how they thought leaders like Nehru or Gandhi were responsible for Partition, how the world would have been better had Partition never happened – a historical wrong which ought to have been righted. Having heard of other Partition-affected families that travelled safely from West Punjab to East Punjab thanks to timely advice and action, we reflected on the significance of the transparent flow of information during times of human crises. Nowhere else in the world had so many people migrated without any sense of security about what lay at the end of their journey on the other side.

I was about eight years old, at boarding school in Sherwood, when I got my first letter. My grandfather wrote elegantly, often using idioms and phrases I did not know then, some in Punjabi. One of his favourites was: *Jo sukh chajju ke chaubare, O na Balkh na Bukhare*, the joy of one's home cannot be found anywhere else, be it Balkh or Bukhara. Among other things, he would write about the sacrifices his generation had to make and emphasized how lucky I was to be born in a free country.'

'Did you understand the significance of these annual letters back then?' I ask.

He shakes his head. 'He would often end his letters with jokes, and because I went to Sherwood, he would play around with the words, calling me a "Wooden Sher" or a "Sher of the Woods". But over the years, I look back at these letters to find strength. It was brave of my grandfather to keep his family together and strong, and not pass on the hatred and pain that traumatized him to his children and grandchildren. But I also think he didn't want us to forget the source of his pain. He'd often quote Burke – "Those who don't know history are destined to repeat it" – and felt obligated to tell his story in that sense. I feel horribly about Partition. My grandfather taught me the value of love, but it was love that left the Indian subcontinent in 1947.'

One year after Harshit and I first meet, as I am almost done writing this book, he informs me that his grandfather, his hero, has passed away. Attaching a photograph of a handwritten page from his family tree, Harshit writes:

> His ancestors followed the tradition of visiting Haridwar and Rishikesh even when they were in Wazirabad. My grandfather was committed to continuing that tradition. Our family's genealogical records are maintained in *bahi-khatas*, the books kept by the pundits of Haridwar. After his demise, as per custom, I too visited Haridwar to record his death. There, in those very books, I found the handwritten notes of my grandfather's father, Tara Chand Kohli, dated to 1933. I wished that my grandfather had seen that page, perhaps the only thing of his father that he'd ever have, something he would have clutched closely to his chest.

THE EATING HABITS of Delhi, the city where I grew up, certainly transformed after the influx of refugees from West Punjab. 'Cuisine was a minor but still a significant casualty,' Anoothi Vishal, the author of *Mrs LC's Table*, writes. 'Tandoori became the food of Delhi', and the bold, tomato-laden flavours of West Punjab replaced the Mughlai cuisine born out of the composite culture of the walled city of Shahjahanabad.[2] In her autobiography, *Climbing the Mango Trees*, along with mentions of the now commonly sighted Punjabi tandoor, Madhur Jaffrey mentions how 'most grocers now carried big wheels of paneer', which is recorded to have been used as far back as at the time of Shah Jahan's Mughal kitchen[3] but became a prominent and popular part of Delhi's culinary landscape after Partition.

On a seemingly unrelated note, during my childhood, Tuesday meant a strictly vegetarian diet, for it was the day of the week dedicated to Lord Hanuman. This inflexible rule is now far more relaxed in our home, but I was surprised to learn that in the years following Partition, the new state of Pakistan *also* observed a vegetarian Tuesday, though for reasons quite different. Two days a week were 'meatless days' – inspiring the title of Sara Suleri's poignant memoir – where the newly forged country strove to conserve the national supply of goats and cattle. In the title essay, Suleri, born in Karachi in the decade following Partition, writes:

> Every Tuesday and Wednesday the butchers' shops would stay firmly closed, without a single carcass dangling from the huge metal hooks that lined the canopies ... [but] the people who could afford to buy meat, after all, were those who could afford refrigeration, so the only thing the government accomplished was to make some people's Mondays very busy indeed.[4]

She goes on to describe how this practice of abstention across the country did not result in the adoption of vegetarianism, but rather the 'acquisition of all things fleshy' for reserve, enough to last a household for the next three days. However, vegetarianism as a result of Partition does come up in a conversation with the 1992-born Vernika Awal, a food writer based in Noida. Her family migrated a few months before Partition was announced, travelling from the larger Rawalpindi area, specifically Campbellpur (now Attock), to Adampur, in Jalandhar district, via Amritsar.

'Back in Pakistan, my great-grandfather owned indigo plantations, and its trade often took him across the oceans to Africa. When the news of Partition broke, he was there and was never able to make it back home. He passed away because of a cardiac arrest. My father tells me that his grandmother used to say, "*Taar aayi thi, ke ab woh nahi hai,*" she received a telegram telling her that her husband had passed. And this was just before their migration, so you can only imagine how she felt – hardly being able to grieve for her husband and having to cross into a new land as a single mother of four children.'

'And they are from Campbellpur,' I confirm.

'Yes, which has been conveniently turned into "Camelpur" over the years,' Vernika chuckles. 'My family are part of a community called the Campbellpur *biradri*, settled all along the Doaba region of Punjab, between Jalandhar and Hoshiarpur. Initially, my great-grandmother was offered land in Sirhind, but refused it in order to stay with the rest of the family in Adampur.'

When I ask her whether that is where she grew up as well, she says, 'My father had a transferable job, so I was brought up across India, but we always returned to Adampur to see cousins and grandparents. I'd say, about 80 per cent of the area is populated by the Campbellpur *biradri*, and so it was a very frequently heard term in my childhood. There was always the sense of being from someplace else, a place that the entire clan had migrated from together. My great-grandmother would tell my father stories about Pakistan – the fact that they had seven wells, *kuan*, which she called *ku* in Punjabi' – Vernika extends the *u* into a nasal sound – 'and how the wealth of the family was calculated based on the number of wells they had: basically, how much land one well could irrigate. And the fact that they were trading between India and Africa also meant that it was a family with means.

'But Partition changed all that, and perhaps the greatest impact was on their eating habits. Even small things like dried fruit that were earlier taken for granted were now a luxury. The entire clan became vegetarian once they migrated to India, simply because they could no longer afford meat. Every single generation since then has been vegetarian, including myself.'

'That's fascinating,' I say, making a note. 'What else changed in their daily life?'

'Language,' she states immediately. 'Before Partition, the family was settled throughout the Majha area, where the dialect of spoken

Punjabi was very different than the Doaba region, from where they had migrated.'

Punjab is divided into three regions based on the flow of its rivers: Malwa, south of the river Sutlej, makes up the majority of the area and covers Punjab as well as parts of Haryana, spreading across the districts of Barnala, Bathinda, Faridkot, Firozpur, Ludhiana, Mansa, Moga, Muktsar, Patiala, Sangrur and parts of Fatehgarh Sahib. The people of this region are known as Malwais and speak the Malwai dialect of Punjabi. During the Mughal era, Malwa was known as Sirhind and was the capital of Mughal administration in eastern Punjab.

Majha, where Vernika's family originally comes from, marks the historical split between East and West Punjab – and India and Pakistan – lying between the rivers Ravi and Beas, and meaning 'central' or the 'heartland'. It spans the districts of Lahore, Sheikhupura, Kasur, Narowal, Okara, Nankana Sahib, Gujrat, Wazirabad, Sialkot, Gujranwala, Tarn Taran, Amritsar, Batala, Dera Baba Nanak, Qadian, Pathankot and Gurdaspur. The prestigious Majhi dialect is spoken in these areas and the people are known as Majhis as well.

Doaba is the third region, falling entirely in Indian Punjab and lying between the rivers Beas and Sutlej. The word Doaba – *do* and *ab* – literally translates to 'the land of two rivers'. Its major cities include Jalandhar, Hoshiarpur, Kapurthala, Phagwara, Nakodar, Phillaur and Goraya. The people of this region are known as Doabia, and their dialect Doabi.

'The family had to not only learn the Doabi dialect of Punjabi,' Vernika continues, 'but also how to speak in Hindi. All of them had studied only in madrasas, and Urdu was their first language. Once in India, they taught themselves Hindi by reading a newspaper called *Hindi Samachar*.'

'Do you understand the Majhi dialect?'

'My father can, but I'm unable to,' she shrugs. 'But just to connect language and food, I want to tell you what my great-grandmother did once they settled in India. She took up work as an ayah in a government school, but because the income was too little to bring up her family, she and the children began a small business of making and selling pakoras. My grandfather would go door to door to sell these, and in the same paper that had been bought to learn Hindi would be wrapped the hot, oily pakoras.'

'The entrepreneurial Punjabi spirit,' I say, having witnessed this in my own family. My grandfather, too, had made his first earnings by reserving and selling seats on trains, delivering items on bullock carts, or selling fountain pens, and only after six years of such work was he able to put down a deposit for a shop of his own.

'Vernika, would you say that Partition was openly discussed in your home?'

'It was probably only in the last five years that I began to ask about it with purpose, and most of my questions centred around food. I would ask why we ate certain things, and my elders would tell me that they had eaten them *there*, "*hum wahan khaate the*". And then I would ask, "There, where? *Wahan, kahan*?" And gradually stories about ingredients and spices, vegetables and roots would emerge. A partition line would be drawn between then and now. An entire palate had been abandoned, newer foods had been adopted and, in some cases, merely eating a familiar meal in an unfamiliar place kept them connected to their culture.' She pauses and then says with a smile, 'It is through food that we consume our geographies.'

Her smile becomes wider as she continues, 'Another interesting dish I want to tell you about is something that is made in my aunt's house to date – bread halwa. Her husband's family also migrated to India during Partition and stayed in refugee camps. During those days, when there was hardly anything positive to look forward to, bread halwa was invented as a sweet for festivals or auspicious occasions like Diwali or Gurupurab. As part of their rations in the camp, they would receive flour, milk, ghee, sugar, salt, potatoes, onions, bread – the basics. Flour, which can be used to make halwa, was generally saved up for rotis. So, bread became the hero ingredient of this ingenious dish, which ultimately felt quite similar to the *kadha* prasad made in gurudwaras.'

Wiggling her fingers, Vernika shows me how to mash and crumble the bread, which takes on the texture of wet flour once soaked in milk. 'To a hot *kadhai* they would add a cup of ghee and the soaked bread mixture and a cup of sugar – or as much as they could spare – and cook it until the ghee began to separate and the mixture looked like a halwa. When we make it now, we add dried fruit and cardamom, but that's an indulgence they couldn't afford in the camp. There is something quite inspiring about this sweet dish; it is emblematic of strength and willpower, and the fact that, as a community, we were able to lift our spirits even in the darkest of times.'

'Is it food, then, that remains the connection to a time before Partition?' I ask.

'It is one of the main things,' she says, thinking about it. 'In a single second, Partition can transform from an event in history to a feeling in the present day. In a single bite, you can be transported to a land you've never seen but your family belongs to. When the food we are eating, the language we are speaking are all remnants of this division, it feels like Partition is woven into our everyday life, and it may remain that way no matter how many generations come after us.'

ONE YEAR AFTER the revocation of Article 370 in the Indian Constitution that granted special status to the state of Jammu and Kashmir, I receive an email from Munazah Khan, who was born in 1999 in Kupwara district. Since she now lives in Srinagar, I propose that we set up a video call, but she tells me that the instability of the internet connection in the Valley may not allow it, and so we settle for a regular phone call. I am quick to assume that she wants to talk about Kashmir and Partition, and when I bring this up, her voice is calm yet reticent, and her response makes me feel almost embarrassed at my haste.

'There is nothing to say that hasn't already been said. The history of politics no longer matters; all I want is peace. I want to see peace in my lifetime.' A few seconds of silence pass, and I cannot tell whether she is reconsidering the conversation or the line has simply disconnected. When she speaks again, her tone feels different. 'If you don't mind, I'd rather not think about politics any more than I have to. But I did want to tell you about my grandfather, and the language he carried across from his home town during Partition.'

'I'd like that very much,' I say with a smile.

'Of the many families divided during Partition, one was my paternal grandfather's. His name was Mohammad Sadiq Khan, he was born in Hazara, Abbottabad, and died a few years ago at the age of ninety-six. At the time of the Second World War, he was posted in Indonesia as part of the British Indian Army. But once Partition happened, he was asked to choose between Pakistan, where his home town now fell, and India, where the family had property in North Kashmir. He chose India, with his parents, but the remainder of the family stayed in Pakistan, and they spoke through letters while they still could. I still have some of these.' As she says this, I am reminded of the fact that to date so many families that were divided between India and Pakistan have little means of communicating with each another. 'Over time, my grandfather got married and started a new life in Kupwara.'

'Did he ever go back to meet his family?' I ask.

'Yes, eventually. He retired from the army soon after 1947 and actually became Jammu and Kashmir's first physical education teacher at a government higher secondary school. But because of his years of service, a visa to Pakistan remained difficult to acquire. When he was finally able to go, too many years had passed, his parents were no longer alive, and the only people who remained were stepsiblings or distant relations. But there were things about his childhood in Abbottabad that he missed dearly – for instance, he often spoke about the poem they would recite during their school assemblies. It was called 'Bachche Ki Dua', written by Allama Iqbal. And the other thing he was particular about was his mother tongue. His language.'

'Kashmiri?'

'Oh, no, he never spoke Kashmiri,' she laughs. 'My grandfather's native tongue was Hindko, which is now spoken mostly in the provinces of Khyber Pakhtunkhwa and Punjab in Pakistan, and he continued to speak that till the day he died. He even wrote poetry in Hindko, under the *thakhalus*, the pen name of "Aasi", but never published.'

Munazah says a short sentence in Hindko, and I am surprised to find that I understand it. 'It sounds like a cousin of Punjabi.'

'It is similar to both Punjabi and Seraiki,' she adds, 'but Hindko is the main language spoken in our house even today, and because I've grown up speaking it, my accent is quite different from the standard accent of the region. Of course, my grandfather spoke a very pure version of Hindko, but over the decades, the influence of other languages has trickled into it – certain words, phrases – and it has adapted to the land it now lives in. Both my grandmother and mother are Kashmiri but have learnt this language over the years because we chose to never give it up.'

'It was a part of your grandfather's identity that he couldn't part with,' I observe.

'He never wanted us to speak Kashmiri in the house. *Hum apni zubaan bolenge*, we will speak our language.' Munazah's voice now becomes seeped in warmth and nostalgia, the kind that accompanies the bestowal of a family treasure. 'I suppose, in a land that wasn't his by birth – even though he had chosen to migrate to it after Partition – his mother tongue became a companion, the one thing that no one could take away. It stood in for the memory of everything he would likely never see again. Hindko was the part of home he could carry.'

Several months later, I stumble upon an interesting essay on Hindko, which makes me feel like even though Munazah's grandfather carried the language on his tongue from a land that is now Pakistan, it is actually equally at home today.

In Vol. 8 (Part I) of the Linguistic Survey of India, published in 1919, George Abraham Grierson ... presented in detail the particulars of a language he called Lahnda ... The south and

west of Lahnda territory he identified as the Seraiki region …
and the northern half as the Hindko region. This was the area,
he stated, where the 'language of the Hindus' (that is what
he interpreted Hindko to mean) was spoken … [However,]
scholars post-Grierson understood Hindko to mean the
'language of the people of Hind, i.e. India' and not the Hindus,
which was a term used for a religious community. And so it has
come to be a language named after India that is now largely
spoken in Pakistan.[5]

But Munazah is not the only one who has inherited a language now
mainly spoken in Pakistan. For the Delhi-based journalist Somya
Lakhani, Seraiki constitutes a large part of her linguistic repertoire.
Both sets of her grandparents migrated from areas of the North-
West Frontier Province (now Khyber Pakhtunkhwa) – Mianwali,
D.I. Khan, Bhakkar.

'For the longest time, I didn't know what dialect my grandparents
spoke. Was it Mianwali or Seraiki? I think it was a mix of both –
they are neighbouring dialects and share many common words,' she
begins. 'The beauty of Seraiki is that it is heavily inspired by Urdu,
and so when I was growing up in Delhi, one of the things that really
confused me was how my nana could speak Hindi, yet not read it.
But he could read and write in Urdu with ease. He would teach me
the alphabet – alif, be, pe, te – so it was never an alien language for
us. Today, the polarization is such that some people in India think
of Urdu as the "other" language, a language that strictly belongs to
the Muslim community. But it will always be my language. It was
what my nana knew and so any time someone refers to Urdu as a
Musalmaan zubaan, I don't quite understand that, because the *real*
irony is that Urdu was born in Delhi,'[6] Somya laughs.

I nod and ask her what Seraiki sounds like.

'Seraiki is a mix of Punjabi and Urdu, so, for instance, my
grandfather would never call a tree *ped*, as we normally would in
Hindi. He would call it *darakht*. He would always call an office a
daftar, so there were words and phrases he used that we were aware

weren't Hindi. The language that everyone in our house spoke, however, was Punjabi. And this was the Punjabi we *never* saw on television – Bollywood just turned Punjabi into a very caricature-ish speech, completely forgetting the beauty of the language. They presented it as a sort of humorous monolith, forgetting the fact that it is highly nuanced, and across the lengths of undivided Punjab, every district or area offers its own dialect of Punjabi. Between my father and mother's side, even with a geographic difference of only a hundred kilometres, I can sense the slight difference in speech.

'But we never saw that on television, *except*' – here, Somya's face breaks into a wide smile – 'except for two instances. The first was in the film *Veer-Zaara*,[7] where Preiti Zinta or Zaara's mum, played by Kirron Kher, uses the word *julso. Tussa julso saadey naal*, a line that my grandmother used, which meant: do you want to leave with us? The other phrase we use is *turra*, or *assi turde payein*, which also means we are leaving. The first time I heard this phrase in the film, I thought to myself, "Finally, this is *our* world!"

'The second time was when my entire family collectively watched a show because it was so close to the language we spoke. This was a few years ago when Zee TV used to still show Pakistani dramas, and the show was called *Aunn Zara*.[8] It was a comedy about a young couple who get married and don't get along at first but then eventually fall in love. A very cute story. But the real joy of that show was that the boy Aunn's grandmother used to speak Seraiki, or at least close to what I thought was Seraiki. The entire time that the show aired, my parents, grandparents, sister and I used to be glued to the television, and you could just see the sheer joy on my grandparents' faces. *This* was the language they missed, this was what they spoke to their relatives and children in, but they never really saw it represented anywhere.'

I smile. 'And I'm sure it meant something for them to see a part of themselves, their history, represented that way. Something that's so personal…'

She nods. 'I have held on to language very tightly. I'm the eldest grandchild of my maternal grandparents, and due to sheer proximity,

I've spent more time with them than my paternal side. Their stories have informed my understanding of Partition, just like the inheritance of their language has allowed me to access a part of their lives on the other side. I know that language is what we use to communicate with people, and we often just take it for granted. But the beauty of the language, the very words we choose and the meaning of those words, the memories we associate with them – they're completely and entirely built upon centuries of cultural and linguistic history.

'There are words or phrases that my grandparents used to use while we were growing up, and now that they are no more, my sister and I have actively begun using them. For instance, if we are at a party somewhere and we want to leave, my sister will just say to me, "Somya, *turra*?" That's it, we just say *turra,* which to another person means nothing, but to us the message is clear. Or sometimes, just playfully, if there is a baby in the family and he or she is crying or bothering us, we just say "*sam po*". Like, "Come on, *sam po*," which basically means: come on, please go to sleep,' she laughs. 'So, on one hand, it does feel like we are protecting these words and phrases from extinction, but on the other hand we are also using them in more innovative ways. I think in our generation, my sister and I make some effort to preserve this language; the rest of the cousins – who are my age or older – understand it, maybe speak it a bit too; but the younger ones definitely don't. I fear that the generation after ours may not inherit even a random assortment of these words or phrases.'

'Do you think language has been your greatest connection to Partition?' I ask.

'Oh, definitely,' Somya is quick to reply. 'And I think it's because I just hated the fact that Bollywood was constantly making a joke of Punjabi. I was never offended; I'm not easily offended. I don't care if you want to make a joke, but I know that in the midst of all this, *my* language was getting lost. I didn't find any representation in terms of the dialects spoken.'

'I'm curious, did your grandparents also teach you the specific dialectical differences within Punjabi?'

'Actually, it was the historian Sohail Hashmi sahib,' she smiles. 'A repository of knowledge, he not only told me that the dialect we speak is Seraiki, but also why it is called so. How all the people on the geographic belt that my grandparents are from used to own *serais*, or rest houses, and several travellers who stayed there either did not speak Urdu or weren't well-versed in it. So, the owners of these *serais* began picking up various languages as well as their scripts, mixing them in with Punjabi or other languages that they normally spoke, and this amalgamated *zubaan* became Seraiki – *serai walon ki zubaan.*[9] When he told me this, I was just fascinated because I'd never heard this origin story and never understood why Seraiki as a word was never even introduced in my family.'

'Later on, as I began to read more about Partition and the refugee experience of people who migrated from Pakistan to India, I began to discern a very particular feeling within my family and the community we came from. You see, in India, there was space for Lahoris, there was space for Peshawaris, there was space for Rawalpindi-*wallahs*. These were the major cities of culture and education on the other side. But what about Bhakkar and Mianwali that were not large centres of … anything at the time? They were half-agrarian, half-commercial, and kind of suburban. So, who was carving out land for these people? How would they get to retain their identity? I know that in Delhi there are colonies called Mianwali Nagar and Derawal Nagar, but nothing more. And so, naturally, there was not just resentment for the lack of representation but also gradual erosion of cultural identity.'

'I think you may already know this, but my paternal grandmother is also from D.I. Khan,' I say and she nods, 'but she doesn't speak a word of Seraiki any more. I think she may still understand fragments if she hears someone else speak, but not on her own. And I don't speak it at all.'

She shrugs, her point proven. 'Several years ago, while working on a story for the *Indian Express*, I spoke to a gentleman who was also from the same area, and we began discussing exactly this sentiment of representation and anger. He must have been over sixty years old, but he concurred with the fact that we had not gotten the same importance in an independent India that other people had, even other Punjabis from more prominent cities.'

'Do your parents speak Seraiki, are they interested in...?' I trail off.

Somya reacts with a kind of part laugh, part sigh. 'They do, but I don't even know if it's justified to have trouble with how little my parents' generation has done to preserve the past. I do feel like they didn't do enough to protect the language for the future generations. But while they were growing up, their parents and grandparents were still putting down roots for a new life, rebuilding their careers and a sense of stability. So, maybe nobody had the time, and I understand that there were three generations before me who worked so hard for me to have this luxury to introspect.' She pauses, and when she speaks again, I can hear her voice crumble, 'But sometimes I really wish that my mother or her siblings or the rest of their clan had worked harder on trying to save the little things.

'My father was born in Jhansi, but his parents and siblings migrated to India from Mianwali in 1947. Sadly, my grandfather and aunt passed away before I was born, and my grandmother when I was only four. My uncle, who retired as the principal of a government school, lived in so many different cities, so we rarely spoke about Partition, and my father didn't say much either. I wish I knew more, and I realize that I must visit my uncle and speak to him, because so much is already lost.'

'I feel like our generation is far more dependent on books and archives to reconstruct our own pasts, particularly if those alive at Partition are no longer around. It's like a jigsaw puzzle, where we often don't know where to begin from, and there will always be pieces missing,' I add.

'And that really breaks my heart,' Somya says as she closes her eyes for a few seconds.

When she opens them again, there is renewed focus. 'For my grandparents, Partition was always something that they didn't like talking about. They spoke about the time before, but actively avoided talking about migration or resettlement. If I prodded them, they would always ask why I was interested in something so old. "*Purani baat hai, ab kyu uchhaal rahe ho?*" I figured early on that this was something that continued to pain them, and that they had made a very conscious effort to assimilate into their adopted landscape – to forget the painful past almost. Whenever they spoke about Pakistan, it was only about happy things, how the house was, or what food was cooked, or the language they spoke. But they actively avoided discussing the violence or migration or suffering with us; *that* we were never privy to.'

'Not even while you were watching films like *Veer-Zaara*?' I ask. 'I know it's not directly about Partition, but so many of the themes resonate.'

She thinks about this for a minute. 'It happened when we took them to watch the film *Pinjar*. I can't explain it, but seeing them cry at many of the scenes, seeing them silently watch onscreen the kind of violence they may have faced themselves, and then, after the film, hearing them say, "*Yeh sab apni aakhon se dekha hai,*" that they had seen these things unfold before their eyes. My nani reached India in a train, hidden in a trunk; my nana used to tell us that he believed the move to India was temporary. Whenever I read anything about Partition, I'd discuss it with them, and again the same phrase, "*kya bataein*", as if to say, "What shall we tell you about what we have seen? You are only reading these things but we have witnessed them." They would allude but never openly detail what they saw.'

'But even in the silence,' I reply, 'even in that phrase, "*kya bataein*", there is a world of horror and pain to be found. The fact that what happened at that time was so unspeakable, so unrepeatable, it cannot even be brought to one's lips ...'

'The word Partition only encapsulates sadness for me,' Somya states. 'Take something as basic as a village, ancestral land. A place where generations of your family have been born and raised. Where is my village, my *gaon*? Every generation before my parents was born in what is now Pakistan. Even my paternal uncle and aunt were born in Pakistan. So, is that where my village is? And if so, then I have no way of getting there, no way of walking past that border and no grandparents left to help me find what may remain of us on that side.

'A few years ago, an advertisement for Google showed two best friends separated by Partition being reunited by their respective grandchildren – one in Lahore, the other in Delhi – thanks to technology.[10] It was the most humane ad I had ever seen. It made Partition feel personal and intimate, rather than political and hostile; it made Pakistanis feel like our own. I wept when I saw that ad, and I showed it to my nana and promised that I would take him back "home". I told him that we would go to his village and find his house, and see the trees that he used to talk about and where they used to tie the cows. I kept thinking that I would take him there, but I never could.'

'Do you think that he wished Partition had never happened?' I ask. The ongoing politics between the countries of the subcontinent has prevented entire generations from attaining any kind of closure.

'I don't know about my nana, but I certainly feel like if Partition had not happened, my personal history would have been different. Geographically, we may still have been in the Frontier Province, the land would have been ours. Maybe life would have been better or maybe it would have been worse, I can't say. But what I can say with certainty is that so many families, including my grandparents', had to rebuild their lives from scratch, in cities that were not their own, finding homes in lanes they didn't recognize, made to speak languages that they didn't speak on a regular basis, adopting customs that were not theirs...' From her tone it sounds like Somya may break down, but she takes a deep breath and continues, just as resolute. 'It must have been so difficult. I *know* it was so difficult. The idea of home for them was growing up in their village, so yes, I think they would have wished that Partition hadn't happened.

'In 2016, my nani fell sick and went into a delirium in the last few months of her life, where I felt for a moment that she thought she was back in Pakistan. She was talking about a home that I didn't understand or recognize, sometimes she would speak about herself as if she was ten years old. Scenes were playing in her head, and

I think they were scenes from when she was young. She was sitting in India, but her mind, her heart, even her bodily gestures were in Pakistan, maybe. She was here, but she was also there. Her stories are all locked up in Dera Ismail Khan.'

'Do you know what really hurts me?' Somya now centres her gaze on me. 'That so many people in India vocalize hate for Pakistan – a land that most of them have never been to, a land that may hold their own history. You can hate the politics of a certain place, but how can you hate an entire land you've never seen, an entire people you've never spoken to, an entire history you lay half ownership over? The fact of the matter is that I can relate more to someone sitting in Pakistan right now than someone from the southern or eastern part of India, because our language is the same, our habits are the same, our food is the same. When it is winter, I know that someone in Dera Ismail Khan or Bakkhar too is making the same *pinnis* as we are, the same *panjiri ladoos*, the same kind of *lassi* and *shira*.'

Her voice is simultaneously impassioned yet helpless.

When I had first proposed this conversation, Somya had shied away, claiming that she didn't know what she could tell me and how much of it would be helpful. As I remind her of this now, she laughs.

'To be completely honest, Partition is my favourite subject to talk about.'

'Why is that?' I ask, curious.

'Well, what Partition did to our families is unforgivable, and I don't think that it should ever be forgotten. What *you* are doing, these conversations, they are vital pieces of our history. Whether it is memory passed down or even memory lost, we have to keep documenting how the consequences of Partition continue to shape us, year after year, generation after generation. I have grown up listening to stories of Partition, so at some point I feel like I've heard everything, like there's nothing left to know. Every single story is a repetition, which is still beautiful because I can listen to the same story over and over. But I want to tell you this one story I heard only this year – after thirty-two years of being alive – for the very first time.

Just to show that Partition memory always finds a way to resurface, no matter how much time has passed.

'My mother was raised in the tight-knit neighbourhood of Krishna Nagar in east Delhi, and some time in the 1980s, one of her neighbours, Mr Gossain, visited Pakistan to see his ancestral home. Incidentally, my mother's family were his neighbours in Mianwali as well as in Delhi, and so my mother's dadi instructed him to see what remained of their house. She described the house, the lane, the locality, the bazaars, eager to know what had remained. Mr Gossain would have been a young man at the time, as old as my parents, and so he was going to a city he'd never been to before, to a house he'd never seen. Anyway, he went to Pakistan and upon his return the entire mohalla – this big Punjabi mohalla of Krishna Nagar – got together to know what he had come back with, what stories he had to tell. "*Gossain Pakistan nu wapas aaya hai, Mianwali ho kar aaya hai*," they said excitedly.

'From him, my mother's dadi learnt that there was nothing left of their old life any more; everything had changed. Forty years had passed, after all. So, there was a bit of disappointment on that front, but my mother remembers that everyone listened to his stories with rapt attention. He talks about the people he met, the lanes, the homes, the bazaars, the food. And then Mr Gossain says that he's brought water from Mianwali. *Ghar ka paani*, he called it, water from home.'

Goosebumps erupt across my arms when I hear this, and my heart feels immediately full. I think about all the times I have carried soil for people back and forth across the border. Sometimes they stored it in jars like collector's items and showed it off to friends and family; other times it was sprinkled on their graves and in their gardens. A piece of home, a part of *their* soil. But this is water, and I wonder whether it would command the same presence.

As if picking up on this thought, Somya continues, her voice now emotional. 'Water, what a thing to bring back. It's something so basic, so rudimentary, so necessary for one's survival. But it's not something you can store, not something that stays. You can't protect it or display it. You will consume it, or you may forget it. It's a bottle of water. But there was something so scared about it. *Ghar ka paani*. That emotion, I can't describe it. The story just left me overwhelmed but brought so much joy.'

She tells me that everyone in the neighbourhood drank a few sips of that water that day. As I hear this, I can't help but think how a part of Mianwali then literally ran through bodies.

My heart still full, I return now to the subject with which we began, the one Somya holds most dear.

'I have just one more question,' I say. 'Why do you continue to speak Seraiki?'

She takes her time to formulate her thoughts, running her forefinger over her lips.

'I had so many conversations with my grandparents but I never once thought to record them – like we are doing now,' she says, gesturing to our set-up. 'What if, now that they are gone, I can no longer hold on to the thread that ties me to where they came from? My sole fear is that if I don't continue to speak their language, I will forget it. That would devastate me, and the generations that come after me, because a vital piece of our being would have been forgotten. Language is my way of retaining my grandparents' memories, and I will always continue to speak in their Seraiki.'

IT IS MONSOON when I call Duaa Amir in Karachi. The morning is bright, but I can hear the rain thrashing outside her window.

'Both sides of my family migrated twice, first in 1947 from India to East Pakistan and then in 1971 from what became Bangladesh to Pakistan, and the interesting thing is that both sides were also originally from Bihar. The fact that they came from the same place allowed for the same rituals to be shared and practised and retained. That, I feel, is something that Partition was unable to erase – people carrying across their culture,' she beams.

Traditions and customs are not akin to luggage or goods; they were not transported in trunks or suitcases on the bogey of a train, a compartment of a ship, or on foot in long caravans. They are embroidered throughout our ancestry, embedded within our skin, in the deepest valves of our heart that cannot be measured in physical units. An intangible culture carried across borders and propagated further down the generations must be understood as an essential part of collective cultural memory. When we speak, Duaa is only nineteen years old, born in 2001, so her innate understanding of this fact leaves an impression on me.

'My first exposure to what Partition must have been was in middle school when I watched the drama *Dastaan*.[11] It was very tragic because from the point of view of a teenager, all I saw was two people who loved one another be separated because of Partition, confined to either side of the border, and that was heartbreaking.'

'Did it inspire you to ask questions at home?'

'Not once,' she laughs sadly. 'Of course, now in retrospect, I find it odd that I didn't. But *Dastaan* also focused on the Partition in Punjab, and so, I suppose, at that age I never made the connection that my family from Bihar had witnessed the same event.'

Duaa admits that it has only been a year since she began actively asking about Partition, but there had always been traces of India woven through her childhood. 'After my father died, we moved in with my maternal grandparents, and every Sunday over breakfast, my grandfather, Reyaz-ul-Huda, would tell us stories about his childhood. He passed away in 2016, but until then each weekend without fail he would begin our conversations by saying, "*Beta, main toh Phulwari Sharif se hoon*, I am from Phulwari Sharif." I vividly recall this opening line being like a mantra or a prayer, and he would then go on to tell us about his life in Bihar, where he was born in the early 1940s.'

'What kind of stories would he tell you?'

'India remained a bittersweet memory for him. His father passed away when he was only a year old, and their financial situation was very dire after that. He would tell us that because they couldn't afford proper shoes, he would tie old bottles to the soles of his feet. But every story would eventually lead back to his father, because

India was the only place where they were together. It's incredible how the human psyche works' – Duaa places her forefinger to her temple – 'because no matter how tragic life was in Phulwari Sharif, my grandfather clung to its memories, considered them his roots.'

'Did his family migrate eastwards during Partition?' I ask, having read that approximately 10 lakh refugees migrated from Bihar to East Pakistan due to the sheer proximality of the region. This exodus began in the aftermath of the 1946 Bihar riots when 'Hindu mobs attacked Muslim families in an attempt to avenge the Noakhali riots in which many Hindu families had been killed'.[12]

'Yes, to Dhaka,' she says, 'but no one ever speaks about the circumstances in which they left. My grandfather always avoided talking about the journey like a memory he didn't want to revisit. But I know they left by train. My grandmother's father was an architect in the British Indian Army, deployed during the Second World War. At the time of Partition, she was very young, but her elder sister was nine or ten years old and she would tell stories of how their neighbour's daughters were made to drown themselves in a well for fear of … well, you know. On that side of the family, the entire conversation was about the scale of brutality. And between extreme silence from my grandfather and extreme violence from my grandmother, I just found myself wondering about the stories in the middle. Stories of daily life, its change and fracture.' She looks at me expectantly.

I nod. 'Partition is too vast an event to be considered only in its most extreme forms. And the fact that there are still traditions from Bihar practised in your family is testament to the ways in which daily life was carried across.'

'Sometimes when there is a wedding or a get-together in the family, it feels like the entire population of Bihar has collected in one place,' Duaa laughs. 'My family may not speak through words about the displacement they went through, but the way in which traditions are performed and protected makes it clear that even seven decades later, the memory of separation from the homeland remains strong.'

'Tell me about these traditions.'

She picks up a beautiful magenta-pink fabric with silver block prints and holds it up for me to see. 'This is called *chhapa* and it's mandatory for every Bihari bride to wear a sari made of this fabric at her *nikkah*.' Bringing it up to her nose, she says, 'It has a very nice and distinct smell too. Interestingly, Indian *chhapa* is in high demand in Pakistan and is considered almost a "cool" thing for a bride to wear a *chhapa* brought in from India.'

'Is *chhapa* not produced in Pakistan?'

Duaa laughs. 'Oh, it is, but ever since I was young, I've been hearing the term Indian *chhapa*, as if it's important for the fabric to have been brought from the homeland, from Bihar. One of the other customs is that the elders sit around the bride and apply scented oil to her hair and comb it. As they carry out these rituals, they sing songs called *tona*, which are similar to the Punjabi *tappe*. The traditional jewellery worn by the bride comprises a pair of large, circular silver earrings, known as *bijli*, adorned with a filigree pattern, and a seven-strand necklace called *jugnu*. Every single bride in my family has also worn this big nose ring, which belonged to my great-grandmother and is definitely from India.

'There are particular words and phrases that my grandparents continued to use that can be attributed to their Bihari upbringing – for instance, the word for eleven in Urdu is *gyarah*, but he always pronounced it as *igyarah*, or not assigning any gender to objects, which is typical of Biharis. I have to admit that, as a child, I used to be almost embarrassed of these idiosyncrasies, I wanted to speak Urdu in a very polished way, but now I find myself adopting everything, trying to use the words he used,' she smiles. 'Try as I might, I cannot ignore or outgrow the things that make me culturally Bihari. They are embedded within me.'

I mirror her smile and ask, 'What about food?'

'Oh, yes,' she says, clapping her hands together, 'we make a lot of Bihari food at home – apart from the special kababs, my grandmother also makes a delicious *bachka*, which is a black chickpea pakora, and a deep-fried sweet dish called *pua*, made with flour, semolina, sugar and milk. One more thing, which may be irrelevant to Partition but relevant to my grandparents and the topic of food, is that I had always seen my grandfather address my grandmother as *dost*, or friend. They were married in East Pakistan, and I guess you really needed a friend through all the turmoil they experienced. So, later on in life, I would often hear him call out to her, "*Dost, aaj pua – ya bachka – khaatey hain.*" She still makes the best Bihari food and a part of me thinks it's a way of holding on to all the things my grandfather loved.'

'Do you know if all these traditions and customs are practised by Indian Biharis as well?'

'Well, how different can we be?' she smiles. 'And if we are able to keep alive these remnants even though we are no longer in Bihar, I'm sure that those still living there have been able to retain them as well. I don't know any Indian Biharis, but I would love to meet them and talk about Patna.'

Then, after a few seconds, she adds, 'I always wondered why my grandfather never told us about Partition and assumed that it was because we were too young to understand such tragedy. But lately I've come to realize that maybe he thought that us growing up with the knowledge of any violence experienced by his family may make us prejudiced against a certain community. As a result, he only told us happy stories about his life in India. He was only a child when he migrated to Dhaka.'

According to the 1951 census, East Bengal was home to 671,000 Bihar refugees, and by 1961 this number had reached 850,000. In the two decades following Partition, it is estimated that about 1.5 million Muslims migrated from Bihar and West Bengal to East Bengal.[13]

'My grandfather's family migrated to Dhaka in 1947 because they already had relatives there,' Duaa recounts. 'And he always maintained that his life changed in Dhaka, he went to school and college, began earning and got married. He could support his single mother who had raised him. But eventually hostility grew towards Urdu-speaking Biharis, who were seen as agents of Pakistani domination. With the creation of Bangladesh in 1971, my grandfather's family had no choice but to escape to Pakistan by flight. My paternal family, on the other hand, came to Pakistan safely through Nepal.'

In *1971: A People's History from Bangladesh, Pakistan and India*, Anam Zakaria writes:

> The Biharis were traditionally seen as pro-Pakistan and the economic leadership in East Pakistan mainly came from amongst them, leading to significant power differences between the Urdu-speaking community and the Bengalis who worked as peasants or in mills, and organizations led by the non-Bengalis. During 1971, Bihari civilians – alongside pro-Pakistan Bengalis – were accused of collaborating with the Pakistan Army.[14]

After the 1971 war, many of the Biharis left behind in Bangladesh became stateless; several began to reside in refugee camps, and some fled to Pakistan. According to the historian Partha Ghosh, approximately 470,000 Biharis out of a total of 700,000 opted to be repatriated to Pakistan through the International Red Cross.[15]

'In those early years,' Duaa says, 'the term "Bihari" was used derogatorily. But my grandfather established himself well as a chartered accountant in Karachi, so my mother was never privy to any unfortunate encounter that may have led her to question her Bihari identity. However, she once heard General Zia-ul-Haq on national television sarcastically referring to Biharis as *bikharis*, or beggars, and quickly realized that though she may have lived a sheltered life because of her parents, there were many others who were targeted because of their identity. As a result, both my parents simply state that they are *muhajir* or Urdu-speaking refugees, not mentioning their Bihari origins. On the contrary, I feel that my generation is attempting to reduce this stigma and is proud of our Bihari ancestry.'

'Do you think that your parents' marriage also happened because of their common identities?'

She nods. 'I think it played an important role, and preference was given to proposals from Bihari families. Even though my paternal and maternal side did not know one another before, there was a commonality to their experiences and that meant something.'

Suddenly, our line is disturbed – outside her window, rain envelops the city of Karachi, and inside her house a baby's distant wails float into our conversation. Duaa apologizes, telling me that she lives in a joint family, and quickly gets up to close the door. When she returns, I ask her whether she feels the inheritance of Partition, whether the years following the death of her grandfather – who was her strongest link to India – have made her feel closer to the land he was born in. She thinks about this for a while.

'You know, towards the end of his life, my grandfather only spoke about Bihar, he longed for it. His country may have been Pakistan, but his homeland was India. And if both sides of my family can trace their history back to that place, can I not trace myself back to Bihar as well? I feel bound to Partition in that way. Also, because we have been displaced by two partitions, the definition of home is quite ... malleable – the fact that we can easily move to new places and call it home.'

'A sense of adaptability, you mean?'

'Adaptability, of course, but duality as well,' she replies, and I ask her to elaborate. 'My grandfather felt proud to be Pakistani and had tremendous respect for Urdu literature. But at the same time he could read Hindi and was fluent in Bangla as well. Wherever he was from, wherever he lived, he picked up parts of that place and left parts of himself behind. I mentioned to you earlier that after my father died, we moved in with my grandparents, but I never really considered this my *home*. It was always my grandparents' home, and it's really strange to connect the dots now, during this conversation, but I've never bought anything for my room that couldn't be packed up into a box. People buy furniture or decorative pieces, but I would always collect keychains, or other small things that could be easily packed up in case I had to move. And if I think about my grandparents leaving their homes in India and migrating to East Pakistan and then to Pakistan, I wonder whether they felt the same – at least at the beginning? Did they also hesitate to buy things because they didn't feel at home? How long did it take them to *adapt* to a place they could now consider home, lay down roots in, have children? I know that my story is not directly related to Partition, as my grandparents' is, but it is a way for me to try to understand and empathize with how they may have felt.'

I nod and then ask, 'When you think of the word Partition, what comes to mind?'

'Bihar,' she beams, 'only Bihar. I don't think it is wrong to say that my understanding of India, my thoughts about Partition are bound to Bihar.'

Duaa exits the frame for a few minutes and I can hear her searching for something. When she returns, she holds up a book. 'Can you see this?'

The title is reversed in the camera, but squinting my eyes I read the words *HIDDEN TREASURE*.

'This is my great-grandfather's, and on the title page are inscribed the words, "This book belongs to Gholam Husnain, Village P.O. Phulwari Sharif, dist. Patna." I have heard of my grandfather's village ever since I was a child, but this was the first time I'd actually seen it written anywhere – not on a map, but handwritten as a place once inhabited. Phulwari Sharif, the words with which he began any and every conversation, could now be touched and traced by me. It was reaffirming to know that the place was real, it was where this book had been read and inscribed – a place I'd never visited but intrinsically understood to be a part of me and my identity.'

SOMETIMES I FEEL that, nearly seven and a half decades later, we are still shedding the detritus of 1947.

On witnessing sentiments of communal hatred among children who had lived through Partition, Begum Anis Kidwai once wrote most prophetically that '...it wasn't only the generations of today that were lost, but future generations had been destroyed too. The coming generations would be even more blind and unfeeling, and if something weren't done now to restore balance, they would plummet into the deepest abyss of all.'[16] The following conversation has become a testament to this feeling, to the creation of a thousand fractures, of limitless partitions, and the boundaries that define and confine us.

'IT WAS DECIDED that the entire family would migrate to Pakistan,' the actor and musician Saba Singh Grewal, known by her stage name Saba Azad, recalls. Her maternal grandmother, Qamar 'Azad' Hashmi, was born in 1926 in Jhansi to Zubaida Khatoon, a woman who spoke several languages and was adept at horse riding and rifle shooting, and Azhar Ali 'Azad', a tehsildar who wrote Urdu prose and Persian poetry. In the summer of 1947, when the Partition plan was announced, Qamar was living in the Timarpur area of Delhi with her parents, a sister and three brothers, one of whom had a family of his own, and another, Asghar Ali Abbasi, who taught English at a polytechnic in Kashmiri Gate.

'Timarpur was safe until June, when a bomb exploded in a house nearby,' she says. 'The decision to leave for Pakistan had already been made and their larger belongings like furniture and trunks sent across by the goods train, so the family quickly packed up the remainder of their life in Delhi and ... I've actually made notes so that I don't forget any step in their journey.' She points to a notebook in her hands and flips the page. 'So, the family got on a bus that drove them to Kashmiri Gate and no further because a curfew had been imposed in the area. They may have been on their way to the Old Delhi Railway Station to catch a train to Pakistan, but because of this curfew, they were stranded. It was there, at Kashmiri Gate, that they were spotted by a gentleman named Hamid Hashmi, or Chacha Hamid, as my mother knew him, who was my would-be grandfather's younger brother.'

'So, the families knew one another?' I ask, making a note.

'Yes, my grandfather's family, the Hashmis, owned one of the largest furniture businesses in Delhi, and they also happened to supply furniture to Asghar Ali Abbasi's English department at the polytechnic. Upon finding the Abbasi family stranded, Chacha Hamid invited them to stay with them for as long as they needed. Kashmiri Gate was peaceful, as a Sikh police officer was in charge of the area, and so all of these young people – my grandparents and their siblings – lived together for a few weeks. They would discuss what was happening in their city, and what the Partition of India would look like. The Hashmi family had been actively involved in the freedom struggle and was popularly known as the "first red family" of Delhi[17] – my grandfather, Haneef, had been jailed during the Quit India Movement and spent almost six months in solitary confinement, and his mother, Amtul Muqeit, had been the president of the Delhi committee of the National Federation of Indian Women – NFIW. Somewhere in these daily discussions, there was a proposition that Qamar and Haneef be married, but it was only a passing comment at the time.'

Saba suddenly looks up from her notes and says, 'It's only a bit of background, but I want to tell you about the furniture business, because it's an inspiring story about friendship and loyalty.'

As I nod for her to go on, she begins, 'There were five people who ran the business – my great-grandfather, Idrees, and his four sons. Idrees Hashmi was an art teacher in Timarpur, who eventually went into business with his best friend, Vermaji, a Hindu. But even before the furniture shop opened, Vermaji passed away, and yet my great-grandfather chose to name their shop Verma–Hashmi. You never hear these stories, you know,' Saba beams. 'They always get swallowed by the communal conflicts of Partition. But I felt it important to put this on record. It was only later that the name was changed to Hashmi Brothers.'

'Had the Hashmi family also decided to migrate to Pakistan?' I ask Saba.

'Actually, one particular incident led them to make that decision. In July 1947, when refugees from West Punjab had already begun trickling into Delhi after escaping the riots, my grandfather's eldest brother was in Connaught Place running an errand. Suddenly, he was surrounded by a mob holding swords. He was a very, very tall and strapping man, and, in the nick of time, was spotted by a friend who ushered him away from the crowd and brought him home. But he could have been badly wounded or, worse, even killed. So far, Idrees Hashmi had not wanted to leave India; he was adamant that he be buried where he was born. But after this incident, the Hashmis and Abbasis talked all night and decided that it would be best for them all to leave at once. From Kashmiri Gate they went to the Purana Qila refugee camp, where thousands of Muslim families were waiting for safe passage to Pakistan. The Hashmis – with the exception of Haneef, my grandfather – left by a flight, but the Abbasis had to wait for their train.

'When the Abbasis did make their way to the Nizamuddin train station, they found the train packed to the brim, with no room to move or breathe. They were travelling with elderly parents and young children, and decided to wait for the next train. As luck would have it, this train was attacked on its way to Lahore and all the passengers were murdered along the way. So, the family escaped death again. They came back to Purana Qila but could not re-enter the camp, having left it once, and were forced to find shelter at the camp in Humayun's Tomb, where they lived from August until November 1947.'[18]

'Through heat and monsoon,' I add, 'from camp to camp, in your own city.'

Saba nods sadly.

'How come your grandfather didn't migrate with his family?'

'The Hashmis were always very politically active, and Haneef was a member of the Communist Party of India, which contributed to his decision to remain here. He was doing relief work with the party during Partition and must have been no older than twenty-five years when he decided to stay, all alone.' Saba heaves a deep sigh. 'The sacrifices that generation had to make – I can't imagine taking such a grave life decision that would separate me from my family this way.'

'I don't think anyone envisioned the border between India and Pakistan becoming as fortified as it did,' I smile sadly. 'A fortnight after the Partition plan had been agreed upon, at one of his prayer meetings, Gandhi claimed that he couldn't imagine India and Pakistan as separate nations. That if he had to go to Punjab or Sindh, he wasn't going to ask for a passport, he would just go walking! A permanent separation was unthinkable, and the public anticipated soft borders.'[19]

Saba chuckles, 'Yes, I think many people imagined that they'd be able to travel back and forth between the two countries more easily.' Biting her lower lip, she continues, 'Anyway, the Abbasis finally migrate to Pakistan by train and live with relatives in Lahore. The sisters begin working – teaching, stitching clothes – in order to start earning for the family, the two brothers who accompanied them move elsewhere to start their lives. At this point, both the Hashmis and Abbasis are in Pakistan, with the exception of my grandfather, who remains in Delhi. A year passes, and the conversation about Qamar and Haneef's marriage is rekindled and it is decided that Qamar will travel *back* to India to be married in Delhi. And the rest, as they say, is history!' Saba smiles.

'So, *both* their families remained in Pakistan?' I confirm.

'To this day,' Saba nods.

'And only the couple lived in India?'

'That's correct. They had five children – Sahiba, Sohail, my mother Shehla, Safdar and Shabnam.'

Her grandfather, Haneef, continued to run the furniture business, but it collapsed in the aftermath of Partition. In an interview, her uncle, the historian Sohail Hashmi, cites 'an unstated boycott of Muslims' as one of the reasons. The family suffered tremendously difficult financial conditions, and soon Haneef moved to Aligarh on the invitation of Dr Zakir Hussain, then vice chancellor of Aligarh University, who requested him to set up a workshop at the university. Meanwhile in Delhi, Qamar completed her Montessori teacher's training. In the mid-1950s, the family reunited in Aligarh and lived there until the mid-1960s. Each of the children grew up with strong political opinions – a trait inherited from their parents.[20] In 1976, Haneef passed away in his fifties, leaving Qamar to recast her life yet again; she died in her late eighties in 2013.

'Did you ever have a chance to speak to your grandmother about Partition?' I ask Saba.

'Oh, yes. When I was a teenager, she published a book called *Panchwa Chirag*, or The Fifth Flame. It was a biography of her late son, Safdar Hashmi, who was wounded fatally by a political mob on 1 January 1989 while performing *Halla Bol*, a street play about the exploitation of factory workers, in Sahibabad. But parts of the book also discuss Partition and family life.'

'And what did you make of her migrations: moving to Pakistan for family, or back to India for love, at a time when the region became so stringently bifurcated on religious grounds?'

'I've only known her to be a fiercely independent woman who did not let religion dictate her life. I believe these values have found their way to us, her grandchildren.' She points inwards, at her heart. 'The thought that you could divide people on the basis of religion, to the point of mass migration, is a concept I will never fathom, because of how inconsequential religion has been to the ideals of my upbringing. My parents come from two different religious backgrounds – my father is Sikh, my mother is Muslim – but neither believes in nor practices any form of religion. Most of the stories from Partition, in my opinion, are no more than the politics of power rearing its ugly head. But for it, half my family wouldn't have been on the other side of the border. But for it, we may have been a society that took pride in our diversity, rather than living in fear of our differences. I despise using the word tolerant, because it insinuates that there are people who belong and there are those who don't and thus need to be tolerated.

'My elders tell me that the promise of a free India was very different – it had hope. The future of India was like this big dream of plurality and secularism. The preamble to our Constitution asserts India as a socialist, secular, democratic republic – ideals that are swiftly fading in to the past. When my mother talks about her childhood in Aligarh, she never once mentions religion, and it's probably because of her communist upbringing. She and her siblings were not really aware of what it meant to be religious or have any value for it in their lives, and yet they celebrated Holi, Diwali, Eid and Dussehra equally. But as I look back at my childhood in Delhi, where I was often questioned about my religious identity or lack thereof, I'm able to draw a direct line from 1947 – things that otherwise, in isolation, may not seem like a consequence of Partition, but once we begin to connect the dots, it's what feels most logical.'

Until now, the conversation has remained confined to the past. As we steer it into the present, Saba maintains that the increasing collision of religion and politics, which has become part of the current rhetoric, once again opens up the scars left by Partition. Scars that the past should have dulled seem fresher than ever.

When I ask her what she means, she offers me her name, Azad.

'It is the simplest way I can explain how the legacy of division lives on in my daily life. My mother is a Hashmi, my father a Grewal. Early on in my school life, I was asked about my religion – "Are you Muslim or Sikh?" – but whatever the answer, I was either othered for it or teased because of it. And so, over a decade ago, I decided to change my name. It may have been for whimsical and artistic reasons at the time, but now, however unintentional, the name carries a lot more weight.'

'What was the reason?' I ask softly.

'I think I was just afraid,' she admits in a small voice. 'On one hand, I was a Muslim made to feel like the other for her identity. But the truth is, the reality of being even a non-practising half-Muslim with an Urdu name is shrouded in fear, uncertainty and discrimination. On the other hand, I was a Sikh who was constantly made fun of with all kinds of sardar jokes. As a child devoid of any kind of religious practices, who didn't know anything at all about what it really meant to be either, I didn't relate to any of it. But the word *azad* felt like my own; I was so torn about my identity that this just fit – Azad, free.' Saba pronounces the word with lightness, releasing it into the room like an offering. 'You see, no matter how much my parents tore themselves away from their religions, to the world, their names, and therefore their identities, remained grounded in them. But Azad was a name not related to either.'

In the subcontinent, a name is enough to unfold one's genealogy.

'When people know your name, they assume they know things about you – religion, caste, origin – so changing my name was also to prevent people from branding me as one thing or the other. I was more than a Hashmi, more than a Grewal. My identity was pluralistic, which is why "Azad" made sense. My father tried to reason with me then, but I had made up my mind, for I was taking on a name that meant freedom – from religious tags, from being identified by my parents' backgrounds. But little did I know then,' she chuckles sadly, 'that I was taking on not just a beautiful-sounding name from the language of poets, Urdu, the language that even my Sikh grandmother grew up reading, but also a minority surname.

'From then till now, so much has changed. India has once again become a place divided, closer to the feelings triggered during Partition than ever before. It was just a few months ago that protests against CAA–NRC* erupted across the streets of this nation, because together they threatened the idea of a secular India. In light of all this, I have become more of a minority than my parents.'

Saba pauses to take a deep breath. '*Even more than my parents*,' she stresses, 'because they use the surname Grewal, which, for now is a "safe" name. I adopted Azad because it was the pen name of my poet great-grandfather Azhar Ali "Azad", which was further adopted as a pen name by my grandmother, Qamar "Azad". I asked her if I could have this name, and she agreed, bequeathing it to me, and I became Saba "Azad". I was also thinking of the freedom fighter Chandrashekhar Azad ... But the realization of what this name meant only happened years later, when I thought I was free but the very word I'd chosen to establish my freedom was tethered to religious nomenclature.'

'Do you regret it?' I ask.

---

* Citizenship Amendment Act and National Register of Citizens.

'No,' she is quick to answer. 'I love my name and I still believe and hope to live in a world where it can be viewed with the same freedom I felt when I took it on. But can I be honest with you?' Her eyes immediately fill with tears, as if they have been waiting to spill over. 'Because of the rising propaganda and hatred towards minorities, particularly Muslims, and the fact that, from time to time, communal riots resonant of Partition are experienced, I have felt the need to cling to my Sikh identity harder than I ever did before. I turn to it for safety.'

Saba now breaks down, tears streaming down her cheeks, and for several seconds this is the only sound between us. When I try to speak, my throat feels scratchy, as if made of sandpaper.

'I'm sorry,' she says finally, wiping her face. 'Look, I've spent my life running from religion, my parents have spent *their* lives rejecting religion. But no matter how much we look away, it's attached to our identity so strongly, and not out of choice. And the very thing I tried to disassociate from – out of fear of ridicule as a child – is what I seek safety in now. It's such a bizarre state of being. I wish I could say that Partition is no longer relevant, but I can't, because despite my privilege, I feel its ghostly tremors every day. It has led us to where we are right now, how I feel at this very moment. Had we not been forced to be divided on the basis of religion during Partition, someone with a minority name may not have felt the fear or the need to hide it, to disguise it, to constantly be vigilant about their *name* – something as basic as their name. I keep returning to the fact that had Partition not happened, we may have been a more inclusive society, and religion may never have played as big a role in political discourse as it does today. Maybe I am naïve or simply wishing out loud.'

Jawaharlal Nehru once said:

The only real long-term policy we can have is to consolidate India by making all the minorities in the country feel completely at home in the State, and indeed by removing all sense of difference from the political point of view between the so-called majorities and minorities.[21]

Keeping these words in mind, I think of Saba's grandmother leaving her home in India and travelling to the promised land across the border during Partition. I then think about her leaving her entire family in Pakistan and making the journey back, only a year later, to rebuild a home. I wonder if she has ever thought about the future, about whether her children or grandchildren would consider the past in the way that Saba is now.

When I bring this up, she reminds me that her experiences are not without precedent. 'Religious differences did not simply disappear after Partition. They may have subsided then, only to emerge at other times. The years 1984, 1992, 2002 are all examples of the remnants of division in India. The legacy of Partition remains alive, threaded into our daily lives. And not just among the nations it impacted, but *within* them too. The fact that I cannot see my family who live in Pakistan because of the border between us, or cannot take pride in a name that I have chosen for myself because it's a discernibly minority name in an increasingly communal nation, means that the tendencies to divide have remained.'

I look at Saba, not sure of what to say next.

She now clears her throat. 'Do *you* think we have learnt from Partition, from history?'

This reminds me of so many conversations over so many years with so many different people, all trying to answer the same question. I shake my head and reply with the words borrowed from Kamleshwar's *Kitne Pakistan*, which I return to often: 'History, which can provide remedial insights into the past, is often cast aside.'[22]

We look at each other, heavy silence on both ends.

'I want to say otherwise.' She pauses. 'But Partition doesn't yet feel like an event of the past.'

'Which is why we are not the generation to forget it,' I concur.

Epilogue

ON 14 AUGUST 2021, Prime Minister of India Narendra Modi announced that the date would henceforth be known as Partition Horrors Remembrance Day, in 'memory of the struggles and sacrifices of our people'.[1] The decision sparked debate in many circles – over the wording, the conflating of history with present-day politics, even the 'standardization of remembering as a national exercise'.[2] But, for someone like me, who thinks and writes about Partition day after day, year after year, the act of memorialization – both tangible and intangible – is essential, when done in a manner that is inclusive and empathetic, taking into consideration the sentiments of those who actually witnessed the trauma that has long defined the nations of the erstwhile British Empire.

For seventy-five years, we have endlessly concerned ourselves with the geopolitical consequences of this historical event, and not nearly enough with how it has registered – through remembering or forgetting – in collective memory and public consciousness. However, the struggles and sacrifices made at Partition were not one-sided, and so while a day of remembrance is welcome, it *cannot* exclusively apply to Indians, and must extend beyond our frontiers, potentially paving the way for cross-border conversations and gradual reconciliation. Even the date chosen, 14 August, Pakistan's Independence Day, further complicates the notion of collective remembrance rather than advocating for it. Perhaps a date like 3

June – when the announcement of Partition was first made in 1947 by Viceroy Lord Mountbatten – may have been more appropriate.

An official day of commemoration should have ideally meant a joint effort between the governments of India, Pakistan and Bangladesh,[3] giving the peoples of a once undivided land the opportunity for their varied experiences to be heard and recognized, acknowledged and honoured – not only by their own countrymen but also their neighbours. Listening to others is perhaps the first step to building empathy towards them, and if the research for this book reveals anything, it is to remember that we originated from a shared history, once experienced a shared pain, and thereby carry through our generations a shared loss.

Lastly and most importantly, such a commemoration cannot only be to recall the horror that was witnessed or communal violence that was unleashed. The aim of a Partition Remembrance Day must also be to look both outwards at our community and inwards within our families in order to understand collective grief, generational trauma, divisive tendency, and how the legacy of Partition 'should be a tool not only to reconstruct the past but also to interpret it'[4] to make sure that such an event does not happen again.

IT IS A new year as I sit down to write this Epilogue. Going through the many interviews in this book, hoping to sew together the seams of Partition, my thoughts return to the words I once wrote in *Remnants*, about how 'memorialization [was] not a passive practice but an active conversation'.[5] It dawns on me then that this archive that all my interviewees and I have created together *is* a commemoration, an act of remembrance. By engaging in gradual, continual, long-term, multigenerational, cross-border conversations, we have actively remembered Partition. Through these chapters, we have acknowledged that the shared history of the region is often crippling and unbearably tangled, but we have neither simplified nor diminished it. We have merely remembered so there can be a record of this remembrance.

That being said, I admit that this has been a very difficult book to write, permeating deeper than I could have imagined, becoming more autobiographical than I had intended. While speaking with survivors, there is a definitive understanding that what you are recording is the past. But in this book of descendants, where the past has bled into the present, and the fault lines from history – personal, political, emotional, physical, familial, spiritual, religious, ethnic – have extended into the current moment, the understanding of the past being the past is harder to substantiate. The sense of a prolonged Partition is felt viscerally and instinctually in every conversation, and I wonder whether any *language of remembering* will do justice to the enormity of trauma that has clearly found a way to exist as a genealogical imprint. The very word 'Partition' has become a feeling, an experience, a history, a memory, a burden, a wound, a war, all at once.

Seventy-five years on, we cannot undo what has been done, for 'India and Pakistan as two separate and sovereign nations is an unalterable reality of history'.[6] So, I try not to hark back to the geography of an undivided land, but rather the relationships that once existed between common people, for human connections are what will inspire any form of peace and reconciliation in the region. And while it may be an ambitious proposition, I do believe that if no official or government organization initiates this process of peace, then the task falls upon writers, artists, oral historians, filmmakers, musicians, cultural ambassadors and the like who engage in and depend on mediums that transcend borders. Thus, it is my hope that the stories of this book will evoke empathy among future generations to imagine a world where a man-made border does not remain an encumberment to forging meaningful ties with those across it, and where citizenships or passports do not assert superiority over humanity.

Notes

Introduction

1. Marianne Hirsch, *The Generation of Postmemory: Writing and Visual Culture After the Holocaust* (New York: Columbia University Press, 2012), p. 4.
2. Ibid., p. 5.
3. Eva Hoffman, *After Such Knowledge: A Mediation on the Aftermath of the Holocaust* (New York: Vintage, 2005), p. 16 [emphasis added].
4. Rita Kothari, 'Speaking of Partition', 14 August 2017, https://www.addastories.org/speaking-of-partition/.
5. Dan Bar-On, *Fear and Hope: Three Generations of the Holocaust* (Cambridge: Harvard University Press, 1995).
6. Lisa has also previously written about her family's experience of Partition and this incident at Sealdah station. See Lisa Ray, *Close to the Bone* (New Delhi: HarperCollins, 2019), pp. 3–5.
7. See The 1947 Partition Archive, The Partition Museum, the Citizens' Archive of India, the Citizens' Archive of Pakistan, Project Dastaan, BBC Radio 4's Partition Voices.
8. Anam Zakaria, *The Footprints of Partition: Narratives of Four Generations of Pakistanis and Indians* (New Delhi: HarperCollins, 2015), pp. 8–9.

1. Beginning

1. See the work of Italian scholar and oral historian Alessandro Portelli.

2. I note this to be an exceptionally perceptive observation on my aunt's part, for when I interviewed my grandfather, Balraj Bahri, he said something quite similar about his migration: 'In those first few moments … a paralysis overcame me and I had the strangest feeling of sudden maturation, as if completely leaving behind my childhood and emerging across the border as an adult, disoriented and overwhelmed…' Aanchal Malhotra, *Remnants of a Separation: A History of the Partition Through Material Memory* (New Delhi: HarperCollins India, 2017, 2018), p. 84.

3. Fikr Taunsvi, trans. Maaz Bin Bilal, *The Sixth River: A Journal from the Partition of India* (New Delhi: Speaking Tiger, 2019), p. 89.

4. Ahmad Salim, *Lahore 1947* (New Delhi: India Research Press, 2002).

5. See Anuj Bahri and Debbie Smith, *Bahrisons: Chronicle of a Bookshop* (New Delhi: India Research Press, 2003), p. 44: After settling into Kingsway Camp, the family 'shared a simple meal. Roti and onions were all we could spare, but we enjoyed it like a feast.'

From pp. 47–50: In those early days, Balraj, his brother Davinder and their cousins would reserve the second-class seats [unreservable, sold on a first-come-first-served basis] in trains and sell them to desperate passengers for a fee of Rs 5, making a profit. On the very first day, they returned to the camp with an unthinkable sum of Rs 5 and 'that night, there was a small celebration', for, along with their daily ration of dal and roti, a plateful of vegetables was prepared. The first earnings had been brought home, and they would 'dine in style'.

On p. 63: After Balraj signs the lease for a shop in Khan Market in 1953, his mother is overjoyed and visits the temple. 'To the shop were attached our dreams of a better, more prosperous and secure future.' Upon her return and upon her son's request, she cooks a 'delicious mutton curry, tandoor roti and kheer'.

2. Belonging

1. For a more comprehensive reading about Shams Manzil, please see Aanchal Malhotra, 'The Light of a House That Stands No More: The Stone Plaque of Mian Faiz Rabbani', *Remnants of a Separation: A History of Partition Through Material Memory* (New Delhi: HarperCollins, 2017, 2018), pp. 141–59. A full account of carrying the plaque to Lahore can be read on Air Commodore Kaiser Tufail's blog: http://kaiser-footloose.blogspot.in/2008/11/our-trip-to-india.html.

2. Excerpts from 'The Partition' (2020) by Puneet Anand, reproduced with permission of the author: https://onepurebliss.home.blog/2021/03/11/the-partition/.

3. See Aanchal Malhotra, 'When the Bubonic Plague Ravaged India', *Mint Lounge*, 26 April 2020, https://www.livemint.com/mint-lounge/features/when-the-1897-bubonic-plague-ravaged-india-11587876174403.html.

4. The Muhajir people are Urdu-speaking Muslim immigrants and their descendants who migrated from various regions of India after the 1947 Partition to settle in the newly created state of Pakistan. The term is most commonly used for those who came from India and settled in Sindh.

5. Pakistan was under martial law from 1977 to 1985. Also see 'How Zia Ruled: 1997–1988', *Dawn*, 2 July 2017.

6. Aanchal Malhotra, 'There Are No More Places to Migrate to', *Departures in Critical Qualitative Research*, Vol. 8, No. 1 (University of California Press, 2019): pp. 42–49.

7. Subhasri Ghosh, 'Representation of forced migrants: a case study of the East Bengali migrants to West Bengal', Conserveries mémorielles [online], #13, 2013: 'Between 1947 and 1950 – the span within which Calcutta witnessed a spate of influx – the root cause of migration from the east remained the persecution of Hindu minorities by the East Pakistani administration in the form of arbitrary requisition of houses of the minorities, absence of Hindu representatives in the decision-making bodies, a partisan police force, rumors of minority massacres … However, from 1950 onwards, hatred took a gory turn as it came to be manifested in a violent manner, with the merciless slaughter of Hindus, together with forced abduction and marriage of Hindu girls, and destruction of Hindu edifices. The watershed was the February Riot of 1950, which was the first major riot to affect East Bengal after the Partition of 1947.'

8. See Tathagata Roy, *My People, Uprooted: The Exodus of Hindus from East Pakistan and Bangladesh* (Kolkata: Ratna Prakashan, 2001), p. 189.

9. Chittagonian is an Indo-Aryan language spoken in the Chittagong Division in Bangladesh and is estimated to have 13 to 16 million speakers. Its sister languages include Sylheti, Rohingya, Chakma, Assamese and Bengali.

10. Tabassum Zaman, 'The Imagined Bengal – When the City Goes Soft', *The Daily Star*, 29 June 2018: 'The most constant element in the social imaginary of two Bengals is a river that never was. The two Bengals

are very often referred to as Epar Bangla and Opar Bangla – meaning this and that bank of a river – by Bengalis from both sides. In both evocations the other Bengal remains the Opar Bangla ... The imaginary river, more than dividing, ironically helps connect the two distinct banks as intimate and organic halves.'

11. Edward W. Said, 'Reflections on Exile', *Reflections on Exile and Other Literary and Cultural Essays* (London: Granta Books, 2001, 2012), p. 173.

12. According to the UNHCR report of December 1992 – 'Muslims attacked and burnt down Hindu temples and shops across Bangladesh and disrupted an India–Bangladesh cricket match following the destruction of the Babri Masjid in India by Hindu fundamentalists. About 5,000 young men with rods and bamboo sticks tried to storm Dhaka National Stadium, but they were beaten back by police firing tear gas and rubber bullets. At least 10 people have died, many Hindu women have been raped, and hundreds of Hindu homes and temples have been destroyed.'

3. Borderlands

1. B.S. Baviskar, D.W. Attwood, *Inside-Outside: Two Views of Social Change in Rural India* (New Delhi: Sage Publications, 2013).

2. To read more about Kehkashan cottage, see Aanchal Malhotra, 'How my book brought together two families, divided by Partition and united by a house', Scroll.in, 27 November 2017, https://scroll.in/magazine/856901/how-my-book-brought-together-two-families-divided-by-partition-and-united-by-a-house.

3. Lord Dalhousie first established the town as a sanatorium – a trauma centre – as the British often suffered from ill health. The first Indian who purchased land in these affluent hills was the Maharaja of Jammu and Kashmir, subsequently awarding his property, Kailash, to Justice Bakshi Tek Chand, who represented him in a legal matter in England. In due course, the British began to invite members of Punjabi aristocracy to purchase land in Dalhousie, and most of these families at the time happened to be Muslim. They further invited acquaintances of repute to populate the hill. The local population, however, consisted of Hindu mountain folk.

4. Muhammad Ahmad, *A Mighty Striving* (Ahmadiyya Anjuman Lahore Publications, UK, 2012), p. 347. The subsequent pages of this book mention the presence of Mian Afzal Husain, who ultimately left

Dalhousie on 27 August in a military convoy sent from Lahore. His family, however, had left right after the Partition line was announced.

5. The Bengal Boundary Commission consisted of justices C.C. Biswas, B.K. Mukherji, Abu Saleh Mohamed Akram and S.A. Rahman. The members of the Punjab Commission were justices Mehr Chand Mahajan, Teja Singh, Din Mohamed and Muhammad Munir.

6. Yasmin Khan, *The Great Partition: The Making of India and Pakistan* (Connecticut: Yale University Press, 2007), p. 126.

7. Neha Banka, 'In West Bengal, Some Villages Celebrate Independence Day After August 15; Here's Why', *The Indian Express*, 16 August 2019, https://indianexpress.com/article/research/west-bengal-partition-india-independence-day-5908464/#:~:text=The%20varying%20dates%20on%20which,officially%20removed%20from%20East%20Pakistan.

8. Bishwanath Ghosh, 'Trailing Blood from the Swan's Belly', *The Hindu*, 6 December 2015, https://www.thehindu.com/thread/politics-and-policy/article7955118.ece.

9. When I write to Abhishek a few months after this interview, he tells me that his mother had come to visit him in Malda and he took her for a walk along the Bangladeshi border. 'She was so happy seeing a glimpse of the land her parents and in-laws came from and about which she must have heard countless stories. The highway gantry with the words "Dhaka 351 km" were particularly poignant, and she kept talking about it for the rest of the day,' he wrote back in the email.

10. Dan McDougall, 'The Forgotten Refugees Who Wait for Justice After 60 Years', *The Guardian*, 5 August 2007, https://www.theguardian.com/world/2007/aug/05/india.theobserver.

11. Karuna Ezara Parikh, *The Heart Asks Pleasure First* (New Delhi: Pan Macmillan India, 2020), p. 207.

12. Adam Taylor, 'Say Goodbye to the Weirdest Border Dispute in the World', *The Washington Post*, 1 August 2015, https://www.washingtonpost.com/news/worldviews/wp/2015/08/01/say-goodbye-to-the-weirdest-border-dispute-in-the-world/.

13. 'INDIA AND BANGLADESH: Land Boundary Agreement, 2015', Ministry of External Affairs, Government of India.

14. See Debabrata Saha, 'The Blue Passport', Museum of Material Memory, 28 June 2020, http://www.museumofmaterialmemory.com/the-blue-passport/.

15. Aanchal Malhotra, 'The Inheritance of Ceremonial Servings: The Khaas Daan of Narjis Khatun', *Remnants of a Separation: A History of the*

Partition Through Material Memory (New Delhi: HarperCollins India, 2017, 2018) p. 171.

16. Kuldip Nayar and Asif Noorani, *Tales of Two Cities* (New Delhi: Lotus, 2008).

17. Pran Nevile, *Lahore: A Sentimental Journey* (New Delhi: Penguin Books India, 2006), p. 189. Also see Raza Rumi, *Delhi by Heart: Impressions of a Pakistani Traveller* (New Delhi: HarperCollins India, 2013), pp. 48–49. The music group The Sufi Gospel Project's Sonam Kalra narrates a similar incident from after the 2011 India–Pakistan World Cup semi-final in Mohali, when the Wagah border's gates were thrown open and she saw a gentleman carrying a placard with Daman's famous verses. (Tanushree Ghosh, 'Looking Back in Hope', *The Indian Express*, 2 August 2018, https://indianexpress.com/article/entertainment/entertainment-others/sonam-kalra-india-pakistan-partition-1947/.)

18. Nirupama Dutt, 'Pakistani Poet Who Decried Partition', *Hindustan Times*, 6 August 2017, https://www.hindustantimes.com/punjab/pakistani-poet-who-decried-partition/story-OrVi8zWLe76fxP6UJ2vbSN.html.

19. Saaz Agarwal, 'The Red India-Pakistan Passport', The Songbird on My Shoulder (blog), 30 May 2014, http://thesongbirdonmyshoulder.blogspot.com/2014/05/the-red-india-pakistan-passport.html.

20. Dr Sadhu Chand Vinayek was also a philanthropist, founder of an orphanage and a home for the blind, recognized by a medal awarded by the Indian Red Cross and presented to him by the President of India, Sarvepalli Radhakrishnan.

21. Anam Zakaria, *The Footprints of Partition: Narratives of Four Generations of Pakistanis and Indians* (New Delhi: HarperCollins India, 2015), p. 28.

22. Ibid, p. 27.

4. Discovery

1. Bapsi Sidhwa, *City of Sin and Splendour: Writings on Lahore* (New Delhi: Penguin Books India, 2005).

2. The haveli of Nau Nihal Singh remains of the finest examples of Sikh architecture in Lahore.

3. On 8 March 1947, the *Pakistan Times* newspaper reported that the Hindu residents of Kucha Mela Ram inside Bhati Gate had signed a petition of non-violence.

4. On 2 March 1947, Premier of Punjab (Unionist Party) Malik Khizar Hayat Tiwana resigned at 10.15 p.m. On 3 March, Sikh leader Master Tara Singh came out on the stairs of the Punjab Assembly, Lahore, and declared that they would not concede to Partition, leading to violent demonstrations and riots across the city. A curfew from 8 p.m. to 7 a.m. was declared on 4 March and extended until 8 March 1947. Also see Ian Talbot, *Khizar Tiwana, the Punjab Unionist Party and the Partition of India* (Curzon Press, 1996), p. 161: '...within less than a week of Khizr's resignation, communal violence had reached alarming proportions and the Congress had demanded the partition of the province. For the first time, violence spread from the cities to the countryside and took on the sinister undertones of "ethnic cleansing". Whole villages in the Jhelum, Attock and Rawalpindi districts were put to the sword.'

5. Sardar Prabha Singh Bhalla lived with his family in B-29 Model Town, Lahore. When his eldest daughter got married, he bought her the plot next door, B-30. This house still stands today.

6. Ishtiaq Ahmed, *The Punjab Bloodied, Partitioned and Cleansed* (New Delhi: Rupa Publications, 2011), p. 296.

7. The social activist Anis Kidwai, who worked in the various refugee camps across Delhi, put the number of people in Purana Qila in the month of September at 80,000 to 100,000. The camp served as a base, both for Muslims who wished to go to Pakistan as well as for Hindus and Sikhs coming into India.

8. See the works of Ritu Menon, Kamla Bhasin and Urvashi Butalia.

9. The 1982 Kenyan coup d'état was a failed attempt to overthrow President Daniel arap Moi's government. At 3 a.m. on Sunday, 1 August 1982, a group of soldiers from the Kenya Air Force took over Eastleigh Air Base just outside Nairobi, and by 4 a.m. the nearby Embakasi air base had also fallen. Following the coup d'état attempt to remove President Moi, many Asian shops and businesses in Nairobi were attacked and pillaged. See also, Alan Cowell, 'A Fearful Reminder Lingers for Asians in Kenya', *The New York Times*, 1 September 1982: 'Many Asians say that in the hiatus between the start of the rebellion led by an air force private and the reassertion of Government control, they came face to face with the unleashed hatred of some of Kenya's 16 million African majority.'

10. Kiran Misra, 'Stop Pretending Caste Doesn't Exist', Justice News (web), 16 May 2020. Also see Suraj Yengde, *Caste Matters* (New Delhi: Penguin Random House, 2019).

11. 'Gazetteer of the Dera Ismail Khan District', 1883, pp. 94–95: 'The languages spoken in the Bhakkar and Leiah tahsils and in the larger part of Dera Ismail Khan, and also in parts of Tank and Kulachi, are a dialect of Panjabi, differing very slightly from that in use all over the south Punjab, *viz.*, in Multan, Jhang, Muzaffargarh, Dera Ghazi Khan, Bahawalpur, Shapur and the Isakhel and Mianwali tahsils of Bannu, and merging in Shahpur, Jhang, ang Montgomery into the northern Punjabi. The grammatical forms of the dialect mark it out very distinctly, and its vocabulary in some points approaches Sindhi. This dialect is also understood by a considerable proportion of the people whose mother tongue is Pashtu. It is commonly called Hindi, sometimes Derawali. The name Punjabi is not in use. The enumerators have generally described it as Hindi Desi or Hindi Mulki, and in the Pashtu speaking parts of the country, it is called Hindko by which name the Pathans know it.'

12. H.A. Rose, *A Glossary of the Tribes and Castes of the Punjab and the NWFP*, Vol. III, L-Z (Lahore: Civil and Military Gazette, 1914).

13. Ibid., p. 41.

14. Ibid., p. 417.

15. Maulvi Nur Muhammad, *Tarikh-i-Jhang Siyal* (Meerut: Ahmad Press, 1865).

16. Ibid., p. 418.

5. Family

1. See Anam Zakaria, *1971: A People's History from Bangladesh, Pakistan and India* (New Delhi: Penguin Random House, 2019), p. xvii.

2. Ibid.

3. The erstwhile Princely State of Hyderabad, then made up of sixteen districts that are now part of present-day Maharashtra, Karnataka and all of Telangana, was one of the largest under British India. Its last Nizam, Mir Osman Ali Khan, was once one of the richest men in the world and a Muslim ruler who presided over a largely Hindu population and wanted to remain autonomous. Following Independence, negotiations between the Indian union and his government began, as Hyderabad was surrounded by India, and a Standstill Agreement was signed in November 1947. However, on 17 September 1948, Hyderabad state was annexed by the Indian government in an invasion known as Operation Polo. The operation led to violence on communal

lines, and a commission known as the Sunderlal Committee, headed by a Hindu Congressman, Pandit Sunderlal, was appointed. Its report, which was finally only released in 2013, concluded that 'in the whole state at least 27 thousand to 40 thousand people lost their lives during and after the police action'. For a more detailed account, please see the work of scholar Yunus Y. Lasania at The Hyderabad History Project.

4. Ferya Ilyas, 'Hyderabadi Heritage: Deccan Diaries', *The Express Tribune*, Pakistan, 1 December 2013.

5. Vazira Fazila-Yacoobali Zamindar, *The Long Partition and the Making of Modern South Asia: Refugees, Boundaries, Histories* (New Delhi: Penguin Viking, 2008), p. 234.

6. The 9th Asian Games were held from 19 November to 4 December 1982 in Delhi.

7. The works of CRCI include architectural documentation, historic building conservation planning, projects related to cultural heritage tourism and management, capacity building and training, etc. Having worked with clients like the Archaeological Survey of India, Government of India, and UNESCO, among others, their significant projects include conservation and revitalization management planning for the Gobindgarh Fort and Grand Trunk Road in Punjab, and conservation plans for historic buildings in the Golden Temple complex, Amritsar.

8. From an interview with Gurmeet Sangha Rai in *Platform* magazine by Soumya Mukerji, https://www.platform-mag.com/design/gurmeet-rai-sangha.html.

9. Lepel H. Griffin, *The Punjab Chiefs: Historical and Biographical Notices of the Principal Families in the Territories under the Punjab Government* (Lahore: T.C. McMarthy, Chronicle Press, 1865), pp. 118–19.

10. Raj Kaur was married to Ranjit Singh, the son of Maha Singh of the Sukarchakia *misl*, then one of the most powerful chiefs in Punjab. Upon the rise of Maharaja Ranjit Singh as the first ruler of the great Sikh Empire, Raj Kaur would come to be known as Maharani Datar Kaur or Mai Nakain. Her son, Maharja Kharrak Singh, and grandson, Maharaja Nau Nihal Singh, would later ascend the throne.

11. Griffin, *The Punjab Chiefs*, pp. 120–21.

12. When the Samjauta Express first began in 1976, it was a daily train between Amritsar and Lahore until 1994.

13. Allama Iqbal had, in fact, personally drafted the 1938 marriage deed or *nikahnama* of M.D. Taseer and Christobel George, also known as Bilqis Taseer. Christobel's sister Alys Faiz married Faiz Ahmad Faiz in 1941.

14. Aatish Taseer, *Stranger to History: A Son's Journey Through Islamic Lands* (New Delhi: HarperCollins India, 2009, ed. 2012), p. 52.

15. The announcement of this revocation was made by the official Twitter handle of the Ministry of Home Affairs, Government of India, on 7 November 2019.

16. See Aatish Taseer, 'I Am Indian. Why Is the Government Sending Me into Exile?', *Time* magazine, 7 November 2019.

17. Taseer, *Stranger to History*, p. 55: 'The governments of the two countries parted ways more decisively than the people.'

18. Ibid., p. 54.

19. Ibid., p. 137.

20. Ibid., p. 57.

6. Fear

1. Urvashi Butalia, *The Other Side of Silence: Voices from the Partition of India* (New Delhi: Penguin Books, 1998), p. 5.

2. Nandita Bhavnani, *The Making of Exile: Sindhi Hindus and the Partition of India* (Chennai: Tranquebar Press, 2014), p. 156.

3. Rita Kothari and Jasbirkaur Thadhani, 'Sindhi Sikhs in India: The Missing People', *Journal of South Asian Studies* 39, no. 4 (2016): p. 2: 'A conglomeration of endogamous groups, the Sindhi Sikhs have regional affiliations to Sindh, which, besides other religio-social emphases, help them identify themselves as Bandai, Nawabshahi, Naichan, etc.'

4. Aanchal Malhotra, 'Witnessing a History of Faith Through a Temple Complex in Pakistan', *Travel + Leisure* magazine, 26 September 2019.

5. Hamida Khanam, then a young lecturer at Lady Brabourne College, recollects seeing the looting on that day. 'In the afternoon … around 5.30, I saw a huge crowd coming towards Park Circus … I saw men carrying electric fans, brass utensils … I realized this was not a simple gathering, there was looting going on … just a few moments later I saw people looting a sweet shop on the other side of the road that belonged to a Hindu family. I realized the situation was very grave.' (Partition Tapes, 69, SOAS.)

See also, Debjani Sengupta, 'A City Feeding on Itself: Testimonies, Histories and Literature on "Direct Action Day", Calcutta, 1946', *The Partition of Bengal: Histories and Fictions, 1940s–1960s* (Centre for Historical Studies, Jawaharlal Nehru University, 2010), p. 18: 'The riot that erupted on 16 August came to an end on 19 August, but sporadic outbursts continued throughout 1946 and in the months leading to the Independence. A statement made by Baidyanath Mullick as late as October 1946 showed that the city was still in the grip of fear: "In Benia Pukur Sub area there were disturbances last night (on 28.10.46) ... The Muslim mob set a number of houses on fire. The police came but could not help. In fact, a Muslim officer came and advised the Hindus to run away. Today most of the Hindus fled away from the area."'

6. In *The Great Partition: The Making of India and Pakistan* (Yale University Press, 2008), historian Yasmin Khan puts the causalities of Direct Action Day at 4,000 dead and over 10,000 injured.

7. Phillips Talbot, *An American Witness to India's Partition* (New Delhi: Sage Publications, 2007), p. 192.

8. Ibid., p. 191: 'To escape the wrath of roving mobs, 150,000 people or more left their homes in panic. Some found military escort as they flowed toward neighborhoods in which their own community was in a majority or toward Howrah railway station, whence they hoped to return to their ancestral villages.'

9. Barney White-Spunner, *Partition: The Story of Indian Independence and the Creation of Pakistan in 1947* (London: Simon and Schuster, 2017), p. 11: 'The worst butchery was in the south of the city. As the soldiers moved in, they had to clear over 150 corpses from one crossroads so that they could get their vehicles past. In one bustee or slum area, they found a house with fifteen bodies in the first room and twelve in the second ... The majority of those killed in Calcutta were Hindus.'

7. Friendship

1. Rajmohan Gandhi, *Patel: A Life* (Ahmedabad: Navajivan Trust, 2011), p. 430.

2. Ibid., p. 428.

3. See Raghvendra Singh, *India's Lost Frontier: The Story of North-West Frontier Province of Pakistan* (New Delhi: Rupa Publications, 2019).

4. As I listen to Garima Kumar list city after city on her grandmother's journey to finding 'home', a place in the world that she can call hers, I am reminded of these lines from Ismat Chugtai's 'Roots': 'Own country? Of what feather is that bird? And tell me, good people, where does one find it? That place one is born in, that soil which has nurtured us, if that is not our country, can an abode of a few days hope to be it? And then, who knows, we could be pushed out of there too, and told to find a new home, a new country … Is it a country or an uncomfortable shoe? If it pinches, exchange it for another!'

5. Nina Sabnani, *Mukand and Riaz* (film), 2005.

6. Aanchal Malhotra, 'The Good Samaritans of 4, Fane Road', *Mint Lounge*, 15 February 2020. This story first appeared in the 'Love Thy Neighbour' issue: The trial for the Lahore Conspiracy Case began on 10 July 1929 in Borstal Jail, Lahore, where Bhagat Singh and twenty-seven others were charged with murder and waging war against King George V. The average age of the revolutionaries was twenty-two. Their case was presided over by judge Rai Sahib Pandit Sri Kishen, and the accused were defended by a body of seven prominent Indian lawyers, among whom was Amolak Ram Kapur.

7. Khurshid Mahmud Kasuri, *Neither a Hawk Nor a Dove* (New Delhi: Penguin Viking, 2015), p. 19.

8. Ibid., pp. 79–81.

9. Ibid., p. 82.

10. Swaran Lata Kapoor's maternal grandfather used to be the leading trader of rice in Lahore, and the family now runs Shyam di Hatti in Khan Market, Delhi.

11. Through a conversation with his great-great-granddaughter, Samrata Diwan, founder of the Family Fables Co., a bespoke publishing company documenting family, personal and institutional history, I learn about Pandit Girdhari Lal Salwan and the Salwan Sanatan Dharam High School, started in Peshawar in 1943, with Mehr Chand Khanna among the first members of the school Managing Committee. During Partition, Pandit Girdhari Lal Salwan was deeply involved in the peacekeeping activities, spearheading the interests of the Hindu and Sikh minorities. After Partition, in 1948, the Salwan School was restarted in Rajendra Nagar, a new resettlement colony named after the first President of India, Dr Rajendra Prasad, where people were largely living in tents on a monthly allowance. This first school for the refugees' children was also started in tents and had over 3,000

students. The school operated in two shifts: the morning one for girls and the evening one for boys. Many of the teachers, including older ones who had migrated from Peshawar, were refugees themselves. The first principal of Salwan Boys School, Dina Nath Dutta, was a refugee. Rajni Kumar, the Chairperson of Springdales Education Society, was the principal of Salwan Girls School.

12. The Citizenship Amendment Act (CAA) was passed by the Parliament of India on 11 December 2019. It amended the Citizenship Act of 1955 by providing a pathway to Indian citizenship for persecuted religious minorities from the neighbouring countries of Afghanistan, Bangladesh and Pakistan who are Hindu, Sikh, Parsi, Buddhist, Jain or Christian, and who arrived in India before the end of December 2014. Notably absent from the list of religions was Islam, which according to the last census of 2011 was the second largest religion of India, practised by 14.2 per cent of the country's population, or roughly 172 million people.

8. Grief

1. Holland Cotter, 'Zarina Hashmi, Artist of a World in Search of Home, Dies at 82', *The New York Times*, 5 May 2020, https://www.nytimes.com/2020/05/05/arts/zarina-hashmi-dead.html. In her memoir, *Directions to My House* (New York: Asian/Pacific/American Institute, New York University, 2018), co-written with Sarah Burney, she writes, 'These memories formed how I think about a lot of things: fear, separation, migration, the people you know, or think you know.'

2. An interview with Zarina Hashmi by Courtney A. Stewart, Senior Research Assistant, Department of Islamic Art, The Metropolitan Museum of Art, 9 February 2017.

3. Zehra Jumabhoy, 'Zarina Hashmi (1937–2020): An Artist Whose Work Is Woven with Ideas of Displacement and Mobility', *Scroll*, 29 April 2020, https://scroll.in/article/960503/zarina-hashmi-1937-2020-an-artist-whose-work-is-woven-with-ideas-of-displacement-and-mobility.

4. Agha Shahid Ali, 'I See Kashmir from New Delhi at Midnight', *The Veiled Suite: The Collected Poems* (New Delhi: Penguin Books, 2010).

5. Fatimah Asghar, *If They Come for Us* (New York: One World, 2018), p. 23.

6. Lawrence L. Langer, 'The Alarmed Vision: Social Suffering and Holocaust Atrocity', in Veena Das, Arthur Kleinman, Margaret M.

Lock (eds.) *Social Suffering* (Berkeley: University of California Press, 1997), pp. 47–66.

7. Report regarding train running and programme on the Eastern Punjab Railway for 3, 4 and 5 November 1947, No.RT/29/1, New Delhi, 4 November 1947, Ministry of Railways, Government of India.

9. Hope

1. The play *Six Degrees of Separation*, written by John Guare, premiered on 16 May 1990 at the Mitzi E. Newhouse Theatre in New York City. It explores the existential premise that everyone in the world is connected to everyone else in the world by a chain of no more than six acquaintances.

2. The Delhi College of Engineering was set up in 1938 at Kashmere Gate, from where it functioned for nearly sixty years until 1996.

3. Visit @thesingingsingh on Instagram to explore stories from The Lost Heer Project.

4. The Ghadar Party was founded on 15 July 1913 in Astoria, Oregon, by early Indian immigrants settled in North America. Their motive was to overthrow British colonialism in India.

5. Tim Harper, *Underground Asia: Global Revolutionaries and the Assault on Empire* (Cambridge: Harvard University Press, 2021), p. 254. Also see George Morton Jack, *The Indian Empire at War: From Jihad to Victory – The Untold Story of the Indian Army in the First World War* (Boston: Little, Brown, 2018), p. 237: '…prosecutions and punishments of Ghadarite Indian soldiers of the 23rd Cavalry … not by traditional court martial but by special tribunal under the Defence of India Act of 1915. [This] gave the Government of India powers to detain without proof suspects of terrorism and political crimes, including inciting hatred and mutiny, and to try them forthwith by special tribunal with no right of appeal to sentences, including death sentences.'

6. In 1905, when Queen Mary visited India as the Princess of Wales, she was invited to a purdah party in the gardens.

7. Harleen adds here that 'majority of its early students were girls from Punjab, who were housed in special hostels set up for them. It was a bold move by many families in Punjab, who sent out their daughters to Delhi. Oftentimes, the entire families relocated to Delhi temporarily. Other times, it was only a male relative who would accompany the girls. In 1924, when the first batch of female doctors graduated from

its college, Punjab got its first female native doctor and Sikhs their first Sikh "doctor-ani".'

8. Gulzar, *Footprints on Zero Line: Writings on the Partition* (New Delhi: HarperCollins India, 2017).

9. The then Information Minister of Pakistan, Mushahid Hussain Syed, had called the then Prime Minister of India Atal Bihari Vajpayee's Minar-e-Pakistan visit the 'biggest event' between India and Pakistan.

10. 'Aman ki Asha', or Hope for Peace, is an initiative that aims to develop peace between India and Pakistan. Established in 2010, it is a joint campaign by two media houses, the Jang Group of Pakistan, and *The Times of India* in India.

11. Beena Sarwar, 'Why Atal Bihari Vajpayee Was a Man of Peace', *Daily O*, 17 September 2018.

10. Identity

1. Roger Pearce, *Once a Happy Valley: Memoirs of an ICS Officer in Sindh, 1938–1948* (Oxford University Press, 2001).

2. I borrow the term 'vanished homeland' from Saaz Agarwal's biography of her family in pre-Partition Sindh titled *Sindh: Stories from a Vanished Homeland* (Pune: Black and White Fountain, 2012).

3. Rita Kothari, *Unbordered Memories: Sindhi Stories of Partition* (New Delhi: Penguin Books, 2009). In the Introduction to the text, Kothari illuminates how 'Sindhi narratives are essentially transborder and are not confined by religious and national identities.'

4. Priya Kumar and Rita Kothari, 'Sindh, 1947 and Beyond', *Journal of South Asian Studies*, Vol. 39, No. 4 (2016): p. 775: 'A large majority of Sindhi Hindus were Nanakpanthis – followers of Guru Nanak [and] … Sindhi tikanas (places of worship) often contained images of Guru Nanak and the Guru Granth Sahib along with those of Hindu deities … there is a lot of evidence that the majority of Hindus in Sindh were murids (followers) of the Sufi pirs (saints) who had played a very important role in Sindhi Islam … Sufism created an ethos for Hindus in which they did not think of Islam as inimical … [And] Sindhi Muslims, in turn, participated in the worship of the samadhi of Hindu saints.'

5. Sheba Remy Kharbanda's *Five Rivers: A Portrait of Partition*, installed at the India Habitat Centre in Delhi, 2014, can be viewed at http://www.shebaremy.com/installation/.

6. *The Vilayati Tarti/Foreign Land Project* by Sheba Remy Kharbanda can be found on vimeo.

7. *Doctor Who*, Season 11, Episode 6 – Demons of the Punjab.

8. Binayak Dutta, 'Lest We Forget: The Many Partitions and Their Legacies in Northeast India', *Partition Studies Quarterly*, No. 01 (25 November 2019).

9. Nitish Sengupta, *Land of Two Rivers: A History of Bengal from the Mahabharata to Mujib* (London: Penguin UK, 2011): Suhrawardy, leader of the Muslim League, was completely unprepared for a Pakistan that may not include the city of Calcutta. 'He appealed to the Hindus to accept his proposal ... [and] announced that "independent Bengal will frame its own constitution and its Legislative Assembly will take the final decision in the matter. We Bengalis have a common mother tongue and common economic interest."' Suhrawardy also addressed a press conference in Delhi on 27 April 1947 to make a case for an undivided and sovereign Bengal.

10. See Samrat Choudhury, *The Braided River: A Journey Along the Brahmaputra* (New Delhi: HarperCollins India, 2021).

11. Sanjib Baruah, 'Partition and the Politics of Citizenship in Assam', in ed. Urvashi Butalia, *Partition: The Long Shadow* (New Delhi: Penguin Random House India, 2015), p. 83.

12. Haimanti Roy, *Partitioned Lives: Migrants, Refugees, Citizens in India and Pakistan, 1947–1965* (New Delhi: Oxford University Press, 2012), p. 64: From a resolution dated 3 April 1948 – 'More frequently, the border severed villages from the markets that served them, forcing villagers of one dominion to cross the border to access items for their daily use ... The local Muslim League condemned the situation in which villagers at the Sylhet border had to travel across the international border to the local bazaar at Dawki to purchase *paan* (betel leaf), and orange, pineapple and rice saplings, where they faced harassment from the Indian border officials.'

13. See Subir Bhaumik, Samir Purkayastha, Samrat Choudhury, 'Media Factsheet on Issues of Citizenship in the Northeast', Calcutta Research Group, 2020.

14. K.C. Chakravarti, 'Assam Disturbances: I, Bongal Kheda Again', *The Economic Weekly*, 30 July 1960.

15. Samrat Choudhury, 'After Amnesia', *RAIOT*, 8 December 2015.

16. The journal can be read at https://partitionstudiesquarterly.org/ and is co-founded by Amrita Gupta Singh, Samrat Choudhury and Binayak Dutta.

17. Since Partition, Muslims have constituted the largest religious minority in India, making up 14.23 per cent of the country, according to the last census in 2011. In Pakistan, as calculated by the most recent census in 2017, Hindus constitute the largest religious majority at 1.73 per cent of the total population.

18. Aatish Taseer, 'India Is No Longer India: Exile in the time of Modi', *The Atlantic*, May 2020.

19. September and October 2008 saw a wave of attacks, by Hindu organizations such as the Bajrang Dal and Sri Ram Sena, directed against Christian churches and prayer halls in Mangalore city and its surrounding areas.

20. Zeba Talkhani, *My Past Is a Foreign Country* (London: Sceptre, Hodder & Stoughton, Hachette, 2019, 2020), p. 96.

21. Ibid., p. 95.

22. Gyanendra Pandey, 'Can a Muslim Be an Indian?' *Comparative Studies in Society and History*, Vol. 41, No. 4 (Cambridge University Press, October 1999): p. 618.

23. Ibid., p. 621.

24. Ibid., p. 624.

25. In a *Hindustan Times* photo piece on Mithi from 10 October 2018, Sunil Kumar, a thirty-five-year-old businessman and resident, says, 'Since I was old enough to reason, I have witnessed fraternity, love and harmony between Hindus and Muslims. That has been going on for generations of our forefathers … it shall go on forever.' Along with a photograph of the Sri Krishna temple, the caption reads that 'not a single guard is employed, in sharp contrast to the Hindu neighbourhoods in the megacity of Karachi, some 300 kilometres away, which are under armed surveillance'.

26. Initial tensions between Sindhis and *muhajirs* grew over the question of language, and eventually, by the late 1970s, over the existing quota system, which facilitated Sindhis gaining government employment and admission to educational institutions. By 1984, Altaf Hussain created the Muhajir Quami Party (MQM), or the Muhajir People's Party, to protect and defend the community's interests from discrimination.

11. Legacy

1. Aanchal Malhotra, 'Exploring the Stories, Legends, and Myths of Lahore', *The Indian Express*, 16 December 2018. Also see Tania Qureshi, 'Partition and Gobind Ram', *Pakistan Today*, 6 August 2017.

2. *Buniyad* is a 1986-87 Indian television serial directed by Ramesh Sippy and Jyoti, and written by Manohar Shyam Joshi. It dealt with the Partition of India in 1947 and its aftermath.

3. Marianne Hirsch, *The Generation of Postmemory: Writing and Visual Culture After the Holocaust* (New York: Columbia University Press, 2012), p. 13.

4. Narayani Basu, *V.P. Menon: The Unsung Architect of Modern India* (New Delhi: Simon & Schuster, 2020).

5. Ibid., p. xi.

6. Narayani Basu, 'How Do You Write a Biography', *Contingent Magazine*, 21 May 2020.

7. Here, Narayani also mentions that many of her other relatives who were married into public families maintained a veneer of silence or privacy when it came to speaking about the events surrounding Independence or Partition. Her grandmother Premilla's elder sister, Bimla, was married to General P.N. Thapar, the fourth chief of staff, Indian Army; elder brother, Narottam Sahgal, a district collector, was married to Sarla, the daughter of Sir J.P. Srivastava; and brother, Gautum, was married to Nayantara Sahgal of the Nehru family. Premilla was married to Anantan, or Angu, VP's eldest son, in 1951. See Basu, pp. 419–20.

8. See the official papers of Vapal Pangunni Menon, accessible at the National Archives of India.

9. V.P. Menon, interview with H.V. Hodson, School of Oriental and African Studies, London, 1965.

10. Basu, pp. 158–59.

11. See H.V. Hodson, *The Great Divide: Britain–India–Pakistan* (London: Hutchinson & Co., 1969).

12. Ibid., p. xii.

13. Here, I am reminded of Kamleshwar's *Partitions*, originally written in Hindi as *Kitne Pakistan* and translated by Ameena Kazi Ansari (New Delhi: Penguin Books India, 2006). On page 95, Kamleshwar writes: 'Jinnah sahib did not create history; history created him ... Don't set the cauldron of religion over the flames of history.'

14. Basu, p. 325.

15. Mehr Chand Mahajan was born on 23 December 1889 in Kangra (present-day Himachal Pradesh), where his father, Lala Brij Lal, was an advocate. Mahajan graduated from Government College, Lahore, in 1910 and earned an LLB degree in 1912, beginning his law career the following year in Dharamsala. His appointments took him to

Gurdaspur and Lahore from 1914 to 1943. He served as the Prime Minister of Jammu and Kashmir from 1947-48, upon the invitation of the maharaja, after which he served as a judge in the Supreme Court from 1948 to 1954, and took final office as the third Chief Justice of India in 1954.

16. See V.N. Datta, 'The Punjab Boundary Commission Award (12 August 1947)', *Proceedings of the Indian History Congress*, Vol. 59 (1998): pp. 850–62.

17. Mehr Chand Mahajan, *Looking Back* (New Delhi: Har Anand Publications Pvt. Ltd, revised ed. 2018), pp. 114–17.

18. When the government neighbourhoods around Khan Market in Lutyens' Delhi were first built, they were known as Maan Nagar and Shaan Nagar, befitting the government officers they were meant to house. They were later renamed Bharati Nagar, after the Tamil poet Subramania Bharati, and Rabindra Nagar, after Nobel laureate Rabindranath Tagore.

19. Yashpal, trans. Anand, *This Is Not That Dawn* (New Delhi: Penguin India, 2010). The English title of Yashpal's original Hindi novel, *Jhootha Sach*, is borrowed from the lines of Faiz Ahmd Faiz's poem 'Subh-e-Azadi', which read, '*Yeh vo sahar toh nahin*'.

20. Karan Mahajan, 'India's Forgotten Feminist Epic,' *New Yorker*, 27 March 2015.

21. Yashpal, p. xvii.

22. Ria and Sanjana Chopra, 'Train to India', Museum of Material Memory, 7 June 2020, https://museumofmaterialmemory.com/train-to-india/.

23. Ibid.

12. Loss

1. Aanchal Malhotra, *Remnants of A Separation: A History of Partition Through Material Memory* (New Delhi: HarperCollins India, 2017, ed. 2018), pp. 10–11.

2. Ibid., p. 29.

3. See Fakir Khana Museum, Google Arts & Culture.

4. Fakir Syed Aijazuddin, *The Resourceful Fakirs: Three Muslim Brothers at the Sikh Court of Lahore* (New Delhi: Variety Book Depot, 2020).

5. Farhan Ahmed Shah, 'Legends of Lahore', *The Express Tribune*, 26 October 2012.

6. Edward Said, *Culture and Imperialism* (New York: Vintage, 1993), p. 336: 'No one today is purely *one* thing ... Yet just as human beings make their own history, they also make their cultures and ethnic identities. No one can deny the persisting continuities of long traditions, sustained habitations, national languages, and cultural geographies, but there seems no reason except fear and prejudice to keep insisting on their separation and distinctiveness, as if that was all human life was about.'

7. Fatima Bhutto, 'From Lahore to Amritsar', *Condé Nast Traveller*, 9 October 2015.

8. See Ali Usman Qasmi and Megan Eaton Robb (eds), *Muslims Against the Muslim League: Critiques of the Idea of Pakistan* (New Delhi: Cambridge University Press, 2017).

9. See Pallavi Raghavan, *Animosity at Bay: An Alternative History of the India–Pakistan Relationship, 1947–1952* (New Delhi: HarperCollins India, 2020).

10. Nehmat Kaur, 'Reimagining Indo-Pak History in a Borderless Place', *The Wire*, 27 May 2018.

11. A large number of Kashmiri Muslims migrated from the Kashmir Valley to the Punjab due to grave conditions such as famine, ill treatment and extreme poverty during the Sikh and Dogra rule. According to the 1911 census, there were 1,77,549 Kashmiri Muslims in the Punjab. Also see, Chitralekha Zutshi, *Languages of Belonging: Islam, Regional Identity and the Making of Kashmir* (London: C. Hurst & Co. Publishers, 2004).

12. Kavita Panjabi, 'A Unique Grace', in Urvashi Butalia (ed.), *Partition: The Long Shadow* (New Delhi: Penguin Books India, 2015), p. 51.

13. Fikr Taunsvi, trans. Maaz Bin Bilal, *The Sixth River: A Journal from the Partition of India* (New Delhi: Speaking Tiger, 2019), p. 94.

14. *Halfway to Freedom: A Report on the New India in the Words and Photographs of Margaret Bourke-White* (New York: Simon and Schuster, 1949), pp. 5–6.

15. See Malhotra, pp. 365–384; Bal K. Gupta, *Forgotten Atrocities: Memoirs of a Survivor of the 1947 Partition of India* (2012); Krishna Mehta, *Chaos in Kashmir* (Calcutta: Signet Press, 1954); Andrew Whitehead, *A Mission in Kashmir* (New Delhi: Penguin Books, 2008).

16. Maximilien-François-Marie-Isidore de Robespierre (born 6 May 1758, Arras, France – died 28 July 1794, Paris) was a Jacobin leader and one of the principal figures in the French Revolution.

17. Ritu Menon and Kamla Bhasin, 'Recovery, Rupture, Resistance: Indian State and the Abduction of Women during Partition, *Economic and Political Weekly* (24 April 1993): p. 2.

18. Urvashi Butalia, 'Women', in *The Other Side of Silence: Voices from the Partition of India* (New Delhi: Penguin Books, 1998), pp. 106–71.

19. Malhotra, p. 368.

20. See Bal K. Gupta.

21. When fighting broke out in Punjab, the ICRC, which had closed down the delegation that it had maintained in British India since the Second World War, had no local representative. When its attention was drawn to the terrible plight of the refugees, it decided, in late 1947, to send Dr Otto Wenger, who had been a delegate in British India from 1943 to 1947, and he carried out many visits to camps for Italian and German prisoners of war and civilian internees. According to lCRC archives, file G 3/37c, Letter No. 6 of 27 February 1948 from Dr Wenger states that his efforts had achieved the following results:

    '1. The immediate dispatch of aid, by the Pakistan Red Cross, and of medical personnel, by the Christian Relief Association, to the Alibeg Camp. The ICRC delegate had visited this camp, situated in "Azad Kashmir" near the border with Pakistan. It housed 1,600 non-Muslims living in appalling conditions.

    2. Pakistan's agreement to arrange for the evacuation through its territory of all non-Muslims trapped in 'Azad Kashmir' who wished to go to India, and its commitment to supply the camps experiencing the most difficult conditions with provisions in the meantime.

    3. The consent of 'Azad Kashmir' to the departure of non-Muslims who wished to leave.

    This agreement covered about 5,000 civilians, some free and some interned, 2,500 of whom were in Muzaffarabad, 1,600 in Alibeg, 125 in Gobindpar and 700–800 in Bagh.' (International Review of the Red Cross, June 1998).

22. This is an edited excerpt from my essay, 'There Are No More Places to Migrate To', *Departures in Critical Qualitative Research*, Vol. 8, No. 1 (University of California Press, Spring 2019): pp. 42–49.

23. Ragini Kashyap's maternal grandfather, Col. R.C. Kapur, was the grandson of Bawa Dinga Singh, one of Lahore's largest businessmen at the time. They lived in a grand haveli with 101 rooms, which is now a state guest house in Lahore. Ragini tells me how her great-grandmother

was widowed during her pregnancy, so her grandfather, born after his father's death, was raised in his maternal home – Bawa Dinga Singh's home. Recently, she joined a Facebook group on the heritage buildings of Lahore and found a photo posted by someone of Bawa Dinga Singh's original, smaller haveli. Ragini commented on it, and the person who responded – a Pakistani Muslim – was from the family who still lived there. The story goes that at the time of Partition, the Singhs gave the haveli to this gentleman's family as trusted custodians of the building (but entirely for their own use). Out of gratitude and respect, the family never got rid of the home temple or changed the structure of the haveli. 'The experience, albeit online, was both surreal and a little chilling, if I'm being honest,' Ragini writes.

24. The Third Culture Cooks, 'Partition 73: Mian Tariq Mustafa on Memories of 1947 and the Birth of Pakistan', YouTube, 9 September 2020.

13. Love

1. The trajectory of Captain Anwar's career, even before he met Susmita Roy, was nothing short of extraordinary. In 1935, he was admitted as a cadet to Dufferin, a British merchant marine training ship, where he was awarded the Sawyer Prize and obtained an 'Extra First Class' certificate. Thereafter, he joined the British India Steam Navigation (BISN) Company. In 1940, he took up flying and joined the Civil Air Reserved Corps as a trainee. In 1941, he received his pilot's 'A License' from the Bihar Flying Club and subsequently became an instructor. In 1945, he received his 'Pilot B Commercial License'. Thereafter, until his death in 1959, he worked as a commercial pilot.

2. Zulfiquar Rahman, 'Remembering Captain Mustafa Anwar', *The Daily Star*, 25 July 2017: 'Captain Anwar's flourishing career came to an untimely end on 14 August 1959, when he died in a plane crash ... At the time of his death, he was forty-one years old. Captain Anwar was laid to rest at the Azimpur graveyard in Dhaka. His death was reported not only locally but also in newspapers such as *The Guardian* and *The New York Times*.'

3. Sudeep Chakravarti, *The Bengalis: A Portrait of a Community* (New Delhi: Aleph, 2017), p. 7: '...hagiography sometimes makes it appear as if nothing of import existed before 1971, the year Bangladesh was born, the year Bongobondhu, Friend of Bengal, won independence from Pakistan on the back of his charisma, an unstoppable momentum

of identity politics that created history over the blood sacrifice of an estimated 3 million Bangladeshis and the generous help of India.'

4. K. Anis Ahmed, 'Why Do Bangladeshis Seem Indifferent Towards Partition?' *The New York Times*, 16 August 2017.

5. Ravinder Kaur, *Since 1947: Partition Narratives Among Punjabi Migrants of Delhi* (New Delhi: Oxford University Press, 2007), p. 99. In an interview with a refugee from D.I. Khan, Kaur notes, 'The ones who could afford their own rations would be allotted Hudson and Reeds Lines barracks, while those who could not would be sent to Edward and Outram Lines. The latter would be housed in cloth tents from World War II, while the former were settled in concrete barracks.'

6. For the duration of this course, she lived in a hostel on Curzon Road, where she met another young woman, Shubh, who remained one of her best friends for life. My grandmother graduated top of her class and, to celebrate, my great-grandmother bought her a Singer sewing machine, which – on her teacher's salary of Rs 150 per month – would have been about five months' savings.

7. L.C. Jain, *Civil Disobedience: Two Freedom Struggles, One Life* (The Book Review Literary Trust, 2011), pp. 70–72.

8. Aanchal Malhotra, *Remnants of A Separation: A History of Partition Through Material Memory* (New Delhi: HarperCollins India, 2017, ed. 2018), p. 8.

Also see, Kuldip Nayar and Asif Noorani, *Tales of Two Cities* (New Delhi: Lotus Collection, Roli Books, 2018): 'It was quite customary for people when meeting someone for the first time to find out from which part of India they had migrated. If they belonged to the same city, the next question was about the locality where they used to live. All such conversations acquired a tinge of nostalgia. Favours were granted to each other. Shops were named after the original cities of the shopkeepers. The trend changed after the sixties, but Karachi has retained outlets like Benares Silk House, Madras Jewellers, Ambala Sweets, Lucknow Chat House, Aligarh Bakery and Pilibhit Oil Depot.'

9. Rizwana Shamshad, *Bangladeshi Migrants in India: Foreigners, Refugees, or Infiltrators?* (New Delhi: Oxford University Press, 2017): 'The refugees from East Bengal were called Bangals by the older natives of Kolkata, while the native West Bengalis were called Ghotis by East Bengalis. This divide is based on the territory of the older East and West Bengal created after the British Partition of 1905. The River Padma is also regarded to be a central geographic boundary by all Bengalis.'

14. Memory

1. The contents of this envelope include: a sepia print of her father, Hari Chand Gulyani, who died when my grandmother was only a child; two photographs of her mother, Lajvanti Gulyani, one taken on either side of the border; a very handsome studio portrait of my grandfather, Balraj, in his youth; a stamped passport picture of Swaran Lata; the tiny sepia photo from Kingsway Camp; and one of her younger siblings, Madan Mohan and Dharam, where they look near identical. I know this last one is taken in D.I. Khan, because Madan died in 1948, shortly after the family migrated to Delhi.

2. Besides Panjab University, several young refugees also took classes at Delhi University, completing degrees that had been left half finished. See L.C. Jain, *Civil Disobedience: Two Freedom Struggles, One Life* (New Delhi: The Book Review Literary Trust, 2011), p. 71: 'There was the case of students who could not finish their degrees in Pakistan. Each camp had a certain number of these students. They were told by Delhi University that if they did social work in any of the relief camps, they would certify the students and give them the degree. So, 400 to 500 youngsters registered as volunteers.'

3. Marianne Hirsch, *The Generation of Postmemory: Writing and Visual Culture After the Holocaust* (New York: Columbia University Press, 2012), p. 34.

4. Edmund de Waal, *The Hare with Amber Eyes: A Hidden Inheritance* (London: Vintage Books, 2011) p. 347.

5. Ibid.

6. Björn Krondorfer, 'Is Forgetting Reprehensible? Holocaust Remembrance and the Task of Oblivion', *The Journal of Religious Ethics*, Vol. 36, No. 2 (June 2008): p. 237.

7. Urvashi Butalia, *The Other Side of Silence: Voices from the Partition of India* (New Delhi: Penguin Books, ed. 2017).

8. Amnah Shaukat, 'A City Under Water', *The Friday Times*, 26 January 2018.

9. Hirsch, p. 2.

10. Hirsch (2012), as cited in Sue Vice, 'Memory Thieves?: Representing Dementia in Holocaust Literature', *English Language Notes*, Vol. 57, No. 2 (1 October 2019): pp. 114–26.

11. See Judy M. Zarit, Nancy K. Orr, and Steven H. Zarit, *The Hidden Victims of Alzheimer's Disease: Families under Stress* (New York: New York University Press, 1985).

12. See Kavita Puri, *Partition Voices: Untold British Stories* (New Delhi: Bloomsbury Publishing, 2019), p. 207: 'In *Rootless*, Dr Veena Dhillion's father says, "Dharam was very unwilling to talk about partition: he was quite traumatised by it. It was only when he developed Parkinson's disease and dementia in the final part of his life that he started to speak of those times."' Also see, Anirudh Kala, *The Unsafe Asylum: Stories of Partition and Madness* (New Delhi: Speaking Tiger Books, 2018); eds. Sanjeev Jain and Alok Sarin, *The Psychological Impact of the Partition of India* (New Delhi: Sage Publications, 2018); John Upchurch, *Mango Dreams* (2016), a film.

13. Securing one of the many trunks that accompanied the Khannas from Multan to Lucknow was an old lock and key, still used to lock their home in Delhi today.

14. See Devika Chawla, *Home, Uprooted: Oral Histories of India's Partition* (New York: Fordham University Press, 2014). The final section of her book is titled 'My Father, My Interlocutor', where she explores the role her father, Sudhakar Chawla, takes on in her field research. It is he who introduces Devika to several people she interviews for the book, either through personal or familial contacts: 'As my now seventy-two-year-old Papa, who was six when the family left Pakistan, partook in the interviews, he himself felt encouraged to remember, eventually taking us both into the crevasses of some of our own family history, portions of which would have remained unremembered but for this project. (p. 34)' Here, the 'father/interlocutor–daughter/ethnographer duo' is what exhumes the memories of Partition together.

15. Pran Nevile, *K.L. Saigal: The Definitive Biography* (New Delhi: Penguin Books, 2011). An advertisement in *The Tribune* in December 1937 invites the public to meet their favourite star, K.L. Saigal, in person at the All India Exhibition at Variety Theatre, Minto Park, Lahore. Interestingly, also present that day was a young Mohammed Rafi, whose singing talent was to be recognized on a grand scale during his performance at the exhibition. It is said that K.L. Saigal had predicted then and there that Rafi would become a singing sensation.

16. Series 2, *Three Pounds in My Pocket*, BBC Radio 4, 2015.

17. 'Partition Voices: The Untold Stories of British Asians and Colonial British Who Witnessed India's Partition', BBC Radio 4 Series, 2017, https://www.bbc.co.uk/sounds/series/b090rrl2.

18. Puri, pp. 254–56.

19. Ibid., p. 258.

20. Sanam Maher, *The Sensational Life and Death of Qandeel Baloch* (New Delhi: Aleph Book Company, 2018). Also see, 'Divided Lands', a panel with Arif Anwar, Sanam Maher and Kavita Puri, chaired by Paul Barclay at the Adelaide Festival, March 2020.

21. Puri, pp. 259–60: Ravi Datt Puri had one last request: that upon his death, all religions, not just Hinduism, must be reflected. At the end of his life, he chose inclusion and not division. Therefore, at the service, a Sikh friend read the 'Mul Mantar', and a British Pakistani friend, Hafeez Sheikh, recited a Muslim prayer. His first boss, Vincent Thomas, a devout Methodist, would often take Puri to church, and so, to mark his influence, Kavita's sister-in-law read a Methodist funeral prayer. Kavita's father-in-law, wearing a yarmulke, spoke the ancient Aramic words of the Kaddish, the Jewish prayer of death.

15. Material Memory

1. 'The Necklace That Divided Two Nations', 'Museum of Lost Objects, presented by Kanishk Tharoor', BBC Radio 4, 15 July 2017.

2. Larry Collins and Dominique Lapierre, *Freedom at Midnight: The Epic Drama of India's Struggle for Independence* (New Delhi: Vikas Publishing House Ltd, 1960), pp. 168–70.

3. 'The Necklace That Divided Two Nations', BBC Radio 4.

4. Ibid.

5. Also see Nayanjot Lahiri, 'The Past Is a Divided Country', *Open* magazine, 10 August 2017: Lahiri details how it was Mortimer Wheeler, who had just completed his term as director general of the ASI in India and had become archeological advisor to the government of Pakistan, who suggested that articles be divided with absolute equity. 'That this suggestion was accepted (with the division being eventually done by Wheeler himself), looking back some seventy years later, was tragic. A magnificent Mohenjodaro necklace [was] ... divided down the middle because a formula was foisted unthinkingly ... Oddly enough, nowhere in the correspondence relating to this is there a sense that the character of these objects was being permanently destroyed. There is, instead, an overriding anxiety about carefully adhering to the arithmetic of division.'

6. Aanchal Malhotra, *Remnants of a Separation: A History of the Partition Through Material Memory* (New Delhi: HarperCollins India, 2017, ed. 2018), p. 4.

7. Ibid, p. 26.

8. Yasmin Khan, *The Great Partition: The Making of India and Pakistan* (London: Yale University Press, 2007), p. 147: 'The Urdu writer Masud Hasan Shahab Dehlvi, who was living in Delhi at the time, was married in the weeks preceding Partition and had to procure curfew passes for his wedding guests, some of whom faced difficulties returning home after the celebrations.' Also see Richard Symonds, *In the Margins of Independence: A Relief Worker in India and Pakistan, 1942–1949* (London: Oxford University Press, 2001), p. 33: 'The Delhi in which I arrived on 11 September appeared physically and nervously shattered. Stabbing and looting had spread from the narrow streets of Old Delhi to the broad boulevards of Lutyens Delhi … There was a rigid curfew after 6 p.m.'

9. Shah Nawaz Khan (January 1914 – 9 December 1983) was an Indian politician who served as an officer in the Indian National Army during the Second World War. After the war, he was tried, convicted for treason, and sentenced to death alongside General Prem Sahgal and Colonel Gurbaksh Singh Dhillon in a public court martial carried out by the British Indian Army at Red Fort, Delhi. The sentence was commuted following unrest and protests in India. Also see, Malhotra, p. 394.

10. Mayank Austen Soofi, 'City Monument – General Shah Nawaz Khan's Grave, Old Delhi', *The Delhi Walla*, 6 February 2021 (web): 'Among those who care for graves of historical people, it is common knowledge that the shrine of Sufi saint Hazrat Sarmad Shahid lies between the Jama Masjid and the Red Fort in Old Delhi. Some might even know that the grave of freedom fighter Maulana Abul Kalam Azad lies between these two monuments as well. But very few will be aware that the area is also home to the grave of General Shah Nawaz Khan.'

11. See www.sabaqizilbash.com.

12. Edmund de Waal, *The Hare with Amber Eyes: A Hidden Inheritance* (London: Vintage, 2011), p. 17.

13. By the time Saba and Mujtaba's *walima* ceremony took place, her mother had had a relapse and needed surgery done only at Apollo Hospital, New Delhi. Saba was due to graduate from RISD and Mujtaba had just finished his degree from UC Berkeley. The pair dropped everything and flew out to New Delhi. Saba's brothers and mother flew in from Lahore. In the meantime, Mujtaba – through his aunt – managed to find the family an annex to rent in Delhi's Maharani Bagh neighbourhood. The landlord lived on the property, and Saba

noticed the mail that would arrive for the tenant on the floor above always bore the title 'Princess'. She recalls it feeling so familiar, yet so different. They stayed at the Apollo Hospital for over a month, and were quite the celebrities there. In a gap week between the treatment, Mujtaba's family organized a *walima* ceremony, akin to a wedding reception. Saba writes to me of the trip: 'Every male cousin from Mujtaba's family came to the airport to receive us. My mother-in-law, in customary Kashmiri fashion, fed my mother *khatais*, plum cakes, walnut pastries.'

14. 'India: Written in Blood', *TIME* magazine, 28 October 1946, p. 42: 'Mobs in the Noakhali district of East Bengal ... burned, looted and massacred on a scale surpassing even the recent Calcutta riots. In eight days an estimated 5,000 were killed.'

15. Notes written by Ruth Robinson Pickett for a speech she delivered on 11 December 1973. In this speech, she also begins by saying that she arrived in India 'via stork route' after her parents had gone out as missionaries to India in 1892. (Courtesy of her great-granddaughter, Margaret Ruth Sagan, and the Pickett family archives.)

16. Art McPhee, *The Road to Delhi: Bishop Pickett Remembered* (Bengaluru: SAIACS Press, 2005).

17. Art McPhee, 'Gospel Ferment in India Among Both Hindus and Christians: Bishop J. Waskom Pickett's Rethinking on 1930s Missions in India', *International Journal of Frontier Missions* (Fall 2002): 'There is good evidence that Pickett, a friend and confidant of H.C. Mookerjee, Vice President of the Constituent Assembly and chair of the session that adopted the religious liberties clause of India's Constitution, was, early on, consulted by Mookerjee on some of the language. Unlike any other constitution, India's specifically gives the right to propagate one's faith.' Article 25 of the Constitution of India grants 'freedom of conscience and free profession, practice and propagation of religion'.

18. Ibid.: 'Following Independence, in 1947, no expatriate in India surpassed Pickett in political influence. He had unusual access to Prime Minister Nehru, knew all the members of his cabinet well, and was a close friend of B.R. Ambedkar, Nehru's Law Minister and Rajkumari Amrit Kaur, his Health Minister.'

19. Ibid.: Donald Ebright, one-time director of the famine relief for the National Christian Council (NCC) of India, wrote that 'Bishop J.W. Pickett ... did more than any one non-government person to organize voluntary relief in Delhi'.

20. Ruth Robinson Pickett, 1973.

21. The Pickett children all went to university in the US. Doug was in India through 1946, graduating Woodstock and travelling to the Kumaon district to help his father with a review of villages with food scarcity. He then went to university at Ohio Wesleyan in Delaware. When he returned as an I-3 Methodist missionary, he was hired by the (Methodist) Board of Missions and began teaching at Picket Junior High School in Khatauli, UP. He also did projects for Church World Service and then returned to the US for graduate school in 1960. His own career would be in international development – Doug was the director of the Peace Corps in India and Nepal by 1972 and then worked for USAID. Elizabeth, his older sister, worked as a missionary in north India in the 1940s and 1950s, and her three elder children were all born in Mussoorie.

22. In an earlier letter dated 12 February 1951, written from Alexandria on the way over, Doug mentions how excited he is that he has received a radio from his sister and brother-in-law: 'It is very powerful, and the reception has been excellent. I can even get All India Radio – as far away as Gibraltar! It should be very functional in Khatauli!'

23. John Wesley Robinson is buried in the graveyard on Kaladhungi Road in Nainital, where he died.

24. See William Dalrymple, *White Mughals: Love and Betrayal in Eighteenth Century India; The Last Mughal: The Eclipse of a Dynasty; Delhi 1857; Return of a King: The Battle for Afghanistan; Kohinoor: The Story of the World's Most Infamous Diamond.*

25. William Dalrymple, 'Kolkata, My Ancestors, and Me', BBC, 22 October 2016.

26. An interview conducted with Captain Scott by Clare Jenkins on 22 July 1996, on behalf of Andrew Whitehead, can be found on his website www.andrewwhitehead.net/partition-voices-sir-paul-scott.

16. Migration

1. Burns Road, where Shweta Notaney's grandmother's family once lived before they migrated to Delhi via Bombay, incidentally now houses the descendants of families who migrated to Karachi from Delhi during Partition. Now owners of the most well-known food joints in the city, they call themselves 'Delhi-wallahs'. Along the length of Burns Road, one can spot Hindu and Sikh symbols on the houses, and in one corner a Hindu temple lies empty.

Also see, William Dalrymple, *City of Djinns: A Year in Delhi* (New Delhi: HarperCollins Publishers, 1993), p. 61.

2. According to the latest Pakistan census of 2017, Hindus made up 2.14 per cent of Pakistan's population, or 4.44 million people. Also see Priya Kumar and Rita Kothari, 'Sindh, 1947 and Beyond', *South Asia: Journal of South Asian Studies*, Vol. 39, No. 4 (2016): pp. 773–89: 'Sindh remains home to 95 per cent of Pakistan's Hindu population of about 2.5 million.'

3. Ibid., p. 787: 'After the initial wave of migration of Sindhi Hindus at the time of Partition, a new wave occurred in the wake of the 1965 Indo-Pakistani war when approximately 8,000 people crossed the border from Sindh's Thar Parkar district.'

4. According to the 1931 census, the population of Sindh was about 4.1 million. Approximately 73 per cent were Muslims, 26 per cent Hindus, and 1 per cent belonged to other religions, mainly Christianity and Sikhism. The Hindu minority was concentrated in the urban areas, whereas the Muslim majority dominated the countryside; most of Sindh's middle class at the time of Partition was Hindu. There were about 1,400,000 Hindu Sindhis, concentrated as a majority in four of Sindh's five major cities, namely, Larkana, Shikarpur, Hyderabad and Sukkur, and as a minority in Karachi. Following Independence, Hindu Sindhis were expected to stay in Sindh, as there were good relations between the Hindu and Muslim Sindhis. Also see Aanchal Malhotra, *Remnants of a Separation: A History of Partition Through Material Memory* (New Delhi: HarperCollins India, 2017, ed. 2018), p. 10, 304.

5. Margaret Bourke-White, *Portrait of Myself* (New York: Simon and Schuster, 1963), p. 275.

6. See also the work of American photographer David Duncan Douglas, who most famously captured B.S. Kesavan, the first national librarian of independent India, dividing the libraries. The iconic photograph, published in *LIFE* magazine on 18 August 1947, was likely staged, but shows the young librarian with a worried look on his face, hands buried in his hair, flanked on either side by stacks of books with placards labelled 'INDIA' and 'PAKISTAN'. However, as Anhad Hundal pointed out in his article for *The Caravan* magazine titled 'The Mystery of an Iconic Partition Photograph', the books in the Imperial Secretariat Library in New Delhi where the photograph was taken were never actually divided, despite there being a proposal to do so, like many other archives and collections that were split between the two nations. Moreover, when the writer Mukul Kesavan showed the photograph

to his father, the librarian just laughed and said, 'You know that this never happened.'

7. Margaret Bourke-White, *Halfway to Freedom* (New York: Simon and Schuster, 1949), p. 3.
8. Ibid., p. 5.
9. V.P. Menon, *The Transfer of Power in India* (London: Longman, 1957) p. 432.
10. Urvashi Butalia, *The Other Side of Silence: Voices from the Partition of India* (New Delhi: Penguin Books India, 1998); Yasmin Khan, *The Great Partition: The Making of India and Pakistan* (London: Yale University Press, 2007, ed. 2008).
11. See Prashant Bharadwaj, Asim Khwaja and Atif Mian, *The Partition of India: Demographic Consequences* (UC San Diego, Harvard KSG and Chicago Booth School of Business, June 2009); William Dalrymple, 'The Great Divide: The Violent Legacy of Indian Partition', *The New Yorker*, 22 June 2015; Steven Brocklehurst, 'Partition of India: "They Would Have Slaughtered Us"', BBC, 12 August 2017.
12. Haimanti Roy, *Partitioned Lives: Migrants, Refugees, Citizens in India and Pakistan, 1947–1965* (New Delhi: Oxford University Press, 2012), p. 3.
13. Malhotra, p. 48.
14. Ravinder Kaur, *Since 1947: Partition Narratives Among Punjabi Migrants of Delhi* (New Delhi: Oxford India Paperbacks, 2018), p. 35: '...the mass arrival of Punjabi refugees dramatically changed the spatial, social, economic and political profile of Delhi'.
15. Anis Kidwai, trans. Ayesha Kidwai, *In Freedom's Shade* (New Delhi: Penguin Random House India, 2011), p. 64.
16. Pippa Virdee, *From the Ashes of 1947* (New Delhi: Cambridge University Press, 2018), p. 75.
17. Leonard Woolf was consistently critical of the reluctance of the British in India to transfer power and authority to Indians. He once wrote: 'I have no doubt that if British governments had been prepared to grant in 1900 what they refused in 1900 but granted in 1920; or to grant in 1920 what they refused in 1920 but granted in 1940; or to grant in 1940 what they refused in 1940 but granted in 1947 – then nine-tenths of the misery, hatred and violence, the imprisonings and terrorism, the murders, flogging, shootings, assassinations, even the racial massacres would have been avoided; the transference of power might well have been accomplished peacefully, even possibly without Partition.'

18. Ahmed Ali, *Twilight in Delhi* (New Delhi: Rupa Publications, 2007), p. xix.

19. Ibid., p. xx.

20. Dalrymple, *City of Djinns*, pp. 62–65.

21. Anam Zakaria, *1971: A People's History from Bangladesh, Pakistan and India* (New Delhi: Penguin Random House India, 2019), p. 59: 'Today then in Bangladesh, unlike in India and Pakistan, 1947 has been forgotten from the collective imagination of the people. Children learn little about it, if at all. [The year] 1947 is only evoked in relation to 1971.'

22. According to the Minority Rights Group International, today Bangladesh's Bihari minority lives in shanty towns that were initially temporary relief camps. The largest settlement is the Geneva Camp with 25,000 residents.

23. Originally known as Africa Concern, the organization was founded in Dublin, Ireland, in 1968 by a small group of people, including John and Kay O'Loughlin Kennedy, who came together to respond to an appeal for aid for the devastating famine in Biafra. In 1970, they were asked to respond to a cyclone in East Pakistan, which is when Concern Africa came to be known simply as Concern.

24. Zakaria, *1971*, p. xi

25. Srinath Raghavan, *1971: A Global History of the Creation of Bangladesh* (Cambridge, Massachusetts: Harvard University Press, 2013), pp. 5–6. Sultan M. Hali, 'Jinnah's Two Nation Theory— Vindicated', *Pakistan Today*, 20 October 2017. In the aftermath of Pakistan's surrender in 1971, then prime minister of India Indira Gandhi said, 'Today, we have sunk Jinnah's two-nation theory in the Bay of Bengal.'

26. Kavita Puri, *Partition Voices: Untold British Stories* (New Delhi: Bloomsbury Publishing, 2019), pp. 3–4.

27. Daniel Naujoks, 'Emigration, Immigration, and Diaspora Relations in India', *Migration Information Source*, the Online Journal of the Migration Policy Institute (15 October 2009).

28. Norman Buchignani, 'South Asian Canadians', *The Canadian Encyclopedia*, Historica Canada (12 May 2010, edited 10 February 2020). Also see 'History of South Asians in Canada: A Timeline', South Asian Studies Institute, University of the Fraser Valley.

29. Originally known as the Ceasefire Line, it was renamed the Line of Control after the signing of the Shimla Agreement in July 1972. It

divides the erstwhile princely state of Jammu and Kashmir into Indian-controlled Jammu and Kashmir and Ladakh (union territories since 2019 but a state prior to that) and Pakistan-administered Kashmir and Gilgit–Baltistan.

30. Jagdeep Raina, 'Everything I Wish You Had Told Me', *Inverse Journal*, 8 February 2021.

17. No Man's Land

1. During the Great War (1914–18), the Jullundur Brigade was part of the Lahore Division of the Indian Army and comprised the 1st Manchesters, 47th Sikhs, and 59th (Scinde) Rifles Frontier Force. The three regiments are now: 1st Battalion the Kings Regiment of the British Army, 5th Battalion the Sikh Regiment of the Indian Army, and 1st Battalion (Scinde) the Frontier Force Regiment of the Pakistan Army.

2. See William Green, Swanborough Gordon and Pushpinder Singh (eds), *The Indian Air Force and Its Aircraft: IAF Golden Jubilee, 1932–82* (London: Ducimus Books, 1983), and Pushpinder Singh, *History of Aviation in India: Spanning the Century of Flight* (New Delhi: Society for Aerospace Studies, 2003).

3. *Nishaan Nagaara* is an illustrated Sikh quarterly journal focusing on the diaspora's commitment to the community's history, heritage, traditions and faith. The inaugural issue was released by Dr Manmohan Singh. The *Vayu Aerospace and Defence Review* is a bimonthly aviation and defence magazine published from New Delhi.

4. For sixty years since Independence, this section of the Radcliffe Line was popularly referred to as 'Wagah Border' – after Wagah village in Pakistan – and it was only in 2007 that the Government of India officially renamed the Indian stretch of the international boundary to 'Attari Border' – after the closest village, Attari, on the Indian side.

5. Aashish Kochhar, 'The Making of the Attari–Wagah Border', Live History India, 11 October 2020. Also see, Bishwanath Ghosh, 'The Officer Who Set Up the "Wagah Border"', *The Hindu*, 15 August 2020.

6. Pushpinder Singh Chopra, *1947– A Soldier's Story from the Records of Maj. Gen. Mohinder Singh Chopra* (New Delhi: The Military Studies Convention, New Delhi, 1997) p. 15: Lt. Col. Mohinder Singh Chopra and his family travelled to the east of India in June 1947. Here, his elder daughter, Deep, recalls the trip: 'The first thing that comes to mind about father's transfer to Shillong in June 1947 is the long, arduous

journey taking us from the Simla hills through virtually the breadth of north India along the great Gangetic plain, barren and dry before the monsoons but slowly turning lush as we reached the Assam hills with their evergreen forests, full of flora seldom seen in the north...'

7. Ibid.

8. The initial conversation with Padam Rosha took place at his home in February 2015. The final interview can be accessed through the archives of The Partition Museum, Amritsar. Within the museum building, it plays in the section on the creation of the new border at Wagah in the Gallery of Divisions.

9. Shriram Iyengar writes in *Cinestaan* (21 September 2016, updated 15 November 2017) about how the composer C. Ramchandra, who had accompanied Lata Mangeshkar to Amritsar, described this meeting in no man's land, where the two women had run towards each other and embraced like long-lost friends, in his biography. 'We who were witness to this divine meet were overwhelmed, and could not stop the tears. Even soldiers on both sides of the border were weeping ... I shall never forget this scene in my life. A great testimony to the fact that music can break any barrier.'

10. Pran Nevile, who first narrated this incident to me when we met in 2014, has also documented it in the Epilogue of his bestselling book *Lahore: A Sentimental Journey* (New Delhi: Penguin Books, 2006), p. 189.

11. An abridged version of this anecdote can be found in the Prologue of Aanchal Malhotra, *Remnants of a Separation: A History of the Partition Through Material Memory* (New Delhi: HarperCollins India, 2017, ed. 2018).

12. Anirudh Kala and Alok Sarin, 'The Partitioning of Madness', in *The Psychological Impact of the Partition of India*, ed. Sanjeev Jain, Alok Sarin (New Delhi: Sage Publications, 2018), p. 16.

13. Mountbatten India Office Records L/PO/6/123 part 3/p.222, Para 56.

14. Ibid., p. 23: '[The] transfer of mental patients took place three years and four months after Partition. It is as if the new countries had forgotten about them, and their fate, in a sense, ranked lower than the division of the material assets of tables and chairs in the scheme of things. The number of patients received from Pakistan was less than half of the number expected. The rest had died during this period.'

15. Saadat Hasan Manto, 'Toba Tek Singh', *Kingdom's End and Other Stories*, trans. Khalid Hasan (New Delhi: Penguin Books, 1989), pp. 11–18.

16. Uday Bhatia, 'Riz Ahmed: No Land's Man', *Live Mint*, 20 March 2020.

17. Riz Ahmed, 'The Long Goodbye: Livestream Edition', The Great American Music Hall, San Francisco, 19 December 2020. This live show was presented by the Manchester International Festival (MIF) and Brooklyn Academy of Music (BAM).

18. BBC, 13 January 1964. See also Mayurakshi Das, 'Calcutta Cauldron: City-Life During the January 1964 Riots', *Proceedings of the Indian History Congress*, Vol. 78 (2017): pp. 1147–54.

19. Ibid.

20. Amitav Ghosh, *The Shadow Lines* (New Delhi: Penguin Books, 1988, ed. 2019), pp. 253–54.

21. Nina Sabnani has written about this incident and her mother's migration in an unpublished short story titled 'Home Sweet Home'.

22. Rita Kothari, *Memories and Movements: Borders and Communities in Banni, Kutch, Gujarat* (Hyderabad: Orient Blackswan, 2013), p. 10.

23. Ibid., p. 51: The author interviews Rajaram Lakhani, 28 February 2009.

24. Nina Sabnani, 'Roots in the Sky', in *Sindhi Tapestry: Reflections on the Sindhi Identity*, ed. Saaz Aggarwal (Pune: Black and White Fountain, 2021), pp. 81–85.

25. Isabel Huacuja Alonso, 'The AIR Urdu Service's "Letters of Longing"', *Radio for the Millions: Hindi–Urdu Broadcasting and the Politics of Sound in Modern South Asia* (unpublished book currently under review, cited with author's permission), p. 263 (of the manuscript shared by the author).

26. Ibid., p. 264.

27. Ibid., p. 263.

18. Pain

1. Bal K. Gupta, *Forgotten Atrocities: Memoirs of a Survivor of the 1947 Partition of India* (2012), p. 19: 'November 25, 1947: Throughout the night, I could hear the incessant ringing of machine guns and heavy artillery as the Pakistani army and Pathans began their final assault on Mirpur.' Mr Dharam Vir Gupta narrates a similar account of the fall of Mirpur in November 1947. The interview was conducted by oral history scholar Prince Tomar on behalf of the 1947 Partition Archive: 'Mr Gupta recalls picking out innumerable bullets from his three-storeyed house. The attacks became consistent, bullets and canons were red. [They] were organized and strategized.'

2.   Bal K. Gupta, 'Death of Mahatma Gandhi and Alibeg Prisoners', *Daily Excelsior*, 30 January 2014: 'The Alibeg Prison was located about two miles from Pakistan's border. It was originally a large gurudwara that was converted into a prison by the Pakistani army to detain Hindu and Sikh prisoners. It was outrageous that a holy shrine was converted into a slaughterhouse.'

3.   While speaking about how both her maternal grandfather and paternal grandmother's father had been slaughtered in front of their family, Sumedha Mahajan recalls a scene from the 2013 film *Bhaag Milkha Bhaag*, directed by Rakeysh Omprakash Mehra, on the life of the Indian athlete and Olympic runner Milkha Singh, 'the flying Sikh'. A rather gory scene is shown in the film, where a young Milkha watches his father being beheaded by attackers during the Partition riots. Sumedha asserts that she was careful never to watch this scene or the film with her grandparents, lest it brought back painful memories.

4.   Sansar Chandra, 'Reliving the Tragedy of Mirpur', *The Tribune*, 25 November 2001: 'The number of survivors from Mirpur who reached Jammu alive was a meagre 3,400.'

5.   Census of India, 1941, Volume XXII, Jammu & Kashmir State, Part III, Village Tables, Srinagar, Jammu and Kashmir Government, 1942.

6.   Christopher Snedden, 'What Happened to Muslims in Jammu? Local Identity, "The Massacre of 1947" and the Roots of the "Kashmir Problem",' *South Asia: Journal of South Asian Studies*, Vol. 14, No. 2 (2001): p. 111.

7.   Ian Stephens, *Pakistan* (London: Ernest Benn Limited, 2nd rev. ed., 1964), p. 200.

8.   Snedden, p. 124: 'In a report titled "Kashmir refugees in Pakistan" by Afzal Mirza, published in *Dawn* on 2 January 1951, Mirza states that Muslim refugees from Jammu and Kashmir started to enter Pakistan at the end of September 1947.'

9.   Sabreet Bhat, 'Jammu Massacre: How a Hindu Journalist Recorded the Muslim Massacre', *Free Press Kashmir*, 3 November 2017: 'By November 1947 ... Muslims in Talab Khatikan area were shifted to the police lines at Jogi gate, where now the Delhi Public School is situated. They were shortly sent to Pakistan ... Several thousands of these Muslims were loaded in about sixty lorries to take them to Sialkot. Many miles into the journey, they were cut short and boarded in buses escorted by Dogra troops ... But no sooner did they reach Chattha on

Jammu–Sialkot Road, a large number of armed goons pounced on these Muslims and slaughtered them mercilessly.'

10. Snedden, p. 122: 'Although the actual number of deaths in these incidents is uncertain, there were sufficient killings to make some Muslims in Jammu Province believe there was a post-partition plot to eliminate them.'

Also see, Ved Bhasin, 'Jammu, 1947', *Kashmir Life*, 17 November 2015. In this transcript of a speech that the veteran journalist gave at Jammu University to commemorate the sixty-eighth anniversary of the Jammu massacres in 2003, he speaks from his own experience of being present at the scene as a seventeen-year-old student and peace activist in 1947.

11. The Ministry of Refugees and Rehabilitation, File No. B132, 169/CF/53, NDC, Islamabad: 'A majority of the non-Muslim population of Sialkot had fled to Jammu during the partition-related disturbances. Sialkot and Jammu were nothing less than twin cities. The north-eastern part of Sialkot was principally inhabited by the Dogra inhabitants. They were closely linked culturally and linguistically with the Hindu Dogras of Gurdaspur on the one side and Jammu on the other. As the Punjab boundary award was announced and the disturbances worsened, about 100,000 Hindu and Sikh refugees from Sialkot migrated to Jammu.'

Also see, Illays Chatta, 'Terrible Fate: "Ethnic Cleansing" of Jammu Muslims in 1947', *Pakistan Vision*, Vol. 10, No. 1, pp. 123–26: 'In Jammu city alone, by mid-September, [Hindus and Sikhs] numbered 65,000 … In the first week of November, the Pakistan government despatched many buses to Jammu city to transport the refugees into Sialkot.'

12. The Rashtriya Swayamsevak Sangh is strengthened by graded training camps called Sangha Shiksha Varga, conducted at regular intervals. The first level is Prathamika Shiksha Varga and is a basic training camp of seven days' duration. It is usually held at the district or zilla level. The second level is Prathama Varsha Shiksha Varga, also known as a first-year training camp of twenty-one days' duration. It is usually held at the provincial level. The third level is Dvitiya Varsha Shiksha Varga, also known as a second-year training camp of twenty-one days' duration. It is usually held at the zonal level. Trutiya Varsha Shiksha Varga is the third-year and highest-level training camp of thirty days' duration. It is organized at the national level in the RSS headquarters at Nagpur. Also see: 'History of Sangh Shiksha Varh' (RSS.org).

13. The word 'Sindh' is derived from the Sanskrit word 'Sindhu', which literally means 'river' and is also a reference to the river Indus which cuts through the province of Punjab. The Greeks, as far back as 325 BCE under Alexander the Great, referred to the land as 'Indós', from which comes the modern name for the river. The ancient Persians referred to everything east of this river as 'Hind' or 'Hindu', cognate with the Sanskrit 'Sindh' or 'Sindhu', since in Persian the consonant 's' has an 'h' sound. For them, the word 'Hindu' had little to do with religion; it referred simply to the culture of the peoples who lived on the other side of the river Sindhu. This combined with the suffix 'stan', cognate with the Sanskrit 'sthan', both meaning 'place', resulted in 'Hindustan', the land on the other side (from Persia's perspective) of the Indus. When the British arrived in the seventeenth century, they adopted the Greek version of the name Sindh, calling the region India. The word 'Hindustan' was in use synonymously with the word 'India' during the British Raj.

14. Aleida Assmann, 'Re-framing Memory: Between Individual and Collective Forms of Constructing the Past', in eds. Karen Tilmans, Frank van Vree and Jay Winters, *Performing the Past: Memory, History, and Identity in Modern Europe* (Amsterdam: Amsterdam University Press, 2010), p. 39: 'The memory boom reflects a general desire to reclaim the past as an indispensable part of the present.'

15. *Border* is a 1997 Hindi war film directed, produced and written by J.P. Dutta. Set during the Indo–Pakistani war of 1971, it is an adaptation of real-life events that happened during the Battle of Longewala in 1971.

16. *Raazi* is a 2018 Hindi spy thriller directed by Meghna Gulzar. The film is an adaptation of Harinder Sikka's novel *Calling Sehmat* (New Delhi: Konark Publishers, 2008; New Delhi: Penguin Random House, 2018), a true account of an Indian RAW (Research and Analysis Wing) agent, who, on her father's request, is married into a family of Pakistani military officials to relay information to India prior to the Indo-Pakistani war of 1971.

17. In *The Idea of Punjabiyat*, Prof. Pritam Singh, Senior Lecturer and Chair of the Economics Field at Oxford Brookes University, Oxford, writes that 'the moment we use the word *Punjabiyat*, it suggests a reference simultaneously to something that is very tangible while still elusive … The tangibility of Punjabiyat derives from the recognition of Punjab as an area that once existed as a sovereign state for the half-century between 1799 and 1849. In addition, it also derives from Punjabi as a language with a rich literary heritage, the Punjabi identity

as a linguistic and regional one within both India and Pakistan ... The elusiveness of Punjabiyat comes from the floating nature of the use of the word itself. In Pakistan, the central drive of the movement is to win the right to use the Punjabi language against the hegemony of Urdu; while in India, Punjabiyat is seen as a project of bringing Sikhs and Punjabi Hindus close to each other against Sikh secessionism and Punjabi Hindu alienation from the community's mother tongue.'

18. Alok Bhalla, 'Memory and History: In Conversation with Krishna Sobti', *Partition Dialogues: Memories of a Lost Home* (New Delhi: Oxford University Press, 2006), p. 138.

19. '*Husna*' by Piyush Mishra, 2018. The first stanza of the song could be translated as:

> I felt like I am in Lahore in the first district and the second subdivision
>
> I felt like I am in that Resham street, in the second colony's fourth house
>
> I felt like I am in Pakistan, that place which they call a different country now
>
> I felt like I was by the side of you Husna, as I write this letter from Hindustan
>
> Source: https://urduwallahs.wordpress.com/2015/06/21/husna-piyush-mishra/.

20. Nikita Takkar, 'A 1947 Partition Song You'd Want to Hear Again and Again', Coca-Cola India, 12 April 2018, https://www.coca-colaindia.com/stories/a-1947-partition-song-youd-want-to-hear-again-and-again-.

21. '*Ki Banu Duniya Da*', performed by Gurdas Maan and Diljit Dosanjh, Coke Studio India, 2015.

19. Regret

1. See Anirudha Dutta, *Half a Billion Rising: The Emergence of the Indian Woman* (New Delhi: Rupa Publications India, 2015).

2. Prithvi 'Lali' Vij was the host and producer of the *Sounds of Asia* TV show in Toronto, Canada, which ran for many years on both Global Television and Citytv. Prior to that, he hosted a radio programme called *Voice of India*, broadcasting in Hindi.

3. Many years after this conversation, my aunt, Vibha, told me that when she was young, her mother shared that she had no baby photographs of herself as everything was lost during migration. The only pictures she

had were from after they family moved to India. 'She looked so sad,' my aunt said, 'that I never brought it up again.'

4. See Ian Talbot, 'A Tale of Two Cities: The Aftermath of Partition for Lahore and Amritsar 1947–1957', *Modern Asian Studies*, Vol. 41, No. 1 (2007): pp. 151–85.

5. Yaqoob Khan Bangash, 'When Christians were Partitioned in the Punjab – II', *The News on Sunday*, 24 November 2019.

6. Ibid.

7. Hilal-e-Pakistan, or Crescent of Pakistan, is the second-highest civilian award and decoration of the Islamic Republic of Pakistan. The award seeks to recognize those people who have made 'meritorious contribution to the national interests of Pakistan, social or cultural contribution, or other significant public or private endeavors'.

8. Najum Latif, 'Justice Cornelius, Father of Pakistan Cricket,' *Scoreline*, 14 November 2020; Patrick Sookhdeo, 'The Impact of Islamization on the Christian Community in Pakistan (PhD thesis)', School of Oriental and African Studies, University of London, 1999, pp. 136–37.

9. The firm was founded in 1975 as Lane & Mufti by partners Terence M. Lane and Afzal H. Mufti. Its name was changed to Cornelius, Lane & Mufti in 1979 when Justice A.R. Cornelius, Hamid Khan and Jawwad S. Khawaja joined. See https://www.clm.com.pk/About.html. On 22 December 2021, Cornelius, Lane & Mufti released a new book on Justice Cornelius titled *Justice A.R. Cornelius: A Constitutionalist*, edited by Asad Ullah Khan and Amna Umar Khan, and published by Jahangir's World Times Publications.

10. Ralph J.D. Braibanti, *Chief Justice Cornelius of Pakistan: An Analysis with Letters and Speeches* (Karachi: Oxford University Press, 1999).

11. *Woman in Gold* (2015), directed by Simon Curtis.

12. Aryan remembered that both Peter and Michael were his grandfather Ashok's age and were at Cambridge at the same time as he was. He recalled the colleges they went to – Saint Catherine's and Clare's College – and contacted their alumni associations, requesting both Peter's and Michael's contact information as family. He received an email address of someone who would later become Uncle Michael, and Aryan kept in touch with him for five years until he died. There had been no contact between him and his family in India from 1953 to 2014, and now Ashok could finally talk to his cousin, Michael. For Aryan, getting them to reconnect was 'unfinished business. And I wanted to do that because my grandfather was sick, he was incapable of doing it himself.'

20. Returning

1. Aanchal Malhotra, *Remnants of a Separation: A History of the Partition Through Material Memory* (New Delhi: HarperCollins India, 2017, ed. 2018), p. xx.

2. Georges Perec, trans. and ed. John Sturrock, *Species of Space and Other Pieces* (New Delhi: Penguin Classics, 2008), p. 91.

3. Gyanendra Pandey, *Remembering Partition: Violence, Nationalism and History in India* (New Delhi: Cambridge University Press, 2011), p. 140: 'When the Purana Qila camp was finally established, allegedly after an appeal by the Pakistani High Commissioner, a Pakistani army contingent was deputed for the defence of the camp. The government of Pakistan sent out hundreds of tents to accommodate at least some of the refugees.' Also see, Anis Kidwai, *In Freedom's Shade*, trans. Ayesha Kidwai (New Delhi: Penguin Random House India, 2011), p. 40: Begum Anis Kidwai put the number of people in the Purana Qila refugee camp in the month of September 1947 at 80,000–100,000, dropping to about 60,000 in the month of October. 'The camp's filth, slush and malodours were intolerable ... As far as the eye could see, tents and tin-roofed shelters were crowded together ... [with] naked children, dishevelled women, bareheaded girls and men burning in defiance and humiliation.'

4. *1942* is a 1951 black-and-white film directed by Hemen Gupta that draws inspiration from the Quit India Movement. It can be watched online (with English subtitles) on Indiancine.ma, an annotated online archive of Indian films.

5. Project Dastaan is a peace-building initiative which examines the human impact of global migration through the lens of the largest forced migration in recorded history, the 1947 Partition (www.projectdastaan. org).

6. Sanam tells me that Burewala Mandi is known as the city of education in West Punjab and produces the highest number of doctors. It is also the ancestral hometown of the actor Rajesh Khanna, whose father was the headmaster of MC Model Town, where Mr Khanna had his early education.

7. Lambardar or Numberdar is a title in India and Pakistan which applies to powerful families of zamindars of the village revenue estate, and it comes with the associated social prestige. Put more simply, the term means the one who holds a certain percentage of the land revenue.

8. Elizabeth Day, 'Raghu Rai – Interview', *The Guardian*, 17 January 2010.

9. During our interview, Raghu Rai remembers that while they stayed in the refugee camp, all that was provided during meals was dal and roti. Disinterested in both, he would refuse to eat until his mother found some milk and sugar and dipped pieces of the roti into it to feed her youngest child.

10. Raghu Rai, *Bangladesh: The Price of Freedom* (New Delhi: Niyogi Books, 2013). Also see raghuraifoundation.org/work/bangladesh/.

11. Krishna Bose, *Lost Addresses: A Memoir of India, 1934-1955*, trans. Sumantra Bose (New Delhi: Niyogi Books, 2015), p. 135.

12. In early 2020, while trying to research the elephants belonging to large ancestral estates in East Bengal, Varun came across a document written by a Bangladeshi professor, Sayyed Misbah Deen (Emeritus Professor of Computer Science at Keele University, United Kingdom), titled 'My Memoir: My Early Life in Bangladesh and Beyond' (2016), self-published on his website. Reading through it, he was shocked to find mention of the family elephant, Kusum. The professor's grandfather owned another zamindari estate not far from Taljanga but would visit the house often, particularly during periods of travel as the railway station was close to the Taljanga estate. The memoir mentions, in very moving prose, how everyone in the entire district knew of Kusum and mourned her loss when she died during the war. They were angry at the British for taking away their beloved elephant. Varun reached out to the professor and they had a long conversation about Kusum, where he even remembered the place where she slept and the size and shape of the links on her chains. In Varun's own words: 'I think that was probably one of the most heart-warming conversations I'd had. The gentleman, whom I had no prior connection to, and I bonded over the fact that we both had stories to tell about the same elephant!'

13. Kavita Panjabi, 'A Unique Grace', in Urvashi Butalia, ed., *Partition: The Long Shadow* (New Delhi: Penguin Books India, 2015), p. 63.

21. Separation and Reunion

1. '1st Queen's at Quetta – The Earthquake', The Queen's Royal Surrey Regimental Association, https://www.queensroyalsurreys.org.uk/reg_in_india/india43_1.shtml.

2. Anuj Bahri and Debbie Smith, *Bahrisons: Chronicle of a Bookshop* (New Delhi: India Research Press, 2003), p. 33.

3. Ibid., p. 32.

4. The family would have likely travelled by the East Bengal Railway, which opened the line from and to Goalundo in 1871. Even after Partition in 1947, the train ran up to 1964, and was the last direct link with Calcutta. From *Goalundo Ghat: From the Hooghly to the Himalayas* (Bombay: The Times Press, 1913): 'If one goes from Calcutta to Dacca, the rail journey is broken at Goalundo and from there to Narayanganj is continued by steamer. The night mail from Calcutta deposits one at Goalundo in the early hours of the morning.'

5. After the first Kashmir war of 1947–48, Haveli tehsil was bifurcated, its northern half in Pakistan and southern half in India.

6. *Mera Pakistani Safarnama*, written originally in Punjabi by Balraj Sahni, was translated into Hindi and published as *Pakistan ka Safar*. For a detailed piece on the actor's long association with Partition, in life and in films, see Ammad Ali, *Balraj Sahni: From the Lacerations of Partition to Garam Hawa* (Indian Cinema Heritage Foundation, 1 May 2021).

7. When Balraj Sahni was returning to India, Ahmed Rahi came to bid farewell to his friend at the railway station. For the remainder of the afternoon, Rahi could not forget the look on Sahni's face when they parted. That night, unable to fall asleep, he wrote a poem dedicated to Balraj Sahni, an extract of which reads:
   'Tere liye pardes hai des mera, mere liye pardes hai des tera ... jerha dard mera o' dard tera. Etho jaandiaan cheeki sir oh teri, otho aaondiaan roya si dil mera. Aidoon waddh ke hor ki dukh hosi teri akh ithay, meri akh uthay. Tuttay dilla da ki shumaar karr'ay, eho jeha ujaaria aahlna nay, Koi kakh ithay, koi kakh uthay.' (Mahmood Awan, 'Politics, Partition and Poetry', *The News on Sunday*, 23 July 2017) A rough translation of the text is, 'What is a foreign land for you is a homeland for me, what is foreign for me is your homeland ... The pain that is mine is also yours. Your soul screams when it leaves here, my heart cried coming back from there. What greater grief could there be when you crave for here and I crave for there? How do we count the broken hearts, a million here, a million there? How brutally the nest was destroyed, a straw here, a straw there.'

22. Silence

1. Sukeshi Kamra, *Bearing Witness: Partition, Independence, End of the Raj* (New Delhi: Roli Books, Lotus Collection, 2002), p. 3: '... the silence of the many who belong to this group does not signal resolution and/or a settling of the past, but rather a culturally required repression of the visible signs of trauma.'

2. Björn Krondorfer, 'Is Forgetting Reprehensible? Holocaust Remembrance and the Task of Oblivion', *The Journal of Religious Ethics*, Vol. 36, No. 2 (June 2008): p. 244.

3. Kamra, p. ix.

4. See also Sukeshi Kamra, 'Engaging Traumatic Histories: The 1947 Partition of India in Collective Memory', ed. Urvashi Butalia, *Partition: The Long Shadow* (New Delhi: Penguin Random House India, 2015), pp. 154–77.

5. Vishwajyoti Ghosh, *This Side, That Side: Restoring Partition – An Anthology of Graphic Narratives* (New Delhi: Yoda Press, 2013), p. 12.

6. See Sadia Saeed, 'Pakistani Nationalism and the State Marginalization of Ahmadiyya Community in Pakistan', *Studies in Ethnicity and Nationalism*, Vol. 7, No. 3 (2007), pp. 132–52.

7. See www.1947partitionarchive.org.

8. This family story also appears in Ritika Popli's own writing, which is currently under review in an academic journal.

9. Karthik Venkatesh, 'A Language buried by Partition', *Mint Lounge*, 24 June 2017: 'Seraiki is spoken by close to 20 million people in Pakistan and about 70,000 people in India ... Long considered a Punjabi dialect ... Seraiki as a language is reckoned by many linguists as closer to Sindhi in some respects, though [it] is more or less intelligible to Punjabi speakers too.'

10. Aliah University (AU) is one of the oldest modern-style educational institutes in Asia and the first in India, set up in 1780 by Warren Hastings, the British governor general of East India Company, near Sealdah in Calcutta. At the time, it was also known as Islamic College of Calcutta, Calcutta Madrasah, Calcutta Mohammedan College, or Madrasah-e-Aliah. It was elevated to the status of a university in 2008.

11. See www.adibphotography.com.

12. The South Asian community in the UK organized the first South Asian Heritage Month in July 2019 and is now campaigning to have Partition

history in the school curriculum. Running from 18 July to 17 August, the South Asian Heritage Month seeks to commemorate and celebrate South Asian culture and the entwined histories of the UK and South Asia.

23. The Other

1. Beach Luxury Hotel, whose construction began before Partition under the proprietorship of a Parsi gentleman, Dinshaw B. Avari – after whom his grandson, who now runs the establishment, is named – officially opened its doors in time for the Zoroastrian New Year in 1948. In an address given by Mr Dinshaw B. Avari, on the occasion of the function held by the Parsi community of Karachi to commemorate his eighty-fifth birthday on 5 November 1987, he said, '[When] Beach Luxury Hotel started construction, Partition took place, and the Sind Government once again requisitioned my Hotel. They said that as a Minority Member I will run away and they needed the building for Government Offices. This was somewhere around December 1947, and I gave them a written assurance that I will open the Hotel by our Zoroastrian New Year, 21st of March 1948.'

2. See Anam Zakaria, *Footprints of Partition: Narratives of Four Generations of Pakistanis and Indians* (New Delhi: HarperCollins India, 2015); *Between the Great Divide: A Journey into Pakistan-administered Kashmir* (New Delhi: HarperCollins India, 2018); *1971: A People's History from Bangladesh, Pakistan and India* (New Delhi: Penguin Random House India, 2019).

3. This incident on the bus, as well as Noorani sahib's memory of illuminations on buildings on the eve of Independence in Bombay, has been mentioned in Kuldip Nayar and Asif Noorani, *Tales of Two Cities* (New Delhi: Lotus, 2018), Kindle edition.

4. Ibid. [Kindle edition]: '...whenever I wrote about the need for friendship between the two countries, I was dubbed an Indian agent. I was warned that there would be a midnight knock someday. But mercifully there never was.' Also see Asif Noorani, 'How a Pakistani Man Realized It's Easy to Be Friends with Indians', *The Quint*, 14 April 2017; and Asif Noorani, 'Stranded in India during the 1965 war: How I Made Friends Among "Enemies"', *Scroll*, 8 September 2016.

5. Between 2010 and '13, Anam Zakaria worked for the non-profit organization The Citizens Archive of Pakistan (CAP). One of the programmes that CAP – dedicated to the historic and cultural

preservation of Pakistan – conducted was the Exchange for Change, which sought to connect schoolchildren in India and Pakistan with the hope of facilitating dialogue and fostering better understanding.

6. Aanchal Malhotra, *Remnants of a Separation: A History of the Partition through Material Memory* (New Delhi: HarperCollins India, 2017, ed. 2018), p. 23.

7. Zakaria, *Footprints of Partition*, p. 224.

8. Anam Zakaria, '70 Years of Partition: India, Pakistan Have Successfully Demonized Each Other in Popular Imagination', *Scroll*, 18 August 2017, https://scroll.in/article/847420/70-years-of-partition-india-pakistan-have-successfully-demonised-each-other-in-popular-imagination.

9. Naveen Kishore, 'The Idea of Culture', at the 2018 History for Peace conference, Kolkata, 3 August 2018.

10. Karuna Ezara Parikh, *The Heart Asks Pleasure First* (New Delhi: Pan Macmillan India, 2020), p. 237.

11. Ibid., pp. 207–10.

24. The Quotidian

1. *Gadar: Ek Prem Katha* is a 2001 Hindi film directed by Anil Sharma, set during the 1947 Partition and loosely based on the tragic love story of Buta Singh and Zainab. To read more about Buta Singh, see Urvashi Butalia, *The Other Side of Silence: Voices from the Partition of India* (New Delhi: Penguin Books, 1998), pp. 127–32.

2. Anoothi Vishal, 'Partition Changed India's Food Cultures Forever', *The Wire*, 14 August 2017, https://thewire.in/food/partition-food-punjab-mughlai-bengal.

3. See Salma Husain, *Nuskha-e-Shahjahani: Pulaos from the Royal Kitchen of Shah Jahan* (New Delhi: Rupa Publications, 2007).

4. Sara Suleri, *Meatless Days* (Chicago: University of Chicago Press, 1989; New Delhi: Penguin Random House India, 2018).

5. Karthik Venkatesh, 'The Strange and Little-known Case of Hindko', *Mint Lounge*, 6 July 2019, https://www.livemint.com/mint-lounge/features/the-strange-and-little-known-case-of-hindko/amp-1562400834033.html.

6. Waaz Laal, *The History of the Urdu Language* (New Delhi: Mujtabai Press, Delhi, 1920), pp. 5–10: 'The word "urdu" itself is Turkish and means "army" or "camp"; our English "horse" is said to be connected with it. The Muslim army stationed in Delhi from 1193 onwards was

known as the *Urdu* or *Urdu e Mu'alla*, The Exalted Army ... The soldiers in Delhi at a very early date gave up the use of Persian among themselves and began to speak a modified form of the vernacular. In Delhi this form of speech, to distinguish it from the usual Khari Baoli (and probably also from Persian), was called Zabān-i Urdū, the language of the army, or Zabān-i Urdū-yi Muallā, the language of the Exalted [or Royal] Army. As the soldiers and the people intermixed and intermarried, the language spread over the city into the suburbs and even into the surrounding districts.'

7. *Veer-Zaara* is a 2004 Hindi film, directed by Yash Chopra and co-produced with his son Aditya Chopra, about an Indian Air Force officer and the daughter of a Pakistani politician who are star-crossed lovers.

8. *Aunn Zara* is a 2013 Pakistani drama series based on Faiza Iftikhar's novel *Hisaar-e-Mohabbat* (Fort of Love) and is directed by Haissam Hussain.

9. Ghulam Raza, 'Etymology of the Saraiki Language Name', *Journal of Linguistics & Literature*, Vol. 1, No. 1 (2016): p. 66: In *Saraiki Zabaan Kaa Irtiqaa*, translated from the Urdu as 'the evolution of Seraiki language', B.A. Zami 'traces the origin of the name Saraiki to the word sarāñ, meaning "hotel" or "inn". The equivalent word for sarāñ in Urdu/Hindi is sarai. In the Multan region, there were many sarai/sarīñ for serving and hosting travellers, merchants and businessmen. In these sarai/sarīñ, people from around the country spoke the local language [Multani] by mixing some words of their own languages and this mixed language started to be called Saraikī, meaning the language of sarai/sarāñ.'

10. 'Reunion' is a Google India advertisement directed by Amit Sharma and written by Sukesh Kumar Nayak. It was released on 13 November 2013 and went viral, having a strong impact in both India and Pakistan, and was viewed more than 1.6 million times before it was officially aired on television on 15 November 2013.

11. *Dastaan* is a 2010 Pakistani drama based on the novel *Bano* by Razia Butt, set in the years between 1947 and '56. It was dramatized by Samira Fazal and directed by Haissam Hussain.

12. Anam Zakaria, *1971: A People's History from Bangladesh, Pakistan and India* (New Delhi: Penguin Random House India, 2019), p. 210.

13. Sultan M. Hali, 'Biharis: Their Crime Was Their Belief in Pakistan', *Global Village Space*, 14 December 2018, https://www.globalvillagespace.com/biharis-their-crime-was-their-belief-in-pakistan-

sultan-m-hali/#:~:text=Former%20PAF%20officer%20calls%20
out,the%20least%20Pakistan%20can%20do.

14. Zakaria, *1971*, p. 106.

15. Hali, 'Biharis'.

16. Anis Kidwai, *In Freedom's Shade*, trans. Ayesha Kidwai (New Delhi: Penguin Books India, 2011), p. 79.

17. Saba tells me that her mother's siblings were all aware of this fact, and it had once even been published in a Party paper. A mention is made in Qamar 'Azad' Hashmi's obituary by the South Asia Citizens Web, 2 February 2013: 'The Hashmis were a political family and the family was called the first red family of Delhi.'

18. Saba tells me that one of her granduncles, Tahir, already living in Dhaka when Partition took place, was very worried about his family upon hearing the news of trains being slashed on both sides of the border. He wrote letters to both Gandhi and Jinnah's offices, inquiring about his missing family. While Jinnah's office did not answer, Gandhi's did with very precise details of when the family had left the refugee camp in Delhi and which train they had boarded in August 1947. However, it was this very train that the family had alighted at Nizamuddin train station, and whose passengers had eventually been massacred en route to Pakistan. Unable to locate the family, Tahir travelled from East to West Pakistan, and they were finally reunited at a relative's home in Lahore.

19. Yasmin Khan, *The Great Partition: The Making of India and Pakistan* (New Haven: Yale University Press, 2007, ed. 2008), p. 194: 'The permanent separation of Indians and Pakistanis from each other, and their inability to cross the new border, was the most long-lasting and divisive aspect of Partition, though it was barely taken into consideration by the politicians at the time ... In the summer of 1947, few could appreciate the full connotations of the division which would ultimately result in some of the harshest border regulations in the world.'

20. From an interview with Sohail Hashmi published by *The New Leam*, 26 July 2020, https://www.thenewleam.com/2020/07/interview-the-idea-of-india-being-projected-today-is-based-on-exclusion-of-minoritiesdalits-and-tribals-says-sohail-hashmi/.

21. Jawaharlal Nehru, *Letters for a Nation: From Jawaharlal Nehru to His Chief Ministers, 1947–1963*, ed. Madhav Khosla (New Delhi: Penguin Random House India, 2015).

22. Kamleshwar, *Partitions*, trans. Ameena Kazi Ansari (New Delhi: Penguin Books India, 2006), p. 83.

Epilogue

1. Tweet from Prime Minister Narendra Modi's official Twitter handle, 14 August 2021. Can be accessed at https://twitter.com/narendramodi/status/1426410192258830341.

2. Fahad Zuberi, 'Memorialising Past', *The Indian Express*, 5 September 2021, https://indianexpress.com/article/opinion/columns/partition-of-india-national-day-of-remembrance-day-7490387/.

3. This thought is also echoed in Karan Thapar's 'Horrors of 1947 Partition: A Selective Remembrance?', *Deccan Chronicle*, 20 August 2021, https://www.deccanchronicle.com/opinion/columnists/190821/karan-thapar-horrors-of-1947-partition-a-selective-remembrance.html: '...should this not be a day when the three countries of the subcontinent remember together the trauma they suffered and never want to repeat?'

4. Robin David, 'Here's How We Can Observe Partition Horrors Remembrance Day', *The Times of India*, 8 September 2021, https://timesofindia.indiatimes.com/blogs/On-the-bounce/heres-how-we-can-observe-partition-horrors-remembrance-day/.

5. Aanchal Malhotra, *Remnants of a Separation: A History of the Partition Through Material Memory* (New Delhi: HarperCollins India, 2017, ed. 2018), p. 9.

6. L.K. Advani, the Indian politician who is one of the founding leaders of the Bharatiya Janata Party and served as the seventh deputy prime minister of India, from 2002 to 2004, migrated from Karachi to Bombay during Partition. This quote is an excerpt from his speech at a function organized by the Karachi Council on Foreign Relations, Economic Affairs and Law on 5 June 2005.

Acknowledgements

ONE OF THE MANY pleasures while writing this book was having the conversations that made it possible. I have learnt that there is exceptional power in cross-border dialogue, which can inspire us to look back and beyond, to a history once shared. And so, for the recollection of memory, for helping me learn or unlearn or relearn, for affirming that violence and brutality *cannot* be the only legacy of a once-undivided land, for inviting me into their homes and histories, and trusting me with their stories, I am indebted to each of my interviewees – including those referred to below only by their initials to maintain anonymity as per their request – and their families. This book belongs to you, and to all the inheritors of Partition:

A, Aatish Taseer, Abdul and Hamza Azim, Abhishek Acharyya, Adib Chowdhury, AJ, Ali Abbasi, Ali Samoo, Dr Ali Usman Qasmi, Amit Tandon, Amitoj Singh, Amrita Das, Amrita Singh, Anam Zakaria, Anirudha Dutta, Dr Anisur Rahman, Anoosha Hameed and Sheikh Abdul Hameed, Aparna Bhattacharya and Saktipada Das, Arjunvir Singh, Arslan Athar, Aryan D'Rozario, Akash Mathias D'Rozario, Shaila Rozario Seth and family, Alicia Cornelius and family, Asif Noorani, Ayushi, Balbir Singh Bir, Gurdeep Kaur, Jasminder Gulati, Bhag Malhotra, Neeraj Oberoi, Tanuj Kapur and Anuj Bahri, Bhavneet Kaur, Bilal Ahmed Ghous and Khaksar, Chayya Syal and Bharath Syal, Dimple Suneja, Dolly Suneja and Raj Kapur Suneja, Dr Sukeshi Kamra, Duaa Amir, Farhan Ahmed Shah, Fatimah Asghar, G, Garima Kumar, Gurmeet Sangha Rai, Avani Rai,

Purvai Rai and Raghu Rai, Harleen Singh Sandhu, Harsh Vardhan Sahni, Harshit Kohli, Hussain Khalid, Ipsa Samaddar, Israa Nasir, Jagdeep Raina, Jasmin Athwal, Kalyani Ray Chowdhury, Karuna Ezara Parikh, Amitesh Ray and Agneesh Ray, Karan Mahajan, Karan Torani, Kastury Gosh and Jashaswi Gosh, Kavita Puri, Kinshu Dang, Kuldeep Kaur, Lisa Ray, M, Maleeha Malik and Farhat Malik, Mayukh Bhattacharya, Md. Anas Khan, Meg Sagan, Mohan Katyal, Padam Rosha, Lady Kishwar Desai and Mallika Ahluwalia, Mrs Sindhu, Munazah Khan, Nagma Nassa, Narayani Basu, Naveen Farhan, Nina Sabnani, Nishant, Nivedita Bobal, Noshina Rohi and Maira Qadir, Pallavi Bhatia, Pranab Akhanda and Arpita Akhanda, Prarna Mansukhani, Shublaxmi Mansukhani and Deepak Mansukhani, Priyanka Pathania, Priyanka Sabarwal, Prof. D.P. Sengupta and Prof. Kundan Sengupta, Proma Huq, Puneet Anand, Amneet Anand, Jasjot Anand and Upkar Singh Anand, Mian Faiz Rabbani, Samar and Air Commodore Kaiser Tufail, Pushpinder Singh Chopra, Rabeya Sen and Bharati Sen, Ragini Kashyap, Rajni Malhotra, Mona Mehra, Jiwan Vohra, Vibha Vohra Bhalla and Vishwa Nath Vij, Ramesh Kumari Dutta, Pratibha Jain and Anju Mehta, Rashi Puri, Ritesh Banglani, Ritika Popli, Roshan Abbas Naqvi, Rukaiya Idrish Siamwala, Saba Azad and Shehla Hashmi Grewal, Saba Qizilbash and Mujtaba Hussain, Sadia Malik, Samrat Choudhury, Sanam Zaman Khan, Inayat Ullah Khan and Aqsa Malik, Sanjana Chopra and Ria Chopra, Sanjiv Nanda, Sayantan Ghosh, Seema Gupta and Sumedha Mahajan, Shafa Tasneem, Sheba Kharbanda, Shreyoshi Saha and Shiny Saha, Shweta Notaney, Sinjini Majumdar, Somya Lakhani, Suhail Nayyar, Sumohini Bhagat, Surangana Makin and Om Prakash Khanna, Tahara Anderson and Dr Muhammad Ashraf Hasan, Tanjima Kar Sekh, Tayyaba Pirzada, Umair Khan, Varun Mallik, Vernika Awal, Sam Dalrymple, William Dalrymple and Olivia Fraser, Yusra Rasool, Z, Zeba Talkhani.

Some of these conversations are also in memory of and dedicated to those who passed away while this book was taking shape – Balbir Singh Bir, Pushpinder Singh Chopra, Kalyani Ray Chowdhary, Ved Kohli, Om Prakash Khanna, Raj Kapoor Suneja, Narender Chopra, Narayan Chandra Pal, Upkar Singh Anand.

I am grateful to Devapriya Roy, Janice Pariat, Amandeep Madra and Aman Raj Khanna for introducing me to interviewees; to Srinivas Jain for sharing his father L.C. Jain's memoir, *Civil Disobedience*, which helped in the research for stories that took place at Kingsway Camp, north Delhi; and to my cousin, Neev Kalia, who explored the area with me. Sumedha Mahajan, for being my guide in Jammu; Sayantan Ghosh, for always taking the time to translate Bengali interviews; and Kumail Hasan, for helping me search for my grandmother's home in Lahore. The project would have certainly taken twice as long without the help of Sanjana Anand, Jayosmita Ganguly and Sanjana Chopra, who transcribed many of the interviews.

For access to the interview with Padam Rosha in Chapter 17 on 'No Man's Land', I would like to thank The Partition Museum and Mallika Ahluwalia. This book also includes excerpts from my pieces that have been previously published in *The Indian Express* ('Exploring the Stories, Legends and Myths of Lahore', December 2018), *Departures in Critical Qualitative Research*, Vol. 8, No. 1, University of California Press ('There Are No More Places to Migrate to', Spring 2019) and *Mint Lounge* ('The Good Samaritans of 4, Fane Road', February 2020; 'When the 1897 Bubonic Plague Ravaged India', April 2020).

This work would have been incomplete without my parents, Rajni Malhotra and Anuj Bahri, and family members Bhag Malhotra, Vishwa Nath Vij, Jiwan Vohra, Neeraj Oberoi, Tanuj Kapur, Mona Mehra and Vibha Vohra-Bhalla, who all patiently sat through many rounds of interviewing. My siblings, Aashna and Aaditya, to whom this book is dedicated. Friends and colleagues who have had meaningful conversations with me on the subject over many years – Naveen Kishore, Jassa Ahluwalia, Mayank Austen Soofi, Somya Lakhani, Malvika Bhatia, Anshul Tewari, Priyanka Pathania, Farhan Ahmed Shah, Sam Dalrymple, Sparsh Ahuja, Rana Safvi, Mujib Mashal and Adil Rana Chhina.

Large sections of this book were written under lockdown and curfew, during a pandemic, and the surmounting grief of the outside world juxtaposed against the inward grief of many of my interviewees was not lost on me. I unravelled on several occasions, and to those who kept me whole and intact, I will forever be thankful – Shruti Brahmbhatt, Navdha Malhotra, Laura Emoke Gabor and Pranav Misra. Kavita Puri, fellow Partition scholar, who remains my sounding board, and Karuna Ezara Parikh, for taking out time to read the mighty first draft and giving me detailed notes.

This is an unusual project, in both format and content, which may not have seen fruition without my agent, David Godwin, who agreed that much still remains to be said about Partition and encouraged me to be the one to say it; my publisher, Ananth Padmanabhan, who has been there since the very beginning; and my editor, Siddhesh Inamdar, for his painstaking and nuanced edits. The discussions that emerged between us during the reading and editing of this text – on the ability of the past to inform the present and shape the future – will remain sacred. I am grateful also to Suchismita Ukil for bringing a fresh set of eyes to the manuscript; Saumya Gupta for taking the cover photograph of a nostalgic afternoon going through old family photographs; and Bonita Vaz-Shimray for the elegant design and thoughtful conversations on image and text, memory and its visual interpretation.

The Partition scholars who have not just inspired me with their work but have, over the years, given me time from their busy schedules and wisdom from the field: my deepest gratitude to Anam Zakaria (who has also very kindly written the Foreword), Ritu Menon, Urvashi Butalia, Ravinder Kaur, Dr Yasmin Khan, Dr Sukeshi Kamra, Rita Kothari, Dr Debjani Sengupta, Dr Devika Chawla, Andrew Whitehead, Kavita Puri, Maaz Bin Bilal, Dr Ishtiaq Ahmed and Dr Isabel Huacuja Alonso, who very generously allowed me to read and cite from the chapter on All India Radio's Urdu programmes from her unpublished manuscript. I encourage everyone to pick up their books as well as the many others cited in the Notes. Also listed are a plethora of films, music, artworks, poetry, works in translation and archival sources that have nourished and informed this text.

Lastly, the title of this book is borrowed from a piece that Sukant Deepak wrote on my work for the Indo-Asian News Service, following a conversation at the Jaipur Literature Festival, 2020.

About the Author

Aanchal Malhotra is an oral historian and writer from New Delhi. She is the co-founder of the Museum of Material Memory and writes extensively on the 1947 Partition and its related topics. Her first book, published in South Asia as *Remnants of a Separation* and internationally as *Remnants of Partition*, was shortlisted for the Sahitya Akademi Yuva Puraskar, British Academy's Nayef Al-Rodhan Prize for Global Cultural Understanding, Hindu Lit for Life Non-fiction Prize, Kamaladevi Chattopadhyay NIF Book Prize and the Shakti Bhatt First Book Prize. *In the Language of Remembering* is her second book.